PEARSON BACCALAUREATE

STANDARD LEVEL

Biology

2nd Edition

ALAN DAMON • RANDY McGONEGAL • PATRICIA TOSTO • WILLIAM WARD

Supporting every learner across the IB continuum

Published by Pearson Education Limited, Edinburgh Gate, Harlow, Essex, CM20 2JE.

www.pearsonglobalschools.com

Text © Pearson Education Limited 2014
Project Management by Alison Nick
Edited by Eva Fairnell
Proofread by Judith Shaw
Indexed by Susan Boobis
Designed by Astwood Design
Typeset by Phoenix Photosetting, Chatham, Kent
Original illustrations © Pearson Education 2014
Illustrated by Tech-Set Ltd and Phoenix Photosetting
Cover design by Pearson Education Limited

The rights of Alan Damon, Randy McGonegal, Patricia Tosto, and William Ward to be identified as authors of this work have been asserted by them in accordance with the Copyright, Designs and Patents Act 1988.

First published 2014

20 19 18 17 16
IMP 10 9 8 7 6 5 4

British Library Cataloguing in Publication Data
A catalogue record for this book is available from the British Library
ISBN 978 1 447 95904 5
eBook only ISBN 978 1447 95905 2

Acknowledgements
The publisher would like to thank the following for their kind permission to reproduce their photographs:

(Key: b-bottom; c-centre; l-left; r-right; t-top)

Alamy Images: 19th era 2 235t, age fotostock Spain, S.L. 261, All Canada Photos 267b, Charles Krebs 27 , Enigma 534b, Ester Van Dam 244, GreenStockCreative 532br, Janusz Gniadek 249, Megapress 496, Robert Morris 540, Tom Uhlman 182, Universal Images Group 234b, 253; **Alan Damon:** 139t, 162, 188, 192r, 231, 234t, 260, 263b, 265b, 269tl, 568; **Corbis:** 2 / Chad Baker / Jason Reed 275 b, 2 / F64 / Ocean 530 , 2 / Ryan McVay / Ocean 532tr, Christian Charisius / Reuters 184, Elmer Frederick Fischer 275t, Marty Snyderman 264, Paul Souders 422, Thomas Marent / Minden 222t, Wilfried Krecichwost 532tc; **Department of Biological Sciences:** 51c, 51b; **DK Images:** Colin Keates 539, Craig Knowles 193, Debbie Maizels 148, Frank Greenaway 299t, Geoff Dann 266, Gerard Brown 183b, Gill Tomblin 187b, Ian O'Leary 206, John Woodcock 135b, Linden Artists 208t, M.I. Walker 174b, 191t, Mick Posen 211, Mike Saunders 208b, Nigel Hicks 183t, Pat Aithe 233, Peter Anderson 550, Peter Bull 319t, 538, Peter Bull 319t, 538 , Peter Gardner 174t, Roy Flooks 218t, Stephen Oliver 207b, Zygote Media Group 288b, 331t, 519b; **Floating Island International, Inc:** 419; **Fotolia.com:** Alejandro Dans 387, alekswolff 453tr, catolla 389, Christian Musat 553, claffra 221b, Dragonimages 215b, gabe9000c 433t, Leysan 269tr, Mark Balyshev 384, Mykhailo Kovtoniuk 118, Olhaafanasieva 385, Patrick J. 228, Photographee.eu 532bl, Robert Kneschke 532cr, SNEHIT 180, tinadefortunata 278; **genome.gov:** 131t; **Getty Images:** Alan John Lander Phillips 382, BSIP / UIG 501, drbimages 531t, E.A. Janes 532c, Gamma-Rapho 532cl, Janis Christie 429, Jeremy Woodhouse 197t, Jon Gibbs 453tl, Mark Raycroft 186 t, Michael Gottschalk 393, Mint Images / Frans 235b, Ralph Lee Hopkins 427, Spike Walker 391t, Steve Gschmeissner 415, Tetra Images 532bc, Travel Ink 532 tl, UIG 215t; **Imagemore Co., Ltd:** 525b, 536; **NASA:** 214tr, 222c, 222b; **Paul Billiet:** 247, 186b; **Pearson Education Ltd:** Jules Selmes 534t, Coleman Yuen 55b; © **Rough Guides:** Paul Whitfield 133; **Science Photo Library**

Ltd: A.B. Dowsett 14, 308t, 399, 416, 543t, 543b, 524, 535, AJ Photo 564, Alfred Pasieka 90, 96b, 98, 56, 68 , 293r, Alice J. Belling 71 , AMI Images 305, Anatomical Travelogue 331b, 315, Anatomical Travelogue 331b, 315, Andrew J. Martinez 434, Bildagentur-Online / OHDE X, 402, Biology Media 20tc, Biophoto Associates 263tl, 290l, 309t, 497, 514b, British Antarctic Survey 218b, C008 / 4381 304t, Christian Darkin 10, Claudia Stocker 243, Claus Lunau 374, 54,Clouds hill Imaging Ltd 388t, CNRI 19b, 138, 302, 313, CNRI 19b, 138, 302, 313, D. Phillips 293l, David Parker 168t, Detlev Van Ravensswaay 533t, Don Fawcett 322, 327, 51t, Don W. Fawcett 22, 537, Doncaster and Bassetlaw hospitals 251, Dr Jeremy Burgess 17, 21br, 47br, 65, 125, 192l, Dr Kari Lounatmaa 20tl, Dr Keith Wheeler 333t, Dr Neil Overy 450, Dr Tim Evans 467b, 58, Dr. Richard Kessel & Dr. Gene Shih, Visuals Unlimited 47bl, Edward Lettau 502, Eye of Science 111t, 127t, 525, 298 t, 303 , F003 / 0988 288c, Frank Fox 267t, Frans Lanting, Mint Images 468t, G200 / 0119 163, Gary Carlson 3, 74, Gerry Pearce 464t, 464b,Gustoimages 176t, 432, 75 , 517 , Hank Morgan 79, Hermann Eisenbeiss 64 , J.C. Revy, ISM 83, 102t, J.C. James King-Holmes 544, Javier Trueba / MSF 541bl, Jeff Lepore 483, John Bavosi 284 , 289 , John Durham 109b, 306, John Greim 398, Juergen Berger 508t, Kevin Curtis 129, Laguna Design 94b, 401, 437, 58t, 81 , Library of Congress 531b, Luis Montanya / Marta Montanya 438, Marc Phares 508 c, Mark Williamson 460, Martin Bond 417cr, Martin Shields 73t, Martyn F. Chillmaid 111b, 391b, Mary Martin 49, Matt Meadows 465, Mehau Kulyk 294 t, Michael W. Tweedie 238t, Monica Schroeder / Science Source 298b, Nancy Hamilton 507, National Library of Medicine 150, Natural history Museum 256, 542, Niaid / CDC 13t, Nigel Cattlin 170br, Pan Xunbin 404br, Pascal Goetgheluck 563, 67, Patrick Landmann 165, Paul D Stewart 257, Peter Gardiner 250, Phantatomix 93t, Prof. David Hall 394, Professors P. Motta & T. Fujita / University La Sapienza, Rome 514t, Professors P. Motta & T. Naguro 104, R. Bick, Poindexter, UT Medical School 519t, Ria Novosti 164, Richard R. Hansen 470b, Robert Brook 470t, Roger Harris 295, 326, Science Source 230, Sciepro 296, 304b, 286 , 307 , Scott Bauer / US Department of Agriculture 472, Sheila Terry 60b, 299b, Simon Fraser 82, Sinclair Stammers 128, Sovereign, ISM 354, Spencer Grant 499 , Steve Allen 521, Steve Gschmeissner 16b, 48b, 301, 316b, 319b, 320t, 469tl, 508 b, Thomas & Pat Leeson 433b, 468b, 485, Thomas Deerinck, NCMIR 2, U.S. Coast Guard 411, US Department of Agriculture 471, Victor Habbick Visions 467t, Visual Science 52, Volker Steger 131b, William Ervin 490, Zephyr 352, 494; **Shirley Burchill:** 152b, 197b, 241, 265t, 152b, 197b, 241, 265t; **Shutterstock.com:** chungking 221t, EpicStockMedia 367, Fotokostic 248t, Igor Sirbu 269br, Martin Fowler 187t, Nicram 269bl, Paul Aniszewski 196, Sashkin 338, Tyler Olson 541tr, Umberto Shtanzman 541br; **Sidney Bailet:** 147b; **vischeck.com:** Alan Damon 159.

Cover images: *Front:* **Getty Images:** Alastair Pollock Photography

All other images © Pearson Education

Every effort has been made to trace the copyright holders and we apologise in advance for any unintentional omissions. We would be pleased to insert the appropriate acknowledgement in any subsequent edition of this publication.

The following have been reproduced from IB documents and past examination papers: Understandings, Applications and skills, Guidance, Essential ideas, some Nature of science, past exam questions, and corresponding mark schemes provided in the eBook. Our thanks go to the International Baccalaureate for permission to reproduce its intellectual copyright.

This material has been developed independently by the publisher and the content is in no way connected with or endorsed by the International Baccalaureate (IB). International Baccalaureate® is a registered trademark of the International Baccalaureate Organization.

There are links to relevant websites in this book. In order to ensure that the links are up to date and that the links work we have made the links available on our website at www.pearsonhotlinks.com. Search for this title or ISBN 9781447959045.

We are grateful to the following for permission to reproduce copyright material:

Figures

Figure on page 51 from *Lehninger principles of biochemistry*, 3rd ed., W. H. Freeman (Nelson, D. and Cox, M. 2000), p. 35, © Don W. Fawcett/ Photo Researchers, reproduced with permission; Figure 1.35 from World Health Organization, *WHO report on the global tobacco epidemic*, WHO, 2008, p.9, http://www.who.int/tobacco/mpower/graphs/en/index.html [accessed 16 June 2014], reproduced with permission of the publisher; Figure 3.23 from http://biomed.emory.edu, reproduced with permission from Dr. Stephanie Sherman; Figure on page 227 from Reducing uncertainty about

Dedications

To my father, the late Dr William A. Damon, a man of principle, an intellectual giant, and a dear friend.

Alan Damon

To my children and grandchildren. You are my future even when I am gone.

Randy McGonegal

I dedicate this book to my husband, who has been my editor and constant support.

Pat Tosto

I dedicate this book to the most important people in my life, my family. You have allowed me to be more than I ever could have been without you.

Bill Ward

Contents

Introduction

Authors' introduction to the second edition

Welcome to your study of International Baccalaureate (IB) Standard Level (SL) biology. This book is the second edition of the market-leading Pearson Baccalaureate SL biology book, first published in 2007. It has been completely rewritten to match the specifications of the new IB biology curriculum, and gives thorough coverage of the entire course content. While there is much new and updated material, we have kept and refined the features that made the first edition so successful. Our personal experience and intimate knowledge of the entire IB biology experience, through teaching and examining, curriculum review, moderating internal assessment, and leading workshops for teachers in different continents, has given us a unique understanding of your needs in this course. We are delighted to share our enthusiasm for learning biology in the IB programme with you!

Content

The book covers the two parts of the IB syllabus: the core and the options, of which you will study one. Each chapter in the book corresponds to a topic or an option in the IB guide, in the same sequence.

The sequence of sub-topics within each chapter is given in the contents page.

Each chapter starts with a list of the Essential ideas from the IB biology guide, which summarize the focus of each sub-topic.

Essential ideas

 3.2 Chromosomes carry genes in a linear sequence that is shared by members of a species.

This is followed by an introduction, which gives the context of the topic and how it relates to your previous knowledge. The relevant sections from the IB biology guide for each sub-topic are then given as boxes showing Understandings, and Applications and skills, with notes for Guidance shown in italics where they help interpret the syllabus.

Understandings:
- Prokaryotes have one chromosome consisting of a circular DNA molecule.
- Some prokaryotes also have plasmids but eukaryotes do not.

Applications and skills:
- Application: Non-disjunction can cause Down syndrome and other chromosome abnormalities.
- Application: Studies showing age of parents influences chances of non-disjunction.
- Skill: Drawing diagrams to show the stages of meiosis resulting in the formation of four haploid cells.
  - *Guidance*
    - *Preparation of microscope slides showing meiosis is challenging and permanent slides should be available in case no cells in meiosis are visible in temporary mounts.*

The text covers the course content using plain language, with all key scientific terms explained in the eBook glossary.

We have been careful to apply the same terminology you will see in IB examinations in all worked examples and questions.

The nature of science

Throughout the course you are encouraged to think about the nature of scientific knowledge and the scientific process as it applies to biology. Examples are given of the evolution of biological theories as new information is gained, the use of models to conceptualize our understanding, and the ways in which experimental work is enhanced by modern technologies. Ethical considerations, environmental impacts, the importance of objectivity, and the responsibilities regarding scientists' code of conduct are also considered here. The emphasis is on appreciating the broader conceptual themes in context. You should familiarize yourself with these examples to enrich your understanding of biology. We have included at least one example in each sub-section, and hope you will come up with your own as you keep these ideas at the surface of your learning.

Key to information boxes

A popular feature of the book is the different coloured boxes interspersed throughout each chapter. These are used to enhance your learning, as explained using the examples below.

 **Nature of science**

This is an overarching theme in the course to promote concept-based learning. Throughout the book you should recognize some similar themes emerging across different topics. We hope they help you develop your own skills in scientific literacy.

 NATURE OF SCIENCE

Most, but not all, organisms assemble proteins from the same 20 amino acids. Virtually every reference concerning amino acids will tell you that there are 20 amino acids in nature. It is true that the universal genetic code (universal indicating that it is used in the vast majority of organisms on Earth) only encodes 20. But in nature there are frequently exceptions, and that includes things that are called 'universal'. If you include all known living organisms then there are 22 amino acids that are used to create polypeptides. In addition to the 20 amino acids whose structures are given in Figure 2.20, there are two additional amino acids called selenocysteine and pyrrolysine.

Even though the first accurate model of DNA was produced by James Watson (American) and Francis Crick (British) in 1953, many other scientists from around the world contributed pieces of information that were instrumental in developing the final model. Erwin Chargaff (Austrian) had determined that the numbers of adenine and thymine bases were equal, as were the numbers of cytosine and guanine bases. Rosalind Franklin (British) and Maurice Wilkins (born in New Zealand) had calculated the distance between the various molecules in DNA by X-ray crystallography.

 International-mindedness

The impact of the study of biology is global, and includes environmental, political, and socio-economic considerations. Examples of this are given to help you see the importance of biology in an international context.

 Utilization

Applications of the topic through everyday examples are described here, as well as brief descriptions of related biological industries. This helps you to see the relevance and context of what you are learning.

 Gene therapy is the process of taking a beneficial gene from a person who possesses it and putting it into a person who does not have it, but who needs it to stay healthy. The challenge is that it is very difficult to get the DNA into the sick person's cells. One way is to force the gene into the patient's cells using a virus to deliver it. Partly because of a lack of understanding of how to use viruses safely to deliver genes, the decision was made to stop all testing of gene therapy on human patients in the USA in 1999, when an 18-year-old patient died after a virus had been injected into his body. However, gene therapy trials are coming back, little by little, notably in helping blind children to regain their eyesight.

In the 1997 science fiction film *GATTACA*, one of the main characters brings a sample of cells to a walk-up window at an establishment that provides anonymous genome services. Within seconds, she gets a full printout and analysis of the genome she is interested in. One objective of science fiction as an art form is to warn society of what might happen in the future if we are not careful. This film raises questions about how far technology will lead us and whether or not we want to go in that direction. Our society will need to make some difficult decisions in the coming years concerning our genomes and who has access to the information contained within them.

  Interesting fact

These give background information that will add to your wider knowledge of the topic and make links with other topics and subjects. Aspects such as historic notes on the life of scientists and origins of names are included here.

 Laboratory work

These indicate links to ideas for lab work and experiments that will support your learning in the course, and help you prepare for the Internal Assessment. Some specific experimental work is compulsory, and further details of this are in the eBook.

 Investigating the factors that affect the rooting of stem cuttings
Design an experiment to assess one factor affecting the rooting of stem cuttings. The basic idea is to cut a few centimetres of stem from a healthy plant and place it into an appropriate medium either sticking up or having it lying flat. Typical plants to try are impatiens, begonias, jade, or African violet.

Who should decide how fast and how far humans should go with our study of DNA and the technology that is rapidly emerging?

  TOK

These stimulate thought and consideration of knowledge issues as they arise in context. Each box contains open questions to help trigger critical thinking and discussion.

Key fact

These key facts are drawn out of the main text and highlighted in bold. This will help you to identify the core learning points within each section. They also act as a quick summary for review.

 There are three main sources for variation in a population:
- **mutations in DNA**
- **meiosis**
- **sexual reproduction.**

Whenever a definition is given for a major concept in biology, in this instance the term 'gene', be sure to memorize its definition word for word. Such definitions have been phrased carefully so that all the important details are included.

  Hints for success

These give hints on how to approach questions, and suggest approaches that examiners like to see. They also identify common pitfalls in understanding, and omissions made in answering questions.

Challenge yourself

These boxes contain open questions that encourage you to think about the topic in more depth, or to make detailed connections with other topics. They are designed to be challenging and to make you think.

CHALLENGE YOURSELF

8 Use the symbols mentioned above to represent all the possible nucleotides of DNA.

eBook

In the eBook you will find the following:

- Animations
- Videos
- Interactive glossary of scientific words used in the course
- Internal assessment advice
- Answers to all exercises in the book
- Worksheets
- Interactive quizzes

For more details about your eBook, see the following section.

Questions

There are three types of question in this book.

1 Worked example with Solution

These appear at intervals in the text and are used to illustrate the concepts covered.

They are followed by the solution, which shows the thinking and the steps used in solving the problem.

Worked example

You are walking outside with a friend who is wearing a red and white shirt. Explain why the shirt appears to be red and white.

Solution

Sunlight is a mixture of all of the wavelengths (colours) of visible light. When sunlight strikes the red pigments in the shirt, the blue and the green wavelengths of light are absorbed, but the red wavelengths are reflected. Thus, our eyes see red. When sunlight strikes the white areas of the shirt, all the wavelengths of light are reflected and our eyes and brain interpret the mixture as white.

2 Exercises

These questions are found throughout the text. They allow you to apply your knowledge and test your understanding of what you have just been reading.

The answers to these are given in the eBook at the end of each chapter.

Exercises

25 Explain why a blue object appears to be blue to the human eye.

26 Explain why black surfaces (like tarmacadam and asphalt) get much hotter in sunlight than lighter surfaces (like stone and concrete).

27 Plants produce sugars by photosynthesis. What do plants do with the sugars after that?

28 Why do most plants produce an excess of sugars in some months of the year?

3 Practice questions

These questions are found at the end of each chapter. They are mostly taken from previous years' IB examination papers. The markschemes used by examiners when marking these questions are given in the eBook, at the end of each chapter.

Practice questions

1   Draw the basic structure of an amino acid, and label the groups that are used in peptide bond formation.

(Total 4 marks)

Answers

Full answers to all exercises and practice questions can be found in the eBook.

 Hotlink boxes can be found at the end of each chapter, indicating that there are weblinks available for further study. To access these links go to www.pearsonhotlinks.com and enter the ISBN or title of this book. Here you can find links to animations, simulations, movie clips and related background material, which can help to deepen your interest and understanding of the topic.

We truly hope that this book and the accompanying online resources help you enjoy this fascinating subject of IB Standard Level biology. We wish you success in your studies.

Alan Damon, Randy McGonegal, Pat Tosto, Bill Ward

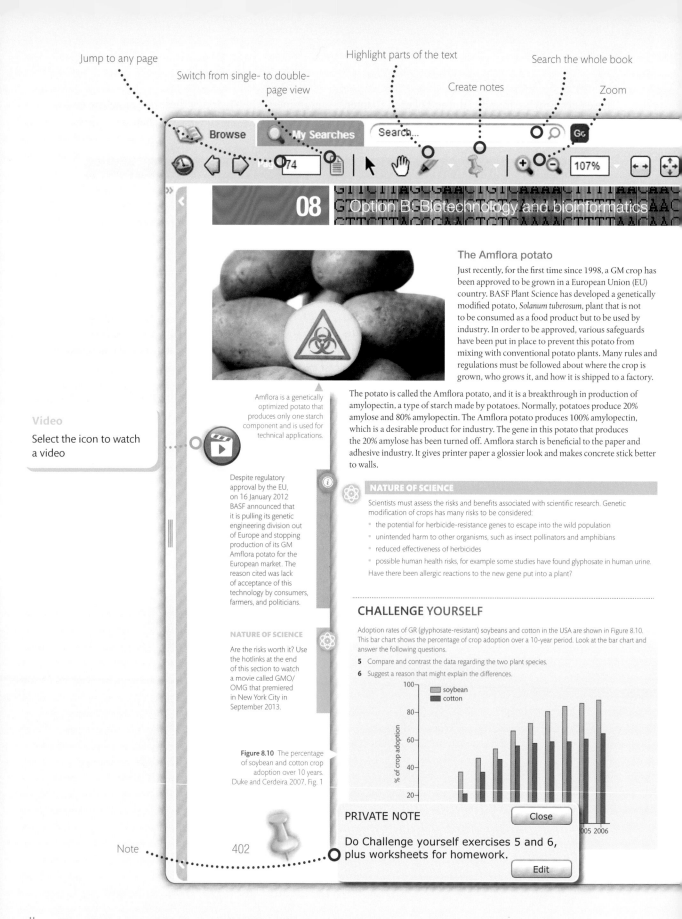

Jump to any page

Switch from single- to double-page view

Highlight parts of the text

Create notes

Search the whole book

Zoom

Browse   My Searches   Search...

Page 74   107%

08 Option B: Biotechnology and bioinformatics

The Amflora potato

Just recently, for the first time since 1998, a GM crop has been approved to be grown in a European Union (EU) country. BASF Plant Science has developed a genetically modified potato, *Solanum tuberosum*, plant that is not to be consumed as a food product but to be used by industry. In order to be approved, various safeguards have been put in place to prevent this potato from mixing with conventional potato plants. Many rules and regulations must be followed about where the crop is grown, who grows it, and how it is shipped to a factory.

The potato is called the Amflora potato, and it is a breakthrough in production of amylopectin, a type of starch made by potatoes. Normally, potatoes produce 20% amylose and 80% amylopectin. The Amflora potato produces 100% amylopectin, which is a desirable product for industry. The gene in this potato that produces the 20% amylose has been turned off. Amflora starch is beneficial to the paper and adhesive industry. It gives printer paper a glossier look and makes concrete stick better to walls.

Amflora is a genetically optimized potato that produces only one starch component and is used for technical applications.

Video
Select the icon to watch a video

Despite regulatory approval by the EU, on 16 January 2012 BASF announced that it is pulling its genetic engineering division out of Europe and stopping production of its GM Amflora potato for the European market. The reason cited was lack of acceptance of this technology by consumers, farmers, and politicians.

NATURE OF SCIENCE

Scientists must assess the risks and benefits associated with scientific research. Genetic modification of crops has many risks to be considered:

- the potential for herbicide-resistance genes to escape into the wild population
- unintended harm to other organisms, such as insect pollinators and amphibians
- reduced effectiveness of herbicides
- possible human health risks, for example some studies have found glyphosate in human urine.

Have there been allergic reactions to the new gene put into a plant?

NATURE OF SCIENCE

Are the risks worth it? Use the hotlinks at the end of this section to watch a movie called GMO/OMG that premiered in New York City in September 2013.

CHALLENGE YOURSELF

Adoption rates of GR (glyphosate-resistant) soybeans and cotton in the USA are shown in Figure 8.10. This bar chart shows the percentage of crop adoption over a 10-year period. Look at the bar chart and answer the following questions.

5 Compare and contrast the data regarding the two plant species.
6 Suggest a reason that might explain the differences.

Figure 8.10 The percentage of soybean and cotton crop adoption over 10 years. Duke and Cerdeira 2007, Fig. 1

soybean
cotton

% of crop adoption

100 — 80 — 60 — 40 — 20 —

2005 2006

PRIVATE NOTE   Close

Do Challenge yourself exercises 5 and 6, plus worksheets for homework.   Edit

Note

402

See the definitions of key terms in the glossary

reate a bookmark

Switch to whiteboard view

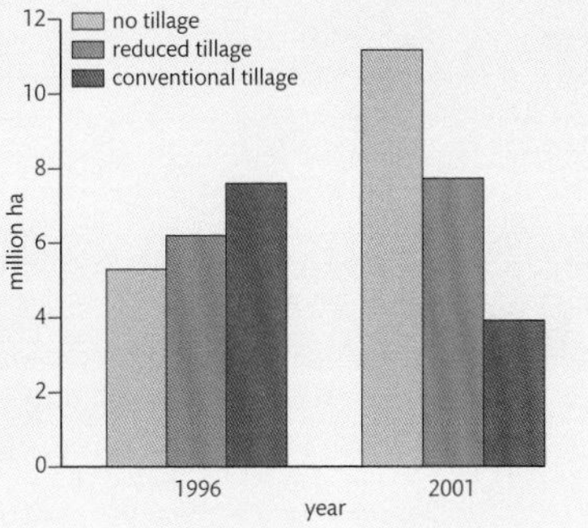

CTTGGCTCCAGCATCGATGAAGAACGCAGCG

Animation

Select the icon to see a related animation

Figure 8.11 Soybean tillage methods by hectares farmed in the USA in 1996 and 2001. Duke and Cerdeira 2007, Fig. 2

Worksheets

Select the icon to view a worksheet with further activities

Topsoil loss caused by tillage (the preparation of soil by mechanical agitation, such as digging, stirring, and overturning) is the most destructive effect of crops planted in rows. Tillage contributes to soil erosion by water and wind, soil moisture loss, and air pollution from dust. Glyphosate-resistant plants reduce tillage. Reduction in tillage improves soil structure, and results in reduced run-off and less pollution of rivers and streams.

Look at Figure 8.11 and answer the following questions.

7 Compare and contrast tillage results from 1996 and 2001.

8 Suggest a reason for these numbers.

9 Explain the environmental impact of these numbers.

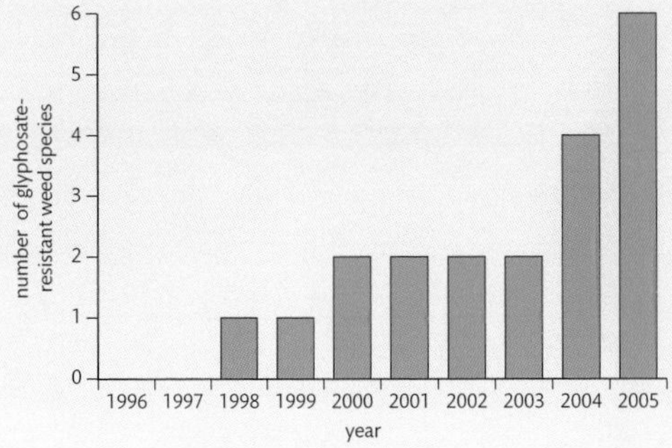

Quiz

Select the icon to take an interactive quiz to test your knowledge

Figure 8.12 Glyphosate-resistant weed species in the USA.

Based on data from 'Facts About Glyphosate-Resistant Weeds', Purdue Extension, www.ces.purdue.edu/extmedia/GWC/GWC-1.pdf.

10 Describe the resistance seen in weed species in the USA to glyphosate.

11 Using the knowledge you have gained about how organisms change over time, describe how this may have occurred.

12 Compare and contrast resistance of weed species from 1996 to 2005.

13 Do some research and find one solution that scientists might suggest in solving this problem. Give one answer, although there may be many.

Answers

Select the icon at the end of the chapter to view answers to exercises in this chapter

! The word 'compare' in a question means you need to write down the similarities and contrast the differences between two or more things.

TOK Discuss the view of Karl Popper that, for science to progress, scientists must question and criticize the current state of scientific knowledge.

403

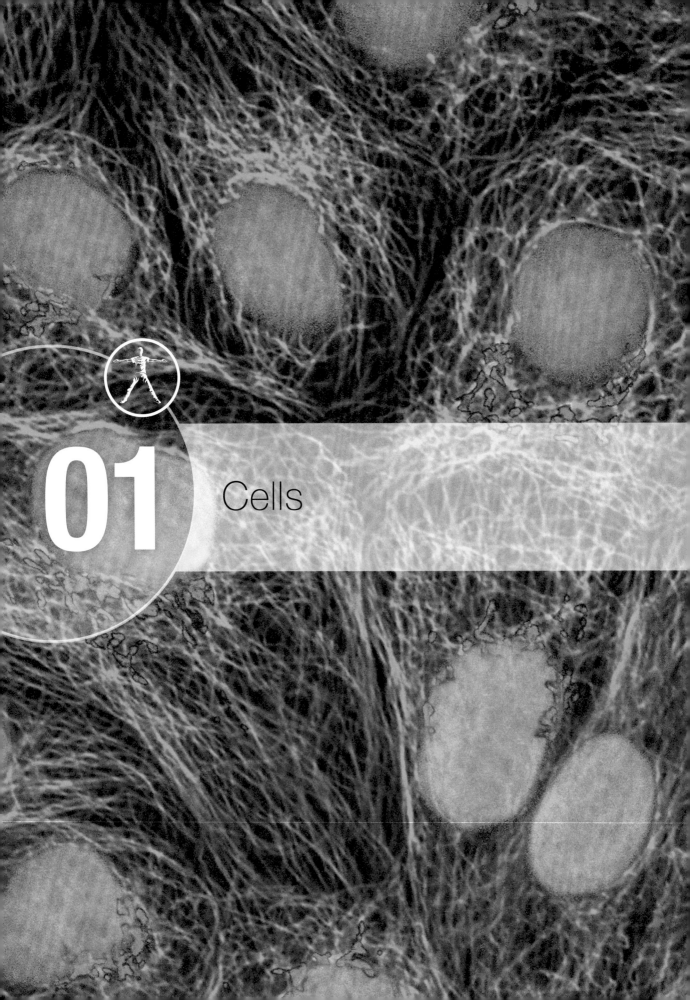

01 Cells

Essential ideas

1.1 The evolution of multicellular organisms allowed cell specialization and cell replacement.

1.2 Eukaryotes have a much more complex cell structure than prokaryotes.

1.3 The structure of biological membranes makes them fluid and dynamic.

1.4 Membranes control the composition of cells by active and passive transport.

1.5 There is an unbroken chain of life from the first cells on Earth to all cells in organisms alive today.

1.6 Cell division is essential but must be controlled.

HeLa cells were the first cells to be successfully cultured on a large scale and have been used extensively in biological research, including the development of the first polio vaccine.

Cytology is the study of all aspects of a cell. As our understanding of the cell has increased, so has our ability to understand all forms of life, including diseases, that occur on Earth. However, there is still much work to be done in order to solve all the mysteries of the cell. Biological research laboratories all over the world are very active in this area.

Whether organisms are extremely small or extremely large, it is vital we understand their smallest functional units. These units are known as cells. Organisms range in size from a single cell to trillions of cells. To understand better all the organisms around us we must study their cells.

In this chapter, we will begin with a look at cell theory. After cell theory we will learn about the differences between prokaryotic and eukaryotic cells. A detailed explanation of cell parts and their functions will then follow. As much attention today is given to cancer, which seems to occur in most organisms and involves abnormal cell reproduction, we will focus on normal cell reproduction. Some time will also be spent on understanding how the most complex cells may have come into existence on our planet.

Look at the picture on the right. Human nerve cells (neurones) are essential to our lives. Because of these cells, we are able to acknowledge and respond to our surroundings. Neurones are usually very efficient but sometimes things go wrong. Can we gain a greater understanding and better treatment of conditions such as depression by learning more about how these cells function?

This is an artist's impression of human nerve cells.
▼

3

1.1 Cell theory, cell specialization, and cell replacement

Understandings:

- According to the cell theory, living organisms are composed of cells.
- Organisms consisting of only one cell carry out all functions of life in that cell.
- Surface area to volume ratio is important in the limitation of cell size.
- Multicellular organisms have properties that emerge from the interaction of their cellular components.
- Specialized tissues can develop by cell differentiation in multicellular organisms.
- Differentiation involves the expression of some genes and not others in a cell's genome.
- The capacity of stem cells to divide and differentiate along different pathways is necessary in embryonic development and also makes stem cells suitable for therapeutic uses.

Applications and skills:

- Application: Questioning the cell theory using atypical examples, including striated muscle, giant algae, and aseptate fungal hyphae.
- Application: Investigation of functions of life in *Paramecium* and one named photosynthetic unicellular organism.
- Application: Use of stem cells to treat Stargardt's disease and one other named condition.
- Application: Ethics of the therapeutic use of stem cells from specially created embryos, from the umbilical cord blood of a newborn baby and from an adult's own tissues.
- Skill: Use of a light microscope to investigate the structure of cells and tissues, with drawing of cells. Calculation of the magnification of drawings and the actual size of structures and ultrastructures shown in drawings or micrographs.

Guidance

- Students are expected to be able to name and briefly explain these functions of life: nutrition, metabolism, growth, response, excretion, homeostasis, and reproduction.
- Chlorella or Scenedesmus are suitable photosynthetic unicells, but Euglena should be avoided as it can feed heterotrophically.
- Scale bars are useful as a way of indicating actual sizes in drawings and micrographs.

Cell theory

It has taken several hundred years of research to formulate the cell theory that is used today. Many scientists have contributed to developing the three main principles of this theory. These three principles are:

1 all organisms are composed of one or more cells
2 cells are the smallest units of life
3 all cells come from pre-existing cells.

Cell theory has a very solid foundation largely because of the use of the microscope. Robert Hooke first described cells in 1665 after looking at cork with a self-built microscope. A few years later Antonie van Leeuwenhoek observed the first living cells and referred to them as 'animalcules', meaning little animals. In 1838, the botanist Matthias Schleiden stated that plants are made of 'independent, separate beings' called cells. One year later, Theodor Schwann made a similar statement about animals.

The second principle continues to gain support today, because so far no one has been able to find any living entity that is not made of at least one cell.

Some very famous scientists, such as Louis Pasteur in the 1880s, have performed experiments to support the third principle. After sterilizing chicken broth (soup) by boiling it, Pasteur showed that living organisms would not 'spontaneously' reappear. Only after exposure to pre-existing cells was life able to re-establish itself in the sterilized chicken broth.

NATURE OF SCIENCE

As with most scientific theories, cell theory is not without areas of concern and problems. A key characteristic of a good scientist is a sceptical attitude towards theoretical claims. To overcome or validate this scepticism, evidence obtained by observation or experimentation is essential. Whenever possible in science, controlled experiments are needed to verify or refute theories. These experiments have a control group and a variable group(s). The groups are kept under similar conditions apart from the factor that is being tested or questioned. The factor being tested is referred to as the independent variable. The dependent factor is measured or described using quantitative or qualitative data. Relatively recent findings that have raised questions about cell theory include observations of striated muscle, giant algae, and aseptate fungal hyphae.

As this chapter develops and more information about the basic characteristics of cells is learned, some recent findings will be discussed.

Functions of life

All organisms exist in either a unicellular or a multicellular form. Interestingly, all organisms, whether unicellular or multicellular, carry out all the functions of life. These functions include:

- metabolism
- growth
- reproduction
- response
- homeostasis
- nutrition
- excretion.

All of these functions act together to produce a viable living unit. Metabolism includes all the chemical reactions that occur within an organism. Cells have the ability to convert energy from one form into another. Growth may be limited but is always evident in one way or another. Reproduction involves hereditary molecules that can be passed to offspring. Responses to stimuli in the environment are imperative for the survival of an organism. These responses allow an organism to adapt to its environment. Homeostasis refers to the maintenance of a constant internal environment. For example, an organism may have to control fluctuating temperature and acid–base levels to create a constant internal environment. Providing a source of compounds with many chemical bonds that can then be broken down to provide an organism with the energy necessary to maintain life is the basis of nutrition. Excretion is essential to life because it enables those chemical compounds that an organism cannot use or that may be toxic or harmful to it to be released from the organism's system.

Two organisms can be used to demonstrate the functions of life: *Paramecium* and *Chlorella*.

Paramecium is a unicellular member of the kingdom known as the Protista. Study the diagram of a *Paramecium* to become familiar with this organism's basic structure.

TOK Theories are developed after the accumulation of a great deal of data via observation and/ or experimentation. Sometimes theories will be abandoned completely because of conflicting evidence.

The functions of life manifest in different ways in different types of organisms. However, all organisms maintain the same general functions that allow them to continue life. You may see different terms for these functions in other sources.

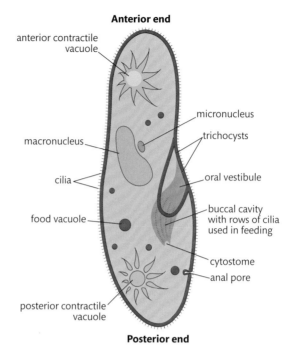

Anterior end

anterior contractile vacuole

micronucleus

macronucleus

trichocysts

cilia

oral vestibule

food vacuole

buccal cavity with rows of cilia used in feeding

cytostome

anal pore

posterior contractile vacuole

Posterior end

CHALLENGE YOURSELF

Answer the following questions about the observations you made in the labs.

1 With the paramecia, the microorganisms should have clustered around the negative pole. Which of the processes of life is demonstrated by this action?

2 You should have seen that when food was added to a culture of paramecia they clustered around the food particles. Which of the functions of life does this represent?

3 After these organisms had used the food particles, what life function would they carry out to get rid of potentially toxic wastes?

4 Two of the structures shown in the diagram of a *Paramecium* (Figure 1.1) are involved in excretion or internal water concentration regulation. They are the anal pore and the contractile vacuole. Conduct some research into the role each of these structures plays in excretion.

Paramecium and the functions of life

Safety alerts: Be cautious of sharp objects. Only use a 9-volt battery as an electric source. Make sure your instructor checks your set-up before you begin. Wash your hands thoroughly with soap and water before and after the procedure.

Paramecium can be used to demonstrate the functions of life in several ways.

1 Place a number of paramecia into a Syracuse dish or an evaporating dish with positive and negative electrodes of low-voltage electrical charge on opposite sides. A simple 9-volt battery will usually trigger a response. Do not use electricity of a higher voltage, otherwise the organism will be harmed. Low-voltage electricity can be applied for several minutes. The dish should be placed on the stage of a dissecting microscope. A strong magnifying lens may also be used. Describe the movement and final location of the largest population of paramecia.

2 Once this activity has ended, remove the electrodes and add several small, but visible, pieces of hard-boiled egg yolk. Again, using the magnifying instrument make observations of the movement and final location of the paramecia.

3 Finally, to a culture of paramecia add a drop of very dilute acetic acid (vinegar). Once again, report on the movement and final location of the paramecia.

4 When you have finished these tests, your teacher will explain what should be done with the organisms. Respect for life is very important in our studies. The IB policy on animal experimentation must be followed at all times.

5 Using what you know about the functions of life, explain why the paramecia moved in the ways you observed.

The next organism we will look at is *Chlorella*. Compared with *Paramecium*, *Chlorella* has a completely different approach to nutrition. *Chlorella* is a single-celled organism that has one very large structure called a chloroplast inside a cell wall. This structure enables the conversion of the energy in sunlight to a chemical energy form called carbohydrate. This carbohydrate provides the major nutritional source for the organism. Study the diagram of a *Chlorella*.

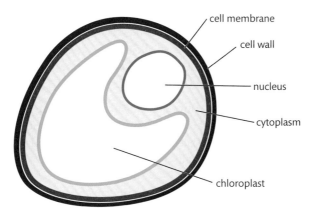

cell membrane

cell wall

nucleus

cytoplasm

chloroplast

Figure 1.2 *Chlorella*. A common freshwater organism. This organism has been used by many researchers to determine the details of, and the factors that affect, a process known as photosynthesis. The structures labelled chloroplasts are especially important in this process.

Chlorella and the functions of life

Safety alerts: Be cautious of sharp objects. Follow classroom rules for use of microscope. Wash your hands thoroughly with soap and water before and after the procedure.

Many classroom practical activities can be carried out with cultures of *Chlorella*. Carry out the following activity.

1 Obtain two depression microscope slides, and place the same number of *Chlorella* organisms in a proper culture medium in each well.

2 Seal a cover slip on each slide with a ring of petroleum jelly.

3 To reduce evaporation further, place each slide in a Petri dish.

4 Place one Petri dish with its slide in sunlight.

5 Place the other Petri dish in complete darkness.

6 Using a microscope, check the numbers of *Chlorella* on each slide for 3 days.

7 Use the functions of life to explain the results observed.

8 An advanced activity can be carried out. Using a culture of *Chlorella*, design an experiment that would allow you to see what colour (wavelength) of light this organism prefers.

Correlation and cause are extremely important in scientific research. A correlation means there is a statistical link relating one variable or factor with another. In the case of a causal relationship, one factor causes another; there must be a scientific process or mechanism connecting the factors with one another.

NATURE OF SCIENCE

Perhaps in the design of the *Chlorella* activity you had an idea based on your previous experiences in science about what the outcome of your procedure would be. This idea is referred to as a hypothesis. Scientists form hypotheses that can be tested by observation and/ or experimentation. These tested hypotheses may ultimately serve to simplify and unify existing scientific ideas.

Controlled experiments are the best way to investigate the relationship between two factors or variables. However, this type of experiment is not always possible. In this case, statistical analysis of the data may indicate a correlation. As time and research proceeds, a causal relationship may be seen. Objective data, both qualitative and quantitative, are used to establish relationships whenever possible. It is essential that repeated measurements are taken and that large numbers of readings are taken so that the data collection is reliable. Scientists spend a lot of time working with people from other disciplines in order to gain a greater understanding of their findings. They also read current scientific articles throughout their career in order to gain further insight into their research. Eventually, a researcher may decide to publish his or her findings in an appropriate scientific journal. For this to happen, an article undergoes a peer-review process, which means several scientists working in the same field read the article before it is published to make sure the methodologies and findings are sound and honest.

Cells and sizes

Cells are made up of a number of different subunits. These subunits are often of a particular size, but all are microscopically small. In most cases the use of microscopes with a high magnification and resolution are needed to observe cells and especially their subunits. Resolution refers to the clarity of a viewed object.

Light microscopes use light, passing through living or dead specimens, to form an image. Stains may be used to make it easier to see any details. Electron microscopes use electrons passing through a dead specimen to form an image and provide us with the greatest magnifications (over 100 000×) and resolution.

Table 1.1 A comparison of light and electron microscopes

Light microscope	Electron microscope
Inexpensive to purchase and operate	Expensive to purchase and operate
Simple and easy specimen preparation	Complex and lengthy specimen preparation
Magnifies up to 2000×	Magnifies over 500 000×
Specimens may be living or dead	Specimens are dead, and must be fixed in a plastic material

Most cells can be up to 100 micrometres (μm) in size. Organelles can be up to 10 μm in size. Bacteria can be up to 1 μm in size. Viruses can be up to 100 nanometres (nm) in size. Cell membranes are 10 nm thick, while molecules are about 1 nm in size. All of these objects are three-dimensional.

Scientists use the International System of Units (SI) for measurements. This system is based on powers of 10 and utilizes bases and prefixes. When describing cell size, the base utilized is the metre. Commonly used prefixes for cell size are:

- 1 centimetre (cm) = 1/100 (10^{-2}) metre
- 1 millimetre (mm) = 1/1000 (10^{-3}) metre
- 1 micrometre (μm) = 1/1 000 000 (10^{-6}) metre
- 1 nanometre (nm) = 1/1 000 000 000 (10^{-9}) metre
- 1 metre = 10^2 cm = 10^3 mm = 10^6 μm = 10^9 nm

Cells and their subunits are so small they are hard to visualize, so it is important to appreciate their relative sizes. Cells are relatively large, and then in decreasing order of size are:

$$\text{organelles} \rightarrow \text{bacteria} \rightarrow \text{viruses} \rightarrow \text{membranes} \rightarrow \text{molecules}$$

If you want to calculate the actual size of a specimen seen with a microscope, you need to know the diameter of the microscope's field of vision. This can be calculated with a special micrometre, or on a light microscope with a simple ruler. The size of the specimen can then be worked out. Drawings or photographs of specimens are often enlarged. To calculate the magnification of a drawing or photograph, a simple formula is used:

$$\text{magnification} = \text{size of image/by size of specimen.}$$

Scale bars are often used with a micrograph or drawing so that the actual size can be determined. Scale bars and magnification will be addressed in more detail in a later practical activity.

Worked example

Most compound light microscopes have a field of vision at a low power of about 1.4 mm. If you are looking at a eukaryotic cell that has a diameter of close to 60% of the field of vision at low power, what would be the diameter of the cell in micrometres?

Solution

As the field of vision is 1.4 mm or 1400 µm, multiply 1400 µm by 0.60:

$$1400 \times 0.60 = 840 \text{ µm}$$

Worked example

The length of an image you are looking at is 50 mm. If the actual length of the subject of the image is 5 µm, what is the magnification of the image you are looking at?

Solution

magnification = 50 mm/5 µm = 50 000 µm/5 µm = 10 000×

Or: magnification = 50 mm/5 µm = 50×10^{-3} m divided by 1×10^{-6} m = 10 000×

Limiting cell size

So, the cell is a small object. You may wonder why cells do not grow to larger sizes, especially as growth is one of the functions of life. There is a principle called the surface area to volume ratio that effectively limits the size of cells. In a cell, the rate of heat and waste production, and rate of resource consumption, are functions of (depend on) its volume. Most of the chemical reactions of life occur inside a cell, and the size of the cell affects the rate of those reactions. The surface of the cell, the membrane, controls what materials move in and out of the cell. A cell with more surface area per unit volume is able to move more materials in and out of the cell, for each unit volume of the cell.

As the width of an object such as a cell increases, the surface area also increases, but at a much slower rate than the volume. This is shown in the following table: the volume increases by a factor calculated by cubing the radius; at the same time, the surface area increases by a factor calculated by squaring the radius.

Sphere formulas:
Surface area = (four)(pi)(radius squared)
Volume = (four-thirds)(pi)(radius cubed)

Table 1.2 Surface area to volume ratios

Factor	Measurement		
Cell radius (r)	0.25	0.50	1.25
Surface area	0.79	3.14	19.63
Volume	0.07	0.52	8.18
Surface area : volume ratio	11.29 : 1	6.04 : 1	2.40 : 1

This means that a large cell, compared with a small cell, has relatively less surface area to bring in materials that are needed and to get rid of waste. Because of this, cells are limited in the size they can reach and still be able to carry out the functions of life. Thus large animals do not have larger cells; instead they have more cells.

Cells that are larger in size have modifications that allow them to function efficiently. This is accomplished with changes in shape, such as being long and thin rather than spherical. Some larger cells also have infoldings or outfoldings to increase their surface area relative to their volume.

Cell reproduction and differentiation

One of the functions that many cells have is the ability to reproduce themselves. In multicellular organisms this allows growth to happen. It also means damaged or dead cells can be replaced.

This is a computer artwork of an egg cell fertilized during in vitro fertilization and now undergoing the first cell division.

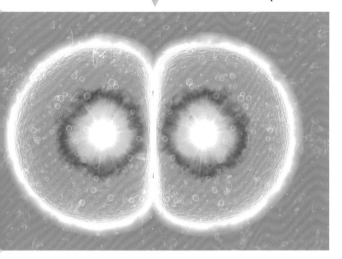

Multicellular organisms usually start their existence as a single cell after some type of sexual reproduction. This single cell has the ability to reproduce at a very rapid rate, and the resulting cells then go through a differentiation process to produce all the required cell types that are necessary for the well-being of the organism. The number of different cell types that can arise from the one original cell can be staggering. This differentiation process is the result of the expression of certain specific genes but not others. Genes, segments of DNA on a chromosome, enable the production of all the different cells in an organism. Therefore, each cell contains all the genetic information needed for the production of the complete organism. However, each cell will become a specific type of cell depending on which DNA segment becomes active.

Cancer cells are examples of cells that undergo extremely rapid reproduction with very little or improper differentiation. The result is a mass of cells (a tumour) with no useful function to the organism.

Some cells have a greatly reduced ability to reproduce once they become specialized, or lose the ability altogether. Nerve and muscle cells are good examples of this type of cell. Other cells, including epithelial cells such as skin, retain the ability to reproduce rapidly throughout their life. The offspring of these rapidly reproducing cells will then differentiate into the same cell type as the parent.

One of the results of cell reproduction and the subsequent differentiation process that occurs in multicellular organisms is emergent properties. These properties depend on the interactions between all the different parts of a particular biological unit, such as the cell. When you look at the function(s) of each part of a cell, it is less than the overall function of the complete cell. In other words, the whole is more than the sum of its parts. To continue with this emergent concept, a whole multicellular organism is capable of carrying out more functions than the sum of the function(s) each cell is specialized in. The ultimate example of emergence is a collection of inert (non-living) molecules that is capable, when functioning together, of creating a living entity that demonstrates the functions of life.

TOK

When discussing the overall functions of a cell, you should focus on the distinctions between living and non-living factors in the environment. It is very useful and productive to refer to the functions of life in such a discussion.

Stem cells

There are populations of cells within organisms that retain their ability to divide and differentiate into various cell types. These cells are called stem cells.

Plants contain such cells in regions of meristematic tissue. Meristematic tissues occur near root and stem tips and are composed of rapidly reproducing cells that produce new cells capable of becoming various types of tissue within that root or stem. Gardeners take advantage of these cells when they take cuttings from stems or roots and use them to propagate new plants.

In the early 1980s, scientists found pluripotent or embryonic stem cells in mice. These stem cells retain the ability to form any type of cell in an organism and can even form a complete organism.

When stem cells divide to form a specific type of tissue, they also produce some daughter cells that stay as stem cells. This enables the continual production of a particular type of tissue. Medical scientists saw the possibilities of using such cells to treat certain human diseases. However, one problem discovered early on in stem cell research was that stem cells cannot be distinguished by their appearance. They can only be isolated from other cells on the basis of their behaviour.

Stem cell research and treatments

Recently some very promising research has been directed towards growing large numbers of embryonic stem cells in culture so that they can be used to replace differentiated cells lost as a result of injury and disease. This involves therapeutic cloning. Parkinson's and Alzheimer's diseases are caused by the loss of proper functioning brain cells, and it is hoped that implanted stem cells could replace many of these lost or defective brain cells, thus relieving the symptoms of the disease. With some forms of diabetes, the pancreas is depleted of essential cells and it is hoped that a stem cell implant in this organ could have positive effects. As at present most of the research on stem cells is being carried out using mice, it will probably be some time before this approach to treatment becomes widespread in humans.

However, there is a type of stem cell treatment that has been used successfully in humans for many years. As well as pluripotent stem cells, there are tissue-specific stem cells. These stem cells reside in certain tissue types and can only produce new cells of that particular tissue. For example, blood stem cells have been introduced routinely into humans to replace the damaged bone marrow of some leukaemia patients.

Stargardt's disease is an example of a human condition that is in the early stages of being treated with stem cells. Stargardt's disease is an inherited disease caused by both parents passing on a gene to their offspring that codes for a defect in the processing of vitamin A. Vitamin A is essential for the light-sensitive cells in the retina to function properly. With Stargardt's disease, within the first 20 years of a patient's life he or she begins to lose his or her central vision. Later on, peripheral vision loss occurs, which eventually leads to blindness.

In March 2010, a stem cell treatment was begun that was designed to protect and regenerate photoreceptors in the retina that are damaged by Stargardt's disease. Currently the particular stem cells being used for this treatment in humans are human embryonic stem cells. The study is ongoing, but the early results are promising.

There are ethical issues involved in stem cell research. The use of pluripotent stem cells is particularly controversial. These cells are obtained from embryos, largely from laboratories carrying out *in vitro* fertilization (IVF). Harvesting these cells involves the death of an embryo, and some people argue that this is taking a human life. Others argue that this research could result in a significant reduction in human suffering, and is, therefore, totally acceptable.

In 2005, stem cells were used successfully to help restore the lost insulation of nerve cells in rats, thus resulting in greater mobility in these animals.

Stem cells are being utilized in a number of ways by scientists around the world. One area of research involves using human embryonic stem cells in order to understand human development better. This research involves studies of cell division and differentiation. Other scientists are using stem cells to test the safety and effects of new drugs. Information in this area is essential to the understanding of how these drugs might affect differentiating cells in existing organisms. Another very interesting area of study involves cell-based therapies, especially as they may have a positive influence on the treatment of diseases and traumas such as Alzheimer's disease, spinal cord injuries, heart disease, diabetes, burns, and strokes.

There has been much sharing of data involving stem cell research. However, many nations have banned or restricted research in this area because of local cultural and religious traditions.

 TOK How the scientific community conveys information concerning its research to the wider society is very important. The information must be accurate, complete, and understandable, so that society can make informed decisions regarding the appropriateness of the research. There is a need to balance the very great opportunities of this type of research with the potential risks. Recently, there has been evidence that some types of cancer may be caused by stem cells undergoing a cancer-like or malignant transformation. Where do you stand in the debate about the nature of stem cell research? How do you feel about the source of pluripotent stem cells?

Exercises

1 How is the excretion of metabolic wastes from cells related to the concept of the surface area to volume ratio?

2 Explain how the function of life known as nutrition differs in *Paramecium* compared with the green alga *Chlorella*.

3 How does specialization in muscle and nerve cells affect their ability to reproduce?

4 What would prevent stem cells from other species being successful in humans?

NATURE OF SCIENCE

Developments in scientific research follow improvements in apparatus: the invention of electron microscopes led to greater understanding of cell structure.

1.2 The ultrastructure of cells

Understandings:

- Prokaryotes have a simple cell structure without compartmentalization.
- Eukaryotes have a compartmentalized cell structure.
- Electron microscopes have a much higher magnification than light microscopes.

Applications and skills:

- Application: Structure and function of organelles within exocrine gland cells of the pancreas and within palisade mesophyll cells of the leaf.
- Application: Prokaryotes divide by binary fission.
- Skill: Drawing of the ultrastructure of prokaryotic cells based on electron micrographs.
- Skill: Drawing of the ultrastructure of eukaryotic cells based on electron micrographs.
- Skill: Interpretation of electron micrographs to identify organelles and deduce the function of specialized cells.

Guidance

- *Drawings of prokaryotic cells should show the cell wall, pili, and flagella, and plasma membrane enclosing cytoplasm that contains 70S ribosomes and a nucleoid with naked DNA.*
- *Drawings of eukaryotic cells should show a plasma membrane enclosing cytoplasm that contains 80S ribosomes and a nucleus, mitochondria and other membrane-bound organelles are present in the cytoplasm. Some eukaryotic cells have a cell wall.*

Becoming familiar with common prefixes, suffixes, and word roots will help you understand biological terms. For example, the word prokaryotic comes from the Greek words 'pro', which means before, and 'karyon', which means kernel, referring to the nucleus.

What is a prokaryotic cell?

After extensive studies of cells, it has become apparent that all cells use some common molecular mechanisms. There are huge differences between different forms of life but cells are the basic unit and different cells have many characteristics in common. Cells are often divided into particular groups based on major characteristics. One such division separates cells into two groups: prokaryotic and eukaryotic cells. Prokaryotic cells are much smaller and simpler than eukaryotic cells. In fact, most prokaryotic cells are less than 1 μm in diameter. Because of this, and many other reasons that will be discussed later, the prokaryotic cells are thought to have appeared on Earth first. As bacteria are prokaryotic cells, you can see that such cells play a large role in the world today.

Bacteria and members of a group referred to as Archaea are made up of prokaryotic cells and are called prokaryotes. The vast majority of these organisms do not cause disease and are not pathogenic (disease-causing).

Features of prokaryotic cells

Study the figure of a prokaryotic cell (Figure 1.3) and make sure you can identify:

- the cell wall
- the plasma membrane
- flagella
- pili
- ribosomes
- the nucleoid (a region containing free DNA).

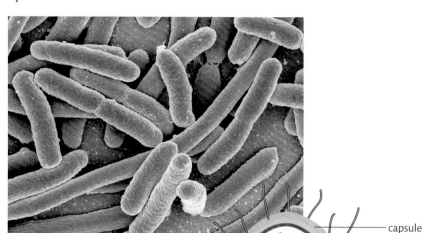

Figure 1.3 This is a false-colour scanning electron micrograph (SEM) of the bacterium *Escherichia coli*. Below is a drawing of a prokaryotic cell.

The cell wall and plasma membrane

The prokaryotic cell wall protects and maintains the shape of the cell. In most prokaryotic cells this wall is composed of a carbohydrate–protein complex called peptidoglycan. Some bacteria have an additional layer of a type of polysaccharide outside the cell wall. This layer makes it possible for some bacteria to adhere to structures such as teeth, skin, and food.

The plasma membrane is found just inside the cell wall and is similar in composition to the membranes of eukaryotic cells. To a large extent the plasma membrane controls the movement of materials into and out of the cell, and it plays a role in binary fission of the prokaryotic cell. The cytoplasm occupies the complete interior of the cell. The most visible structure with a microscope capable of high magnification is the chromosome or a molecule of DNA. There is no compartmentalization within the cytoplasm because there are no internal membranes other than the plasma membrane. Therefore, all cellular processes within prokaryotic cells occur within the cytoplasm.

If there is no compartmentalization within prokaryotic cells, chemical reactions are not isolated from one another. This may limit the cell's development and efficiency because of possible interference between the reactions.

The importance of plasmids in prokaryotic cells will be discussed fully in Chapter 3. Plasmids have very important roles to play in some techniques involving genetic engineering/modification.

Some types of bacteria go through binary fission every 20 minutes when conditions are ideal. This results in huge populations and greater potential for infections. Refrigeration of foods is often used to reduce ideal conditions for bacteria. This results in lower bacterial counts in our food and less chance of infection/food poisoning.

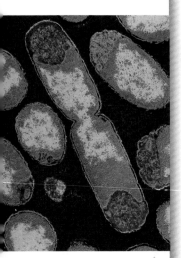

This is a false-colour transmission electron micrograph (TEM) showing *Escherichia coli* dividing by binary fission.

Pili and flagella

Some bacterial cells contain hair-like growths on the outside of the cell wall. These structures are called pili and can be used for attachment. However, their main function is joining bacterial cells in preparation for the transfer of DNA from one cell to another (sexual reproduction).

Some bacteria have flagella (plural) or a flagellum (singular), which are longer than pili. Flagella allow a cell to move.

Ribosomes

Ribosomes occur in all prokaryotic cells and they function as sites of protein synthesis. These small structures occur in very large numbers in cells that produce a lot of protein, and, when numerous, they give a granular appearance to an electron micrograph of a prokaryotic cell.

The nucleoid region

The nucleoid region of a bacterial cell is non-compartmentalized and contains a single, long, continuous, circular thread of DNA, the bacterial chromosome. Therefore this region is involved with cell control and reproduction. In addition to the bacterial chromosome, bacteria may also contain plasmids. These small, circular, DNA molecules are not connected to the main bacterial chromosome. The plasmids replicate independently of the chromosomal DNA. Plasmid DNA is not required by the cell under normal conditions but it may help the cell adapt to unusual circumstances.

Binary fission

Prokaryotic cells divide by a very simple process called binary fission. During this process, the DNA is copied, the two daughter chromosomes become attached to different regions on the plasma membrane, and the cell divides into two genetically identical daughter cells. This divisional process includes an elongation of the cell and a partitioning of the newly produced DNA by microtubule-like fibres called FtsZ.

Very often in IB, laboratory tests and examinations will require you to draw an object or organism. Follow the guidelines given below when completing any drawing.
- The size should be appropriate for the complexity of the drawing.
- Correct positioning of structures is essential.
- The outline of structures should be continuous unless gaps or pores are present in the actual border or structure.
- Proportions are important.
- The relative numbers of parts are important.
- Draw in pencil first so that mistakes can be corrected. Write on or label the final drawing in black ink.
- Labelling must be included on all drawings unless the question tells you not to.
- Lines from labels to parts on a drawing should be straight and should never cross.
- In IB exams, boxes are provided for drawings. Do not draw or write outside the box as this area will not be scanned or marked.

Summary

Here is a list of the major distinguishing characteristics of prokaryotic cells.

- Their DNA is not enclosed within a membrane and forms one circular chromosome.
- Their DNA is free; it is not attached to proteins.
- They lack membrane-bound organelles. Ribosomes are complex structures within the plasma membrane, but they have no exterior membrane.
- Their cell wall is made up of a compound called peptidoglycan.
- They usually divide by binary fission, a simple form of cell division.
- They are characteristically small in size, usually between 1 and 10 μm.

What is a eukaryotic cell?

Whereas prokaryotic cells occur in bacteria, eukaryotic cells occur in organisms such as algae, protozoa, fungi, plants, and animals. Examine the following diagrams and pictures.

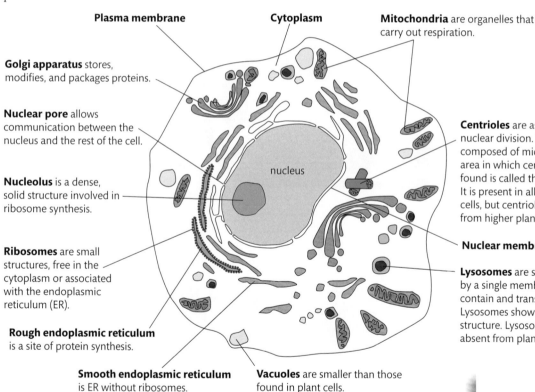

Plasma membrane

Cytoplasm

Mitochondria are organelles that carry out respiration.

Golgi apparatus stores, modifies, and packages proteins.

Nuclear pore allows communication between the nucleus and the rest of the cell.

Nucleolus is a dense, solid structure involved in ribosome synthesis.

Ribosomes are small structures, free in the cytoplasm or associated with the endoplasmic reticulum (ER).

Rough endoplasmic reticulum is a site of protein synthesis.

Smooth endoplasmic reticulum is ER without ribosomes.

Vacuoles are smaller than those found in plant cells.

nucleus

Centrioles are associated with nuclear division. They are composed of microtubules. The area in which centrioles are found is called the centrosome. It is present in all eukaryotic cells, but centrioles are absent from higher plant cells.

Nuclear membrane

Lysosomes are sacs bounded by a single membrane. They contain and transport enzymes. Lysosomes show little internal structure. Lysosomes are usually absent from plant cells.

Eukaryotic cells range in diameter from 5 to 100 μm. A 'kernel' or nucleus is usually noticeable in the cytoplasm. Other organelles may be visible within the cell if you have a microscope with a high enough magnification and resolution. Organelles are non-cellular structures that carry out specific functions (a bit like organs in multicellular organisms); different types of cell often have different organelles. These structures enable compartmentalization in eukaryotic cells, which is not a characteristic of prokaryotic cells. Compartmentalization enables different chemical reactions to be separated, which is especially important when adjacent chemical reactions are incompatible. Compartmentalization also allows chemicals for specific reactions to be isolated; this isolation results in increased efficiency.

CHALLENGE YOURSELF

5 Prepare a drawing of the ultrastructure of a prokaryotic cell based on electron micrographs. Make sure you follow the guidelines given for drawings.

Figure 1.4 Look at this drawing of a typical animal cell and compare it with Figure 1.5.

The term 'eukaryote' comes from the Greek word 'eukaryon' meaning true kernel or true nucleus.

Endoplasmic reticulum (ER) is a network of tubes and flattened sacs. ER connects with the plasma membrane and the nuclear membrane and may be smooth or have attached ribosomes (rough ER).

Central vacuole has storage and hydrolytic functions

Cytoplasm contains dissolved substances, enzymes, and the cell organelles.

Nucleus contains most of the cell's DNA.

Nuclear pore

Chloroplasts are specialized plastids containing the green pigment chlorophyll. They consist of grana within the colourless stroma. They are the sites for photosynthesis.

Nucleolus

Nuclear membrane is a double-layered structure.

Cell wall is a semi-rigid structure composed mainly of cellulose.

Ribosomes are small (20 nm) structures that manufacture proteins. They may be free in the cytoplasm or associated with the surface of the endoplasmic reticulum.

Plasma membrane is inside the cell wall.

Golgi apparatus

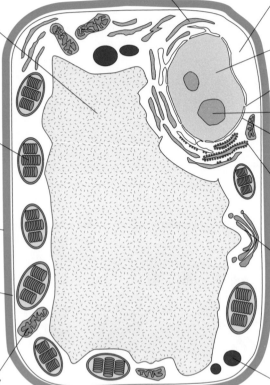

Mitochondria are bounded by a double membrane. They are energy transformers.

Starch granules are composed of carbohydrate stored in amyloplasts.

Figure 1.5 What is different and what is similar between this typical plant cell and Figure 1.4?

A TEM of a pancreatic exocrine cell. Can you tell this is an animal cell? Locate as many of the structures of an animal cell as you can. How do the structures of this cell reflect the overall functions of the pancreas?

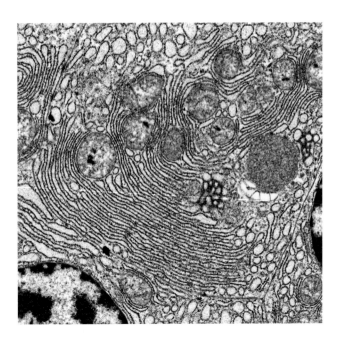

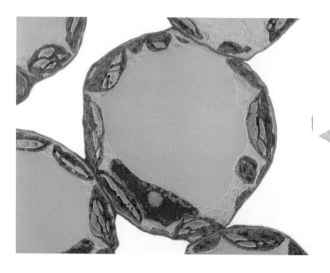

A TEM of a cell from the mesophyll region of a leaf. How do you know this is a plant cell? Locate as many of the structures of a plant cell as you can. What cell structures reflect most the unique abilities of a plant cell?

As you read about the organelles of eukaryotic cells below, refer back to the figures above and on page 16 and add more names of organelles. Also, be certain to note which organelles are common to both types of cells and which organelles occur in only one of the two types.

Organelles of eukaryotic cells

Common organelles include the following (see Figures 1.4 and 1.5):

- endoplasmic reticulum
- ribosomes
- lysosomes (not usually found in plant cells)
- Golgi apparatus
- mitochondria
- nucleus
- chloroplasts (only in plant and algal cells)
- centrosomes (in all eukaryotic cells, but centrioles are not found in some plant cells)
- vacuoles.

The microscope has given us an insight into the structure and function of the following eukaryotic cell organelles and characteristics.

Cytoplasm

All eukaryotic cells have a region called the cytoplasm that occurs inside the plasma membrane or the outer boundary of the cell. It is in this region that the organelles are found. The fluid portion of the cytoplasm around the organelles is called the cytosol.

Endoplasmic reticulum

The endoplasmic reticulum (ER) is an extensive network of tubules or channels that extends most everywhere in the cell, from the nucleus to the plasma membrane. Its structure enables its function, which is the transportation of materials throughout the internal region of the cell. There are two general types of ER: smooth ER and rough ER. Smooth ER does not have any of the organelles called ribosomes on its exterior surface. Rough ER has ribosomes on its exterior.

TOK

Visual illusions are the result of sensory-derived images that differ from objective reality. M. C. Escher's *Waterfall* is a prime example of an optical illusion. In his print water seems to flow downhill on its way to the 'top' of the waterfall. How can the repeating of experiments in science decrease the chances of an illusion? Do you feel modern technology is decreasing the chances of these visual illusions occurring in modern-day science research?

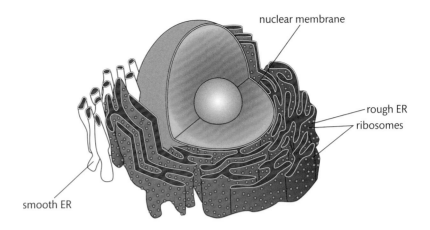

Figure 1.6 Smooth ER and rough ER.

Smooth ER has many unique enzymes embedded on its surface. Its functions are:

- the production of membrane phospholipids and cellular lipids
- the production of sex hormones such as testosterone and oestrogen
- detoxification of drugs in the liver
- the storage of calcium ions in muscle cells, needed for contraction of muscle cells
- transportation of lipid-based compounds
- helping the liver release glucose into the bloodstream when needed.

Rough ER has ribosomes on the exterior of the channels. These ribosomes are involved in protein synthesis. Therefore, this type of ER is involved in protein development and transport. These proteins may become parts of membranes, enzymes, or even messengers between cells. Most cells contain both types of ER, with the rough ER being closer to the nuclear membrane.

Ribosomes

Ribosomes are unique structures that do not have an exterior membrane. They carry out protein synthesis within the cell. These structures may be found free in the cytoplasm or they may be attached to the surface of ER. They are always composed of a type of RNA and protein. You will recall that prokaryotic cells also contain ribosomes. However, the ribosomes of eukaryotic cells are larger and denser that those of prokaryotic cells. Ribosomes are composed of two subunits. These subunits together equal 80S. The ribosomes in prokaryotic cells are also composed of two subunits, but they only equal 70S.

Lysosomes

Lysosomes are intracellular digestive centres that arise from the Golgi apparatus. A lysosome does not have any internal structures. Lysosomes are sacs bounded by a single membrane that contain as many as 40 different enzymes. The enzymes are all hydrolytic and catalyse the breakdown of proteins, nucleic acids, lipids, and carbohydrates. Lysosomes fuse with old or damaged organelles from within the cell to break them down, so that recycling of the components can occur. Lysosomes are also involved in the breakdown of materials that may be brought into a cell by phagocytosis. Phagocytosis is a type of endocytosis that is explained on page 37 in Section 1.4. The interior environment of a functioning lysosome is acidic; this acidic environment is necessary for the enzymes to hydrolyse large molecules.

The letter S used in the measurement of ribosomes refers to Svedberg units, which indicate the relative rate of sedimentation during high-speed centrifugation. The higher the S value, the quicker the structure will become part of the sediment and the more mass it will have.

Golgi apparatus

The Golgi apparatus consists of what appears to be flattened sacs called cisternae, which are stacked one on top of another. This organelle functions in the collection, packaging, modification, and distribution of materials synthesized in the cell. One side of the apparatus is near the rough ER, called the *cis* side. It receives products from the ER. These products then move into the cisternae of the Golgi apparatus. They continue to move to the discharging or opposite side, the *trans* side. Small sacs called vesicles can then be seen coming off the *trans* side. These vesicles carry modified materials to wherever they are needed inside or outside the cell. This organelle is especially prevalent in glandular cells, such as those in the pancreas, which manufacture and secrete substances.

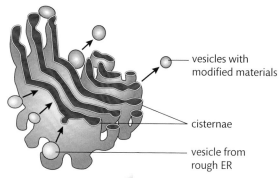

vesicles with
modified materials

cisternae

vesicle from
rough ER

Figure 1.7 In this drawing of the Golgi apparatus, the movement of the vesicles is shown by arrows. Can you identify which side is the *cis* side and which is the *trans* side?

Mitochondria

Mitochondria (singular mitochondrion) are rod-shaped organelles that appear throughout the cytoplasm. They are close in size to a bacterial cell. Mitochondria have their own DNA, a circular chromosome similar to that in bacterial cells, allowing them some independence within a cell. They have a double membrane: the outer membrane is smooth, but the inner membrane is folded into cristae (singular crista). Inside the inner membrane is a semi-fluid substance called the matrix. An area called the inner membrane space lies between the two membranes. The cristae provide a huge surface area within which the chemical reactions characteristic of the mitochondria occur. Most mitochondrial reactions involve the production of usable cellular energy called adenosine triphosphate (ATP). Because of this, the mitochondria are often called the powerhouse of a cell. This organelle also produces and contains its own ribosomes; these ribosomes are of the 70S type. Cells that have high energy requirements, such as muscle cells, have large numbers of mitochondria.

Figure 1.8 Compare this drawing of a mitochondrion with the false-colour TEM of a mitochondrion.

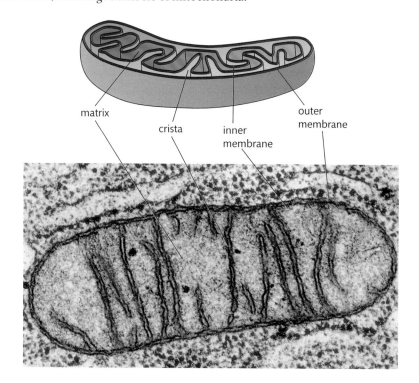

matrix

crista

inner
membrane

outer
membrane

Nucleus

The nucleus in eukaryotic cells is an isolated region where the DNA resides. It is bordered by a double membrane referred to as the nuclear envelope. This membrane allows compartmentalization of the eukaryotic DNA, thus providing an area where DNA can carry out its functions without being affected by processes occurring in other parts of the cell. The nuclear membrane does not provide complete isolation because it has numerous pores that allow communication with the cell's cytoplasm.

Figure 1.9 The nucleus has a double membrane with pores and contains a nucleolus.

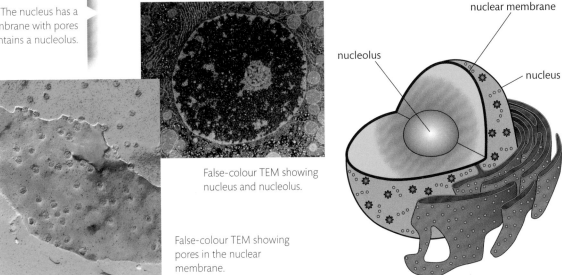

False-colour TEM showing nucleus and nucleolus.

False-colour TEM showing pores in the nuclear membrane.

The DNA of a eukaryotic cell often occurs in the form of chromosomes; chromosomes vary in number depending on the species. Chromosomes carry all the information that is necessary for the cell to exist; this allows an organism to survive, whether it is unicellular or multicellular. The DNA is the genetic material of the cell. It enables certain traits to be passed on to the next generation. When the cell is not in the process

Figure 1.10 This drawing shows how DNA is packaged into chromosomes.

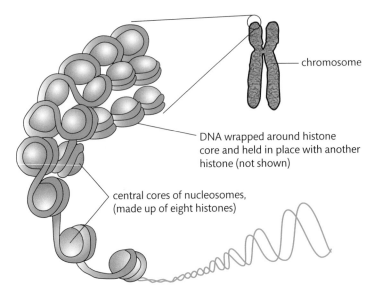

of dividing, the chromosomes are not present as visible structures. During this phase the cell's DNA is in the form of chromatin. Chromatin is formed of strands of DNA and proteins called histones. The DNA and histone combination often results in structures called a nucleosome. A nucleosome consists of eight spherical histones with a strand of DNA wrapped around them and secured with a ninth histone. This produces a structure that resembles a string of beads. A chromosome is a highly coiled structure of many nucleosomes.

The nucleus is often located centrally within the cell's cytoplasm, although in some cell types it is pushed to one side or the other. The side position is characteristic of plant cells because these cells often have a large central vacuole. Most eukaryotic cells possess a single nucleus, but some do not have a nucleus at all, and some have multiple nuclei. Without a nucleus, cells cannot reproduce. The loss of reproductive ability is often paired with increased specialization to carry out a certain function. For example, human red blood cells do not have nuclei: they are specialized to transport respiratory gases. Most nuclei also include one or more dark areas called nucleoli (singular nucleolus). Ribosome molecules are manufactured in the nucleolus. The molecules pass through the nuclear envelope before assembling as ribosomes.

Chloroplasts

Chloroplasts occur only in algae and plant cells. The chloroplast contains a double membrane and is about the same size as a bacterial cell. Like the mitochondrion, a chloroplast contains its own DNA and 70S ribosomes. The DNA of a chloroplast takes the form of a ring.

You should note all the characteristics that chloroplasts and mitochondria have in common with prokaryotic cells.

As well as DNA and ribosomes, the interior of a chloroplast includes the grana (singular granum), the thylakoids, and the stroma, which are labelled in Figure 1.11. A granum is made up of numerous thylakoids stacked like a pile of coins. The thylakoids are flattened membrane sacs with components necessary for the absorption of light. Absorption of light is the first step in the process of photosynthesis. The fluid stroma is similar to the cytosol of the cell. It occurs outside the grana but within the double membrane. Stroma contains many enzymes and chemicals that are necessary to complete the process of photosynthesis. Like mitochondria, chloroplasts are capable of reproducing independently of a cell.

Figure 1.11 Compare the drawing of a chloroplast with this TEM of a chloroplast.

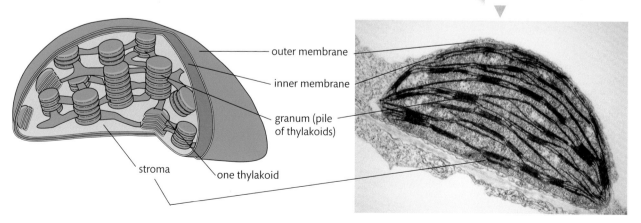

outer membrane
inner membrane
granum (pile of thylakoids)
stroma
one thylakoid

Centrosome

The centrosome occurs in all eukaryotic cells. Generally, it consists of a pair of centrioles at right angles to one another. These centrioles are involved with the assembly of microtubules, which are important to a cell because they provide structure and allow movement. Microtubules are also important for cell division. Cells from higher plants, plants that are thought to have evolved later, produce microtubules even though they do not have centrioles. The centrosome is located at one end of the cell close to the nucleus.

Vacuoles

Vacuoles are storage organelles that are usually formed from the Golgi apparatus. They are membrane-bound and have many possible functions. They occupy a very large space inside the cells of most plants. They may store a number of different substances, including potential food (to provide nutrition), metabolic waste and toxins (to be expelled from the cell), and water. Vacuoles enable cells to have higher surface area to volume ratios even at larger sizes. In plants, they allow the uptake of water, which provides rigidity to the organism.

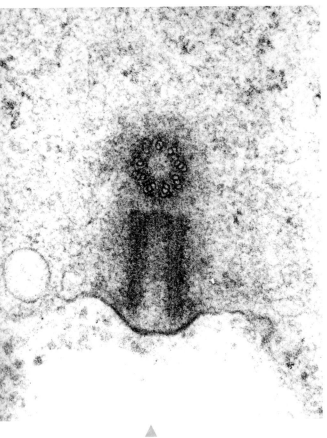

This TEM shows the two centrioles of a centrosome.

Summary of eukaryotic cell organelles and areas

Table 1.3 A summary of eukaryotic cells

Name	Main function	Cell type
Cytoplasm	Contains the organelles	Plant and animal
Endoplasmic reticulum (ER)	Transportation	Plant and animal
Rough ER	Protein transportation and processing	Plant and animal
Smooth ER	Lipid synthesis and transportation	Plant and animal
Ribosomes	Protein synthesis	Plant and animal
Lysosomes	Intracellular digestion	Animal and some plants
Golgi apparatus	Storage, packaging, and transport	Plant and animal
Mitochondria	ATP formation	Plant and animal
Nucleus	Control centre housing chromosomes	Plant and animal
Chloroplasts	Photosynthesis	Plant
Centrosome	Region that aids in cell division	All (but no centrioles in plant)
Vacuole	Storage	Most prominent in plant, smaller in animal when present

A comparison of prokaryotic and eukaryotic cells

A table is a good way to summarize the differences between prokaryotic and eukaryotic cells.

When comparing items, be certain to state the characteristic of each type of item, as shown in the table for prokaryotic and eukaryotic cells.

Table 1.4 Comparing prokaryotic and eukaryotic cells

Prokaryotic cells	Eukaryotic cells
DNA in a ring form without protein	DNA with proteins as chromosomes/chromatin
DNA free in the cytoplasm (nucleoid region)	DNA enclosed within a nuclear envelope (nucleus)
No mitochondria	Mitochondria present
70S ribosomes	80S ribosomes
No internal compartmentalization to form organelles	Internal compartmentalization present to form many types of organelles
Size less than 10 μm	Size more than 10 μm

If asked to state the similarities between the two types of cells, make sure you include the following:

* both types of cell have some sort of outside boundary that always involves a plasma membrane
* both types of cell carry out all the functions of life
* DNA is present in both cell types.

A comparison of plant and animal cells and their extracellular components

We will now look at how to compare two general types of eukaryotic cell: plant and animal cells. A table like the one below can be used to highlight the differences. However, do not forget to also recognize the similarities between the two cell types.

Table 1.5 Comparing plant and animal cells

Plant cells	Animal cells
The exterior of the cell includes an outer cell wall with a plasma membrane just inside	The exterior of the cell only includes a plasma membrane. There is no cell wall
Chloroplasts are present in the cytoplasm area	There are no chloroplasts
Large centrally located vacuoles are present	Vacuoles are not usually present or are small
Carbohydrates are stored as starch	Carbohydrates are stored as glycogen
Do not contain centrioles within a centrosome area	Contain centrioles within a centrosome area
Because a rigid cell wall is present, this cell type has a fixed, often angular, shape	Without a cell wall, this cell is flexible and more likely to be a rounded shape

Most cell organelles are present in both plant and animal cells. When an organelle is present in both types of cell, it usually has the same structure and function. For example, both cell types contain mitochondria that possess cristae, a matrix, and a double membrane. Also, in both cell types, the mitochondria function in the production of ATP for use by the cell.

The outermost region of various cell types is often unique to that cell type, as shown by the following table.

Table 1.6 Outermost parts of different cells

Cell	Outermost part
Bacteria	Cell wall of peptidoglycan
Fungi	Cell wall of chitin
Yeasts	Cell wall of glucan and mannan
Algae	Cell wall of cellulose
Plants	Cell wall of cellulose
Animals	No cell wall, instead a plasma membrane that secretes a mixture of sugar and proteins called glycoproteins that forms the extracellular matrix

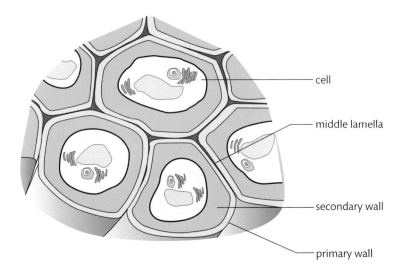

Figure 1.12 This drawing of a section through plant cells shows the primary walls, middle lamella and secondary walls.

cell

middle lamella

secondary wall

primary wall

Whenever a cell wall is present, it is involved in maintaining cell shape. It also helps regulate water uptake. Because of its rigidity it will only allow a certain amount of water to enter the cell. In plants, when an adequate amount of water is inside the cell, there is pressure against the cell wall. This pressure helps support the plant vertically.

The extracellular matrix (ECM) of many animal cells is composed of collagen fibres plus a combination of sugars and proteins called glycoproteins. These form fibre-like structures that anchor the matrix to the plasma membrane. This strengthens the plasma membrane and allows attachments between adjacent cells. The ECM allows cell-to-cell interactions, possibly altering gene expression and enabling the coordination of cell actions within the tissue. Many researchers think the ECM is involved in directing stem cells to differentiate. Cell migration and movement also appear to be, at least partially, the result of interactions in this area.

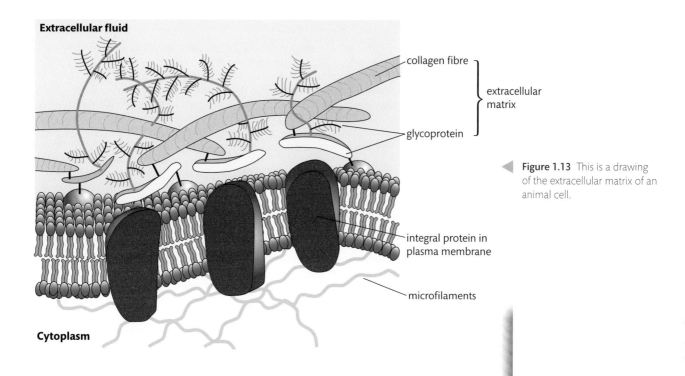

Extracellular fluid

collagen fibre

extracellular matrix

glycoprotein

Figure 1.13 This is a drawing of the extracellular matrix of an animal cell.

integral protein in plasma membrane

microfilaments

Cytoplasm

The use of a light microscope to investigate cells and cell structure sizes
Safety alerts: Be very cautious with sharp instruments. Wash your hands thoroughly with soap and water before and after handling cell sources. Follow all additional teacher safety directives.

This practical will develop your skill in using a microscope, allow you to observe some common cells microscopically, and demonstrate ways to calculate the size of cells and cell parts. There are many different types of compound light microscope. Before beginning this practical, it is essential you understand how to use your school's microscopes properly. As well as a microscope, other materials necessary for this practical include microscope slides, cover glasses, methylene blue in a dropper bottle, water in a dropper bottle, a plastic ruler, toothpicks, and several sources of cells.

1 Determine the total magnification of each objective lens

Because you are using a compound microscope, there are two types of lens present. One is the ocular lens and the other is the objective lens. Each of these lenses has a number on it followed by an ×. These numbers represent the magnification of that particular lens. To determine the total magnification of an object being examined with the microscope, multiply the power of the ocular lens by the power of the objective lens. Carry out this procedure for each of the microscope objective lenses you use and record the information required in the following table.

Table 1.7 Microscope total magnification and diameter of field of view

Power of ocular lens	Power of objective lens	Total magnification	Diameter of field of view (mm)	Diameter of field of view (μm)
Low				
Medium				
High				

2 Determine the diameter of the field of view

The field of view (field of vision) is the circular area you can see when you look through the ocular lens of a microscope. It is important to know its diameter. One way to determine this is to place a plastic ruler under the low-power objective lens so that it crosses the diameter of the field of view. Observe and record the diameter in millimetres in the above table. Repeat the same procedure for the next two objectives to determine the diameter of their field of view. Instead of using a ruler for the two higher power objectives, you can use proportions to determine the field of view by comparing their diameters with the diameter determined for the lowest power. Convert millimetre (mm) measurements to microns (micrometres; µm):

$$1 \text{ mm} = 1000 \text{ µm}$$

3 Observing and determining the sizes of cells

(a) You will now look at several types of cells. Prepared slides may be used or you can make your own wet-mount slides. Your teacher will provide the information you need to produce a wet mount.

(b) Some ideas for producing your own wet-mount slides include: the inside epidermal layer from the bulb of an onion; *Elodea* leaf cells; *Anabaena* (an aquatic cyanobacterium); cheek cells from inside your mouth; scraped soft banana tissue.

(c) Whatever cells are used, study them carefully, noting any internal structures, and their size in relation to the rest of the cell and its visible parts. Using a stain such as methylene blue or iodine often means you can see the parts of a cell more clearly. Use any resources available, including texts and the internet, to identify any structures you can see.

(d) For each cell type you observe, complete the following steps.

(i) Using a pencil, draw several typical cells seen in the field of view. Label any visible cell structures.

(ii) Carefully and accurately make a scale drawing of these cells and any visible internal parts.

(iii) Beside each drawing include the:

- total magnification
- diameter of the field of view
- estimated length of an individual cell.

To figure out the length of one cell, divide the diameter of the field of view by the number of cells that cross the diameter of the field of view. This value should be recorded in microns (µm).

Another way to determine the size of objects in the field of view of a microscope is to use an eyepiece graticule. Graticules must be calibrated. To calibrate a graticule, a plastic millimetre ruler or a graduated slide can be used. While using the lowest power objective lens, move the graduated slide until the graticule scale and the graduated slide scale align. The size of the graticule units can now be determined. You can follow the same procedure to calibrate the other two objectives, or you can calculate the other calibrations. Once you have calibrated the graticule, it can be used to take accurate measurements of the object being viewed.

4 Microscope magnification and cell size

We will complete this activity with some problems involving cell size and magnification. Use this general formula for calculating magnification:

$$\text{magnification} = \text{drawing size}/\text{actual size}$$

(a) An organism has an actual length of 0.01 mm. If you draw a diagram that is 50 mm, what is the magnification of your drawing?

(b) Scale bars are lines added to a micrograph (the photograph of an image under a microscope) or a drawing to represent the actual size of the structures. For example, a 25-µm bar would represent the size of a 25-µm image. The picture on page 27 shows an image of several *Volvox* seen in a microscope field of view. Use the scale bar to determine the approximate size of the three central, fully shown *Volvox*.

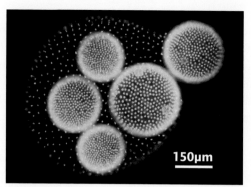

150μm

(c) An organism has an actual length of 0.05 mm. If you use a scale of 1 : 200, what will the size of your drawing of the organism be?

(d) You should look at more images of micrographs on the internet to develop your skills in determining the sizes of cells and cell structures. Be certain to include electron micrographs in your practice.

Exercises

5 What is a disadvantage to prokaryotic cells of having their DNA free in the cytoplasm without a nuclear membrane?

6 What structures are involved in sexual reproduction in prokaryotic cells?

7 Dental plaque involves the presence of bacteria. Explain how the bacteria are able to attach firmly to teeth such that the bacteria can only be removed with scraping.

8 Why do muscle cells have a large number of mitochondria?

9 Name two organelles that are similar to prokaryotic cells.

10 If plant cells have chloroplasts for photosynthesis, why do they also need mitochondria?

11 What is the importance of scale bars on micrographs?

1.3 Membrane structure

Understandings:

- Phospholipids form bilayers in water due to the amphipathic properties of phospholipid molecules.
- Membrane proteins are diverse in terms of structure, position in the membrane, and function.
- Cholesterol is a component of animal cell membranes.

Applications and skills:

- Application: Cholesterol in mammalian membranes reduces membrane fluidity and permeability to some solutes.
- Skill: Drawing of the fluid mosaic model.
- Skill: Analysis of evidence from electron microscopy that led to the proposal of the Davson–Danielli model.
- Skill: Analysis of the falsification of the Davson–Danielli model that led to the Singer–Nicolson model.

Guidance

- *Amphipathic phospholipids have hydrophilic and hydrophobic properties.*
- *Drawings of the fluid mosaic model of membrane structure can be two-dimensional rather than three-dimensional. Individual phospholipid molecules should be shown using the symbol of a circle with two parallel lines attached. A range of membrane proteins should be shown including glycoproteins.*

To learn more about prokaryotic and eukaryotic cells, and the features of bacterial cells, go to the hotlinks site, search for the title or ISBN, and click on Chapter 1: Section 1.2.

NATURE OF SCIENCE

Using models as representations of the real world: there are alternative models of membrane structure.

Falsification of theories, with one theory being superseded by another: evidence falsified the Davson–Danielli model.

TOK

Using models is a way in which scientists explain complex structures such as cellular membranes. Models are based on the knowledge available at the time a theory is suggested. Even though the early models of cell membranes were later proved wrong (because of new data), they helped in the development of the presently accepted model of cell membranes. Discuss why it is important to learn about theories that are later discredited.

Membrane structure

As early as 1915 scientists were aware that the structure of membranes isolated from cells included proteins and lipids. Further research established that the lipids were phospholipids. Early theories were mostly concerned with phospholipids forming a bilayer with proteins, forming thin layers on the exterior and interior of the bilayer. The Davson–Danielli model, proposed by Hugh Davson and James Danielli in 1935, used this lipid bilayer model, suggesting it was covered on both sides by a thin layer of globular protein.

In 1972, Seymour J. Singer and Garth L. Nicolson proposed that proteins are inserted into the phospholipid layer and do not form a layer on the phospholipid bilayer surfaces. They believed that the proteins formed a mosaic floating in a fluid layer of phospholipids. There were several reasons why Singer and Nicolson proposed a model that was different from the Davson–Danielli model. These reasons included the following.

- Not all membranes are identical or symmetrical, as the first model implied.
- Membranes with different functions also have a different composition and different structure, as can be seen with an electron microscope.
- A protein layer is not likely because it is largely non-polar and would not interface with water, as shown by cell studies.

Much of the evidence used to change the Davson–Danielli model was gathered with the use of the electron microscope. Another source of evidence was the study of cells and their actions in various environments and solutions. The ability to culture cells in the laboratory allowed many of these studies. Since 1972 further evidence has been gathered about membranes, and slight changes to the Singer–Nicolson model have been made.

The current agreed model for the cellular membrane is the fluid mosaic model. It is shown in the following diagram. All cellular membranes, whether plasma membranes or organelle membranes, have the same general structure.

Figure 1.14 In the fluid mosaic model of the cell membrane there is a double layer of lipids (fats) arranged with their tails facing inwards. Proteins are thought to 'float' in the lipid bilayer.

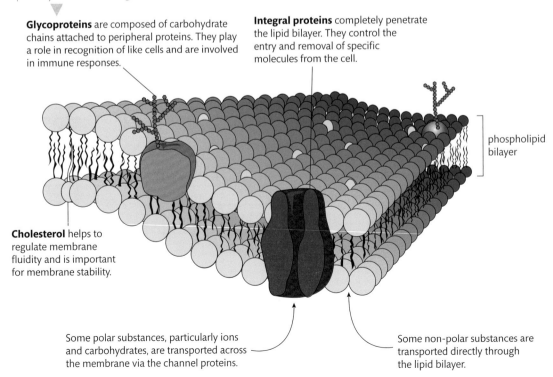

Glycoproteins are composed of carbohydrate chains attached to peripheral proteins. They play a role in recognition of like cells and are involved in immune responses.

Integral proteins completely penetrate the lipid bilayer. They control the entry and removal of specific molecules from the cell.

phospholipid bilayer

Cholesterol helps to regulate membrane fluidity and is important for membrane stability.

Some polar substances, particularly ions and carbohydrates, are transported across the membrane via the channel proteins.

Some non-polar substances are transported directly through the lipid bilayer.

Phospholipids

In Figure 1.14 note that the 'backbone' of the membrane is a bilayer produced from huge numbers of molecules called phospholipids. Each phospholipid is composed of a three-carbon compound called glycerol. Two of the glycerol carbons have fatty acids. The third carbon is attached to a highly polar organic alcohol that includes a bond to a phosphate group. Fatty acids are not water soluble because they are non-polar. In contrast, because the organic alcohol with phosphate is highly polar, it is water soluble. This structure means that membranes have two distinct areas when it comes to polarity and water solubility. One area is water soluble and polar, and is referred to as hydrophilic (water-loving). This is the phosphorylated alcohol side. The other area is not water soluble and is non-polar. It is referred to as hydrophobic (water-fearing).

Figure 1.15 This is a model of a phospholipid.

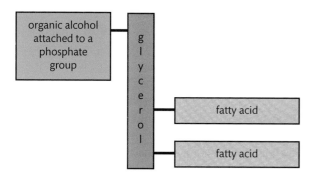

The hydrophobic and hydrophilic regions cause phospholipids to align as a bilayer if there is water present and there is a large number of phospholipid molecules. Because the fatty acid 'tails' do not attract each other strongly, the membrane tends to be fluid or flexible. This allows animal cells to have a variable shape and also allows the process of endocytosis (which is discussed below) to take place. What maintains the overall structure of the membrane is the tendency water has to form hydrogen bonds.

Figure 1.16 This model of a phospholipid bilayer shows how phospholipid molecules behave in two layers. Both layers have the phosphorylated alcohol end of the molecules towards the outside and the fatty acid tails oriented towards each other in the middle.

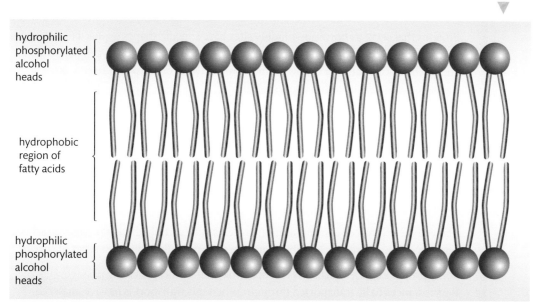

Cholesterol

Membranes must be fluid to function properly. They are a bit like olive oil in their consistency. At various locations in the hydrophobic region (fatty acid tails) in animal cells are cholesterol molecules. These molecules have a role in determining membrane fluidity, which changes with temperature. The cholesterol molecules allow membranes to function effectively at a wider range of temperatures than if they were not present. Plant cells do not have cholesterol molecules; they depend on saturated or unsaturated fatty acids to maintain proper membrane fluidity.

Proteins

The last major component of cellular membranes comprises the proteins. It is these proteins that create the extreme diversity in membrane function. Proteins of various types are embedded in the fluid matrix of the phospholipid bilayer. This creates the mosaic effect referred to in the fluid mosaic model. There are usually two major types of proteins. One type is referred to as integral proteins and the other type is referred to as peripheral proteins. Integral proteins show an amphipathic character, with both hydrophobic and hydrophilic regions within the same protein. These proteins will have the hydrophobic region in the mid-section of the phospholipid backbone. Their hydrophilic region will be exposed to the water solutions on either side of the membrane. Peripheral proteins, on the other hand, do not protrude into the middle hydrophobic region, but remain bound to the surface of the membrane. Often these peripheral proteins are anchored to an integral protein. Look at the drawing of the fluid mosaic model (Figure 1.14) to see the location of these proteins.

Membrane protein functions

As you will recall, it is the membrane proteins that impart different functions to the different membranes. There are many different proteins, which have six general functions:

- sites for hormone-binding
- enzymatic action
- cell adhesion
- cell-to-cell communication
- channels for passive transport
- pumps for active transport.

Proteins that serve as hormone-binding sites have specific shapes exposed to the exterior that fit the shape of specific hormones. The attachment between the protein and the hormone causes a change in the shape of the protein, which results in a message being relayed to the interior of the cell.

Cells have enzymes attached to membranes that catalyse many chemical reactions. The enzymes may be on the interior or the exterior of the cell. Often they are grouped so that a sequence of metabolic reactions, called a metabolic pathway, can occur.

Cell adhesion is provided by proteins that can hook together in various ways to provide permanent or temporary connections. These connections, referred to as junctions, can include gap junctions and tight junctions.

Many of the cell-to-cell communication proteins have carbohydrate molecules attached. They provide an identification label that represents the cells of different types of species.

Some proteins contain channels that span the membrane, providing passageways for substances to be transported through. When this transport is passive, material

Make sure you can draw and label all the parts of a membrane as described in this section for the fluid mosaic model. Follow the directions given earlier for making a good drawing. In the drawing, the phospholipids should be shown using the symbol of a circle with two parallel lines attached. It is also important to show a wide range of proteins with various functions and locations.

moves through the channel from an area of high concentration to an area of lower concentration.

In active transport, proteins shuttle a substance from one side of the membrane to another by changing shape. This process requires the expenditure of energy in the form of ATP. It does not require a difference in concentration to occur.

A passive process does not need the cell to provide any energy for it to occur. If energy is needed for a process to occur, that process is called active and the form of energy most often used is a type of nucleic acid called adenosine triphosphate or ATP.

Exercises

12 Explain the orientation of the bilayer of phospholipid molecules in the plasma membrane using the terms hydrophobic and hydrophilic.

13 Why does a diet high in plants and plant products have relatively low cholesterol levels compared with a diet involving high amounts of animal products?

14 What type of properties do amphipathic phospholipids possess?

15 What do many of the proteins of the plasma membrane involved with cell-to-cell communication have attached to them?

Membrane transport

NATURE OF SCIENCE

Experimental design: accurate quantitative measurements in osmosis experiments are essential.

Understandings:

- Particles move across membranes by simple diffusion, facilitated diffusion, osmosis, and active transport.
- The fluidity of membranes allows materials to be taken into cells by endocytosis or released by exocytosis. Vesicles move materials within cells.

Applications and skills:

- Application: Structure and function of sodium–potassium pumps for active transport and potassium channels for facilitated diffusion in axons.
- Application: Tissues or organs to be used in medical procedures must be bathed in a solution with the same osmolarity as the cytoplasm to prevent osmosis.
- Skill: Estimation of osmolarity in tissues by bathing samples in hypotonic and hypertonic solutions.

Guidance
- Osmosis experiments are a useful opportunity to stress the need for accurate mass and volume measurements in scientific experiments.

Passive and active transport

There are two general types of cellular transport:

- passive transport
- active transport.

As mentioned previously, passive transport does not require energy (in the form of ATP), but active transport does. Passive transport occurs in situations where there are areas of different concentrations of a particular substance. Movement of the substance occurs from an area of higher concentration to an area of lower concentration. Movement is said to occur along a concentration gradient.

When active transport occurs, the substance is moved against a concentration gradient, so energy expenditure must occur.

Passive transport: diffusion and osmosis

Examine Figure 1.17. It shows chemical diffusion.

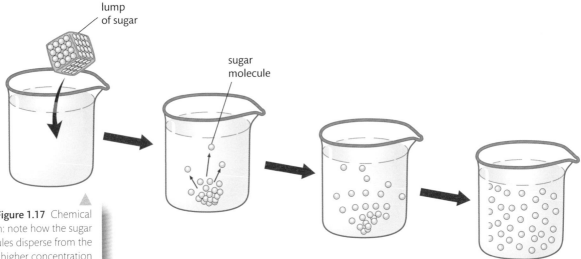

lump of sugar

sugar molecule

Figure 1.17 Chemical diffusion: note how the sugar molecules disperse from the area of higher concentration to the area of lower concentration.

Diffusion

Diffusion is one type of passive transport. Particles of a certain type move from a region of higher concentration to a region of lower concentration. However, in a living system, diffusion often involves a membrane. For example, oxygen gas moves from outside a cell to inside that cell. Oxygen is used by the cell when its mitochondria carry out respiration, thus creating a relatively lower oxygen concentration inside the cell compared with outside the cell. Oxygen diffuses into the cell as a result. Carbon dioxide diffuses in the opposite direction to the oxygen because carbon dioxide is produced as a result of mitochondrial respiration.

Facilitated diffusion

An example of a disease involving facilitated diffusion is cystinuria. This occurs when the protein that carries the amino acid cysteine is absent from kidney cells. The result is a build-up of amino acids in the kidney, resulting in very painful kidney stones.

Facilitated diffusion is a particular type of diffusion involving a membrane with specific carrier proteins that are capable of combining with the substance to aid its movement. The carrier protein changes shape to accomplish this task but does not require energy.

It should be evident from this explanation that facilitated diffusion is very specific depending on the carrier protein. The rate of facilitated diffusion will level off when total saturation of the available carriers occurs.

Osmosis

Osmosis is another type of passive transport: movement occurs along a concentration gradient. However, osmosis involves only the passive movement of water across a partially permeable membrane. A partially permeable membrane is one that only allows certain substances to pass through (a permeable membrane would allow everything through). A concentration gradient of water that allows the movement to occur is the result of a difference between solute concentrations on either side of a partially permeable membrane. A hypertonic (hyperosmotic) solution has a higher concentration of total solutes than a hypotonic (hypo-osmotic) solution. Water therefore moves from a hypotonic solution to a hypertonic solution across a partially permeable membrane (study Figure 1.18). If isotonic solutions occur on either side of a partially permeable membrane, no net movement of water is evident.

Table 1.8 summarizes diffusion and osmosis (passive transport) across cellular membranes.

Table 1.8 Diffusion and osmosis

Type of passive transport	Description of membrane
Simple diffusion	Substances other than water move between phospholipid molecules or through proteins that possess channels
Facilitated diffusion	Non-channel protein carriers change shape to allow movement of substances other than water
Osmosis	Only water moves through the membrane using aquaporins, which are proteins with specialized channels for water movement

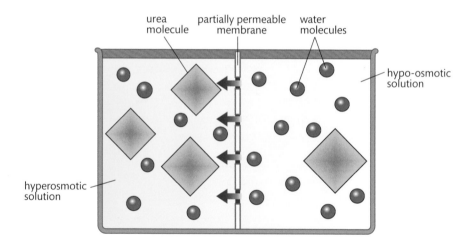

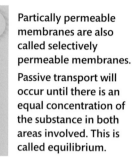

Partically permeable membranes are also called selectively permeable membranes.

Passive transport will occur until there is an equal concentration of the substance in both areas involved. This is called equilibrium.

An aid to remembering the difference between diffusion and osmosis is 'H₂Osmosis', linking the solvent water to osmosis.

Figure 1.18 The partially permeable membrane between two solutions of different osmotic concentrations allows water molecules to pass from the hypo-osmotic solution to the hyperosmotic solution.

Size and charge

The size and polarity of molecules determine the ease with which various substances can cross membranes. These characteristics and the ability of molecules to cross membranes are arranged along a continuum like this:

small and non-polar molecules cross membranes easily ⟷ large and polar molecules cross membranes with difficulty

How easily a substance can move across a membrane passively depends on two major factors: size and charge. Substances that are small in size and non-polar will move across a membrane with ease. Substances that are polar, large in size, or both, do not cross membranes easily. Examples of small, non-polar substances are gases such as oxygen, carbon dioxide, and nitrogen. Ions such as chloride ions, potassium ions, and sodium ions have a great deal of difficulty crossing membranes passively, as do large molecules such as glucose and sucrose. Molecules such as water and glycerol are small, uncharged polar molecules that can cross membranes fairly easily.

A practical example of diffusion and osmosis is kidney dialysis. Many people have problems regulating blood solutes (solutes are substances that are dissolved in a solvent, in this case blood, to form a solution).

Solutions occur throughout the body in various types of spaces: intracellular spaces occur inside cells; extracellular spaces occur outside cells; interstitial spaces occur between cells; intravascular spaces occur within blood vessels.

Problems in regulating the solutes in the many body spaces can arise as the result of some sort of irregularity in the function of the kidneys. This can ultimately threaten a person's life because of the lack of homeostatic levels of solutes. To re-establish homeostasis, a process called haemodialysis may be carried out.

In this process, blood is passed through a system of tubes composed of selectively permeable membranes. These tubes are surrounded with a solution that is referred to as the dialysate. The dialysate contains key solutes at levels close to the patient's normal blood levels. Wastes are kept at a low level in the dialysate. As blood moves through the tubes, the dialysate is constantly replaced to maintain ideal levels.

Dialysis is also an example of how cell or tissue osmolarity (the concentration of osmotically active particles) can be estimated. If cells are placed in a solution of known osmolarity, there are three possibilities: the cells may gain mass, the cells may lose mass, or the cells may remain at the same mass.

CHALLENGE YOURSELF

Use your knowledge of osmosis, diffusion, membrane transport, and kidney dialysis to answer the following questions.

6 When solutes move from the blood through the selectively permeable membrane into the dialysate, what process is occurring?

7 Why is the process that allows wastes to move from the blood to the dialysate referred to as passive?

8 What is the importance of constantly changing the dialysate?

9 Name some characteristics of solutes in blood that would affect their rate of movement through the selectively permeable membrane.

10 Haemodialysis also allows regulation of water concentrations within the blood. What process is occurring when water moves through the tube membranes into the dialysate?

11 What factors might affect the time necessary for dialysis to bring about homeostatic blood levels of solutes and wastes?

12 If a group of cells are placed in a hypotonic solution, what will happen to their mass? Explain your answer.

13 One way to stop undesirable plants growing at a specific location is to apply a solution of water with a high concentration of sodium chloride (table salt). Why does this kill the plants and prevent their return for a period of time?

Determining the osmolarity of tissues
Safety alerts. Use safety goggles and lab aprons. Be cautious of cork borers and any other sharp instruments used. Wash your hands thoroughly with soap and water after each day's procedures.

Follow these instructions to determine the osmolarity of tissues by bathing samples in hypotonic, isotonic, and hypertonic solutions. The instructions use potatoes as a source of tissue, but other tissues could be used.

1 With a cork borer, cut six cores from a potato. The cores should all be as close to the same length as possible: 30–50-mm cores are recommended. Each core should be kept separate and identified as core A, core B, core C, core D, core E, and core F.

2 Before continuing, produce a table that will show the volume and mass of the potato cores before and after being placed in solutions of six different sucrose molarities. The molarities to be used are 0.0 M, 0.2 M, 0.4 M, 0.6 M, 0.8 M, and 1.0 M.

3 Using an appropriately sized graduated cylinder approximately one-half filled with water, determine the volume of each core using fluid displacement. Record this information.

4 Once each core is removed from the graduated cylinder, blot it dry with a paper towel and determine its mass using a laboratory balance. Record your results in the table.

5 Place each core in a different test tube labelled with the core's identification letter and the molarity of the sucrose solution to be placed in the tube.

6 Add a labelled molar solution to each test tube until the core is covered. Place foil or plastic wrap over each tube and store for 24 hours.

7 On the next day, repeat steps 3 and 4. Record your 24-hour results in the table.

8 Data processing
  • Produce a table to record the processed data involving the percentage change in mass and core volume.
  • Calculate the percentage change in mass, and the percentage change in volume, at the end of 24 hours, for each core. Record your results in the processed data table.
  • Construct an appropriate graph, with the independent variable of sucrose molarity on the x-axis and the dependent variable of mass percentage change on the y-axis.
  • Construct a similar graph showing volume percentage change.

9 Analysis
  • What is the osmolarity of the potato tissue? Explain how you determined this.
  • Explain the importance of accurate mass and volume measurements in this procedure, and in all scientific experiments.
  • Suggest some ways in which this procedure could be altered so that more reliable data could be attained.

Active transport and the cell

As you will remember, active transport requires work to be performed. This means energy must be used, so ATP is required. Active transport involves the movement of substances against a concentration gradient. This process allows a cell to maintain interior concentrations of molecules that are different from exterior concentrations. Animal cells have a much higher concentration of potassium ions than their exterior environment, whereas sodium ions are more concentrated in the extracellular environment than in the cells. The cell maintains these conditions by pumping potassium ions into the cell and pumping sodium ions out of it. Along with energy, a membrane protein must be involved for this process to occur.

The sodium–potassium pump

The mechanism for actively moving sodium and potassium ions, the sodium–potassium pump, has five stages.

1 A specific protein binds to three intracellular sodium ions.

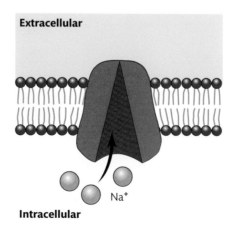

Figure 1.19 Stage 1: A protein in a phospholipid bilayer opens to the intracellular side and attaches three sodium ions.

2   The binding of sodium ions causes phosphorylation by ATP. ATP has three attached phosphates. When it carries out phosphorylation, one phosphate is lost resulting in a two-phosphate compound called ADP. ATP and ADP are discussed in more detail in Chapter 2.

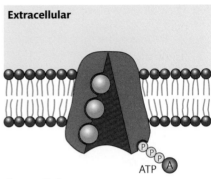

Figure 1.20 Stage 2: ATP attaches to the protein.

3   The phosphorylation causes the protein to change its shape, thus expelling sodium ions to the exterior.

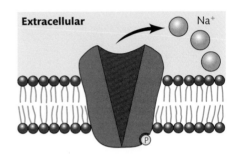

Figure 1.21 Stage 3: The carrier opens to the exterior of the cell and the sodium ions are released. ADP is released, leaving a phosphate group attached to the protein.

4   Two extracellular potassium ions bind to different regions of the protein, and this causes the release of the phosphate group.

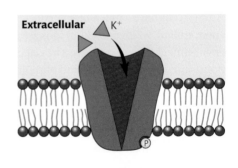

Figure 1.22 Stage 4: Extracellular potassium ions attach to the protein.

5   The loss of the phosphate group restores the protein's original shape, thus causing the release of the potassium ions into the intracellular space.

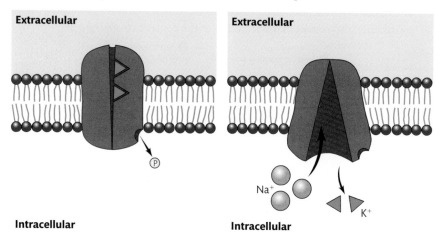

Figure 1.23 Stage 5: The protein opens towards the cell interior again and releases the potassium ions into the interior.

The sodium–potassium pump shows how important and active specific proteins are in the active transport of particular substances. It is also clear how ATP plays a crucial role in active transport.

There are many other examples of active transport in cells besides the sodium–potassium pump. Liver cells use active transport to accumulate glucose molecules from blood plasma even though the liver has a higher glucose concentration.

Endocytosis and exocytosis

Endocytosis and exocytosis are processes that allow larger molecules to move across the plasma membrane. Endocytosis allows macromolecules to enter the cell, while exocytosis allows molecules to leave. Both processes depend on the fluidity of the plasma membrane. It is important to recall why the cell membranes are fluid in consistency: the phospholipid molecules are not closely packed together, largely because of the rather 'loose' connections between the fatty acid tails. It is also important to remember why the membrane is quite stable: the hydrophilic and hydrophobic properties of the different regions of the phospholipid molecules cause them to form a stable bilayer in an aqueous environment.

Endocytosis occurs when a portion of the plasma membrane is pinched off to enclose macromolecules or particulates. This pinching off involves a change in the shape of the membrane. The result is the formation of a vesicle that then enters the cytoplasm of the cell. The ends of the membrane reattach because of the hydrophobic and hydrophilic properties of the phospholipids and the presence of water. This could not occur if the plasma membrane did not have a fluid nature.

Exocytosis is essentially the reverse of endocytosis, so the fluidity of the plasma membrane and the hydrophobic and hydrophilic properties of its molecules are just as important as in endocytosis. One example of cell exocytosis involves proteins produced in the cytoplasm of a cell. Protein exocytosis usually begins in the ribosomes of rough ER and progresses through a series of four steps, outlined below, until the substance produced is secreted to the environment outside the cell.

Cystic fibrosis is a human genetic disease in which the membrane protein that transports chloride ions is missing. This causes high concentrations of water inside the cells that line the lungs, and abnormally thickened mucus production. It is a very serious condition.

1   Protein produced by the ribosomes of the rough ER enters the lumen, inner space, of the ER.

2   Protein exits the ER and enters the *cis* side or face of the Golgi apparatus; a vesicle is involved.

Examples of endocytosis include:

- phagocytosis, the intake of large particulate matter
- pinocytosis, the intake of extracellular fluids.

3 As the protein moves through the Golgi apparatus, it is modified and exits on the *trans* face inside a vesicle.

4 The vesicle with the modified protein inside moves to and fuses with the plasma membrane; this results in the secretion of the contents from the cell.

Figure 1.24 How the Golgi apparatus functions.

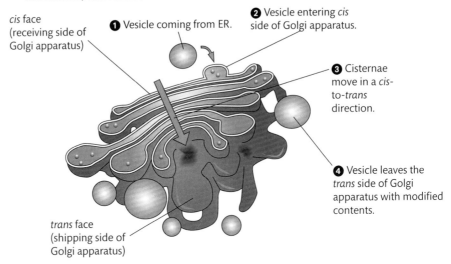

cis face (receiving side of Golgi apparatus)

❶ Vesicle coming from ER.

❷ Vesicle entering *cis* side of Golgi apparatus.

❸ Cisternae move in a *cis*-to-*trans* direction.

❹ Vesicle leaves the *trans* side of Golgi apparatus with modified contents.

trans face (shipping side of Golgi apparatus)

Examples of exocytosis occur when:

- pancreas cells produce insulin and secrete it into the bloodstream (to help regulate blood glucose levels)
- neurotransmitters are released at synapses in the nervous system.

The fluidity of the plasma membrane is essential to allow fusion and subsequent secretion of the vesicle contents. At this point the vesicle membrane is actually a part of the plasma membrane.

Summary of membrane transport processes

Table 1.9 Passive processes

Process	Source of energy	Description	Example
Diffusion	Kinetic energy of molecules	Movement along a concentration gradient	Oxygen moving through plasma membrane
Facilitated diffusion	Kinetic energy of molecules	Diffusion using a carrier	Glucose moving into cells
Osmosis	Kinetic energy of molecules	Diffusion of water through a partially permeable membrane	Movement of water in and out of cells through aquaporins

Table 1.10 Active processes

Process	Source of energy	Description	Example
Active transport	ATP	Movement through a membrane against a concentration gradient	Sodium–potassium pump
Exocytosis	ATP	Vesicles fuse with plasma membrane and eject contents from the cell	Secretion of insulin from pancreatic cells
Endocytosis	ATP	Vesicles form from the cell exterior creating vesicles that move inwards	Phagocytosis and pinocytosis

16 Why is the term equilibrium used with passive but not active transport?

17 What type of amino acids will be present where integral proteins attach to cell membranes?

18 Why are exocytosis and endocytosis known as examples of active transport?

1.5 The origin of cells

Understandings:

- Cells can only be formed by division of pre-existing cells.
- The first cells must have arisen from non-living material.
- The origin of eukaryotic cells can be explained by the endosymbiotic theory.

Applications and skills:

- Application: Evidence from Pasteur's experiments that spontaneous generation of cells and organisms does not now occur on Earth.

Guidance
- Evidence for the endosymbiotic theory is expected. The origin of eukaryote cilia and flagella does not need to be included.
- Students should be aware that the 64 codons in the genetic code have the same meanings in nearly all organisms, but that there are some minor variations that are likely to have accrued since the common origin of life on Earth.

Cell theory

The cell theory was discussed in Section 1.1. We mentioned that the current theory has three main parts:

1 all organisms are composed of one or more cells

2 cells are the smallest units of life

3 all cells come from other pre-existing cells.

We also mentioned that there are some problems with and exceptions to the current cell theory. These exceptions will now be discussed. Scientists use the term theory to represent a well-substantiated explanation of a natural phenomenon that incorporates tested hypotheses and laws. Because of this, a theory is an extremely valuable endpoint of science that represents understandings that have developed from extensive observation, experimentation, and logical inferences. Cell theory is a prime example of this. It has been modified during the years since it was first proposed in the 1800s. It will continue to be modified as cellular research progresses in the future.

One obvious missing component of cell theory is how the first cell arose. There is no evidence that new cells arise from non-living material today. However, the first cells must have been formed in this way. As already mentioned, in the 19th century the famous French scientist Louis Pasteur showed that bacteria could not spontaneously appear in sterile broth. Here is an overview of his experiment.

1 He boiled a nutrient broth.
2 The now sterile nutrient broth was then placed in three flasks, as shown below. Incubation over a period of time was then allowed.

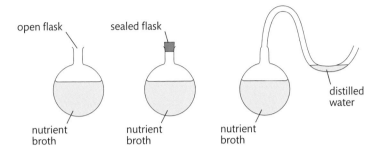

Figure 1.25 Pasteur's broth experiment.

open flask   sealed flask

distilled water

nutrient broth   nutrient broth   nutrient broth

3 A sample of each flask was then transferred to a plate containing solid medium and incubated.

The only flask sample that showed the presence of bacteria was the opened one. The other two did not show any bacterial growth. This indicated to Pasteur that the concept of spontaneous generation was wrong.

The Italian scientist Francesco Redi also questioned the concept of spontaneous generation, nearly 200 years before Pasteur, and conducted an experiment using raw meat in jars. Many other experiments have been done since the work of these two science pioneers, casting further doubt on the idea of spontaneous generation.

Moving on to the exceptions to the current cell theory, these include:

• the multinucleated cells of striated muscle cells, fungal hyphae, and several types of giant algae
• very large cells with continuous cytoplasm that are not compartmentalized into separate smaller cells
• viruses
• the problem of explaining the 'first' cells without spontaneous generation.

These examples represent exceptions to the 'normal' cells that we see in most of the organisms on Earth today. Continued research is needed to see how these exceptions 'fit' in with the current cell theory.

A common origin for all cells on Earth requires an explanation of how a cell could progress from a simple, non-compartmentalized prokaryote to a complex, highly compartmentalized eukaryote. This is currently explained by the endosymbiotic theory. This theory was presented by Lynn Margulis in 1981. Key points of the theory include:

• about 2 billion years ago a bacterial cell took up residence inside a eukaryotic cell
• the eukaryotic cell acted as a 'predator', bringing the bacterial cell inside
• the eukaryotic cell and the bacterial cell formed a symbiotic relationship, in which both organisms lived in contact with one another
• the bacterial cell then went through a series of changes to ultimately become a mitochondrion.

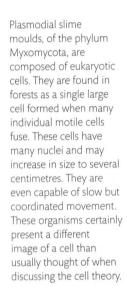

Plasmodial slime moulds, of the phylum Myxomycota, are composed of eukaryotic cells. They are found in forests as a single large cell formed when many individual motile cells fuse. These cells have many nuclei and may increase in size to several centimetres. They are even capable of slow but coordinated movement. These organisms certainly present a different image of a cell than usually thought of when discussing the cell theory.

NATURE OF SCIENCE

Now is an ideal time to have a classroom discussion about cell characteristics, the functions of life, and exceptions to the current cell theory. In the discussion be open to the ideas of others, remembering that this is a key characteristic of a successful scientist.

In this process, the eukaryote helped the bacteria by providing protection and carbon compounds. The bacteria, after a series of changes, became specialized in providing the eukaryote with ATP. There is a lot of evidence to support this theory. Mitochondria:

- are about the size of most bacterial cells
- divide by fission, as do most bacterial cells
- divide independently of the host cell
- have their own ribosomes, which allows them to produce their own proteins
- have their own DNA, which more closely resembles the DNA of prokaryotic cells than of eukaryotic cells
- have two membranes on their exterior, which is consistent with an engulfing process.

In addition to the mitochondria, chloroplasts in plant cells also provide evidence for the theory of endosymbiosis. A modern-day protist called *Hatena* normally fulfils its nutritional needs by ingesting organic matter. However, when it behaves as a predator and ingests a green alga, it switches its method of fulfilling its nutritional needs to one that uses sunlight to convert organic molecules, a process known as photosynthesis. The two organisms, the *Hatena* and the green alga, continue to thrive in a symbiotic relationship.

Another organism, *Elysia chlorotica*, demonstrates a similar situation. *Elysia* is a slug found in salt and tidal marshes and creeks. Its early stage of life, referred to as its juvenile stage, characteristically involves movement and it derives its nutrition by ingesting nutrients from its surroundings. During this juvenile stage it is brown. As it develops, if *Elysia* comes into contact with a specific type of green algae, it will enter its adult phase, in which chloroplasts from the ingested algae will be retained in its digestive tract. The adult stage of *Elysia* is therefore green in colour. The symbiotic relationship between *Elysia* and the green algae allows the adult form of *Elysia* to take on a more sedentary lifestyle, depending on light being available to carry out photosynthesis.

The final bit of evidence for endosymbiotic theory is DNA. DNA provides a code made up of 64 different 'words'. Interestingly, this code has the same meaning in nearly all organisms on Earth and is said to be 'universal'. There are only slight variations, which can be explained by changes since the common origin of life on our planet. As mentioned above, the mitochondria of eukaryotic cells have a DNA code that more closely resembles bacteria than eukaryotic cells. Most scientists believe that the more DNA two organisms have in common, the more closely related they are to one another.

Exercises

19 Why did bacteria grow in the broth of the flask that was left open by Pasteur?

20 Provide an explanation for how a nucleus might have come to exist within eukaryotic cells.

21 How does the example of *Hatena* and the alga represent an emergent explanation of life?

22 From the evidence presented in this section, explain why many scientists feel there has been an unbroken chain of life from the first cells on Earth to all cells in organisms alive today.

CHALLENGE YOURSELF

14 On a sheet of paper produce a series of drawings that represent how two membranes could have come to exist on mitochondria and chloroplasts through an engulfing process involving endocytosis.

TOK

Biology is concerned not only with life, but also anything that affects life. When studying organisms, it is possible to take two approaches. One approach, often referred to as reductionism, reduces the complex phenomena of organisms to the interaction of their parts. Essentially, this viewpoint says it is the sum of the parts that make up the complex system, the organism. Another approach is that of holism or of looking at systems. This approach has the central belief that the whole is greater than the sum of its parts. Discuss how both approaches have allowed the accumulation of the body of knowledge we now possess in biology. Attempt to utilize both approaches to explain the functions of life as demonstrated by a single cell.

NATURE OF SCIENCE

Serendipity and scientific discoveries: the discovery of cyclins was accidental.

1.6 Cell division

Understandings:

- Mitosis is division of the nucleus into two genetically identical daughter nuclei.
- Chromosomes condense by supercoiling during mitosis.
- Cytokinesis occurs after mitosis and is different in plant and animal cells.
- Interphase is a very active phase of the cell cycle with many processes occurring in the nucleus and cytoplasm.
- Cyclins are involved in the control of the cell cycle.
- Mutagens, oncogenes, and metastasis are involved in the development of primary and secondary tumours.

Applications and skills:

- Application: The correlation between smoking and incidence of cancers.
- Skill: Identification of phases of mitosis in cells viewed with a microscope or in a micrograph.
- Skill: Determination of a mitotic index from a micrograph.

Guidance

- *The sequence of events in the four phases of mitosis should be known.*
- *Preparation of temporary mounts of root squashes is recommended but phases in mitosis can also be viewed using permanent slides.*
- *To avoid confusion in terminology, teachers are encouraged to refer to the two parts of a chromosome as sister chromatids, while they are attached to each other by a centromere in the early stages of mitosis. From anaphase onwards, when sister chromatids have separated to form individual structures, they should be referred to as chromosomes.*

The cell cycle

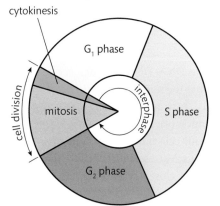

Figure 1.26 The cell cycle in eukaryotes.

The cell cycle describes the behaviour of cells as they grow and divide. In most cases, the cell produces two cells that are genetically identical to the original. These are called daughter cells. The cell cycle integrates a growth phase with a divisional phase. Sometimes, cells multiply so rapidly that they may form a solid mass of cells called a tumour. We refer to this disease state as cancer. It appears that any cell can lose its usual orderly pattern of division, because we have found cancer in almost all tissues and organs.

You may wonder what causes a cell to go out of control. To answer this question, we must first understand the ordinary cell cycle. Usually, the life of a cell involves two major phases. In one phase, growth is the major process. In the other phase, division is the major process. The cell cycle begins and ends as one cell, so it can be represented by a circle divided into various named sections, as shown in Figure 1.26.

Interphase

The largest phase of the cell cycle in most cells is interphase. This is the longest and most variable of the cell-cycle phases. Interphase includes three smaller phases: G_1, S, and G_2. During G_1, the major event is growth of the cell. At the beginning of G_1, the cell is the smallest it will ever be. After G_1 comes the S phase, in which the main activity is replication of the DNA of the cell, the chromosomes. This phase is sometimes referred to as the synthesis phase. Once the chromosomes have been replicated, the cell enters its second growth phase, called G_2. During this phase, the cell grows and makes preparations for mitosis, the M phase. During G_2, organelles may increase in number, DNA begins to condense from chromatin to chromosomes, and microtubules may begin to form.

Cyclins are a group of proteins that control the cell's progression through the cell cycle. The cyclins bind to cyclin-dependent protein kinases (CDKs), enabling them to act as enzymes. These activated enzymes then cause the cell to move from G_1 to the S phase and from G_2 to the M phase. The points where the cyclin-activated CDKs function are called checkpoints in the cell cycle. Some cells will pause during G_1 and enter a separate phase, the G_0 phase. G_0 is a non-growing state and certain cells stay in G_0 for varying periods of time. Some cells, such as nerve and muscle cells, never progress beyond the G_0 phase.

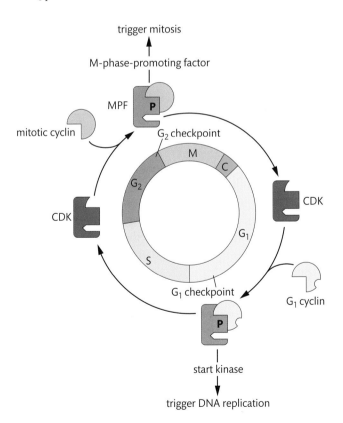

NATURE OF SCIENCE

Tim Hunt and Joan Ruderman were studying gene expression in early embryos. While doing so they found three proteins that varied in concentrations at different times of the cell cycle. These were eventually called cyclins. This illustrates that scientists must always be observant, to spot unplanned and surprising discoveries. This example of 'accidental' discovery is common in science.

Figure 1.27 Two cyclins are extremely important to the cell cycle: G_1 cyclin and mitotic cyclin. Note their location in the cell cycle and that they must combine with a CDK to become active.

Table 1.11 A summary of the events of interphase

Phases of interphase	Major events
G_1	Growth of cell and increase in number of organelles
S	Replication of chromosomes, with copies remaining attached to one another
G_2	Further growth occurs, organelles increase in number, DNA condenses to form visible chromosomes, microtubules begin to form
Overall	Cell is performing the tasks appropriate to its type, e.g. a cell of the pancreas may be actively secreting insulin to lower high glucose levels in the body

Mitosis

Once all the preparatory processes have taken place, and the DNA has replicated, the cell moves into mitosis or the M phase. During mitosis the replicated chromosomes separate and move to opposite poles of the cell, thus providing the same genetic material at each of these locations. When the chromosomes are at the poles of the cell, the cytoplasm divides to form two cells distinct from the larger parent. These two cells have the same genetic material and are referred to as daughter cells.

Mitosis involves four phases. They are, in sequence:

- prophase
- metaphase
- anaphase
- telophase.

To remember the correct order of phases in the cell cycle and mitosis, remember the word 'shipmate'. If you take away the word 'she', you get 'ipmat': these letters give you the order of interphase, prophase, metaphase, anaphase, and telophase.

Before considering a detailed description of these phases, it is essential you understand the chromosome. As you will recall, during the second growth phase, G_2, the chromatin (elongated DNA and histones) begins to condense. This condensation is accomplished via a process called supercoiling. First, the DNA wraps around histones to produce nucleosomes. The nucleosomes are further wrapped into a solenoid. Solenoids group together in looped domains, and then a final coiling occurs to produce the chromosome.

Eukaryotic cells contain chromosomes that, before replication in the S phase of the cell cycle, are composed of one molecule of DNA. After replication, the chromosome includes two molecules of DNA. These two identical molecules are held together by the centromere, and each molecule is referred to as a chromatid. Together, they are called sister chromatids. The chromatids will eventually separate during the process of mitosis. When they do, each is then called a chromosome and each has its own centromere.

Once you are familiar with the structure of a chromosome, you can understand the four phases of mitosis. Remember, when a cell enters the phases of mitosis, replication of DNA has already occurred. Therefore, the chromosomes at this stage are each composed of two sister chromatids.

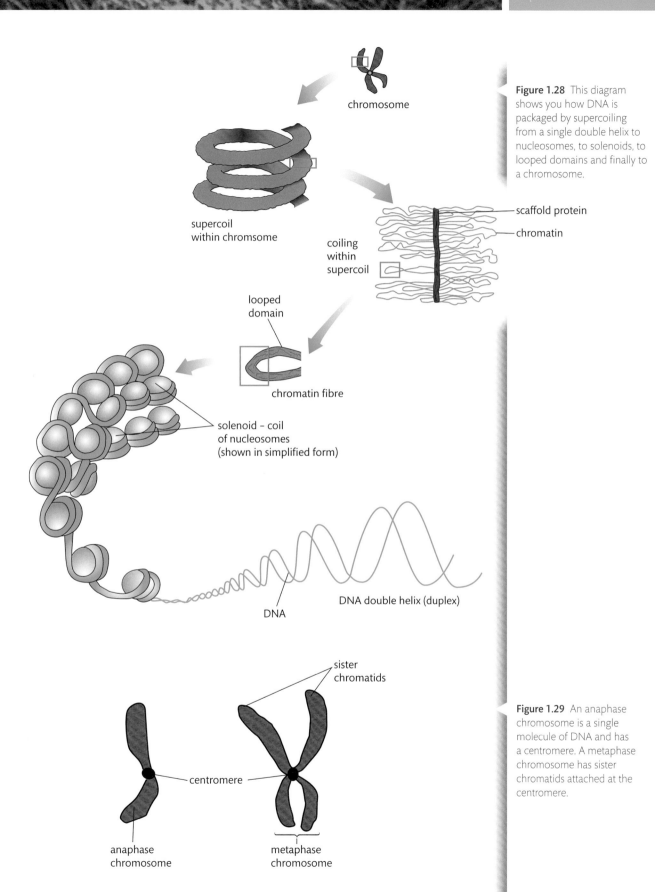

chromosome

supercoil
within chromsome

coiling
within
supercoil

scaffold protein

chromatin

looped
domain

chromatin fibre

solenoid – coil
of nucleosomes
(shown in simplified form)

DNA

DNA double helix (duplex)

Figure 1.28 This diagram shows you how DNA is packaged by supercoiling from a single double helix to nucleosomes, to solenoids, to looped domains and finally to a chromosome.

sister
chromatids

centromere

anaphase
chromosome

metaphase
chromosome

Figure 1.29 An anaphase chromosome is a single molecule of DNA and has a centromere. A metaphase chromosome has sister chromatids attached at the centromere.

Prophase

Examine the figure below.

1 The chromatin fibres become more tightly coiled to form chromosomes.
2 The nuclear envelope disintegrates and nucleoli disappear.

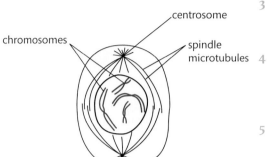

3 The mitotic spindle begins to form and is complete at the end of prophase.
4 The centromere of each chromosome has a region called the kinetochore that attaches to the spindle.
5 The centrosomes move towards the opposite poles of the cell as a result of lengthening microtubules.

Figure 1.30 This animal cell is in prophase. For clarity, only a small number of chromosomes is shown.

Metaphase

Examine the figure below.

1 The chromosomes move to the middle or equator of the cell. This is referred to as the metaphase plate.
2 The chromosomes' centromeres lie on the plate.
3 The movement of chromosomes arises as the result of the action of the spindle, which is made of microtubules.
4 The centrosomes are now at the opposite poles.

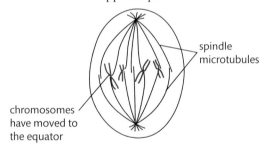

Figure 1.31 The cell is now in metaphase. Again, only a small number of chromosomes is shown.

Anaphase

Examine the figure at the top of the next page.

1 This is usually the shortest phase of mitosis. It begins when the two sister chromatids of each chromosome are split.
2 These chromatids, now chromosomes, move towards the opposite poles of the cell.
3 The chromatid movement arises as a result of the shortening of the microtubules of the spindle.
4 Because the centromeres are attached to the microtubules, they move towards the poles first.
5 At the end of this phase, each pole of the cell has a complete, identical set of chromosomes.

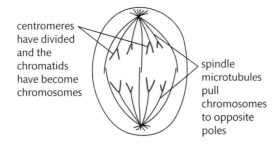

centromeres have divided and the chromatids have become chromosomes

spindle microtubules pull chromosomes to opposite poles

Figure 1.32 The cell is now in anaphase. Again, only a small number of chromosomes is shown.

Telophase

Examine the figure below.

1   The chromosomes are at each pole.
2   A nuclear membrane (envelope) begins to re-form around each set of chromosomes.
3   The chromosomes start to elongate to form chromatin.
4   Nucleoli reappear.
5   The spindle apparatus disappears.
6   The cell is elongated and ready for cytokinesis.

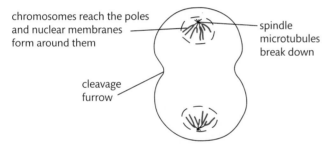

chromosomes reach the poles and nuclear membranes form around them

spindle microtubules break down

cleavage furrow

Figure 1.33 Finally, the cell enters telophase.

Cytokinesis

As you can see, the phases of mitosis involve nuclear division. It appears that the process of mitosis occurs in discrete stages. But this is not in fact true: the stages occur along a continuum. We only use the separate stages to help us understand the overall process.

Once nuclear division has occurred, the cell undergoes cytokinesis. Cytokinesis in animal cells involves an inward pinching of the fluid plasma membrane to form cleavage furrows. However, plant cells have a relatively firm cell wall and they form a cell plate. The cell plate occurs midway between the two poles of the cell and moves outwards towards the sides of the cell from a central region. Both processes result in two separate daughter cells that have genetically identical nuclei.

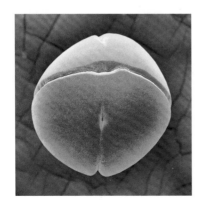

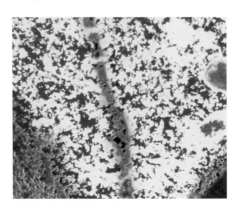

Left:
Frog embryo showing cells dividing to form the 4-cell stage.
Right:
Micrograph showing the telophase stage of mitosis in the root tip cell of maize.
Most noticeable is the cell wall being formed that will separate the daughter cells in cytokinesis.

Figure 1.34 Cytokinesis in animal and plant cells.

cleavage furrow

daughter cells

contractile ring of microfilaments

Cleavage of an animal cell (SEM)

vesicles forming cell plate

cell plate

new cell wall

wall of parent cell

daughter cells

Cell plate formation in a plant cell (TEM)

Table 1.12 A summary of the two types of cytokinesis

Cell example	Description of cytokinesis
Animal	Cell membrane pinches inwards forming cleavage furrows that ultimately separate the two cells
Plant	Cell plate forms from the inside producing the rigid cell walls that separate the two cells

The growth of organisms, development of embryos, tissue repair, and asexual reproduction all involve mitosis. Mitosis does not happen by itself. It is a part of the cell cycle.

Study the micrographs below and on page 49 to note the main events of the stages of mitosis and to note the differences between plant and animal cells in mitosis. Note that A is from a plant cell and B is from an animal cell.

A Micrograph of root tip cells from an onion undergoing mitosis. From top left to bottom right: the chromosomes condense and appear as long thread-like structures (prophase). They then align along the centre of the cell (metaphase). Each chromosome consists of two identical sister chromatids that separate and are pulled to opposite ends of the cell (anaphase). Nuclear membranes then form around the two daughter nuclei as the chromosomes de-condense (telophase). The cell then divides (cytokinesis).

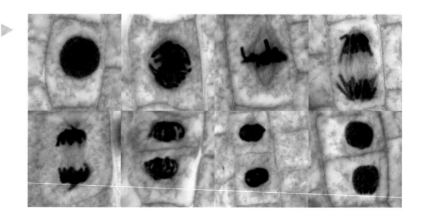

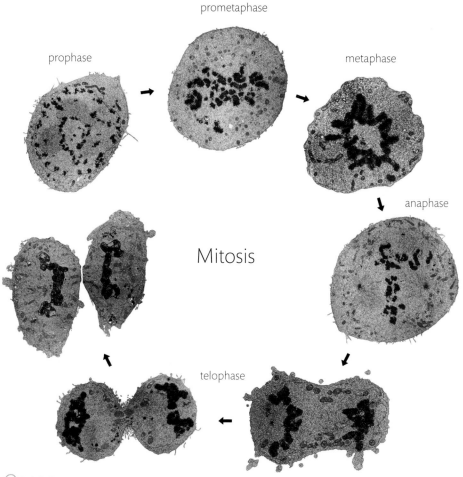

prophase

prometaphase

metaphase

anaphase

Mitosis

telophase

Cancer

As mentioned earlier, cancer occurs when a cell's cycle becomes out of control. The result is a mass of abnormal cells referred to as a tumour. A primary tumour is one that occurs at the original site of a cancer. A secondary tumour is a metastasis, a cancerous tumour that has spread from the original location to another part of the organism. An example of metastasis is a brain tumour that is in fact composed of breast cancer cells. In some cases the metastasis of the primary tumour cells is so extensive that secondary tumours are found in many locations within the organism.

Laboratories all over the world are busy researching causes and treatments for all known types of cancers. Sharing of information is a common occurrence amongst these laboratories and their researchers.

The mitotic index is an important tool for predicting the response of cancer cells to chemotherapy. It is the ratio of the number of cells in a tumour or tissue type undergoing mitosis compared with the number of cells not undergoing mitosis. A higher mitotic index indicates a more rapid proliferation of cells of a certain type. It is likely that tumours with higher mitotic indices will be more difficult to control, and a patient with such a tumour may be given a poorer prognosis than a patient with a tumour that has a lower mitotic index.

A question to consider here is how or why a primary tumour forms. Most organisms have sections of genes that may mutate or may be expressed at abnormally high levels. These sections of genes, called oncogenes, contribute to converting a normal cell into a cancer cell. The oncogenes may start to change or go through mutation because they are triggered by an outside agent referred to as a mutagen. One such potential mutagen is cigarette smoke. There is a correlation between smoking and the incidence of cancer. This has been shown consistently in many independent studies. Examine the graph from the World Health Organization shown in Figure 1.35 and note the positive correlation.

TOK This is an appropriate time to discuss the unethical actions of the tobacco industry in the suppression of results linking smoking with cancer. A global perspective should be included in this discussion.

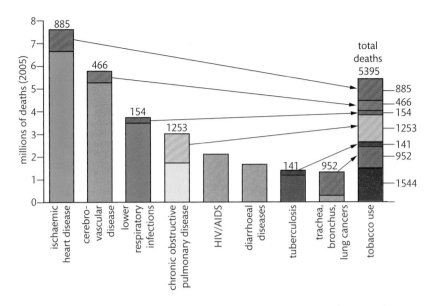

Figure 1.35 Examine this graph from the World Health Organization noting tobacco use as a risk factor for eight leading causes of death in the world. Especially note the information provided concerning trachea, bronchus, and lung cancers. Darker areas indicate proportions of deaths that are related to tobacco use and are coloured according to the column of the respective cause of death. WHO, http://www.who.int/tobacco/mpower/graphs/en/index.html

A very interesting activity is to find micrographs on the internet of various human tissues going through cell division. Determine the mitotic index of these various types of tissue. Attempt to find micrographs of the same types of tissue that are cancerous and determine their mitotic index. This comparison will show quite effectively the more rapid cell division found in cancer tissues.

CHALLENGE YOURSELF

Cancer cells have a higher rate of mitotic division than normal cells. Because of this, cancer tissue has a higher mitotic index than normal tissue. This is why cancer cells can grow and spread very rapidly.

15 If a microscopic field of 1000 normal cells has 900 cells in interphase, estimate the number of cells in interphase when 1000 cells of the same type are from tissue that is cancerous.

16 If the normal cells have an average cell cycle time of 600 minutes, estimate the average, relative cell cycle time of the cancer cells.

17 How does this information affect the mitotic index of the two sets of cells?

Exercises

23 A chemical called colchicine disrupts the formation of microtubules. What effect would this drug have on a cell going through mitosis?

24 If a parent cell has 24 chromosomes, how many chromatids would be present during metaphase of mitosis?

25 Explain when cytokinesis occurs within the cell cycle.

26 Compare cytokinesis in plant and animal cells.

27 What is the value of the mitotic index?

To learn more about the mitotic phases, go to the hotlinks site, search for the title or ISBN, and click on Chapter 1: Section 1.6.

1   The micrograph on the right shows an adult human stem cell.

   (a) The cell cycle can be divided into two parts: interphase and mitosis.

       (i) Identify, with a reason, whether the stem cell in the micrograph
            is in interphase or mitosis.   (1)

       (ii) Deduce **two** processes that occur in human cells during this
            part of the cell cycle, but not during the other part.   (2)

   (b) State **two** characteristics of stem cells that can be used to
        distinguish them from other body cells.   (2)

   (c) Outline **one** therapeutic use of stem cells.   (3)

                                                              (*Total 8 marks*)

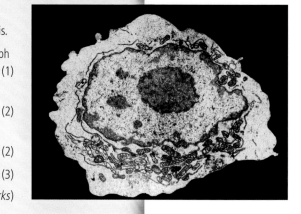

2   To the right is a micrograph of an *E. coli* bacterium
    undergoing reproduction.

    In the diagram what does label X identify?

    A Nucleoid   **C** Histones
           region
                             D Endoplasmic
    B Chromatin   reticulum

                              (*Total 1 mark*)

3   Which of the following is **not** a function performed
    by a membrane protein?

    A Hormone-   **B** Cell adhesion   **C** Enzyme   **D** Pumps for
           binding sites   synthesis   active transport

                                                                          (*Total 1 mark*)

4   Which of the following take(s) place during either interphase or mitosis in animal cells?

    I.   Re-formation of nuclear membranes.

    II. Pairing of homologous chromosomes.

    III. DNA replication.

    A I only.   **B** I and II only.   **C** II and III only.   **D** I and III only.

                                                                          (*Total 1 mark*)

5 **(a)** The scanning electron micrograph on the right shows the surface of the nuclear
       envelope with numerous nuclear pores.

       (i) Calculate the power of magnification of the image.   (1)

       (ii) State the diameter of the pore labelled X.   (1)

   (b) List **two** examples of how human life depends on mitosis.   (1)

   (c) Describe the importance of stem cells in differentiation.   (3)

                                                              (*Total 6 marks*)

   Adapted from Nelson and Cox 2000,
   © Don W. Fawcett/Science Source

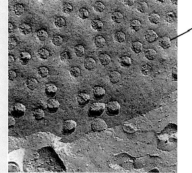

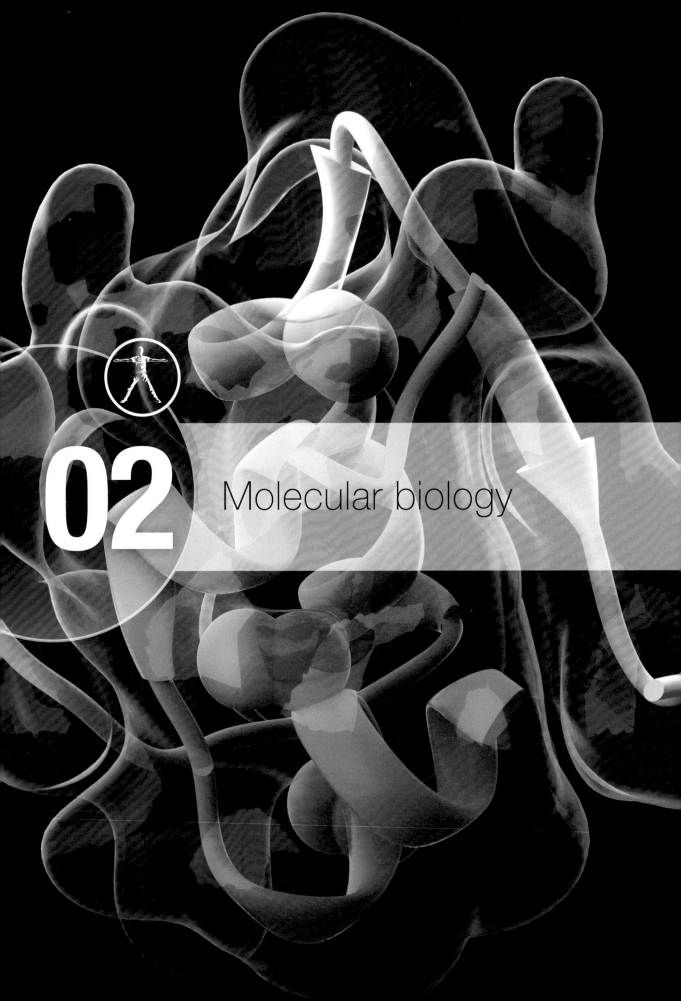

02 Molecular biology

Essential ideas

2.1 Living organisms control their composition by a complex web of chemical reactions.

2.2 Water is the medium of life.

2.3 Compounds of carbon, hydrogen, and oxygen are used to supply and store energy.

2.4 Proteins have a very wide range of functions in living organisms.

2.5 Enzymes control the metabolism of the cell.

2.6 The structure of DNA allows efficient storage of genetic information.

2.7 Genetic information in DNA can be accurately copied and can be translated to make the proteins needed by the cell.

2.8 Cell respiration supplies energy for the functions of life.

2.9 Photosynthesis uses the energy in sunlight to produce the chemical energy needed for life.

Computer image of an insulin molecule. Insulin is a peptide (protein) hormone that helps to regulate glucose levels between the bloodstream and the cytoplasm of cells.

Organic chemistry is the chemistry of carbon compounds. Biochemistry is the branch of organic chemistry that attempts to explain the chemistry characteristics of living organisms. Even though biochemistry can be amazingly complex and varied, there are common patterns that are well known. For example, all living organisms are made up of molecules that can be classified into one of four types:

- carbohydrates
- lipids
- proteins
- nucleic acids.

In addition, biochemical processes in living organisms follow certain common pathways for which we can study the common pattern. So, when we study cell respiration or photosynthesis as biochemical processes, we do not need to study a completely different process for each organism or species.

This chapter will introduce you to some of the more common biochemically important molecules and processes.

2.1 Molecules to metabolism

Understandings:
- Molecular biology explains living processes in terms of the chemical substances involved.
- Carbon atoms can form four covalent bonds, allowing a diversity of stable compounds to exist.
- Life is based on carbon compounds, including carbohydrates, lipids, proteins, and nucleic acids.
- Metabolism is the web of all the enzyme-catalysed reactions in a cell or organism.
- Anabolism is the synthesis of complex molecules from simpler molecules, including the formation of macromolecules from monomers by condensation reactions.
- Catabolism is the breakdown of complex molecules into simpler molecules including the hydrolysis of macromolecules into monomers.

NATURE OF SCIENCE

Falsification of theories: the artificial synthesis of urea helped to falsify vitalism.

Applications and skills:

- Application: Urea as an example of a compound that is produced by living organisms but can also be artificially synthesized.
- Skill: Drawing molecular diagrams of glucose, ribose, a saturated fatty acid, and a generalized amino acid.
- Skill: Identification of biochemicals such as sugars, lipids, or amino acids from molecular diagrams.

Guidance
- Only the ring forms of D-ribose, alpha-D-glucose, and beta-D-glucose are expected in drawings.
- Sugars include monosaccharides and disaccharides.
- Only one saturated fat is expected, and its specific name is not necessary.
- The variable radical of amino acids can be shown as R. The structure of individual R-groups does not need to be memorized.
- Students should be able to recognize from molecular diagrams that triglycerides, phospholipids, and steroids are lipids. Drawings of steroids are not expected.
- Proteins or parts of polypeptides should be recognized from molecular diagrams showing amino acids linked by peptide bonds.

Aquaporins are channels that allow water molecules to pass through the membrane.

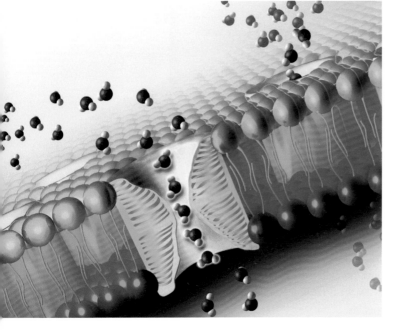

Molecular biology is the chemistry of living organisms

The majority of molecules within all living organisms can be categorized into one of four biochemical groupings. Those groupings are carbohydrates, lipids, proteins, and nucleic acids. In turn, these four groupings of molecules interact with each other in a wide variety of ways in order to carry out the metabolism of each cell.

Consider the following example of metabolism in order to see how living processes are actually chemical substances interacting in predictable patterns. Insulin is a protein hormone that facilitates the movement of glucose from the bloodstream to the interior of cells. Insulin does this by interacting with protein channels in body cell plasma membranes, thereby opening those channels to glucose. As long as glucose is in a higher concentration outside the cell compared with inside the cell, glucose will continue to move through the open channel by diffusion. The plasma membrane is largely composed of a type of lipid called a phospholipid. Because of molecular polarity differences, phospholipids will not allow glucose to pass through the membrane without going through the protein channels. Both insulin and the channels within the plasma membrane are proteins, therefore they must both be coded for by deoxyribonucleic acid (DNA) within the cells of the organism in which they are working.

Glucose is a carbohydrate, the phospholipid molecules are lipids, both insulin and the membrane channels are proteins, and DNA is a nucleic acid. Each molecule has a specific function and collectively they all work together in order to ensure that body cells have access to glucose for their energy needs. All the biochemistry within all living organisms can be 'broken down' into smaller interactions similar to the above example.

Carbon-based life

Organic chemistry is the study of compounds that contain carbon. Some compounds
that contain carbon are not classified as organic, including carbon dioxide. Despite
this important exception, there are very many molecules containing carbon that are
classified as organic. The molecules already mentioned above (carbohydrates, proteins,
lipids, and nucleic acids) are all organic molecules. These are the molecules from which
all living things are composed, thus the element carbon can be considered to be the
keystone element for life on Earth. This is the reason why you sometimes hear life on
Earth being described as 'carbon based'.

You may recall from your introductory chemistry course that each carbon atom has an
atomic number of six. Directly this means that carbon has six protons, but indirectly
it also means that carbon has six electrons. Two of these six electrons form the stable
inner shell, and four are found in the second and unfilled shell. Carbon's way of 'filling'
this second shell of electrons is to share four electrons with other atoms in order to
create a stable configuration of eight electrons in total. Each time carbon shares one of
its electrons, a covalent bond is formed, and carbon always forms four covalent bonds.

There are many other elements found within the molecules of living organisms.
In addition to carbon, the following elements are common: hydrogen, oxygen,
nitrogen, and phosphorus. These elements are used in the molecular structures of
carbohydrates, proteins, lipids, and nucleic acids by forming covalent bonds with
carbon, and very often by forming covalent bonds with each other.

Carbon dioxide is one of the
very few carbon-containing
substances that is not classified
as organic. In this model the
black, centre, atom is the
carbon atom, and the two red
atoms are the oxygen atoms.

Carbon's name is derived
from the Latin word
'carbo', meaning charcoal.

TOK You will notice that
virtually all the images
you see of atoms and
molecules are in the
form of models. Why are
models used? What do the
real atoms and molecules
look like?

The structure and bonding
of an ethanol molecule.
The atoms shown in black
are carbon, the red atom
is oxygen, and all the white
atoms are hydrogen.

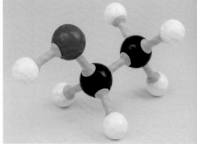

Biochemical compounds that are important to living organisms

Living things are composed of an amazing array of molecules. We can start to
make sense of all of these molecules by classifying them into different types.
Molecules of the same type have certain qualities in common and become fairly
easy to recognize with a little practice. Table 2.1 shows some of the more common
biochemically important molecules and their subcomponents (or building blocks).

Table 2.1 Types of molecules

Molecule	Subcomponents (building blocks)
Carbohydrates	Monosaccharides
Lipids	Glycerol, fatty acids, phosphate groups
Proteins (polypeptides)	Amino acids
Nucleic acids	Nucleotides

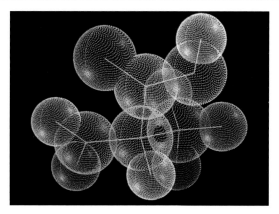

This is a colour-coded molecular model of the amino acid alanine. Green = carbon; pink = oxygen; blue = nitrogen; white = hydrogen.

As you study biochemistry, you will soon learn to recognize and classify common biochemical molecules into appropriate categories. Table 2.2 shows some of the common categories and examples of molecules.

Table 2.2 Common categories of molecules

Category	Subcategory	Example molecules
Carbohydrates	Monosaccharides	Glucose, galactose, fructose, ribose
	Disaccharides	Maltose, lactose, sucrose
	Polysaccharides	Starch, glycogen, cellulose, chitin
Proteins		Enzymes, antibodies, peptide hormones
Lipids	Triglycerides	Fat stored in adipose cells
	Phospholipids	Lipids forming a bilayer in cell membranes
	Steroids	Some hormones
Nucleic acids		Deoxyribonucleic acid (DNA), ribonucleic acid (RNA), adenosine triphosphate (ATP)

The ways in which these molecules interact with each other in living organisms is amazingly diverse and interesting. All of these interactions are referred to as metabolism and that is the focus of the next section.

Metabolism: reactions controlled by enzymes

If you were to visualize zooming into the inside of a cell down to the molecular level, you would see thousands of molecules colliding with each other as they move through their aqueous (water-based) environment. Many of these collisions do not result in any action other than the molecules changing direction and thus heading into new collisions. But sometimes these molecular collisions provide enough energy to specific molecules, the reactants, for those reactants to undergo a chemical reaction of some type. That single chemical reaction would be one of the millions of reactions that occur within that cell that comprise that cell's metabolism. In a multicellular organism, all of the reactions within all of the cells (and fluids such as blood) comprise the metabolism of the organism.

When two molecules collide, a large number of factors determines whether a reaction occurs or not. Some of these factors include the:

• identity of the colliding molecules
• orientation of the colliding molecules (where they hit each other)
• the speed of the molecules when they collide.

Cells use enzymes in order to increase the likelihood that a collision will lead to a useful reaction. Enzymes are protein molecules that have a specific shape into which a reactant(s) can fit, at a molecular location called the active site of the enzyme. By having an active site, the enzyme increases the likelihood of a reaction.

Let's look at an example of one reaction that makes up part of a typical cell's metabolism. The reaction we will consider is one in which adenosine triphosphate (ATP) is formed or synthesized. ATP is the most common molecule used by cells when chemical energy is required. ATP is synthesized from the bonding of adenosine diphosphate (ADP) to a phosphate (P) group. This reaction requires energy, and that energy may come originally from food (cell respiration) or sunlight (photosynthesis). Put simply, the reaction can be summarized as:

$$ADP + P_i \rightarrow ATP$$

adenosine diphosphate plus inorganic phosphate yields adenosine triphosphate

The odds of these two reactants ($ADP + P_i$) colliding at a very high speed, at exactly the correct orientation, leading to a new covalent bond forming between them, is extremely small. That is where an enzyme comes into play: the enzyme acts as a catalyst for the reaction. The catalyst will not be used up and so the enzyme will be available to act as a catalyst many times over. The ADP reactant fits into part of the enzyme's active site, and the inorganic phosphate group reactant fits perfectly oriented next to it, and, within a small fraction of a second, the two reactants become covalently bonded to each other. So, in effect, three molecules are involved in the collision but only two of them result in the production of ATP. The ATP is then released from the active site and the enzyme is ready for another collision with another ADP and phosphate group. The catalysis provided by the enzyme enables this reaction to occur at a much higher reaction rate and with less collisional energy compared with the same reaction occurring without the enzyme.

All of your metabolism is based on this fundamental scenario. A multitude of reactions are occurring inside each living organism's cells at any given moment. Most of these reactions are being catalysed by enzymes. These are the reactions that make up your overall metabolism, and include diverse sets of reactions, including:

• replication of DNA, in preparation for cell division
• synthesis of RNA, allowing chemical communication between the nucleus and cytoplasm

Metabolism is best thought about from a molecular perspective. Often, people think only of physiological parameters, such as heart rate and digestion, as their metabolism. But remember that metabolism is all of the reactions within all of the cells of an organism.

The 'collisional energy' referred to in this section is called activation energy. An enzyme is often defined as an organic catalyst that lowers the activation energy of a reaction.

- synthesis of proteins, including bonding of one amino acid to another
- cell respiration, with nutrients being converted into ATP
- photosynthesis, with light energy being used to create carbohydrates
- and many, many more.

Metabolism = catabolism + anabolism

It is very common for people to use some form of the word metabolism in everyday conversations, for example: 'I wish I had a higher metabolic rate so that I could eat more without putting on weight'. When people say something like that, they are usually thinking of factors like their heart rate. There is actually a great deal more than this involved in metabolism. As described in the previous section, your metabolism is the sum total of all the enzyme-catalysed reactions taking place within you. Some of these enzyme-catalysed reactions function to convert large, complex molecules (like many of the foods that we eat) to smaller, simpler molecular forms. This is called catabolism. Other enzyme-catalysed reactions carry out the reverse: they convert small, simple molecules into a larger, more complex molecules. This is called anabolism. These molecular conversions are done for a variety of reasons, and we will look at a couple of examples in this section. You will find more examples later as you study the various biochemical and physiological processes common to living organisms.

Many organisms, including all animals, rely on the foods that they eat to obtain the building block molecules that make up their larger molecules. When animals eat foods, the food is digested (or hydrolysed) into the building blocks (catabolism). After these building blocks are transported to body cells, they are bonded together to form larger molecules once again (anabolism).

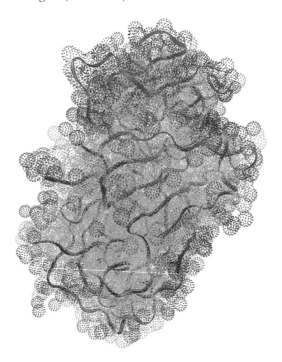

Let's explore what happens to ingested foods. Foods are chemically digested in your alimentary canal. The digestive enzymes that accomplish this are hydrolysing

Many of the carbon atoms found in the food that you eat (such as carbohydrates) will be eliminated from your body in the molecules of carbon dioxide that you breathe out.

This computer graphic image shows pepsin, an enzyme that helps to digest proteins. Pepsin is an example of a hydrolysing enzyme.

enzymes. Each reaction is called a hydrolysis and requires a molecule of water as a reactant. This is a good way to recognize hydrolysis reactions: water is always 'split' as part of the reaction. Below are four examples of hydrolysis reactions.

1   Hydrolysis of a disaccharide to two monosaccharides (see Figure 2.1).

lactose + water → glucose + galactose

Figure 2.1 Hydrolysis of the disaccharide lactose to form the two monosaccharides galactose and glucose. The difference between galactose and glucose is shown in the blue areas.

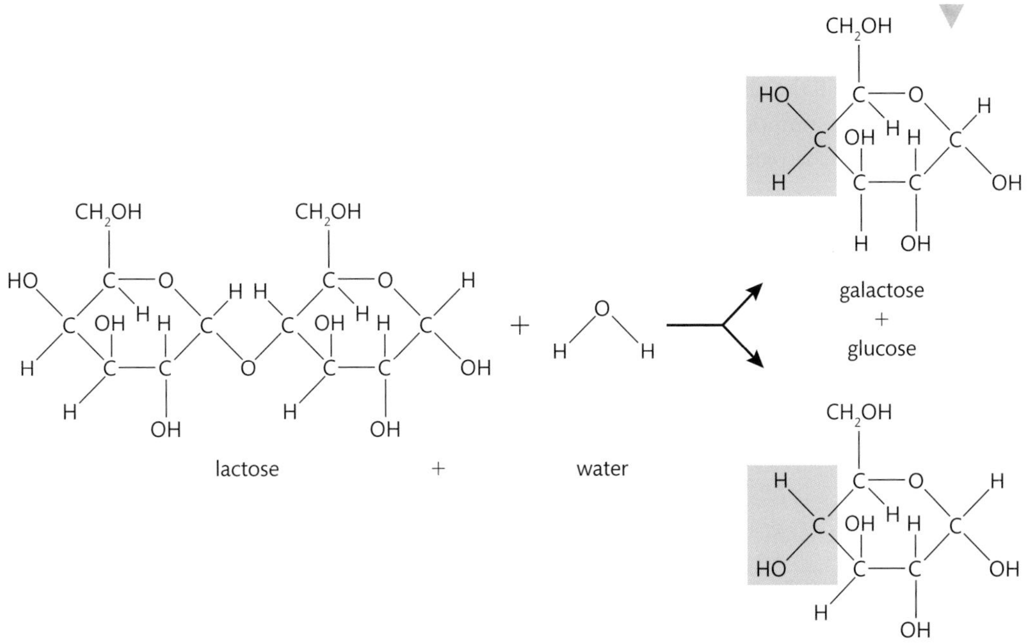

lactose   +   water

galactose
+
glucose

2   Hydrolysis of a polysaccharide to many monosaccharides.

starch + (many) water → (many) glucose

3   Hydrolysis of a triglyceride lipid to glycerol and fatty acids (see Figure 2.2).

triglyceride + 3 water → glycerol + 3 fatty acids

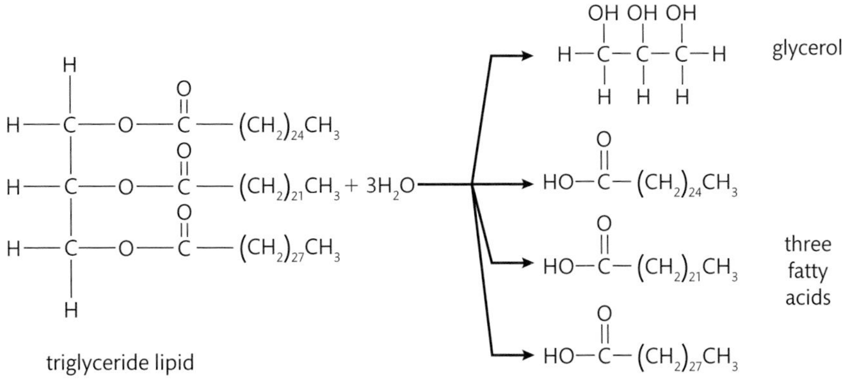

triglyceride lipid

glycerol

three
fatty
acids

Figure 2.2 Hydrolysis of a triglyceride lipid to form glycerol and three fatty acid molecules.

4   Hydrolysis of a polypeptide (protein) to amino acids.

protein + (many) water → (many) amino acids

Condensation reactions are, in many ways, the reverse of hydrolysis reactions. In cells, condensation reactions occur to re-form the larger, biochemically important, molecules. In the four examples given above, simply reverse the reaction arrow and each example shows a condensation reaction. For example:

- condensation of amino acids to form a polypeptide

(many) amino acids → protein + (many) water

Notice that in condensation reactions, water molecule(s) are products rather than reactants. Condensation reactions require a different type of enzyme, one that is capable of catalysing reactions in which covalent bonds are created rather than broken.

In summary, remember that an organism's metabolism comprises all of the reactions that occur within all of its cells. Thus metabolism can also be thought of as the sum of all the reactions that work to hydrolyse large biochemical substances into smaller subcomponents (catabolism), plus all those reactions that rebuild large, more complex biochemical substances from the smaller subcomponents (anabolism).

Molecular model of urea. The large grey atom is carbon. Each of the two blue side-chains is an amine functional group and the red atom is a double-bonded oxygen atom.

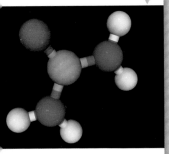

NATURE OF SCIENCE

It is difficult for people growing up and learning in today's world to truly appreciate the scientific ideas of the past. One of the philosophies that was widely held nearly two centuries ago was called vitalism. Vitalism was the belief that living organisms and inanimate things differed fundamentally because living organisms contained a non-physical or vitalistic element, and were subject to different principles of nature compared with non-living things. A part of this philosophy even suggested that the organic molecules that are characteristic of living organisms could only be produced within living organisms.

One example of an organic molecule is urea. Urea is produced in some living organisms as a nitrogenous waste product. In mammals, including humans, urea is produced in the liver, enters the bloodstream, and is then filtered out of the bloodstream by the kidneys, and becomes a component of urine. The fundamentals of this process were known in the early 1800s, and it was assumed, because of the widely held principle of vitalism, that this was the only way urea could be produced.

In 1828, Friedrich Wöhler, a German physician and chemist, made a discovery that helped change the thinking behind vitalism. In his laboratory, Wöhler had mixed two inorganic substances, cyanic acid and ammonium, in a beaker. He noticed the formation of a crystalline substance that looked familiar to him. After testing, he confirmed that the crystals were urea. He had previously only come across urea crystals in the study of the compounds that are characteristic of urine. For perhaps the first time in a controlled setting, an organic molecule was synthesized from inorganic substances.

Wöhler did not fully appreciate the meaning and consequences of his findings at the time, but, as it turned out, his published work was soon used as evidence that vitalism should be questioned as a scientific theory. It was not long before other substances, such as amino acids, were synthesized from inorganic precursors in various laboratories.

What does this show about the nature of science?

- Scientific theories undergo modifications over time. Some are just modified, while some are proved to be completely false.

- Frequently, important discoveries are made 'accidently'. Dr Wöhler did not add the two inorganic substances together with the intention of making urea.

- Frequently, a scientific discovery is not appreciated immediately for its importance. This is one of the reasons why discoveries need to be published. This allows the entire scientific community to fit new knowledge into the bigger picture of science, and sometimes that only happens much later.

The German physician and chemist Friedrich Wöhler.

CHALLENGE YOURSELF

2 Drawing molecular diagrams of common biochemical substances is easier than you might think, especially with a little practice. You will be expected to be able to draw the following molecules from memory:

- alpha-D-glucose
- beta-D-glucose
- ribose
- an unnamed saturated fatty acid
- a generalized amino acid.

When drawing these, and other complex organic molecules, it helps to draw them in a sequential pattern. That sequence is given below.

(a) Draw the carbons first (this is called the carbon backbone of the molecule).

(b) Then add in any functional groups that are found as part of the molecule.

(c) 'Fill in' with hydrogen atoms, to ensure that all the carbon atoms are showing four covalent bonds.

(d) Look over your entire structure, to make sure that all of the different atom types are showing the correct number of covalent bonds for that type of element.

(e) If you know or have been given the chemical formula of the substance, count the number of each type of atom and check that number against the known formula.

Here is how it would work for the monosaccharide sugar called alpha-D-glucose, a substance that we know has the chemical formula of $C_6H_{12}O_6$.

(a)

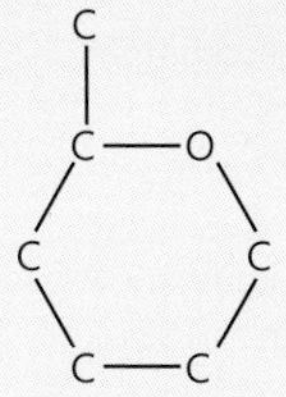

Figure 2.3 The carbon backbone of alpha-D-glucose.

(b)

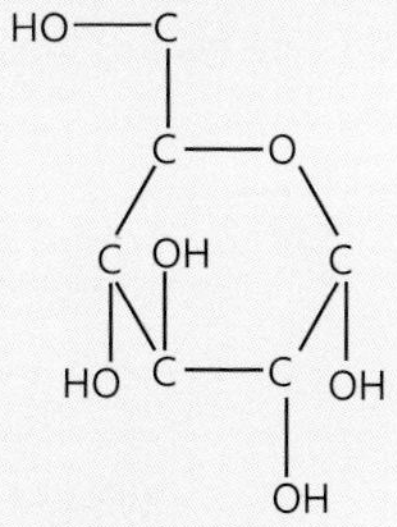

Figure 2.4 The alcohol groups added.

(c)

Figure 2.5 The hydrogens added.

Note: Be sure to count the covalent bonds around each element, and make sure that the number is appropriate for each. You should also count the number of each type of atom and check that against the known formula of $C_6H_{12}O_6$.

Beta-D-glucose has exactly the same chemical formula as alpha-D-glucose and the two are, in fact, isomers of each other. Alpha-D-glucose and beta-D-glucose differ only in how a few of the atoms within the structure are oriented in space in relation to each other. Here is the finished molecular diagram of beta-D-glucose:

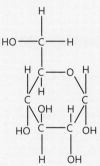

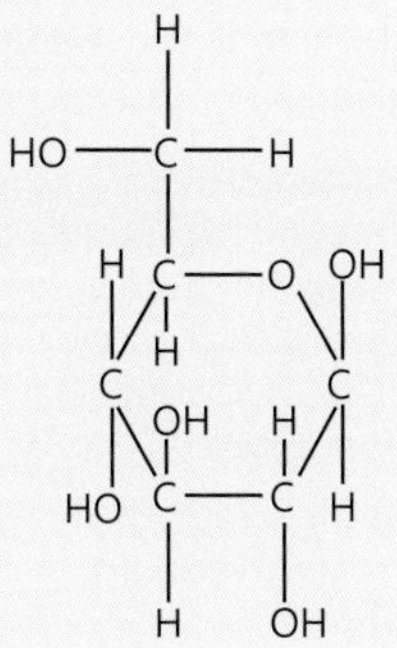

Figure 2.6 Beta-D-glucose.

Trying to draw complex organic molecules by somehow memorizing the entire intact structure is frustrating and impossible for most people. Instead, always use the sequence of steps shown on the previous page, of laying out the carbon backbone, adding the functional groups, and then filling in with hydrogen(s) as needed. This will not only help you learn the molecules you need to know, but it will also enable you to look at large, complex biochemical molecules from a new and more useful perspective.

Here are the completed molecular diagrams of another three molecules that you need to learn to draw from memory. Get out some paper and a pencil and practise drawing the two glucose molecules shown on the previous page and the three molecules shown below. Don't practise drawing them in their entirety, but use the step-by-step process as shown above. Do this until you are confident that you know each one very well.

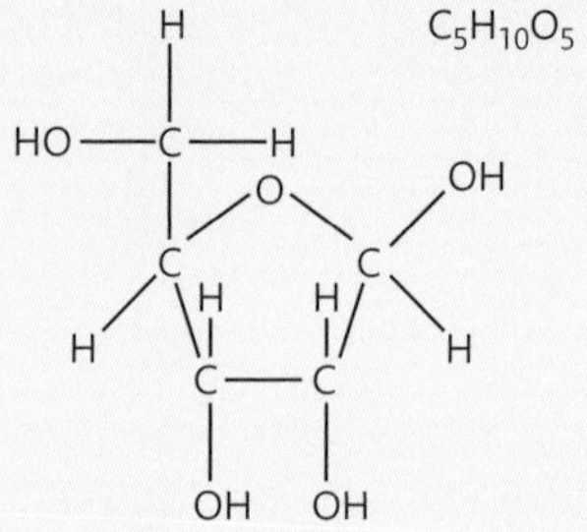

$C_5H_{10}O_5$

Figure 2.7 D-ribose.

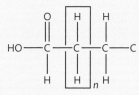

Figure 2.8 A generalized fatty acid.

Where n = any number between 3 and 29 (11–23 are the most common)

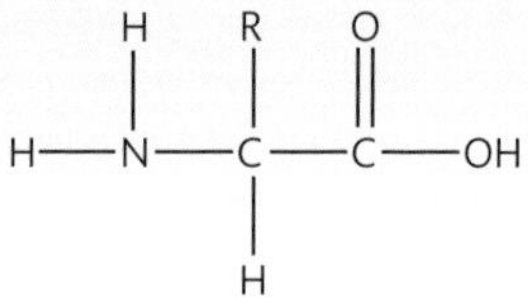

Figure 2.9 A generalized amino acid.

Where R = 1 of 20 variable groups

Section summary

- Carbon atoms form four covalent bonds, leading to an incredible variety of organic molecules.
- Organic compounds within living organisms include carbohydrates, lipids, proteins, and nucleic acids.
- All of the enzyme-catalysed reactions in living things are collectively called metabolism.
- Anabolism is the portion of metabolism where monomers are formed into macromolecules.
- Catabolism is the portion of metabolism where macromolecules are formed into monomers.

Exercises

1 One way to check whether organic molecules are drawn correctly is to make a sketch based on the information given and then count the number of atoms of each element using a given or known formula. Draw each of the molecules described below and then check each against the formula given in the answers.

 (a) Sketch a single carbon atom, add an alcohol group, fill in with hydrogen atoms. Give the formula of the molecule.

 (b) Sketch a single carbon atom, add an amine group, add a carboxyl group, fill in with hydrogens. Give the formula of the molecule.

2 Give the products of each of the following reactions:

   (a) the complete hydrolysis of a starch molecule

   (b) the condensation reaction between glucose and galactose

   (c) the complete hydrolysis of a triglyceride lipid.

3 Briefly describe the two aspects of metabolism.

2.2 Water

NATURE OF SCIENCE

Use theories to explain natural phenomena: the theory that hydrogen bonds form between water molecules explains the properties of water.

Understandings:

- Water molecules are polar and hydrogen bonds form between them.
- Hydrogen bonding and dipolarity explain the cohesive, adhesive, thermal, and solvent properties of water.
- Substances can be hydrophilic or hydrophobic.

Applications and skills:

- Application: Comparison of the thermal properties of water with those of methane.
- Application: Use of water as a coolant in sweat.
- Application: Modes of transport of glucose, amino acids, cholesterol, fats, oxygen, and sodium chloride in blood in relation to their solubility in water.

Guidance

- *Students should know at least one example of a benefit to living organisms of each property of water.*
- *Transparency of water and maximum density at 4°C do not need to be included.*
- *Comparison of the thermal properties of water and methane assists in the understanding of the significance of hydrogen bonding in water.*

The structure of water molecules and the resulting polarity

Water is the solvent of life. Living cells typically exist in an environment in which there is water within the cell (cytoplasm) and also water in the surrounding environment (intercellular fluid, fresh or salt water, etc.). We refer to all solutions as aqueous solutions if water is the solvent, no matter what mixture of substances make up the solutes. Thus, cytoplasm and water environments such as the oceans are all aqueous solutions.

In order to understand the many properties of water, and the importance of those properties to living organisms, we must first consider the structure of water molecules.

The covalent bonds between the oxygen atom and the two hydrogen atoms of a single water molecule are categorized as polar covalent bonds. You should remember from fundamental chemistry that covalent bonds form when two atoms share electrons. As electrons are negatively charged and the nucleus of an atom (because of the protons) is positively charged, any electrons that are shared equally create a bond and, because the charges cancel, this is called a non-polar covalent bond. The bond between two carbons is a good example of this type of bond. Polar covalent bonding results from an unequal sharing of electrons. In water, the single oxygen atom is bonded to two different hydrogen atoms. Each oxygen–hydrogen bond is a polar covalent bond, and results in a slight negative charge

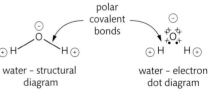

water – structural diagram

water – electron dot diagram

Figure 2.10 The shared electrons between oxygen and hydrogen are not shared equally, thus they are polar covalent bonds. This gives rise to the polarity of water.

at the oxygen end of the molecule and a slight positive charge at the end with the two hydrogens. Because of the triangular shape of a water molecule, the two ends of each molecule have opposite charges, with the oxygen side being somewhat negative and the hydrogen side being somewhat positive. This is why water is a polar molecule: it has different charges at each end and so exhibits dipolarity. Because of this dipolarity, water molecules interact with each other and other molecules in very interesting ways. Many of these interactions are explained by the usually ephemeral (short-lived) attractions between either two water molecules or between water and another type of charged atom (or ion). These typically short-lived attractions are called hydrogen bonds and will be explained further in the following sections.

Figure 2.11 In liquid water, water molecules form 'split second' hydrogen bonds with other water molecules (dotted line), despite the fact that water continues to move in many different directions. These short-lived hydrogen bonds give rise to many of the interesting properties of water.

Cohesive properties

Water molecules are highly cohesive. Cohesion is when molecules of the same type are attracted to each other. As mentioned earlier, water molecules have a slightly positive end and a slightly negative end. Whenever two water molecules are near each other, the positive end of one attracts the negative end of another; this is hydrogen bonding. When water cools below its freezing point, the molecular motion has slowed to the point where these hydrogen bonds become locked into place and an ice crystal forms. Liquid water has molecules with a much faster molecular motion, and the water molecules are able to influence each other, but not to the point where molecules stop their motion. The ephemeral hydrogen bonding between liquid water molecules explains a variety of events, including:

- why water forms into droplets when it is spilt
- why water has a surface tension that allows some organisms to 'walk on water' (for some this is 'run on water')
- how water is able to move as a water 'column' in the vascular tissues of plants.

You can float a paper clip on water because of the surface tension of water. Make sure you maximize the surface area of the paper clip on the water if you try this.

A water strider making use of the high surface tension of water.

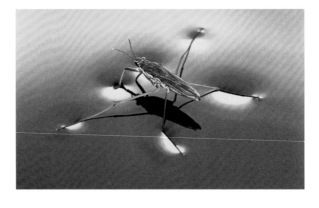

Basilisk lizards may be as long as 0.8 m, but they can run across the surface of bodies of water. The relatively large surface area of their toes does not break through the surface tension of the water as long as they keep running.

Adhesive properties

Water molecules are certainly not the only molecules in nature that exhibit polarity. Any attraction between two unlike molecules is called adhesion. Thus when water molecules are attracted to cellulose molecules by hydrogen bonding, the attraction is an example of adhesion because the hydrogen bonding is between two different kinds of molecules. Where is this important in nature? One example is the column of water in plant vascular tissue, mentioned above. Cohesion and adhesion are both at work, because the water molecules exhibit cohesion to each other, and they also exhibit adhesion to the inside of the vascular tubes, which are partially composed of cellulose. When the column of water is 'pulled up', cohesion moves each molecule up a bit; when the column is not being 'pulled up', adhesion keeps the entire column from dropping down within the tube. The same phenomenon occurs when water is placed in a capillary tube; in fact, you can think of the vascular tissue in plants as being biological capillary tubes.

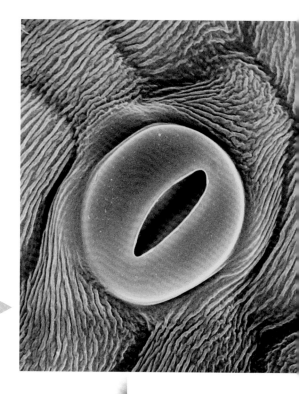

Water evaporates from leaves through small openings called stomata. As shown here, each stoma has two cells, called guard cells, that surround it. When the guard cells swell with water, the stoma appears between the cells, and water evaporates through the stoma. One benefit to the plant of this is the cooling effect that evaporation provides.

Thermal properties

Water has thermal properties that are important to living things. One of those thermal properties is high specific heat. In simple terms, this means that water can absorb or give off a great deal of heat without changing temperature very much. Think of a body of water on a very cold night: even though the air may be very cold, the body of water is relatively stable in temperature. All living things are composed of a great deal of water, and so you can think of your water content as a temperature stabilizer. Water also has a high heat of vaporization. This means that water absorbs a great deal of heat when it evaporates. Many organisms, including ourselves, use this as a cooling mechanism. Your internal body heat results in perspiration, and the perspiration then evaporates from your skin. Much of the heat that turned the water molecules from the liquid phase to the vapour phase came from your body, and thus sweating not only makes you feel cooler, it really does lower your temperature.

Solvent properties

Water is an excellent solvent of other polar molecules. You may remember from earlier science classes that like dissolves like. The vast majority of molecules typically found inside and outside most cells are also polar molecules. This includes carbohydrates, proteins, and nucleic acids (DNA and RNA). Most types of lipids are relatively non-polar and thus most organisms have special strategies to deal with the transport and biochemistry of lipids.

Because water is an excellent solvent for biochemically important molecules, it is also the medium in which most of the biochemistry of a cell occurs. A cell contains a wide variety of fluids, all of which are primarily water. We refer to such solutions as aqueous solutions. Table 2.3 shows some common aqueous solutions in which specific biochemical reactions take place.

The word 'stoma' comes from a Greek word meaning mouth or opening. In medicine, stoma is a surgically created opening in the body that replaces a normal opening.

Specific heat is the amount of heat per unit mass required to raise the temperature one degree Celsius.

Heat of vaporization is the amount of heat required to convert a unit mass of liquid into vapour with no increase in temperature.

Table 2.3 Common aqueous solutions

Aqueous solution	Location	Common reactions
Cytoplasm	Fluid inside cells but outside organelles	Glycolysis/protein synthesis reactions
Nucleoplasm	Fluid inside nuclear membranes	DNA replication/ transcription
Stroma	Fluid inside chloroplast membranes	Light-independent reactions of photosynthesis
Blood plasma	Fluid in arteries, veins, and capillaries	Loading and unloading of respiratory gases/clotting

Examples of water as a solvent in plants and animals

The properties of water make it an excellent medium for transport. Vascular tissue in plants carries water and a variety of dissolved substances. More specifically, xylem carries water and dissolved minerals up from the root system to the leaves of a plant. Phloem then transports dissolved sugars from the leaves to the stems, roots, and flowers of a plant.

Blood is the most common transport medium in animals, and is largely made up of water. The liquid portion of blood is called blood plasma. Some of the more common solutes in blood plasma are:

- glucose (blood sugar)
- amino acids
- fibrinogen (a protein involved in blood clotting)
- hydrogen carbonate ions (as a means of transporting carbon dioxide).

Water 'loving' or water 'fearing' substances

Molecules in living systems interact with water in a variety of ways. Remember that water is the solvent of life, and living cells typically have an aqueous environment both inside and outside their plasma membrane.

Molecules, such as water, that are polar substances are said to be hydrophilic, or water 'loving'. The majority of substances that are biochemically important are polar. Polar molecules easily dissolve in water, because a polar solvent will dissolve polar solutes. It is not difficult to recognize most of the molecules that are hydrophilic, as these molecules typically contain functional groups that result in the molecules being polar. Carbohydrates are a good example of polar molecules; their relative solubility in water is attributed to their multiple hydroxyl (alcohol) functional groups.

Molecules that are classified as non-polar are said to be hydrophobic, or water 'fearing'. Organic substances that are non-polar are typically composed of just carbons and hydrogens (hydrocarbons) or have large areas of the molecule where there are only carbons and hydrogens. Methane (CH_4) is an example of a hydrophobic molecule; it is composed of only one carbon and four hydrogens. Methane will not dissolve in water. Examples of biochemically important molecules that are predominantly non-polar are the fatty acids found in triglyceride lipids and phospholipids. In addition to a carboxyl functional group at one end, a fatty acid consists of a long chain of carbons

TOK

Try doing a web search on the topic of 'memory of water'. Are any of the claims you find examples of pseudoscience rather than science?

with only hydrogens. The carboxyl group gives the fatty acid slight polarity at that end, but the chain of hydrocarbons is so long that the majority of the molecule is non-polar and thus hydrophobic.

Protein molecules can be differentially polar depending on the arrangement of their amino acids. Some amino acids are relatively polar and some are non-polar. The location of each type of amino acid is important within the three-dimensional structure of the protein. Good examples are the proteins that attach into and extend out of a cell membrane. The amino acids making up the portion of the protein that attaches to (and extends down into) the membrane are hydrophobic and easily mix with the hydrophobic fatty acid 'tails' of the membrane phospholipid molecules. The portion of the protein that extends out of the membrane is predominately made up of hydrophilic amino acids that easily mix with the water environment either inside or outside the cell or organelle.

This photo shows what happens when a hydrophobic substance encounters water. The two types of molecules do not mix because they are not soluble.

Figure 2.12 A comparison of water and methane.

NATURE OF SCIENCE

You probably already know the freezing point (0°C) and boiling point (100°C) of water. You may not already know the phase change temperatures for methane: the freezing point of methane is –183°C and the boiling point is –162°C.

It is interesting to think about why these two substances have such very different phase change temperatures. Consider the structure and polarity of these two molecules.

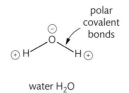

water H$_2$O

methane CH$_4$

The polar covalent bonds within water give rise to the polarity of the molecule. All of the covalent bonds within methane are non-polar and so methane is a non-polar substance. All molecules composed of just carbons and hydrogens (hydrocarbons) are non-polar.

When methane undergoes a phase change, because of its lack of polarity, there are no hydrogen bonds that influence the change of phase. You have probably realized that methane has a very low (cold) freezing point and also a very low boiling point. When methane changes from a liquid to a gas at –162°C there are no hydrogen bonds attracting the molecules to each other. Thus they 'escape' from each other with only a relatively small amount of molecular motion needed. That is not true for water molecules: each water molecule is constantly forming, breaking, and almost instantly reforming hydrogen bonds with other water molecules. When water changes from a liquid to a gas at 100°C, the high temperature is necessary to create the relatively high rate of molecular motion needed to enable the molecules to 'escape' from each other.

When methane changes from its liquid phase to its solid phase (at its freezing point, –183°C), the change in phase is explained by the fact that methane no longer has enough molecular motion to exist as a liquid. Water makes this phase change at a much higher temperature (0°C) because, when the molecular rate of motion becomes low enough, hydrogen bonding locks water molecules into stable geometric forms known as ice crystals.

We cannot actually see the hydrogen bonds. However, the theory that is used to explain hydrogen bonding is largely supported by many pieces of evidence, including those described above. Sometimes, in the nature of science, a theory helps explain a phenomenon and then multitudes of similar phenomena support the theory.

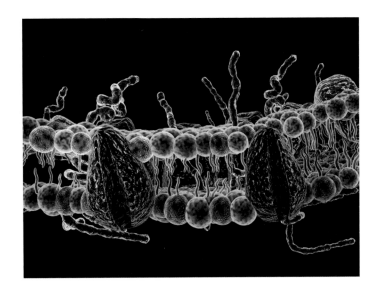

An artist's drawing of a cell membrane with proteins. The portions of the proteins found within the bilayer of phospholipids are composed of relatively non-polar amino acids, whereas those outside the bilayer are composed of many polar amino acids.

A typical person might be able to survive about 3 weeks without food. However, a typical person would only survive 1 week or less without any water intake.

How does solubility in water affect the mode of transport of molecules in organisms?

Water in living organisms acts as a mode of transport for the variety of molecules that must be moved about both within cells and between cells. Just think of the various water-based fluids you already know, such as cytoplasm, intercellular fluid, blood, and digestive juices. Because of their different polarities, each type of substance has a different solubility in whatever aqueous environment it is found in, including blood plasma. Table 2.4 summarizes the various relative polarities of a few selected molecules and shows whether or not an alternative mode of transport is needed as that substance circulates in the bloodstream.

Table 2.4 Polarity of different molecules

Substance	High or low relative solubility in water	Mode of transport in an aqueous environment (no special mode means the substance dissolves directly and easily into water)
Glucose	Polar molecule/high solubility	No special mode of transport needed/dissolves directly in aqueous plasma
Amino acids	Varying polarity but all are reasonably soluble	No special mode of transport needed/dissolve directly in aqueous plasma
Cholesterol	Largely non-polar/very low solubility	Transported by blood proteins that have polar amino acids on the outer portion to give water solubility, and non-polar amino acids internally to bind the non-polar cholesterol
Fats	Non-polar fatty acid components/very low solubility	Transported by blood proteins that have polar amino acids on the outer portion to give water solubility, and non-polar amino acids internally to bind the non-polar fatty acid molecules
Oxygen	Travels as diatomic O_2/low solubility	Relatively low solubility in water is exacerbated by the relatively high temperature of warm-blooded animals (oxygen is less soluble in warm aqueous solutions)/haemoglobin is used to bind and transport oxygen molecules reversibly
Sodium chloride	Ionizes/high solubility	No special mode of transport needed/sodium chloride is an ionic compound, it ionizes into separately charged Na^+ and Cl^- ions in aqueous plasma

Humans and other animals have difficulty absorbing relatively large triglycerides and their digested form (fatty acids) from the intestine into the bloodstream. Chylomicrons are very small particles made up primarily of fat and some protein. Chylomicrons are produced in the alimentary canal and then transported into the bloodstream. They are used to transport fats to the liver and other tissues in the body. If your doctor orders a lipid blood test, chylomicrons are some of the low-density lipoproteins (LDL) that are measured. If their levels in the blood are elevated, they are referred to as the 'bad lipoproteins'.

Section summary

- Many of the properties of water are attributed to the polarity of water molecules.
- Hydrogen bonding occurs between water molecules, and between water molecules and other polar substances.
- Water is a very good solvent for molecules that are important to living organisms, as most of those molecules are also polar.
- Any substance that readily dissolves in water is called hydrophilic, and any substance that does not dissolve readily in water is called hydrophobic.

Exercises

4 Choose any specific aquatic or terrestrial animal and make a list of all the ways in which water is important to that animal.

5 How are the properties of water involved in any item of your list?

2.3 Carbohydrates and lipids

NATURE OF SCIENCE

Evaluating claims: health claims made about lipids in diets need to be assessed.

Understandings:

- Monosaccharide monomers are linked together by condensation reactions to form disaccharides and polysaccharide polymers.
- Fatty acids can be saturated, monounsaturated, or polyunsaturated.
- Unsaturated fatty acids can be *cis* or *trans* isomers.
- Triglycerides are formed by condensation from three fatty acids and one glycerol.

Applications and skills:

- Application: Structure and function of cellulose and starch in plants and glycogen in humans.
- Application: Scientific evidence for health risks of *trans* fats and saturated fatty acids.
- Application: Lipids are more suitable for long-term energy storage in humans than carbohydrates.
- Application: Evaluation of evidence and the methods used to obtain the evidence for health claims made about lipids.
- Skill: Use of molecular visualization software to compare cellulose, starch, and glycogen.
- Skill: Determination of body mass index by calculation or use of a nomogram.

Guidance
- *The structure of starch should include amylose and amylopectin.*
- *Named examples of fatty acids are not required.*
- *Sucrose, lactose, and maltose should be included as examples of disaccharides produced by combining monosaccharides.*

Monosaccharides: the building blocks of disaccharides

Biochemically important molecules can be extremely large and complex but they are always made of smaller monomer (building block) molecules. The monomers of carbohydrates are the monosaccharides. At the beginning of this chapter you were introduced to hydrolysis reactions and an opposite set called condensation reactions. Condensation reactions are key to that part of your metabolism called anabolism, where larger molecules are synthesized from smaller monomer units. As the monomer units of carbohydrates are monosaccharides, we will start by looking at their structure. Monosaccharides can be classified according to how many carbon atoms they contain. The three most common monosaccharides are:

• trioses, containing 3 carbons and with the chemical formula $C_3H_6O_3$
• pentoses, containing 5 carbons and with the chemical formula $C_5H_{10}O_5$
• hexoses, containing 6 carbons and with the chemical formula $C_6H_{12}O_6$.

You may have noticed a common pattern in the formulas of these three simple sugars: monosaccharides typically fit the formula $C_nH_{2n}O_n$, where n equals the number of carbon atoms.

Let's look at a detailed example of a condensation reaction occurring between two monosaccharides. The example in Figure 2.13 shows the formation of the disaccharide sucrose from the reaction between the two monosaccharides glucose and fructose.

In similar reactions, other disaccharides are formed by different monosaccharides undergoing a condensation reaction. Figure 2.14 shows the condensation reaction that forms the disaccharide maltose from two alpha-D-glucose molecules. In a very similar way, the disaccharide lactose is formed by the condensation reaction between alpha-D-glucose and the monosaccharide galactose.

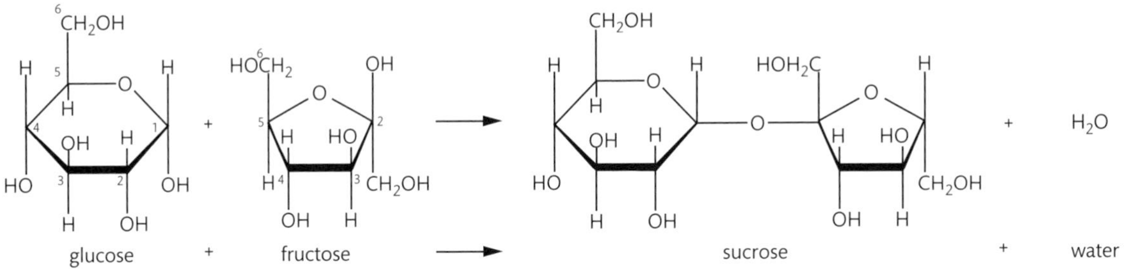

Some textbooks will refer to condensation reactions as dehydration synthesis reactions. The names condensation and dehydration synthesis are both good reminders that water is always one of the products of these reactions.

Figure 2.13 The condensation reaction between glucose and fructose to form the disaccharide sucrose and a water molecule. Each corner of the sugar rings has an 'unshown' carbon atom. Each carbon atom is numbered in the reactants. Glucose and fructose are isomers of each other because they have the same chemical formula, $C_6H_{12}O_6$.

Figure 2.14 A condensation reaction showing the formation of the disaccharide maltose. Notice that water is always a product of a condensation reaction and that one of the two monosaccharides 'donates' a hydroxide ion (^-OH) and the other monosaccharide 'donates' a hydrogen ion (H^+), which combine to form the water molecule. The bond that is freed up is used to form the covalent bond between the two monosaccharides. All condensation reactions occur in a very similar way.

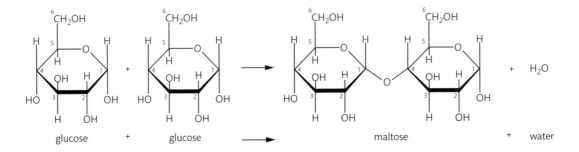

glucose + glucose → maltose + water

Monosaccharides: the building blocks of polysaccharides

Condensation reactions can be used to synthesize even larger molecules by accomplishing the same or a similar reaction on more than one area of a monomer such as a monosaccharide. Repeatedly bonding glucose monosaccharides produces a variety of very large molecules or polymers. Some examples are cellulose, starch, and glycogen; Table 2.5 summarizes their functions.

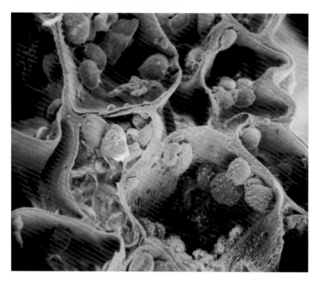

Scanning electron micrograph (SEM) of sliced open plant cells. The plant cell walls composed largely of cellulose are clearly visible, and in the interior of the cells are chloroplasts, which produce and store carbohydrates such as starch.

Table 2.5 The functions of major polysaccharides

Polysaccharide	Summary of functions
Cellulose	Major component of plant cell walls, helps give rigidity/support to plant parts such as roots, stems, and leaves
Starch	Organic products of photosynthesis are stored in plants as starch, typically as starch granules in chloroplasts or in plant storage areas such as roots or root structures
Glycogen	Animals store excess glucose in this form. Glycogen is stored in the liver and in muscle tissue

At the end of this section, use the hotlinks to view and manipulate three-dimensional models of cellulose, starch, and glycogen. When viewing these structures online, take note of the following.

- Cellulose, starch, and glycogen are all polysaccharides of the same monomer unit, glucose.
- The bonding mentioned with each molecule, such as 1,4 linkages, refers to the carbon numbers of the glucose molecules that create the covalent bond.
- Starch has two subcomponents, amylopectin and amylose.
- Amylose is the only one of the three glucose polysaccharides that is a linear molecule with no side branching.
- All three polysaccharides can be composed of many thousands of glucose monomers.

Fatty acids

Although they have similarities in their molecular structure, not all fatty acids are identical. All fatty acids have a carboxyl group (–COOH) at one end and a methyl group (CH₃–) at the other end. In between is a chain of hydrocarbons (hydrogen atoms and carbon atoms) that is usually between 11 and 23 carbons long (12–24 carbons when counting the carbon of the methyl group as well).

Saturated fatty acids

In Figure 2.15, the yellow zone on the left is the carboxyl group, the white zone in the middle is the hydrocarbon chain (shown much shorter than any fatty acid in the human body), and the green zone on the right is where the methyl group is located.

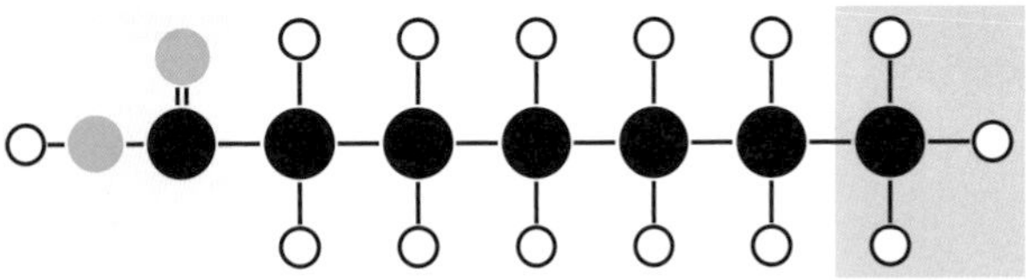

Figure 2.15 The three sections found in all fatty acids: the carboxyl group at one end, the long hydrocarbon chain in the middle, and the methyl group at the other end. The end with the methyl group is also called the omega end.

omega end

Saturated fatty acids are called that because the carbons are carrying as many hydrogen atoms as they can, in other words they are saturated with hydrogen atoms. These molecules are typically found in animal products such as butter, bacon, and the fat in red meat. These fats are generally solid at room temperature. Because the carbons are carrying as many hydrogen atoms as possible, saturated fatty acids have no double bonds between the carbon atoms. The shape of the molecule is straight: there are no kinks or bends along the chain.

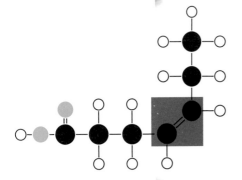

Monounsaturated fatty acids

If one double bond exists in the chain of hydrocarbons, the fatty acid is not saturated any longer: it has two empty spaces where hydrogen atoms could be. This type of unsaturated fatty acid is referred to as monounsaturated.

In Figure 2.16, the double bond between two carbons in the hydrocarbon chain is highlighted. Notice how the absence of two consecutive hydrogen atoms on the same side of the carbon atom chain causes the molecule to bend at the zone where the double bond is.

Figure 2.16 The highlighted zone in the middle of the fatty acid shows that it has a single double bond in the hydrocarbon chain. This creates a bend or kink in the shape of the molecule. Note: Fatty acids typically have more carbons than the one shown for this illustration.

Polyunsaturated fatty acids

Polyunsaturated fatty acids have at least two double bonds in the carbon chain. They typically come from plants (olive oil is an example). These fatty acids are called polyunsaturated because two or more carbons are not carrying the maximum number of hydrogen atoms (another way of saying this is that two or more carbons are double bonded to each other). Lipids that contain polyunsaturated fatty acids tend to be liquids at room temperature.

Imagine a hydrocarbon chain several times longer than any shown in the figures so far, with several more double bonds. The molecule may have so many bends/kinks that it starts to curve over onto itself or twist around itself. This frequently happens with polyunsaturated fatty acids.

Hydrogenation: *cis* and *trans* fatty acids

In many heavily processed foods, polyunsaturated fats are often hydrogenated or partially hydrogenated as part of the processing. This means the double bonds (and hence the kinks) are eliminated (or partly eliminated) by adding hydrogen atoms. Hydrogenation straightens out the natural bent shape of unsaturated fatty acids. Naturally curved fatty acids are called *cis* fatty acids, and the hydrogenated, straightened ones are called *trans* fatty acids. The vast majority of *trans* fatty acids are the result of chemical transformations in food-processing factories. They are usually only partially hydrogenated and thus still contain one or more double bonds.

One category of *cis* fatty acids is called omega-3. The name comes from the fact that the first carbon double bond to be found in this molecule is at the third carbon atom counting backwards from the omega end (see Figure 12.17). Fish are a good source of omega-3 fats.

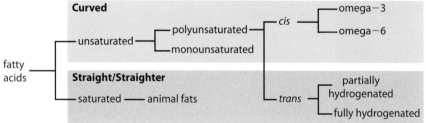

Part of the ingredients list of a bought cake. 'Partially hydrogenated' means that this is a product that contains *trans* fats.

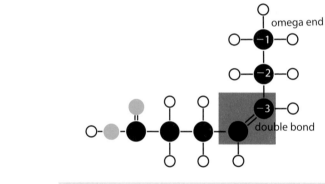

Figure 2.17 This sketch shows how the name omega-3 is derived for some fatty acids. Starting at the omega carbon, count the carbons until you reach the first double bond.

Figure 2.18 Summary of fatty acid types.

Condensation reactions result in the formation of triglyceride lipids

The component molecules of triglyceride lipids (fats in animal cells and oils in plant cells) are glycerol and three fatty acids. The identity and thus characteristics of the three fatty acids in each triglyceride will determine the overall characteristics of the fat or oil. Triglycerides vary greatly from each other, including their relative healthiness in our diet. Figure 2.19 is a representation of the condensation reaction that creates the covalent bonds between the glycerol portion and the three fatty acids of a triglyceride lipid. Notice that, as in all condensation reactions, a water molecule is created from each of the three reactions.

Condensation and hydrolysis reactions in biochemistry are so common that you will encounter information concerning those two types of reactions throughout your study of biology. Take the time to learn the basics of these two reaction types.

Figure 2.19 Condensation reaction showing the four reactants necessary to form a triglyceride lipid. Notice that there are four products: the three water molecules as well as the triglyceride.

glycerol

three fatty acids

triglyceride lipid

NATURE OF SCIENCE

Now that you are familiar with the terminology and basic chemical structure of lipids and fatty acids, you are ready to read and evaluate some information concerning various types of lipids in your foods. Try to evaluate the information given by researching the following.

Use a search engine to research consumer information reported by food companies concerning lipids. Try:

- one or more of your favourite fast food restaurants (or at least some you know) and couple the restaurant name with 'nutrition information'
- the company and snack name of one or more of your favourite snacks plus 'nutrition information'
- other searches that you can think of that may or may not give you reasonably reliable information.

Diets characteristic of people in various areas of the world appear to have a huge influence on health and longevity.

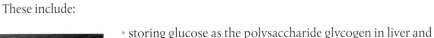

Energy storage solutions in humans

Humans and many other organisms have developed chemical strategies to store molecules in reserve to use for ATP production during the process of cell respiration. These include:

- storing glucose as the polysaccharide glycogen in liver and muscle tissues
- storing triglyceride lipids within adipose (fat) cells.

Triglyceride lipids, when needed, can be hydrolysed into two carbon segments that can enter into cell respiration at a chemical sequence point that is very efficient for the production of ATP. Thus lipids have about twice the energy content per gramme compared with other molecules, such as carbohydrates and proteins, that are also used for cell respiration.

Lipids have another advantage as a long-term energy storage molecule: they are insoluble in water (such as in the aqueous environments of cytoplasm, intercellular fluid, and blood plasma), and so they do not upset the osmotic balance of solutions. If humans were to store large concentrations of glucose in certain cells of the body for long-term energy storage, those cells would swell to ridiculous proportions because the glucose would attract water into the cells due to the surrounding hypotonic fluids.

This drawing shows a fat cell (adipocyte) becoming larger as lipids are stored in it.

Calculating the body mass index

The use of an indexed value known as the body mass index (BMI) as an indicator of healthy weight has recently become popular. The BMI is a number that reflects both the weight and the height of a person. The idea is that people who are taller should weigh more. There are three ways that you can determine your BMI:

• using a formula, based on either metric or imperial measurements of weight and height
• using a graph known as a nomogram to read the BMI value from a central intersection point between weight and height measurements
• using an online calculator that outputs the BMI after the height and weight measurements have been input.

Each of the methods used to determine the BMI must be correlated with information concerning the BMI that shows whether a value reflects someone being underweight, normal in weight, overweight, or obese. Such charts often come with a caution that states children and pregnant women should not use them. Table 2.6 shows the data provided by the Centers for Disease Control and Prevention (CDC).

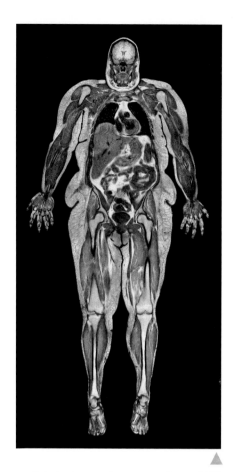

Colorized magnetic resonance image (MRI) of a woman with a very high BMI. Among a myriad of other possible problems, the extra body mass present in obese patients puts a strain on their heart and lungs.

Some, but not all, countries make a concerted effort to inform their citizens of the health risks and benefits of certain foods/diets. This is why good scientific research on the consequences and benefits of certain food types is essential.

Table 2.6 Interpreting BMI values

BMI	Description category
Below 18.5	Underweight
18.5–24.9	Normal weight
25.0–29.9	Overweight
30.0 and above	Obese

Here are the two formulas for calculating BMI:

• formula 1, metric units, BMI = weight (kg)/[height (m) × height (m)]
• formula 2, imperial units, BMI = weight (lb)/[height (in) × height (in)] × 703

Example 1 (metric): for someone who is 1.70 m and weighs 58 kg, his or her BMI = 58/(1.7 × 1.7) = 20.1. Therefore this person is categorized as having a normal weight.

Example 2 (imperial): for someone who is 5′10″ (5′10″ = 70″) and weighs 235 lb, his or her BMI = 235/(70 × 70) × 703 = 33.7 . This person is categorized as obese.

CHALLENGE YOURSELF

3 Calculate the BMI of a person who is 1.64 m tall and weighs 79 kg. Using Table 2.6, which category would be used to describe him or her?

4 Calculate your own BMI after measuring your height and current weight.

At the end of this section, use the hotlinks to go to a website that includes a nomogram and online calculator for determining BMI.

5 Use the online calculator to confirm your own BMI calculation.

6 Use the nomogram to confirm your own BMI calculation.

Section summary

- Carbohydrates are found in nature in three forms: monosaccharides, disaccharides, and polysaccharides.
- Two specific monosaccharides are covalently bonded together to form a specific disaccharide.
- As many as thousands of glucose molecules are bonded together to form a variety of polysaccharides.
- Triglycerides are formed from one glycerol and three fatty acids.
- Saturated fatty acids have no double bonds between carbons in a long chain, whereas unsaturated fatty acids have one or more double bonds between carbons.
- Cellulose and starch are polysaccharides formed within plant cells; glycogen is a polysaccharide formed in some animal cells.
- As a result of solubility properties and high energy content, lipids make good long-term energy storage molecules in many animal cells.

To learn more about the three-dimensional models of cellulose, starch, and glycogen, and calculating BMI, go to the hotlinks site, search for the title or ISBN, and click on Chapter 2: Section 2.3.

Exercises

6 Write the word equation for the condensation reactions that would produce a triglyceride lipid from its four molecular subcomponents.

7 Rank these fatty acids types from the least to the most healthy: saturated fatty acid; unsaturated fatty acid; *trans* fatty acid.

8 Why is BMI a better reflection of a person's health compared with body mass alone?

NATURE OF SCIENCE

Looking for patterns, trends, and discrepancies: most but not all organisms assemble proteins from the same amino acids.

2.4   Proteins

Understandings:

- Amino acids are linked together by condensation to form polypeptides.
- There are 20 different amino acids in polypeptides synthesized on ribosomes.
- Amino acids can be linked together in any sequence, giving a huge range of possible polypeptides.
- The amino acid sequence of polypeptides is coded for by genes.
- A protein may consist of a single polypeptide or more than one polypeptide linked together.
- The amino acid sequence determines the three-dimensional conformation of a protein.
- Living organisms synthesize many different proteins with a wide range of functions.
- Every individual has a unique proteome.

Applications and skills:

- Application: Rubisco, insulin, immunoglobulins, rhodopsin, collagen, and spider silk as examples of the range of protein functions.
- Application: Denaturation of proteins by heat or by deviation of pH from the optimum.
- Skill: Drawing molecular diagrams to show the formation of a peptide bond.

Guidance

- *The detailed structure of the six proteins selected to illustrate the functions of proteins is not needed.*
- *Egg white or albumin solutions can be used in denaturation experiments.*
- *Students should know that most organisms use the same 20 amino acids in the same genetic code, although there are some exceptions. Specific examples could be used for illustration.*

Formation of polypeptides

Cells use the naturally occurring 20 amino acids to synthesize polypeptides. They do this under the control of DNA, each polypeptide being created under the control of a specific area of a specific DNA molecule called a gene. In a multicellular organism, every cell of that organism has the same set of chromosomes and thus the same DNA. Each cell that has differentiated to have a specific function in a specific tissue of the body only uses the genes that are necessary for that cell type. Some of those genes are almost universal, such as the genes that code for proteins involved in common cell functions. A good example of this would be the protein components that make up ribosomes, as all cells need ribosomes. In addition, each specific cell type then uses the genes that help accomplish the specific activities necessary for that cell type. A cell of the human pancreas would 'turn on' the gene for synthesis of the peptide hormone insulin, whereas most cells would not activate that gene even though the gene is present in all human cells. The total number of (possibly) active genes in any living organism is difficult to determine with accuracy. A current estimate for human beings is somewhere between 20 000 and 25 000 genes in each of our cells. This is nothing to brag about though, as a high gene count falls somewhere between grape plants (which have about 30 000 genes) and chickens (which have about 17 000 genes). This shows why it would be a mistake to correlate the number of genes with organism complexity. Table 2.7 shows a selection of organisms and their approximate gene count.

Table 2.7 Selected organisms and their approximate number of genes

Common name of the organism	Approximate number of genes in the organism's genome
Yeast (single-celled fungi)	6 000
Drosophila (fruit fly)	14 000
Rice plant	51 000
Laboratory mouse	30 000
Domestic dog	19 000
Humans	20–25 000

No matter how many genes an organism has within its genome, all genes are the genetic code for the possible polypeptides found within that organism, and all polypeptides are synthesized from the same monomers, specifically amino acids. Although there are a few exceptions to this, virtually all organisms use the same genetic code, and they use the same 20 amino acids to construct their polypeptides.

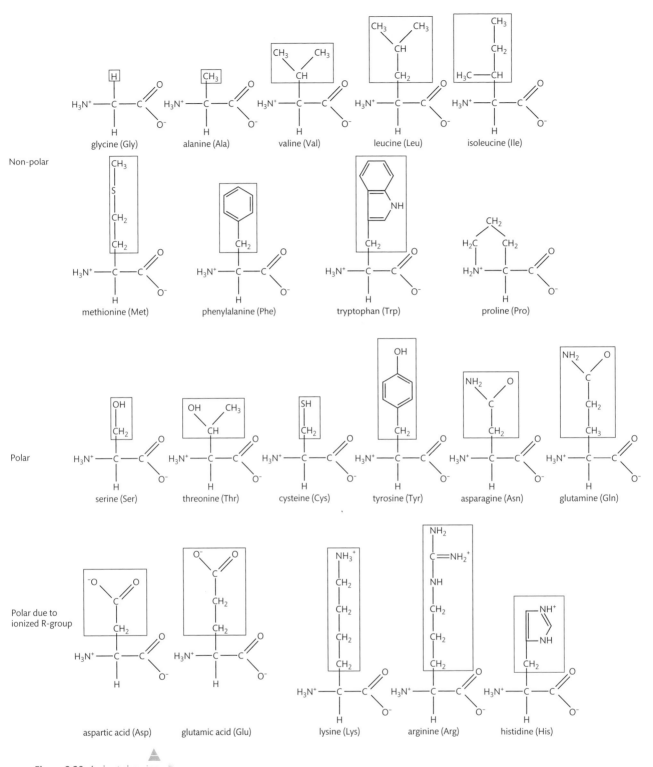

Non-polar

glycine (Gly)   alanine (Ala)   valine (Val)   leucine (Leu)   isoleucine (Ile)

methionine (Met)   phenylalanine (Phe)   tryptophan (Trp)   proline (Pro)

Polar

serine (Ser)   threonine (Thr)   cysteine (Cys)   tyrosine (Tyr)   asparagine (Asn)   glutamine (Gln)

Polar due to ionized R-group

aspartic acid (Asp)   glutamic acid (Glu)   lysine (Lys)   arginine (Arg)   histidine (His)

Figure 2.20 A chart showing the structures of the 20 amino acids. The boxed areas shown are the R-groups of the amino acids. Note how each amino acid is identical except for the variable R-group.

Figure 2.21 Condensation reaction between the amino acids alanine and valine. Note that for simplicity the amine and carboxyl groups are being shown in a non-ionized form. This reaction looks the same for any two amino acids, as the only change would be to the R (variable) groups.

alanine   new covalent (peptide bond)   valine

Each of the 20 amino acids differs from the others in one bonding location around the central carbon atom; that difference in structure is called the R or variable group of the amino acid (Figure 2.20). You do not need to memorize the R-groups but you do need to memorize the general structure that applies to all amino acids.

When amino acids are in an aqueous solution, such as cytoplasm or blood plasma, the amine and carboxyl functional groups ionize, as shown in Figure 2.20. This ionization does not alter the covalent bonding pattern but it does make the functional groups look a little different as each carboxyl group has 'lost' a hydrogen ion and each amine group has gained a hydrogen ion.

When polypeptides are synthesized at ribosomes under the control of genes, the reaction that is occurring is a condensation reaction. The sequence of the amino acids is determined precisely by the DNA, but the condensation reactions are virtually identical.

Polypeptides are highly variable

The condensation reactions described above do not occur between any two amino acids randomly. The order of the amino acids is always determined by triplets of nucleotides along nucleic acid molecules (DNA and RNA), and is directed by a ribosome. As there are 20 amino acids, there is a large choice for the sequence of the amino acids as well as the total number of amino acids to use within a polypeptide. Each polypeptide that has been selected for a specific purpose has not only its own amino acid sequence, but also its own three-dimensional shape; that shape has a dominant influence on the function of the polypeptide. Even a change in a single amino acid in the overall sequence of a polypeptide can have drastic effects on its function.

Computer graphic representation of the structure of bradykinin, a polypeptide that is active in human metabolism. Despite the apparent complexity, this is a relatively short peptide consisting of only nine amino acids.

Levels of polypeptide and protein structure

Proteins serve a tremendous variety of functions in cells and organisms; Table 2.8 shows you just a few examples.

Table 2.8 Some examples of proteins and their functions

Rubisco	The short-hand name for the enzyme that catalyses the first reaction of the carbon-fixing reactions of photosynthesis
Insulin	A protein hormone produced by the pancreas that results in a decrease of blood sugar levels and an increase of sugar inside body cells
Immunoglobulin	Another name for an antibody that recognizes an antigen(s) as part of the immune response
Rhodopsin	A pigment found in the retina of the eye that is particularly useful in low light conditions
Collagen	The main protein component of connective tissue, which is abundant in skin, tendons, and ligaments
Spider silk	A fibrous protein spun by spiders for making webs, drop lines, nest building, and other uses

Given the myriad of functions of proteins, they have to be capable of assuming many forms and structures. The function of any particular protein is closely related to its structure. There are four levels of organization to protein structure: primary, secondary, tertiary, and quaternary.

- Primary protein structure: the sequence of amino acids within the protein; this sequence determines the three-dimensional shape, as shown below.
- Secondary protein structure: repetitive shapes of either a helix (a spiral staircase shape) or a pleated sheet (a sheet with corrugated folds), e.g. spider silk.
- Tertiary structure: a shape often described as globular, e.g. enzymes.
- Quaternary: two or more polypeptides combined together to make a single functional protein, e.g. haemoglobin.

Figure 2.22 Simplistic example of a polypeptide's primary structure.

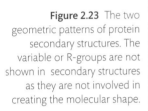

Figure 2.23 The two geometric patterns of protein secondary structures. The variable or R-groups are not shown in secondary structures as they are not involved in creating the molecular shape.

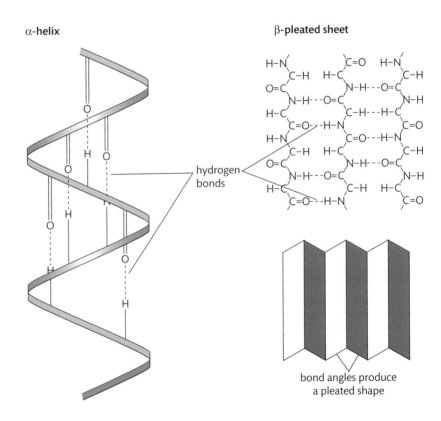

α-helix

β-pleated sheet

hydrogen bonds

bond angles produce a pleated shape

When trying to identify individual amino acids within a large, complex polypeptide, try to identify the peptide bonds between each of the covalently bonded amino acids. That bond will always be a nitrogen atom bonded to a carbon atom, with that carbon atom also doubled bonded to an oxygen.

Figure 2.24 Molecular model of the protein structure of haemoglobin. Each haemoglobin molecule is considered to be a single protein. Each contains four polypeptide chains held together in a quaternary structure. Some of the same types of bonds important for creating the tertiary structure also help to hold quaternary structure proteins together.

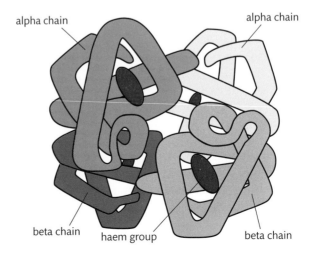

alpha chain

alpha chain

beta chain

haem group

beta chain

Some proteins are more than one polypeptide

Frequently, the terms polypeptide and protein are used interchangeably. In fact, based on the biochemistry of proteins, the two terms do have a slightly different meaning. A protein is an organic substance consisting of covalently bonded amino acids, and it is ready to carry out its function. If the protein is an enzyme, it is ready to catalyse a reaction. If the protein is an antibody (immunoglobulin), it is ready to bond to an antigen as part of an immune response. The point is, a protein is able to carry out its intended function. That may or may not be true for a polypeptide.

A polypeptide is a single amino acid chain with its own primary structure. It has a single *c*-terminal end and a single *n*-terminal end. If the single polypeptide is able to carry out its function as it is, then that polypeptide is considered to be a protein.

Some polypeptides cannot serve a biochemical function until they combine with one or more other polypeptide(s). If you recall, this is what is called a quaternary structure. When two or more polypeptides bond together and then are ready to accomplish their function, together they are considered to be a single protein.

Your unique proteome

Over the last few decades we have come to know that each individual organism of a species is genetically different from all other organisms. This is especially true for organisms that reproduce by sexual reproduction. The specific DNA sequence that is unique to one individual is called a genome. As DNA is the genetic code for proteins, this means that each individual has a unique set of proteins that he or she is capable of synthesizing. Thus each individual is said to have a unique proteome as well as a unique genome.

Proteins can be denatured by heat and alteration of the pH environment

The intra-molecular bonds of proteins that hold together their secondary, tertiary, and quaternary structures are susceptible to alterations in normal temperature and pH; the intra-molecular bonds can be disrupted. When a protein takes on a three-dimensional shape, it does this because of the interactions of the amino acids with each other.

When protein molecules are placed into a temperature environment that is higher than their physiological optimum, the increased molecular motion puts a great deal of stress on many of the relatively weak intra-molecular bonds. This can result in the primary structure remaining intact (the sequence of amino acids connected by peptide bonds) but the hydrogen bonds often cannot stay in place under the stress caused by the increased molecular motion. The result is that the protein loses its normal three-dimensional shape and function. A protein's function is directly dependent on its shape; in most instances, as long as the covalent bonds (like peptide bonds) remain intact, the protein will return to its normal shape and function if it is returned to its normal temperature.

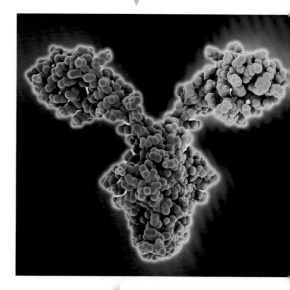

This is a protein found in the ribosomes of some bacteria. The computer model of the protein clearly shows that the protein is composed of two polypeptides. Each of the polypeptides would require a different gene within the bacteria's genome to code for its synthesis.

For centuries people have been selectively breeding both crops and animals to increase their food value. Recently, some companies have begun genetically modifying foods using biotechnology. The jury is still out regarding whether this approach will ultimately be both beneficial and safe.

Technically, a proteome is the collection of proteins found within a particular cell type at a specified time under a specific set of environmental circumstances. Cells in multicellular organisms differentiate and thus do not produce the same proteins even though they contain the same genome.

A similar phenomenon occurs when a protein is placed in a pH environment that is not close to its optimum pH. A protein will lose its normal three-dimensional shape, and thus lose its functionality, in these circumstances. When a fluid environment such as cytoplasm, blood plasma, etc., is flooded with either H^+ ions (an acid) or ^-OH ions (a base), the extra charges can prevent normal hydrogen bonding. Thus the protein will not take on its 'normal' shape and will not function normally.

NATURE OF SCIENCE

Most, but not all, organisms assemble proteins from the same 20 amino acids. Virtually every reference concerning amino acids will tell you that there are 20 amino acids in nature. It is true that the universal genetic code (universal indicating that it is used in the vast majority of organisms on Earth) only encodes 20. But in nature there are frequently exceptions, and that includes things that are called 'universal'. If you include all known living organisms then there are 22 amino acids that are used to create polypeptides. In addition to the 20 amino acids whose structures are given in Figure 2.20, there are two additional amino acids called selenocysteine and pyrrolysine.

Some living organisms have evolved proteins and other molecules that remain stable and functional at very high temperatures. This is a hot spring called Morning Glory in Yellowstone National Park, USA. The brilliant colours you see in the water are primarily the result of the growth of cyanobacteria that can live in water temperatures as high as 165°C.

Section summary

- Numerous amino acids are bonded together by condensation reactions to form polypeptides.
- There are 20 different amino acids that differ from each other in only one of the molecules, an area called the variable or R-group.
- Because polypeptides can differ in both the number and sequence of amino acids, a huge number of polypeptides exist in nature.
- Amino acids do not bind to other amino acids in a random order: their number and sequence is determined by a cell's genetic code.
- A protein is a molecule that has a function. Some proteins are composed of a single polypeptide and some are composed of two or more polypeptides.
- Amino acids within a protein interact with each other to form internal bonds that shape the molecule.
- Each cell synthesizes a set of proteins. That set of proteins is known as the proteome of that cell.

Exercises

9 Study the amino acid chart (Figure 2.20) and find the amino acids that meet the following criteria.

   (a) The single amino acid whose non-R-group shape is slightly different compared with all the others.
   (b) The two amino acids that contain sulfur atoms.
   (c) The five amino acids that contain either a carboxyl or an amine group as part of their R-group.

10 How many peptide bonds would be found in a polypeptide that contains 76 amino acids?

11 Considering only the usual 20 naturally occurring amino acids, how many combinations of amino acids would be possible if four amino acids were to bond together in a random order?

2.5 Enzymes

NATURE OF SCIENCE

Experimental design: accurate, quantitative measurements in enzyme experiments require replicates to ensure reliability.

Understandings:

- Enzymes have an active site to which specific substrates bind.
- Enzyme catalysis involves molecular motion and the collision of substrates with the active site.
- Temperature, pH, and substrate concentration affect the rate of activity of enzymes.
- Enzymes can be denatured.
- Immobilized enzymes are widely used in industry.

Applications and skills:

- Application: Methods of production of lactose-free milk and its advantages.
- Skill: Design of experiments to test the effect of temperature, pH, and substrate concentration on the activity of enzymes.
- Skill: Experimental investigation of a factor affecting enzyme activity.

Guidance

- *Lactase can be immobilized in alginate beads, and experiments can then be carried out in which the lactose in milk is hydrolysed.*
- *Students should be able to sketch graphs to show the expected effects of temperature, pH, and substrate concentration on the activity of enzymes. They should be able to explain the patterns or trends in these graphs.*

Enzymes are organic molecules that act as catalysts

Enzymes are proteins. Thus enzymes are long chains of amino acids that have taken on a very specific three-dimensional shape. Think of a flexible metal wire that can be bent many times into what is called a globular shape. This shape is complex and at first glance appears to be random, but in enzymes (and other globular proteins) the complex shape is not random: it is very specific. Somewhere in the three-dimensional shape of the enzyme is an area that is designed to match a specific molecule known as that enzyme's substrate. This area of the enzyme is called the active site. The active site of an enzyme matches the substrate in a similar way to a glove fitting a hand. In this analogy, the glove represents the active site and the hand represents the substrate.

Another analogy that is very commonly used for enzyme–substrate activity is a lock and key. In this analogy, the lock represents the enzyme's active site and the key represents the substrate. Because the three-dimensional shape of the internal portion of the lock is complex and specific, only one key will fit. The same principle is generally true for enzymes and their substrates: they are specific for each other.

It is not enough for an enzyme's substrate(s) to just enter an active site. The substrate(s) must enter with a minimum rate of motion that will provide the energy necessary for the reaction to occur. Enzymes do not provide this energy, they simply lower the energy minimum that is required. The energy being referred to is called the activation energy of the reaction. Thus enzymes lower the activation energy of reactions. Enzymes

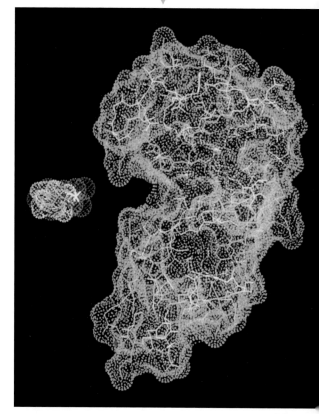

This computer graphic shows an enzyme (the larger molecule on the right) and its substrate. Notice the active site on the left-hand side of the enzyme.

are not considered to be reactants and are not used up in the reaction. An enzyme can function as a catalyst many, many times. In addition, an enzyme cannot force a reaction to occur that would not otherwise happen without the enzyme; however, the reaction may be much more likely to occur with an enzyme because the input of energy (activation energy) required will be lower with the enzyme present.

Factors affecting enzyme-catalysed reactions

When you are considering the various environmental factors that affect enzyme-catalysed reactions, you must first remember that all chemical reactions are fundamentally molecules colliding. If the molecules that are colliding do so at a high enough rate of speed and the molecules have the capability of reacting with each other, then there is a chance that a reaction will occur. Enzymes cannot change those fundamentals.

Effect of temperature

Imagine an enzyme and its substrate floating freely in a fluid environment. Both the enzyme and substrate are in motion and the rate of that motion is dependent on the temperature of the fluid. Fluids with higher temperatures will have faster moving molecules (more kinetic energy). Reactions are dependent on molecular collisions and, as a general rule, the faster molecules are moving, the more often they collide, and with greater energy. Reactions with or without enzymes will increase their reaction rate as the temperature (and thus molecular motion) increases. Reactions that use enzymes do have an upper limit, however (see Figure 2.25). That limit is based on the temperature at which the enzyme (as a protein) begins to lose its three-dimensional shape because the intra-molecular bonds are being stressed and broken. When an enzyme loses its shape, including the shape of the active site, it is said to be denatured. Denaturation is frequently temporary, as in many instances the intra-molecular bonds will re-establish when the temperature returns to a suitable level.

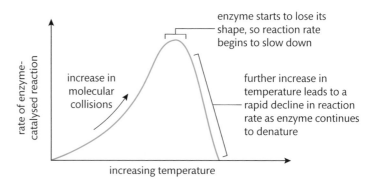

Whether or not an enzyme is permanently destroyed by denaturation is largely dependent on whether covalent bonds (such as peptide bonds) have broken. DNA determines the order of amino acids, and they have no way of reassembling properly if they become detached from each other.

Figure 2.25 The effect of increasing temperature on the rate of an enzyme-catalysed reaction.

Effect of pH

The active site of an enzyme typically includes many amino acids of that protein. Some amino acids have areas that are charged either positively or negatively. The negative and positive areas of a substrate must match the opposite charge when the substrate is in the active site of an enzyme, in order for the enzyme to have catalytic action. When a solution has become too acidic, the relatively large number of hydrogen ions (H^+) can bond with the negative charges of the enzyme or substrate, and prevent proper charge matching between the two. A similar scenario occurs when a solution has become too basic: the relatively large number of hydroxide ions ($^-$OH) can bond with the positive charges of the substrate or enzyme, and once again prevent proper charge matching between the two. Either of these scenarios will result in an enzyme becoming less efficient, and in extreme situations becoming completely inactive. One further possibility is that the numerous extra positive and negative charges of acidic and basic solutions can result in the enzyme losing its shape and thus becoming denatured.

There is no one pH that is best for all enzymes (see Figure 2.26). Many of the enzymes active in the human body are most active when in an environment that is near neutral. There are exceptions to this, however; for example, pepsin is an enzyme that is active in the stomach. The environment of the stomach is highly acidic and pepsin is most active in an acidic pH.

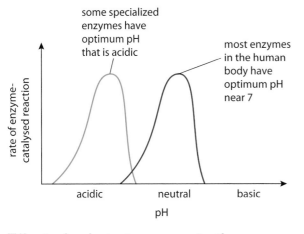

Figure 2.26 The effect of pH on the rate of an enzyme-catalysed reaction. This illustrates that there is no single pH that is best for all enzymes.

Effect of substrate concentration

If there is a constant amount of enzyme, as the concentration of a substrate increases, the rate of reaction will increase as well (see Figure 2.28). This is explained by the idea of increased molecular collisions. If you have more reactant molecules, there are more to collide. There is a limit to this, however, because enzymes have a maximum rate at which they can work. If every enzyme molecule is working as fast as possible, adding more substrate to the solution will not increase the reaction rate further (see Figure 2.28).

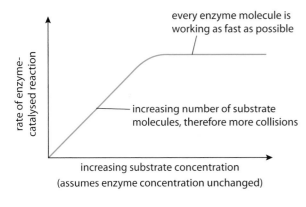

Figure 2.28 The effect of increasing the substrate concentration on the rate of an enzyme-catalysed reaction.

Use of immobilized enzymes in industry

Cells are not the only 'factories' that make good use of enzymes. In the last 50 years, many industrial applications have been developed that make use of these catalytic proteins. However, there are major problems that have to be overcome. For example,

	pH
strongly acidic	1
	2
	3
	4
weakly acidic	5
	6
neutral	7
weakly alkaline	8
	9
strongly alkaline	10
	11
	12
	13
	14

Figure 2.27 The pH scale. Most fluids within the human body are close to neutral. The pH of blood plasma is typically 7.4, making it very slightly alkaline.

The pH scale is a logarithmic scale. This means that each whole number on the pH scale represents an increase or decrease by a power of 10. Thus a solution with a pH of 4 has 10 times more relative hydrogen ions compared with a solution with a pH of 5. That same solution with a pH of 4 has 100 times more relative hydrogen ions compared with a solution with a pH of 6.

if you want to catalyse one particular reaction, you need a pure enzyme, not a mixture as found in cells. Extracting or producing pure enzymes in the large quantities needed for industrial use is expensive. Because of their cost, enzymes in industry need to be reused repeatedly. The problem is that it is difficult to remove enzymes from liquid products in solutions so that the enzymes can be used further. One answer to this problem is to invent ways to trap the enzymes in place and prevent them from getting washed out with the products. Researchers found that an enzyme could be held in place in tiny pores on beads of a substance called calcium alginate. Those enzymes trapped in the pores are said to be immobilized. As long as the alginate beads are recovered in the industrial process, the enzymes are also recovered and can be reused.

Use of immobilized lactase to produce lactose-free milk

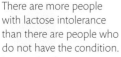

It has been found that there is an extremely high incidence of lactose intolerance in some ethnic groups and a relatively low incidence in others. This is a good example of natural variation in a population.

There are more people with lactose intolerance than there are people who do not have the condition. In genetics, lactose intolerance is called the wild-type (the most common phenotype in a natural population).

The majority of humans are born with the ability to digest lactose, one of the most common sugars found in milk. The reason for this is that we are born with the ability to produce the enzyme lactase in our digestive tract. Lactase is the enzyme that digests the disaccharide lactose into two monosaccharides (glucose and galactose); the monosaccharides are much more readily absorbed into the bloodstream. Most people lose the ability to produce lactase as they get older, and by adulthood no longer produce any significant amount of lactase. These people are said to be lactose intolerant. Normal milk and milk products enter their digestive tract and are not digested; instead the normal bacterial colonies in their intestines feed directly on the lactose. In effect, these bacterial colonies are being overfed. This leads to symptoms such as cramping, excessive gas, and diarrhoea.

In order to avoid these unpleasant symptoms, people who are lactose intolerant can eat milk and milk products that have been treated with lactase before consumption. With this treatment, the nutrients in the milk are not affected but the disaccharide lactose has been pre-digested, so a lactose-intolerant person is able to absorb the monosaccharide sugars.

One of the ways to pre-digest milk products on a large industrial scale is to use the method described above. Specifically, lactase enzyme molecules are trapped in the small pores of alginate beads and then milk and milk products are exposed to these beads for enough time for pre-digestion to occur.

Investigation of factors affecting enzyme activity
Safety alerts: Eye protection and lab aprons should be worn for all stages of these experiments.

Enzymes are protein catalysts. The catalytic ability of an enzyme can be optimized in certain pH and temperature environments, as well as by increasing the substrate concentration available to the enzyme. Because enzymes are proteins, they are subject to the same denaturing factors that affect all other proteins, including pH environments that are far from their optimum, and temperature environments that put stress on their internal bonds that help shape the molecule.

Note: This lab is designed for a class to be divided into three groups, each assigned one of the following questions.

1 What is the effect of altering the pH environment on the activity of the enzyme lactase? Hypothesis for question 1: the optimum pH environment for lactase will be slightly acidic (pH 6.0–6.5).

2 What is the effect of altering the temperature environment on the activity of the enzyme lactase? Hypothesis for question 2: the optimum temperature environment for lactase will be 25°C.

3   What is the effect of altering the concentration of substrate (lactose) on the activity of the enzyme lactase? Hypothesis for question 3: the optimum substrate concentration for lactase will be a ratio of 20 parts lactose by mass to 1 part lactase by mass.

- The following locally available reagents will need to be purchased: lactose powder (available from food shops), lactase powder or tablets, and glucose test strips (available from pharmacies). An alternative to using glucose test strips is to use Benedict's reagent, following standard protocols. An alternative for lactose powder is milk; use powdered milk if you want to compare the ratio of lactose mass to lactase mass, as in question 3.

- In addition, pH strips or another means of measuring the pH of solutions will be needed for the pH group, as well as buffered solutions for the desired pH. Bulb thermometers will be needed for the temperature group, and a mass scale for the substrate concentration group.

- Standard glassware and supplies, such as stirring rods, spatulas, test tubes, beakers, etc., will also be needed, based on your chosen techniques for carrying out the tests.

- To make the enzyme solution (lactase), crush and add one lactase tablet to 200 ml water. Stir well until completely dissolved.

- To make the substrate solution (lactose), starting with powdered milk, follow the instructions given with the powder, and then decant the volumes needed.

- To carry out a negative control test (one that is designed to purposely give negative results), test the lactose solution using either a glucose test strip or Benedict's reagent (to show the absence of glucose).

- To carry out a positive control test (one that is designed to purposely give positive results), in a test tube add 2 ml of liquid milk and 1 ml of enzyme solution. Immediately mix well and start a timer. Test the solution for the presence of glucose after each 1-minute time period until the test is positive for glucose. Record the time necessary to achieve this positive result.

Each group will need to use the above standard procedures to design and carry out their own investigation by altering the solution pH, solution temperature, or the ratio of the mass of substrate to mass of enzyme (this mass ratio investigation should be based on the mass of the substrate and enzyme when in powder/tablet form). The dependent variable in each investigation will be the time necessary to achieve a positive glucose test.

Commercially available lactase has been formulated to still be active in the stomach and so is not sensitive to alterations in various acidic pH environments. Thus this investigation should attempt to start at a slightly acidic pH and have various increments to (safe) alkaline solutions.

Commercially available lactase is also quite temperature tolerant and will not completely denature until boiled for about 30 minutes.

Section summary

- Reactions that are catalysed by enzymes involve molecular collisions between the substrate(s) and the active site of the enzyme.
- Each enzyme has its own optimum pH and temperature environment in which it is most efficient.
- Reactions catalysed by enzymes are sensitive to changes in pH, temperature, and substrate concentration.
- Temperatures and pH environments that are far from optimum for an enzyme may result in the enzyme losing its three-dimensional shape, thus losing its activity. This is known as denaturing an enzyme.
- Modern industries sometimes make use of enzymes immobilized on alginate beads in order to facilitate recovery of the enzymes for future use.

To learn more about enzymes, go to the hotlinks site, search for the title or ISBN, and click on Chapter 2: Section 2.5

Exercises

12 Briefly explain why enzymes and substrates are specific for each other.

13 Why are enzymes considered to be catalysts of reactions?

14 How much more acidic is a solution of pH 3 compared with a solution of pH 6?

NATURE OF SCIENCE

Using models as representations of the real world: Crick and Watson used model making to discover the structure of DNA.

2.6 Structure of DNA and RNA

Understandings:
- The nucleic acids DNA and RNA are polymers of nucleotides.
- DNA differs from RNA in the number of strands present, the base composition, and the type of pentose.
- DNA is a double helix made of two antiparallel strands linked by hydrogen bonding between complementary base pairs.

Applications and skills:
- Application: Crick and Watson's elucidation of the structure of DNA using model making.
- Skill: Drawing simple diagrams of the structure of single nucleotides of DNA and RNA, using circles, pentagons, and rectangles to represent phosphates, pentoses, and bases.

Guidance
- *In diagrams of DNA structure, the helical shape does not need to be shown, but the two strands should be shown antiparallel. Adenine should be shown paired with thymine, and guanine with cytosine, but the relative lengths of the purine and pryimidine bases do not need to be recalled, nor the numbers of hydrogen bonds between the base pairs.*

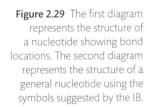

For many years most scientists all over the world believed it was protein, not DNA, that contained our genetic information. Research conducted in the first few decades of the 20th century demonstrated that DNA contains our genetic blueprint.

Nucleotides are the building blocks of nucleic acids

As you learned earlier in this chapter, nucleic acids are one of the major carbon-based groups. There are three major examples of nucleic acids in nature. They are adenosine triphosphate (ATP), deoxyribonucleic acid (DNA), and ribonucleic acid (RNA). ATP functions as an energy storage compound. Other nucleic acids function as coenzymes. In this section we will focus on DNA and RNA. DNA and RNA are involved with the genetic aspects of the cell.

Both DNA and RNA are polymers of nucleotides. Individual nucleotides are referred to as monomers and always consist of three major parts: one phosphate group, one 5-carbon monosaccharide, and a single nitrogenous base. Chemical bonds occur at specific locations in order to produce a functional unit. Look at Figure 2.29.

Figure 2.29 The first diagram represents the structure of a nucleotide showing bond locations. The second diagram represents the structure of a general nucleotide using the symbols suggested by the IB.

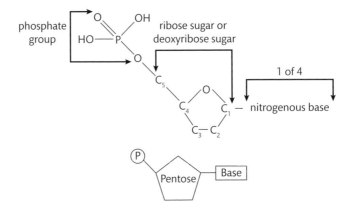

It is important to note that in the diagram circles are used to represent phosphates, pentagons are used to represent 5-carbon sugars (also called pentoses), and rectangles are used to represent nitrogenous bases. All IB drawings involving nucleotides should use these symbols.

All the bonds within the nucleotide involve the sharing of electrons, and are therefore referred to as covalent bonds. The phosphate group is the same in DNA and RNA. However, there are five possible nitrogenous bases, which are shown in Table 2.9.

Table 2.9 The five nitrogenous bases

RNA nitrogenous bases	DNA nitrogenous bases
Adenine (A)	Adenine (A)
Uracil (U)	Thymine (T)
Cytosine (C)	Cytosine (C)
Guanine (G)	Guanine (G)

The base uracil only occurs in RNA, not DNA, and the base thymine only occurs in DNA, not RNA. When drawing nucleotides, it is common practice to put the capitalized first letter of the base inside the rectangle.

The sugar differs in the nucleotides of DNA and RNA. DNA nucleotides contain the pentose known as deoxyribose and RNA nucleotides contain ribose. In Figure 2.30, you can see that they are very similar molecules.

Monomers into polymers

Monomers (single nucleotides) in both DNA and RNA may bond together to produce long chains or polymers. An example of such a chain is shown in Figure 2.31.

In Figure 2.31, each adjoining nucleotide has been drawn in a different colour to emphasize the nucleotide structure. Notice that the chain has an alternating pentose–phosphate backbone, with the nitrogenous bases extending outward. The importance of the order of these nitrogenous bases will be discussed later in conjunction with the genetic code. The nucleotides attach to one another to form a chain as a result of condensation reactions forming connecting covalent bonds.

Single strand or double strand

RNA is composed of a single chain or strand of nucleotides, while DNA consists of two separate chains or strands of nucleotides connected to one another by weak hydrogen bonds. The strands of both DNA and RNA may involve very large numbers of nucleotides. For the two strands of DNA, imagine a double-stranded DNA molecule as a ladder (see Figure 2.32). The two sides of the ladder are made up of the phosphate and deoxyribose sugars. The rungs of the ladder (what you step on) are made up of the nitrogenous bases. Because the ladder has two sides, there are two bases making up each rung. The two bases making up one rung are said to be complementary to each other. The complementary base pairs are adenine (A)–thymine (T) and cytosine (C)–guanine (G).

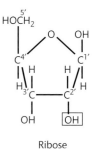

Figure 2.30 Nucleotide sugars.

Deoxyribose

Ribose

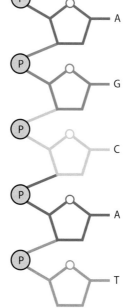

CHALLENGE YOURSELF

8 Use the symbols mentioned on page 88 to represent all the possible nucleotides of DNA. Once you have done that for DNA, do the same for RNA.

Figure 2.31 Five nucleotides bonded to form a very small section of a strand of DNA or RNA.

CHALLENGE YOURSELF

9 Examine the first diagram in Figure 2.29 representing the general structure of a nucleotide. Notice that the carbons of the pentose are numbered. These numbers are always placed in this way for both ribose and deoxyribose. Now look at Figure 2.31, in which five nucleotides are connected together. Answer the following.
  (a) In the polymer, which numbered carbons are always attached to the phosphate group?
  (b) In a monomer, what number carbon is always attached to the phosphate group?
  (c) Which carbon is always attached to the nitrogenous base?

Figure 2.32 A small section of a double-stranded DNA molecule showing hydrogen bonds between complementary nitrogenous bases. The two single strands that make up the double-stranded molecule run in opposite directions to each other. The term that describes this is 'antiparallel'. Thus we say that the two strands of the double helix are antiparallel and complementary to each other.

Even though the first accurate model of DNA was produced by James Watson (American) and Francis Crick (British) in 1953, many other scientists from around the world contributed pieces of information that were instrumental in developing the final model. Erwin Chargaff (Austrian) had determined that the numbers of adenine and thymine bases were equal, as were the numbers of cytosine and guanine bases. Rosalind Franklin (British) and Maurice Wilkins (born in New Zealand) had calculated the distance between the various molecules in DNA by X-ray crystallography.

TOK

Even though some information was exchanged, the development of the first accurate model of DNA was highly competitive. Several groups in different parts of the world were trying to make sense of shared knowledge to produce an appropriate model. Some scientists did not share their research or findings. How is this 'anti-scientific'? Discuss what can be done to increase the sharing of personal knowledge in scientific research.

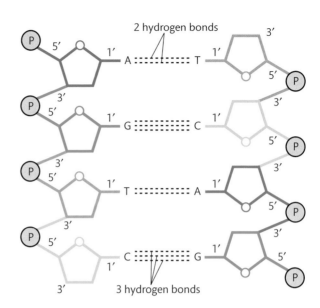

We can now use all of this information to construct a simple, yet accurate, drawing of DNA. In Figure 2.32, it is essential to note that one strand of DNA has the 5-carbon, often referred to as the 5-prime (5′) carbon, unattached and on top. At the bottom of

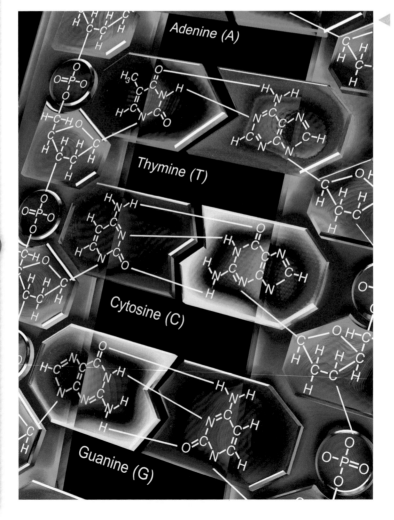

Figure 2.33 This artwork shows complementary base pairs and hydrogen bonding in DNA. Note that thymine and cytosine are much smaller molecular structures than adenine and guanine.

that same strand notice that the 3- or 3-prime (3′) carbon is unattached. If you look at the opposite strand of deoxyribose and phosphates, you will notice it is the opposite: the 3′ carbon is at the top and the 5′ carbon is at the bottom. These two strands are therefore said to be antiparallel to one another. Electrical charges related to the molecules of the two strands cause a characteristic twisting action of the DNA ladder to produce the double helix shape that Watson and Crick described in the model they proposed in the early 1950s.

CHALLENGE YOURSELF

10 In order to better understand the basic structures of RNA and DNA, it is useful to compare and contrast their characteristics. They are actually quite similar. When comparing two compounds, using a *t*-chart or a table is recommended. *t*-charts may take many forms, but all allow a direct comparison between related items or materials. In this case, complete the table below, which allows a comparison of the two compounds.

Feature	RNA	DNA
Number of strands		
Bases present		
Pentose present		
Name of monomers		

Table 2.10

Section summary

- The subcomponents or 'building block' units of DNA are called DNA nucleotides.
- Each DNA nucleotide is composed of a phosphate group, deoxyribose sugar, and one of four nitrogenous bases.
- The four nitrogenous bases within DNA nucleotides are adenine, thymine, cytosine, and guanine.
- DNA is a double-stranded molecule, with each strand composed of nucleotides where the sugar of one nucleotide is covalently bonded to the phosphate group of the next nucleotide.
- The two strands of DNA are held together by hydrogen bonding between the complementary base pairs cytosine–guanine and adenine–thymine.
- DNA is described as having two antiparallel strands because the two strands are aligned in opposite directions.
- RNA is another nucleic acid. It is composed of only one strand. Its RNA nucleotides differ from DNA nucleotides in that they contain a different pentose: ribose in place of deoxyribose. RNA nucleotides also contain the nitrogenous base uracil, which takes the place of thymine in DNA nucleotides.

To learn more about DNA structure, go to the hotlinks site, search for the title or ISBN, and click on Chapter 2: Section 2.6.

NATURE OF SCIENCE

Obtaining evidence for scientific theories: Meselson and Stahl obtained evidence for the semi-conservative replication of DNA.

Exercises

15 Why do researchers often give DNA information as the sequence of nitrogenous bases without indicating the presence of the phosphate group and sugar component of each nucleotide?

16 Starting with a blank piece of paper, practise drawing a ladder diagram of DNA in which the nitrogenous base sequence of one strand is C, T, G, G, A, T. Be sure to include a representation of the phosphate groups and deoxyribose sugar in each nucleotide.

2.7 DNA replication, transcription, and translation

Understandings:

- The replication of DNA is semi-conservative and depends on complementary base pairing.
- Helicase unwinds the double helix and separates the two strands by breaking hydrogen bonds.
- DNA polymerase links nucleotides together to form a new strand, using the pre-existing strand as a template.
- Transcription is the synthesis of mRNA copied from the DNA base sequences by RNA polymerase.
- Translation is the synthesis of polypeptides on ribosomes.
- The amino acid sequence of polypeptides is determined by mRNA according to the genetic code.
- Codons of three bases on mRNA correspond to one amino acid in a polypeptide.
- Translation depends on complementary base pairing between codons on mRNA and anticodons on tRNA.

Application and skills:

- Application: Use of *Taq* DNA polymerase to produce multiple copies of DNA rapidly by the polymerase chain reaction (PCR).
- Application: Production of human insulin in bacteria as an example of the universality of the genetic code allowing gene transfer between species.
- Skill: Use a table of the genetic code to deduce which codon(s) corresponds to which amino acid.
- Skill: Analysis of Meselson and Stahl's results to obtain support for the theory of semi-conservative replication of DNA.
- Skill: Use a table of mRNA codons and their corresponding amino acids to deduce the sequence of amino acids coded by a short mRNA strand of known base sequence.
- Skill: Deducing the DNA base sequence for the mRNA strand.

Guidance

- *The different types of DNA polymerase do not need to be distinguished.*

DNA replication involves 'unzipping'

Cells must prepare for a cell division by doubling the DNA content of the cell in a process called DNA replication. This process doubles the quantity of DNA and also ensures that there is an exact copy of each DNA molecule. In the nucleus of cells are two types of molecules that are particularly important for the process of DNA replication; they are:

- enzymes needed for replication, which include helicase and a group of enzymes collectively called DNA polymerase

- free nucleotides, which are nucleotides that are not yet bonded and are found floating freely in the nucleoplasm, some contain adenine, some thymine, some cytosine, and some guanine.

One of the early events of DNA replication is the separation of the double helix into two single strands. You should remember that the double helix is held together by the hydrogen bonds between complementary base pairs (adenine and thymine, cytosine and guanine). The enzyme that initiates this separation into two single strands is called helicase. Helicase begins at a point in or at the end of a DNA molecule, and moves one complementary base pair at a time, breaking the hydrogen bonds so the double-stranded DNA molecule becomes two separate strands.

Helicase can catalyse the unzipping of DNA at a rate measured in hundreds of base pairs per second.

The unpaired nucleotides on each of these single strands can now be used as a template to help create two double-stranded DNA molecules identical to the original. Some people use the analogy of a zipper for this process. When you pull on a zipper, helicase is like the slide mechanism. The separation of the two sides of the DNA molecule is like the two opened sides of a zipper. See Figure 2.34.

Helicase (currently at about the half-way point in this image of a DNA double helix being unzipped) would have started on the left and be moving towards the right.

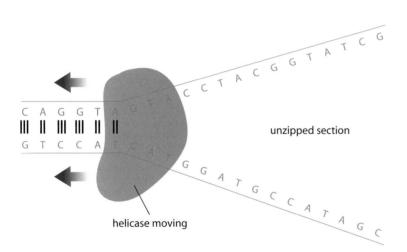

helicase moving

unzipped section

Figure 2.34 The first step of DNA replication is helicase unzipping the double-stranded DNA molecule, forming a section with two single strands.

Formation of two complementary strands

As shown in Figure 2.34, once DNA has become unzipped, the nitrogenous bases on each of the single strands are unpaired. In the environment of the nucleoplasm, there are free-floating nucleotides. These nucleotides are available to form complementary pairs with the single-stranded nucleotides of the unzipped molecule. This does not happen in a random fashion. A free nucleotide locates on one opened strand at one end, and then a second nucleotide can join the first. This requires these two nucleotides to become covalently bonded together, because they are the beginning of a new strand. The formation of a covalent bond between two adjoining nucleotides is catalysed by one of the DNA polymerase enzymes that are important in this process.

A third nucleotide then joins the first two, and the process continues in a repetitive way for many nucleotides. The other unzipped strand also acts as a template for the formation of another new strand. This strand forms in a similar fashion, but

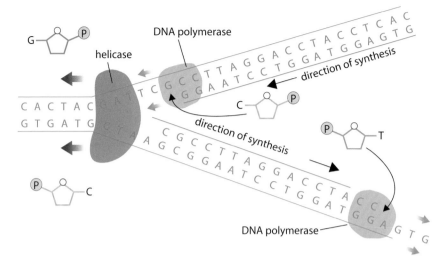

Figure 2.35 DNA replication.

in the opposite direction to the first strand. In Figure 2.35, notice that one strand is replicating in the same direction as helicase is moving and the other strand is replicating in the opposite direction.

The significance of DNA replication is that it ensures that two identical copies of DNA are produced from one original. The diagram illustrates a very small section of DNA replicating.

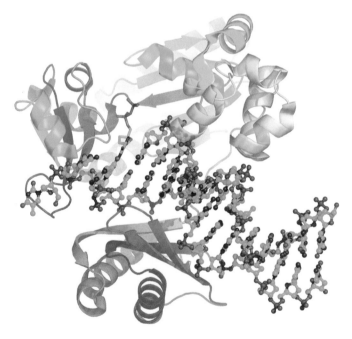

Figure 2.36 A small section of DNA (shown in the centre of this artwork) is seen in a DNA polymerase enzyme.

Notice that in the area where replication has already taken place, the two strands are absolutely identical to each other. This is because the original double-stranded molecule had complementary pairs of nucleotides and it was the complementary nucleotides that used the unzipped single-stranded areas as templates.

This also means that no DNA molecule is ever completely new. After replication, every DNA molecule consists of a strand that is 'old' paired with a strand that is 'new'. DNA replication is described as a semi-conservative process because half of a pre-existing DNA molecule is always conserved (saved).

CHALLENGE YOURSELF

11 The experimental work that determined that DNA replication was semi-conservative is often called 'the most beautiful experiment in biology'. This experiment was carried out by Matthew Meselson and Frank Stahl, with their results published in 1958. An overview of the experiment and the data obtained follows.

- Two separate cultures of *Escherichia coli* bacteria were grown with the presence of either a 'heavy' isotope of nitrogen, ^{15}N, or an ordinary 'light' isotope of nitrogen, ^{14}N.

- After many generations, the DNA in each bacteria culture contained either the heavy form or the light form of nitrogen. The nitrogen was part of the nucleotides' nitrogenous bases.

- Bacteria of each culture were treated to release their DNA into a solution.

- The solution with DNA from both cultures was then centrifuged at high speed.

- The result was two bands of DNA, the band that was lower in solution contained the ^{15}N, the band that was higher contained the ^{14}N.

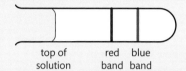

top of   red   blue
solution   band   band

Figure 2.37 Meselson and Stahl's experiment.

- In Figure 2.37, you can see the two bands. The lower, blue, band had the heavier nitrogen, ^{15}N.

- This first tube represented a 'standard' to which future results could be compared.

- A new culture of *E. coli* was grown in the ^{15}N medium for many generations, to ensure all the DNA present was ^{15}N. A DNA sample was obtained and centrifuged. This became generation 0.

- At the same time as generation 0 was obtained, some of the bacteria were placed in a ^{14}N culture medium and allowed to grow for 20 minutes, which is the generation time for *E. coli* grown in optimal conditions.

- A sample was then taken, processed, and centrifuged to produce generation 1. This same process was continued so that four generations were obtained, each being processed and centrifuged.

- Figure 2.38 represents the results obtained.

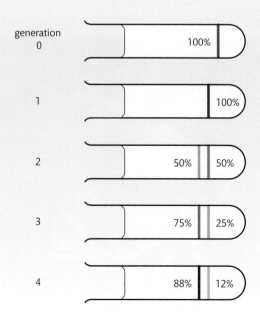

Figure 2.38 Meselson and Stahl's results.

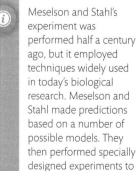

Meselson and Stahl's experiment was performed half a century ago, but it employed techniques widely used in today's biological research. Meselson and Stahl made predictions based on a number of possible models. They then performed specially designed experiments to gather data to support one of these models.

Answer these questions from the results obtained.
(a) In semi-conservative replication, the new molecule of DNA has one strand from the original molecule and one new strand produced from nucleotides in the surrounding environment. How does generation 1 support this model?
(b) Why does generation 2 support the semi-conservative model?

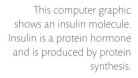

parent

products of first replication

The results of Meselson and Stahl's experiment are summarized in Figure 2.38. Notice the colours of the original strand of DNA and how one 'parent strand' becomes one of each of the new strands produced by replication.

DNA replication summary

- Cells replicate their DNA in preparation for a cell division.
- Helicase is an enzyme that separates the double-stranded DNA molecule into two single strands.
- Free-floating (unattached) nucleotides provide the building block units for synthesizing a new DNA strand.
- Existing DNA strands are used as a template for new strands of DNA by making use of complementary base pairing.
- DNA replication is called semi-conservative because each resulting DNA molecule is actually an 'old' strand now paired with a 'new' strand.

Figure 2.39 This figure demonstrates the general process of semi-conservative replication of DNA.

Protein synthesis

The control that DNA has over a cell is determined by a process called protein synthesis. In simple terms, DNA controls the proteins produced in a cell. Some of the proteins produced are enzymes. The production (or lack of production) of a particular enzyme can have a dramatic effect on the overall biochemistry of the cell. Thus DNA indirectly controls the biochemistry of carbohydrates, lipids, and nucleic acids with the production of enzymes.

This computer graphic shows an insulin molecule. Insulin is a protein hormone and is produced by protein synthesis.

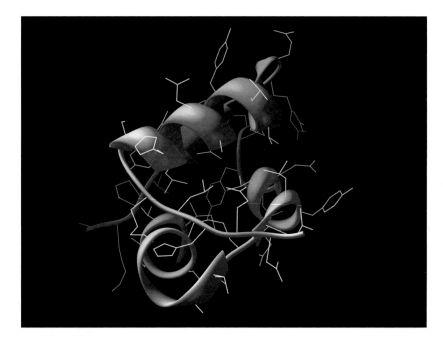

Protein synthesis involves two major sets of reactions, transcription and translation. Both either produce or require a type of nucleic acid called RNA, which was discussed in Section 2.6.

Transcription produces RNA molecules

The sections of DNA that code for polypeptides are called genes. Any one gene is a specific sequence of nitrogenous bases found in a specific location in a DNA molecule. Molecules of DNA are found within the confines of the nucleus, yet proteins are synthesized outside the nucleus in the cytoplasm. This means that there has to be an intermediary molecule that carries the message of the DNA (the code) to the cytoplasm where the enzymes, ribosome, and amino acids are found. This intermediary molecule is called messenger RNA (mRNA).

The nucleoplasm (fluid in the nucleus) contains free nucleotides, as mentioned earlier. In addition to the free nucleotides used for DNA replication, the nucleoplasm also contains free RNA nucleotides. Each of these is different from the DNA counterpart, because RNA nucleotides contain the sugar ribose not deoxyribose. Another major difference is that no RNA nucleotides contain thymine; instead there is a nitrogenous base unique to RNA, called uracil.

The transcription process

The process of transcription begins when an area of DNA of one gene becomes unzipped (see Figure 2.40). This is very similar to the unzipping process involved in DNA replication, but in this case only the area of the DNA where the particular gene is found is unzipped. The two complementary strands of DNA are now single-stranded in the area of the gene. Recall that RNA (which includes mRNA) is a single-stranded molecule. This means that only one of the two strands of DNA will be used as a template to create the mRNA molecule. An enzyme called RNA polymerase is used as the catalyst for this process.

As RNA polymerase moves along the strand of DNA acting as the template, RNA nucleotides float into place by complementary base pairing. The complementary base pairs are the same as in double-stranded DNA, with the exception that adenine on the DNA is now paired with uracil on the newly forming mRNA molecule. Consider the following facts concerning transcription:

- only one of the two strands of DNA is 'copied,' the other strand is not used
- mRNA is always single-stranded and shorter than the DNA that it is copied from, as it is a complementary copy of only one gene
- the presence of thymine in a molecule identifies it as DNA (the presence of deoxyribose is another clue)
- the presence of uracil in a molecule identifies it as RNA (the presence of ribose is another clue).

Figure 2.40 Transcription (synthesis of an RNA molecule). RNA polymerase has helicase-like activity as it plays a role in opening the DNA double helix. It also catalyses the addition of free RNA nucleotide to the growing mRNA strands.

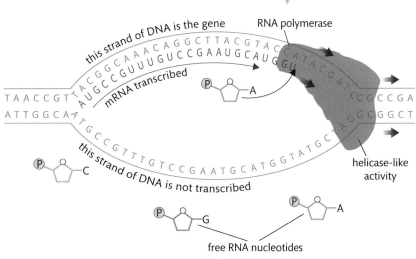

The genetic code is written in triplets

$$\text{DNA triplet} \rightarrow \text{(transcription)} \rightarrow \text{mRNA (codon)}$$

The mRNA molecule produced by transcription represents a complementary copy of one gene of DNA. The sequence of mRNA nucleotides is the transcribed version of the original DNA sequence. This sequence of nucleotides making up the length of the mRNA is typically enough information to make one polypeptide. As you will recall, polypeptides are composed of amino acids covalently bonded together in a specific sequence. The message written into the mRNA molecule is the message that determines the order of the amino acids. Researchers found experimentally that the genetic code is written in a language of three bases. In other words, a set of three bases contains enough information to code for one of the 20 amino acids. Any set of three bases that determines the identity of one amino acid is called a triplet. When a triplet is found in an mRNA molecule, it is called a codon or codon triplet. This is shown in the model below.

Translation results in the production of a polypeptide

There are three different kinds of RNA molecule. They are all single-stranded and each is transcribed from a gene (a section of DNA).

In this model, you can see mRNA (upper right) and tRNA (the clover shape). The amino acid that would be bonded to the tRNA is not shown.

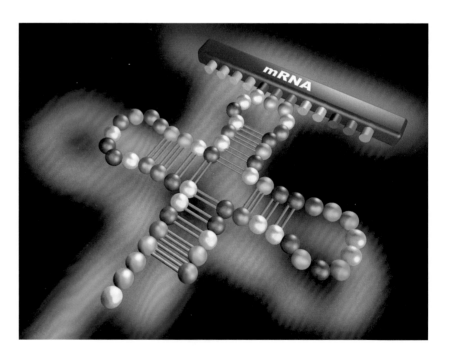

Here is a quick summary of each RNA type:

- mRNA, messenger RNA, as described above, each mRNA is a complementary copy of a DNA gene and has enough genetic information to code for a single polypeptide
- rRNA, ribosomal RNA, each ribosome is composed of rRNA and ribosomal protein
- tRNA, transfer RNA, each type of tRNA transfers one of the 20 amino acids to the ribosome for polypeptide formation.

Figure 2.41 shows a typical tRNA molecule. Notice that the three bases in the middle loop are called the anticodon bases, and they determine which of the 20 amino acids is attached to the tRNA.

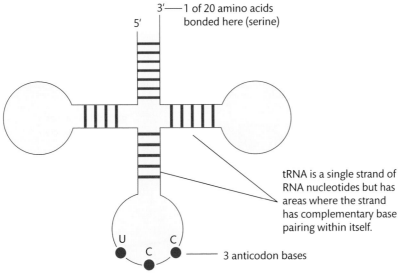

3'——1 of 20 amino acids bonded here (serine)
5'

tRNA is a single strand of RNA nucleotides but has areas where the strand has complementary base pairing within itself.

U   C
C
3 anticodon bases

Figure 2.41 Structure of a tRNA 3' molecule.

Once an mRNA molecule has been transcribed, the mRNA detaches from the single-strand DNA template and floats free in the nucleoplasm. At some point, the mRNA will float through one of the many holes in the nuclear membrane (nuclear pores) and will then be in the cytoplasm.

The translation process

The mRNA will locate a ribosome and align with it, so that the first two codon triplets are within the boundaries of the ribosome.

A specific tRNA molecule now floats in: its tRNA anticodon must be complementary to the first codon triplet of the mRNA molecule. Thus the first amino acid is brought into the translation process. It is not just any amino acid: its identity was originally determined by the strand of DNA that transcribed the mRNA being translated. While the first tRNA 'sits' in the ribosome holding the first amino acid, a second tRNA floats in and brings a second (again specific) amino acid. The second tRNA matches its three anticodon bases with the second codon triplet of the mRNA. As you can see in Figure 2.42, two specific amino acids are now being held side by side. An enzyme then catalyses a condensation reaction between the two amino acids, and the resulting covalent bond between them is called a peptide bond.

The next step in the translation process involves breaking the bond between the first tRNA molecule and the amino acid that it transferred in. This bond is no longer needed, as the second tRNA is currently bonded to its own amino acid, and that amino acid is covalently bonded to the first amino acid. The first tRNA floats away into the cytoplasm and invariably reloads with another amino acid of the same type. The ribosome that has only one tRNA in it now moves one codon triplet down the mRNA molecule. This, in effect, puts the second tRNA in the ribosome position that the first originally occupied, and creates room for a third tRNA to float in, bringing with it a third specific amino acid. The process now becomes repetitive: as another

The process of producing proteins utilizes a DNA code that is universal in all organisms. Because of this, researchers have successfully inserted the human gene that codes for the production of human insulin into bacteria. The result of this is bacteria that produce human insulin that can be used to treat humans with diabetes.

TOK

Who should decide how fast and how far humans should go with our study of DNA and the technology that is rapidly emerging?

peptide bond forms, the ribosome moves on by another triplet, and so on. The process continues until the ribosome gets to the last codon triplet. The final codon triplet will be a triplet that does not act as a code for an amino acid, instead it signals 'stop' to the process of translation. The entire polypeptide breaks away from the final tRNA molecule, and becomes a free-floating polypeptide in the cytoplasm of the cell.

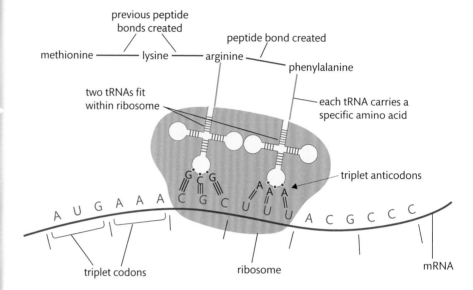

Figure 2.42 Events of translation (synthesis of a polypeptide).

Polymerase chain reaction and *Taq* DNA polymerase

Polymerase chain reaction, also known as PCR, was developed in the 1970s. It is a means by which DNA replication can be carried out artificially in a laboratory setting. However, it can only replicate rather short segments of DNA. By replicating DNA segments, scientists can produce huge numbers of these segments to study and analyse. It is often used in forensic situations when only a limited amount of the original DNA has been recovered at a crime scene.

An enzyme is used in PCR that is stable at relatively high temperatures. This enzyme was discovered in 1985 from a bacterium called *Thermus aquaticus* (*Taq*). This bacterium occurs naturally in hot springs, and its enzymes are not denatured at high temperatures, including the specific DNA polymerase that it possesses. This DNA polymerase has been named *Taq* polymerase and its use has greatly increased the number of discoveries in the field of gene technology.

Protein synthesis summary

- The genetic information of living organisms (the genetic code) is stored within the nitrogenous base sequences of DNA.
- RNA molecules of three different types are involved in the use of the DNA genetic code for the purpose of synthesizing proteins.
- DNA and RNA are both composed of nucleotides, but have many differences in both structure and function.
- Transcription is the process whereby a gene of DNA is used to create a sequence of single-stranded RNA nucleotides (most often this is mRNA).
- Each three-base sequence of nucleotides along an mRNA molecule is called a triplet codon.

CHALLENGE YOURSELF

12 Imagine that an mRNA leaves the nucleus of a eukaryotic cell with the following base sequence: AUGCCCCGCACGUUUCC AAGCCCCGGG.

Find an mRNA codon chart and answer the following.
(a) Determine in sequence the amino acids that are coded for by the above mRNA molecule.
(b) Determine the DNA code sequence that gave rise to the above mRNA codons.
(c) What would the amino acid sequence be if the first cytosine of the mRNA molecule was replaced with a uracil? (This would be the result of a change occurring in the DNA molecule that transcribed this mRNA.)

- The genetic code is written in a pattern whereby each three-base set (known as a triplet) codes for one of the 20 amino acids within a protein.
- Translation is the process whereby the triplet codons of an mRNA molecule are used to synthesize a specific protein (polypeptide).
- Translation requires an mRNA, a ribosome, tRNA, amino acids, and enzymes.
- With some exceptions, one gene of DNA provides enough genetic information to synthesize one polypeptide.

To learn more about DNA replication and transcription, and to find a codon chart, go to the hotlinks site, search for the title or ISBN, and click on Chapter 2: Section 2.7.

Exercises

17 What type of bonds does helicase act upon?

18 What is the difference between a codon and a triplet?

19 What are the two major sets of reactions in protein synthesis?

20 What are the three major parts of all nucleotides?

2.8 Cell respiration

NATURE OF SCIENCE

Assessing the ethics of scientific research: the use of invertebrates in respirometer experiments has ethical implications.

Understandings:

- Cell respiration is the controlled release of energy from organic compounds to produce ATP.
- ATP from cell respiration is immediately available as a source of energy in the cell.
- Anaerobic cell respiration gives a small yield of ATP from glucose.
- Aerobic cell respiration requires oxygen and gives a large yield of ATP from glucose.

Applications and skills:

- Application: Use of anaerobic cell respiration in yeasts to produce ethanol and carbon dioxide in baking.
- Application: Lactate production in humans when anaerobic respiration is used to maximize the power of muscle contractions.
- Skill: Analysis of results from experiments involving measurement of respiration rates in germinating seeds or invertebrates using a respirometer.

Guidance
- Details of the metabolic pathways of cell respiration are not needed but the substrates and final waste products should be known.
- There are many simple respirometers that could be used. Students are expected to know that an alkali is used to absorb carbon dioxide, so reductions in volume are due to oxygen use. Temperature should be kept constant to avoid volume changes due to temperature fluctuations.

Cell respiration is used by all cells to produce ATP

Organic molecules contain energy in their molecular structures. Each covalent bond in a glucose, amino acid, or fatty acid represents stored chemical energy. When we burn wood in a fire, we are releasing the stored chemical energy in the form of heat and light. Burning is the release of chemical energy called rapid oxidation.

Cells break down (or metabolize) their organic nutrients by slow oxidation. A molecule, such as glucose, is acted on by a series of enzymes. The function of these enzymes is to catalyse a sequential series of reactions in which the covalent bonds are broken (oxidized) one at a time. Each time a covalent bond is broken, a small amount of energy is released. The ultimate goal of releasing energy in a controlled way is to trap the released energy in the form of ATP molecules. If a cell does not have glucose available, other organic molecules may be substituted, such as fatty acids or amino acids.

This is a computer graphic of glucose. The backbone of the molecule is shown in stick form. The spheres represent the relative sizes of the individual atoms ($C_6H_{12}O_6$).

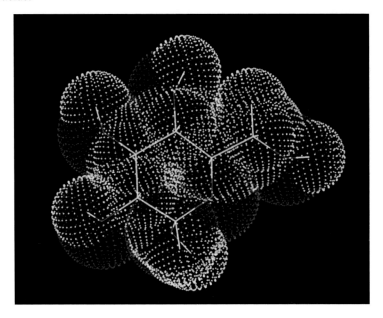

Glycolysis is the first step in the cell respiration process

Assuming that glucose is the organic nutrient being metabolized, all cells begin the process of cell respiration in the same way. Glucose enters a cell through the plasma membrane and floats in the cytoplasm. An enzyme modifies the glucose slightly, then a second enzyme modifies this molecule every more. This is followed by an entire series of reactions that ultimately cleaves the 6-carbon glucose into two 3-carbon molecules. Each of these 3-carbon molecules is called pyruvate. Some, but certainly not all, of the covalent bonds in the glucose are broken during this series of reactions. Some of the energy that is released from the breaking of these bonds is used to form a small number of ATP molecules. Notice in Figure 2.43 that two ATP molecules are needed to begin the process of glycolysis and a total of four ATP molecules are formed. This is referred to as a net gain of two ATP (a gain of four ATP minus the two ATP needed at the start).

Some cells use anaerobic respiration for ATP production

Figure 2.43 A simplified version of the events of glycolysis.

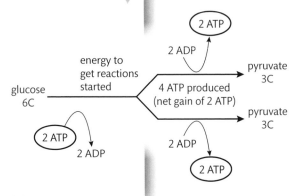

The term 'cell respiration' refers to a variety of biochemical pathways that can be used to metabolize glucose. All of the pathways start with glycolysis. In other words, glycolysis is the metabolic pathway that is common to all organisms on Earth. Some organisms derive their ATP completely without the use of oxygen and are referred to as anaerobic. The breakdown of organic molecules for ATP production in an anaerobic way is also called fermentation. There are two main anaerobic pathways, which will be discussed here separately: alcoholic fermentation and lactic acid fermentation.

Alcoholic fermentation

Yeast is a common single-cell fungus that uses alcoholic fermentation for ATP generation when oxygen is not present (see Figure 2.44). You will recall that all organisms use glycolysis to begin the cell respiration sequence. Thus yeast cells take in glucose from their environment and generate a net gain of two ATP by glycolysis. The organic products of glycolysis are always two pyruvate molecules. Yeast then converts both of the 3-carbon pyruvate molecules to molecules of ethanol. Ethanol is a 2-carbon molecule, so a carbon atom is 'lost' in this conversion. The 'lost' carbon atom is given off in a carbon dioxide molecule. Both the ethanol and carbon dioxide that are produced are waste products from the yeast and are simply released into the environment. Bakers' yeast is added to bread products for baking because the generation of carbon dioxide helps the dough to rise. It is also common to use yeast in the production of ethanol as alcohol to be drunk.

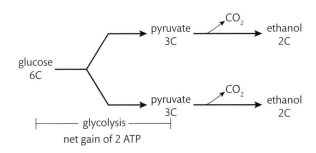

 Most types of yeast are facultatively anaerobic, which means they only carry out alcoholic fermentation when oxygen is not available. If oxygen is present they actually carry out a different type of respiration, in which ethanol and carbon dioxide are not produced. Yeast cells are eukaryotic and do possess mitochondria.

Figure 2.44 A simplified version of the events of alcoholic fermentation.

Lactic acid fermentation

Organisms that normally use a cell respiration pathway that involves oxygen sometimes find themselves in a metabolic situation where they cannot supply enough oxygen to their cells. A good example of this is a person exercising beyond his or her normal pattern or routine. In this situation, the person's pulmonary and cardiovascular systems (lungs and heart) supply as much oxygen to the body's cells as is physically possible. If the person's exercise rate then exceeds his or her body's capacity to supply oxygen, at least some of the glucose entering into cell respiration will follow the anaerobic pathway called lactic acid fermentation. See Figure 2.45.

 All alcohol that is sold to be drunk is ethanol. Beer, wine, and spirits contain different proportions of ethanol, plus other ingredients for flavouring.

Once again, recall that glycolysis is used by all cells to begin the cell respiration sequence. Also remember that glycolysis:

• takes place in the cytoplasm
• results in the net gain of two ATP molecules per glucose molecule
• results in the production of two pyruvate molecules.

Cells that are aerobic normally take the two pyruvate molecules and metabolize them further in an aerobic series of reactions. But if a cell is not getting a sufficient amount of oxygen for the aerobic pathway, i.e. is in a low-oxygen situation, excess pyruvate molecules are converted into lactic acid molecules. Like pyruvate, lactic acid molecules are 3-carbon molecules, so there is no production of carbon dioxide. What benefit does this serve? Lactic acid fermentation allows glycolysis to continue with a small gain of ATP in addition to the ATP that is generated through the aerobic pathway.

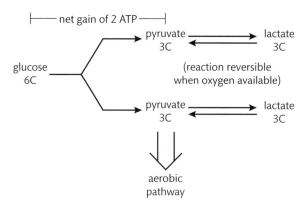

Figure 2.45 A simplified version of the events of lactic acid fermentation.

Aerobic cell respiration is the most efficient pathway

Cells that have mitochondria usually use an aerobic pathway for cell respiration. This pathway also begins with glycolysis, and thus has a net gain of two ATP as well as generating two pyruvate molecules. The two pyruvate molecules then enter a mitochondrion and are metabolized further.

This high-resolution, false-colour SEM shows a single mitochondrion. Any cell containing mitochondria uses aerobic cell respiration as its primary cell respiration pathway.

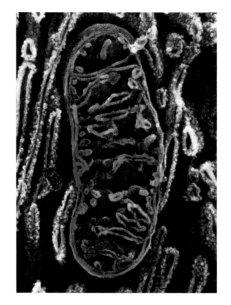

Each pyruvate first loses a carbon dioxide molecule and becomes a molecule known as acetyl-CoA. Each acetyl-CoA molecule enters into a series of reactions called the Krebs cycle. During this series of reactions, two more carbon dioxide molecules are produced from each original pyruvate molecule that entered it. The Krebs cycle is said to be a cycle because it is a series of chemical reactions that begin and end with the same molecules. This reacquisition of the beginning molecule allows this series of chemical reactions to be repeated over and over again (see Figure 2.46).

Some ATP is generated directly during the Krebs cycle and some is generated indirectly through a later series of reactions directly involving oxygen. Aerobic cell respiration breaks down (or completely oxidizes) a glucose molecule and the end-products are carbon dioxide and water plus a much higher number of ATP molecules than anaerobic respiration yields.

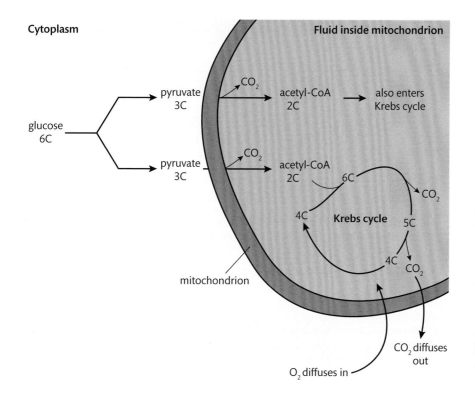

Cytoplasm

Fluid inside mitochondrion

glucose
6C

pyruvate
3C

CO_2

acetyl-CoA
2C

also enters
Krebs cycle

pyruvate
3C

CO_2

acetyl-CoA
2C

6C

Krebs cycle

4C

5C

CO_2

4C

CO_2

mitochondrion

CO_2 diffuses
out

O_2 diffuses in

Figure 2.46 Aerobic cell respiration. Notice that the 4C molecule of the Krebs cycle combines with the 2C molecule called acetyl-CoA. The resulting 6C molecule then goes through a series of reactions in which two carbons are lost in the form of carbon dioxide. This restores the 4C molecule that can begin the cycle all over again.

Worked example

Respirometers are devices used to measure an organism's rate of respiration by measuring the oxygen rate of exchange. They are sealed units in which any carbon dioxide produced is absorbed by an alkali such as soda lime or potassium hydroxide. Absorbing the carbon dioxide allows an accurate measurement of oxygen exchange. These devices may work at a cellular level or at a whole-organism level. Look at the graph and answer the questions. The y-axis of the graph represents the relative amount of oxygen used.

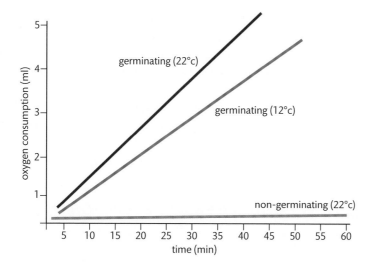

germinating (22°c)

germinating (12°c)

non-germinating (22°c)

oxygen consumption (ml)

time (min)

Figure 2.47 Oxygen consumption by germinating and non-germinating pea seeds at 12°C and 22°C.

1 In the germinating pea seeds, what type of respiration is occurring? What is the evidence for this answer?

2 Why is the oxygen consumption of non-germinating pea seeds very low?

3 Why would the germinating seeds show a greater oxygen consumption at 22°C than at 12°C?

4 Predict how the graph would look for non-germinating seeds at 12°C.

Solutions

1 Aerobic. There is a significant amount of oxygen consumption occurring.

2 They are not carrying out respiration and have a low metabolic rate.

3 At 22°C the rate of respiration is faster than at 12°C. Therefore, there is a greater oxygen consumption at the higher temperature.

4 The line of the graph would be almost right on the non-germinating (22°C) line that exists now. A prediction that it would be just slightly lower is best.

NATURE OF SCIENCE

It is tempting to places invertebrates in respirometers to determine oxygen consumption. However, the use of invertebrates in such experiments has ethical implications. It is essential to refer to the IB animal experimental policy before carrying out any procedures on animals. A discussion of the ethics of animal use in respirometer experiments would be wise at this point.

Section summary

• Cells obtain energy by the slow oxidation of organic molecules such as glucose in a series of reactions referred to as cell respiration.

• The first stage of cell respiration is called glycolysis and occurs in the cytoplasm of all cells.

• During glycolysis, glucose is broken down (oxidized) into two 3-carbon molecules called pyruvate.

• Glycolysis yields a net gain of two ATP molecules per molecule of glucose oxidized.

• Organisms that use an anaerobic form of cell respiration called alcoholic fermentation convert pyruvate into ethanol.

• Aerobic organisms under anaerobic conditions use a form of cell respiration known as lactic acid fermentation. Each pyruvate molecule is temporarily converted into a molecule of lactic acid.

• Aerobic cell respiration completely oxidizes glucose into carbon dioxide and water, and is by far the most efficient cell respiration pathway (it produces the most ATP per glucose oxidized).

• Organisms that have mitochondria within their cells are capable of aerobic cell respiration.

To learn more about aerobic cell respiration, go to the hotlinks site, search for the title or ISBN, and click on Chapter 2: Section 2.8.

Exercises

21 Which stage of cell respiration is common to all types of cell respiration?

22 Where does this stage of cell respiration occur in a cell?

23 Why does that make sense?

24 Why do we inhale oxygen and exhale carbon dioxide?

NATURE OF SCIENCE

Experimental design: controlling relevant variables in photosynthesis experiments is essential.

Understandings:

- Photosynthesis is the production of carbon compounds in cells using light energy.
- Visible light has a range of wavelengths, with violet the shortest wavelength and red the longest.
- Chlorophyll absorbs red and blue light most effectively, and reflects green light more than other colours.
- Oxygen is produced in photosynthesis from the photolysis of water.
- Energy is needed to produce carbohydrates and other carbon compounds from carbon dioxide.
- Temperature, light intensity, and carbon dioxide concentration are possible limiting factors on the rate of photosynthesis.

Applications and skills:

- Application: Changes to the Earth's atmosphere, oceans, and rock deposition due to photosynthesis.
- Skill: Drawing an absorption spectrum for chlorophyll, and an action spectrum for photosynthesis.
- Skill: Design of experiments to investigate the effect of limiting factors on photosynthesis.
- Skill: Separation of photosynthetic pigments by chromatograph.

Guidance

- *Students should know that visible light has wavelengths between 400 and 700 nm, but they are not expected to recall the wavelengths of specific colours of light.*
- *Water free of dissolved carbon dioxide for photosynthesis experiments can be produced by boiling and cooling water.*
- *Paper chromatography can be used to separate photosynthetic pigments but thin layer chromatography gives better results.*

Photosynthesis converts light energy into chemical energy

Plants and other photosynthetic organisms produce foods that start food chains. We count on the Sun as a constant energy source for both warmth and food production for all of our planet. However, the sunlight that strikes Earth must be converted into a form of chemical energy in order to be useful to all non-photosynthetic organisms. The most common chemical energy produced from photosynthesis is the molecule glucose. If you recall, glucose is also the most common molecule that organisms use for fuel in the process of cell respiration.

Plants use the pigment chlorophyll to absorb light energy

The vast majority of plant leaves appear green to our eyes. If you were able to zoom into leaf cells and look around, you would see that the only structures in a leaf that are actually green are the chloroplasts. Plants contain a variety of pigments in chloroplasts. The photosynthetic pigment that dominates in most plant species is the molecule chlorophyll.

Separation of photosynthetic pigments by chromatograph

Safety alerts: Fumes from the chemicals used in this procedure are dangerous. Use the chemicals in a well-ventilated area or under an exhaust or fume hood. Wear goggles and a lab apron throughout the procedure. Follow all your teacher's specific instructions.

As stated above, many plants contain a variety of pigments. A procedure known as paper chromatography can separate the pigments present in most modern plants. The pigment called chlorophyll *a* is the principal pigment. Chlorophyll *b*, carotenes, and xanthophylls act as accessory pigments by absorbing light at different wavelengths, and passing this energy on to chlorophyll *a* to be used in photosynthesis.

- Spinach, *Spinacia oleracea*, or kale, *Brassica oleracea*, leaves are recommended for this procedure. A chromatography solvent that consists of an organic solvent, such as a type of alcohol, acetone, or petroleum ether, will be used. Be very careful with the solvent, it is highly flammable and should be worked with under some type of a fume or exhaust hood. A strip of chromatography paper must be used for this lab as well.

- Place a line of pigment from the leaf on a strip of chromatography paper using a 'ribbed' coin. This line should be dark in colour and as thin as possible. Several repeated applications with the coin at the same place on the paper should result in a dark-coloured line.

- The paper, with a pencil mark where the pigment was placed, is then positioned inside a closed chromatography chamber filled with a shallow layer of chromatography solvent. This solvent layer should reach between the tip of the paper and the pencil line for the pigment. The paper is then placed in the closed chromatography chamber until the solvent comes to within 1–2 cm of the top of the paper.

- When the solvent has reached this position on the paper, remove the paper from the chamber, keeping all parts under the exhaust or fume hood, and immediately mark the position of the solvent line. Mark the positions of the different coloured pigments on the paper.

- Now calculate the R_f value for each of the separated pigments.

R_f refers to retention factor or relative mobility factor. R_f = distance moved by pigment/distance moved by solvent. Record your results below.

Table 2.11 Lab results

Pigment colour	Distance solvent moved	Distance pigment moved	R_f value
Carotene (orange)			
Xanthophylls (yellow)			
Light green (chlorophyll *a*)			
Green (chlorophyll *b*)			

1 Explain why the four pigments moved at different rates through the chromatography paper.

2 Would any leaf from any plant have each of the pigments that are present in spinach or kale? How would this affect the chromatograph of these different leaves?

3 A procedure known as thin layer chromatography would give even better results than chromatography paper. Research and explain the difference between thin layer chromatography and paper chromatography.

Plants make use of the same part of the electromagnetic spectrum that our eyes are able to see. We call this the visible portion of the spectrum. Sunlight is actually a mixture of different colours of light. You can see these colours when you let sunlight pass through a prism.

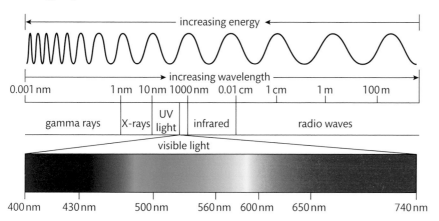

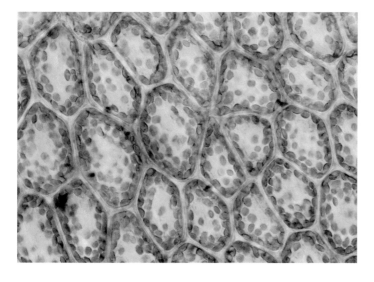

Figure 2.48 The electromagnetic spectrum. Notice that the visible light portion of this spectrum has colours with wavelengths of between 400 nm and 740 nm.

Inside each of these plant leaf cells are many green chloroplasts. Each chloroplast is loaded with chlorophyll.

The visible light spectrum includes many colours, but, for the purpose of considering how chlorophyll absorbs light energy, we are going to consider three regions of the spectrum:

- the red end of the spectrum
- the green middle of the spectrum
- the blue end of the spectrum.

Substances can do one of only two things when they are struck by a particular wavelength (colour) of light. They can:

- absorb that wavelength (if so, energy is being absorbed and may be used)
- reflect that wavelength (if so, the energy is not being absorbed and you will see that colour).

You are walking outside with a friend who is wearing a red and white shirt. Explain why the shirt appears to be red and white.

Solution

Sunlight is a mixture of all of the wavelengths (colours) of visible light. When sunlight strikes the red pigments in the shirt, the blue and the green wavelengths of light are absorbed, but the red wavelengths are reflected. Thus, our eyes see red. When sunlight strikes the white areas of the shirt, all the wavelengths of light are reflected and our eyes and brain interpret the mixture as white.

Let's apply this information to how chlorophyll absorbs light for photosynthesis. Chlorophyll is a green pigment. This means that chlorophyll reflects green light and therefore must absorb the other wavelengths of the visible light spectrum. When a plant leaf is hit by sunlight, the red and blue wavelengths of light are absorbed by chlorophyll and used for photosynthesis. Almost all the energy of the green wavelengths is reflected, not absorbed.

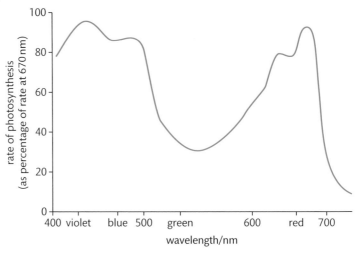

Figure 2.49 This action spectrum of photosynthesis indicates that most photosynthesis occurs in the blue and the red wavelength areas. Note the lower rate of photosynthesis with the green wavelength.

Photosynthesis occurs in two stages

Photosynthesis produces sugar molecules as a food source for the plant. Sugars, such as glucose, are held together by covalent bonds. It requires energy to create those covalent bonds, and the source of that energy can ultimately be traced back to the Sun.

The first stage of photosynthesis is a set of reactions that 'trap' light energy and convert it to the chemical energy of ATP. The second stage of photosynthesis is a set of reactions in which ATP is used to help bond carbon dioxide and water molecules together to create a sugar, such as glucose.

The first stage of photosynthesis

The first stage of photosynthesis is a set of reactions typically referred to as the light-dependent reactions (see Figure 2.50). In this set of reactions, chlorophyll (and other photosynthetic pigments) absorb light energy and convert that energy to a form of chemical energy, specifically ATP. In addition, light energy is used to accomplish a reaction that is called photolysis of water. In this reaction, a water molecule is split into its component elements: hydrogen and oxygen.

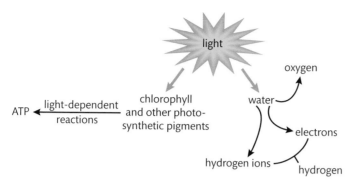

light

oxygen

ATP ← light-dependent reactions ← chlorophyll and other photo-synthetic pigments   water

electrons

hydrogen ions   hydrogen

Figure 2.50 Functions of light during photosynthesis.

This is an SEM (with false colour added) of an upper leaf section. These cells are very active in photosynthesis, as is shown by the large number of chloroplasts.

▼

The oxygen that is split away due to the photolysis of water is typically released from the plant leaf as a waste product. From the plant's perspective, the useful products formed during this stage of photosynthesis are ATP and hydrogen.

The second stage of photosynthesis

The second stage of photosynthesis is a series of reactions collectively referred to as the light-independent reactions. ATP and hydrogen are used as forms of chemical energy to convert carbon dioxide and water into useful organic molecules for the plant. Glucose, a typical product of photosynthesis, is an organic molecule. It requires six inorganic carbon dioxide molecules to form one glucose molecule.

$$6CO_2 + 6H_2O \rightarrow C_6H_{12}O_6 + 6O_2$$

This conversion of an inorganic form of an element to an organic form is known as fixation. Therefore, photosynthesis can be described as a series of reactions in which carbon dioxide and water are fixed into glucose, and oxygen is produced as a by-product.

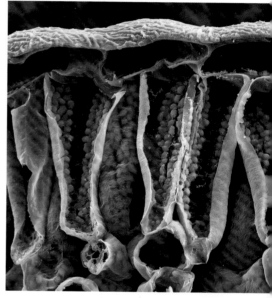

The fixation reaction described above requires energy. The energy to create the glucose comes directly from the ATP and hydrogen created in the first stage of photosynthesis. Ultimately, this energy can be traced back to sunlight. It is also important to note that glucose is only one of the many possible organic molecules that can be formed from photosynthesis.

Measuring the rate of photosynthesis

Look again at the summary reaction for photosynthesis:

$$6CO_2 + 6H_2O \rightarrow C_6H_{12}O_6 + 6O_2$$

This balanced equation shows us that carbon dioxide molecules are reactants and oxygen molecules are products of photosynthesis. If you recall some of the information you learned earlier about cell respiration, you will see that the reverse is true for that process. In other words, for cell respiration oxygen is a reactant and carbon dioxide is a product.

At any given time of year, any one plant has a fairly consistent rate of cell respiration. Not only is this rate consistent throughout the day and night, it is also at a relatively low level. Plants need ATP for various biochemical processes, but the level is typically far lower than any animal needs.

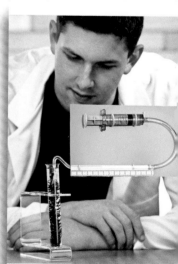

This student is measuring oxygen produced by an aquatic plant. The rate of oxygen produced is a direct reflection of the rate of photosynthesis.

The same consistency is not true regarding the rate of photosynthesis. The photosynthetic rate is highly dependent on many environmental factors, including the intensity of light and air temperature. During the daytime, especially on a warm sunny day, the rate of photosynthesis may be very high for a particular plant. If so, the rate of carbon dioxide taken in by the plant and the rate of oxygen released will also be very high. Because the plant is also carrying out cell respiration, a correction needs to be made for the carbon dioxide and oxygen levels. At night, the rate of photosynthesis may drop to zero. At that time, a particular plant may be giving off carbon dioxide and taking in oxygen to maintain its relatively low and consistent rate of cell respiration (see Figure 2.51).

Figure 2.51 A graph showing the oxygen given off and taken in by a hypothetical plant over a 48-hour period. When the line intersect is at 0, the oxygen generated by photosynthesis is equal to the oxygen needed for cell respiration.

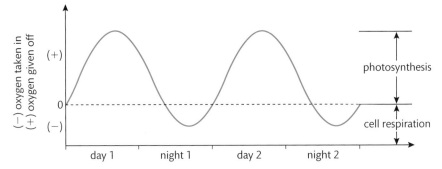

Measuring the rate of oxygen production or carbon dioxide intake is considered to be a direct measurement of photosynthetic rate as long as a correction is made for cell respiration. Another common method for measuring photosynthesis is to keep track of the change in biomass of experimental plants. However, the mass of plants is considered to be an indirect reflection of photosynthetic rate, as an increase or decrease in biomass may be caused by a whole variety of factors as well as the photosynthetic rate.

The effects of changing environmental factors on the rate of photosynthesis

Look now at the patterns that can be seen when three common environmental factors are varied, and how these factors are predicted to change the rate of photosynthesis in a generalized plant (Figures 2.52–54).

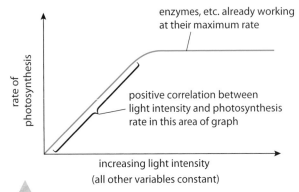

Figure 2.52 The effect of increasing light intensity on the rate of photosynthesis.

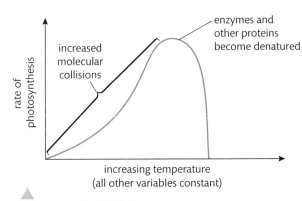

Figure 2.53 The effect of increasing temperature on the rate of photosynthesis.

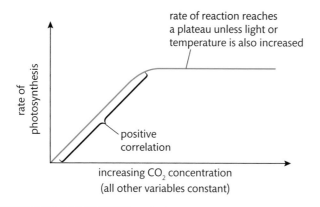

rate of reaction reaches a plateau unless light or temperature is also increased

positive correlation

rate of photosynthesis

increasing CO_2 concentration
(all other variables constant)

Figure 2.54 The effect of increasing carbon dioxide concentration on the rate of photosynthesis.

CHALLENGE YOURSELF

13 Many scientists have been involved in the development of the concept of limiting factors. They include Justus von Leibig, F. F. Blackmann, and Walter Taylor. A limiting factor is described as a factor that would most directly affect the rate of a physiological process. In photosynthesis, the limiting factor is the one that affects the rate of the photosynthetic process regardless of the effects of other factors. In many cases, it is the one factor that is in 'shortest' supply. Use Figures 2.52–2.54 to answer the following questions about photosynthesis and limiting factors.

(a) When examining the effect of light intensity on the rate of photosynthesis in Figure 2.52, why is the early part of the graph labelled as a positive correlation?

(b) In Figure 2.53, why does the denaturing of enzymes and other proteins at high temperatures dramatically lower the rate of photosynthesis?

(c) In Figure 2.54, what could possibly cause a change from the plateau shown to an increasing rate?

(d) Design a procedure to investigate the effect of one of the limiting factors mentioned above on the rate of photosynthesis. Some useful information to use in your planning is that water for photosynthesis experiments can be made to be free of dissolved carbon dioxide by boiling and then cooling it.

Section summary

- Photosynthetic organisms produce organic molecules such as glucose to begin food chains.
- Photosynthetic pigments, including chlorophyll, are used to absorb light energy to begin the process.
- Most plants are green because chlorophyll reflects the green wavelengths of light and absorbs the red and blue wavelengths.
- Photosynthesis occurs in two stages: the light-dependent reactions and the light-independent reactions.
- The light-dependent reactions produce chemical energy in the form of ATP and hydrogen, and also the 'waste product' oxygen.
- The light-independent reactions 'fix' carbon dioxide and water into organic molecules (such as glucose) using the ATP and hydrogen molecules produced during the light-dependent reactions.
- The rate of photosynthesis can be measured directly by measuring either the rate of production of oxygen or the rate of uptake of carbon dioxide.
- The rate of photosynthesis can be measured indirectly by measuring the biomass increase of a plant.
- Varying the temperature, light intensity, and carbon dioxide concentration all affects the rate of photosynthesis in plants.

To learn more about photosynthesis, go to the hotlinks site, search for the title or ISBN, and click on Chapter 2: Section 2.9.

Exercises

25 Explain why a blue object appears to be blue to the human eye.

26 Explain why black surfaces (like tarmacadam and asphalt) get much hotter in sunlight than lighter surfaces (like stone and concrete).

27 Plants produce sugars by photosynthesis. What do plants do with the sugars after that?

28 Why do most plants produce an excess of sugars in some months of the year?

Practice questions

1 What causes water to have a relatively high boiling point?

   A Hydrogen bonds between water molecules.

   B Hydrogen bonds between hydrogen and oxygen within water molecules.

   C Cohesion between water molecules and the container in which the water is boiled.

   D Covalent bonds between hydrogen and oxygen within water molecules.

(Total 1 mark)

2 Outline the significance to organisms of the different properties of water.

(Total 5 marks)

3

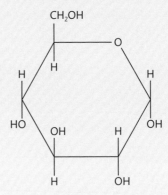

Which of the following terms correctly describe(s) the molecule above?

   I.   Monosaccharide.

   II. Glucose.

   III. Component of triglyceride.

   A I only.   **B** I and II only.   **C** II and III only.   **D** I, II, and III.

(Total 1 mark)

4 Draw the basic structure of an amino acid, and label the groups that are used in peptide bond formation.

(Total 4 marks)

5 The reaction below shows the energy changes in a chemical reaction.

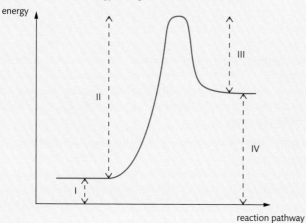

What would happen to the changes in energy if this reaction was controlled by an enzyme?

A I would increase.

B II would decrease.

C I and IV would decrease.

D II and III would decrease.

(Total 1 mark)

6 The percentage of thymine in the DNA of an organism is approximately 30%. What is the percentage of guanine?

A 70%   **B** 30%   **C** 40%   **D** 20%

(Total 1 mark)

7 The effect of temperature on photosynthesis was studied in sweet orange, *Citrus sinensis*, using leaf discs. The production of oxygen was used to measure the rate of photosynthesis.

Gross photosynthesis refers to the sum of net photosynthesis and respiration. Net photosynthesis was calculated by subtracting the rate of respiration in the dark from gross photosynthesis.

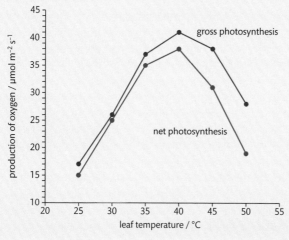

Ribeiro et al. 2006

(a) Identify the optimum temperature for photosynthesis in this plant. (1)

(b) Determine the difference between gross photosynthesis and net photosynthesis at 40°C and 50°C. (2)

(c) Deduce what happens to the rate of respiration as the temperature increases between 40°C and 50°C. (1)

(d) (i) Describe the general pattern of change in photosynthesis in sweet orange as the temperature increases. (1)

(ii) Compare the effect of temperature on photosynthesis with the effect of temperature on respiration in sweet orange. (2)

(Total 7 marks)

8 What sequence of processes is carried out by the structure labelled X during translation?

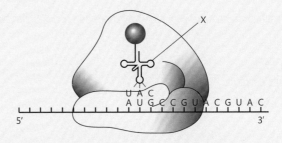

A Combining with an amino acid and then binding to an anticodon.

B Binding to an anticodon and then combining with an amino acid.

C Binding to a codon and then combining with an amino acid.

D Combining with an amino acid and then binding to a codon.

(Total 1 mark)

9 Which of the following is the best definition of cell respiration?

A A process needed to use energy, in the form of ATP, to produce organic compounds.

B A process used to provide oxygen to the atmosphere.

C A controlled release of energy, in the form of ATP, from organic compounds in cells.

D A controlled release of energy in the production of food from organic compounds.

(Total 1 mark)

10 The diagram below shows part of the respiratory pathway. The number of carbon atoms in each molecule is indicated.

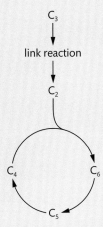

(a) (i) Label pyruvate and acetyl coenzyme A on the diagram above. (1)

   (ii) Indicate **two** places where decarboxylation occurs on the diagram. (1)

   (iii) List **one** product other than carbon dioxide formed in this stage of respiration. (1)

(b) State precisely where in a cell this stage of respiration is occurring. (1)

(Total 4 marks)

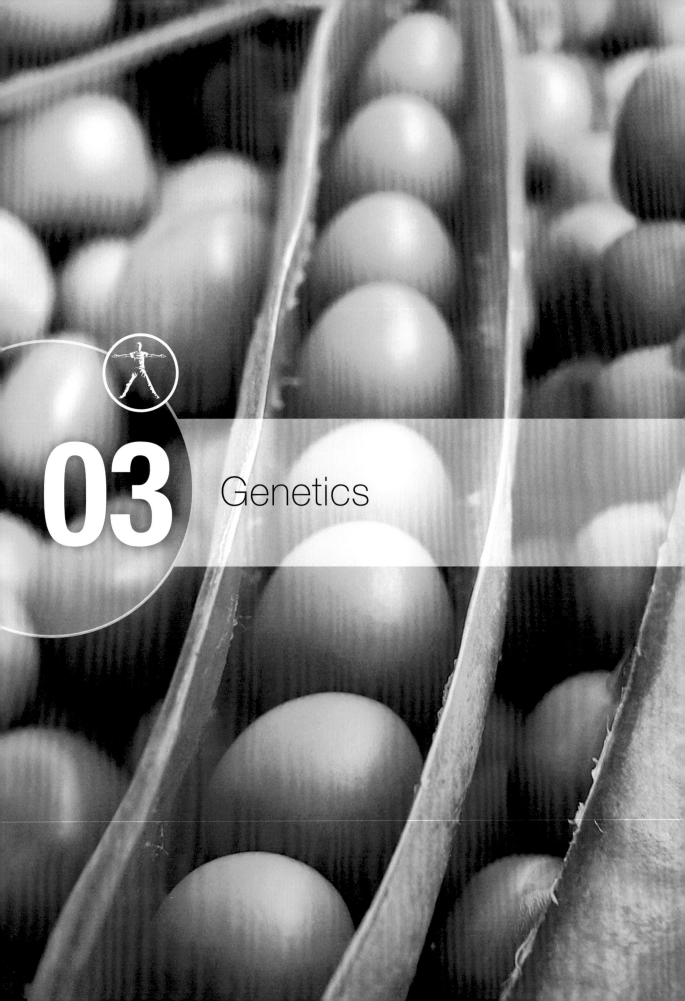

03 Genetics

Essential ideas

3.1 Every living organism inherits a blueprint for life from its parents.

3.2 Chromosomes carry genes in a linear sequence that is shared by members of a species.

3.3 Alleles segregate during meiosis allowing new combinations to be formed by the fusion of gametes.

3.4 The inheritance of genes follows patterns.

3.5 Biologists have developed techniques for artificial manipulation of DNA, cells, and organisms.

One of the most famous experiments in biology was Gregor Mendel's pea-breeding investigations, which revealed important insights into the secrets of genetics.

- What will my first baby look like?
- Will my children be able to see the difference between red and green, even though I cannot?
- How can we find out who was at a crime scene by analysing their DNA?
- How can crops be genetically changed to improve their quality and quantity?
- Is it possible to clone humans?
- How many genes do I have?
- If I find a gene that has medical value, can I patent it and make money from my discovery?

In order to answer these questions, the mechanisms of genetics must be understood. Genetics is the science of how inherited information is passed on from one generation to the next using the genetic material of genes and deoxyribonucleic acid (DNA).

3.1 Genes

NATURE OF SCIENCE

Developments in scientific research follow improvements in technology: gene sequencers are used for the sequencing of genes.

Understandings:

- A gene is a heritable factor that consists of a length of DNA and influences a specific characteristic.
- A gene occupies a specific position on a chromosome.
- The various specific forms of a gene are alleles.
- Alleles differ from each other by one or only a few bases.
- New alleles are formed by mutation.
- The genome is the whole of the genetic information of an organism.
- The entire base sequence of human genes was sequenced in the Human Genome Project.

Applications and skills:

- Application: The causes of sickle cell anaemia, including a base substitution mutation, a change to the base sequence of mRNA transcribed from it, and a change to the sequence of a polypeptide in haemoglobin.
- Application: Comparison of the number of genes in humans with other species.
- Skill: Use of a database to determine differences in the base sequence of a gene in two species.

Guidance

- *Students should be able to recall one specific base substitution that causes glutamic acid to be substituted by valine as the sixth amino acid in the haemoglobin polypeptide.*
- *The number of genes in a species should not be referred to as genome size as this term is used for the total amount of DNA. At least one plant and one bacterium should be included in the comparison, and at least one species with more genes and one with fewer genes than a human.*
- *The GenBank® database can be used to search for DNA base sequences. The cytochrome c gene sequence is available for many different organisms and is of particular interest because of its use in reclassifying organisms into three domains.*
- *Deletions, insertions, and frame shift mutations do not need to be included.*

What is a gene?

Have you ever heard people say 'she looks just like her mum' or 'that kind of thing skips a generation'? Although those people might not have known it, they were talking about genetics.

CHALLENGE YOURSELF

1 Look at the list of characteristics below and think about which ones are determined by DNA and which are not. Are there some that can be influenced by both DNA and a person's environment? For example, most people who have inherited a light skin colour can darken their skin by tanning in the sun.

- Skin colour
- Freckles
- Number of fingers on each hand
- Blood type
- Colour blindness
- Sex (male/female)
- Ability to digest lactose
- Reflexes
- Type of ear wax (wet or dry)
- A scar from an accident
- Ability to speak
- Ability to speak Spanish
- Height
- Personality
- Intelligence

What about this: if a man had to have his left foot removed because of a war injury, would his future children be born with only one foot? Before scientists understood the mechanisms of genetics, it was believed that acquired characteristics could be passed on from one generation to the next. This idea has been refuted. The classic debate of nature versus nurture is a good topic for a Theory of knowledge discussion.

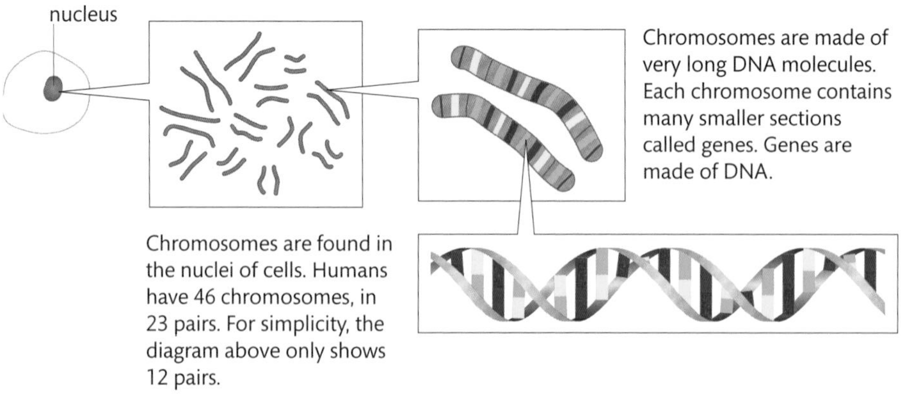
nucleus
Chromosomes are made of very long DNA molecules. Each chromosome contains many smaller sections called genes. Genes are made of DNA.
Chromosomes are found in the nuclei of cells. Humans have 46 chromosomes, in 23 pairs. For simplicity, the diagram above only shows 12 pairs.

Figure 3.1 Zooming into a cell reveals where DNA is found.

Whenever a definition is given for a major concept in biology, in this instance the term 'gene', be sure to memorize its definition word for word. Such definitions have been phrased carefully so that all the important details are included.

Genes

A gene is a heritable factor that consists of a length of DNA and influences a specific characteristic. 'Heritable' means passed on from parent to offspring, and 'characteristic' refers to genetic traits such as your hair colour or your blood type. The estimated 21 000 genes that you possess are organized into chromosomes.

A gene is found at a particular locus on a chromosome

A gene for a specific trait occupies a corresponding place, called a locus (plural loci), on a chromosome (see Figure 3.2; there will be more about chromosomes in Section 3.2).

When geneticists map out the sequences of DNA, they carefully map the locus of each sequence. When further research reveals that a particular sequence controls a certain heritable factor, the locus of the gene is noted for further reference. For example, scientists now know that the locus of the gene controlling a protein called transducin that enables colour vision is found on chromosome 1. A mutation of this gene stops a person from being able to make the protein transducin properly, which is necessary to transmit information about colour from the eye to the brain; as a result, the person will not see in colour. This is an extremely rare genetic condition called complete achromatopsia. When we say 'the ability to see in colour is a genetic trait' we mean one of two things is happening with someone's DNA: either that person has the DNA code for making colour vision possible or that person does not have it. This is illustrated in Figure 3.3.

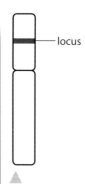

Figure 3.2 The locus is the specific position of a gene on a chromosome.

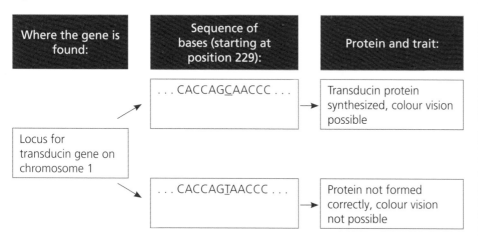

Where the gene is found:	Sequence of bases (starting at position 229):	Protein and trait:
Locus for transducin gene on chromosome 1	. . . CACCAG<u>C</u>AACCC . . .	Transducin protein synthesized, colour vision possible
	. . . CACCAG<u>T</u>AACCC . . .	Protein not formed correctly, colour vision not possible

Figure 3.3 The presence of a C or a T makes a big difference in colour vision.

You will recall that you possess two copies of each gene in your body: one copy from your mother and one from your father. As a result, if you could look at the locus of the transducin gene on one of the two copies of your first chromosome, for example, you would find the same gene at the same locus on the other copy of chromosome 1. One copy would be the one your mother gave you and the other would be the copy your father gave you. Would those genes be identical? Not necessarily, because genes can come in different forms.

Alleles: versions of genes

Variations or versions of a gene are called alleles. An allele is one specific form of a gene, differing from other alleles by one or a few bases. In the example of transducin and colour vision above, a single base pair difference between the most common allele (with a C at position 235) and the rare mutated allele (with a T at position 235) is all that is takes to determine whether you can distinguish colours or not. These different forms allow for a single trait, such as the trait for the ability to see in colour, to have variants, in this example either colour or grey-scale vision.

CHALLENGE YOURSELF

Table 3.1 Comparison of the number of genes in humans and other species

Organism	Scientific name	Number of bases	Number of genes
Virus (bacteriophage)	phiX174 *	5400	11
Bacterium	*Escherichia coli* (type K-12)	4 639 000	4377
Nematode (roundworm)	*Caenorhabditis elegans*	100 292 000	20 000
Human	*Homo sapiens*	3 000 000 000	21 000
Asian rice	*Oryza sativa*	430 000 000	up to 56 000
Baker's yeast	*Saccharomyces cerevisiae*	12 495 000	5770
Mouse-ear cress	*Arabidopsis thaliana*	135 000 000	25 000
Fruit fly	*Drosophila melanogaster*	122 654 000	27 407
Japanese canopy plant	*Paris japonica***	150 000 000 000	Unknown

*First genome ever sequenced (in 1977).
**Largest plant genome sequenced so far.

2

(a) Which species has the largest number of genes?

(b) Which species has the smallest number of genes?

(c) Which species has the most similar number of genes to humans?

(d) Some people are tempted to say that the more genes an organism has, the more advanced it is. Discuss this idea: what kinds of arguments support it and what arguments refute it?

Table 3.2 Examples of possible alleles

Gene or trait	Examples of possible alleles
Colour vision	Allele to produce transducin (the protein necessary for colour vision); allele that does not code correctly for transducin
Skin pigmentation	Allele to make pigments; allele that cannot make pigments (in other words an allele for albinism, see Section 3.4)
Blood type	Allele for type A; allele for type B; allele for type O

Another example of the difference between two alleles of the same trait is the difference that causes the genetic condition cystic fibrosis.

Cystic fibrosis

Maintaining a proper balance of fluids in the body is essential for good health. One such fluid is mucus, a thick, slippery, substance used in many parts of the body, including the lungs and intestines. A gene called *CFTR*, found on chromosome 7, plays a key role in the production of mucus. The standard version of this gene (the standard allele) allows a person's mucus-producing cells to function properly, whereas an allele generated by a mutation of the *CFTR* gene causes cystic fibrosis. People with this genetic condition produce abnormally excessive quantities of mucus in various organs and have difficulties with their respiratory and digestive systems, among other complications. In this example, the trait is for mucus production; one allele is for a balanced mucus production, the other for excessive mucus production that leads to cystic fibrosis. We will see later how to calculate the chances of a child inheriting this condition from his or her parents.

One base can make a big difference

From the sections on transcription and translation of DNA, you will remember how important it is for each letter in the genetic code to be in a specific place. If, for whatever reason, one or more of the bases (A, C, G, or T) is misplaced or substituted for a different base, the results can be dramatic. As we have seen with cystic fibrosis, the difference between one version of a gene and another (the mutated and non-mutated alleles of the *CFTR* gene) can mean the difference between healthy organs and organs hampered by an overproduction of mucus.

Another example of a change of bases can be seen in the gene *ABCC11*, which determines several things, one of them being whether or not the cerumen (ear wax) that you produce is wet or dry. Some people produce dry cerumen, which is flaky and crumbly with a grey colour, while others produce earwax that is more fluid and has an amber colour. The gene that determines this is on chromosome 16 and has two alleles: the G variant codes for dry cerumen, the A variant codes for wet cerumen. The allele containing G for wet earwax is much more common in European and African populations, while the allele containing A is much more common among Asians. Why is this of interest to geneticists? For one thing, it can reveal a lot about how populations have migrated and interbred in the past, but it can also reveal other things about our health. As curious as it may seem, the *ABCC11* gene is also partly responsible for the smell of underarm sweat, as well as the production of breast milk, and could potentially have a link to breast cancer. Most women probably would not care whether or not they have the gene for dry or fluid earwax, but if they could find out whether they had an allele that could reduce their chances of having breast cancer, they might be much more interested.

How are such differences in genes generated in populations? We will now look at how mutations work.

How new alleles are produced

Worked example

Look at the two sequences of DNA below, which are from the coding strand of a section of genetic information that helps in the formation of haemoglobin, found in red blood cells. Look carefully at the two sequences. Identify the difference between the two and complete the following phrase.

DNA sequence 1: GTG   CAC   CTG   ACT   CCT   GAG   GAG

DNA sequence 2: GTG   CAC   CTG   ACT   CCT   GTG   GAG

'Codon number __ along the first sequence has the letter __ in position number __, whereas the codon in the same position in sequence 2 has the letter __ instead.'

Solution

Codon number 6 along the first sequence has the letter A in position number 2, whereas the codon in the same position in sequence 2 has the letter T instead.

Now look at the effect this has on the mRNA sequences produced from the template strand that is found opposite the coding strand when the DNA is unzipped for transcription:

mRNA sequence 1: GUG CAC CUG ACU CCU GAG GAG

mRNA sequence 2: GUG CAC CUG ACU CCU GUG GAG

Using Figure 3.4 and the mRNA sequences above, showing which codons are associated with which amino acids, fill in the names of the missing amino acids (a) to (h) in Figure 3.5.

First base	Second base: U	Second base: C	Second base: A	Second base: G	Third base
U	UUU, UUC – Phenyl-alanine UUA, UUG – Leucine	UCU, UCC, UCA, UCG – Serine	UAU, UAC – Tyrosine UAA – Stop codon UAG – Stop codon	UGU, UGC – Cysteine UGA – Stop codon UGG – Tryptophan	U C A G
C	CUU, CUC, CUA, CUG – Leucine	CCU, CCC, CCA, CCG – Proline	CAU, CAC – Histidine CAA, CAG – Glutamine	CGU, CGC, CGA, CGG – Arginine	U C A G
A	AUU, AUC, AUA – Isoleucine AUG – Methionine start codon	ACU, ACC, ACA, ACG – Threonine	AAU, AAC – Asparagine AAA, AAG – Lysine	AGU, AGC – Serine AGA, AGG – Arginine	U C A G
G	GUU, GUC, GUA, GUG – Valine	GCU, GCC, GCA, GCG – Alanine	GAU, GAC – Aspartic acid GAA, GAG – Glutamic acid	GGU, GGC, GGA, GGG – Glycine	U C A G

Figure 3.4 Codons and their associated amino acids. For example, RNA coding for lysine is AAA.

Sequence 1:	valine	–	histidine	–	(a)______	–	(b)______	–	(c)______	–	(d)______	–	glutamic acid

Sequence 2:	valine	–	histidine	–	(e)______	–	(f)______	–	(g)______	–	(h)______	–	glutamic acid

Figure 3.5 Using Figure 3.4 and the mRNA sequences above, can you find the missing amino acids for boxes (a) to (h)?

Solution

Sequence 1:	valine	–	histidine	–	leucine	–	threonine	–	proline	–	glutamic acid	–	glutamic acid

Sequence 2:	valine	–	histidine	–	leucine	–	threonine	–	proline	–	valine	–	glutamic acid

Figure 3.6 Is this what you found? We will need these sequences later when we explore sickle cell disease.

Notice how the error of only one letter in the original DNA code changed the composition of amino acids in sequence 2. This would change the composition and the structure of the resulting protein, in the same way that changing the shapes and compositions of some of the bricks used to build a house would change the shape (and therefore the structural integrity) of the house. This kind of change in the DNA code is produced by a mutation.

Mutations

A mutation is a random, rare change in genetic material. One type involves a change of the sequence of bases in DNA. If DNA replication works correctly, this should not happen (see Section 2.7). But nature sometimes makes mistakes. For example, the base thymine (T) might be put in the place of adenine (A) along the DNA sequence. When this happens, the corresponding bases along the messenger RNA (mRNA) are altered during transcription.

As we have seen with the example of cystic fibrosis, mutated genes can have a negative effect on a person's health. Sometimes, however, mutations can have a positive effect that is beneficial to an organism's survival.

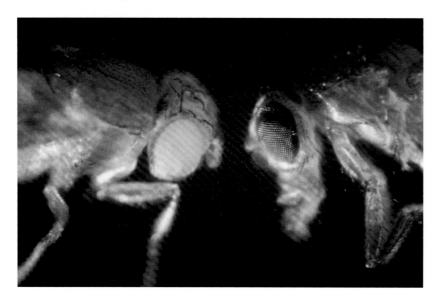

On the left, a white-eyed mutant fruit fly, and on the right the kind of fruit fly typically found in nature, called the wild-type.

Are mutations good or bad for us?

LRP5 is a gene that helps immune system cells make a certain type of protein that acts as a receptor on their surfaces. Research indicates that this receptor is used by the human immunodeficiency virus (HIV) to infect the cells (see Section 6.3 for a description of HIV). People with a mutation of *LRP5* cannot make this receptor protein on their immune system's cells and, as a result, HIV cannot infect them. This means that people with a mutated allele of *LRP5* are naturally immune to HIV. Such a mutation is very rare in the human population.

A mutation that provides an individual or a species with a better chance for survival is considered to be a beneficial mutation, and there is a good chance that it will be passed on to the next generation. In contrast, mutations that cause disease or death are detrimental mutations, and they are less likely to be passed on to future generations, because they decrease the chances of an individual's survival. In addition to beneficial and harmful mutations, there are neutral mutations that do not have an effect on a species' survival.

When a mutation is successfully passed on from one generation to the next, it becomes a new allele: it is a new version of the original gene. This is how new alleles are produced. You and everyone you know possess many mutations. Whether they are harmful, beneficial or neutral depends on what they are and what kind of environment you need to survive in.

Table 3.3 A summary of different types of mutations: not all mutations are negative

Type of mutation	Example in plants	Example in animals
Detrimental	A mutation that does not allow a plant to produce a chemical that it secretes against insect attacks, thereby making it vulnerable	A mutation that makes it impossible to produce a certain digestive enzyme, thereby making digestion difficult and therefore compromising the ability of the organism to survive
Neutral	A single base substitution in a gene for chlorophyll that does not change the amino acid coded for, and therefore does not modify the chlorophyll (e.g. GUA and GUG both code for valine)	A single base substitution in a gene for haemoglobin that does not change the amino acid coded for, and therefore does not modify the haemoglobin (e.g. GAG and GAA both code for glutamic acid)
Beneficial	A mutation giving a plant the ability to make a protein that increases its frost resistance, which would be beneficial in colder climates	A mutation changing the shape or size of the lens of the eye, giving the animal more acute vision for finding prey

A gene to help digestion

For most of our existence, humans have been hunter-gatherers and our genes are generally well adapted for this lifestyle. Originally, as for all mammals, the only age at which we drank milk was when we were infants. By the time our ancestors reached adulthood, their bodies had stopped being able to digest milk; more precisely, humans could not break down the disaccharide in milk called lactose. This continues to be the case for most of the human population today: more than half of the human population has lactose intolerance and those people can only digest lactose in their infancy. In the past 10 000 years, however, many human populations have adopted an agricultural-based lifestyle, raising animals for milk and consuming dairy products on a daily basis. In their genetic makeup, many agricultural societies show a higher frequency of the genetic code that allows humans to digest lactose throughout adulthood. From an evolutionary point of view, this advantage has increased humans' ability to survive harsh climatic conditions. As European human populations spread out and established populations outside Europe, notably in North America, they brought their lactose tolerance (and their livestock) with them.

Gene therapy is the process of taking a beneficial gene from a person who possesses it and putting it into a person who does not have it, but who needs it to stay healthy. The challenge is that it is very difficult to get the DNA into the sick person's cells. One way is to force the gene into the patient's cells using a virus to deliver it. Partly because of a lack of understanding of how to use viruses safely to deliver genes, the decision was made to stop all testing of gene therapy on human patients in the USA in 1999, when an 18-year-old patient died after a virus had been injected into his body. However, gene therapy trials are coming back, little by little, notably in helping blind children to regain their eyesight.

Who decides whether an experiment is safe? Is the loss of life for some patients participating in trials necessary in order to find a cure? If years of research had not been delayed because human trials had been stopped, wouldn't we have made much more progress by now in curing genetic diseases?

Base substitution mutation

The type of mutation that results in a single letter being changed is called a base substitution mutation. The consequence of changing one base could mean that a different amino acid is placed in the growing polypeptide chain. This may have little or no effect on the organism, or it may have a major influence on the organism's physical characteristics.

Sickle cell disease

In humans, a mutation is sometimes found in the gene that codes for haemoglobin in red blood cells. This mutation gives a different shape to the haemoglobin molecule. The difference leads to red blood cells that look very different from the usual flattened disc with a hollow in the middle.

The mutated red blood cell, with a characteristic curved shape, made its discoverers think of a sickle (a curved knife used to cut tall plants). The condition that results from this mutation is therefore called sickle cell disease, also known as sickle cell anaemia.

The kind of mutation that causes sickle cells is a base substitution mutation. If you look back at the two sequences given previously in the worked example on page 123, the first is for the section of the haemoglobin gene's DNA that codes for standard-shaped red blood cells, whereas the second sequence shows the mutation that leads to the sickle shape. In this case, one base is substituted for another so that the sixth codon in this sequence of haemoglobin, GAG, becomes GTG. As a result, during translation, instead of adding glutamic acid, which is the intended amino acid in the sixth position of the sequence, valine is added there instead. Again, refer back to the worked example to see this mutation.

Because valine has a different shape and different properties compared with glutamic acid, the shape of the resulting polypeptide chain is modified. As a result of this, the haemoglobin molecule has different properties that cause the complications associated with sickle cell disease.

The symptoms of sickle cell disease are weakness, fatigue, and shortness of breath. Oxygen cannot be carried as efficiently by the irregularly shaped red blood cells. In addition, the haemoglobin tends to crystallize within the red blood cells, causing them to be less flexible. The affected red blood cells can get stuck in capillaries, so blood flow can be slowed or blocked, a condition that is painful for the sufferer.

People affected by sickle cell anaemia are at risk of passing the mutated gene on to their offspring. From a demographic point of view, the mutated gene is mostly found in populations originating from West Africa or from the Mediterranean.

The advantages of sickle cell disease

Although sickle cell disease is a debilitating condition, those who have it are very resistant to malaria infection. Malaria is an infectious disease that occurs in tropical regions. A parasite called *Plasmodium* is transmitted to human blood by an infected female *Anopheles* mosquito feeding on the blood. The parasite attacks the person's red blood cells and produces symptoms of high fever and chills, and can result in death.

In terms of the shapes of human red blood cells, we all carry two copies of the gene for the shape of our red blood cells, one copy that we inherited from our mother and the other that we inherited from our father. People born with two copies for standard disc-shaped cell have only disc-shaped cells and are highly susceptible to malaria infection. People who have one gene that is for disc-shaped cells and one for sickle-shaped cells

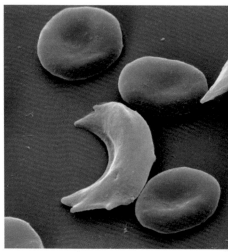

Three standard, disc-shaped red blood cells, and one sickle-shaped cell.

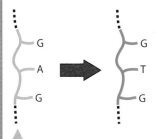

Figure 3.7 A mutation where base A is replicated by base T; GAG codes for glutamic acid and GTG codes for valine.

127

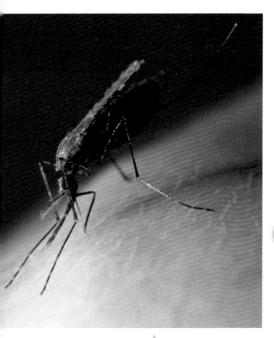

have what is called sickle cell trait. They have some sickle-shaped cells and some disc-shaped cells in their bloodstream but in most cases they do not suffer from anaemia. Anaemia is the result of low red blood cell levels and is characterized by a paleness of skin and low energy levels. People with sickle cell trait have a better resistance to malaria because of chemical imbalances that make the survival of *Plasmodium* in their blood more difficult. The insufficient quantities of potassium in sickle-shaped cells cause *Plasmodium* to die. Lastly, people who inherit a sickle cell gene from both their mother and their father can produce only sickle-shaped cells and suffer from severe anaemia that can sometimes be fatal. On the other hand, they have the highest resistance to malaria.

 When we look at where sickle cell disease is most common in the world, there appears to be a significant overlap with the places where malaria occurs. Is this just a coincidence? Or is there a reason for this? Scientists and statistics experts often say that 'correlation does not mean causality', meaning that just because two things occur in the same place at the same time does not necessarily mean that one causes the other. How can we tell the difference between causality and correlation? The answer is that there must be some kind of mechanism that could explain how one could cause the other. From what you have read about sickle cell disease and malaria in this chapter, what do you think? Are they merely correlated or is there also causality?

Malaria can be transmitted by the female *Anopheles* mosquito, which is therefore one of the deadliest animals on Earth.

Table 3.4 Different types of genetic conditions

Condition	Example
1 Chromosomal anomaly	Caused by an extra chromosome, such as Down syndrome (chromosome 21) (see page 147)
2 Autosomal genetic disease	Caused by a gene found on one of the 22 non-sex chromosomes, such as cystic fibrosis (chromosome 1) (see page 140)
3 Sex-linked genetic disease	Caused by a gene found on the X or Y chromosome, such as colour blindness found on the X chromosome (see page 159)

The first type is generally considered to be a one-time error in the distribution of chromosomes, whereas the second and third types are passed on generation after generation.

A genome

How do we know all that we do about genes? How do we know where they are and what they do? Before answering these questions, it is important to appreciate the point that, although we have made considerable progress in the past few decades, our maps of human chromosomes are still far from complete, and there are many DNA sequences for which we do not know the function. As an analogy, think of the maps produced by cartographers and explorers in the Middle Ages; many parts of the globe remained uncharted and had the words *terra incogn*ita (Latin for 'unknown land') inscribed on them.

Sequencing DNA

In order to find out which gene does what, a list must be made showing the order of all the nucleotides in the DNA code. Researchers use highly specialized laboratory equipment including sequencers to locate and identify sequences of bases. The complete set of an organism's base sequences is called its genome.

A short fragment of a sequence looks like this: GTGGACCTGACTCCTGAGGAG. Each letter represents one of the four bases in the DNA code. This short fragment contains seven codons with a total of 21 bases represented by letters. Now imagine 3 billion of those letters: what would that look like? If you printed out 3000 base letters per page, it would need 1 million pages, which would stack about 100 m high. That's an impressive quantity of information, especially considering that you can keep it all in the nucleus of a typical cell in your body.

The complete genomes of some organisms have been worked out. Among those organisms are the fruit fly, *Drosophila melanogaster*, and the bacterium, *Escherichia coli*, because these two organisms have been used extensively in genetics experiments for decades.

How do geneticists work out the complete genome?

Many steps are necessary. Here is a summary of one way of doing it: the Sanger technique (see Figure 3.8).

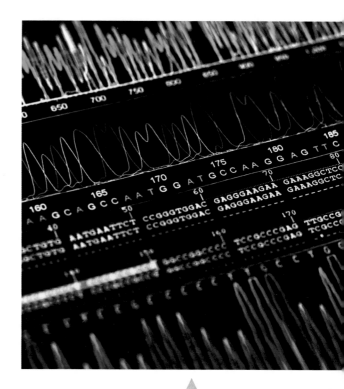

Computers are used to speed up the sequencing process.

- Once a DNA sample has been taken, it is chopped up into fragments and copies are made of the fragments. A primer sequence is added to help start the process.
- To determine the sequence, a DNA polymerase enzyme attaches to one copy of the first fragment (let's call it fragment 1). Then it will start to add free nucleotides following the principle of complementary base pairing. Two kinds of nucleotides will be added.
- Some free nucleotides are standard ones and others are special dideoxynucleotide triphosphates (ddNTPs; labelled ddA, ddT, ddC, and ddG in Figure 3.8) added as DNA chain terminators, meaning that when one is reached, the elongation of the strand is stopped. These have been previously marked with fluorescent markers to identify them. Sometimes the chain termination happens all the way at the end of fragment 1, but most of the time the process stops before it reaches the end. This process happens on each of the many copies of fragment 1.
- The result is a series of new strands, some dozens of bases long, others only a handful of bases long, and some that have all the bases of fragment 1.
- Now everything is ready for the sequencing: the multiple chains of varying lengths (each with a fluorescently marked end) are placed in order from longest to shortest. This is done using a technique called gel electrophoresis, which will be explained in Section 3.5.
- To recognize each letter, a laser activates the fluorescent markers on the nucleotides as they go through the process. A sensor hooked up to a computer analyses the wavelength of the light and determines whether it represents an A, T, C, or G.
- The process must be repeated many times: for A, T, C, and G. Repetitions make sure there are no errors. Fortunately, many copies of fragment 1 were made, so this is easy to check.

Thanks to modern communication technologies, it is possible for scientists working all over the world to collaborate and contribute to a scientific endeavour such as sequencing the genome of plants that help feed the world. Rice is one example: biologists from 10 countries contributed to sequencing the first rice genome.

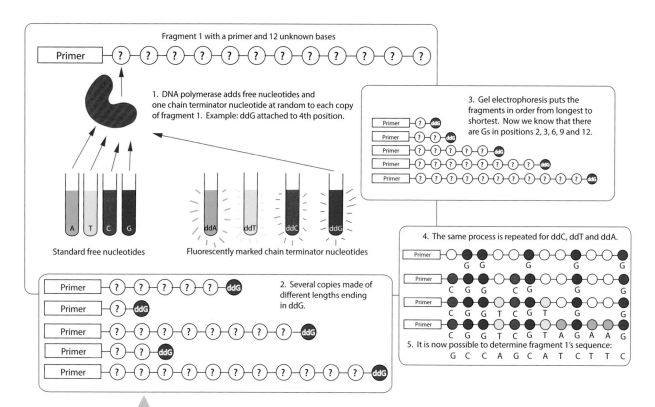

Figure 3.8 One method of DNA sequencing is called the Sanger technique.

In the 1997 science fiction film *GATTACA*, one of the main characters brings a sample of cells to a walk-up window at an establishment that provides anonymous genome services. Within seconds, she gets a full printout and analysis of the genome of the man she wants to know about. He is not aware that she is doing this. One objective of science fiction as an art form is to warn society of what might happen in the future if we are not careful. This film raises serious questions about how far technology will lead us and whether or not we want to go in that direction. Our society will need to make some difficult decisions in the coming years concerning our genomes and who has access to the information contained within them.

- Once fragment 1 is done, the lab technicians must process fragment 2, fragment 3, and so on, until all the fragments of the original sequence have been processed.
- At this stage, the challenge is to put all the sequenced fragments of code together. When the original sequence was chopped up to make all these fragments, they became mixed up and out of order. Now that we know what their sequences are, we need to know the order in which to put them. This daunting task has been made easier by computers, but it consists of lining up any overlapping segments until they all match.

Since the Sanger technique was invented, many techniques have been developed to analyse each fragment only once, making it unnecessary to make multiple copies of each. This reduces the time and the cost of sequencing a genome. The objective of developing new sequencing techniques is to have a fast, inexpensive way to map anyone's genome.

The Human Genome Project

In 1990, an international cooperative venture called the Human Genome Project set out to sequence the complete human genome. Because the genome of an organism is a catalogue of all the bases it possesses, the Human Genome Project hoped to determine the order of all the bases A, T, C, and G in human DNA. In 2003, the Project announced that it had succeeded in achieving its goal. Now, scientists are working on deciphering which sequences represent genes and which genes do what. The human genome can be thought of as a map that can be used to show the locus of any gene on any one of the 23 pairs of chromosomes.

There is another international connection with the Human Genome Project in the sense that this project is a good example of scientists from all over the world working together. Dozens of nationalities participated in the project, and the results are available for free access worldwide thanks to online databases open to the public.

Delving into human genetics confirms two major themes:

* we are all the same
* we are all different.

On the one hand, the Human Genome Project has shown that there are only a very small number of DNA bases that make one person different from any other person in the world. This creates a feeling of unity, of oneness with all people. From peanut farmers in West Africa, to computer technicians in California, to fishermen in Norway, to businesswomen in Hong Kong, all humans carry inside them a common genetic heritage.

On the other hand, the Human Genome Project has shown that the small differences that do exist are important ones that give each person his or her uniqueness in terms of skin colour, facial features and resistance to disease, for example. These differences should be appreciated and celebrated as strengths. Unfortunately, they are often the basis of discrimination and misunderstanding.

Can one genetic group be considered genetically superior to another? History has shown that many people think so, yet genetics shows that this is not the case. All human populations, whatever slight differences their genomes may have, deserve equal esteem as human beings.

Before the Human Genome was mapped, fewer than 100 loci were known for genetic diseases. After the mapping was completed, more than 1400 were known, and today the number is in the thousands and increasing.

In addition, by comparing the genetic makeup of populations around the world, countless details can be revealed about our ancestries and how human populations have migrated and mixed their genes with other populations over time. Without knowing it, you are carrying around in each one of your cells a library of information about your past.

Many companies offer genome sequencing for private citizens willing to pay the price. Some of the products offered are revelations about ancient family origins and risk factors for some health problems, such as the chances of developing certain types of cancer or heart disease. Would you want to know if there was a chance that your life could be suddenly shortened by the presence or absence of a certain gene? Would you tell your family and friends? Would you want your parents to do such a test? Should people tell their employer or each other about any health-related issues revealed by a genomic analysis? Or, on the contrary, is this a private, personal thing that no one else needs to know about? How accurate and reliable are these analyses? Should we believe everything they say? **TOK**

Using DNA to make medicines

Another advantageous use of the human genome is the production of new medications. This process involves several steps:

* find beneficial molecules that are produced naturally in healthy people
* find out which gene controls the synthesis of a desirable molecule
* copy that gene and use it as instructions to synthesize the molecule in a laboratory
* distribute the beneficial therapeutic protein as a new medical treatment.

This is not science fiction: genetic engineering firms are finding such genes regularly. One current line of research is dealing with genes that control ageing. How much money do you think people would be willing to pay for a molecule that could reverse the effects of ageing and prolong life by several decades?

Dr Francis Collins, one of the leaders of the Human Genome Project team.

Dr Craig Venter, one of the leaders of the Human Genome Project team.

131

What if a biotech company finds a useful human gene in your body? For example, a gene that produces a protein to help balance cholesterol levels in the body and prevent heart problems. Can the company patent that gene in order to protect its discovery and in order to earn money from it? With a patent, the company could charge pharmaceutical manufacturers that wanted to use the gene to make new medicines. In many countries there are few if any laws about such things because the techniques are so new.

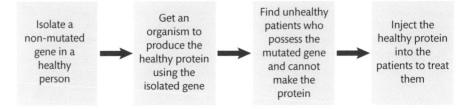

Figure 3.9 The process of protein therapy, a promising use of genetically modified organisms.

CHALLENGE YOURSELF

3 Cytochrome *c* is a protein found in mitochondria and it plays a key role in cell respiration by shuttling electrons from one place to another. If an organism did not have the genetic code to make cytochrome *c*, it could not survive. By comparing the genetic sequence used to produce this protein in various species, scientists were able to see how mutations accumulate over time. The differences between a horse's base sequence for this protein and a zebra's is much smaller than the differences between a horse's and a lizard's. Humans and chimpanzees have identical cytochrome *c* amino acid sequences, whereas the yeast *Candida krusei* has 51 amino acid differences compared with humans.

For this exercise, find the relevant PDF file in the hotlinks at the end of this section. Follow the instructions to compare the genetic sequences for various organisms for the gene that makes cytochrome *c*.

Use the hotlinks to find ancient sequences of base pairs to compare between species of prokaryotes. Can you find a correlation between the numbers of mutations and the evolutionary distance between species?

NATURE OF SCIENCE

Why are scientists interested in comparing the genetic codes of various species? For one thing, when looking at a gene that every living thing should have, such as a gene for how to make ribosomes, the number of mutations a species has in that gene compared with another species gives insight into how closely they are related to each other.

Because of a certain number of differences in metabolism and genetic makeup in types of single-celled organisms that looked similar to bacteria, the biologist Carl Woese proposed the domain Archaea to distinguish them from bacteria (prokaryotes) and eukaryotes. Although Archaea do not have a nucleus, they have enough differences compared with prokaryotes to set them apart from other bacteria. Among the species in this group are single-celled organisms that thrive in very salty conditions, some that live in hot springs at extreme temperatures, and many others that live in the soil or in the ocean: some might be living in you or on you right now.

It took decades for Woese's proposal to be accepted, but the overwhelming evidence in Archaea's favour made it very difficult for opponents of the idea to argue against it.

Can human genes be patented?

In the spring of 2013, the United States Supreme Court heard a landmark case between a biotech company, Myriad Genetics (the defendant), and the Association for Molecular Pathology, AMP (the plaintiff), a group of genetics experts who specialize in many things, including the diagnosis of genetic diseases and disorders. Myriad had a patent on naturally occurring human genes called *BRCA*, which can be used to tell whether a woman has a genetically increased chance of breast cancer or ovarian cancer, two of the most common and deadly cancers in Western society today. AMP was taking Myriad to court because they thought the *BRCA* gene sequences should be available freely for diagnosing cancer. AMP thought that it was unfair that clinical teams could not access the *BRCA* genes to do their own testing and diagnosis. They argued that a company such as Myriad should not be able to put an industrial patent on genes, because DNA sequences occur naturally and are not invented by a company: therefore, they are not patentable objects.

Myriad's argument was that, although DNA is found in nature, genes are all connected to each other, whereas the isolated sequences for which they had patents could only be the product of a biotech laboratory using sophisticated equipment to do the separation and identification: therefore, the DNA sequences in question were not in their natural form. The researchers at Myriad were the first to patent these fragments of DNA and recognize their usefulness. They patented their *BRCA* genes just as any pharmaceutical company would patent a new molecule that they thought would make a useful medicine. These patents, and the diagnostic tests associated with them, have made Myriad a very successful and profitable company. Because it is their intellectual property, anyone who wants a genetic test for breast cancer or ovarian cancer must go to them. Myriad argued that taking away their patents would take away their livelihood because it would allow any company to develop and perform their own diagnostic tests.

A patent is an authorization for a person or a company to make, use, or sell an invention, and it makes it illegal for anyone else to make, use, or sell it. For example, Thomas Edison had more than 1000 patents for the many things he invented, such as his improved electric light bulb and his phonograph. In the medical field, it is common to patent new pharmaceutical molecules developed in laboratories so that only the initial company that invented the drug can manufacture and sell it. Typically, a patent filed today is limited to 20 years.

Biotechnology is posing a rising number of challenges to the legal institutions of the world.

Another argument from the plaintiff was that, because Myriad was the sole company to administer *BRCA* diagnostics, it was impossible for a patient to get a second opinion, a key step in the diagnosis and treatment of a medical condition as serious as cancer. Also, Myriad could charge high fees because they had no competition in the market. Myriad's justification for the cost of the tests was that biotech research requires very expensive laboratory equipment and highly trained professionals, so the money earned from the diagnostic tests helps the company invest in new developments to advance scientific knowledge and continue putting new diagnostic tools in place.

In the end, the US Supreme Court found it unconstitutional to patent a DNA sequence found in nature. Justice Clarence Thomas wrote 'A naturally occurring DNA segment is a product of nature and not patent eligible merely because it has been isolated.'

Section summary

- Living organisms get their DNA from their parents.
- The locus of a chromosome is a specific position where a gene (a heritable unit of DNA that codes for a specific trait) is found.
- One allele (a version of a gene) can differ from another allele by one or more DNA bases.
- The Human Genome Project has allowed scientists to map the positions of genes and their mutations.

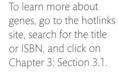

To learn more about genes, go to the hotlinks site, search for the title or ISBN, and click on Chapter 3: Section 3.1.

Exercises

1 What is the difference between an allele and a gene?

2 Give an example of a mutation in an eagle's offspring that could be considered a beneficial mutation.

3 Explain why eukaryotic chromosomes always come in pairs.

NATURE OF SCIENCE

Developments in research follow improvements in techniques: autoradiography was used to establish the length of DNA molecules in chromosomes.

3.2 Chromosomes

Understandings:

- Prokaryotes have one chromosome consisting of a circular DNA molecule.
- Some prokaryotes also have plasmids but eukaryotes do not.
- Eukaryote chromosomes are linear DNA molecules associated with histone proteins.
- In a eukaryote species there are different chromosomes that carry different genes.
- Homologous chromosomes carry the same sequence of genes but not necessarily the same alleles of those genes.
- Diploid nuclei have pairs of homologous chromosomes.
- Haploid nuclei have one chromosome of each pair.
- The number of chromosomes is a characteristic feature of members of a species.
- A karyogram shows the chromosomes of an organism in homologous pairs of decreasing length.
- Sex is determined by sex chromosomes and autosomes are chromosomes that do not determine sex.

Applications and skills:

- Application: Cairns' technique for measuring the length of DNA molecules by autoradiography.
- Application: Comparison of genome size in T2 phage, *Escherichia coli*, *Drosophila melanogaster*, *Homo sapiens*, and *Paris japonica*.
- Application: Comparison of diploid chromosome numbers of *Homo sapiens*, *Pan troglodytes*, *Canis familiaris*, *Oryza sativa*, and *Parascaris equorum*.
- Application: Use of karyograms to deduce sex and diagnose Down syndrome in humans.
- Skill: Use of databases to identify the locus of a human gene and its polypeptide product.

  ### Guidance
  - *The terms karyotype and karyogram have different meanings. Karyotype is a property of a cell: the number and type of chromosomes present in the nucleus, not a photograph or diagram of them.*
  - *Genome size is the total length of DNA in an organism. The examples of genome and chromosome number have been selected to allow points of interest to be raised.*
  - *The two DNA molecules formed by DNA replication prior to cell division are considered to be sister chromatids until the splitting of the centromere at the start of anaphase. After this, they are individual chromosomes.*

The chromosome in prokaryotes

You will recall from Chapter 1 that the nucleoid region of a bacterial cell contains a single, long, continuous, circular thread of DNA. Therefore, this region is involved with cell control and reproduction.

Notice how the presence of a single circular chromosome is a very different situation from all the cells we looked at in Section 3.1, which always had chromosomes in pairs. Why is this? Prokaryotes can reproduce using binary fission (dividing), whereas organisms such as plants and animals more frequently use sexual reproduction (involving a male and a female). Any time two parents are involved, the offspring will have pairs of chromosomes rather than single chromosomes. Because prokaryotes have only one parent, they have only one chromosome.

Figure 3.10 The DNA in prokaryotes can be found in the circular chromosome or in plasmids.

Plasmids

Escherichia coli, like many prokaryotes (bacteria), have small loops of DNA that are extra copies of some of the genetic material of the organism. These loops are called plasmids. These small, circular, DNA molecules are not connected to the main bacterial chromosome. The plasmids replicate independently of the chromosomal DNA. Plasmid DNA is not required by the cell under normal conditions, but it may help the cell adapt to unusual circumstances. Plasmids can be found in Archaea as well as in bacteria.

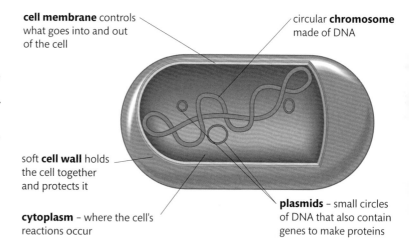

cell **membrane** controls what goes into and out of the cell

circular **chromosome** made of DNA

soft **cell wall** holds the cell together and protects it

cytoplasm – where the cell's reactions occur

plasmids – small circles of DNA that also contain genes to make proteins

As we will see later in Section 3.5, these loops can be used in genetic engineering. Genetic manipulation using plasmids is not possible in eukaryotes such as plants and animals, because they do not have plasmids. Other techniques must be used for genetically modified (GM) crops and animals, which we will discuss later (also in Section 3.5).

Eukaryote chromosomes

The DNA of eukaryotic cells most often occurs in the form of chromosomes. Chromosomes carry information necessary for the cell to exist. This allows the organism, whether unicellular or multicellular, to survive. DNA is the genetic material of the cell. It enables certain traits to be passed on to the next generation. When the cell is not dividing, the chromosomes are not visible structures. During this phase, the cell's DNA is in the form of chromatin. Chromatin is formed of strands of DNA and proteins called histones.

Figure 3.11 This drawing shows how DNA is packaged into chromosomes.

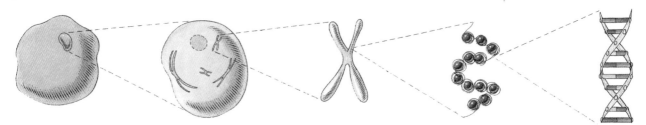

When looking at unfolded DNA with an electron microscope, you can see what looks like beads on a string. Each of the beads is a nucleosome. A nucleosome consists of two molecules of each of four different histones. The DNA wraps twice around these eight protein molecules. The DNA is attracted to the histones because DNA is negatively charged and the histones are positively charged. Between the nucleosomes is a single string of DNA. There is often a fifth type of histone attached to the linking string of DNA near each nucleosome. This fifth histone leads to further wrapping (packaging) of the DNA molecule and eventually to the highly condensed or supercoiled chromosomes.

When DNA is wrapped around the histones and then further wrapped in even more elaborate structures, it is inaccessible to transcription enzymes. Therefore, the wrapping or packaging of DNA regulates the transcription process. This allows only certain areas of the DNA molecule to be involved in protein synthesis.

Multiple chromosomes

As shown in Table 3.5, eukaryotes have more than one chromosome. Most eukaryotes have multiple pairs of chromosomes, and each chromosome will carry a different set of instructions for the cell.

Table 3.5 A comparison of eukaryote chromosomes and prokaryote chromosomes

	Prokaryote	Eukaryote
Number of chromosomes	1	2 or more*
Shape	Circular	Linear
Histones	Not present**	Present
Presence of plasmids	Sometimes	Never
Organized into pairs	No	Yes

* It is rare for eukaryotes to have one chromosome, but some can, such as male bees, wasps, and ants.

** Among prokaryotes, archaeans have the same properties as bacteria (prokaryotes) in this table, with the exception that histones are present in archaean DNA but not in bacterial DNA.

Homologous chromosomes: same genes but not always the same alleles

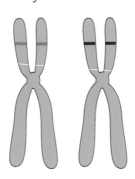

Figure 3.12 Homologous chromosomes. Although these are the same size and shape, and carry the same genes, the different coloured bands on the short arms of each chromosome reveal that they do not carry the same allele of the gene at the locus shown.

In a typical human cell, the 46 chromosomes can be grouped into 23 pairs of chromosomes called homologous chromosomes. Homologous means similar in shape and size, and it means that the two chromosomes carry the same genes. The example in Figure 3.12 shows one of the 23 pairs of homologous chromosomes found in humans.

Remember that the reason there are two of each chromosome is that one came from the father and the other from the mother. Although a pair of homologous chromosomes carries the same genes, they are not identical because the alleles for the genes from each parent could be different. In Figure 3.12, we can see that the locus shown contains different coloured bands, revealing that this individual got a different allele from his or her mother than from his or her father for this particular gene.

It is important to note that the shapes you see in Figure 3.12 represent two chromosomes together as a single pair, but that each chromosome has been doubled as a result of DNA replication. Chromosomes only look like this when the cell they are in is getting ready to divide. At this stage, the two blue-banded zones are part of two connected sister chromatids forming a single chromosome attached at the centromere. Likewise, the two red-banded zones belong to two sister chromatids. Each chromatid includes the long arm as well as the short arm (the one that contains the coloured bands in this example). This will be important to remember later, when we watch the sister chromatids split during cell division. When the chromatids separate, they become two identical chromosomes. But as long as they are attached at the centromere, they are considered to be part of a single chromosome.

Examining chromosomes in root tips

Safety alerts: The chemicals in this lab, as well as the risk of breaking glass during the squashing process, require vigilance and caution. Ask your teacher what precautions to consider.

There are two options for doing this lab, depending on time and materials available. You can either prepare your own root tip squashes from plant material grown in the laboratory, or you can examine pre-made root tip preparations from a laboratory supply company.

For the first option, carry out the following.

- Over a beaker full of water, suspend a plant that will produce roots in the water, for example garlic, onion, or potato. Use toothpicks to support it.

- Leave it for 2–5 days until little white roots have pushed their way down into the water. Top up the water periodically if it gets low.

- Cut off the roots and place them first into ethanoic acid for 10 min, then into 1 M HCl for 10 min, then rinse them with water.

- Cut off 2 mm of the tips, and place these segments on a microscope slide.

- Stain them with orcein, allowing it to soak in for a few minutes.

- To spread the cells out on the slide, use a mounted needle.

- Place a cover slip over the root tips, and place several layers of paper towel over the slide and cover slip. Push down firmly to squash the tissue.

- If you have the time and materials, you can compare the chromosomes in your root tips with professionally prepared slides.

Diploid and haploid cells

The term diploid is used to describe a nucleus that has chromosomes organized into pairs of homologous chromosomes. Most cells in the human body are diploid cells, and in such cells the nucleus contains a set of 23 chromosomes from the mother and 23 from the father. There is a category of cells that only contain 23 chromosomes in total: the sex cells, also called gametes. Because the chromosomes in sperm and egg cells do not come in pairs, but rather only have a single chromosome from each pair, they are said to be haploid.

The adult form of animal cells is rarely haploid, but there are exceptions, for example male bee, wasp, and ant cells are haploid. Generally speaking, the vast majority of cells in sexually reproducing organisms are diploid, and only the gametes are haploid.

CHALLENGE YOURSELF

4 Use the karyogram in the photo below to determine whether the child is a boy or a girl. How do you know? Does the child's karyotype include any anomalies? If so, describe what you see.

The variable n represents the haploid number, and it refers to the number of sets of chromosomes that a nucleus can have. For a human egg cell, $n = 23$. When an egg cell is fertilized by a sperm cell (a sperm is also haploid and therefore contains 23 chromosomes), a zygote is formed and the two haploid nuclei fuse together, matching up their chromosomes into pairs. Hence humans generally have a total of 23 + 23 = 46 chromosomes. This means that in humans, $2n = 46$, so diploid cells in humans have 23 pairs of chromosomes making a total of 46 chromosomes. Compare this number with some of the other species in Table 3.6.

Table 3.6 A comparison of types of cells and chromosome numbers

Species	Types of cells and chromosome numbers	
	Haploid = n	Diploid = $2n$
Human, *Homo sapiens*	23	46
Chimpanzee, *Pan troglodytes*	24	48
Domestic dog, *Canis familiaris*	39	78
Rice, *Oryza sativa*	12	24
Roundworm, *Parascaris equorum*	1	2

This is a karyogram showing all 23 pairs of chromosomes. What can we learn about the individual's karyotype from this figure? This karyogram was prepared using false colour imagery.

Chromosome number: a defining feature

As you can see, the number 46 for humans is very different compared with the number for a worm. One of the best-studied worms in genetics laboratories is *Caenorhabditis elegans*, whose genome was first sequenced in 1998. It has six chromosomes, meaning its diploid number, $2n$, is 6, and therefore its haploid number, n, is 3. It would be expected that all the cells in *C. elegans* would have six chromosomes, and, likewise, that all cells in humans would have 46. Although this is true for most cells, we have already seen the exception of haploid cells (n), and we will see later that some people can be born with chromosomes missing (45 or fewer) or with extra chromosomes (47 or greater), but these remain exceptions. In addition, some cells do not contain a nucleus and have no chromosomes to show, such as red blood cells. Generally speaking, however, the number of chromosomes is a characteristic feature of the cells of a species.

Karyograms and karyotypes

A karyogram is a representation of the chromosomes found in a cell arranged according to a standard format, as in the example in the photo to the left. The chromosomes are placed in order according to their size and shape. The shape depends mainly on the position of the centromere. A karyogram is used to show a person's karyotype, which is the specific number and appearance of the chromosomes in his or her cells.

How is such an image obtained? Once the cells of an organism have been collected and grown in culture, a karyogram is made following the steps below. For an explanation of how the cells are collected, see Section 3.3.

1   The cells are stained and prepared on a glass slide, to see their chromosomes under a light microscope.

2   Photomicrograph images are obtained of the chromosomes during a specific phase of cell division called the mitotic metaphase (see Section 1.6).

3   The images are cut out and separated, a process that can be done using scissors or using a computer.

4   The images of each pair of chromosomes are placed in order by size and the position of their centromeres. Generally speaking, the chromosomes are arranged in order by decreasing length. The exception is in the 23rd pair of chromosomes, which can contain one or two X chromosomes, which are considerably larger than the chromosomes in the 22nd pair (see the chromosome pair marked X in the photo on page 138).

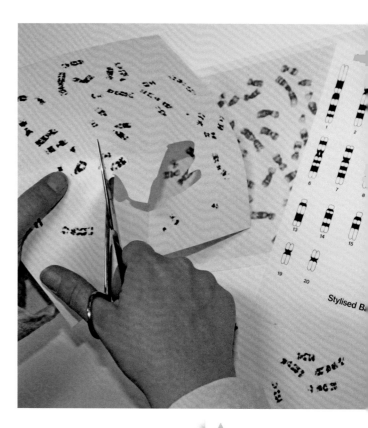

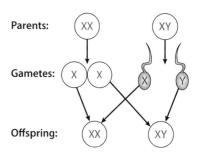
Images of chromosomes are cut out and pasted to make a karyogram.

Sex determination

The 23rd pair of chromosomes are called the sex chromosomes because they determine whether a person is a male or a female. The X chromosome is longer than the Y chromosome, and contains many more genes. Unlike the other 22 pairs of chromosomes, this is the only pair in which it is possible to find two chromosomes that are very different in size and shape.

In human females there are two X chromosomes. When women produce gametes, each egg will contain one X chromosome. Human males have one X chromosome and one Y chromosome. When males produce sperm cells, half of them contain one X chromosome and half contain one Y chromosome. As a result, when an egg cell meets a sperm cell during fertilization, there is always a 50% chance that the child will be a boy and a 50% chance that the child will be a girl (see Figure 3.13):

• XX = female

• XY = male.

The chances remain the same no matter how many boys or girls the family already has.

Any chromosome that is not a sex chromosome is called an autosome, or autosomal chromosome. Humans have 22 pairs of autosomes and one pair of sex chromosomes (see Figure 3.14).

Figure 3.13 How sex is determined: will the baby be a boy or a girl?

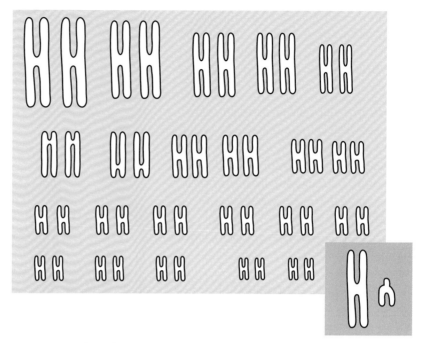

Figure 3.14 Human chromosomes: grey = autosomes, purple = sex chromosomes.

If a trait or gene is described as autosomal, its locus is on one of the 22 pairs of autosomes, not on the sex chromosomes. Where a gene is located determines whether or not the trait it controls is more common in males or females. When a trait is more common in one sex than the other, there is a good chance that the trait is sex-linked, and that the locus of the gene is on either the X chromosome or the Y chromosome (see sex linkage in Section 3.4). If there is no pattern to the frequency of a trait between females and males, it is most likely to be an autosomal trait.

Autoradiography

Autoradiography is a technique in which radiation from a substance is captured on photographic film or by a camera sensor. Unlike an X-ray, during which the film or sensor is exposed to an external source of radioactivity, autoradiograms (the images formed by autoradiography) are exposed to radioactive particles being given off by the substance itself. This technique has been described as structures such as DNA being able to 'take their own pictures'. It is used in genetics work to obtain images of DNA strands so that their lengths can be measured.

Cairns' technique involves injecting radioactive materials into the DNA samples that will expose the film faster. Such materials are called radio markers. In the case of measuring the lengths of DNA strands, the DNA forming during replication is given a radioactive form of a molecule called thymidine. Thymidine is a component of a DNA nucleotide made up of a pentose sugar bonded to thymine; it is represented by the letter T in the genetic code. The radioactive form added in the experiment is called ^{3}H-thymidine, in which the ^{3}H is the radioactive isotope of hydrogen. An isotope is a version of an atom with a different atomic mass compared with other versions of the same atom, usually because it has more neutrons. The radioactive ^{3}H molecule is used as a radio marker to keep track of where those thymidine molecules are, because it leaves traces of its presence on photographic film.

This technique was used by John Cairns in 1962 to demonstrate that a bacterium's chromosome is made up of a single circle of DNA and that it is replicated by being unzipped. The photos he took using autoradiography looked like the image below, and Cairns called them theta structures because they were reminiscent of the Greek letter theta (θ).

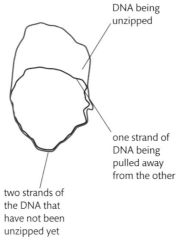

DNA being unzipped

one strand of DNA being pulled away from the other

two strands of the DNA that have not been unzipped yet

Figure 3.15 A diagram of what Cairns saw when the circular DNA chromosome of *E. coli* was being unzipped for replication.

CHALLENGE YOURSELF

5   Scientists have long dreamed of the moment when they can see the mysterious secret code of life. For example, discovering the code behind something as wonderfully useful as insulin, the protein in your blood that helps regulate blood sugar, was the dream for many decades. Wouldn't it be nice to be able to read the code, copy it, and use the copy to make insulin in a laboratory? In the early 1980s, a small company called Genentech was the first to make laboratory-synthesized insulin available to patients who needed it to treat their diabetes. The company went on to many other projects in the field of biotechnology and, three decades later, the company was worth tens of billions of dollars.

Today, a lot of the discoveries that took months or years to make are just a few clicks away, because they are available for everyone to consult. The online genetic database at the National Center for Biotechnology Information (NCBI), for example, has many genes that you yourself can look up. Interested in insulin or haemoglobin? Search for those words or their genes (*INS* for insulin or *HBB* for one of the subunits of haemoglobin). At the end of this section, use the hotlinks to see if you can find out at what position and on what chromosome you can find the secret code for these valuable molecules of life. If you ask for the FASTA data (pronounced 'Fast A'), you can see every A, T, C, and G that makes up a gene coding for a protein. Also, check out the NCBI 1000 Genome Browser, an online map of human genes chromosome by chromosome. If you get lost, they have video tutorials to help.

Section summary

- Chromosomes are made of DNA, which contains a linear sequence of bases that code for each organism's traits.
- The chromosome number is characteristic of a certain species.
- Thanks to binary fission, a prokaryote has one parent cell and possesses a single circular DNA molecule as its chromosome.
- Organisms that reproduce sexually have two parents and as a result tend to have pairs of chromosomes in the nuclei of their cells. The pairs consist of homologous chromosomes that carry the same genes but not necessarily the same versions of those genes (alleles).
- Plasmids are circles of extra copies of DNA and can be found in some prokaryotes but not in eukaryotes.
- Eukaryotes and archaeans have histones associated with their DNA, whereas bacteria do not. Haploid = n, diploid = $2n$.

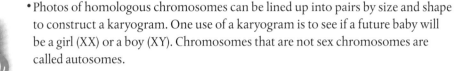

To learn more about chromosomes, go to the hotlinks site, search for the title or ISBN, and click on Chapter 3: Section 3.2.

• Photos of homologous chromosomes can be lined up into pairs by size and shape to construct a karyogram. One use of a karyogram is to see if a future baby will be a girl (XX) or a boy (XY). Chromosomes that are not sex chromosomes are called autosomes.

Exercises

4   Draw and label a chromosome. Include the following labels: chromatid, centromere. Indicate an example of a locus.

5   Explain why prokaryotes are never diploid.

3.3   Meiosis

Understandings:

• One diploid nucleus divides by meiosis to produce four haploid nuclei.
• The halving of the chromosome number allows a sexual life cycle with fusion of gametes.
• DNA is replicated before meiosis so that all chromosomes consist of two sister chromatids.
• The early stages of meiosis involve pairing of homologous chromosomes and crossing over followed by condensation.
• Orientation of pairs of homologous chromosomes prior to separation is random.
• Separation of pairs of homologous chromosomes in the first division of meiosis halves the chromosome number.
• Crossing over and random orientation promotes genetic variation.
• Fusion of gametes from different parents promotes genetic variation.

Applications and skills:

• Application: Non-disjunction can cause Down syndrome and other chromosome abnormalities.
• Application: Studies showing age of parents influences chances of non-disjunction.
• Application: Description of methods used to obtain cells for karyotype analysis, e.g. chorionic villus sampling and amniocentesis, and the associated risks.
• Skill: Drawing diagrams to show the stages of meiosis resulting in the formation of four haploid cells.

Guidance
• *Preparation of microscope slides showing meiosis is challenging and permanent slides should be available in case no cells in meiosis are visible in temporary mounts.*
• *Drawings of the stages of meiosis do not need to include chiasmata.*
• *The process of chiasmata formation need not be explained.*

Producing four haploid nuclei

The vast majority of cells in a person's body each contains 46 chromosomes. Gametes (sperm cells and egg cells) cannot contain 46 chromosomes for the simple reason that, if they did, when they fused together during fertilization, the baby that would be formed would have a total of 92 chromosomes, and each new generation would double its chromosome number, making an impossibly large amount of DNA to deal with. To avoid this problem of accumulating too many chromosomes, humans and other animals produce egg cells and sperm cells in such a way that the number of chromosomes in their nuclei is halved. Hence, sperms and eggs only contain 23 chromosomes, one from each pair, rather than complete pairs. In order to make such special cells with half the chromosomes, a special type of cell division is needed: meiosis. Such a splitting is called a reduction division.

Figure 3.16 How the chromosome number is halved. More details about the specific stages of meiosis appear later in this chapter.

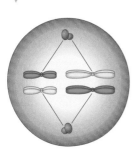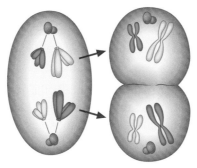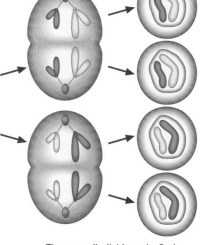

Each chromosome makes an identical copy of itself. The two copies stay in contact with each other.
The chromosomes line up in pairs. Each pair codes for the same characteristics.

The cell divides in two. One chromosome from each pair goes into each new cell. (This means there are no pairs of chromosomes in the new cells.)

The new cells divide again. Each chromosome splits in two. Each half goes into a new cell. This makes four haploid cells. These develop into gametes.

The halving of the chromosome number

Whereas mitosis produces diploid ($2n$) nuclei containing 46 chromosomes (organized into 23 pairs), meiosis produces haploid (n) nuclei that contain 23 chromosomes, each representing half of one pair. Notice in Figure 3.16, from a single cell on the left, four cells were produced on the right. Notice also that the number of chromosomes in the example is 4 in the parent cell at the start (so $2n = 4$), because there are 2 in each pair. In contrast, the number of chromosomes at the end is only 2 ($n = 2$), because each 'pair' is not a pair anymore but rather a single representative from each pair. In the testes and ovaries, respectively, meiosis produces haploid sperms and eggs, so that, when fertilization occurs, the zygote will receive 23 + 23 = 46 chromosomes; half from the mother, and half from the father. This is how the problem of changing chromosome number is avoided. As a result, the human number of 46 is preserved by the sexual life cycle.

DNA is replicated before meiosis

The reason why chromosomes are represented as having the shape reminiscent of the letter 'X' or 'H', as used in the previous section, is because at this stage in the chromosome's existence, the DNA has been replicated so that a full copy of the original DNA has been produced.

As a result, the single chromosome comprises two sister chromatids side-by-side and joined in the middle at the centromere (see Figure 3.18).

In reality, before the chromosomes start preparing for the cell to divide, they are all uncoiled and are not visible in the nucleus. This is one of the reasons why, when looking at cells under a microscope, it is not usually possible to see chromosomes all coiled up. It is only in the early stages of the preparation for cell division that condensation happens and the chromosomes coil up into the shapes you are being shown in this chapter.

Figure 3.17 How chromosome number is maintained in the sexual life cycle.

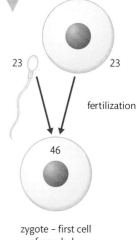

23   23

fertilization

46

zygote – first cell of new baby

Figure 3.18 An artist's conception of a single chromosome before and after DNA replication.

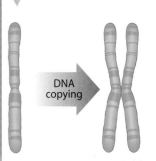

DNA copying

143

Pairing of homologous chromosomes and crossing over

Meiosis is a step-by-step process by which a diploid parent cell produces four haploid daughter cells. Before the steps begin, DNA replication allows the cell to make a complete copy of its genetic information during interphase. This results in each chromatid having an identical copy, or sister chromatid, attached to it at the centromere.

In order to produce a total of four cells, the parent cell must divide twice: the first meiotic division makes two cells, and then each of these divides during the second meiotic division to make a total of four cells.

One of the characteristics that distinguishes meiosis from mitosis (see Section 1.6) is that, during the first step, called prophase I, there is an exchange of genetic material between non-sister chromatids in a process called crossing over (see Figure 3.19). This trading of segments of genes happens when sections of two homologous chromatids break at the same point, twist around each other, and then each connects to the other's initial position.

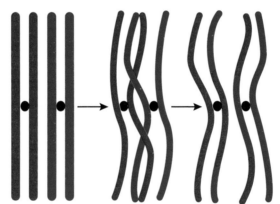

Figure 3.19 Crossing over occurring in a pair of homologous chromosomes.

Crossing over allows DNA from a person's maternal chromosomes to mix with DNA from the paternal chromosomes. In this way, the recombinant chromatids that end up in the sperm or the egg cells are a mosaic of the two parent cells' original chromatids. This helps increase the variety among offspring from the same two parents, and so increases the chances of survival of some offspring if one combination of alleles is more favourable for survival than others.

Meiosis I takes place in order to produce two cells, each with a single set of chromosomes (see Figure 3.20).

Random orientation

Figure 3.20 shows that, during metaphase I, the homolgous pairs of chromosomes line up along the centre of the cell. The way that they happen to line up is by chance, and that is why it is called random orientation. As seen with crossing over, this is another adaptation that increases variety in the offspring. The result of random orientation is that a male will only very rarely produce two sperm cells that are identical. Likewise, for a female, it is highly likely that she will never produce the same egg twice in her lifetime. These are among the reasons why a couple will never have the same offspring twice. The only way that a male and a female can naturally have the same offspring twice is by producing identical twins, but, in this case, it is two children from the same egg cell and the same sperm cell.

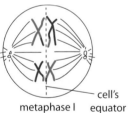

pair of homologous chromosomes

prophase I

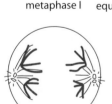

metaphase I

cell's equator

anaphase I

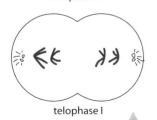

telophase I

Figure 3.20 The stages of meiosis I.

Halving the chromosome number

Prophase I

1 Chromosomes become visible as the DNA becomes more compact.
2 Homologous chromosomes, also called homologues, are attracted to each other and pair up: one is from the individual's father, the other from the mother.
3 Crossing over occurs.
4 Spindle fibres made from microtubules form.

Metaphase I

1 The homologous chromosomes line up across the cell's equator by random orientation.
2 The nuclear membrane disintegrates.

Anaphase I

Spindle fibres from the poles attach to chromosomes and pull them to opposite poles of the cell.

Telophase I

1 Spindles and spindle fibres disintegrate.
2 Usually, the chromosomes uncoil and new nuclear membranes form.
3 Many plants do not have a telophase I stage.

At the end of meiosis I, cytokinesis happens: the cell splits into two separate cells. The cells at this point are haploid because they contain only one chromosome of each pair. However, each chromatid still has its sister chromatid attached to it, so no S phase is necessary.

Now meiosis II takes place in order to separate the sister chromatids (see Figure 3.21).

Prophase II

1 DNA condenses into visible chromosomes again.
2 New meiotic spindle fibres are produced.

Metaphase II

1 Nuclear membranes disintegrate.
2 The individual chromosomes line up along the equator of each cell in no special order; this is called random orientation.
3 Spindle fibres from opposite poles attach to each of the sister chromatids at the centromeres.

Anaphase II

1 Centromeres of each chromosome split, releasing each sister chromatid as an individual chromosome.
2 The spindle fibres pull individual chromatids to opposite ends of the cell.
3 Because of random orientation, the chromatids could be pulled towards either of the newly forming daughter cells.

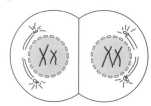

prophase II

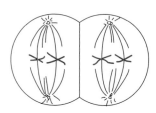

metaphase II

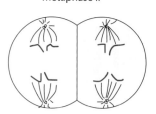

anaphase II

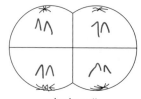

telophase II

Figure 3.21 Meiosis II.

145

4   In animal cells, cell membranes pinch off in the middle, whereas in plant cells new cell plates form to demarcate the four cells.

Telophase II

1   Chromosomes unwind their strands of DNA.
2   Nuclear envelopes form around each of the four haploid cells, preparing them for cytokinesis.

Fertilization and variation

As can be seen with siblings from the same mother and father who are not identical twins, crossing over during prophase I and random orientation during metaphase I allow variation in the offspring. There is one other way that genetic variation is also promoted: fertilization. When the egg and sperm cells meet, there is a great deal of chance involved. For example, a man can produce millions of different sperm cells, each with a unique combination of half his DNA.

How is this calculated? If only the number of chromosomes in each haploid cell (n) is considered, the calculation is 2^n because there are two possible chromosomes in each pair (maternal and paternal) and there are n chromosomes in all. For humans, the number is 2^{23} because there are 23 chromosomes in each gamete. So the probability that a woman could produce the same egg twice is 1 in 2^{23} or 1 in 8 388 608. Even this calculation is an oversimplification, however, because it does not take into consideration the additional variety that results from crossing over.

In addition, the calculation 2^n only considers one gamete. To produce offspring, two gametes are needed, and the chances that both parents produce two identical offspring (apart from identical twins) is infinitesimal.

A   B   C

Figure 3.22 Rows A, B, and C show three of the sixteen possible orientations for four pairs of homologous chromosomes. In humans there are 23 pairs with more than 8 million possible orientations.

Extra or missing chromosomes

Sometimes errors occur during meiosis and a child can receive an atypical number of chromosomes, such as 47 instead of 46. One such anomaly is called Down syndrome, and it happens when there is an extra chromosome in the 21st pair. The extra chromosome results from a phenomenon called non-disjunction, which can happen at different times but most often occurs when the 21st pair of homologous chromosomes fails to separate during anaphase I. Hence, the egg the woman produces has two 21st chromosomes instead of one. And when a sperm cell fertilizes the egg, the total number of 21st chromosomes is three.

NATURE OF SCIENCE

Researchers wanted to find out what influences affected the frequency of Down syndrome. Studies were done by collecting statistics on the many different characteristics of the parents and families of children born with Down syndrome. Such studies are called epidemiological studies, and they look at trends in populations, often examining thousands of cases. Many graphs were made to see if there was a correlation between various factors. The factor that gave the most conclusive results was the age of the mother, as can be seen in the results of one such study shown in Figure 3.23.

The error giving an extra chromosome to the 21st pair can happen during meiosis I or meiosis II, which is why the graph shows both, but the majority of cases are meiosis I. Thanks to such a graph, what advice can doctors give women who wish to avoid this syndrome in their children?

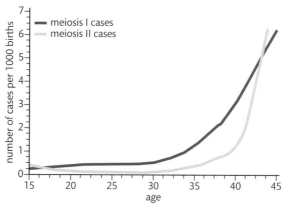

http://biomed, emory.edu/reproduced with permission

Figure 3.23 Correlation of age of mother and occurrence of Down syndrome in children.

The two boys in this photo are fraternal twins. The one on the right received an extra 21st chromosome and has Down syndrome.

CHALLENGE YOURSELF

Parents who are concerned that they might have a high risk of producing a baby with a chromosomal anomaly (for example a karyotype with 45 or 47 chromosomes instead of 46) may be interested in having a karyogram prepared of the unborn baby's genetic material. This tool has allowed specialists called genetic counsellors to advise parents about their future baby. Genetic counsellors can analyse the karyogram and tell the parents about any chromosomal anomalies such as Down syndrome.

6 What would a genetic counsellor look for in a karyogram to find out if an unborn child has Down syndrome?

Parents who find out that their future child will have a chromosomal disorder that would lead to learning disabilities have a choice to make: some may choose to terminate the pregnancy and try for another child without any anomalies, whereas other parents may decide that they will keep the child no matter what.

7 What factors do parents use to make such a difficult decision?

Here is another difficult issue that raises ethical concerns: because a karyogram can be used to determine whether the future baby is a boy or a girl, some parents use this to choose whether they will have the baby. For example, in cultures where having a boy is considered to be more valuable than having a girl (notably in countries where the law prohibits couples from having more than one child), parents might be tempted to terminate pregnancies when the baby is not the sex they want.

8 What would a genetic counsellor look for to determine the gender of the unborn child?

9 In your country, is this an acceptable use of technology?

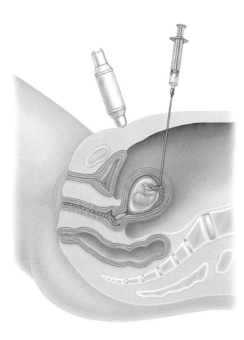

Figure 3.24 Finding an unborn baby's chromosomes by collecting cells from the chorionic villus with a hypodermic needle. The probe on the lower part of the future mother's abdomen is the sonogram probe. An amniocentesis is similar except that the needle would extract cells from the liquid surrounding the embryo.

CHALLENGE YOURSELF

10 Without looking back at the drawings showing them, can you draw the stages of meiosis? Start with a single cell that has two pairs of chromosomes, each having two sister chromatids. In the end, you should have four cells with two single chromosomes in each.

Obtaining cells for karyotyping

An unborn baby's cells can be extracted in one of two ways: either by a process called amniocentesis or by removing cells from the chorionic villus. Amniocentesis involves using a hypodermic needle to extract some of the amniotic fluid around the developing baby. Inside the liquid, some of the baby's cells can be found and used for the preparation of a karyotype. For the second method, cells are obtained by chorionic villus sampling, which involves obtaining a tissue sample from the placenta's finger-like projections into the uterus wall.

In either case, among the cells collected are foetal cells that are then grown in the laboratory. The preparation of a karyotype is an expensive and invasive procedure. It is usually used for seeing whether an unborn baby has any chromosomal anomalies, e.g. 45 or 47 chromosomes instead of 46. If the parents or doctors are concerned about the chromosomal integrity of an unborn child (for example, if an expectant mother is over the age of 35), a karyotype is recommended.

Section summary

- Meiosis allows for the shuffling of alleles, greatly increasing variety in the offspring. Meiosis is a reduction division, producing four haploid sex cells (gametes) from one diploid parent cell. During meiosis, the two sister chromatids that were formed during DNA replication are pulled apart.
- Genetic variety can be maximized in three ways: (1) random orientation of homologous pairs during metaphase I; (2) the process of crossing over during prophase I; and (3) sexual reproduction, where there is a certain amount of chance in which sperm cell encounters which egg.
- In the first division of meiosis, the chromosome number is halved (from $2n$ to n).
- Later, when the gametes fuse during fertilization, the typical chromosome number will be re-established: $n + n = 2n$.

Exercises

6 Look at Figure 3.23. Although the graph clearly shows an increase in the risk of non-disjunction as the mother's age increases, many babies with Down syndrome are born to mothers under the age of 35. Think about it. Can you explain why?

7 Why is meiosis referred to as a reduction division?

8 Explain why meiosis rather than mitosis is necessary for gamete production.

9 State the name of a type of cell in your body that is haploid.

10 Draw and label the stages of meiosis II.

3.4 Inheritance

NATURE OF SCIENCE

Making quantitative measurements with replicates to ensure reliability: Mendel's genetic crosses with pea plants generated numerical data.

Understandings:

- Mendel discovered the principles of inheritance with experiments in which large numbers of pea plants were crossed.
- Gametes are haploid so contain only one allele of each gene.
- The two alleles of each gene separate into different haploid daughter nuclei during meiosis.
- Fusion of gametes results in diploid zygotes with two alleles of each gene that may be the same allele or different alleles.
- Dominant alleles mask the effects of recessive alleles but co-dominant alleles have joint effects.
- Many genetic diseases in humans are due to recessive alleles of autosomal genes, although some genetic diseases are due to dominant or co-dominant alleles.
- Some genetic diseases are sex linked. The pattern of inheritance is different with sex-linked genes due to their location on sex chromosomes
- Many genetic diseases have been identified in humans but most are very rare.
- Radiation and mutagenic chemicals increase the mutation rate and can cause genetic diseases and cancer.

Applications and skills:

- Application: Inheritance of ABO blood groups.
- Application: Red–green colour blindness and haemophilia as examples of sex-linked inheritance.
- Application: Inheritance of cystic fibrosis and Huntington's disease.
- Application: Consequences of radiation after nuclear bombing of Hiroshima and accident at Chernobyl.
- Skill: Construction of Punnett grids for predicting the outcomes of monohybrid genetic crosses.
- Skill: Comparison of predicted and actual outcomes of genetic crosses using real data.
- Skill: Analysis of pedigree charts to deduce the pattern of inheritance of genetic diseases.

Gregor Mendel (1822–1884) studied the genetics of garden pea plants.
▼

Guidance
- *Alleles carried on X chromosomes should be shown as superscript letters on an upper case X, such as X^h.*
- *The expected notation for ABO blood group alleles is:*

Phenotypes	O A B AB	Genotypes	**ii** I^AI^A or I^Ai I^BI^B or I^Bi I^AI^B

Mendel's experiments with pea plants

Who was Gregor Mendel?

In 1865, an Austrian monk named Gregor Mendel published the results of his experiments on how garden pea plants passed on their characteristics. At the time, the term 'gene' did not exist (he used the term 'factors' instead) and the role that DNA played would not be discovered for nearly another century. Some of the questions Mendel asked were:

- How can I be sure that I will get only smooth peas and no wrinkled ones?
- How can I be sure that the resulting plants will be short or tall?
- How can I be sure to obtain only flowers of a certain colour?

NATURE OF SCIENCE

Gregor Mendel used artificial pollination in a series of experiments in which he carefully chose the pollen of various plants to fertilize other individuals of the same species. He used a small brush to place the pollen on the reproductive parts of the flowers, thus replacing the insects that do it naturally. This technique takes away the role of chance because the experimenter knows exactly which plants are fertilized by which pollen.

In one cross, he wanted to see what would happen if he bred tall plants with short plants. The result was that he got all tall plants (see the last row of Table 3.7). But then when he crossed the resulting tall plants with each other, some of the offspring in the new generation were short.

Table 3.7 also shows some of the other characteristics he tried to cross. The × in the first column shows a cross between one variety of pea plant and another. The expected ratio after two generations of crosses is 3:1 (for every 3 of the first type of plant, we would expect 1 of the other type): look how close Mendel got.

Table 3.7 Mendel's results

Characteristics in parents	First generation produced	Second generation produced	Ratio of results seen in second generation
Round × wrinkled seeds	100% round	5474 round 1850 wrinkled	2.96:1
Yellow × green seeds	100% yellow	6022 yellow 2001 green	3.01:1
Green × yellow pods	100% green	428 green 152 yellow	2.82:1
Tall × short plants	100% long	1787 long 277 short	2.84:1

Can you identify the independent variable and dependent variable in each experiment? What about the controlled variables: which things did Mendel make sure were the same from one experiment to the other so that the investigation was a fair test? Does this experiment have the expected characteristics of repeatability and verifiability? Could you do the exact same experiments today, over a century and a half later, and get similar results?

Key terminology

In order to understand the science of genetics, you first need to know the following terminology.

Genotype – The symbolic representation of the pair of alleles possessed by an organism, typically represented by two letters.

Examples: **Bb**, **GG**, **tt**.

Phenotype – The characteristics or traits of an organism.

Examples: five fingers on each hand, colour blindness, type O blood.

Dominant allele – An allele that has the same effect on the phenotype whether it is paired with the same allele or a different one. Dominant alleles are always expressed in the phenotype.

Example: the genotype **Aa** gives the dominant **A** trait because the **a** allele is masked; the **a** allele is not transcribed or translated during protein synthesis.

Recessive allele – An allele that has an effect on the phenotype only when present in the homozygous state.

Example: **aa** gives rise to the recessive trait because no dominant allele is there to mask it.

Co-dominant alleles – Pairs of alleles that both affect the phenotype when present in a heterozygote.

Example: a parent with curly hair and a parent with straight hair can have children with different degrees of hair curliness, because both alleles influence hair condition when both are present in the genotype.

Locus – The particular position on homologous chromosomes of a gene (as seen in Figure 3.2 and labelled in Figure 3.25). Each gene is found at a specific place on a specific pair of chromosomes.

Homozygous – Having two identical alleles of a gene (see Figure 3.25).

Example: **AA** is a genotype that is homozygous dominant, whereas **aa** is the genotype of someone who is homozygous recessive for that trait.

Heterozygous – Having two different alleles of a gene (see Figure 3.26). This results from the fact that the paternal allele is different from the maternal one.

Example: **Aa** is a heterozygous genotype.

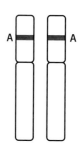

Figure 3.25 This drawing shows you a pair of chromosomes showing a homozygous state, **AA**.

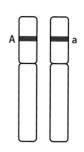

Figure 3.26 This drawing shows you a pair of chromosomes showing a heterozygous state, **Aa**.

Carrier – An individual who has a recessive allele of a gene that does not have an effect on the phenotype.

Example: **Aa** carries the gene for albinism (like the penguin in the photo below) but has pigmented skin, which means an ancestor must have been albino and some offspring might be albino; if both parents are unaffected by a recessive condition yet both are carriers, some of their progeny could be affected (because they would be **aa**).

Test cross – Testing a suspected heterozygote plant or animal by crossing it with a known homozygous recessive (**aa**). Because a recessive allele can be masked, it is often impossible to tell whether an organism is **AA** or **Aa** unless they produce offspring that have the recessive trait. An example of a test cross is shown later in this section when we explore three generations of pea plants.

Gametes have only one allele of each gene

Constructing a Punnett grid

Figure 3.27 shows a Punnett grid. A Punnett grid can be used to show how the alleles of parents are split between their gametes and how new combinations of alleles can show up in their offspring.

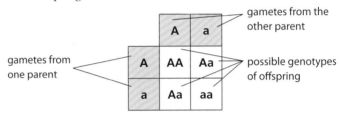

Figure 3.27 A Punnett grid.

The purpose of a Punnett grid is to show all the possible combinations of genetic information for a particular trait in a monohybrid cross. A monohybrid cross is one in which the parents have different alleles and that shows the results for only one trait.

The two alleles of each gene separate

Let's consider a condition called albinism. Most animals are unaffected by albinism and have pigmented skin, hair, eyes, fur, or feathers. But some animals lack pigmentation. An individual with little or no pigmentation is called an albino. For the sake of this illustration, we will assume albinism is controlled by a single gene with two alleles.

Albino animals lack pigmentation, so this penguin does not have the black markings characteristic of most penguins.

In reality, the genetics of albinism is more complex, notably because there are multiple types of albinism. However, using our simplification, **A** will represent the allele for pigmentation and **a** will represent the allele for albinism. We can trace the inheritance of albinism with a Punnett grid.

In order to set up a Punnett grid, the following steps must be followed.

1 Choose a letter to show the alleles.

Use the capital and lower case versions of the letter to represent the different alleles. Usually, a capital letter represents the dominant allele and the lower case letter represents the recessive allele. For example:

- **A** = dominant allele, allows pigments to form
- **a** = recessive allele, albinism, allows few or no pigments to form.

Get used to saying 'big A' and 'little a' when reading alleles and genotypes. Also, do not mix letters: for example, you cannot use **P** for pigmented and **a** for albino. Once you have chosen a letter, write down what it means so that it is clear which allele is which.

2 Determine the parents' genotypes.

To be sure that no possibilities are forgotten, write out all three possibilities and decide by a process of elimination which genotype or genotypes fit each parent.

The three possibilities here are:

- homozygous dominant (**AA**) – in this case, the phenotype shows pigmentation
- heterozygous (**Aa**) – in this case, the phenotype shows pigmentation but the heterozygote is a carrier of the albino allele
- homozygous recessive (**aa**) – in this case, the phenotype shows albinism.

The easiest genotype to determine by simply looking at a person or animal is **aa**. The other two are more of a challenge. To determine whether an individual is **AA** or **Aa**, we have to look for evidence that the recessive gene was received from an albino parent or was passed on to the individual's offspring. In effect, the only way to produce an albino is for each parent to donate one **a**.

3 Determine the gametes that the parents could produce.

An individual with a genotype **AA** can only make gametes with the allele **A** in them. Heterozygous carriers can make **A**-containing gametes or **a**-containing gametes. Obviously, individuals whose genotype is **aa** can only make gametes that contain the **a** allele. So you can record and label with **A** or **a** all the possible gametes.

4 Draw a Punnett grid.

Once all the previous steps have been completed, drawing the actual grid is simple. The parents' gametes are placed on the top and side of the grid. As an example, consider a cross involving a female carrier **Aa** crossed with a male albino **aa**.

You might guess that, because there are three **a** alleles and only one **A**, there should be a three out of four chance of seeing offspring with the recessive trait. But this is not the case. Figure 3.28 is a grid with the parents' gametes.

	a	a
A		
a		

Now you can fill in the empty squares with each parent's possible alleles by copying the letters from the top down and from left to right. When letters of different sizes end up in the same box, the big one goes first.

Be careful when choosing letters. Nearly half the letters of the alphabet should in fact be avoided because they are too similar in their capital and lower case forms. Don't use Cc, Ff, Kk, Oo, Pp, Ss, Uu, Vv, Ww, Xx, Yy, Zz.

When answering questions about genetic outcomes for offspring, it is sometimes tempting to go straight to the Punnett grid and forget about steps 1–3. The problem is that if you do not think carefully about the information going into the Punnett grid, you could put in the wrong information.

Figure 3.28 Punnett grid showing the parents' gametes.

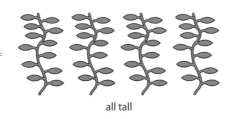

Figure 3.29 Punnett grid with all the possible genotypes filled in.

	a	a
A	Aa	Aa
a	aa	aa

5 Work out the chances of each genotype and phenotype occurring.

In a grid with four squares, each square can represent one of two possible statistics:

• the chance that these parents will have offspring with that genotype, here each square represents a 25% chance

• the probable proportion of offspring that will have the resulting genotypes, this only works for large numbers of offspring.

Fusion of gametes

The results from the above example show the following: there is a 50% chance of producing offspring with genotype **Aa** and a 50% chance of producing offspring with genotype **aa**. Because humans tend to produce a small number of offspring, this is the interpretation that should be used. If the example was about plants that produce hundreds of seeds, the results could be interpreted in the following way: 50% of the offspring should be **Aa** and the 50% should be **aa**.

No matter what the outcome, each offspring is the result of two alleles coming together when the gametes fuse. In this process, the two haploid sex cells join to make a single diploid cell called a zygote. This is the first cell of the new offspring.

Finally, the phenotypes can be deduced by looking at the genotypes. For example, **Aa** offspring will have a phenotype showing pigmentation so they will not be affected by albinism, whereas all the **aa** offspring will be albinos.

Dominant alleles and co-dominant alleles

Using the five steps of the Punnett grid method, we are going to examine the theoretical chances of genetic traits being passed on from one generation to the next.

Short or tall pea plants?

Let's first consider a cross that Gregor Mendel did with his garden pea plants. He took purebred tall plants and crossed them with purebred short plants. Purebred means that the tall plants' parents were known to be all tall, and the short plants' parents were known to be all short. In other words, he knew that none of the plants was heterozygous. He wanted to find out whether he would get all tall plants, some tall and some short, or all short.

Figure 3.30 First cross: tall parent × short parent gives all tall offspring.

The answer took months for Mendel to confirm, but a Punnett grid can now be used to get the answer in seconds: the result was 100% tall plants. Why? Because in garden pea plants, the allele for tall is dominant over the allele for short plants, thus masking the short trait in heterozygotes.

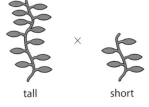

tall × short = all tall

The name given to the generation produced by a cross such as this is the first filial generation, usually referred to as the F_1 generation. What would happen if tall plants from the F_1 generation were crossed to make a second filial generation (F_2)?

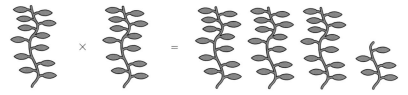

Figure 3.31 This is what happened when Mendel crossed the F_1 plants.

A Punnett grid can give us the results.

	T	t
T	TT	Tt
t	Tt	tt

Figure 3.32 A second filial generation.

This grid can be interpreted in two ways:

- there is a 75% chance of producing tall offspring and a 25% chance of producing short offspring
- 75% of the offspring will be tall and 25% of the offspring will be short.

Although 75% of the plants are tall, they have differing genotypes. Some tall plants are homozygous dominant and others are heterozygous.

Also, in a real experiment, it is unlikely that exactly 25% of the offspring would be short plants. The reason is essentially due to chance. For example, if 90 F_2 peas were produced and all of them were planted and grew into new plants, there is no mathematical way that exactly 25% of them would be short. At the very best, 23 out the 90 plants would be short , which is 25.56%; that is as close as it is possible to get to 25% in this case.

Even if a convenient number of plants was produced, such as 100 plants, farmers and breeders would not be surprised if they got 22, 26 or even 31 short plants instead of the theoretical 25. If the results of hundreds of similar crosses were calculated, the number would probably be very close to 25%. The same phenomenon can be seen in the sex of human children. Although the theoretical percentage is calculated to be 50% girls and 50% boys, in reality few families have exactly half and half. The actual result is due to chance.

Test cross

A plant breeder might need to know whether a specific tall plant from the F_2 generation is a purebred for tallness (homozygous dominant, **TT**) or whether it will not breed true for tallness (heterozygous **Tt**). To find out, she would cross the tall plant (whose genotype is not known) with a plant whose genotype is definitely known: a short plant that must be homozygous recessive, **tt**. By looking at the resulting plants, the test cross can reveal the genotypes of the tall plant as either **TT** or **Tt**.

If she gets a mix of tall and short plants as a result of the cross, she can conclude that the tall plant is heterozygous. The Punnett grid in Figure 3.34 explains her reasoning.

The five steps of the Punnett grid method.

- **Step 1** – Choose a letter.

  T = allele for a tall plant.

  t = allele for a short plant.

- **Step 2** – Parents' genotypes.

  TT for the purebred tall parent.

  tt for the purebred short parent.

- **Step 3** – Determine gametes.

  The purebred tall parent can only give **T**.

  The purebred short parent can only give **t**.

- **Step 4** – Draw a Punnett grid.

	t	t
T	Tt	Tt
T	Tt	Tt

Figure 3.33 A Punnett grid for **TT** and **tt**.

- **Step 5** – Interpret grid.

  100% **Tt** and will be tall, so 0% will be short.

	t	t
T	Tt	Tt
t	tt	tt

Figure 3.34 Test cross between a heterozygous tall plant and a homozygous recessive short plant.

If, on the other hand, all the offspring are tall, without exceptions, she can conclude that the tall plant is **TT**. The Punnett grid would be identical to the one in Figure 3.33. There is another possible interpretation to these results, however. The tall plant could, in fact, be **Tt** but by chance it only passed on **T** and never passed on **t**. Although this is possible, it is unlikely in cases where many offspring are produced.

Multiple alleles

So far, only two possibilities have been considered for a gene: dominant, **A**, or recessive, **a**. With two alleles, three different genotypes are possible, which can produce two different phenotypes. However, genetics is not always this simple; sometimes there are three or more alleles for the same gene. This is the case for the alleles that determine the ABO blood type in humans.

Blood type: an example of multiple alleles

The ABO blood type system in humans has four possible phenotypes: A, B, AB and O. To create these four blood types there are three alleles of the gene. These three alleles can produce six different genotypes.

The gene for the ABO blood type is represented by the letter **I**. To represent more than just two alleles (**I** and **i**) superscripts are introduced. As a result, the three alleles for blood type are written as follows: I^A, I^B and **i**. The two capital letters with superscripts represent alleles that are co-dominant:

- I^A = the allele for producing proteins called type A antigens, giving type A blood
- I^B = the allele for producing proteins called type B antigens, giving type B blood
- **i** = the recessive allele that produces neither A nor B antigens, giving type O blood.

Crossing these together in all possible combinations creates six genotypes that give rise to the four phenotypes listed earlier:

- $I^A I^A$ or I^A**i** gives a phenotype of type A blood
- $I^B I^B$ or I^B**i** gives type B blood
- $I^A I^B$ gives type AB blood (because of co-dominance, both types of antigens are produced)
- **ii** gives type O blood.

Notice how the genotype $I^A I^B$ clearly shows co-dominance. Neither allele is masked: both are expressed in the phenotype of type AB blood.

Is it possible for a couple to have four children, each child showing a different blood type?

Solution

There is only one way for this to happen: one parent must have type A blood but be a carrier of the allele for type O blood, and the other parent must have type B blood and also be a carrier of the allele for type O blood (if necessary, remind yourself of the blood group alleles, as shown above).

The cross would be $I^A i \times I^B i$ and the grid is shown in Figure 3.35. See if you can determine the phenotype of each child before reading on.

	I^A	i
I^B	$I^A I^B$	$I^B i$
i	$I^A i$	ii

Figure 3.35 A Punnet grid for blood type alleles.

So, would it be possible for this couple to have four children and all of them have a different blood group? In theory, yes.

Would it be possible for the same couple to have four children and all of them have type AB blood? In theory, yes, but it would not be likely. This question is similar to asking 'Could a couple have 10 children, all of them girls?' It is possible but statistically unlikely.

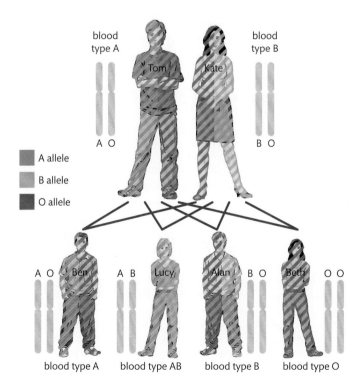

Figure 3.36 How the ABO blood groups can be inherited.

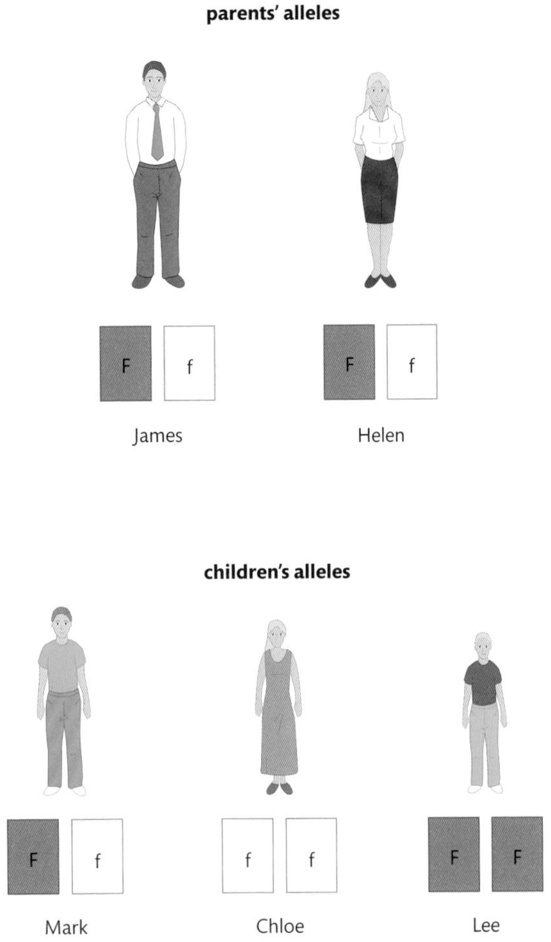

parents' alleles

F	f

James

F	f

Helen

children's alleles

F	f

Mark

f	f

Chloe

F	F

Lee

Figure 3.37 Cystic fibrosis inheritance.

Autosomal genetic diseases in humans

How is it possible for two healthy parents to have a child who suffers from a genetic disease? You should understand enough about how genetics works to be able to answer this: it's because the disease is recessive and both healthy parents must be carriers of the allele that causes the disease. For example, in the case of cystic fibrosis, let's call **F** the allele that leads to healthy production of mucus and **f** the allele for cystic fibrosis. In Figure 3.37, showing a family that has cystic fibrosis, the parents James and Helen are carriers (**Ff**). The only way to have the disease is to have the genotype **ff**, so James and Helen do not suffer from cystic fibrosis but they can pass it on to their children. If you set up a Punnett grid for these parents, you will see that there is a 1 in 4 chance (25%) that they will have a child with cystic fibrosis, and there are three possibilities for the genotypes in their children: Mark is **Ff**, Chloe is **ff**, and Lee is **FF**.

Such diseases are called autosomal recessive diseases because they are caused by recessive alleles, and the locus of their gene is found on one of the first 22 pairs of chromosomes but not on the sex chromosomes X or Y. The following are examples of autosomal recessive diseases:

- albinism
- cystic fibrosis
- phenylketonuria (PKU)
- sickle cell disease and sickle cell trait
- Tay Sachs disease
- thalassemia.

Genetic diseases are rare

You have probably heard of some of the conditions listed above, but not all, and it is unlikely that you will encounter any more than a handful of people with these diseases in your lifetime, because they are so rare in the general population. Even the most frequently occurring autosomal recessive diseases only affect about 1 in 2000 people in a given population, others typically as few as 1 in 10 000 or 20 000 people.

NATURE OF SCIENCE

Students sometimes get the impression that genetics is only about diseases. This is not true. It's just that more is known about disease-causing genes than about things such as eye colour genes, because researchers spend their time and funds studying things that can help society. Studying diseases and discovering their genetic causes is more useful to medicine than studying eye colour. Governments and university laboratories investing money in research want their work and their discoveries to lead to healthier lives for people. Getting a return on their investment also motivates them. Fundamental research ('I would like to study this just to find out how it works') does not attract funding as much as applied research ('I would like to find out how this disease is caused so that we can find better medical treatments for it').

Diseases caused by sex-linked genes or co-dominant alleles

Genes carried on the sex chromosomes

Because the Y chromosome is significantly smaller than the X chromosome, it has fewer loci and therefore fewer genes than the X chromosome. This means that sometimes alleles present on the X chromosome have nothing to pair up with. For example, a gene whose locus is at an extremity of the X chromosome would have no counterpart on the Y chromosome because the Y chromosome does not extend that far from its centromere.

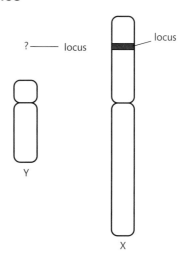

Figure 3.38 Since the Y chromosome is smaller than the X chromosome, there are fewer loci. As a result, the locus marked with a red bar on the X chromosome does not exist on the Y chromosome.

Sex linkage

Any genetic trait whose gene has its locus on the X or the Y chromosome is said to be sex linked.
Often genetic traits that show sex linkage affect one sex more than the other. Two examples of genetic traits that have this particularity are colour blindness and haemophilia.

- Colour blindness is the inability to distinguish between certain colours, often green and red. To people who are colour blind, these two colours look the same; they would not see a difference between a green apple and a red apple, for example.

- Haemophilia is a disorder in which blood does not clot properly. For most people, a small cut or scrape on their skin stops bleeding after a few minutes and eventually a scab forms. This process is called clotting. People with haemophilia have trouble with blood clotting and are at risk of bleeding to death from what most people would consider to be a minor injury such as a bruise, which is a rupture of many tiny blood vessels. Such bleeding can also occur in internal organs. Medical treatments such as special injections help give people affected by haemophilia a better quality of life.

Red and green apples (top) and as a person with red–green colour blindness would see them (bottom). vischeck.com

Alleles and genotypes of sex-linked traits

Because the alleles for both colour blindness and haemophilia are found only on the X chromosome, the letter X is used when representing them:

- X^b = allele for colour blindness
- X^B = allele for the ability to distinguish colours
- X^h = allele for haemophilia
- X^H = allele for the ability to clot blood
- Y = no allele present on the Y chromosome.

The letters X and Y refer to chromosomes and not to alleles, so terms such as dominant and recessive do not apply. X and Y should be considered as entire chromosomes rather than alleles of a gene. In sex-linked alleles, the letter that indicates the allele is the superscript after the X or Y. An absence of a superscript means that no allele for that trait exists on that chromosome.

159

As there is no allele on the Y chromosome, Y is written alone without any superscript. Here are all the possible genotypes for colour blindness:

- X^BX^B gives the phenotype of a non-affected female
- X^BX^b gives the phenotype of a non-affected female who is a carrier
- X^bX^b gives the phenotype of an affected female
- X^BY gives the phenotype of a non-affected male
- X^bY gives the phenotype of an affected male.

In the above list, ^{B} and ^{b} could be replaced by ^{H} and ^{h} to show the genotypes for haemophilia. Notice how only one sex can be a carrier.

The pattern of inheritance with sex-linked genes

Carriers of sex-linked traits

Sex-linked recessive alleles such as X^b are rare in most populations of humans worldwide. For this reason, it is unlikely to get one and much less likely to get two such alleles. This is why so few women are colour blind: their second copy of the gene is likely to be the dominant allele for full colour vision and will mask the recessive allele. The same is true for haemophilia.

As you have seen, there are three possible genotypes for females but only two possible genotypes for males. Only women can be heterozygous, X^BX^b, and, as a result, they are the only ones who can be carriers.

Because men do not have a second X chromosome, there are only two possible genotypes, X^BY or X^bY, for them in relation to colour blindness. With just the one recessive allele **b**, a man will be colour blind. This is contrary to what you have seen up to now concerning recessive alleles: usually people need two to have the trait, and, with one, they are carriers. In this case, the single recessive allele in males determines the phenotype. Men cannot be carriers for X-linked alleles.

As well as colour blindness and haemophilia, more examples of sex-linked traits in humans and other animals include:

- Duchene muscular dystrophy
- white eye colour in fruit flies
- calico–tortoiseshell fur colour in cats.

 Because the scientist John Dalton had red–green colour blindness, the condition is sometimes referred to as Daltonism and people who have it are said to be Daltonian. Dalton asked for his eyes to be dissected after his death (he died in 1844) to verify his hypothesis that the liquid inside them was blue. It was not. However, his eyes were kept for study, and, a century and a half later, scientists used the tissue samples to identify the gene for colour blindness.

The term 'pedigree' refers to the record of an organism's ancestry. Pedigree charts are diagrams that are constructed to show biological relationships. In genetics, they are used to show how a trait can pass from one generation to the next. Used in this way for humans, a pedigree chart is similar to a family tree, complete with parents, grandparents, aunts, uncles, and cousins.

To build such a chart, symbols are used to represent people. Preparing a pedigree chart helps prepare Punnett grids for predicting the probable outcome for the next generation.

Example 1: Huntington's disease

Huntington's disease (Huntington's chorea) is caused by a dominant allele that we will refer to by the letter **H**. This genetic condition causes severely debilitating nerve damage but the symptoms do not show until the person is about 40 years old. As a result, someone who has the gene for Huntington's disease may not know it for certain until they have started a career and possibly started a family.

The symptoms of Huntington's disease include difficulty walking, speaking, and holding objects. Within a few years of starting the symptoms, the person loses complete control of his or her muscles and dies an early death. Because it is dominant, all it takes is one **H** allele in a person's genetic makeup to cause the condition.

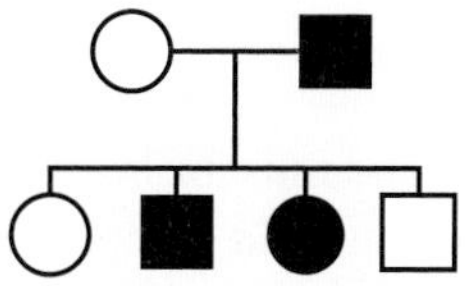

Figure 3.39 This is a pedigree chart showing members of a family affected by Huntington's disease.

1 Give a full description of the six individuals in Figure 3.39, saying who is affected and who is not.
2 State the genotype for each individual.

Solutions

1 The symbols indicate that the unaffected members of the family are the mother, the first child (a girl) and the fourth child (a boy). Those who are affected are the father, the second child (a boy) and the third child (a girl).
2 To work out if the father is **HH** or **Hh**, consider the fact that some of his children do not have the trait. This proves that he must have given one **h** to each of them. Hence, he can only be **Hh** and not **HH**. The mother is not affected so she must be **hh**. This is also true for the first daughter and the last son. Since the mother always gives an **h**, the two middle children must have at least one **h**, but, because they are affected, they are **Hh**.

Example 2: co-dominance in flower colour

Co-dominance in certain flowers can create more than two colours, so a pedigree chart can help keep track of how the offspring got their phenotypes. For example, in purebred snapdragon flowers, sometimes white × red = pink.

The system of letters for showing colour in snapdragon flowers uses a prefix **C**, which refers to the gene that codes for flower colour, plus a superscript, which refers to the specific colour, **R** (red) or **W** (white).

These are the symbols used in pedigree charts.

○ empty circle = female

❑ empty square = male

● filled-in circle = a female who possesses the trait being studied

■ filled-in square = a male who possesses the trait being studied

| vertical line = the relationship parents and offspring

− horizontal line between a man and a woman = they are the parents who had the offspring

So the alleles for co-dominant flower colour are:

- C^R for red flowers
- C^W for white flowers.

The genotypes and their phenotypes are:

- $C^R C^R$ makes red flowers
- $C^W C^W$ makes white flowers
- $C^R C^W$ makes pink flowers.

For co-dominant traits, grey is used in pedigree charts rather than black or white.

1 Using the pedigree chart below, state the genotypes for all the plants A to K.
2 What evidence is there that genetic characteristics can sometimes skip a generation?

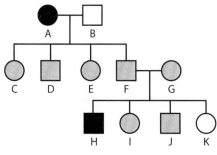

Figure 3.40 This pedigree chart shows how pink flowers can arise in purebred snapdragon plants. Black shapes represent snapdragon plants with red flowers, white shapes represent white-flowered plants, and grey shapes represent plants with pink flowers.

Solutions

1 A and H produce red flowers and must be homozygous for red, $C^R C^R$, because any other combination would give pink or white. B and K produce white flowers and must be homozygous for white, $C^W C^W$, because any other combination would give pink or red. C to G as well as I and J are pink and must be heterozygous, $C^R C^W$, because they have one of each allele from each parent plant.

2 It would be impossible for either the colour red or the colour white to be in the middle generation in this diagram. These colours skip a generation and show up again in the last row.

Colour variation in snapdragon flowers.

Table 3.8 A summary of different types of alleles

Type of genetic cross	Example	Associated alleles
Standard monohybrid cross following Darwinian rules of genetics	Albinism (recessive)	**A** or **a**
Multiple alleles showing co-dominance	ABO blood type	I^A, I^B, **i** (co-dominance shown in AB blood type $I^A I^B$)
Sex-linked traits showing a different distribution in males than in females	Haemophilia (gene only present on the X chromosome)	X^H, X^h, **Y** (notice how the Y does not carry a letter H or h).

Some possible causes of mutations, genetic diseases, and cancer

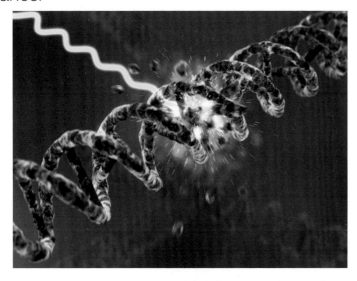

An artist's conception of how DNA can be damaged by radiation.

In principle, DNA is not supposed to be modified during the lifetime of an individual. Normally, the code should be preserved. However, there are exceptions, and exposure to radiation or to carcinogens (cancer-causing chemicals) can sometimes modify the code and cause serious health threats.

NATURE OF SCIENCE

When and how did we find out that X-rays were not a safe and healthy way of performing prenatal (during pregnancy) examinations?

Dr Alice Stewart was particularly talented with numbers. She knew the power of statistical analysis in determining correlation and was horrified by what she found when studying the records of infants dying of cancer. Her statistical analysis in the early 1950s demonstrated that children whose mothers had prenatal X-rays were twice as likely to die of cancer than children whose mothers did not have prenatal X-rays. Although the studies were scientifically sound and the statistics were reliable, doctors did not accept them at first and continued to use X-rays on pregnant women for more than two decades. Stewart was criticized for her work and had trouble getting funding for subsequent projects. Only in the 1970s did other scientists repeat studies similar to hers, with the same results, and finally X-rays were replaced with non-radioactive techniques such as ultrasound sonograms.

What does this case study reveal about the nature of science? And about the importance of repeatability and verifiability? What prevented doctors from taking action immediately and stopping the use of X-rays on pregnant women in the 1950s? Often people use expressions like 'the numbers don't lie' when talking about statistics. Is this always the case? Looking back, it might be tempting to say that doctors using X-rays on pregnant women after Stewart's report were acting unethically: what do you think?

Although it is beyond the scope of this chapter, it is interesting to note that the science of epigenetics challenges the idea that genetics is unchangeable during the lifetime of an individual. In some cases, environmental factors during an organism's lifetime can have an influence in turning on or turning off certain genes.

Other causes of cancer and disease

Diseases such as cancer can sometimes be caused by mutagenic chemicals. Chemistry teachers will tell you that the list of products they are allowed to use with their students today is different compared with when they were students: products such as benzene, which were commonly used in laboratories in the past, are now restricted or forbidden because of their cancer-causing or mutagenic properties. Such chemicals, in high concentrations and with long exposure times, can cause mutations and cancer just as radioactivity can: in a silent and invisible way.

Should we be worried? Toxic things in our environment are regulated by government standards. Normally, as long as the concentrations and exposure times are respected, the danger to your health is very limited. The problem is, sometimes people do not know or do not follow the recommendations for the products they use. Also, companies often test a product alone but not necessarily in conjunction with other products. A pesticide that a woman puts on her vegetable garden may not cause cancer in the doses she inhales or gets on her skin, but if she smokes and she works at the radiology department in the local hospital, and she uses a cell phone many hours a day, and she goes to the tanning salon regularly, and she lives in a city with severe air pollution … Could all those repeated non-lethal daily doses of possible cancer-causing things add up? Or compound each other? These are complex questions that require conclusive evidence in order to be able to say one way or the other.

Marie Curie, who discovered the radioactive elements polonium and radium, did not benefit from the safety standards we have today and died at the age of 66 from her exposure to radioactivity.

DNA and radiation

As the early experimenters with radium found out, radioactivity can cause cancer. Not knowing of the dangers when she was studying radium, the pioneer Marie Curie, the first person to win two Nobel prizes, carried samples of radioactive materials around with her, and kept them on laboratory tables without any precautions. Not surprisingly, she died of leukaemia, and her laboratories, which you can visit in Paris, still show radioactive contamination today.

The world saw the terrifying effects of radiation poisoning on people when the city of Hiroshima was the target of the first atomic bomb used in warfare in August 1945. It is estimated that 100 000 people died at its impact or shortly after, but it is difficult to estimate how many died later from the effects of radiation in the city.

When radiation hits a DNA molecule, it can sometimes knock one or more base pairs out of place, modifying the genetic code. This causes a mutation that, as we have seen, can sometimes be benign (not harmful), but at other times it can be harmful to an organism. When the DNA mutation leads to cancer, as happened to Marie Curie, the organism's health is in jeopardy. However, Marie Curie's husband, Pierre Curie, did not die of cancer, but of something equally dangerous: he slipped in the street and was run over by a horse-drawn carriage in Paris in 1906.

Besides nuclear bombs, another source of radiation is nuclear power plants. As long as they are safe and secure, there should not be any risk of radiation leaking out into the environment. There have been some cases in recent history, however, that have revealed the potential dangers of nuclear power plants: Chernobyl in 1986 and Fukushima in 2011 are two such examples. In both situations, radioactive material was leaked out into the environment and the zones around the out-of-commission power plants were evacuated of all human populations within a radius of tens of kilometres.

Ecology experts studying the area around Chernobyl.

Ecologists are studying the area around Chernobyl to see how nature has responded to the presence of radiation. In some instances, the scientists have been pleasantly surprised to find that nature seems to be doing fine despite the dangerously high radiation levels. In other instances, they have confirmed the presence of mutations in the plants and animals that have colonized the abandoned zone. Cancer studies in the peripheral zones where people are allowed to live, beyond 30 km from the shut-down Chernobyl reactor, suggest that there has been an increase in cancer frequencies. The nuclear power industry has made an effort to isolate the abandoned nuclear power plant at Chernobyl by encasing it in a dome of cement. The hope is that the cement will be thick enough to stop the radiation from continuing to escape into the environment.

Section summary

- Mendel's experiments with pea plants revealed that the inheritance of genes follows certain patterns.
- Haploid gametes resulting from meiosis contain single alleles of each gene that were separated during anaphase II. These alleles will be reunited with alleles from the other parent when a diploid zygote is formed.
- When two alleles are matched up, several things can happen to the phenotype: dominant genes can be masked by recessive genes thereby not allowing one of the parent's traits to show, or co-dominant genes can have an additive effect.
- Genes on the sex chromosomes are said to be sex-linked genes and conditions such as colour-blindness are more common in males than in females because its gene is found on the X chromosome.
- Genes found on any of the other 22 pairs of autosomal chromosomes are referred to as autosomal genes and many genetic diseases are autosomal traits.
- Mutations and cancers can be caused if DNA is modified by radiation.

Exercises

11 Explain why more men are affected by colour blindness than women.

12 Using the C^R and C^W alleles for co-dominance in snapdragon flower colour, show how two plants could have some white-flowered offspring, some pink-flowered offspring, and some red-flowered offspring within one generation.

	X^H	Y
X^H	$X^H X^H$	$X^H Y$
X^h	$X^H X^h$	$X^h Y$

13 Draw a pedigree chart of the two generations described in question 12.

14 Look at the grid to the left showing the chances that a couple's children might have haemophilia.

  (a) State the genotype of the mother and father.
  (b) State the possible genotypes of the girls and boys.
  (c) State the phenotypes of the girls and boys.
  (d) Who are the carriers in this family?
  (e) What are the chances that the parents' next child will be a haemophiliac?

3.5 Genetic modification and biotechnology

Understandings:

- Gel electrophoresis is used to separate proteins or fragments of DNA according to size.
- PCR can be used to amplify small amounts of DNA.
- DNA profiling involves comparison of DNA.
- Genetic modification is carried out by gene transfer between species.
- Clones are groups of genetically identical organisms, derived from a single original parent cell.
- Many plant species and some animal species have natural methods of cloning.
- Animals can be cloned at the embryo stage by breaking up the embryo into more than one group of cells.
- Methods have been developed for cloning adult animals using differentiated cells.

Applications and skills:

- Application: Use of DNA profiling in paternity and forensic investigations.
- Application: Gene transfer to bacteria using plasmids makes use of restriction endonucleases and DNA ligase.
- Application: Assessment of the potential risks and benefits associated with genetic modification of crops.
- Application: Production of cloned embryos produced by somatic-cell nuclear transfer.
- Skill: Design of an experiment to assess one factor affecting the rooting of stem cuttings.
- Skill: Analysis of examples of DNA profiles.
- Skill: Analysis of data on risks to monarch butterflies of Bt crops.

  ### Guidance
  - *Students should be able to deduce whether or not a man could be the father of a child from the pattern of bands on a DNA profile.*
  - *Dolly can be used as an example of somatic-cell transfer.*
  - *A plant species should be chosen for rooting experiments that forms roots readily in water or a solid medium.*

Exploring DNA

DNA is at the very core of what gives animals and plants their uniqueness. We are now going to look at the astounding genetic techniques, developed during the past few decades, that enable scientists to explore and manipulate DNA. These include:

- copying DNA in a laboratory – the polymerase chain reaction (PCR)
- using DNA to reveal its owner's identity – DNA profiling
- mapping DNA by finding where every A, T, C, and G is – gene sequencing, including the Human Genome Project
- cutting and pasting genes to make new organisms – gene transfer
- cloning cells and animals.

These techniques offer new hope for obtaining treatments and vaccines for diseases; for creating new plants for farmers; for freeing wrongly convicted people from prison by proving their innocence with DNA tests.

Techniques such as gene transfer and cloning have sparked heated debates. Is it morally and ethically acceptable to manipulate nature in this way? Are the big biotech companies investing huge sums of money into this research to help their fellow citizens, or are they just in it for the economic profit? Concerning cloning and stem cell research, is it morally and ethically acceptable to create human embryos solely for scientific research?

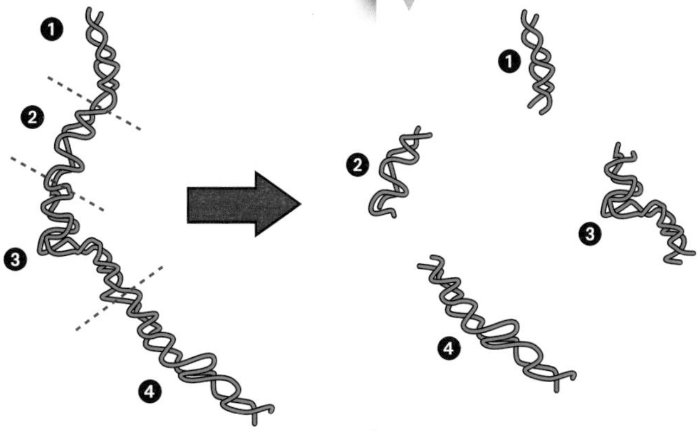

Part of being a responsible citizen is making informed decisions relating to these difficult questions. It is not just technical complexity that makes these questions difficult, it is also because we have never had to face them before.

Figure 3.41 A DNA strand can be cut into several pieces of varying size.

Gel electrophoresis

This laboratory technique is used to separate fragments of DNA in an effort to identify its origin. Enzymes are used to chop up the long filaments of DNA into varying sizes of fragments.

The DNA fragments are placed into small wells (holes) in the gel, which are aligned along one end. The gel is exposed to an electric current, positive on one side and negative on the other.

The effect is that the biggest, heaviest, and least charged particles do not move easily through the gel, so they get stuck very close to the wells they were in at the beginning. The smallest, least massive, and most charged particles pass through the gel to the other side with little difficulty. Intermediate particles are distributed in between. In the end, the fragments leave a banded pattern of DNA like the one shown in the photo overleaf.

As seen in Figure 3.42, gel electrophoresis can stop there or a hybridization probe can be added. A probe, in this case for sickle cell disease, is a known sequence of a complementary DNA sequence that binds with a DNA strand in the gel, revealing the presence of the gene we are interested in.

Figure 3.42 Gel electrophoresis is used to separate DNA fragments so that they can be analysed.

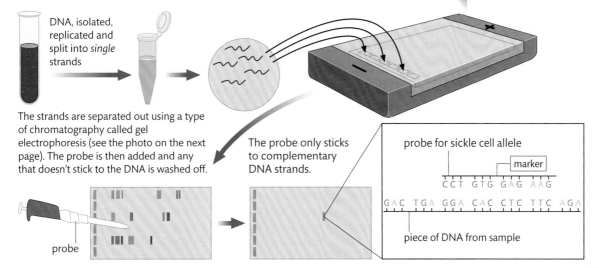

DNA, isolated, replicated and split into *single* strands

The strands are separated out using a type of chromatography called gel electrophoresis (see the photo on the next page). The probe is then added and any that doesn't stick to the DNA is washed off.

The probe only sticks to complementary DNA strands.

probe for sickle cell allele

marker

C C T   G T G   G A G   A A G

G A C   T G A   G G A   C A C   C T C   T T C   A G A

piece of DNA from sample

probe

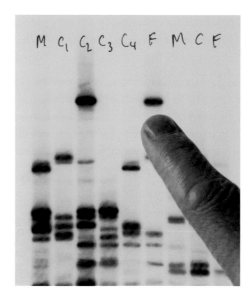

This autoradiogram (or autoradiograph) shows banded lines that were formed from nine different DNA samples during gel electrophoresis. The black traces are left by the radioactivity of the materials used in marking the DNA samples.

CHALLENGE YOURSELF

11 Based on the evidence shown in the autoradiogram to the right, deduce which child (C_1, C_2, or C_3) is most likely to be the child of the father whose track is being pointed to (F). The mother is in the first track on the far left. Justify your answer.

PCR: how to make lots of copies of DNA

Polymerase chain reaction (PCR)

PCR is a laboratory technique using a machine called a thermocycler that takes a very small quantity of DNA and copies all the nucleic acids in it to make millions of copies of the DNA (see Figure 3.43). PCR is used to solve the problem of how to get enough DNA to be able to analyse it.

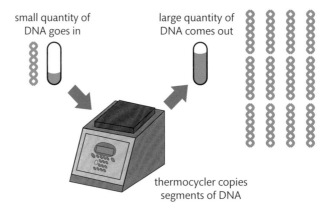

small quantity of DNA goes in

large quantity of DNA comes out

thermocycler copies segments of DNA

Figure 3.43 Analysis is impossible with the DNA from just one or a few cells. PCR is a way of ensuring that enough DNA for analysis can be generated.

When collecting DNA from the scene of a crime or from a cheek smear, often only a very limited number of cells are available. By using PCR, forensics experts or research technicians can obtain millions of copies of the DNA in just a few hours. Such quantities are large enough to analyse, notably using gel electrophoresis.

DNA profiling

The process of matching an unknown sample of DNA with a known sample to see if they correspond is called DNA profiling. This is also sometimes referred to as DNA fingerprinting because there are some similarities with identifying fingerprints, but the techniques are very different.

If, after separation by gel electrophoresis, the pattern of bands formed by two samples of DNA fragments are identical, it means that both most have come from the same individual. If the patterns are similar, it means that the two individuals are probably related.

Applications of DNA profiling

DNA profiling can be used in paternity suits when the identity of someone's biological father needs to be known for legal reasons.

At a crime scene, forensics specialists can collect samples such as blood or semen, which contain DNA. Gel electrophoresis is used to compare the collected DNA with that of suspects. If they match, the suspect has a lot of explaining to do. If there is no match, the suspect is probably not the person the police are looking for. Criminal cases are sometimes reopened many years after a judgment was originally made, in order to consider new DNA profiling results. In the USA, this has led to the liberation of many individuals who had been sent to jail for crimes they did not commit.

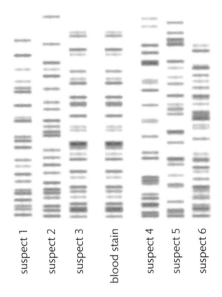

CHALLENGE YOURSELF

12 Using the DNA profiles below from six suspects, can you identify which one matches the DNA profile of the blood stain found at the crime scene?

These seven tracks were produced by gel electrophoresis to allow investigators to analyse and match DNA samples.

DNA profiling is used in other circumstances too, for example in studies of ecosystems, when scientists use DNA samples taken from birds, whales, and other organisms to clarify relationships. This has helped establish a better understanding of social relationships, migrating patterns, and nesting habits, for example. In addition, the study of DNA in the biosphere has given new credibility to the ideas of evolution: DNA evidence can often reinforce previous evidence of common ancestry based on anatomical similarities between species.

How DNA profiles are analysed

In the photo on page 168, showing gel electrophoresis of nine samples of DNA, the line marked C_2 (child number 2) and the one being pointed to, F (father), show similarities in their banding patterns. However, the children marked C_1, C_3, and C_4 do not show many similarities.

From this DNA evidence, it should be clear that person F is much more likely to be the father of child number 2 than of any of the other children. Similar techniques are used to analyse the similarities and differences between DNA collected at a crime scene and DNA samples taken from suspects.

TOK
- How do you think a child would feel if she were to find out from DNA profiling that her father was not her biological father?
- How would a man feel if he found out he was not his child's father?
- What effect would such a result have on the relationships between siblings or between spouses?
- What kind of emotions might someone feel after spending 18 years in prison, and then being freed thanks to a DNA test?

The techniques have been perfected to a point where it is possible to determine the identity of someone by examining cells found in the traces of saliva left on the back of a postage stamp on a letter.

 TOK How do we decide when evidence is reliable or not? Often when DNA evidence is used in a courtroom trial, it has a certain credibility as scientific fact, and yet we know from our own experience in lab work that there is a degree of error in any procedure. Whether it be in the laboratory or in a courtroom, it is difficult to imagine evidence that can be considered 100% certain. When a scientist comes up with new evidence, old theories can be challenged or even overturned. But how do we decide which evidence is to be accepted and which evidence is to be discarded?

Genetic modification: gene transfer between species

Gene transfer

The technique of taking a gene out of one organism (the donor organism, e.g. a fish) and placing it in another organism (the host organism, e.g. a tomato) is a genetic engineering procedure called gene transfer. Just such a transfer was done to make tomatoes more resistant to cold and frost.

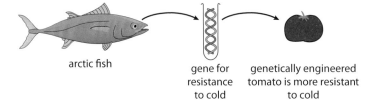

arctic fish

gene for resistance to cold

genetically engineered tomato is more resistant to cold

Figure 3.44 Genetically engineering a frost-resistant tomato.

It is possible to put one species' genes into another's genetic makeup because DNA is universal: as you will recall (Section 2.6), all known living organisms use the bases A, T, C, and G to code for proteins. The codons they form always code for the same amino acids, so transferred DNA codes for the same polypeptide chain in the host organism as it did in the donor organism. In the example above, proteins used by fish to resist the icy temperatures of arctic waters are now produced by the modified tomatoes to make them more resistant to cold.

Another example of gene transfer is found in Bt corn, which has been genetically engineered to produce toxins that kill the bugs that attack it. The gene, as well as the name, comes from a soil bacterium, *Bacillus thuringiensis*, which has the ability to produce a protein that is fatal to the larvae of certain crop-eating pests.

Pests such as this corn earworm, *Helicoverpa zea*, are responsible for reduced yields in traditional corn crops.

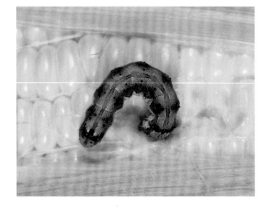

Figure 3.45 Genetically engineering a pest-resistant corn.

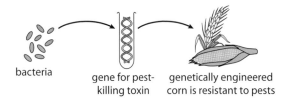

bacteria

gene for pest-killing toxin

genetically engineered corn is resistant to pests

The manipulation of genes raises some challenging questions. For many of these questions, there is not enough conclusive scientific data to reach a satisfactory answer.

TOK

- Is it ethically acceptable to alter an organism's genetic integrity?
- If the organism did not have that gene in the first place, could there be a good reason for its absence?
- Why are people so worried about this new technology? In selective breeding, thousands of genes are mixed and matched. With genetically modified organisms (GMOs), only one gene is changed. Is that not less risky and dangerous than artificial selection?
- Would strict vegetarians be able to eat a tomato that has a fish gene in it?
- Does research involving genetically modified (GM) animals add a whole new level to animal cruelty and suffering in laboratories?
- If Bt crops kill insects, what happens to the local ecosystem that relies on the insects for food or pollination?

Clones

Cutting, copying, and pasting genes

Although the laboratory techniques are complex, the concepts are not difficult.

Cutting and pasting DNA

The 'scissors' used for cutting base sequences are enzymes. Restriction enzymes called endonucleases find and recognize a specific sequence of base pairs along the DNA molecule. Some can locate target sequences that are sets of four base pairs, others locate sets of six pairs. The endonucleases cut the DNA at specified points. If both the beginning and the end of a gene are cut, the gene is released and can be removed from the donor organism. For pasting genes, the enzyme used is called DNA ligase. It recognizes the parts of the base sequences that are supposed to be linked together, called the sticky ends, and attaches them.

Copying DNA (DNA cloning)

Copying DNA is more complex, because a host cell is needed in addition to the cutting and pasting enzymes described above. Although yeast cells can be used as host cells, the most popular candidate in genetic engineering is the bacterium *Escherichia coli*.

enzyme and a
strand of DNA

enzyme recognises
specific sequence

DNA cut in two

Figure 3.46 Endonuclease cuts DNA at a specific point.

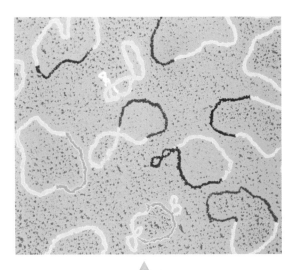

This is a false-colour electron micrograph of plasmids.

Like other prokaryotes, most of the genetic information for *E. coli* is in the bacterium's single chromosome. However, some DNA is found in structures called plasmids. Plasmids are small circles of extra copies of DNA floating around inside the cell's cytoplasm. To copy a gene, it must be glued into a plasmid.

To do this, a plasmid is removed from the host cell and cut open using a restriction endonuclease. The gene to be copied is placed inside the open plasmid. This process is sometimes called gene splicing. The gene is pasted into the plasmid using DNA ligase. The plasmid is now called a recombinant plasmid and it can be used as a vector, a tool for introducing a new gene into an organism's genetic makeup.

Figure 3.47 Gene splicing involves introducing a gene into a plasmid, and it is one of the techniques used in genetic engineering to make a genetically modified organism.

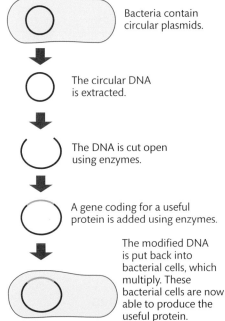

Bacteria contain circular plasmids.

The circular DNA is extracted.

The DNA is cut open using enzymes.

A gene coding for a useful protein is added using enzymes.

The modified DNA is put back into bacterial cells, which multiply. These bacterial cells are now able to produce the useful protein.

In the final step needed for copying (or cloning) the gene, the vector is placed inside the host bacterium and the bacterium is given its ideal conditions in which to grow and proliferate. This is done by putting the bacterium into a bioreactor, a vat of nutritious liquid kept at a warm temperature.

Not only does the host cell make copies of the gene as it reproduces, but because the gene is now in its genetic makeup, the modified *E. coli* cell expresses the gene and synthesizes whatever protein the gene codes for. This process has been used successfully to get *E. coli* to make human insulin, a protein needed to treat diabetes (see Section 2.7). The older technique for obtaining insulin involves extracting it from cow and pig carcasses from the meat industry, but this has caused allergy problems. Using recombinant human DNA avoids that problem.

Genetically modified organisms

A genetically modified organism (GMO) is one that has had an artificial genetic change made using the techniques of genetic engineering, such as gene transfer or recombinant DNA as described above. One of the main reasons for producing a GMO is so that it can be more competitive in food production. Another common reason is to 'teach' a bacterium to produce proteins that are useful in medical applications, as we saw with insulin.

Transgenic plants

The simplest kind of genetically modified (GM) food is one in which an undesirable gene has been removed. In some cases, another, more desirable, gene is put in its place, while in other cases only the introduction of a new gene is needed, no DNA has to be removed.

Whichever technique is applied, the end result is either that the organism no longer shows the undesired trait or that it shows a trait that genetic engineers want. The first commercial example of a GM food was the Flavr Savr tomato. It was first sold in the USA in 1994, and had been genetically modified to delay the ripening and rotting process so that it would stay fresher longer. Although it was an ingenious idea, the company lost so much money from the project that it was abandoned a few years later.

Another species of tomato was modified by a bioengineering company to make it more tolerant to higher levels of salt in the soil. This made it easier to grow in areas with high salinity. One of the claims of the biotech industry is that GM foods will help solve the problem of world hunger, by allowing farmers to grow foods in various, otherwise unsuitable, environments. Critics point out that the problem of hunger in the world is one of food distribution, not food production.

Another plant of potential interest to the developing world is a genetically modified rice plant that has been engineered to produce beta carotene in the rice grains. The aim is that the people who eat this rice will not be deficient in vitamin A (the body uses beta carotene to form vitamin A).

Transgenic animals

One way of genetically engineering an animal is to get it to produce a substance that can be used in medical treatments. Consider the problem faced by people with haemophilia. The reason their blood does not clot is because they lack a protein called factor IX. If such people could be supplied with factor IX, their problem would be solved. The least expensive way of producing large amounts of factor IX is to use transgenic sheep. If a gene that codes for the production of factor IX is associated with the genetic information for milk production in a female sheep, she will produce that protein in her milk.

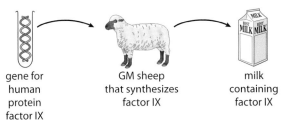

gene for human protein factor IX → GM sheep that synthesizes factor IX → milk containing factor IX

Figure 3.48 Producing factor IX using a transgenic sheep.

In the future, a wide variety of genetic modifications may be possible, perhaps inserting genes to make animals more resistant to parasites, to make sheep produce pre-dyed wool of any chosen colour, to produce prize-winning show dogs, faster racehorses … The possibilities seem almost boundless, and it is difficult to imagine what the future might be like.

Natural methods of cloning

Nature invented cloning long before humans did. Certain plants, such as strawberry plants, can send out horizontal structures to allow a new strawberry plant to grow a short distance from the original plant. The new plant will be an exact genetic copy of the first one, because only one parent was involved and no meiosis and fertilization was used to add variety to the genetic makeup of the plant.

It is possible to 'clone' a strawberry plant by asexual reproduction. The stems and leaves planted in the smaller pot will grow into a new plant.

If planted in the ground, a potato will grow into a new plant. The plant will be genetically identical to (will be a clone of) the original potato plant. This is an advantage for the plant, because there is no need to rely on pollen to fertilize the flowers, but it can be a disadvantage, because if all potato plants in a population are clones, it means that not only do they have the same good qualities, they also have the same weaknesses. If the population is attacked by a pathogen such as potato blight, it could wipe out the population. Historians will tell you of the dangers of this, notably in Ireland in the middle of the 19th century, when 1 million people died of starvation. Of course, historians will also tell you that there were other causes; history is complex, but the potato blight was a major factor in the famine.

A hydra is capable of natural cloning called budding.

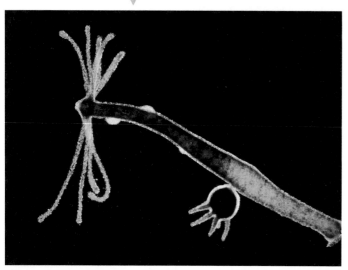

What about animals: can they clone themselves the way plants sometimes do? Although this is extremely rare, and exceptional, among certain invertebrates, one animal that is capable of reproducing asexually by making clones of itself is the hydra, *Hydra vulgaris*. This freshwater organism is in the same phylum as sea jellies, sea anemones, and coral polyps. If food sources are plentiful, small buds will form on its body, develop into adults, and break off to form new, genetically identical, hydra. This process is called budding, and you may have observed this in electron micrographs of yeast cells. Similar to the plant examples (strawberries and potatoes), hydra are also capable of sexual reproduction.

Investigating the factors that affect the rooting of stem cuttings

Design an experiment to assess one factor affecting the rooting of stem cuttings. The basic idea is to cut a few centimetres of stem from a healthy plant and place it into an appropriate medium either sticking up or having it lying flat. Typical plants to try are impatiens, begonias, jade, or African violet.

Be sure to do some research to find a plant species that forms roots easily in either water or a solid medium. Take into account your geographical location and try to find plants that can be acquired locally and that will be in season in your area at the time you are carrying out the experiment.

Some possibilities to consider for your designed investigation are:

- the application of hormones such as ethylene, auxin, or gibberellins (be aware of the fact that certain types of auxins can be destroyed by light or by soil bacteria)

- abiotic factors such as light, temperature, and water (note that for light, not only could the intensity be changed, but the duration could be altered to simulate long days/short nights or short days/long nights)

- the medium in which the roots form, such as soil, sand, agar, or water

- the presence/absence of leaves on the stem

- horticultural techniques, such as wounding or girdling.

Once you carry out your experiment, any successful new plants that grow will be clones of the original plant.

There are ethical and legal considerations to consider: in certain circumstances, it is illegal to copy a plant in this way. Plants bought at a garden centre or nursery are often the result of many years of work on the part of horticulturalists and they can have intellectual property rights on their creative work. It could be argued that the purpose of your cloning exercise is educational and not for profit, but still, it is best to consider the intellectual property issues involved before choosing your plant.

Animals cloned from embryos

The definition of a clone is a group of genetically identical organisms, or a group of cells artificially derived from a single parent. In either case, the resulting cells or organisms were made using laboratory techniques. In farming, clones have been made for decades by regenerating plant material or by allowing an *in vitro* fertilized egg to divide to make copies of itself. When cloning happens naturally in animals (including humans), identical twins are produced.

The first evidence of an experimental attempt to make artificial clones was performed by Hans Dreisch in the 1890s with sea urchin embryos. He was able to separate cells from a single sea urchin embryo and grow two identical embryos. The aim of his experiment was not to create clones but, looking back, we can say that he serendipitously invented a new technique. Serendipity is a good concept to understand in science. It refers to an unexpected but positive discovery and happens when someone is looking for the answer to one question and accidentally finds the answer to a completely different question.

With the correct laboratory equipment, it is possible to separate cells from a growing embryo of an animal, and place the separated cells in the uterus of a female of that species and get artificial twins, triplets, quadruplets, etc., depending on how many cells were separated. Remember that embryonic cells are undifferentiated cells so there is nothing exceptionally astounding about this kind of cloning. Remember, nature has been doing this for a long time by forming identical twins.

Animal clones from adult cells

Clones and cloning

Until recently, cloning was only possible using genetic information from a fertilized egg cell. After dividing many times, some of the cells will specialize into muscle cells, others into nerves, others into skin, and so on, until a foetus forms. For a long time, it was thought that once a cell has gone through differentiation, it cannot be used to make a clone. But then there was Dolly.

This is Dolly with Ian Wilmut, a member of her cloning team.

Cloning using a differentiated animal cell

In 1996, a sheep by the name of Dolly was born. She was the first clone whose genetic material did not originate from an egg cell. Here is how researchers at the Roslin Institute in Scotland produced Dolly (see Figure 3.49).

1   From the original donor sheep to be cloned, a somatic cell (non-gamete cell) from the udder was collected and cultured. The nucleus was removed from a cultured cell.

2   An unfertilized egg was collected from another sheep and its nucleus was removed.

3   Using an electrical current, the egg cell and the nucleus from the cultured somatic cell were fused together.

4   The new cell developed *in vitro* in a similar way to a zygote, and started to form an embryo.

5   The embryo was placed in the womb of a surrogate mother sheep.

6   The embryo developed normally.

7   Dolly was born, and was presented to the world as a clone of the original donor sheep.

This kind of cloning is called reproductive cloning because it makes an entire individual. The specific technique of reproductive cloning is called somatic cell nuclear transfer, because it uses a cell that is not an egg cell (therefore it is a somatic cell), and it has had its nucleus removed and replaced by another nucleus.

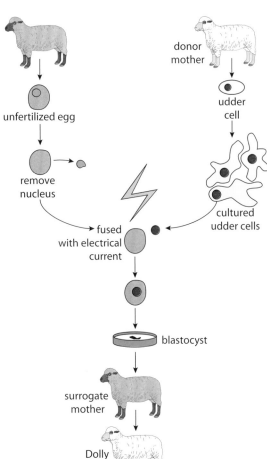

donor mother

unfertilized egg

udder cell

remove nucleus

cultured udder cells

fused with electrical current

blastocyst

surrogate mother

Dolly

Figure 3.49 The step-by-step process of how the clone Dolly was made.

Cloning using undifferentiated cells

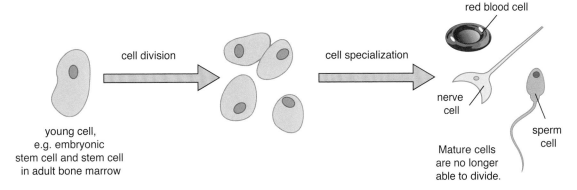

young cell,
e.g. embryonic
stem cell and stem cell
in adult bone marrow

cell division

cell specialization

red blood cell

nerve cell

Mature cells are no longer able to divide.

sperm cell

Figure 3.50 How undifferentiated embryonic stem cells could be cultured and grown into stem cells for research purposes. These steps can be repeated, providing researchers with a valuable resource.

In some cases, scientists are not interested in making an organism but simply in making copies of cells. This second type of cloning is called therapeutic cloning, and its aim is to develop cells that have not yet gone through the process of differentiation. As the first technique in this area involved using embryos, the cells are referred to as embryonic stem cells, and the branch of laboratory work that investigates therapeutic cloning is called stem cell research.

Ethical issues surrounding therapeutic cloning

Because therapeutic cloning starts with the production of human embryos, it raises fundamental issues of right and wrong. Is it ethically acceptable to generate a new human embryo for the sole purpose of medical research? In nature, embryos are created only for reproduction, and many people believe that using them for experiments is unnatural and wrong.

However, the use of embryonic stem cells has led to major breakthroughs in the understanding of human biology. What was once pure fiction is coming closer and closer to becoming an everyday reality, thanks to stem cell research. Some of the aims of current research are to be able to grow:

• skin to repair a serious burn
• new heart muscle to repair an ailing heart
• new kidney tissue to rebuild a failing kidney.

With very rare exceptions, the vast majority of researchers and medical professionals are against the idea of reproductive cloning in humans. However, there is a growing popularity for therapeutic cloning because the potential of stem cell research is so enticing.

The idea of cloning often provokes strong negative reactions from people, especially when the only information they have comes from science fiction or horror films.

TOK

When making ethical decisions about what is good and bad, or right and wrong, it is important to be as well informed as possible.

In dealing with the ethical issues of cloning, it should be stressed that there are two distinct forms of cloning:

• reproductive cloning, making copies of entire organisms
• therapeutic cloning, making copies of embryonic stem cells.

Some people think that both are unacceptable, others think both are fine, and some are in favour of one but not the other. Where do you stand?

Section summary

- In recent decades, biotech laboratories have invented ingenious methods for cutting, copying, pasting, and analysing DNA sequences to rewrite an organism's genetic code or learn about connections and uses for genes.

- PCR, used for copying DNA sequences, and gel electrophoresis, used for analysing DNA or protein sequences, are just two such techniques that have revolutionized our understanding of the code of life.

- By comparing DNA sequences, it is possible to identify the organism or individual to whom a fragment of DNA belongs. This technique, DNA profiling, can be used in criminal investigations, paternity suits, or ecological studies.

- Because the DNA code is universal, genes can be transferred from one individual to another or one species to another. This is observed in nature when bacteria perform gene transfer, or in the laboratory when one gene is inserted into the genome of another species (e.g. from a bacterium to corn, to make Bt corn).

- Natural cloning occurs in plants (e.g. asexual reproduction of potatoes) and in some invertebrate animals (e.g. budding of the hydra). A clone is an identical genetic copy of an organism. Only in very recent decades have researchers been able to clone adult animals (such as Dolly the sheep) from differentiated cells. Such experiments raise ethical issues that society needs to debate.

To learn more about gene transfer, go to the hotlinks site, search for the title or ISBN, and click on Chapter 3: Section 3.5.

Exercises

15 Explain why PCR is necessary.

16 Explain the central ethical issue concerning stem cell research.

17 Justify whether the benefits outweigh the risks in genetically modifying plants and animals.

18 Look at the foods in your house. Are food labels today effective at indicating whether or not the food is genetically modified? Justify your answer.

Practice questions

1 What conclusion can be made from the following evidence from an analysis of DNA fragments?

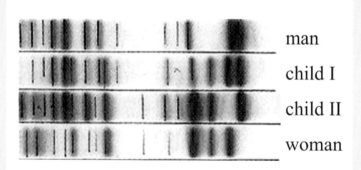

A Both children are related to both parents.

B Child I is related to the man but child II is not.

C Both children are unrelated to either of the parents.

D Child II is related to the man but child I is not.

(Total 1 mark)

2 What evidence is given in the pedigree chart below to establish that the condition is caused by a dominant allele?

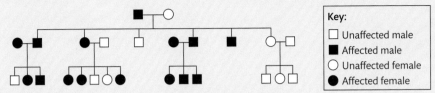

Key:
☐ Unaffected male
■ Affected male
○ Unaffected female
● Affected female

A Two unaffected parents have unaffected children.

B Two affected parents have affected children.

C An affected parent and an unaffected parent have affected children.

D Two affected parents have an unaffected child.

(Total 1 mark)

3 Which of the following is an inherited disease that is due to a base substitution mutation in a gene?

A Trisomy 21

B Sickle cell anaemia

C AIDS

D Type II diabetes

(Total 1 mark)

4 Outline some of the outcomes of the sequencing of the human genome. *(Total 3 marks)*

5 Describe the role of sex chromosomes in the control of gender and inheritance of haemophilia.

(Total 7 marks)

6 What does the karyotype below correspond to?

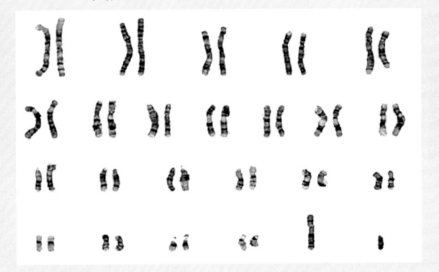

A A normal male.

B A normal female.

C A female with Down syndrome.

D A male with Down syndrome.

(Total 1 mark)

7 Describe the inheritance of ABO blood groups. *(Total 9 marks)*

8 Explain why carriers of sex-linked (X-linked) genes must be heterozygous. *(Total 2 marks)*

04 Ecology

Essential ideas

4.1 The continued survival of living organisms, including humans, depends on sustainable communities

4.2 Ecosystems require a continuous supply of energy to fuel life processes and to replace energy lost as heat.

4.3 Continued availability of carbon in ecosystems depends on carbon cycling.

4.4 Concentrations of gases in the atmosphere affect climates experienced at Earth's surface.

This colourful vegetation and blue sky are a stark contrast to what we would see on the surface of our inhospitable neighbours, the Moon, Mars, or Venus. Our planet shows complex interactions between the atmosphere, water, and living organisms.

Could you live on the Moon or on another planet such as Mars? If you had to make a list of what you would need, there would be some obvious things, such as liquid water, food, and oxygen gas to breathe. But is it possible to maintain life for a long period of time outside established ecosystems?

For example, if you brought bottles of oxygen gas with you to breathe, eventually they would run out. What could you bring with you that could supply oxygen regularly? The same questions can be asked about food and water.

A group of researchers tried such an experiment here on Earth by building a sealed living space called Biosphere II in the desert of Arizona, complete with a rainforest, a miniature ocean, land for growing food, and livestock to provide eggs and milk. A small group of people lived inside for 2 years in the early 1990s, and they learnt a great deal about sustaining life in a closed system. Such an experiment helps us to learn how we might set up a base on the Moon or perhaps Mars but, more importantly, it helped the people living inside appreciate what a delicate balance there is between air, water, and life: a balance that is complex and can be disrupted by actions with unintended consequences.

4.1 Species, communities, and ecosystems

NATURE OF SCIENCE

Looking for patterns, trends, and discrepancies: plants and algae are mostly autotrophic but some are not.

Understandings:

- Species are groups of organisms that can potentially interbreed to produce fertile offspring.
- Members of a species may be reproductively isolated in separate populations.
- Species have either an autotrophic or heterotrophic method of nutrition (a few species have both methods).
- Consumers are heterotrophs that feed on living organisms by ingestion.
- Detritivores are heterotrophs that obtain organic nutrients from detritus by internal digestion.
- Saprotrophs are heterotrophs that obtain organic nutrients from dead organisms by external digestion.
- A community is formed by populations of different species living together and interacting with each other.
- A community forms an ecosystem by its interactions with the abiotic environment.
- Autotrophs obtain inorganic nutrients from the abiotic environment.
- The supply of inorganic nutrients is maintained by nutrient cycling.
- Ecosystems have the potential to be sustainable over long periods of time.

Applications and skills:

- Skill: Classifying species as autotrophs, consumers, detritivores, or saprotrophs from a knowledge of their mode of nutrition.
- Skill: Setting up sealed mesocosms to try to establish sustainability.
- Skill: Testing for association between two species using the chi-squared test with data obtained by quadrat sampling.
- Skill: Recognizing and interpreting statistical significance.

Guidance

- *Mesocosms can be set up in open tanks, but sealed glass vessels are preferable because entry and exit of matter can be prevented but light can enter and heat can leave. Aquatic systems are likely to be more successful than terrestrial ones.*
- *To obtain data for the chi-squared test, an ecosystem should be chosen in which one or more factors affecting the distribution of the chosen species varies. Sampling should be based on random numbers. In each quadrat the presence or absence of the chosen species should be recorded.*

The interdependence of living organisms

In 1980 there was a major volcanic catastrophe at Mount Saint Helens on the west coast of the USA. After the massive eruption, little was left of the forest and rivers that had existed on and around the mountain. The blast from the eruption knocked over massive adult trees as if they were straws.

Forest fires and hot gases burned everything in sight. Volcanic ash rained down, smothering the destroyed forest and covering the carcasses of the animals that died there. Many species that could escape fled the area. Although thousands of people were evacuated, a few did die that day; some of those who died were photographers trying to get the photo of a lifetime.

Yet, within months of the eradication of the ecosystem, life was back. Seeds, dropped by birds or blown in by the wind, germinated in the fertile volcanic ash. Little by little, insects, then birds, then small mammals, moved in. Within a couple of decades, a grassland and shrub ecosystem had reappeared. Today, thousands of species flourish in what had been a desolate landscape.

These trees were knocked down by the Mount Saint Helens eruption in 1980. The ecosystems on the mountain were destroyed.

What is a species?

The definition of a species is a group of organisms that can interbreed and produce fertile offspring. Members of the same species have a common gene pool (i.e. a common genetic background).

Species is the basic unit for classifying organisms. It is one of those words everyone thinks they know, but it is not an easy concept. A species is made up of organisms that:

- have similar physiological and morphological characteristics that can be observed and measured
- have the ability to interbreed to produce fertile offspring
- are genetically distinct from other species
- have a common phylogeny (family tree).

There are challenges to this definition, however. Sometimes, members of separate but similar species mate and succeed in producing hybrid offspring. For example, a horse and a zebra, or a donkey and a zebra, can mate and produce offspring that are called zebroids. In these examples, the parents are both equines (they belong to the horse family, Equidae), so they are related, but they are certainly not the same species. They do not possess the same number of chromosomes, which is one of the reasons why the hybrid offspring produced are usually infertile.

Other challenges to our definition of species include the following.

- What about two populations that could potentially interbreed, but do not because they are living in different niches or are separated by a long distance?
- How should we classify populations that do not interbreed because they reproduce asexually? (The definition above is clearly aimed at sexually reproducing organisms, and cannot be applied to bacteria or archaeans.)
- What about infertile individuals? Does the fact that a couple cannot have a child exclude them from the species? What about the technique of *in vitro* fertilization? What challenges does that pose to the definition of species?

The answers to these questions are beyond the scope of this book and the IB programme. However, you should always think critically about any definition: at first glance it may appear to be straightforward, but on closer scrutiny it can be cause for debate.

Domesticated dogs are all the same species: *Canis familiaris*. In theory, that means that any two dogs from anywhere in the world can mate and have puppies that will grow up and be able to mate with any other dogs, and have more puppies.

This giant panda has characteristics that set its species apart; it cannot breed with other species that are not giant pandas.

All domesticated dogs are the same species.

Hybrids

To understand the idea of fertile offspring, think about what happens when two different but similar species mate and produce offspring. For example, a female horse and a male donkey can mate and produce a mule. However, mules cannot usually mate to make more mules. Because the offspring (the mules) are not fertile, no new species has been created. Instead, a mule is called an interspecific hybrid. When a male lion and a female tiger are crossed, a liger is the name of the hybrid formed.

Hybrids face several challenges to continue as a population. For one thing, the vast majority of animal and plant hybrids are infertile. Even if one generation of hybrids is produced, a second generation is highly unlikely. This presents a genetic barrier between species.

Some examples of animal hybrids are:

• female horse + male donkey = mule
• female horse + male zebra = zorse
• female tiger + male lion = liger.

A liger is a hybrid between a lion and a tiger, and is considerably larger than either parent animal.

Populations can become isolated

If a group from a species is separated from the rest of the species, it might find itself evolving in a different way compared with the rest of the population. For example, mice have inadvertently crossed oceans after going on board ships looking for food, and found themselves hundreds if not thousands of kilometres away from where their parent population lived, perhaps on an island far from any mainland. Two or more mice can mate and have litters of mice that then form a new population on the island. This new population is reproductively isolated from the original population of mice. Compared with the original population on the mainland, an island population of mice may end up with different frequencies of certain alleles for a trait such as fur colour, with the result that the mice in the island population only have black fur, while the mice in the original mainland population can have either brown or black fur.

As well as bodies of water, there are other ways in which populations of the same species can be isolated from each other, such as mountain ranges or deep canyons. There are tree snails in Hawaii, for example, that are present on one side of a volcanic mountain but not the other. But physical objects are not always responsible for separating populations of a species. Think of a group of birds that migrate: if some of those birds arrive early in the springtime and start nesting before the others arrive, the early birds' genes will be isolated from the birds that arrive and nest later. If some birds in a population develop a mating call that is different from the others, this could also potentially separate one population into two groups: one that likes the old call and one that likes the new call. Over time, this might lead to speciation: a new species is formed from an old one.

Autotrophs and heterotrophs

A sheep eating grass is an example of a heterotroph (the sheep) feeding on an autotroph (the grass).

Autotrophs

Some organisms are capable of making their own organic molecules as a source of food. These organisms are called autotrophs, and they synthesize their organic molecules from simple inorganic substances. This process involves photosynthesis. In other words, autotrophs can take light energy from the Sun, combine it with inorganic substances, and obtain a source of chemical energy in the form of organic compounds. Because autotrophs make food that is often used by other organisms, they are called producers.

Examples of autotrophs include:

• cyanobacteria   • algae   • grass   • trees.

Heterotrophs

Heterotrophs cannot make their own food from inorganic matter, and must obtain organic molecules from other organisms. They get their chemical energy from autotrophs or other heterotrophs. Because heterotrophs rely on other organisms for food, they are called consumers. Heterotrophs ingest organic matter that is living or has been recently killed.

Examples of heterotrophs include:

• zooplankton   • fish   • sheep   • insects.

Consumers

Organisms that are not capable of synthesizing their own food from inorganic components of their environment need to get their nourishment by ingesting (eating) other organisms. For example, humans are heterotrophs: we cannot simply lie out in sunlight to get our food the way phytoplankton and plants can. We are consumers: we need to eat other living organisms, whether they are products of autotrophs, such as fruits and vegetables, or products of heterotrophs, such as meat, eggs, honey, and dairy products. Consumers take the energy-rich carbon compounds, such as sugars, proteins, and lipids, synthesized by other organisms in order to survive. The only component in our diet that we can synthesize, by exposure to sunlight, is vitamin D. There are precursors in human skin that absorb ultraviolet (UV) light waves and

CHALLENGE YOURSELF

1 From the photo, identify the following:
- **(a)** non-living inorganic components, both visible and non-visible (these are referred to as abiotic components)
- **(b)** living components, both visible and non-visible (living organisms are referred to as biotic components)
- **(c)** autotrophs present, both visible and non-visible
- **(d)** heterotrophs present, both visible and non-visible.

Can you identify the biotic and abiotic components in this photo?

produce vitamin D. But in order to get all the other types of molecules needed to keep us healthy, we need to consume other living things.

Detritivores

The minotaur beetle, *Typhaeus typhoeus*, is a detritivore.

Some organisms eat non-living organic matter. Detritivores eat dead leaves, faeces, and carcasses. Earthworms, woodlice, and dung beetles are detritivores found in the soil community. Many, but not all, bottom feeders in rivers, lakes, and oceans are detritivores.

Saprotrophs

Organisms called saprotrophs live on or in non-living organic matter, secreting digestive enzymes and absorbing the products of digestion. Saprotrophs play an important role in the decay of dead organic materials. The fungi and bacteria that are saprotrophs are also called decomposers, because their role is to break down waste material. A mushroom growing on a fallen tree is secreting enzymes into the dead tissue of the tree trunk, in order to break down the complex molecules within the tree tissue, and then the mushroom absorbs the simpler energy-rich carbon compounds that are released by the action of the enzymes. Slowly, over time, the tree trunk decomposes as the molecules inside the wood are liberated and reused.

Table 4.1 A summary of trophic level terminology

Autotrophs	Consumers			
Producers	Consumers of living or freshly killed organisms		Consumers of dead material	
	Herbivores	Omnivores	Decomposers	
			Detritivores	Saprotrophs

Communities

A community is a group of populations living and interacting with each other in an area. Examples include the soil community in a forest, and the fish community in a river.

In ecology, the term 'interacting' can mean one population feeding on another, or being eaten. It can mean that one species provides vital substances for another, as in the case of symbiotic bacteria, which help certain plants get nitrogen while the bacteria grow in the plant root nodules. It can also mean that one species gets protection from another, as in the case of aphids being protected by ants from attacks by predators. Interacting can mean that one species relies on another for its habitat, as is the case for parasites living on or inside the bodies of other animals.

Fungi are saprotrophs. Although edible mushrooms are found in the fruit and vegetable section of your local supermarket, they are not classified as plants by biologists. It is arguable that they should be with other consumers in the meat section.

CHALLENGE YOURSELF

2 From Figure 4.1, pick three organisms and determine how many other organisms each one depends on. Which organisms depend on them? What about environmental factors? Which ones does each organism contribute to, and which ones does each depend on?

Figure 4.1 A tropical rainforest contains many interactions between living organisms and their environment.

An example of an easily identifiable plant to use for the fieldwork lab; in this case the plant is yarrow.

Ecosystems

The term abiotic refers to components of the environment that are non-living, such as water, air, and rocks. When abiotic measurements are taken of an environment, they can include temperature, pH, light levels, and the relative humidity of the air. Such things are often measured using electronic probes and data-logging techniques. Although these factors are not living entities, they are often of great interest to biologists because of the interactions that living things have with them. Temperature and humidity, for example, have a large influence on the types of plant life found in a community; an open marsh will not have the same kinds of plants as a dense forest. To find out to what extent a particular abiotic factor influences a species' distribution, many measurements must be taken, of both the abiotic and biotic (living) aspects of the environment. One technique used to determine the frequency and distribution of a species is random sampling.

Fieldwork

To understand random sampling, try this lab using quadrats. A quadrat is a square of a particular dimension that can be made of a rigid material such as metal, plastic, or wood. In this example, each group will use a 1-m² quadrat. Other materials you will need are: a table of random numbers from 1 to 99, a pencil, and something on which to record your data.

- Pick a well-defined area, such as a fenced-in pasture, public park, or a sports field with natural grass (be sure you have permission to work there first).
- Choose a species of plant that grows there that is easy to identify and that is widespread throughout the area, but not so numerous that counting the number of individuals growing in a square metre would take more than a minute or two. Possible examples are dandelions, docks, and yarrow, but the choice will depend on where you live and when you carry out the lab.
- Each group should start in a different part of the area and spin a pencil to determine a random direction. Then, with your group, look at the first number on the random number table and walk in the designated direction that number of steps. If the border of the area is reached before the designated number of steps has been taken, you should 'bounce' off the border like a ray of light off a mirror, and continue in the direction dictated by an angle of incidence that is the same as the angle of reflection.
- Place the quadrat down on the ground at the point determined by the number of steps, and decide which of the four sides will be the 'top' and 'right' of the quadrat.
- Identify and count the number of individuals of the chosen species found inside the borders of the quadrat at that position. If it is zero, record the result as such. Any plants touching the top or right should be considered 'in' and should be counted. Any plants touching the bottom or left side of the quadrat should be considered 'out' and not counted.
- Repeat this as many times as possible in, say, an hour: the more quadrats, the better. However, a typical sports field might be 5000 m², so there is no way a group can sample all 5000 m² and cover the entire field: that is why random sampling is used.
- Before leaving the area you are working in, measure its dimensions so that its total surface area can be determined. This might be challenging for an irregularly shaped pasture or park, in which case online aerial views of the area might be useful. In that case, note the scale of the image.
- Now you will carry out some data processing. Determine how many plants you hit per square metre, then use the surface area calculation to estimate the total number of individuals of that plant that are living in that area: (plants per m²) × (surface area in m²) = (population estimation).

If this experiment is done for two species of plants, are there any calculations you could do to compare the two? See the Mathematics, and information and communication chapter for more about statistical tests.

Alternative: if weather or space forces a group to do this indoors, the activity can be simulated with disks of paper or sticky notes scattered around a gymnasium. In such a case, use a smaller quadrat, maybe one that is 50 cm². An advantage of this alternative lab is that the person scattering the disks or sticky notes knows how many there are in total, and it is interesting to see how close the groups' estimations are to the known number.

Systematic sampling techniques

There is another way of using a quadrat rather than the random sampling described in the lab above: systematic sampling using a transect. A transect is a line traced from one environment to another, such as from a grassland into a woodland, or from an ocean's intertidal zone over dunes. The line might be 10, 25, or 50 m long, and can be made using a long tape measure or piece of string or rope. This method involves laying down a quadrat either every metre along the transect, or at specific intervals along the transect, for example every 2 m, 5 m, or 10 m, and then counting the organisms that hit each quadrat and then counting the organisms found within each quadrat. Notice how, unlike the example of the quadrats used in the fieldwork lab, there are no random numbers. Because the distances are measured carefully, this is especially interesting in cases where we want to see if there is a relationship between the distribution of organisms that live along the transect and an abiotic factor that changes along the transect, such as temperature, humidity, and light levels.

Figure 4.2 Two ways of sampling with quadrats: ten quadrats on the left using random sampling and ten quadrats on the right using systematic sampling along a transect line.

Worked example

Let's suppose a group of students has been working in a forest in late summer and they have measured several abiotic factors, including light intensity in two distinct areas: a heavily wooded area and an open prairie. Not surprisingly, they recorded major differences in light intensity between one area and the next. They identified a particular species of fern that grows in both areas but appears to prefer shaded areas compared with areas exposed to direct sunlight. After collecting their data, they wanted to see if the presence of ferns was statistically significantly larger in the shaded areas (the woodland) compared with the areas in direct sunlight (the prairie). The group was divided into two teams: one for the woodland and the other for the prairie. They used random sampling with 1-m² quadrats to get their data. If they found the fern growing in their quadrat, they recorded a 1, if not, a 0. Table 4.2 shows what their data looked like after 20 quadrats had been thrown by each group.

Quadrat	Shade (woodland)	Sunlight (prairie)	Quadrat	Shade (woodland)	Sunlight (prairie)
1	0	1	11	1	0
2	1	1	12	1	0
3	1	0	13	0	0
4	1	0	14	1	1
5	1	0	15	0	0
6	0	1	16	1	1
7	1	0	17	1	1
8	1	1	18	1	0
9	0	0	19	0	0
10	1	0	20	1	0

Table 4.2 Quadrat data for a fern species. Legend:
1 = presence of ferns in quadrat,
0 = absence of ferns in quadrat

Apply the chi-squared test to these data to decide whether the shade had an influence or not on the distribution of the fern. (See page 561 for an explanation of what the chi-squared test is, how it works, and what the values for the degrees of freedom should be.)

1 State the null hypothesis in this calculation.

2 Determine the number of degrees of freedom in this calculation.

3 Determine the critical value in order to obtain a 95% certainty that there is a statistically significant difference between these two sets of numbers.

4 Calculate the chi-squared value for these data.

5 Interpret this value. Does it mean we can accept or reject the null hypothesis?

6 Is there a statistically significant difference between these two sets of data?

7 Are there enough data to be confident of the results?

Solutions

1 The null hypothesis is 'the two categories (presence of fern and presence of shade) are independent of each other'. In other words, the distribution of this fern species is not related to shade.

2 Because there are two possible outcomes (fern present or fern not present), the number of degrees of freedom is $2 - 1 = 1$.

3 According to the chi-squared table (see Table 5 on page 560), the critical value in order to obtain a 95% certainty is 3.84. This value is found under the column 0.05, which corresponds to a 95% certainty, and it is found in the row that has the degree of freedom of 1.

4 The chi-squared value is calculated to be 4.91. This is obtained using the following values in the contingency tables.

Table 4.3 The table of observed values

	Shade (woodland)	Sun (prairie)	Grand total
Fern absent	6	13	19
Fern present	14	7	21
Grand total	20	20	40

Below, the expected value of 9.5 is from the calculation: $(20 \times 19) \div 40$ and the expected value of 10.5 is from the calculation $(20 \times 21) \div 40$.

Table 4.4 The table of expected values

	Shade (woodland)	Sun (prairie)	Grand total
Fern absent	9.5	9.5	19
Fern present	10.5	10.5	21
Grand total	20	20	40

See page 561 of the Mathematics, and information and communication chapter for help with this calculation.

5 Because 4.91 is greater than the critical value of 3.84, this means we can reject the null hypothesis.

6 Yes, the two categories are related to each other. We can be 95% sure that there is a relationship between the fern distribution and amount of sunlight. In other words, it would be very unlikely that they are independent of each other.

You can be asked about the chi-square test in IB biology exams. Be sure you know when the chi-square test can be used, the steps of how to do it, and how to interpret the results.

7 Twenty quadrats sounds a bit small. In a random sample, there is always the chance that the sampling is not representative of the zone studied. If the zone in the sunlight was the size of a sports field, for example, it would have a surface area of approximately 5000 m². Twenty 1-m² quadrats represents 20 m² of that surface, meaning that only 0.4% of the field was actually sampled. The same can be said for the shaded area in the woods.

Where do autotrophs get their nutrients?

Unlike consumers, who need to eat organic food from plants and animals, autotrophs can make the food they need from their inorganic surroundings. Photosynthetic organisms, such as phytoplankton, cyanobacteria, and plants, are able to produce food by using carbon dioxide, water, and sunlight. They make food from air using sunlight energy. It is a truly remarkable process, and no consumers could survive on this planet without the initial production of food by autotrophs. Because of this ability to make food from inorganic substances, autotrophs are referred to as producers, and they are the start of food chains, which will be explored later in Section 4.2.

Nutrient cycling

When organisms such as trees need minerals to grow and stay healthy, where do they get them from? Even though tonnes of space dust fall on Earth each year, there is not enough to meet the mineral needs of all the organisms in the biosphere. As a result, ecosystems must recycle the carbon, nitrogen, and other elements and compounds necessary for life to exist. For this, organisms must find what they need within the materials available in their own habitat. The problem is that organisms absorb valuable minerals and organic compounds and use them to build their cells. These resources are then locked up and unavailable to others, except, of course, through feeding and decomposition.

Earth has various systems that interact.

Biosphere = where all living things are found.

Atmosphere = where all the gases in the air are found.

Lithosphere = where all the rocks are found.

Hydrosphere = where all the water is found.

Each one of these systems is closely linked with the others, and some, such as the biosphere, cannot exist in their current form without the other three.

Long before plants evolved on Earth, cyanobacteria were photosynthesizing. Cyanobacteria have been producers for many ecosystems.

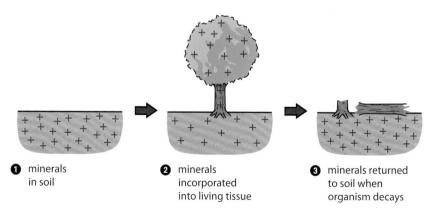

❶ minerals in soil

❷ minerals incorporated into living tissue

❸ minerals returned to soil when organism decays

Figure 4.3 How minerals are absorbed into living trees and then returned to the soil when the organism dies and decays.

Decomposers

An effective way to unlock the precious nutrients stored in the cells of plants and animals is through decay. Decomposers (saprotrophs and detritivores) break down the body parts of dead organisms. The digestive enzymes of decomposers convert the

When talking about the health of Planet Earth, we often use words like 'pollution' and 'waste'. Ecologists studying ecosystems noticed very quickly that what one organism considers to be waste is what another organism considers to be a valuable resource. For example, the nitrogen compounds found in rotting flesh or animal excrement are extremely useful for plant growth. In other words, 'pollution' can be considered to be simply misplaced resources. If we can figure out a system that makes waste useful, then it will be a sustainable system, and all the waste will be put to a new use as part of a cycle. If we cannot find a use for the waste we produce, then we truly are polluting our environment.

organic matter into a more usable form for themselves and for other organisms. For example, proteins from a dead organism are broken down into ammonia (NH_3) and, in turn, ammonia can have its nitrogen converted into useful nitrates (NO_3^-) by bacteria.

In this way, decomposers recycle nutrients so that they are available to other organisms and are not locked inside the bodies or waste products of organisms in the ecosystem. Decomposers play a major role in the formation of soil, without which plant growth would be greatly impaired, if not impossible. The rich black layer of soil called humus is made up of organic debris and nutrients released by decomposers. In a vegetable garden, a compost pile is used to convert plant waste from the garden and kitchen into rich humus that can then be used to grow new vegetables. The organisms doing the work inside the compost pile are decomposers.

CHALLENGE YOURSELF

3 For each organism below, identify which type of nutrition is used: heterotroph; heterotroph that is a saprotroph; heterotroph that is a detritivore; autotroph.
   (a) The bacterium *Rhizobium*.
   (b) Fungi on a dead log.
   (c) Cyanobacteria floating where there is sunlight.
   (d) A snail scraping algae off a rock.

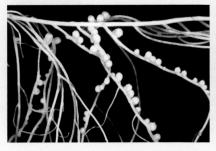

Rhizobium lives in the root nodules of legumes and fixes atmospheric nitrogen. These bacteria are symbiotic and receive carbohydrates and a favourable environment from their host plant.

Fungi on a dead log.

The sustainability of ecosystems

Thanks to this recycling of nutrients, ecosystems can continue to be productive and successful for long periods of time. The producers take simple inorganic compounds, such as carbon dioxide (CO_2), from their environment and convert them into energy-rich sugars, such as glucose ($C_6H_{12}O_6$). Those simple sugars can then be transformed into complex carbohydrates to make cellulose, to build up plant cell walls. Other nutrients can be added to form complex organic molecules such as lipids and proteins.

Consumers will then come along and eat the producers, and digest the complex organic compounds into simpler building blocks, such as amino acids and sugars, for growth and energy. When those consumers die, their cells and tissues are broken down by decomposers, and the minerals are returned to the soil. Producers can once again absorb the nutrients from the soil, and grow new sources of food. The cycle is complete. This process is sometimes informally referred to as the circle of life, but the more scientific term is nutrient cycling.

One example of nutrient cycling is the nitrogen cycle. Nitrogen is extremely important to living organisms, as it is one of the elements needed in nucleotides and amino acids, the building blocks of life. Without this element, organisms would not be able to make DNA or proteins, and thus life would be impossible. Nitrogen starts the cycle in gas form in the atmosphere, as N_2. Plants and animals are incapable of using nitrogen gas but some bacteria are able to transform it into useful forms, such as nitrates, in a process called nitrogen fixation. These usable nitrates are absorbed by plant roots (which is why some plants host the nitrogen-fixing bacteria in their root nodules, as seen in the Challenge yourself photo on page 192), and so the plants pass on nitrogen-rich nutrients when they are consumed by animals. Both plants and animals return the nitrogen to the soil in a variety of ways. Urine and faeces, for example, contain nitrogen compounds, which is why farmers often put animal manure on the fields where they grow crops. When plants and animals die, the nitrogen compounds are returned to the ground by decomposition. Going back to the question at the start of the chapter, about what you would bring to the Moon to live there, would you have listed decomposers? What about nitrogen-fixing bacteria?

A miniature world in a plastic bottle

You can set up your own ecosystem of microbes in a plastic bottle at home or in the lab. This is a long-term project, so make sure you have somewhere that you can leave the bottle for many weeks or months. The experiment you're going to set up is called a Winogradsky column.

For this lab, you will need some dark, wet mud. If you get it near a pond, be sure to take some pond water separately as well. Make sure you have permission to take the samples.

You will need an empty, clean, transparent, plastic drinks bottle that will hold 2 or 3 litres, mud (nice, slimy, stinky, mud works the best), shredded newspaper, crushed egg shells and raw egg yolk.

* Place the last three ingredients in about half a litre of mud, removing any large pieces from the mud such as sticks and stones. Mix the ingredients up and pour them into the bottom of the bottle. A funnel might be necessary. Add more mud on top of that until the bottle is two-thirds full. Add some water, but be sure to leave about 5 cm of air at the top of the bottle. Be sure there are no air bubbles in the mud.

* Place the cap on the bottle and leave it for many weeks near a sunny window: the microorganisms in the bottle need sunlight. It is a good idea to take a photo at the beginning of the experiment, and then one every week or so. These photos will show you the changes that occur over time. Make sure you carefully label your experiment so that no one throws it away thinking it is rubbish.

Variations on the experiment include using: a glass container that can be sealed at the top; different types of mud; different sources of carbon dioxide instead of the egg shells; different sources of sulfur instead of the raw egg yolk.

To interpret the results you will have to do a bit of research to find out what the different colours mean. Each one represents a different kind of bacterial colony in the mud, and each of those transforms molecules for the others to use. As long as there is light entering the system, the column will continue to maintain a healthy microbial ecosystem for many months.

If you have the materials, the time, and the ambition, it is also possible to set up a more complex aquatic ecosystem that is hermetically sealed. Go to the hotlinks for suggestions of websites that explain how to do this. Otherwise, do a search for keywords such as 'make your own ecosphere' or 'sealed terrarium'.

Ethical considerations: in accordance with the IB policy on the use of living organisms in experiments, it is best to avoid putting sentient beings in your ecosphere or mesocosm. Before adding snails or shrimp, for example, you would need to decide if you can justify exposing such organisms to things they would not encounter in their natural habitat, such as low oxygen levels or low food supplies. Fish, tadpoles, or invertebrates bigger than a few millimetres are probably not appropriate.

Two major events in the modern environmental movement were the first photographs of Planet Earth from space, during the Apollo missions in the late 1960s and early 1970s, and the publication in 1962 of *Silent Spring* by Rachel Carson, a book imagining a future with no more birds.

In the decades since those events, more and more people have become concerned about our ability as a species to have enough space, water, and food for everyone. Ecologists who study human interactions with the other forms of life on Earth, and interactions with the non-living components of the environment, are concerned about our future, and think that international cooperation is necessary to solve complex global issues such as insufficient drinking water supplies, overfishing, global climate change, loss of forests and topsoil, bleaching of coral reefs, and the depletion of countless other natural resources. Their plea is that we need to adopt international policies to limit human impact and maintain sustainable practices.

Governments and societies are going to need to think about what is necessary for this to happen. Several paths could be explored, such as better education, international agreements and policies, higher taxation of unsustainable activities, or discussions of population control to limit human impacts. All of these have advantages and disadvantages and would need to be debated. One phrase that often comes up when looking for ways in which we can help our planet is 'act locally, think globally'. This could be a possible topic for discussion in your biology class or TOK class.

Section summary

- As there is a limited number of resources on Earth, sustainability is crucial for the survival of species in an ecosystem.
- In order to be considered a species, a group of organisms needs to be able to mate and produce fertile offspring. There are many challenges to this definition, such as organisms that reproduce asexually and organisms that are reproductively isolated.
- Autotrophs make their own food through processes such as photosynthesis. Heterotrophs, also known as consumers, such as detritivores and saprotrophs need to get their food from the environment.
- When populations of different species live together and interact together, they form a community. By interacting with abiotic surroundings such as air and water, they form an ecosystem.
- One key factor that allows an ecosystem to be sustainable is the fact that the nutrients in it are recycled. Energy, on the other hand, cannot be recycled. Fortunately, new energy arrives from the Sun every day.

To learn more about micro-ecosystems and setting up sealed mesocosms, go to the hotlinks site, search for the title or ISBN, and click on Chapter 4: Section 4.1.

4.2 Energy flow

NATURE OF SCIENCE

Use theories to explain natural phenomena: the concept of energy flow explains the limited length of food chains.

Understandings:

- Most ecosystems rely on a supply of energy from sunlight.
- Light energy is converted to chemical energy in carbon compounds by photosynthesis.
- Chemical energy in carbon compounds flows through food chains by means of feeding.
- Energy released from carbon compounds by respiration is used in living organisms and converted to heat.
- Living organisms cannot convert heat to other forms of energy.
- Heat is lost from ecosystems.
- Energy losses between trophic levels restrict the length of food chains and the biomass of higher trophic levels.

Applications and skills:

- Skill: Quantitative representations of energy flow using pyramids of energy.

Guidance

- Pyramids of number and biomass are not required. Students should be clear that biomass in terrestrial ecosystems diminishes with energy along food chains, due to loss of carbon dioxide, water, and other waste products, such as urea.
- Pyramids of energy should be drawn to scale and should be stepped, not triangular. The terms producer, first consumer, and second consumer, and so on should be used, rather than first trophic level, second trophic level, and so on.
- The distinction between energy flow in ecosystems and cycling of inorganic nutrients should be stressed. Students should understand that there is a continuous but variable supply of energy in the form of sunlight but that the supply of nutrients in an ecosystem is finite and limited.

The importance of sunlight to ecosystems

The best studied ecosystems are those found on Earth's surface, whether they are on land or in surface water. Such systems rely on sunlight, and they will be the main focus of this section. Be aware, however, that there are other, less well-studied, ecosystems that exist in total darkness, such as those in deep ocean water and those found deep underground, but these are not well understood because they are so difficult to access.

All life that you see around you on Earth's surface relies either directly or indirectly on sunlight. If a person eats an omelette for breakfast, for example, the eggs were made indirectly with energy from sunlight. How? The hen that laid the eggs probably ate some kind of grain in order to get the energy to make the eggs, and the plant material eaten by that hen was from a producer, and the producer used sunlight to transform carbon dioxide and water into energy-rich carbon compounds. Take away the sunlight from this scenario, and the eggs could not have been produced because the hen would not have had any grains to eat.

The role of photosynthesis

As seen in Section 4.1, photosynthetic organisms such as phytoplankton and plants take simple inorganic carbon dioxide, CO_2, and convert it into energy-rich sugar, $C_6H_{12}O_6$. The addition of minerals allows the producers to synthesize complex molecules such as cellulose, proteins, and lipids. Notice what is happening in this process: light energy from the Sun is being converted into chemical energy (food). Chemical energy refers to the fact that organic compounds, such as carbohydrates, proteins, and lipids, are rich in energy, thanks to the chemical bonds that exist between the carbon atoms and other atoms. This is what makes fruits, grains, and vegetables good food sources. Consumers cannot 'eat' sunlight and air, but they can eat carbohydrates, proteins, and lipids. The chemical energy in these organic compounds can be measured in calories or kilocalories, which we see listed on food packaging. One way to release the chemical energy from organic compounds is to digest the food, another way is to burn it. Burning wood in a fire is a good example of turning chemical energy in the organic compounds of the wood into light energy (and heat energy).

Sunlight is the initial source of energy for all vegetation.

Food chains

By feeding on producers, consumers can utilize the chemical energy to grow and stay healthy. For example, a cow (the consumer) grazing in a field of grass (the producer) is taking chemical energy from the grass and digesting the organic compounds to help build meat or milk inside its own body. Humans can consume the meat or milk from the cow to benefit from the chemical energy the cow has obtained from the grass. Such a pattern of feeding is called a food chain. The process of passing energy from one organism to another through feeding is referred to as the flow of energy through a food chain.

When studying feeding habits, it is convenient to write down which organism eats which by using an arrow. Thus, herring → seal indicates that the seal eats the herring. When the seal's eating habits are investigated and the herring's diet is considered, new organisms can be added to the chain: copepods (a common form of zooplankton) are eaten by the herring, and great white sharks eat seals. Lining up organisms with arrows between them is how food chains are represented. Here are three examples of food chains from three different ecosystems.

Grassland ecosystem:

grass → grasshoppers → toads → snakes → hawk

River ecosystem:

algae → mayfly larvae → juvenile trout → kingfisher

Marine ecosystem:

diatoms → copepods → herring → seals → great white shark

The definition of a food chain is a sequence showing the feeding relationships and energy flow between species. In other words, it answers the question 'What eats what?' The direction of the arrow shows the direction of the energy flow.

Biologists use the term trophic level to indicate how many organisms the energy has flowed through.

The first trophic level is occupied by the autotrophs or producers. The next trophic level is occupied by the primary consumers (organisms that eat the producers), and the trophic level after that is occupied by secondary consumers (organisms that eat primary consumers).

Three trophic levels can be seen in this photograph: a producer, a primary consumer, and a secondary consumer.

Cellular respiration and heat

In the example of the grass and the grasshoppers, inside a grasshopper chemical energy is used for cellular respiration. Glucose originally produced by the grass is converted by the grasshopper's cells into carbon dioxide and water. This chemical reaction generates a small amount of heat in each of the grasshopper's cells. Any heat generated by cellular respiration is lost to the environment. Although this might be more obvious in mammals, which can give off considerable amounts of heat, even grasshoppers will lose heat to the environment. If the grasshopper is eaten, some of the chemical energy in its body (in the form of protein, for example) is passed on to the next organism (a toad, for example). If the grasshopper dies and is not eaten, detritivores and decomposers will use its available energy.

The cells of decomposers also carry out cellular respiration and, as a result, any heat produced this way will also be lost to the environment. This is just one source of energy loss from one trophic level to the next, as we will see.

How many trophic levels are shown in this Peruvian scene?

Heat cannot be recycled

This section has mentioned heat being lost, but what does it mean when heat is 'lost'? As you may already know from other science courses, there is a law about energy stating that energy cannot be created or destroyed, only converted from one form to another. We have seen that light energy can be converted into chemical energy by the process of photosynthesis. We have also seen that during the process of cell respiration, not all the energy is converted into useful energy (ATP) by the cell: some of it is converted to heat energy. Although this keeps mammals warm, once the heat leaves an organism's body, it cannot be used again as a biological energy resource. So, for the organism, this energy is 'lost'. It has not disappeared, however; it has simply been converted into a form that the organism can no longer use as a source of energy.

Where does the heat go?

Because ecosystems are made up of lots of respiring organisms, each losing heat, heat is lost from the ecosystem. Once the heat has radiated into the surrounding environment, the ecosystem cannot take back that heat to use it. Notice how this is very different from nutrient cycling with substances such as nitrogen and carbon. Unlike nutrients, energy cannot be recycled. It is passed from one trophic level to the next, and when it leaves the ecosystem it is not reusable. Is this a problem? Usually no, because the Sun is constantly providing new energy to producers. The energy is converted to chemical energy and passed on from one trophic level to the next.

Table 4.5 Examples of recyclable and non-recyclable resources

Examples of what ecosystems can recycle	Examples of what ecosystems cannot recycle
Minerals, nitrogen, and carbon can be recycled. There is a limited supply so they are constantly cycled through organisms.	Energy cannot be recycled. It is passed from one trophic level to the next until it is lost to the environment.

The most popular theory for the mass extinction that wiped out the dinosaurs (and many other organisms) at the end of the Cretaceous period, is that the Sun's energy was blocked by particles in the air after a large object smashed into Earth. The darkened skies meant that producers could not get enough sunlight to continue making enough food to feed the consumers.

However, if, for some reason, the Sun stops shining, because it is blocked from Earth by clouds or particles in the sky (as happens after large volcanic eruptions), then the food chain is affected.

Only chemical energy can be used by the next trophic level (see Figure 4.4), and only a small amount of the energy that an organism absorbs is converted into chemical energy. In addition, no organism can use 100% of the energy present in the organic molecules of the food it eats. Typically, only 10–20% of the energy available is used from the previous step in a food chain. This means that as much as 90% is lost at each level.

Here are the main reasons why not all of the energy present in an organism can be used by another organism in the next trophic level.

- Not all of an organism is swallowed as a food source, some parts are rejected and will decay.
- Not all of the food swallowed can be absorbed and used in the body, for example owls cough up the hair and bones of the animals they eat, and undigested seeds can be found in the faeces of fruit-eating animals.
- Some organisms die without having been eaten by an organism from the next trophic level.
- There is considerable heat loss as a result of cellular respiration at all trophic levels (shown by the wavy arrows in Figure 4.4), although the loss of heat varies from one type of organism to the next. Most animals have to move, which requires much

more energy than a stationary plant needs. Warm-blooded animals need to use a considerable amount of energy to maintain their body temperature.

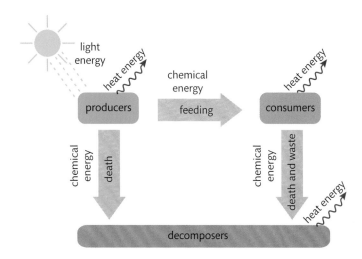

Figure 4.4 Energy flow and energy loss.

Pyramid of energy

A pyramid of energy is used to show how much and how fast energy flows from one trophic level to the next in a community (see Figure 4.5). The units used are energy per unit area per unit time: kilojoules per square metre per year ($kJ\ m^{-2}\ yr^{-1}$). Because time is part of the unit, energy pyramids take into account the rate of energy production, not just the quantity.

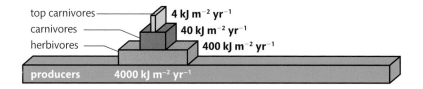

top carnivores — **4 kJ m^{-2} yr^{-1}**
carnivores — **40 kJ m^{-2} yr^{-1}**
herbivores — **400 kJ m^{-2} yr^{-1}**
producers **4000 kJ m^{-2} yr^{-1}**

Figure 4.5 Pyramid of energy.

Because energy is lost, each level is always smaller than the one before. It would be impossible to have a higher trophic level wider than a lower trophic level, for example, because organisms cannot create energy, they can only transfer it inefficiently.

Be careful not to confuse pyramids of energy with pyramids of numbers: pyramids of numbers show the population sizes of each trophic level, not the energy.

Food webs and energy levels in trophic levels

If you look back at the three examples of food chains earlier in this chapter, you will notice that they are all either four or five organisms long. Although some food chains can have up to six trophic levels, most have four. The number of levels is limited by how much energy enters the ecosystem. Because so much is lost at each level, low energy at the start will quickly be lost, whereas abundant energy at the start can sustain several trophic levels. So the number of organisms in the chain as well as the quantity of light available at the beginning will determine how long the chain is.

Whereas nutrients are constantly cycled in ecosystems, energy is not. The cycles of growth, death, and decomposition show how nature recycles nutrients, but energy pyramids show that energy flows through a system and is lost. This is why new energy must arrive in the form of sunlight in order to keep the system going.

Worked example

Using the following information, construct a pyramid of energy. Try your best to make it to scale.

In an ecosystem, the producers make 10 000 kJ m^{-2} yr^{-1}. 1000 kJ m^{-2} yr^{-1} of energy is passed on to the herbivores. In the third trophic level, the carnivores absorb 100 kJ m^{-2} yr^{-1} and the top predators who eat them get 10 kJ m^{-2} yr^{-1}.

Solutions

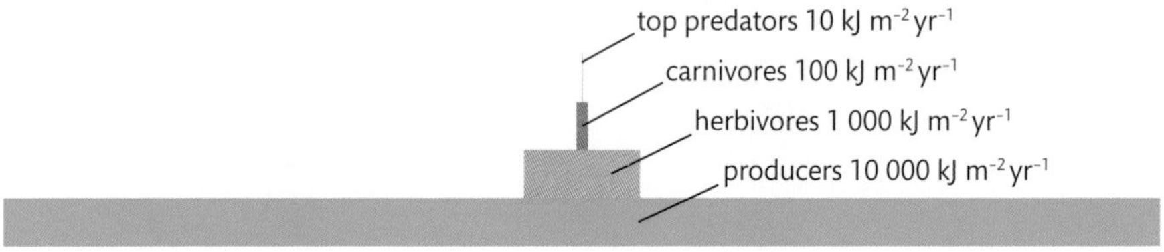

top predators 10 kJ m^{-2} yr^{-1}
carnivores 100 kJ m^{-2} yr^{-1}
herbivores 1 000 kJ m^{-2} yr^{-1}
producers 10 000 kJ m^{-2} yr^{-1}

Figure 4.6 A pyramid of energy showing a 90% loss of energy at each trophic level.

The biomass of a trophic level is an estimate of the mass of all the organisms within that level. It is expressed in units of mass, but also takes into account area or volume. For example, in terrestrial ecosystems, fields of wheat might produce 1 tonne acre^{-1} yr^{-1} in one area of the world, whereas another area might produce 3 tonnes acre^{-1} yr^{-1}. Although there may be other factors, the amount of sunlight reaching the fields will influence the biomass, so that sunnier parts of the world can produce more wheat. In contrast, cooler climates or ones with fewer hours of sunlight per year have a lower biomass and therefore cannot support as many organisms. The fields of wheat could be the start of a food chain that consists of field mice, snakes, and hawks. Some molecules along the food chain cannot participate in the accumulating biomass because they are lost in various forms: carbon dioxide is lost from the organisms during cellular respiration, water is lost during transpiration and evaporation from the skin, and waste products including urea are excreted. So, just as not all energy gets passed on from one trophic level to the next, not all biomass gets passed on either.

Look at the food chains in Figure 4.7 showing a river ecosystem. Notice how the trophic levels link together into a food web. Sometimes it is necessary to describe a food web, rather than a food chain, because an organism such as a juvenile trout eats not only caddis fly larvae but also the larvae of other species. Notice that the trophic levels are labelled with the letter T, and think about the biomass in each: did you ever wonder how scientists estimate the total biomass in each trophic level? That question goes beyond the scope of this section, but, if you are interested, use the hotlinks at the end of this section to find more information.

NATURE OF SCIENCE

The statements about what limits the length of a food chain and prevents one from going beyond a certain number of trophic levels can be explained by the energy pyramids shown earlier. Because so much energy is lost at each level (90%), the only way to have more energy available for the top level is to increase the energy going into the bottom level for the producers. As the energy collected by producers is limited by the amount of sunlight reaching Earth's surface, it is difficult to increase it.

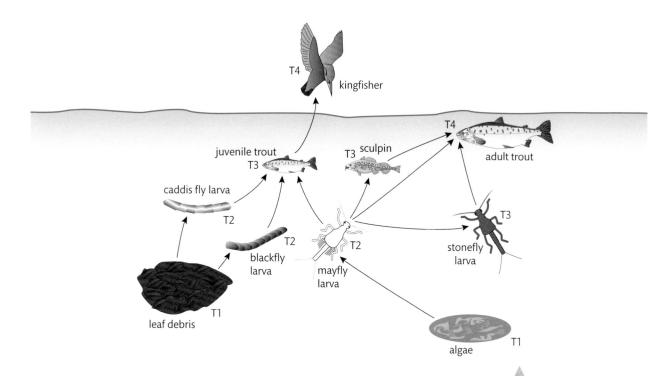

Figure 4.7 A food web from
a river ecosystem showing
trophic (T) levels.

Ever since Thomas Malthus predicted in the late 18th century that humans would eventually
run out of food, scientists and researchers have wondered how big the human population can
get before the amount of biomass available as food becomes insufficient to feed everyone.
Techniques of food production have changed dramatically since Malthus' time, and we have
not yet reached the tipping point he predicted. The industrialization of agriculture, as well
as the invention of artificial fertilizers, brought about the Green Revolution, allowing farmers
to produce many times more biomass than ever before on the same farms. Today, in some
countries, tonnes of grain sit and rot in silos, while in other countries people go hungry. Are
questions of world hunger simply questions of technology and biomass production? Do we
need to produce more food to feed the hungry? Will the Malthusian catastrophe eventually
come about: will we run out of food for our species some day? Or should we be confident that
countries will work together to find the best solution? What questions do scientists still need to
answer in order to guide policy makers, and how will they answer those questions?

Section summary

• The best-studied ecosystems get their initial energy from sunlight. Photosynthetic
  organisms convert light energy into chemical energy in the form of carbon
  compounds such as sugar and starch.
• Herbivores get their energy by eating these carbon compounds, and the carnivores in
  turn get their energy from the organic compounds in the herbivores.
• Ways to show how energy is passed on from one organism to another is through
  food chains, food webs, and pyramids of energy.
• Because of energy being lost as heat, only 10–20% of the energy available in one level
  (called a trophic level) is passed on to the next one.

To learn more about
biomass, go to the hotlinks
site, search for the title
or ISBN, and click on
Chapter 4: Section 4.2.

4 Look at these food chains again. Name the trophic levels (as producer or consumer) for each organism listed.

   (a) Grassland ecosystem:
   grass → grasshoppers → toads → snakes → hawk
   (b) River ecosystem:
   algae → mayfly larvae → juvenile trout → kingfisher
   (c) Marine ecosystem:
   diatoms → copepods → herring → seals → great white shark

5 From the following information, construct a food web:

   • grass is eaten by rabbits, grasshoppers, and mice
   • rabbits are eaten by hawks
   • grasshoppers are eaten by toads, mice, and garter snakes
   • mice are eaten by hawks
   • toads are eaten by hognose snakes
   • hognose snakes are eaten by hawks
   • garter snakes are eaten by hawks.

6 From the food web you have drawn, what is the trophic level of the toad?

4.3 Carbon cycling

Understandings:

• Autotrophs convert carbon dioxide into carbohydrates and other carbon compounds.
• In aquatic ecosystems carbon is present as dissolved carbon dioxide and hydrogen carbonate ions.
• Carbon dioxide diffuses from the atmosphere or water into autotrophs.
• Carbon dioxide is produced by respiration and diffuses out of organisms into water or the atmosphere.
• Methane is produced from organic matter in anaerobic conditions by methanogenic archaeans and some diffuses into the atmosphere or accumulates in the ground.
• Methane is oxidized to carbon dioxide and water in the atmosphere.
• Peat forms when organic matter is not fully decomposed because of acidic and/or anaerobic conditions in waterlogged soils.
• Partially decomposed organic matter from past geological eras was converted either into coal or into oil and gas that accumulate in porous rocks.
• Carbon dioxide is produced by the combustion of biomass and fossilized organic matter.
• Animals such as reef-building corals and molluscs have hard parts that are composed of calcium carbonate and can become fossilized in limestone.

Applications and skills:

• Application: Estimation of carbon fluxes due to processes in the carbon cycle.
• Application: Analysis of data from air monitoring stations to explain annual fluctuations.
• Skill: Construct a diagram of the carbon cycle.

Guidance
• Carbon fluxes should be measured in gigatonnes.

Carbon

As seen in Chapter 2, the element carbon is the cornerstone of life as we know it. Carbon is such a crucial element to living organisms that it is part of the definition of a living thing. You will recall that the term 'organic' implies that carbon is present. Hence, life on Earth is referred to as carbon-based life.

NATURE OF SCIENCE

Making accurate, quantitative measurements: it is important to obtain reliable data on the concentration of carbon dioxide and methane in the atmosphere.

Not only is carbon found in the biosphere in organic molecules such as carbohydrates, proteins, lipids, and vitamins, it is also found in the atmosphere as carbon dioxide and in the lithosphere as carbonates and fossil fuels in rocks. The biosphere refers to all the places where life is found, and the lithosphere is all the places where rocks are found. Petroleum, from which products such as gasoline, kerosene, and plastics are made, is rich in carbon because it originated from partially decomposed organisms that died millions of years ago.

Figure 4.8 The carbon cycle on Earth.
▼

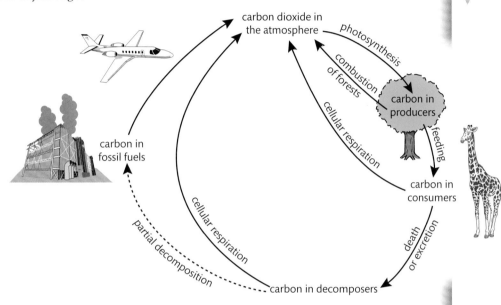

As seen in Figure 4.8, carbon is constantly being cycled between living organisms and inorganic processes that allow the carbon to be available. The carbon atoms that make up the cells of the flesh and blood of the giraffe, for example, came from the vegetation the giraffe ate. Eating organic material provides newly dividing cells in the giraffe's body with a fresh supply of carbon-based energy-rich molecules with which the cells can carry out work. When cellular respiration is complete, carbon dioxide is released into the atmosphere, and when the giraffe dies, its body will be eaten by scavengers and the remains broken down by decomposers. Some of the carbon from the giraffe's body will go back into the atmosphere as carbon dioxide when the decomposers perform cellular respiration. This section will look at some of the many different forms carbon can take as it is cycled by nature.

The role of autotrophs in the carbon cycle

Let's start with food. Photosynthetic autotrophs take carbon dioxide from the atmosphere and convert it into carbohydrates. Here is the unbalanced chemical equation for photosynthesis.

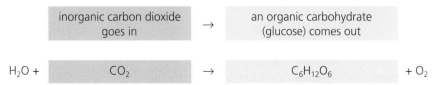

inorganic carbon dioxide goes in	→	an organic carbohydrate (glucose) comes out	
H_2O + CO_2	→	$C_6H_{12}O_6$	+ O_2

Figure 4.9 The unbalanced equation for photosynthesis.

The sugar on the right-hand side of the equation (in green) is a source of food, not only to the autotroph synthesizing it, but also to the organisms that feed on the autotrophs.

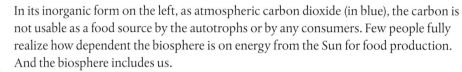

In its inorganic form on the left, as atmospheric carbon dioxide (in blue), the carbon is not usable as a food source by the autotrophs or by any consumers. Few people fully realize how dependent the biosphere is on energy from the Sun for food production. And the biosphere includes us.

From the $C_6H_{12}O_6$ molecules, autotrophs can manufacture other compounds. Fructose and galactose are other sugars that can be made by plants from glucose. Connecting the sugars together into a long chain can make starch; plants can store energy for a future season or a future generation in the form of starch granules, tubers, or seeds. Plants and algae need to build their cell walls with cellulose, which is also made from long chains of glucose. Glucose is the starting point for making other organic compounds that are not carbohydrates, such as lipids and amino acids. These compounds are necessary to make useful things such as cell membranes and proteins such as enzymes. To synthesize these non-carbohydrates, other elements such as nitrogen must be added to the glucose.

Do you use cellulose in your life? You are probably wearing cellulose right now, because any textiles made of cotton are made of plant cellulose. Books are printed on cellulose, because paper pulp is from plant material. And if you use a car or a bus that runs on biofuel, that vehicle is being powered by cellulose.

Carbon in aquatic ecosystems

As you know from drinking fizzy drinks or carbonated water, carbon dioxide can dissolve in water. Although the oceans, lakes, and rivers of the world are not as fizzy as a carbonated drink, they contain dissolved carbon dioxide because carbon dioxide from the atmosphere can be absorbed by the water. Remember also that organisms living in water produce carbon dioxide through cellular respiration. As the carbon dioxide is dissolved in the water, it forms an acid. The pH of water decreases as the amount of carbon dioxide increases. This is why carbonated water has an acidic taste.

$$CO_2 + H_2O \rightarrow H_2CO_3 \text{ (carbonic acid)}$$

$$H_2CO_3 \rightarrow H^+ + HCO_3^- \text{ (hydrogen carbonate ion)}$$

When dissolved in water, the carbonic acid forms the H^+ in the equation above, which is an ion that can influence pH. But what is of interest to us is the hydrogen carbonate ion, HCO_3^-, because this is a good example of an inorganic carbon-based molecule that participates in the carbon cycle.

Figure 4.10 The forms of carbon available in aquatic ecosystems: dissolved carbon dioxide and hydrogen carbonate ions.

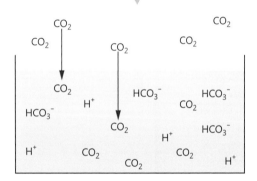

Carbon is available to photosynthetic organisms as carbon dioxide gas in the air or dissolved in water. It is available to consumers in the form of carbohydrates, proteins, and lipids, but can also be absorbed in the form of ions such as carbonate ions.

Cycling of carbon dioxide

Carbon dioxide is absorbed by photosynthetic autotrophs such as photosynthetic bacteria, phytoplankton, plants, and trees. As you will recall, these producers are eaten by consumers, which use the carbon in their bodies. Cellular respiration from all trophic levels, including decomposers, produces carbon dioxide, which is released back into the environment. This carbon dioxide diffuses into the atmosphere or into the water, depending on whether the organism is terrestrial or aquatic.

Methane in the carbon cycle

Other carbon compounds are produced by microbes such as archaeans. Members of the Archaea include methanogens, which are anaerobic (they live in environments with no oxygen). When these methanogenic archaeans metabolize food, they produce methane (CH_4) as a waste gas. You should be familiar with methane because it is the same gas used in laboratories (the flame of Bunsen burners) and in homes for cooking and heating.

These microbes are also common in wetlands, where they produce marsh gas, which can sometimes glow mysteriously at night, but they are also responsible for producing methane gas in the digestive tracts of mammals, including humans. With large herds of cattle being raised worldwide, there is a concern that the quantities of methane they produce are contributing to the greenhouse effect, which will be discussed in the next section.

Figure 4.11 Methane gas production.

The oxidation of methane

How does the burning of fossil fuels produce carbon dioxide? Look at the chemical reaction below, showing methane burning in oxygen gas:

$$CH_4 + 2O_2 \rightarrow 2H_2O + CO_2$$

Methane is the main ingredient in the fossil fuel we call natural gas. As you can see from the formula, this chemical reaction involves oxygen gas from Earth's atmosphere. When the methane is oxidized, the two molecules produced are water vapour and carbon dioxide gas.

The carbon found in the molecule CH_4 was borrowed from a CO_2 molecule that was removed from the atmosphere millions of years ago during photosynthesis. It then took the methane gas millions of years to form and accumulate underground. When we burn natural gas provided by the petroleum industry, we return that carbon to the atmosphere in the form of carbon dioxide. Normally, we would think that this is just part of a balanced cycle. The problem is, one part of the cycle takes millions of years and the other part, the burning of fossil fuels, is very rapid.

Peat as a fossil fuel

Another organic substance that can be used as a fossil fuel is partially decomposed plant material called peat. Peat is a kind of waterlogged soil found in certain types of wetlands, such as mires and bogs, which can be found in the British Isles, Scandinavia, northern Russia, some eastern European countries, northern Canada, northern China, the Amazon River basin, Argentina, northern USA (notably Alaska) and parts of Southeast Asia. Peat is very dark in colour and only certain types of vegetation can grow on its surface, such as sphagnum moss. Although peat is a heterogeneous mixture of many things, at least 30% of its dry mass must be composed of dead organic material for it to be called peat. The soil that forms peat is called a histosol, and a layer of peat is typically between 10 and 40 cm thick.

In her description of living in Biosphere II, a hermetically sealed experimental facility developed in Arizona, USA, researcher Jane Poynter said she had a new appreciation of the air she was breathing. In an interview on the TED Radio Hour in 2013 she said, 'The most profound experience I had in the biosphere was the experience of not only being completely dependent on my biosphere, but being absolutely a part of my biosphere in a very literal way. I mean, as I walked through the biosphere, I was incredibly conscious of the fact that the plants surrounding me were providing me with the oxygen that I needed to breathe, and that I was providing them some of the carbon dioxide they needed to grow.' She says we need to think about this when we are living in Biosphere I, which, in case you hadn't worked it out, is Planet Earth.

Slabs of peat left to dry in Scotland.

Walking on peatlands can be a bit of a challenge because they are very spongy. The high levels of water on peatland force out the air that would normally be between the soil particles. As a result, anaerobic conditions are created, which allows certain types of microorganisms to grow but prevents the growth of microorganisms that would normally help in the decomposition of plant material. Hence many of the energy-rich molecules that would have been fed upon by decomposers are left behind and transformed, over thousands of years, into in energy-rich peat.

Another characteristic of peatlands is the pH of the waterlogged histosol: it is very acidic. Just as with low oxygen levels, if the acidity is not conducive to the decomposers, they will not be able to do their work. High acidity contributes to the fact that non-decomposed material accumulates. In the pools of acidic water that can be found on these wetlands, certain types of organisms can be found that are not found anywhere else, such as some species of aquatic beetles.

In order for it to be usable as a fuel, cut peat is dried out to reduce its high levels of humidity. It is cut into slabs, granules, or blocks, and moved to where it is needed. Like all fossil fuels, however, peat takes a very long time to form and is not considered to be a renewable source of energy. Once all the peat in a wetland has been harvested it is gone; it is unrealistic to wait for new peat to form, so new sources of fuel are needed.

In economic periods when oil prices are high, peat can be a competitive energy source, but when oil prices are low this is not the case, and there have been decades during which many countries decided to drain their wetlands to replace them with forests and farmland. In some cases, environmental concerns about the preservation of wetlands, because they are an important part of the ecosystem and a habitat for unique species, have prevented the digging and drainage of peatlands. Another reason to preserve wetlands is that pollen trapped in deep layers of the bogs thousands of years ago can provide evidence of what the climate was like in the past, giving us 'libraries' of biotic information.

Oil and gas as fossil fuels

In some cases, when left in the correct conditions, partially decomposed peat can be further transformed into coal. Over millions of years, sediments can accumulate above the peat, and the weight and pressure of those sediments compresses the peat. Under conditions ideal for the formation of coal, the sedimentation continues until the carbon-rich deposits are not only under huge pressure but also exposed to high temperatures because they have been pushed far below Earth's surface. The pressure and heat cause chemical transformations associated with lithification, which is the transformation of sediments into solid rock. During lithification, the molecules are compacted and rearranged. What is of great interest to industries using coal is the hydrocarbons, the long chains of carbon atoms attached to hydrogen atoms (see Figure 4.12).

▲ **Figure 4.12** A hydrocarbon chain.

The C–H bonds hold a significant amount of energy, and, because there are many of them in long chains, each hydrocarbon molecule is rich in energy ready to be released by burning.

In order to use coal for energy, it must be extracted from below the ground, which is why mining is necessary. Coal is found in seams, where the layers of sediments were deposited, covered, and then transformed and often twisted and deformed by geological forces over millions of years.

A lump of coal.

In addition to coal, chemical transformations underground can produce other petroleum products, such as crude oil and, as we have seen, natural gas.

For this, we have to go far back in time, before dinosaurs roamed Earth. During the Carboniferous period, hundreds of millions of years ago, some places in the world that are now dry land were underwater and hosted abundant aquatic or marine life, including algae and zooplankton. For example, the dry deserts of Saudi Arabia used to be under the Tethys Ocean, back when all the continents were still stuck together in the supercontinent called Pangaea.

At that distant time in Earth's past, under conditions ideal for the formation of petroleum products, the dead remains of the organisms' in the water did not fully decompose at the bottom of the ocean, and instead formed layers of sediment along with silt. In conditions lacking oxygen (anoxic conditions), the decaying material started to form sludge, as some parts of the organisms' cells decayed while others did not. One component of dead algae and zooplankton that is not easily broken down is the lipid component of their cells. Accumulated lipids that are trapped in sediments at the bottom of an ocean form a waxy substance called kerogen. It, too, is rich in hydrocarbons and, like the formation of other fossil fuels, is transformed by pressure and heat as sediments accumulate above it and cause its molecules to rearrange.

The natural production of kerogen is a long process, and the right conditions have only occurred in certain parts of the world. Over millions of years, and after geological transformation, the kerogen in porous sedimentary rock becomes crude oil or, if it is in a gas state, natural gas. Both of these petroleum products are less dense than rock, so they tend to rise through cracks in the rocks towards the surface. Figure 4.13 shows some of the places where crude oil has been found in the world.

Figure 4.13 World deposits of crude oil.

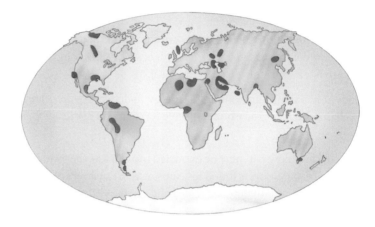

Figure 4.14 Formation of gas and oil.

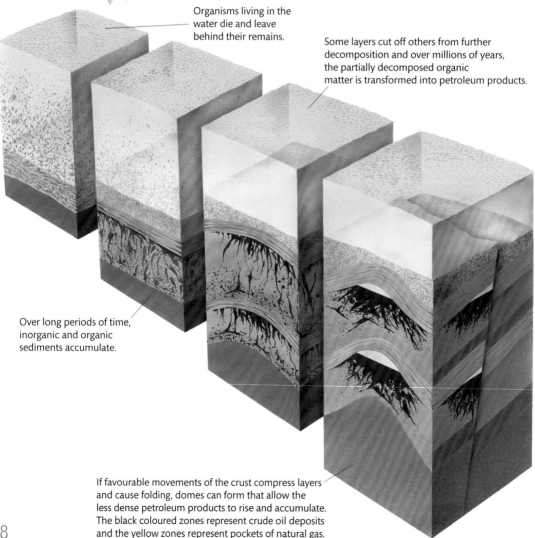

Organisms living in the water die and leave behind their remains.

Some layers cut off others from further decomposition and over millions of years, the partially decomposed organic matter is transformed into petroleum products.

Over long periods of time, inorganic and organic sediments accumulate.

If favourable movements of the crust compress layers and cause folding, domes can form that allow the less dense petroleum products to rise and accumulate. The black coloured zones represent crude oil deposits and the yellow zones represent pockets of natural gas.

In order to be used by humans, petroleum products must be trapped and pooled under a non-porous rock, preferably one that is bent by tectonic movement into a dome, as seen in Figure 4.14. This kind of formation allows large quantities of useful gas and oil to collect together in a productive reservoir. Geologists study the porosity and deformations of rock layers in order to determine which parts of the world might contain exploitable gas and oil reserves.

When an oil field is discovered and crude oil is pumped out of the ground, it is sent to refineries to be separated into the various products that we use every day, using an apparatus called a fractionating tower. Such an apparatus allows the heaviest, most dense molecules with the longest hydrocarbon chains to accumulate at the bottom, and the lightest, least dense molecules with the shortest hydrocarbon chains to accumulate at the top. Look at Figure 4.15 and see how many of these petroleum products you rely on every day.

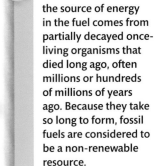

The term 'fossil fuel' refers to the fact that the source of energy in the fuel comes from partially decayed once-living organisms that died long ago, often millions or hundreds of millions of years ago. Because they take so long to form, fossil fuels are considered to be a non-renewable resource.

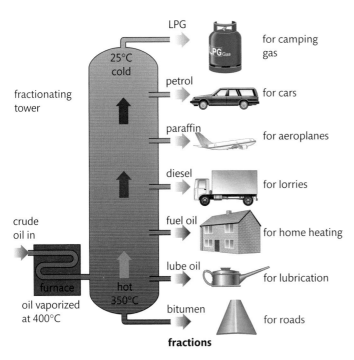

fractions

short chains
low boiling points, runny, volatile and easily ignited

long chains
high boiling points, viscous, non-volatile and not easily ignited

Figure 4.15 The many uses of petroleum products in our everyday lives. How many of these products do you rely on every day? One fraction that is not shown in the diagram is naphtha, which is the main ingredient used to make plastics.

Crude oil has the nickname 'black gold'. Oil and gas companies are prepared to go to the most inaccessible places in the world to dig out the black gold, whether it is in the hot sands of deserts or at the bottom of icy cold oceans. And it is worth all that trouble. In 2012, more than a third of the 50 companies with the highest revenues worldwide were oil and gas companies, four of which had revenues exceeding $400 000 000. Such a number is difficult to grasp, but it is higher than the gross domestic product (GDP) of most countries in the world.

Carbon dioxide is produced when fossil fuels are used

Just as we saw with methane previously, substances rich in hydrocarbons can be oxidized using oxygen gas from the atmosphere when they are burned. If you have ever made a fire on a beach or at a campsite, you know that organic material such as wood is capable of releasing a considerable amount of energy in the form of light and heat. Wood is not the only fuel of biological origin that can be burned: many people living in non-industrialized areas of the world use biomass in the form of animal dung as a source of energy. The dried dung of domesticated animals such as cows can be burned and used for various purposes, including cooking. Fresh, wet dung can be mixed with other refuse from a farm and put into a large container, where methane-producing microorganisms will decompose and ferment the material to produce flammable methane gas, as seen in Figure 4.16. Unlike fossil fuels, biofuels made in a biogas generator like this do not take millions of years to form.

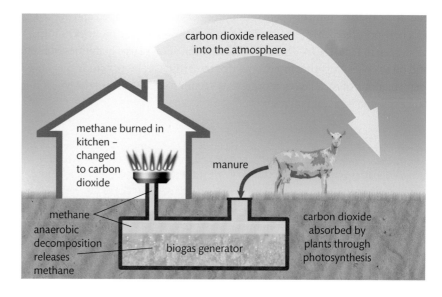

Figure 4.16 Biogas production and use.

In an effort to reduce fossil fuel consumption, some countries, such as the USA and Brazil, have introduced biofuel programmes using ethanol made from crops such as corn and soybeans. The plant material is fed to microorganisms that ferment it and in the process release ethanol. The ethanol is added to gasoline for vehicles, and contributes to a reduction in gasoline use. Standard vehicles cannot use more than 25% ethanol and need 75% or more gasoline (this mix can also be called gasohol), but vehicles specially adapted for biofuels can run solely on ethanol.

Using a different technique, biodiesel can be made from vegetable oils or animal fat. Some people have even modified their cars so that they run on the waste oil from deep-fat fryers at fast food restaurants.

Although it can be argued that using biofuels allows countries to reduce their dependence on imported fossil fuels, the burning of any biomass still releases carbon dioxide into the atmosphere. The difference is that, unlike fossil fuels, the carbon dioxide from biofuels was removed from the atmosphere by plants just a few months or years before the biofuel was used.

Limestone

Marine organisms take dissolved carbon out of the water and use some of it to make their carbonate shells. As we saw earlier in this chapter, the carbon can be in the form of carbon dioxide dissolved in the water or it can be in the form of hydrogen carbonate ions. The organisms that build coral reefs are called coral polyps, and they absorb two ions from the seawater to build the reef: hydrogen carbonate ions and calcium ions. When combined, molecules of calcium carbonate ($CaCO_3$) are formed. This molecule is the basis of the coral reef, and it is sturdy like rock. Below is the chemical equation for making calcium carbonate:

$$Ca^{2+} + 2\,HCO_3^- \rightarrow CaCO_3 + CO_2 + H_2O$$

Other organisms as well as coral polyps use calcium carbonate to build shells around their bodies. Molluscs (from the phylum Mollusca), such as snails, clams, oysters, and mussels, build up their shells with calcium carbonate and, when they die, the shells accumulate at the bottom of the ocean.

Some farmers in the world are growing crops that are not destined for human food nor for animal feed but rather for fuel to power cars and city buses. Brazil and the USA have been innovators in this practice, and it is a way of cycling carbon that depletes fewer fossil fuel reserves. There is a down side to it, however: some questions arise about the morality of such a practice. In the countries where this policy has been put in place, there are people starving. Is it acceptable to use food crops as fuel for motor vehicles instead of making it available for humans to eat? Critics point out that allocating farmland for this use might drive up the price of food crops.

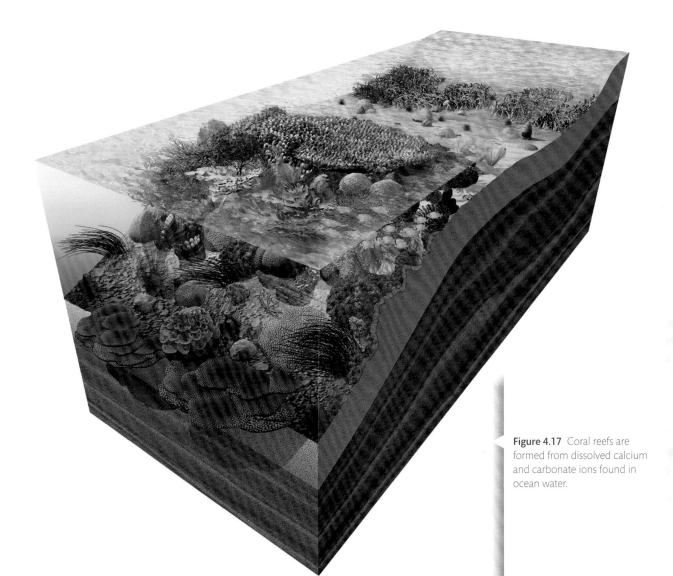

Figure 4.17 Coral reefs are formed from dissolved calcium and carbonate ions found in ocean water.

Microscopic foraminifera usually live on the ocean floor and are also very good at building shells, albeit very small ones. Because they are so numerous, however, and they have been around for hundreds of millions of years, their shells have accumulated in sediments, and when the sediments go through the process of lithification, they form limestone. Limestone has long been used by humans as a building material (the Great Pyramid at Giza and Notre Dame cathedral in Paris are two examples), and is a major ingredient in modern cement.

The process of taking carbon out of the environment and 'locking it up' in a substance for an extended period of time is called carbon sequestration, and when it happens naturally it is called biosequestration. This is one way balance is maintained in the carbon cycle.

Through biosequestration, an accumulation of foraminifera shells as sediments at the bottom of the ocean can trap carbon in limestone for millions of years. When cement is made by humans for construction, limestone is used and, in the process, some of the carbon is released back into the atmosphere as carbon dioxide, cancelling out the biosequestration.

CHALLENGE YOURSELF

4 Using Table 4.6, draw a flowchart showing the exchange of carbon between the atmosphere, the oceans, and the biosphere. Such exchanges are called fluxes and carbon fluxes in this table are expressed in gigatonnes of carbon per year (GtC yr⁻¹). You can do the drawing by hand but there are many flowchart tools available, both online and probably as part of the software on the computer you use.

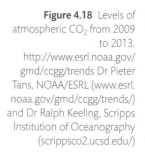

Table 4.6 Carbon exchange into and out of the atmosphere

Carbon fluxes	Quantity of carbon (GtC yr⁻¹)
Examples of fluxes into the atmosphere	
Respiration of terrestrial organisms	120
Respiration of marine organisms at the surface of the ocean	92
Burning of fossil fuels (such as transport)	7.7
Changes in land use (such as deforestation)	1.5
Examples of fluxes out of the atmosphere	
Absorption of carbon dioxide into the water at the surface of the ocean	90
Gross primary production (GPP), photosynthesis of terrestrial organisms	90
Photosynthesis of marine organisms	40
Changes in land use (such as growing crops in prairies)	0.5
Weathering, carbon dioxide being incorporated into rocks and soils	0.2

Worked example

You be the scientist: have a look at this graph from the website of the National Oceanic and Atmospheric Administration (NOAA), showing atmospheric carbon dioxide levels in recent years. This one is from October 2013, but you might be able to find a more recent one if you do a web search for the title.

Figure 4.18 Levels of atmospheric CO_2 from 2009 to 2013. http://www.esrl.noaa.gov/gmd/ccgg/trends Dr Pieter Tans, NOAA/ESRL (www.esrl.noaa.gov/gmd/ccgg/trends/) and Dr Ralph Keeling, Scripps Institution of Oceanography (scrippsco2.ucsd.edu/)

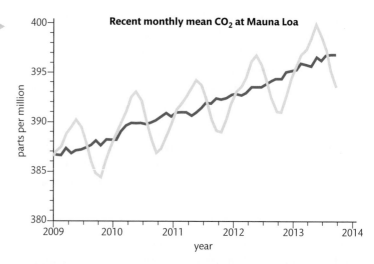

The up-and-down pattern shown in light blue is caused by seasonal fluctuations in carbon dioxide levels. The dark blue line shows the trend corrected for these seasonal fluctuations.

1 (a) Work out how the years are divided up on the *x*-axis of the graph.

(b) Estimate the level of atmospheric carbon dioxide in January of 2010 and in October of 2013 using the corrected values on the dark blue trend line.

(c) Look at the first four lowest values on the light blue line. There is one per year. Determine the month of the year during which this low point most often occurs. Do the same for the high points.

2 (a) In terms of cellular respiration and photosynthesis rates in the northern hemisphere, explain the yearly downward fluctuations from May to October.

(b) Do the same for the upward fluctuations from October to May of the following year.

3 Describe the overall trend shown by the graph for the years shown, giving quantitative data in your description.

Solutions

1 (a) The years are divided into quarters: Jan/Feb/Mar, Apr/May/Jun, Jul/Aug/Sep and Oct/Nov/Dec.

(b) 388 p.p.m. and 397 p.p.m., respectively. It is important to include the units.

(c) Lows are in October and highs in May.

2 (a) As plants, phytoplankton, and photosynthetic bacteria are generally more active in the spring and summer months, more carbon dioxide is extracted from the atmosphere and levels drop. During this time, cellular respiration is contributing large quantities of carbon dioxide to the atmosphere, but not as fast as photosynthesis is taking it out.

(b) Conversely, when photosynthesis is less intense during the autumn and winter months, carbon dioxide levels rise and, although organisms are generally less active at colder times of the year, their cellular respiration rates put more carbon dioxide into the air than the photosynthetic organisms can remove.

3 The trend shows an increase from 387 p.p.m. at the beginning of 2009 to a 397 p.p.m. in October 2013. This 10 p.p.m. increase represents a percentage change of +2.6% for the period shown.

Section summary

- A key part of understanding how Earth functions as a complex system is knowing how carbon is cycled.
- Living organisms release carbon dioxide after performing cellular respiration.
- Burning vegetation can release carbon into the atmosphere.
- Organic matter that is incompletely decomposed can hold on to carbon for thousands or millions of years in the form of peat, coal, crude oil, or methane gas.
- Methane gas can also be produced by certain microorganisms, such as those living in marshes or in the guts of cattle.
- Bioreactors can use decomposing organic material to make methane gas for homes. When methane or any other organic fuel source is burned, carbon dioxide is released into the atmosphere.
- Carbon is available to living organisms in the form of carbon dioxide in the air or dissolved carbon dioxide in water. There are other carbon compounds in water, including hydrogen carbonate ions.
- One example of an organism that relies on carbon in the ocean is coral polyps, which make their reefs from calcium carbonate found in the ocean.

7 Study Figure 4.19.

(a) Using the blue trend line, determine the atmospheric carbon dioxide concentration for 1965 and 2001.

(b) Calculate the percentage change from 1965 to 2001.

(c) Why do the measurements have a high point and a low point for each year?

(d) The photo insert shows the station where the measurements were taken, at the top of a volcanic island in the Pacific that is part of a USA state. Which state is the station in, and why did scientists decide to put the station there?

8 From what inorganic molecules can aquatic organisms get their carbon?

9 Give the names of the hydrocarbon-rich substances that are described below.

(a) A kind of waterlogged soil found in wetlands and made of partially decomposed plant material.

(b) A hard black rock that can be burned to make electricity or direct heat.

(c) A waxy substance formed from accumulated lipids trapped in sediments at the bottom of oceans.

(d) Of all the commonly used petroleum products, this one has the smallest density.

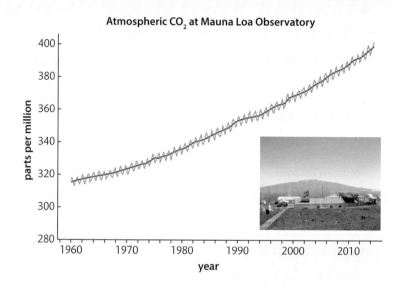

Atmospheric CO_2 at Mauna Loa Observatory

y-axis: **parts per million** (280, 300, 320, 340, 360, 380, 400)
x-axis: **year** (1960, 1970, 1980, 1990, 2000, 2010)

Figure 4.19 The National Aeronautics and Space Administration (NASA) data on carbon dioxide levels in the atmosphere 1958–2014. The up-and-down pattern is caused by seasonal fluctuations in activities such as photosynthesis.
http://www.esrl.noaa.gov/gmd/ccgg/trends
Dr Pieter Tans, NOAA/ESRL (www.esrl.noaa.gov/gmd/ccgg/trends/) and
Dr Ralph Keeling, Scripps Institution of Oceanography (scrippsco2.ucsd.edu/)

NATURE OF SCIENCE

Assessing claims: assessments of the claims that human activities are not producing climate change.

4.4 Climate change

Understandings:

- Carbon dioxide and water vapour are the most significant greenhouse gases.
- Other gases including methane and nitrogen oxides have less impact.
- The impact of a gas depends on its ability to absorb long-wave radiation as well as on its concentration in the atmosphere.
- The warmed Earth emits longer wavelength radiation (heat).
- Longer wave radiation is absorbed by greenhouse gases that retain the heat in the atmosphere.
- Global temperatures and climate patterns are influenced by concentrations of greenhouse gases.
- There is a correlation between rising atmospheric concentrations of carbon dioxide since the start of the industrial revolution 200 years ago and average global temperatures.
- Recent increases in atmospheric carbon dioxide are largely due to increases in the combustion of fossilized organic matter.

Applications and skills:

- Application: Threats to coral reefs from increasing concentrations of dissolved carbon dioxide.
- Application: Correlations between global temperatures and carbon dioxide concentrations on Earth.
- Application: Evaluating claims that human activities are not causing climate change.

Guidance

- *Carbon dioxide, methane, and water vapour should be included in discussions.*
- *The harmful consequences of ozone depletion do no need to be discussed and it should be made clear that ozone depletion is not the cause of the enhanced greenhouse effect.*

The atmosphere

We live at the bottom of an ocean of air we call the atmosphere. It is so natural to us that we don't even think about it unless, for some reason, we are without it. When we go up in an airplane, for example, the cabin needs to be pressurized so that we can keep breathing, and so that we do not freeze to death 10 000 m above the ground. The atmosphere plays a vital role in regulating the temperature of Earth's surface.

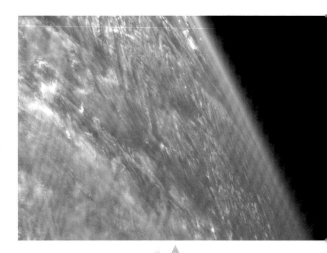

Earth's surface has an average temperature of about 14°C; fluctuations only very rarely go lower than −80°C (in Antarctica) or higher than +50°C (in North Africa). In contrast, the Moon, which is the same distance from the Sun as Earth is, has temperature swings that typically go from −150°C to +120°C, depending on where sunlight is hitting the surface. This is because the Moon has almost no atmosphere. It is estimated that if Earth had no atmosphere, the average temperature would be 32°C colder (−18°C), making the possibility of life very different. We will see in this section how Earth's atmosphere acts as a kind of blanket, keeping us warm at night and sheltering us from excessive heat during the day.

Seen from space along the edge of Earth's curve, the atmosphere is a surprisingly thin, almost insignificant looking, layer of gases.

The roles of carbon dioxide and water vapour in the greenhouse effect

The consequence of the Moon having little or no atmosphere is that it has no greenhouse effect. The greenhouse effect refers to a planet's ability to use its atmosphere to retain heat and keep warm even when no sunlight is hitting the surface. To understand the greenhouse effect, you need to know how a greenhouse works. The walls and roof of a greenhouse are made of glass. Sunlight penetrates through the glass and warms up the plants inside. Sunlight itself, which is made up of short wavelengths, is not warm; the temperature of outer space between the Sun and Earth is hundreds of degrees below freezing.

It is only when sunlight hits an object that some of its energy is transformed into heat. Heat energy, otherwise known as infrared radiation, has longer wavelengths than energy in the form of light. When sunlight goes through the glass of the greenhouse, it warms up the objects inside: the plants, the ground, and anything else inside. The objects inside radiate their heat to the air inside the greenhouse, but the glass of the greenhouse is not as transparent to heat energy as it is to light energy, so some of the heat is then trapped inside the greenhouse. The glass also plays a major role in preventing warm air from rising through convection to dissipate the heat. The result is that the temperature inside the greenhouse is warmer than outside. This helps plants to grow better when it is cold outside, which is one of the main reasons why farmers and gardeners use greenhouses.

The inside of a greenhouse.

Even if you have never been inside a greenhouse, you have probably felt the greenhouse effect when getting into a car that has been sitting in the sunshine with its windows closed on a hot day. The

Governments all over the world have been looking at various possibilities for preventing climate change from getting worse. Over the years, efforts such as the Rio Summits in 1992 and 2012, and the Kyoto Protocol in 1997, have tried to establish goals for carbon emissions. More recently, ideas of a 'carbon tax' or 'cap and trade' policies have been put forward, so that countries compensate for their excessive carbon emissions. Fast-growing economies such as China and India have been under scrutiny for their exponential increases in energy needs, and have been criticized by industrialized nations for using non-renewable energy sources such as coal, which produce excessive carbon dioxide emissions.

It can be considered curious that industrialized countries that for centuries have built their economies on carbon dioxide-emitting fossil fuels would tell countries that are more recently following such economic development that they cannot do the same. It will be interesting to see whether countries all over the world will continue to burn fossil fuels until the last lump of coal or the last drop of crude oil is gone. Then again, perhaps international agreements will curb fossil fuel use and prevent climate change from getting worse.

greenhouse effect on a planet is not caused by glass windows, but by its atmosphere's ability to retain heat in a similar way to that of the glass of a greenhouse or car.

Greenhouse gases (GHGs), such as water vapour and carbon dioxide in Earth's atmosphere, can be thought of as the glass of a greenhouse, although, like many models, this is not a very accurate representation of the natural phenomenon. GHGs have the ability to absorb and radiate infrared radiation (heat). When such gases are present, they keep the atmosphere near Earth's surface warm by absorbing heat from the warmed surface and re-radiating it in all directions, including back down towards the surface. In addition to carbon dioxide and water vapour, methane and nitrogen oxides also contribute to Earth's greenhouse effect, but to a lesser extent.

Climate experts at the International Panel on Climate Change (IPCC) have confirmed that Earth is undergoing global warming because of an enhanced greenhouse effect, also known as the runaway greenhouse effect. Increasing levels of some of the main greenhouse gases (as a result of human activities, such as burning fossil fuels) are causing the atmosphere to retain more and more heat. There will be more about how this works later.

Different gases, different impacts

Different gases in the atmosphere have different impacts on the greenhouse effect on Earth. There are two main factors that determine how much of an influence a gas will have on the greenhouse effect:

- the ability of the gas to absorb long-wave radiation (heat)
- the concentration of that gas in the atmosphere.

Methane, for example, actually has a much greater potential to warm the planet than carbon dioxide, but methane has a relatively short lifetime in the atmosphere: approximately 12 years. Carbon dioxide has an estimated lifetime of 50–200 years in the atmosphere. This is because methane can be broken down into other molecules, whereas carbon dioxide is not very reactive and so can stay in the atmosphere for much longer.

Studies of increases in carbon dioxide and methane gases over time have revealed that carbon dioxide concentrations have increased by approximately 40% since 1750, while methane concentrations have increased by more than 150% in the same time period. However, methane concentrations in Earth's atmosphere are about 1700 p.p.b. (parts per billion) whereas carbon dioxide concentrations are about 400 p.p.m. (parts per million), meaning that the concentration of carbon dioxide is more than 200 times greater than that of methane.

This huge difference is the main reason why environmental groups and government policy makers are much more interested in carbon dioxide concentrations than methane concentrations, although both need to be taken into account in discussions about global climate change. Nitrogen oxides represent just over 320 p.p.b., so they are about a fifth the concentration of methane and, even though they have a global warming potential more than 100 times that of carbon dioxide, their concentration in the atmosphere is more than 1000 times smaller than carbon dioxide concentrations, so they are less of a concern.

Table 4.7 Concentrations of GHGs in Earth's atmosphere

	Concentration in p.p.b. or p.p.m.	Equivalent in %
Carbon dioxide	400 p.p.m.	0.04
Methane	1700 p.p.b.	0.00017
Nitrogen oxides	320 p.p.b.	0.000032

Planet Earth gives off heat

As we have seen with a greenhouse, when sunlight touches an object inside, some of the light energy is absorbed and converted into heat energy, also known as long-wave infrared radiation. On Earth, the mountains, forests, rivers, and oceans absorb some of the sunlight and are warmed. Most of the sunlight bounces off the surface and goes back into space. This is what makes photos such as the one at the top of page 215 possible. Only a small amount is converted into infrared to warm up the surface.

The ability of a surface to reflect light is called its albedo. Light-coloured objects, such as ice and white sand, have a high albedo, so very little light is absorbed and such objects do not heat up as much as dark objects such as dark-coloured rocks and black sand. Think about walking barefoot on light-coloured cement on a hot and sunny day, compared with walking barefoot on black asphalt on the same day. Dark-coloured substances such as the asphalt have a low albedo, and absorb lots of light and convert it into heat.

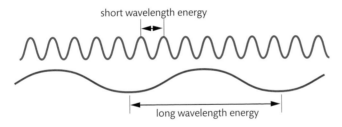

Figure 4.20 Different wavelengths of energy have different properties.

How greenhouse gases heat the atmosphere

If Earth had no atmosphere, the heat radiating from low albedo objects on its surface would simply radiate back into space, and at night we would see temperatures plunge to ones similar to the extremely cold temperatures on the Moon.

Table 4.8 Temperatures on Earth and the Moon

Temperature ranges on Earth (with a natural greenhouse effect)	from −80°C to +50°C
Temperature ranges on the Moon (without a natural greenhouse effect)	from −150°C to +120°C

The reason that this does not happen is because the greenhouse gases absorb and retain the infrared radiation coming from the surface. The greenhouse gases can then re-radiate the heat in all directions, the way a radiator does in a cold room. Some of this heat will be lost to space, but some of the long-wave radiation will be directed down to the surface, keeping it warm. The rest will radiate within the atmosphere, preventing it

Because the greenhouse effect is often misunderstood, be sure to master the scientific vocabulary and concepts. This is challenging for students and adults alike. Few people can explain it precisely, too often saying something incorrect such as 'sunlight is trapped in the air'.

from getting extremely cold at night when no more sunlight is present. When the Sun rises again in the morning, the surface will heat up and the whole process starts again.

During the winter season, the days are shorter and the angle of sunlight is less direct, so Earth's surface cannot warm up as much. This is why it is colder in the winter. In the summer, days are longer and the sunlight hits Earth's surface more directly and intensely. Earth's surface can get very hot, and, during heat waves, the nights are not cool enough to cause the daytime temperatures to lower.

Fortunately, certain gases in the atmosphere filter out some of the more harmful radiation from the Sun, such as UV radiation. Because the atmosphere filters the sunlight, not all of it reaches the surface. This prevents the surface from getting as hot as the Moon's maximum temperature of +120°C, even on the hottest of summer days. So you can see how the atmosphere acts as a kind of blanket around the planet: at night it keeps the planet warm, and during the day it provides a barrier protecting life from too much solar radiation.

Figure 4.21 A summary of the greenhouse effect: short-wave radiation (shown in yellow) hits the surface and some is converted into long-wave radiation (shown in orange). Some of this infrared heat escapes into space but some (shown in red) is radiated back by greenhouse gases.

Global climate change is affected by greenhouse gases

Climate refers to the patterns of temperature and precipitation, such as rainfall, that occur over long periods of time. Whereas weather can change from hour to hour, climates usually do not change within a human's lifetime: climate changes generally occur over thousands or millions of years. Climatologists and palaeoclimatologists collect data about atmospheric conditions in recent decades and the distant past, respectively. As thermometers have only been around for a few hundred years, temperatures on Earth from thousands or millions of years ago must be inferred from proxies.

NATURE OF SCIENCE

How can scientists determine a quantitative value for something that is not directly measurable? The answer is by using a proxy, which is a measurement that is used in place of another one. Because it is impossible to go back in time and measure the temperature of the atmosphere 15 000 years ago, climatologists use proxies, such as tree rings, coral reef growth, and the presence of fossils of temperature-sensitive organisms, to estimate the climate back then. By digging in layers of sediment 15 000 years old and looking at the kinds of bones, shells, coral reefs, plant fossils, and even pollen grains, climatologists can work out what the climate was like at that time in the past. Certain species of foraminifera microfossils, for example, can reveal temperature changes via slight changes in the chemical compositions of their shells.

An ice core being removed from the drilling apparatus.

Layers found in thick sheets of ice that have been formed by annual snowfall can also be used in a similar way as tree rings and ocean sediments. By drilling into the ice and taking cylinder-shaped samples, called ice cores, scientists can study the substances trapped in the layers, such as air bubbles from the year when the layer was deposited. Researchers at Vostok Station in Antarctica have collected layers of ice from more than 3000 m down, yielding climate information going back more than 400 000 years. One indication of temperature is the frequency of different types of isotopes (versions of atoms) found in the air bubbles. Oxygen atoms, for example, are usually found in their most abundant isotope, which is oxygen-16, but can also be found in their 'heavier' form, oxygen-18, which has a greater mass because it has two extra neutrons. When glaciations happen, the oceans have a slightly higher ratio of oxygen-18, and the glaciers that form have a slightly higher ratio of oxygen-16. By examining these ratios in ice and in the shells of marine fossils, climatologists can trace the colder and warmer periods of the past.

Proxy data show that, in the northern hemisphere 15 000 years ago, it was very cold, and Earth was undergoing a glaciation, or ice age. Ice ages were periods of significant change in climate that produced sheets of ice hundreds of metres thick in regions where today there are thriving cities. For example, in the geographical location that is now Berlin in Germany, there would have been an ice sheet similar to the ones still sitting on Greenland and Antarctica today. The last ice age ended about 10 000 years ago, and we are now in an interglacial period associated with warmer temperatures. It does not take much of a temperature drop to produce a glaciation: it is estimated that the last ice age was caused by a global average temperature reduction of 5°C. By looking at deeper ice cores, we know that there has been a succession of ice ages over millions of years.

CHALLENGE YOURSELF

5   The graph below shows the results of collecting data representing thousands of years trapped in ice core samples.

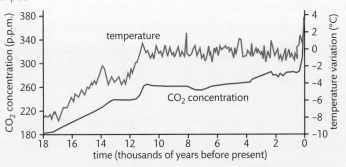

The red line on the graph shows carbon dioxide concentrations that were measured from air bubbles trapped in the ice.

The blue line shows fluctuations between warmer temperatures that are close to zero (representing no change from modern climatic conditions) and colder temperatures several degrees below what they are today.

(a) Is there a strong or a weak correlation between carbon dioxide levels and atmospheric temperatures over the last 400 000 years?

(b) Can scientists conclude that there is causality from this graph: that rising carbon dioxide levels cause global temperatures to go up?

(c) What further evidence would be necessary to confirm or refute causality?

Figure 4.22 Ice core data.

Earth has shown many fluctuations in global temperatures over millions of years. Such fluctuations happened long before humans started producing excessive greenhouse gases. The changes being observed now are alarming scientists because they cannot be explained by natural phenomena.

Many factors are thought to contribute to global temperature changes over time, for example volcanic activity and particles suspended in the air, the quantity of radiation from the Sun, the position of the continents (which move on plates over millions of years), oscillations in ocean currents, fluctuations in Earth's orbit and the inclination of its axis, and probably other phenomena that are yet to be discovered. However, in this chapter we are only going to focus on the influence of changes in the composition of the atmosphere, notably the presence of greenhouse gases.

As shown in Figure 4.22, there appears to be a strong correlation between temperature increase and carbon dioxide increase. Knowing the properties of greenhouse gases, as discussed earlier, it is clear that an increase in carbon dioxide levels will lead to warming of the atmosphere, because it would increase the greenhouse effect. Having said this, closer inspection of the data shows that the increase in temperature (in blue) happens first and then the carbon dioxide concentration (in red) rises. This lag time is partly explained by the fact that, as oceans warm up, they release carbon dioxide, because gases dissolve less well in warm water than in cold water. A positive feedback loop leads to further increases in temperatures over time: warmer temperatures → more carbon dioxide → even warmer temperatures → even more carbon dioxide, and so on.

NATURE OF SCIENCE

Want to see the data for yourself? One of the principles of science, especially research funded by taxpayers, is to make data available to the public. This is to allow verification, critique, and sharing of data, so that scientists with many different approaches can combine their findings and advance our understanding of the topics being studied.

One organization that does this is NOAA. If you go to the NOAA Earth System Research Laboratory Global Monitoring Division's website (see the hotlinks at the end of this section), you will find maps, graphs, and databases of measurements of carbon dioxide and other atmospheric gases over many decades. Check out the section called Products.

The industrial revolution

Ever since machines started replacing hand tools in Europe in the 1800s, humans have produced increasing quantities of carbon dioxide from factories, transport, and other processes using fossil fuels, notably coal and oil. In addition, burning forests to make way for farmland and burning wood for cooking and heating has contributed to this increase.

Figure 4.23 Two hundred years of atmospheric changes.

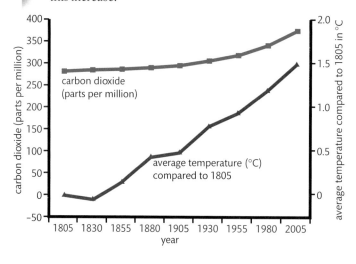

Over the decades, human activities have produced enough carbon dioxide to considerably raise the percentage of this gas in the planet's atmosphere. Estimates suggest that the level of carbon dioxide in the atmosphere has increased by more than 35% compared with its pre-industrial revolution levels.

How do scientists know that the current situation is exceptional, that the changes in Earth's atmosphere are being caused by human activities and are not just part of a natural phenomenon?

Recent increases in atmospheric carbon dioxide are largely due to increases in the combustion of fossilized organic matter

The gases produced by human activity that retain the most heat are among the ones we have already identified as greenhouse gases: carbon dioxide, methane, and oxides of nitrogen. The concentrations of these gases in the atmosphere are naturally low, which normally prevents too much heat retention.

The number one source of carbon emissions as a result of human activity is transport that is based on fossil fuels: cars, lorries, diesel trains, and airplanes. Other human activities that put carbon dioxide into the air include the following: deforestation, heating homes by burning fossil fuels, maintaining a diet high in meat (the meat industry is highly dependent on fossil fuels), purchasing goods that have to be transported long distances from where they are produced to where they will be used, travelling long distances between work and home, purchasing foods that are grown out of season in greenhouses heated by fossil fuels.

Human activities contribute to the production of other greenhouse gases. Again, diet has an impact here, this time with the production of methane. Remember that methane is produced by anaerobic microorganisms present in the guts of animals. Mass consumption of meat, especially in the USA, where people eat the most meat per person per year, has led to an increase in the number of cattle being raised. Cattle are responsible for producing large amounts of methane that escape into the atmosphere.

Each vehicle produces its own mass in carbon dioxide every year.

Lastly, oxides of nitrogen (NO_x) are produced by human activities such as:

• burning fossil fuels (e.g. gasoline in cars) and using catalytic converters in exhaust systems
• using organic and commercial fertilizers to help crops grow better
• industrial processes (e.g. the production of nitric acid).

Consumer demands push industries to produce more, which means burning more energy and releasing increasing amounts of greenhouse gases.

! Do not confuse the greenhouse effect with the depletion of ozone. Although both are the result of human activity, and both influence the atmosphere, they are not interchangeable phenomena. They have different causes and different effects on the environment.

Consumer demands for wood products such as housing, firewood, furniture, and paper lead to massive deforestation.

The problem is that human production of greenhouse gases shows little sign of slowing. As consumer demands for fuel and food increase, so the excess production of waste gases increases.

 NATURE OF SCIENCE

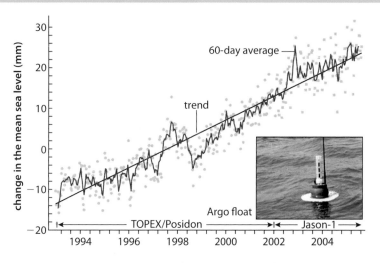

Figure 4.24 NASA data on sea level and the Argo marker, which is used to make the measurements.

How do scientists collect data to see climate change? Look at the various types of data on this page. What kinds of technology are necessary in order to collect the data? How do these data contribute to our understanding of climate change? Large portions of this chapter have dealt with carbon dioxide concentrations: how and where are they collected? Do stations in different parts of the world agree or disagree about trends in carbon dioxide emissions?

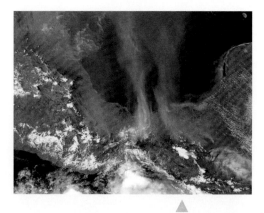

This is a satellite photo of forest fires in the Yucatan peninsula in 1998. The forests were drier than usual that year. Forest fires release large quantities of carbon dioxide into the atmosphere.

Threats to coral reefs

The organisms that build coral reefs are very sensitive to the following: water temperature, water acidity, and the depth of the water. Unfortunately, all three factors are changing in the oceans of the world as a result of human activities. Increased carbon dioxide concentrations in the air lead to increased dissolved carbon dioxide in the oceans, which lowers the pH of seawater. When it is intense, ocean acidification leads to the death of coral polyps and algae, and when they die the reefs are not built up anymore. As a result, the colour of the reef goes from being richly multi-coloured to being as white as bone. This coral reef death is called bleaching and it interrupts the food chain, causing many of the organisms that live there to seek food and shelter elsewhere. Similar to a forest that has lost all its leaves because of acid rain, a bleached coral reef can no longer support the rich ecosystem that once lived there.

Are humans causing global climate change?

Not everyone is convinced that climate change is happening, or that it is caused by human activity. Such critics are sometimes referred to as 'climate change deniers', and they have a number of criticisms about the IPCC's findings.

How do scientists respond to such criticism? What arguments and justifications do they use in response? Table 4.9 presents a few.

Table 4.9 Opinions of climatologists and their critics

Challenges from critics	Possible responses from climatologists
Climate change as a result of human activity is just a theory, not a fact.	Evidence clearly shows temperature increases since the industrial revolution. Decades-old predictions of extreme weather events, record temperatures, and receding glaciers are being confirmed day after day. Climate change is not a debate or a controversy: it is well-supported by an increasing volume of data. The findings of the IPCC state, 'The largest contribution to total radiative forcing is caused by the increase in the atmospheric concentration of CO_2 since 1750.' The term 'radiative forcing' means the difference between the energy arriving at the surface and the energy being lost into space. And the increase in CO_2 referred to is clearly traced to human activity.
There is disagreement within the scientific community about human-induced climate change. Many scientists disagree and have published research showing that climate change is not due to human activity.	The vast majority of recent publications from climatologists confirm anthropogenic climate change; there is a consensus in the scientific community. Often the dissenting scientists who are quoted by critics are not climatologists, or they are quoting out-of-date or refuted data. In other instances, scientists only disagree on the quantity of change or on the amount of responsibility of human activity.
Your models predicted even more of a temperature increase than is actually happening. How can you explain that? Human activities such as burning fossil fuels are increasing, so why aren't the temperatures increasing equally as fast?	Like any science, climatology is complex and we are learning new things all the time. For example, human activities such as transport produce particles in the air that remain in suspension, and some of these aerosols can diffuse sunlight, causing a reduction in the amount of short-wave solar radiation reaching the surface. Less solar radiation hitting Earth means lower temperatures because there are fewer rays of short-wave radiation reaching the surface to be converted into infrared. This phenomenon is cancelling out some of the predicted warming.

Challenges from critics	Possible responses from climatologists
There have been huge fluctuations in climate in the past, and the current changes that we are seeing in recent decades are natural. For example, the Sun is currently in a phase of high-energy output. Wouldn't that be a more logical explanation?	Although it is true that Earth's climate has seen warming and cooling in the past, those changes were relatively slow, taking place over thousands or millions of years. The changes that we are seeing now are happening on a scale of decades, and the speed and magnitude at which CO_2 levels and temperature are increasing are unprecedented. One concrete example of the consequences are so-called 100-year storms that, instead of happening once every century, are occurring several times within the same decade. As for the Sun's output: yes, it is currently in a high-output phase, but that extra energy has only a small fraction of the effect that human-induced global warming has. Also, the most recent hottest years on record happened during a period of lower solar output.
Insisting that climate change is caused by human activity means that, to solve the problem, we are going to need to reduce CO_2 emissions. That will have a severe negative economic effect, as many carbon-based industries will lose revenue.	The alternative, if we let people introduce more and more greenhouse gases into the atmosphere, will exacerbate the already highly destructive patterns we are seeing, and the cost of fixing these new problems is difficult to imagine. Enormous economic burdens are presented by problems such as the damage caused by an increase in extreme weather events, such as super storms and hurricanes, rising sea levels, droughts as well as flooding, a reduction of snow at high altitudes influencing melt water supplies downstream, to name a few.

In the end, climatologists make a clear distinction between what is politically controversial and what is scientifically controversial. The political debate is often driven by non-scientific arguments. One way to spot non-scientific arguments is to look for whether or not the proponent's comments are motivated by economic arguments, notably when they are motivated by their affiliation with industries that produce large quantities of carbon dioxide. As such industries would potentially lose revenue if limits were put on carbon dioxide emissions, it is in their interest to promote doubt and controversy.

NATURE OF SCIENCE

Climate change raises many issues about how science works. Here are four to consider.

1 The fact that there are sceptics and critics of the IPCC reports on global climate change is a good thing. Science encourages constructive criticism and verification, and is open to modification if the criticisms are valid. Often errors and misinterpretations of data are spotted when many people read a publication, and this pushes scientists to be more precise and to be better communicators.

2 The IPCC report is filled with qualifying statements such as 'likely', 'highly likely', 'extremely likely' about the future. Why can't IPCC just make up its mind and say that something is sure to happen? Because systems such as global climate are complex, scientists do not fully understand how they work and, although they are regularly gaining further insights, sometimes they are wrong. For example, the predictions of how fast global temperatures will increase seem to have been confirmed for some years but not for others.

3 Climate change deniers will grab onto such inaccurate predictions and say, 'See? Your models are wrong. Therefore, no one should listen to you.' This is an example of cherry picking, something both sides of the debate are accused of doing. Cherry picking is a form of confirmation bias that consists of only looking at the evidence supporting your side of the argument, and ignoring or downplaying the evidence that hurts your argument. Both sides of the debate have been accused of following blind faith rather than objectively assessing the evidence.

4 Scientists need money for their work, and they often get that money from grants offered by governments and industries. If a scientist is getting funding from an organization that promotes the preservation of nature, the chances are reasonably good that that scientist will tend to look for evidence of human-induced climate change, whereas a scientist whose funding comes from industries highly reliant on fossil fuels will probably tend to look for evidence against human-induced climate change. Journalists and citizens need to be vigilant about this, and double-check where the interpretations of the data are coming from.

CHALLENGE YOURSELF

6 Do you know your carbon footprint? This is the amount of carbon dioxide you as an individual are contributing to the atmosphere. There are many online 'Footprint calculators' available, notably from the Nature Conservancy and WWF. Use the hotlinks at the end of this section to try one: what do you get, and how do you compare with the rest of the world? In what ways are you willing to try to reduce your carbon footprint: diet, transport, home energy use? The website that calculates commuters' itineraries on the Metro system in Paris, France, also calculates how much carbon is saved by not burning fossil fuels for the same commute. Does your public transport system's website have a similar calculator?

Too often people think that climate change is someone else's doing, that their personal day-to-day decisions do not have an impact.

When playing a board game with family or friends, cheating is frowned upon. If one player took more turns or more points than the rules allowed, that person would be considered a cheater and might be asked to leave the table. If everyone around the table started cheating, the game would break down completely. Are there similar situations in society? For example, if a few people break the law, they are often treated as criminals and punished; but if everyone cheated all the time, society would break down. Are there any parallels with pollution? If people are knowingly polluting and not doing anything to reduce their carbon footprint, are they treated by society as cheaters?

There are enough warning signs to lead experts to invoke the precautionary principle. This is an ethical theory that says that action should be taken to prevent harm even if there is not sufficient data to prove that the activity will have severe negative consequences. It also stipulates that if people wish to engage in an activity that may cause changes in the environment, they must first prove that it will not do harm.

Without the precautionary principle, industries and consumers tend to proceed with their activities until it becomes clear that harm is being done to the environment. When irrefutable proof is provided, usually action is taken to reduce the activity in question. For example, the use of the pesticide DDT was prohibited in North America when it was proven to accumulate in ecosystems and reduce populations of birds of prey such as the bald eagle. That decision saved the bald eagle from extinction. How can we 'prove' that something is safe for the environment?

With regards to global warming, tenets of the precautionary principle say that preventative action should be taken now to reduce carbon emissions and greenhouse gas production before it is too late. In addition, the principle holds that those who wish to continue producing excess greenhouse gases should prove that there are no harmful effects before continuing.

In response, farmers, manufacturers, and transport providers, among others, wonder why they should invest money in new techniques that reduce greenhouse gases if scientists are not 100% sure how an enhanced greenhouse effect is going to be harmful to the environment. Industries that make the effort to invest in such measures may find themselves less economically viable than their polluting competitors.

Consequently, unless preventative measures are taken across the board by countries worldwide, there will always be polluting competitors who can offer products at a lower price. The risk is that they will drive the ecologically conscious companies out of business because they do not use any of their capital on ecological measures.

Ideally, well-informed consumers could choose products or services that are provided by ecologically minded companies. If this is done on a massive scale, companies would provide eco-friendly products and services to attract customers, and those companies that did not would be shunned as rogue companies by consumers and be driven out of business.

To learn more about NOAA and carbon footprints, go to the hotlinks site, search for the title or ISBN, and click on Chapter 4: Section 4.4.

Section summary

- Earth's atmosphere acts in a similar way as glass in a greenhouse, keeping the temperature warmer.
- Shorter wavelength energy from the Sun goes through the atmosphere and hits Earth's surface, warming it up.

- Some of the heat, which is a type of long-wave radiation, is trapped by greenhouse gases (GHGs) such as carbon dioxide, water vapour, nitrogen oxides, and methane. Some GHGs are better at absorbing heat than others, and some are more concentrated in the atmosphere than others.
- The flux of carbon into the atmosphere is increasing as a result of human activities over the past two centuries, such as the burning of fossil fuels and deforestation.
- Excess carbon dioxide is causing an increase in the intensity of the greenhouse effect. This is correlated with an increase in global temperatures.
- Instead of spending their time and energy on finding solutions to the challenges that global climate change is creating, some sceptics prefer to doubt that there is a problem at all and ignore the findings of climate experts.

Exercises

10 Distinguish between how a garden greenhouse works and how the greenhouse effect on Earth works.

11 Of the greenhouse gases discussed in this chapter, state which one has a warming potential approximately 100 times that of carbon dioxide. Why aren't scientists talking more about this if it has such a potential to increase the greenhouse effect?

12 In what ways could you reduce your consumption of fossil fuels on a day-to-day basis?

13 A scuba diver returns to her favourite coral reef only to find it empty of life and all the corals turned white. She asks you if you know what this phenomenon is: what do you tell her?

Practice questions

1 What is a community?

   A A group of producers and consumers living and interacting in an area.

   B A group of species living and interacting in an area.

   C A group of organisms living and interacting in an area.

   D A group of populations living and interacting in an area. *(Total 1 mark)*

2 The scarlet cup fungus, *Sarcoscypha coccinea*, obtains its nutrition from decaying wood by releasing digestive enzymes into the wood and absorbing the digested products. Which of the following terms describe(s) the fungus?

   I. Autotroph   II. Heterotroph   III. Saprotroph

   A III only.   **B** II and III only.   **C** I and III only.   **D** I, II, and III.

   (Total 1 mark)

3 Why do food chains in an ecosystem rarely contain more than five organisms?

   A Nutrients are recycled by the decomposers back to the producers.

   B Nutrients are lost from the ecosystem when organisms die.

   C The conversion of food into growth by an organism is not very efficient.

   D Energy is recycled by the decomposers back to the producers. *(Total 1 mark)*

4 Several greenhouse gases occur in the atmosphere. Carbon dioxide (CO_2) is one of them but so are methane (CH_4) and oxides of nitrogen (NO_x). Why are oxides of nitrogen classed as greenhouse gases?

   A They trap some of the long-wave radiation emitted by Earth's surface.

   B They prevent short-wave radiation from reaching Earth's surface.

   C They dissolve in rainwater to produce acid rain.

D They are only produced by human activity whereas CO_2 and CH_4 are also
produced naturally. *(Total 1 mark)*

5 Explain the shape of the pyramids of energy that are constructed by ecologists to
represent energy flow in an ecosystem. *(Total 3 marks)*

6 This diagram represents a simple food chain. In which ways is energy lost between the
trophic levels?

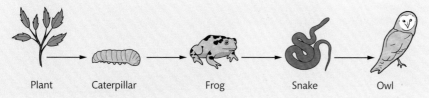

| Plant | Caterpillar | Frog | Snake | Owl |

    I.   Heat loss through cell respiration.

    II.   Material not consumed.

    III. Material not assimilated.

A I and II only.   **B** I and III only.   **C** II and III only.   **D** I, II, and III.

(Total 1 mark)

7 Describe the relationship between the rise in the concentration of atmospheric carbon
dioxide and the enhanced greenhouse effect. *(Total 5 marks)*

8 Variations in the concentration of carbon dioxide in the atmosphere can be studied using
ice cores. An ice core record covering the last 400 000 years has been obtained from
Vostok in the Antarctic. The graph below shows the carbon dioxide concentrations that
were measured at different depths in the ice. Atmospheric temperatures are also shown
on the graph. These were deduced from ratios of oxygen isotopes. The upper line on the
graph shows CO_2 concentrations and the lower line shows temperature.

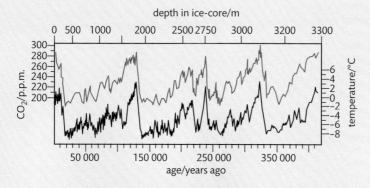

Kump 2002. Reprinted by permission from
Macmillan Publishers Ltd. Copyright © 2002

(a) (i) State the highest carbon dioxide concentration shown on the graph. (1)

    (ii) State the highest temperature shown on the graph. (1)

(b) Using the data in the graph, deduce the relationship between atmospheric carbon
dioxide concentration and temperature. (1)

(Total 3 marks)

9 Outline the precautionary principle. *(Total 2 marks)*

05

Evolution and biodiversity

Essential ideas

5.1 There is overwhelming evidence for the evolution of life on Earth.

5.2 The diversity of life has evolved and continues to evolve by natural selection.

5.3 Species are named and classified using an internationally agreed system.

5.4 The ancestry of groups of species can be deduced by comparing their base or amino acid sequences.

Lemurs arrived on the Comoro Islands and Madagascar about 6.5 million years ago and have adapted to the many habitats available there. They used to be common on mainland Africa but natural selection, notably competition with other primates, has eliminated them from the continent.

There are almost 2 million species on Earth that have been catalogued and given a scientific name, the biggest number being insects. However, there are many more species as yet unidentified, and it is impossible to know exactly how many there are in the biosphere: 5 million? 10 million? 20 million? Even more overwhelming is trying to imagine how many species there were in the past that have now gone extinct. The organisms on Earth today represent much less than 1% of all life forms that have ever existed. How life has changed over time and how we make sense of the living world around us is the focus of this chapter. Understanding the mechanisms by which species evolve by natural selection is arguably one of the most important and influential concepts in biology. So much can be explained by natural selection, from why zebras have stripes, to why new bacterial populations that are resistant to antibiotics are being found in hospitals.

5.1 Evidence for evolution

Understandings:
- Evolution occurs when heritable characteristics of a species change.
- The fossil record provides evidence for evolution.
- Selective breeding of domesticated animals shows that artificial selection can cause evolution.
- Evolution of homologous structures by adaptive radiation explains similarities in structure when there are differences in function.
- Populations of a species can gradually diverge into separate species by evolution.
- Continuous variation across the geographical range of related populations matches the concept of gradual divergence.

Applications and skills:
- Application: Development of melanistic insects in polluted areas.
- Application: Comparison of the pentadactyl limb of mammals, birds, amphibians, and reptiles with different methods of locomotion.

NATURE OF SCIENCE

Looking for patterns, trends, and discrepancies: there are common features in the bone structure of vertebrate limbs despite their varied use.

Charles Darwin (1809–82).

Darwin and Wallace

At the age of 22, Charles Darwin had the opportunity to travel on board the HMS *Beagle* for a scientific exploration mission starting in 1831 and lasting for 5 years. Little did he know that it would allow him to see nature in a new way and come up with what would become one of the most important, controversial, and misinterpreted ideas in biology: evolution by natural selection.

Darwin was not the only person to develop a theory to explain evolution. Darwin was surprised to discover in 1858 that Alfred Russel Wallace had independently developed a nearly identical theory. The two men presented their ideas jointly to the Linnaean Society in 1858.

What is evolution?

Evolution is defined as the process of cumulative change in the heritable characteristics of a population. The word heritable means that the changes must be passed on genetically from one generation to the next, which implies that evolution does not happen overnight. The word cumulative is in the definition to stress the fact that one change is usually not enough to have a major impact on a species. Finally, the word population is in the definition because the changes do not affect just one individual.

Over time, if enough changes occur in a population, a new species can arise in a process called speciation. The members of the new population will be different enough from the pre-existing population that they came from that they will no longer be able to interbreed. Such a process is rarely observable during a human lifetime. However, once you begin to understand evolution, it should become clear that all of life on Earth is unified by its common origins.

It has been argued that once evolution by natural selection is understood, many of the mysteries of nature are revealed. Although there are others, we will examine three phenomena that provide evidence for evolution by natural selection: the fossil record, animal breeding, and homologous structures. Later, we will also look at DNA evidence. When the role of DNA in inheritance (genetics) became understood, it appeared to some to contradict evolution by natural selection; such contradictions often arise with new developments in science. In fact, DNA evidence provides new support for natural selection beyond anything Darwin could have dreamt of, and is referred to as the modern synthesis or neo-Darwinism, a combination of Darwin's ideas with a newer one, the idea of genetics that Mendel started, that was only confirmed long after both men had died.

Darwin's theory of evolution by natural selection	+	Mendel's work confirmed by later understanding of DNA and genetics	=	Modern synthesis or neo-Darwinism used by evolutionary biologists today

The fossil record and evolution

It is impossible to travel back in time, and the best clues scientists have about what life was like thousands or millions of years ago come from fossils. Fossils are the petrified remains or traces of animals and plants, and the fossil record is the accumulation of evidence from these remains and traces, such as skeletons and footprints. Palaeontologists have been collecting and classifying fossils in an organized fashion for almost two centuries.

If you have ever been to a museum full of fossils classified by their age, you may have noticed a few things that palaeontologists have discovered that provide convincing evidence for Earth's evolutionary past.

- Overall, the life that existed more than 500 million years ago was vastly different in appearance from life today.
- Although planet Earth has had extensive oceans for most of its existence, fish fossils have only been found in rocks 500 million years old or younger (less than 15% of the 3.5-billion year existence of life on our planet).
- Although most of the top predators today are mammals such as bears, orcas, big cats, and wolves, none of them existed at the time of the dinosaurs or before.
- Apart from organisms such as certain types of sharks, cockroaches, and ferns, the majority of living organisms today have no similar form in the fossil record.

One conclusion that can be drawn from studying fossils is that life on Earth is constantly changing. However, most of the changes have occurred over huge timescales (hundreds of thousands or millions of years); timescales that humans find difficult to grasp.

Fossil hunting is the job of palaeontologists, and the best palaeontologists are willing to travel around the globe searching for bones, footprints, and plant remains. Some countries have policies controlling fossils to make sure that scientifically significant fossils are kept in museums or university collections. Other countries do not have such policies (or the policies are ignored by smugglers), and fossil hunters can sell fossils for profit to people wanting to add them to their personal collections. Should fossils be protected and conserved, or should they be considered as a commodity that can be bought and sold? What international organization should decide on and enforce such policies?

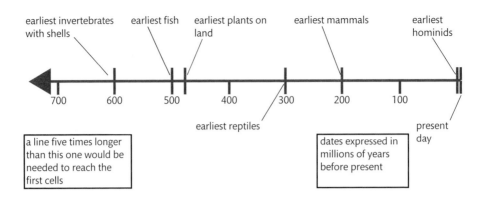

earliest invertebrates with shells

earliest fish

earliest plants on land

earliest mammals

earliest hominids

earliest reptiles

present day

a line five times longer than this one would be needed to reach the first cells

dates expressed in millions of years before present

Figure 5.1 Timeline of a few of the earliest traces of various types of living organisms. Things really started to get interesting in the fossil record around 580 million years ago, when organisms started making body parts that were solid enough to leave clear fossils. For most of the history of life (the 3 billion years not shown on this line), organisms had soft bodies that were not favourable to the formation of fossils, so their remains are more difficult to find.

Ageing fossils

The age of a rock can be determined by carefully examining differences in the ratios of isotopes. Isotopes are versions of atoms that are heavier or lighter than other versions of the same atom (carbon-14 has more mass than carbon-12). If a fossil of a bone or shell has a high level of carbon-14, for example, it is younger than a bone or shell that has a very low level of carbon-14. This is because carbon-14, also written ^{14}C, is radioactive but slowly loses its radioactivity; as it gives off its radioactivity, it transforms into another atom, nitrogen-14. This process of a radioactive parent isotope changing into a stable daughter isotope is called decay. The speed at which this happens is expressed as an isotope's half-life. Half-life is defined as the time it takes for half of the parent isotope to decay into a stable daughter isotope.

The half-life of ^{14}C is 5730 years, meaning that, when an animal dies, its bones will have lost half their ^{14}C after 5730 years. After 11 460 years, half of that amount (now 25% of the original amount) will have decayed. Why is this important? Because by looking at the ratio of radioactive ^{14}C to stable ^{14}N, it is possible to determine the age of a fossil. If there is 12.5% of the radioactive isotope and 87.5% of the stable isotope, that means that three half-lives have gone by and the fossil is 17 190 years old. After a certain number of half-lives, there are so few ^{14}C atoms left that it is difficult to determine the age of the fossil with any accuracy.

Fortunately, if there is insufficient ^{14}C, there are other radioactive isotopes that have much longer half-lives, such as ^{40}K (potassium-40). When the minerals in rocks crystallize from magma, they contain a certain percentage of ^{40}K ions. Once the minerals have hardened and crystallized, no more ^{40}K ions can be added. However, the number reduces as the radioisotope decays

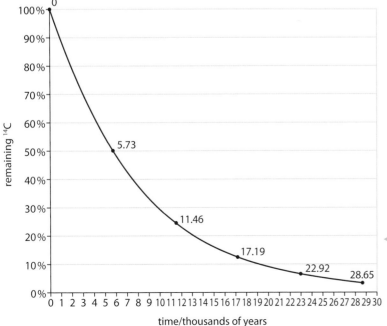

Figure 5.2 The effect of time on the proportion of radioisotope present in material containing carbon-14. The numbers on the curve show the passage of time (in thousands of years) through each successive half-life.

into more stable forms. Just as with ^{14}C, ^{40}K radiometric dating can be a useful tool in determining the age of a sample studied in a laboratory. Radiometric techniques with ^{40}K can be used to measure the age of rocks that formed from magma or lava between 100 000 years and 4.6 billion years ago.

Artificial selection and evolution

The fossil record is far from complete, but the science of breeding domesticated animals, for example cattle, horses, dogs, sheep, and pigeons, provides a good record of recent changes in heritable characteristics.

By watching which males mate with which females, animal breeders can see which characteristics the offspring will have. Of the offspring produced, not all will be equally valuable in the eyes of a breeder. Some cows produce better milk, other cows produce better meat; one breeder may be interested in better milk, another in better meat. Over the years, breeders have learned to choose the males and females with the most desirable genetic characteristics and breed them together.

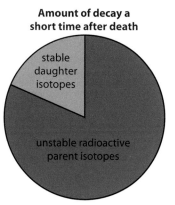
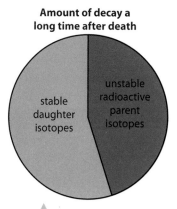

Figure 5.3 The proportions of radioisotopes and stable daughter isotopes in a once-living organism indicate the passage of time since the organism died. The higher the proportion of stable daughter isotopes, the older the fossil.

This cow has been bred to have a straight back for easier birthing and long legs for better milking by mechanical pumps. She is a product of artificial selection by humans and she never existed in this form before human intervention.

After practising selective breeding for dozens and sometimes hundreds of generations, farmers and breeders realized that certain varieties of animals now had unique combinations of characteristics that did not exist before. Today, the meat or milk available to us is very different from that which was produced a few generations ago, thanks to the accumulation of small changes in the genetic characteristics of livestock chosen by breeders.

Although this is evidence that evolution is happening as a result of an accumulation of small changes over time, the driving force is, of course, human choice. The farmers and breeders choose which animals will reproduce and which will not. This is called artificial selection and it should be obvious that it is certainly not the driving force of evolution in natural ecosystems.

Evolution of homologous structures by adaptive radiation

This is the front right fin of a southern right whale showing five articulated fingers.

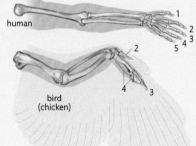

Other evidence for evolution comes from homologous anatomical structures, which are similar in form but which are found in seemingly dissimilar species. One of the most striking examples of this is the five-fingered limb found in animals as diverse as humans, whales, and bats. Such limbs are called pentadactyl limbs because 'penta' means five and 'dactyl' refers to fingers. Although the shape and number of the bones may vary, the general format is the same, despite the fact that the specific functions of the limbs may be very different. Darwin explained that homologous structures were not just a coincidence but evidence that the organisms in question have a common ancestor.

They may be of different sizes, and show varied morphology (shape), but the basic shape and position of the limb bones are the same. This would suggest that all five-fingered organisms have a common ancestor.

Whales, for example, could probably swim just as well with a different number of fingers in their front fins, so the fact that there are five suggests that there is a reason other than swimming efficiency: that of a common ancestry with other five-fingered organisms.

Homologies of the forelimb in six vertebrates

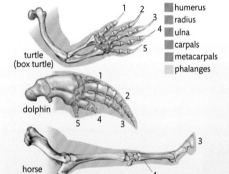
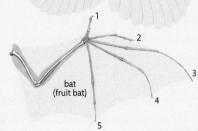

humerus
radius
ulna
carpals
metacarpals
phalanges

turtle (box turtle)

dolphin

horse

human

bird (chicken)

bat (fruit bat)

Figure 5.4 Pentadactyl forelimbs from various animals.

CHALLENGE YOURSELF

1 (a) Look at Figure 5.4 and complete Table 5.1.

Table 5.1

Characteristic	Bat	Bird	Human	Horse	Dolphin	Turtle
Number of digits (fingers)						
Description of phalanges (finger bones) (short/long, wide/narrow)						
Type of locomotion that the limb is best adapted for						

(b) There are two animals in Table 5.1 that have reduced their number of digits over the course of evolution. For these two animals, explain why it would have been a disadvantage to have kept all 5 digits. Limit your answer to the type of locomotion.

(c) Compare and contrast the salamander's forelimbs (Figure 5.5) to the organisms in Table 5.1. Be sure to address the idea of number of digits and locomotion.

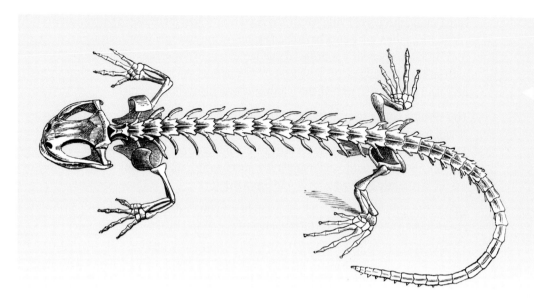

Species divergence

The process of an evolving population changing significantly enough so that the production of offspring with the original population becomes impossible is called speciation. In short, two populations of a species have diverged (separated), and a new species has evolved from an old one; both species will then continue on their separate ways.

Adaptive radiation

Adaptive radiation occurs when many similar but distinct species evolve relatively rapidly from a single species or from a small number of species. This happens as variations within a population allow certain members to exploit a slightly different niche in a more successful way. A niche is a position or role within a community of an ecosystem. By natural selection and the presence of some kind of barrier, a new species can evolve. A barrier separating populations might be a mountain range or a body of water.

An example of this are the primates found in Madagascar and the Comoro Islands off the south-east coast of Africa. Millions of years ago, without competition from monkeys or apes, lemurs on these islands were able to proliferate. Large numbers of offspring meant a greater chance for diversity.

Among the wide range of variation in lemur species, some are better adapted for living on the ground instead of in trees. Others are better adapted for living in lush rainforests, while some can survive in the desert. Most lemurs are active during the day (diurnal) but some are nocturnal. The reason why there are so many different species of lemur with different specialties is because of adaptive radiation.

Recall that a species must be able to freely interbreed with members of the same species to produce fertile offspring. If there has been a significant enough difference in two separated populations and they can no longer interbreed, a speciation has occurred.

Lemurs are primates found in Madagascar. They are a good example of adaptive radiation.

Not a single species of living lemur has been found anywhere else in the world. And yet fossils of their ancestors have been found on the continents of Africa, Europe, and Asia. What happened? It is believed that lemurs were not successful in competing with apes and monkeys, because as soon as traces of the latter start to become more prevalent in the fossil record, the lemur-like organisms become rare.

This would explain why continents and islands tend to have either prosimians (such as lemurs) or anthropoids (such as monkeys and apes), but not both types of primate. This is being confirmed today because more than a dozen species of lemur have become extinct recently, and many more are endangered, as a result of the activities of the most recently evolved anthropoid: humans.

Other examples of adaptive radiation can be seen in birds such as Darwin's finches (described in Section 5.2) on the Galapagos Islands and the Hawaiian honeycreepers. The honeycreepers have a wide variety of beak shapes, some of which are adapted exclusively to sip the nectar of flowers found only on Hawaii. It is believed that all the Hawaiian honeycreepers are the result of the adaptive radiation of a few members of one species that arrived on the islands.

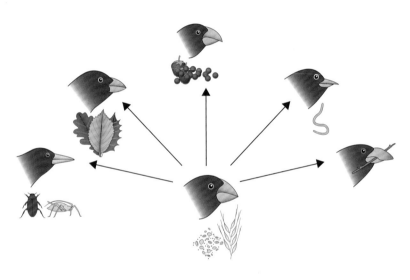

Figure 5.6 Adaptive radiation seen in Darwin's finches on the Galapagos Islands. An original species arrived on the island (bottom centre) but, over time, many species evolved, each one specializing in different food sources and habitats. Adapted from http://www.personal.psu.edu/staff/d/r/drs18/biscilmages/adaptiveRadiation2.png

Continuous variation and the concept of gradual divergence

In Figure 5.7, species A, B, C, and D come from a common ancestor. If any two of the species tried to mate, they would not successfully produce fertile offspring.

Figure 5.7 illustrates how one species can have various splits over time, creating a greater diversity between species. In some cases, the branches of the phylogenetic tree can become spaced so far apart that the species, although once closely related, do not physically resemble each other anymore. For example, when comparing a bird that has a long, thin beak to another with a short, fat beak, it is difficult to imagine that they are both descendants from the same species. And yet biologists have observed this in many species, notably ones that are spread over a wide geographical area.

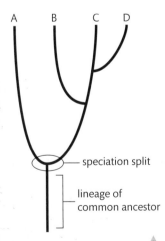

Figure 5.7 Speciation split shown on a phylogenetic tree.

NATURE OF SCIENCE

There is a species of plant that grows in coastal saltwater marshes called saltmarsh cordgrass, *Spartina alterniflora*. It plays an important role in providing habitat for organisms both above and below the water. The following investigation was carried out to determine whether differences in this plant along the eastern coast of the USA were the result of genetic variations or not. To test this, a group of scientists, led by Denise Seliskar, took samples of the cordgrass from three different states from different latitudes:

- Massachusetts (41° 34′ N)
- Delaware (38° 47′ N)
- Georgia (31° 25′ N).

They grew the plants in the same location at a research facility in Delaware and compared their growth in Delaware with how these plants grow in their native habitats. Notice how only one population is growing in its native state: the one from Delaware. The others have been moved either north or south of their native state. The investigators measured the growth of the plants over a 5-year period in various ways, including:

- biomass (how much dry organic material is produced in a year)
- height
- stem diameter.

The hypothesis was that, if there is no genetic variation within this species, then the three populations of plants from different latitudes will have similar growth patterns when grown in Delaware, because they are all given the same growing conditions of soil, water, light, and temperature.

The results, published in the *Journal of Ecology*, February 2002, were as follows. The population that originated from the south (Georgia) grew the most robustly. It showed the greatest biomass, height, and stem diameter. This is typical of plant growth in populations in southern latitudes where the climate is warmer. The northern-most population showed the least robust growth, matching values that were recorded in populations of its native Massachusetts. The population originally from Delaware showed no significant difference in growth from other populations in Delaware.

What can be concluded from this? Before you read on, can you reach your own conclusion? Look back at the hypothesis and decide if the data confirm or refute it.

Answer: the difference in growth refutes the hypothesis. The plants showed growth patterns similar to their native locations, suggesting that their DNA has a significant influence on their growth. The DNA imported from the southern latitude instructed the plants to grow larger, the DNA imported from the northern latitude instructed the plants to grow smaller. This indicates that there is variation in genetics from one geographical location to another.

This may not be the only explanation; perhaps there are others. However, in science, generally the principle of parsimony is applied: we look for the simplest, least convoluted explanation. For example, if we wanted to introduce the idea that an extra-terrestrial visitor came down to the experimental marsh where the plants were growing in order to somehow influence their growth with a special ray gun, we could. But that would not be parsimonious: it would be convoluted and would not be scientific because there is no evidence for it.

When scientific investigations are completed, usually they generate new questions or new ideas for further investigation. What do you think the investigators of the cordgrass would like to find out next?

From the example of the saltmarsh grass in the Nature of Science box, it is possible to see that, within a species that has a wide geographical distribution, there can be measurable differences in DNA. This is because the climate and soil are different in different locations. As a result, the populations adapt to the conditions available to them, and some versions of genes will be selected for and others will be selected against so that the populations are best adapted to their areas. This is called selective pressure. If this phenomenon continues to produce genetic differences over a long enough time, it is not difficult to imagine a point at which the differences between two separated populations are so great that they no longer belong to the same species. There comes a tipping point beyond which the differences outweigh the similarities and the two populations in question can no longer freely reproduce together. For example, if pollen from a northern species of marsh grass was used to pollinate flowers from a southern population, and no seeds or fertile offspring were produced, a speciation would have taken place.

Transient polymorphism

Within a population there is often more than one common form. Different versions of a species are referred to as polymorphisms (meaning many shapes) and can be the result of a mutation. One example of such an organism is *Biston betularia*, the peppered moth, which lives in temperate climates.

This species of moth can have a peppered (grey) form or a melanic (black) form; the melanic form is a rare mutation that usually affects less than 1% of a population. The grey form is well camouflaged against light-coloured surfaces, such as tree branches covered with lichens. One of the reasons why they are much more numerous in the population is that black moths are seen more easily against light-coloured lichens and thus are more frequently preyed upon by birds.

On close examination, you should be able to see two moths on the tree trunk covered with lichen.

Figure 5.8 A map of the distribution of light-coloured and dark-coloured peppered moths in Great Britain under the influence of industrial pollution.

Around the time of Darwin (1860s), a phenomenon was underway that continued for over a century: the industrial revolution. The melanic form of the peppered moth, called *carbonaria*, was increasing in number. Lichens, like the ones pictured on the tree in the photo, are very sensitive to air pollution, and the industrial revolution was producing chemicals, such as sulfur dioxide, that kill lichens. In addition, the air was filled with black soot from the large quantities of coal being burnt. As a result of this, the lichen-free, soot-darkened branches were a more difficult place for light-coloured peppered moths to hide: their camouflage simply did not work anymore. Birds eat moths and visual predation is facilitated when camouflage is poorly adapted.

In places near industrial centres, the *carbonaria* moths accounted for 95–100% of all the peppered moths observed. Today, the percentages of *carbonaria* in a population rarely go above 30% and are often 0%. This is because of a significant improvement in air quality thanks to measures such as the UK Clean Air Act of 1956. These changes in the peppered moth population over time, from light-coloured to dark-

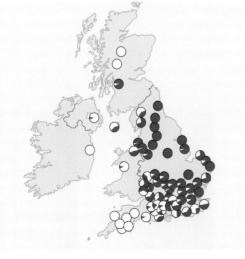

○ light form

● dark form

coloured and then back again, is an example of transient polymorphism, temporary changes in the form of a species.

Worked example

Using the map in Figure 5.8 and the information presented about peppered moths during and after the industrial revolution in the UK, answer the following questions.

1 Statistics for peppered moths in the 1700s do not exist. Predict what the percentage of peppered moths would have been a century before Darwin lived, before the effects of the industrial revolution on trees.

2 (a) In the 1700s in a relatively non-polluted area where lichen is still growing on trees and soot is not a problem, a flock of birds comes to an area where there is a large number of grey peppered moths and only a very small number of black peppered moths. Explain why it is the black ones that have a higher chance of being eaten.

  (b) What influence does this have on the population of dark-coloured moths?

3 Many decades later, the pollution has taken its toll on the lichen, and the soot in the air has blackened trees near industrial areas. Now when a flock of birds arrive to eat the moths; which kind gets eaten and why?

4 (a) Explain how it is possible that, by the 1900s, when the map in Figure 5.8 was made, most of the moths were dark-coloured.

  (b) Explain how it is possible that now, in the 2000s, the population is back to being light-coloured.

Solutions

1 Because the mutation for melanism is very rare, it would be expected that the percentage of dark-coloured moths would be very low, certainly less than 10% and probably closer to 1%.

2 (a) The black ones will be eaten because they are easy to spot against a light background.

  (b) This keeps the population of mutated dark moths at very low levels.

3 Now that the background colour has changed, the light-coloured moths will get eaten. This is because they are no longer able to hide against the darkened background.

4 (a) Because they were able to escape being eaten by birds, *carbonaria* moths were able to survive and pass on their genes to the next generation, something that was not possible before. In contrast, because the light-coloured moths were being spotted and eaten, they could no longer pass on their genes to the next generation. Over many generations, this process reduced the number of light-coloured genes from the population and favoured the allele for dark coloration. The same process happened for dozens of other species of moth.

  (b) Ever since the Clean Air Act was passed in 1956, air quality around industrial zones of the UK has improved: there are fewer sulfur dioxides and less soot in the air. This has allowed the pollution-sensitive lichen population to return and allowed the bark on tree trunks and branches to return to their non-blackened colour. Now that the light-coloured moths can hide better and avoid being eaten, their numbers have increased. In contrast, *carbonaria* moths are no longer effectively camouflaged and get spotted and eaten by birds, reducing their presence in the population.

TOK Is the peppered moth a good example of evolution? The story of the peppered moth is a long one, involving many ups and downs. The data have been criticized, questions have been raised about whether bird predation is the only reason for the population change, and most of the photos of moths trying to rest or hide on tree trunks have been revealed as being staged: they are of dead moths stuck to the trunks for the purpose of the photo. Also, the idea of industrial melanism has been criticized as an example of evolution because no new species is formed: we started with a peppered moth and we finished with a peppered moth.

Although it is one of the most cited examples of modern evolution by natural selection, it has been suggested by some critics that it should be removed from textbooks because it is not a valid example and is based on sloppy science. Research this debate and trace the story's ups and downs. What are the arguments for and against the peppered moth as an example of evolution by natural selection? Should it continue to be used in classrooms as an illustration of how evolution works? When there are disagreeing sides, which one should we believe? What have you learned in Theory of Knowledge to help you to make your decision?

One of the most energetic proponents of neo-Darwinian ideas is the evolutionary biologist Richard Dawkins. In his writing, he points out the difficulty of applying the term species to organisms that lived in the past. For example, he asks his readers to picture a modern-day rabbit and imagine the rabbit's parents. There is no doubt that both of the parents and the offspring are all three of the same species, despite the fact that the offspring is not identical to its parents. We could probably be safe in taking this thought experiment back many generations and assume that, even though there are variations in each generation, there comes a time when the ancestor was significantly different from the modern rabbit. But how far do we go? It is difficult to know how many thousands of generations in the past we would need to study in order to declare that, at that point, that ancestor was, in fact, a different species.

Trying to find out what happened in the past is the job of both historians and evolutionary biologists. Do they use the same methods to infer and deduce what the past was like? What counts as knowledge for an evolutionary biologist, and how is that similar or different from what counts as knowledge for a historian?

Natural scientists often use experimentation in laboratories to test out their hypotheses. And yet, it is impossible to carry out investigations such as breeding experiments with organisms that have gone extinct. How is the scientific method different for a scientist who studies fossils and evolution compared with a scientist who studies genetic traits in contemporary organisms?

Section summary

- Evolution by natural selection is one of the most important ideas in biology.
- The evidence of evolution in the past can be seen in cases of adaptive radiation, such as in Darwin's finches, or in fossils, notably in homologous structures such as the pentadactyl limb.
- In more recent centuries, evidence can be seen in the modifications of domesticated animals by selective breeding (artificial selection).
- Generally speaking, the changes in frequencies of certain traits within a population determine how much evolution has taken place.
- Over time, if enough continual gradual change takes place, a speciation split could occur whereby some members of the population form a new species that can no longer reproduce with the other members.

Exercises

1 Define the term evolution.

2 Concerning species on Earth, describe two overall trends that can be seen in the fossil record.

3 Explain how selective breeding can be a good example of evolution by selection, even though it is not natural selection.

4 List two examples of adaptive radiation.

5.2 Natural selection

Understandings:

- Natural selection can only occur if there is variation amongst members of the same species.
- Mutation, meiosis, and sexual reproduction cause variation between individuals in a species.
- Adaptations are characteristics that make an individual suited to its environment and way of life.
- Species tend to produce more offspring than the environment can support.
- Individuals that are better adapted tend to survive and produce more offspring while the less well adapted tend to die or produce fewer offspring.
- Individuals that reproduce pass on characteristics to their offspring.
- Natural selection increases the frequency of characteristics that make individuals better adapted and decreases the frequency of other characteristics, leading to changes within the species.

Applications and skills:

- Application: Changes in beaks of finches on Daphne Major.
- Application: Evolution of antibiotic resistance in bacteria.

Guidance
- Students should be clear that characteristics acquired during the lifetime of an individual are not heritable. The term Lamarckism is not required.

The mechanism for evolution

Besides providing evidence for evolution, Darwin and Wallace suggested a mechanism for evolution: natural selection. How does this work? It all starts with the overproduction of offspring and the presence of natural variation in the population; then there is a struggle between competing varieties that leads to survival for some and death for others. This section will look at how evolution works through natural selection.

Variation within populations

Organisms such as bacteria reproduce simply by making a copy of their genetic information and then splitting into two using the process of binary fission. The result is that the second generation is identical to the first. In fact, many future generations will be identical or show very little change. There is little chance for the DNA to be modified.

The story is very different for species that reproduce sexually. When a cat has kittens, for example, each one is slightly different, or when a population of guinea pigs interbreeds there can be a wide variety of offspring.

NATURE OF SCIENCE

Use theories to explain natural phenomena: the theory of evolution by natural selection can explain the development of antibiotic resistance in bacteria.

Variation can be seen in this population of guinea pigs.

Variation and success

Variation is closely related to how successful an organism is. A baby bird that has pigments that give it a colour matching its surroundings will have a better chance of not being seen by a predator. A fish with a slightly different shaped mouth might be able to feed from parts of a coral reef that other fish are not able to access. A plant that produces a different shaped flower might have a better chance of attracting insects for pollination.

It might seem obvious that a young bird with a colour that makes it very conspicuous to predators has little chance of surviving to adulthood. On the other hand, it might be more attractive to mates. A fish with an oddly shaped mouth may, in fact, be incapable of feeding adequately and die of starvation. A plant that produces flowers that are not attractive to insects will not have its flowers pollinated and will not produce any offspring.

As we have seen with the peppered moth, how frequent an allele is can change over time because of changes in the environment. This is only possible if there is more than one form of the allele. If the peppered moth did not have a mutation giving some members a dark colour, it is possible that certain populations would have been completely wiped out when their camouflage no longer worked against a dark background. In contrast, in bacteria, for example, there are essentially no differences within a population: all members of the population are genetically identical copies of each other. This means that if an adverse change happened in the environment, such as a change in pH, if one bacterium is susceptible to the change in pH and dies, they in fact all die because they all have the same vulnerability. In species where there is variation, a change in the environment will eliminate some but not all members of the population. This is why variation is a strength and not a weakness in a population. We will see how this works as this section continues.

Mutation, meiosis, and sexual reproduction

There are three main mechanisms that give organisms in a species their variation:

- mutations in DNA
- meiosis
- sexual reproduction.

Mutation

Mutations can sometimes produce genes that lead to genetic diseases, and can have devastating effects on the survival of some individuals in a species. However, sometimes a mutation can produce a characteristic that is advantageous, perhaps a slightly faster growth rate for a tree or better frost resistance for a plant. A beneficial mutation for a bird or insect might result in a different camouflage that better matches a changing habitat. In each generation, only a few genes mutate, and most mutations produce effects that are neither useful nor harmful. As a result, sexual reproduction is a much more powerful source of variation in a population because thousands of genes are mixed and combined. But sexual reproduction is only possible thanks to meiosis.

Meiosis

Meiosis, you will recall from Section 3.3, enables the production of haploid cells to make gametes (sperm cells and egg cells). At the end of meiosis, four cells are produced that are genetically different from each other and only contain 50% of the parent cell's

The idea of eugenics is that, if human breeding is controlled, it could improve the population by favouring desirable characteristics and eliminating undesirable ones. This is highly controversial, and historical applications of it have been widely criticized. Trying to breed a 'superior race' where everyone has the same characteristics is contradictory to the concept Darwinian evolution is based on: variety. The resilience of a species is highly dependent on variety.

genome. An individual that reproduces sexually can produce huge numbers of possible combinations of half the genetic material it possesses, thanks to meiosis. For example, in a woman's lifetime, it is nearly impossible for her to produce the same egg twice. This is why, no matter how many pregnancies she has, she will never have the same child twice from two different pregnancies. The only way identical humans have ever been formed is when two embryos are formed from a single egg, i.e. identical twins, and even then there are slight genetic differences between the siblings.

The variety in gametes comes mainly from the process of random orientation during metaphase I. The lining up of chromosomes in a random order is like shuffling a deck of cards, and it greatly promotes variety in the egg cells or sperm cells produced. In addition to this, the process of crossing-over contributes to the shuffling of genetic material and further increases the genetic variety.

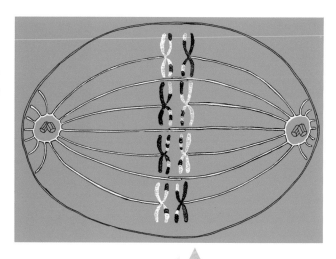

Figure 5.9 Random orientation during metaphase I and crossing-over (shown by banding on sister chromatids) promote variety in the gametes. Each sister chromatid will separate into separate haploid cells at the end of meiosis (see Section 3.3).

Sexual reproduction

As we have seen, asexual reproduction such as binary fission in single-celled organisms does not promote variety in the population. Generally speaking, in an asexually reproducing population, all the members of the population are identical. There may be rare exceptions of mutations or gene transfer, but overall such populations can remain identical generation after generation. The consequence for this is that natural selection only leaves two choices for the population: survive or die. One of the causes of the Great Famine in Ireland in the mid-1800s was that the potatoes had been produced asexually and were all clones, making them all susceptible to the same infection by a microorganism that causes potato blight. This also illustrates that if there is no variety in a population, there is a very limited number of outcomes: the whole population either survives or dies. This is why variety is so important to natural selection. More possibilities lead to more possible outcomes: some members of the population survive without any adverse effects, others may be affected in a negative way but still survive, and others may die. Variety in the population allows some individuals to be better adapted to whatever change in the environment is harmful to others.

Part of what determines whether or not a female animal becomes pregnant is that all the conditions must be right inside her body, and that sperm cells must be present at the opportune moment when an egg is ready. Of the many sperm cells that may be present, only one will penetrate the egg. In determining exactly which sperm cell and egg will meet and fuse together, a certain amount of chance and luck are involved. In non-human primate species, such as chimpanzees, for example, when a female is fertile, many males may copulate with her to try to impregnate her. In such a scenario, it is impossible to guess which male's sperm cells will successfully fertilize her egg. It is largely up to chance. In flowering plants, which bees will land on which flower of a population, with what pollen from another flower in that population, is also a matter of chance.

Which of these yellow pollen grains on the bee's body will pollinate the next flower it visits?

There are three main sources for variation in a population:
- **mutations in DNA**
- **meiosis**
- **sexual reproduction.**

Although it is possible for some organisms to adapt to changes in their environment within their lifetimes, this is not the kind of adaptation referred to in evolution. For example, just because an individual hare can shed its brown fur and grow white fur for the winter in order to be better camouflaged against the snow, does not mean that the individual has 'evolved' from one season to the next. Evolution happens to populations and its effects are only visible over many generations.

But make no mistake, although these two mechanisms for increasing variety (meiosis and sexual reproduction) rely on chance, it would be unfair to conclude that all of life is just a game of chance. As we will see, natural selection has another side to it that has little to do with chance and allows for systematic accumulations of small changes to produce highly adapted forms of life.

To adapt or not to adapt?

The adjective adaptation and the verb to adapt are freely used when talking about evolution. However, the terms have very precise meanings within the framework of natural selection and should not be confused with other uses of the term, notably for human behaviour. For example, humans can consciously decide to adapt to a situation: think of a student learning the language of a country he or she has just moved to, or of a person who is used to driving his or her car on the right-hand side of the road and rents a vehicle in a country where driving is done on the left-hand side and so adapts very quickly to left-hand driving. These are conscious adaptations made by individuals. In nature, the vast majority of adaptations referred to in evolution and natural selection are unconscious adaptations made by populations rather than by individuals.

One example we have already seen is the adaptation of the peppered moth populations over time before and after the industrial revolution. On light-coloured backgrounds, the grey moths were better adapted, whereas on dark-coloured backgrounds, the black moths were better adapted. Another example is that a giraffe's neck is well adapted for reaching leaves high up in trees. If a giraffe was born with a mutation that gave it a short neck, it would have trouble competing with other giraffes to get leaves. A short neck is an example of a characteristic that is not well adapted for a giraffe's lifestyle.

An organism that has characteristics that are well adapted for its environment is said to be fit. The characteristics it possesses fit well into its environment.

Natural selection tends to eliminate from a population individuals that show low fitness, whereas the fittest individuals in a population have a higher likelihood of surviving. Although there are rare exceptions, individuals are usually incapable of changing themselves to adapt. For example, a giraffe born with a short neck cannot stretch its neck to get a longer one. Rather, because it will have difficulty feeding itself and surviving, the chances are very low that it will find a mate and reproduce to be able to pass on its genes to the next generation. Hence the alleles for making a short neck are not found in the giraffe population.

Figure 5.10 The giraffe's long neck explained by natural selection.

Ancient population with variation in neck lengths. Giraffes with longer necks can reach more food and have a better chance of survival. Those born with shorter necks find less food and have lower chances of survival.

After many generations, the genes for longer necks are passed down more successfully than the genes for shorter necks. The population sees more and more long-necked giraffes and fewer and fewer short-necked giraffes until they all have long necks.

Too many offspring

Darwin noticed that plants and animals produce far more offspring than could ever survive. Plants often produce hundreds or thousands more seeds than necessary to propagate the species. Mushrooms produce millions more spores than ever grow into new mushrooms. A female fish lays hundreds or thousands of eggs but only a handful survive to adulthood.

This seems paradoxical, because the production of seeds, spores, and eggs involves using energy and nutrients that also are vital to the parents' survival. Why are such valuable resources squandered on so many excess cells that are never going to give rise to viable offspring? The answer is to maximize the chances of some offspring surviving, even if the survival rate is less than 1%.

Having too many offspring and not enough resources is a problem of supply and demand. There is high demand for water, space, nutrients, and sunlight, but there is a limited supply. The consequence is competition for these resources in order to stay alive. This is called the struggle for survival.

Many species of animal are territorial and possessive of their food supplies: they spend a great deal of time and energy defending their resources. Trees, too, defend their resources, by having active compounds such as tannins and alkaloids in their trunks to ward off attackers such as insects. All these adaptations make it difficult for a new arrival to find enough resources. As a result, parents send out dozens, hundreds, or thousands of potential offspring into the world. Parent organisms that do not produce as many may find the probability of their genes being passed on greatly reduced.

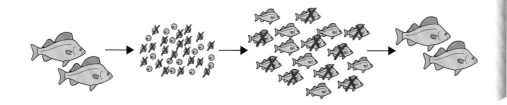

CHALLENGE YOURSELF

2 One quantitative study done over a 30-year period by Rosemary and Peter Grant showed differences in beak sizes of ground finches, *Geospiza fortis*, from two islands of the Galapagos: Daphne Major and Santa Cruz. You can learn more about this study through an online exercise including analysis of the data they collected. You can find a link to this activity in the hotlinks box at the end of this section.

Figure 5.11 A male and female fish can produce hundreds of fertilized eggs, of which several may hatch into juvenile fish but only a very small number will reach adulthood. The vast majority will be eaten or will die before they mature, and many will possess variations of traits that are not well adapted to their environment. Some that died may have possessed 'ice age' alleles helpful for surviving in cold weather, but because we are in an interglacial period these alleles are not fit for the current environment.

Adaption and survival

Evolution is not just based on chance. In a situation where there are too many organisms for limited resources, it is obvious that some individuals will succeed in accessing those resources and the rest will fail. In other words, there is a selection. Exactly which individuals survive and which ones do not is not based on chance alone but determined by their surroundings and the compatibility of their characteristics with those surroundings. The steps of evolution by natural selection are outlined below.

- Overproduction of offspring and, in those offspring, natural variation as a result of genetic differences (e.g. body size, morphology, pigmentation, visual acuity, resistance to disease). In the offspring:
  - useful variations allow some individuals to have a better chance of survival (e.g. hiding from predators, fleeing danger, or finding food)
  - harmful variations make it difficult to survive (e.g. inappropriate colour for camouflage, heavy bones for birds, having such a big body size that there is not enough food to survive).
- Individuals with genetic characteristics that are poorly adapted for their environment tend to be less successful at accessing resources and have less chance of surviving to maturity.
- Individuals with genetic characteristics that are well adapted for their environment tend to be more successful at accessing resources and have a better chance of surviving to maturity. Such individuals are said to have better fitness.
- Because they survive to adulthood, the successful organisms have a better chance of reproducing and passing on their successful genetic characteristics to the next generation.
- Over many generations, the accumulation of changes in the heritable characteristics of a population results in evolution: the gene pool has changed.

As you can see, it is impossible to sum up all these concepts in one catchy phrase such as 'the law of the jungle'. Although Darwin himself eventually adopted the phrase 'survival of the fittest', the idea of evolution by natural selection is more complex than that. In addition, many people have the misconception that what Darwin said was 'only the strongest survive'. This is simply not true.

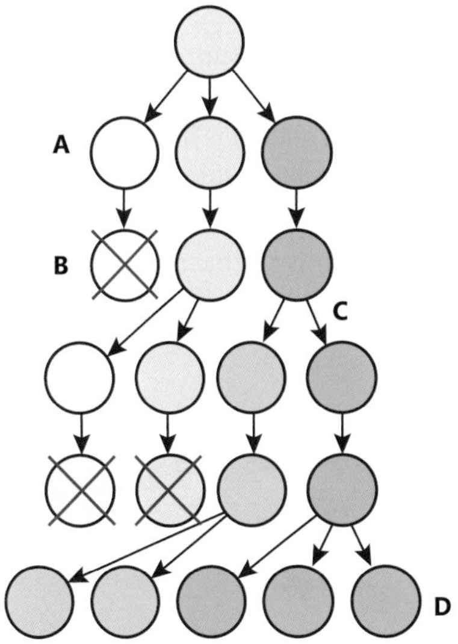

Figure 5.12 A Overproduction of offspring + variation in the population. **B** Poorly adapted variations lead to lower success for individuals who possess them. **C** Individuals with better fitness are more likely to pass on their traits to the next generation. **D** Over many generations, there is an accumulation of change in the heritable characteristics: the population has evolved. Adapted from http://commons.wikimedia.org/wiki/File:Mutation_and_selection_diagram.svg

The theory of evolution by natural selection is full of subtleties. This could be one of the reasons why it is so widely misunderstood by the general public. For example, an organism that is well adapted to its environment is not guaranteed success, it simply has a higher probability of survival than another that is less well adapted. Dinosaurs such as the sauropods were the biggest, strongest animals ever to walk the planet. But they did not survive the environmental changes that drove them to extinction. In fact, the fossil record indicates that more than 99.99% of all life that has ever existed on Earth is now extinct.

In the photo of plover eggs, the colours and speckles act as effective camouflage, making these eggs difficult to spot by predators. Plover chicks are also speckled for camouflage. If a mutation caused a shell to be bright white and/or the chicks to be bright yellow, the mutation would be unlikely to be an advantage to this species. On the contrary, a white egg or yellow-bodied chick would attract the attention of a predator, the egg or chick would be eaten, and the possibility of passing on the mutation to the next generation would be zero.

Passing on successful characteristics

It should be obvious that an individual that never reaches maturity will not be able to pass on its genes to the next generation. An individual that is poorly adapted to its environment, such as an insect with deformed mouthparts that make it impossible to feed, is not likely to survive to adulthood and be able to reproduce.

On the other hand, an individual showing high fitness has a better chance of surviving until adulthood and reaching maturity. Individuals that reach maturity have the possibility of reproducing and passing on their genetic material. Again, there is no guarantee that fitness will allow survival or that survival will allow reproduction, but, in order to reproduce, one thing is certain: survival must come first. Remember the example of the giraffes: those who were born with the alleles to make necks long enough to access better food sources had a greater chance of surviving and passing on those alleles, whereas those with short-neck genes had more trouble finding enough food and were less frequently able to survive to pass on their alleles.

Natural selection and the frequency of characteristics

Pesticide resistance in rats and multiple antibiotic resistance in bacteria are both carefully studied modern examples of natural selection. What is striking about these examples is their rapidity. Although evolution is generally considered to be a long-term process, the mechanism of natural selection can sometimes be quick, taking place over months, years or decades, rather than millennia. As you read the descriptions, see if you can identify the main features of how natural selection works: variation in the population making some individuals better suited for their environment than others,

It is crucial that you remember Darwin's steps of how natural selection leads to evolution. Be sure to memorize the following: (1) overproduction of offspring; (2) variation within the population, as a result of meiosis, sexual reproduction, and mutations; (3) struggle for survival, because there are not enough resources for all members of the population; (4) differential survival, those individuals best fit for their environment tend to survive better; and (5) reproduction, those who survive can pass on their genes to the next generation. It is through these steps that populations evolve. Remember that, even though the changes can be observed in individuals from generation to generation, what is of importance is what happens at the level of populations rather than at the individual level.

overproduction of offspring leading to a struggle for survival, differentiated survival because some die and some live, and, finally, the passing on of successful traits to the next generation.

Pesticide resistance in rats

Pesticides are chemicals that kill animals that are regarded as pests. Farmers use them to eradicate pests, such as rats that eat their crops.

A farmer spraying pesticide on crops.

Consider the following scenario.

1   Once applied in the fields, pesticides kill all the rats … or so the farmer thinks.
2   As a result of natural variation, a few rats from the population on the farm are slightly different and are not affected by the poison.
3   The resistant rats are better adapted to survive in the presence of the pesticides and now, thanks to the farmer's actions, have no other rats to compete with for a food supply. Hence, they thrive and reproduce, making a new population in which some or all of the members possess the genes that give resistance to the pesticide.
4   Seeing rats again, the farmer puts out more of the original poison; this time fewer rats die. Because the characteristic of poison resistance was favoured in the rat population, it is now much more common in the population.
5   To kill the resistant rats, a new pesticide must be used.

Figure 5.13 How populations of pests such as rats develop resistance by natural selection. Notice the difference in the number of resistant rats (coloured brown) before the pesticide application and after the application.

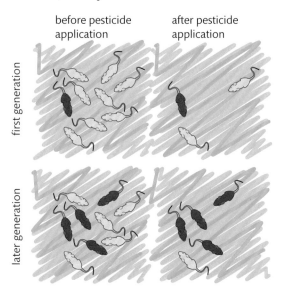

It is important to note that, in this example, we cannot say that the rats become immune to the poison. Although the term 'immunity' is sometimes interchangeable with the term 'resistance', that is not the case here. Immunity develops within the lifetime of an individual; pesticide resistance is a change that evolves in a population from one generation of rats to the next generation. The evolution happened in the population, not in any single rat. A rat is either born with a susceptibility to be killed by the pesticide or is born with resistance to it. An individual rat cannot adapt and evolve into a resistant rat.

It is also important to note that the characteristics that change and evolve over time must be heritable (passed on by genes). An example of this is that farmers have been cutting off the tails of sheep for many centuries and yet sheep continue to be born with long tails. In other words, characteristics acquired during an organism's lifetime cannot be passed on to the next generation and so do not have a part in the theory of evolution by natural selection.

Sheep are still born with long tails, despite being removed by farmers for countless generations.

Antibiotic resistance in bacteria

Antibiotics are medications such as penicillin that kill or inhibit the growth of bacteria. They are given to patients suffering from bacterial infections. They are also sometimes given to people who are suffering from something else and, because their immune system is weak, are at a greater risk of a bacterial infection. However, overuse of antibiotics can lead to the production of resistant strains of bacteria.

Antibiotic resistance in bacteria develops in several steps. Consider the following scenario.

1   A woman gets a bacterial infection such as tuberculosis.
2   Her doctor gives her an antibiotic to kill the bacteria.
3   She gets better because the bacteria are largely destroyed.
4   By a modification of its genetic makeup, however, one bacterium is resistant to the antibiotic.
5   That bacterium is not killed by the antibiotic and it later multiplies in the patient's body to make her sick again.

6   She goes back to the doctor and gets the same antibiotic.

7   This time, no result: she is still sick and asks her doctor what is wrong.

8   The doctor prescribes a different antibiotic that (hopefully) works. But if the population of bacteria continues to acquire mutations, new strains could show resistance to all the antibiotics available.

Because bacteria reproduce asexually, genetically they generally do not change very often. However, there are two sources of possible change in the genetic makeup of bacteria:

• mutations (as seen in Section 3.1)

• plasmid transfer.

Plasmid transfer involves one bacterium donating genetic information to another in a ring of nucleotides called a plasmid. Both the donating and receiving cells open their cell walls so that the genetic material can pass from the donor to the receiver.

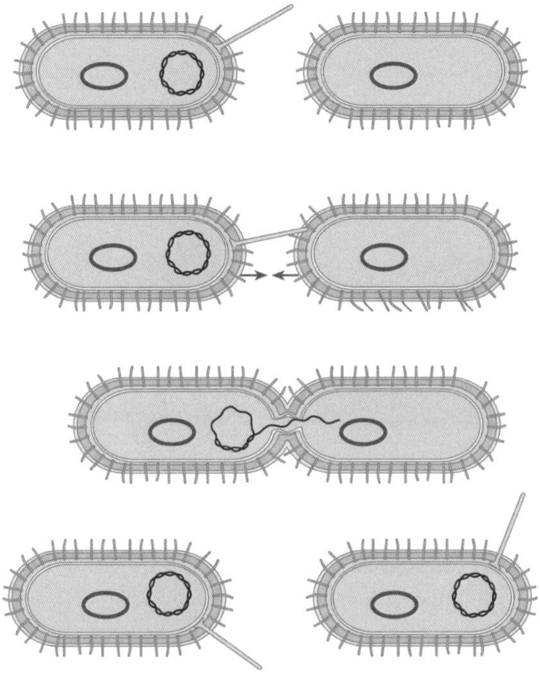

Figure 5.14 The bacterium on the left is passing genetic information to the bacterium on the right in a process called plasmid transfer.

Antibiotic-resistant pathogens such as MRSA are causing hospitals and clinics all over the world to rethink their standards of hygiene. MRSA stands for methicillin-resistant *Staphylococcus aureus*. Health officials are concerned that, without internationally coordinated efforts, these super bugs could be spread from one country to another as patients get transferred across borders for treatment. What kinds of international regulations exist concerning antibiotic use, quarantine, and other such practices, that either encourage or limit the spread of resistant bacteria?

The development of antibiotic-resistant bacteria has happened in several cases. New strains of syphilis, for example, have adapted to antibiotics and show multiple resistance. Some strains of tuberculosis are resistant to as many as nine different antibiotics. There is no cure for people who get sick from such super-resistant germs, and they must rely on their immune system to save them.

Finding new antibiotics would only be a temporary solution, and pharmaceutical companies cannot find new medications fast enough to treat these super-resistant germs. As a result, the best way to curb their expansion is to make sure that doctors minimize the use of antibiotics and that patients realize that antibiotics are not always the best solution to a health problem.

Notice how the two examples above are good illustrations of how we can use a scientific theory to explain observed phenomena. As stated at the beginning of the section on evolution, once the theory of natural selection is understood, it allows us to understand a variety of natural phenomena.

NATURE OF SCIENCE

A *Staphylococcus* bacterium discovered in a hospital is suspected of being resistant to a certain number of antibiotics. To test this hypothesis, the bacterium is introduced into a Petri dish along with small disks of paper that are soaked in different types of antibiotic. In an experiment like this, when the colonies of bacteria grow close to the disks, they show resistance to the antibiotic, whereas when wide, clear circles of inhibited bacterial growth are present, they show that the antibiotic is stopping the bacteria the way it should. Can you interpret the results of the experiment shown in the photo?

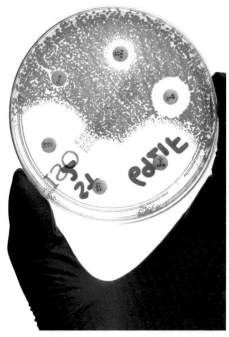

Testing for antibiotic resistance.

In the photo, the four disks of different antibiotics nearest the technician's hand show rings of growth inhibition, suggesting an effective control of the colony of bacteria by the medications. However, the two disks at the top furthest away from the hand (top centre and top left) have allowed the bacterial colony to grow dangerously close. This suggests that this strain of *Staphylococcus* is resistant to those two antibiotics and cannot be stopped by them. Doctors use such tests to help decide which medications to prescribe. In this case, they should prescribe the antibiotics that the bacteria do not show a resistance to, preferably the three at the bottom of the image.

This resistant bacterium is part of a growing number of super bugs, among which we find MRSA. They have evolved because of the way humans use antibiotics.

Evolution by natural selection is a multi-step process. Some steps involve chance, such as variation in a population, or certain aspects of sexual reproduction, such as which gametes participate in fertilization and which do not. However, the presence of a particular characteristic in a population is not purely up to chance. It's not just lucky, for example, that falcons have excellent vision or that dolphins are capable of echolocation. It's not by pure happenstance that flowers have adaptations perfectly suited to their insect pollinators, or that certain bacteria become resistant to the antibiotics we try to fight them with. Natural selection favours useful adaptations and selects against harmful ones in a way that is not based on luck and chance, but on fitness. Heritable changes are passed on from generation to generation, and accumulate over time so that each population either fits its environment, adapts accordingly, or dies out.

TOK In some countries, there is a very intense debate about whether the concept of evolution should be taught in schools. To support the critics of evolution, there are thousands of websites and publications that carefully try to dismantle and disprove the arguments of evolutionary biologists. What criteria are used to determine whether these criticisms are valid or not? What kind of evidence would be necessary to refute Darwin's theory?

Design an experiment simulating natural selection

Safety alerts: When choosing objects used for simulating mouthparts or food, avoid objects that are too sharp, such as certain types of tweezers or thumb tacks. Also, if several competing organisms are trying to get food from the same food source, such as a tray or plate, you should not peck at your competition with your mouthparts.

In order to simulate natural selection between organisms obtaining food, design a lab in which some form of pinchers or clips are used as 'mouthparts' and a variety of small objects are used as 'food'. Some form of 'stomach' needs to be established, such as a Petri dish placed at a particular distance from the food source.

- Examples for mouthparts: tweezers, clothespins, wooden tongs, or even chopsticks.
- Examples for food: dry chickpeas or kidney beans, dry grains of rice, marbles, paper clips, or coins. To make it more challenging, calorie values could be given so that the most difficult food to pick up is worth the most calories.

The investigation should involve participants simulating organisms using their mouthparts (the tweezers, for example) to fill their stomachs with food. Those who attain a minimum requirement of food are allowed to continue to the next round; those who do not are eliminated by natural selection. In effect, the simulated organism dies of hunger.

The designed investigation must show a certain amount of variation of mouthparts within the population of feeding organisms. The investigation must also limit the time and the resources available. Natural selection should be demonstrated by determining a minimum amount of food collected in the organism's stomach within the time limit. Rules must be established to avoid cheating such as holding the stomach under the desk and pushing food into it.

Just as with any designed investigation, be sure to start with the aim, research question, and three types of variables, before establishing the step-by-step method. See the Internal assessment chapter in the eBook for help with variables. Some trial runs will probably be necessary to refine your method.

Section summary

- Evolution by natural selection consists of several steps:
  - overproduction of offspring
  - variation within the population
  - struggle for survival
  - differential survival depending on fitness
  - differential reproduction, whereby those organisms with successful gene combinations have a higher chance of passing on their genes to the next generation.
- The variations within the population are generated by mutations, shuffling of genes during meiosis, and the chances involved in determining which eggs meet which sperm cells during sexual reproduction.
- Fitness is how well a population's characteristics match the requirements of its environment.
- Adaptations are combinations of inherited genetic traits allowing a population to cope with changes in its environment. Although changes can be seen at the level of the individual, evolution occurs in populations and species rather than in individuals.
- Natural selection allows for adaptations that fit the environment the best to be selected for, and for those that are not advantageous to be selected against.

To learn more about evolution, go to the hotlinks site, search for the title or ISBN, and click on Chapter 5: Section 5.2.

Exercises

5   Besides mutation, list two factors that are responsible for increasing variation in a population.

6   Distinguish between artificial selection and natural selection.

7   Ground-nesting birds such as grouse lay their eggs in a nest made on the ground. The eggs of this species are generally speckled dark brown. If a mutation occurred causing the eggs to be brightly coloured, how would the change in colour affect their chances of survival?

8   Explain how a population of insects could develop resistance to the insecticides sprayed on them.

5.3 Classification of biodiversity

NATURE OF SCIENCE

Cooperation and collaboration between groups of scientists: scientists use the binomial system to identify a species rather than the many different local names.

Understandings:

- The binomial system of names for species is universal among biologists and has been agreed and developed at a series of congresses.
- When species are discovered they are given scientific names using the binomial system.
- Taxonomists classify species using a hierarchy of taxa.
- All organisms are classified into three domains.
- The principal taxa for classifying eukaryotes are kingdom, phylum, class, order, family, genus, and species.
- In a natural classification, the genus and accompanying higher taxa consist of all the species that have evolved from one common ancestral species.
- Taxonomists sometimes reclassify groups of species when new evidence shows that a previous taxon contains species that have evolved from different ancestral species.
- Natural classifications help in identification of species and allow the prediction of characteristics shared by species within a group.

Applications and skills:

- Application: Classification of one plant and one animal species from domain to species level.
- Application: Recognition features of Bryophyta, Filicinophyta, Coniferophyta, and Angiospermophyta.
- Application: Recognition features of Porifera, Cnidaria, Platylhelmintha, Annelida, Mollusca, Arthropoda, and Chordata.
- Application: Recognition of features of birds, mammals, amphibians, reptiles, and fish.
- Skill: Construction of dichotomous keys for use in identifying specimens.

  ### Guidance
  - *Archaea, Eubacteria and Eukaryote should be used for the three domains.*
  - *Members of these domains should be referred to as archaeans, bacteria, and eukaryotes.*
  - *Students should know which plant phyla have vascular tissue, but other internal details are not required.*
  - *Recognition features expected for the selected animal phyla are those that are most useful in distinguishing the groups from each other, and full descriptions of the characteristics of each phylum are not needed.*
  - *Viruses are not classified as living organisms.*

The binomial system of names for species

You have a name that you were given when you were born, but you also have a scientific name based on your species: *Homo sapiens*. This system of naming organisms using two names is called binomial nomenclature. 'Bi' means two, 'nomial' means name and 'nomenclature' refers to a system used to name things.

Myrmecophaga tridactyla is a name that literally means 'eater of ants' plus 'with three fingers'. In case you have not guessed, it refers to an anteater, and this one happens to be the giant anteater of Central and South America. In fact, the animal really has five fingers, but they are hard to see because the animal walks on its front knuckles.

Figure 5.15 The giant anteater, *Myrmecophaga tridactyla*.

30 cm

The first name in the binomial nomenclature system is always capitalized and it refers to the genus; the second name always begins with a small letter and refers to the species. Both are always written in italics when typed, or underlined when written by hand. Most words used in binomial nomenclature are Latin or Greek in origin. For example, *Lepus arcticus* is the scientific name for the Arctic hare; both terms come from Latin. This is why the term Latin name is often used, although this is an oversimplification because other languages are also involved.

This system of naming organisms was consolidated and popularized by the dynamic Swedish naturalist Carolus (Carl) Linnaeus. In his book *Systema Naturae* (*The Natural World*, 1735), he listed and explained the binomial system of nomenclature for species that had been brought to him from all over the world. Although he was not the first to use the idea of genus (plural genera), he popularized its use along with the species name in a consistent way.

Today, there are hundreds of specialists who, like Linnaeus, describe and name new species. When it comes to classifying animals, for example, every 4 years the International Congress of Zoology takes place in a different city; it is an event during which animal experts from all over the world share and discuss their findings about animal behaviour, genetics, and classification. The dates and locations of the 19th–22nd congresses are:

- 2004 Beijing, China (XIX)
- 2008 Paris, France (XX)
- 2012 Haifa, Israel (XXI)
- 2016 Japan (XXII).

Zoologists started these conferences in Paris in 1889, on the occasion of the World Fair that year, the one that inaugurated the Eiffel Tower. Although many things are discussed as such congresses, one of the topics that comes up is the binomial nomenclature system. Decisions need to be made about new organisms that have been recently discovered or old organisms that might need reclassifying because of new evidence about their ancestry.

There are three main objectives to using binomial nomenclature and its associated rules: (1) to be sure that each organism has a unique name that cannot be confused with another organism; (2) so that that the names can be universally understood, no matter what nationality or culture is using the name; and (3) so that there is some stability in the system by not allowing people to change the names of organisms without valid reasons.

One result of discussions between many zoologists has been the International Code of Zoological Nomenclature (ICZN), which makes the rules about how to classify and name animals. There are also rules about how to use the names and properly cite them in research papers. In cases where two different animal species have been given the same name, there is a rule that the oldest valid publication of the name should be used. This is referred to as the principle of priority and is taken very seriously. This principle is applied when the same species is accidentally named twice by two different experts with two different names; again the first one gets priority.

In the days when there were fewer rules, some scientists named unsightly or offensively smelling organisms after people they considered to be their enemies. This is no longer allowed.

In addition to these zoological congresses to discuss animals, there are international congresses for many forms of life, including algae, fungi, plants, and bacteria, and each one has their own code for nomenclature. In this way, when a biologist discovers a new organism, he or she has detailed guidance from such codes about where to place the organism in the tree of life, a metaphor used to denote the branches leading back to a common ancestor.

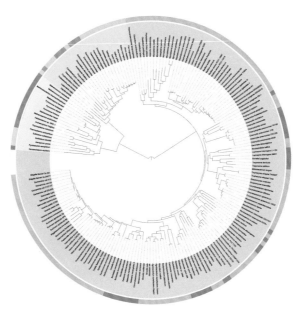

Figure 5.16 A diagram from the interactive Tree of Life online tool. Notice how, unlike other 'tree' diagrams, there is no summit on this circular diagram. All organisms alive today have evolved for the same number of years: we are all survivors. Species names are given around the outside of the circle. Find out more about this by going to the hotlinks site and clicking on Chapter 5: Section 5.3.

Naming new species

Humans like to see similarities and differences in the objects that surround them: hot or cold, delicious or foul-tasting, dangerous or safe, and so on. In the early days of classification, all known organisms were classified into only two kingdoms: plants and animals.

As the centuries went by, and as the study of biology became more systematic, tens of thousands of new species were discovered in forests, deserts, and oceans, some of which showed characteristics of both plants and animals, and some of which were not like either plants or animals. For example, mushrooms grow on the forest floor the way plants do, and yet they do not have leaves or roots and they do not photosynthesize: they get their energy from digesting dead organic matter. So mushrooms cannot be classified as plants, because they are not autotrophs, but they are certainly not animal-like either, one reason being that they have cell walls made of chitin.

With the invention of the microscope in the mid-1600s, many new creatures were discovered that were nothing like plants or animals. In effect, the microscope revealed that there is an entire world of invisible organisms living throughout the biosphere.

If a botanist finds a new species of orchid, for example, he or she would have to describe the plant, describe the location it was found in, name it using the proper rules of binomial nomenclature as set out by the International Code of Botanical Nomenclature (ICBN), and publish the findings in a publically accessible publication. In addition, it is important to put a sample specimen in a public location where other botanists can examine it. Such an example specimen is called a holotype. One of the rules of nomenclature is that a scientific name is not considered valid if a specimen is not available for verification. In some circumstances, a precise illustration is acceptable, but it is always better to make a holotype available. Proposing a name for mythical creatures no one has ever captured, for example, is not accepted.

On the other hand, it is perfectly acceptable to name a well-described organism that no longer exists, such as an extinct dinosaur. Usually the holotypes of fossilized species are kept in museums, but simply finding a fossil, labelling it and putting it on display

International cooperation and communication are key concepts in science. It is important that scientists are able to share their ideas, discuss developments, and make decisions together about how to communicate better and share knowledge. The continuing development of the binomial nomenclature system is an example of scientists recognizing and overcoming the confusion that would occur if each biologist used the local names of species in his or her own language. Although the original purpose of the internet was to serve military needs, the first major non-military group of individuals to see the usefulness of such a system was scientists.

in a museum does not count as officially naming it. Again, the name would have to be published along with a description in a reputable scientific publication.

This fossil skull was discovered by Mary Leakey in 1959 at Olduvai Gorge, Tanzania. It is the holotype for the extinct hominid species *Paranthropus boisei* and the skull is now at the Natural History Museum in London.

Examples of binomial nomenclature

Sometimes scientific names for organisms are relatively easy to decipher because they contain their common names:

- *Amoeba amazonas*
- *Equus zebra*
- *Gekko gecko* (this lizard gets its name from the sounds it makes).
- *Gorilla gorilla*
- *Paramecium caudatum* (caudate means having a tail).

Sometimes, it is more difficult to guess their common name:

- *Apis mellifera* (honeybee, although you might have guessed this if you know that beekeeping is also called apiculture)
- *Aptenodytes patagonicus* (king penguin, although you can probably guess where it lives from its species name)
- *Loxodonta cyclotis* (African forest elephant)
- *Malus domestica* (apple tree).

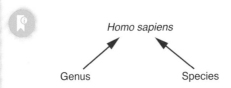

The rules about writing binomial nomenclature names are that:

- the genus name is capitalized but the species name is not
- both are written in italics when typed, or underlined when handwritten
- in addition, after these two names, often the last name of the person who first published the name in a scientific journal is given (but not italicized), and the date when it was published, for example *Equus zebra* Linnaeus, 1758.

Scientists naming organisms sometimes have a sense of humour. Here are a few examples.

- *Albunea groeningi* Boyko, 2002. This sea snail was named after the cartoonist who created 'The Simpsons': Matt Groening.
- *Agra schwarzeneggeri* Erwin, 2002. This Costa Rican ground beetle was named after Arnold Schwarzenegger because of the insect's large biceps.
- *Dracula vampira* Luer, 1978. This orchid in Ecuador got its name from the fact that the petals on the flower look like a bat's wings.
- *Spongiforma squarepantsii* Desjardin, Peay & T.D. Bruns, 2011. This orange-coloured mushroom from Borneo gets its name from the children's cartoon character SpongeBob SquarePants.

A hierarchy of taxa

The term taxa (singular taxon) refers to the categories that scientists have generated names for. You can think of taxa as being like folders for organizing your school papers. Just as you would not (or should not) file your history notes in your maths folder, so biologists do not put birds in the same category as mammals. Likewise, within your history folder, you might have subfolders for homework, notes, tests, and so on. Within the category of plants, biologists have smaller categories for flowering plants, conifers, spore-producing plants, etc. Thus a hierarchy of taxa is used to classify species into many subcategories that are found within larger categories. There are specific names for these categories.

Three domains of life

At the top of the hierarchy are the three largest groupings for organisms, called domains. The names of these three domains are the Archaea domain, the Eubacteria domain and Eukaryote domain. All living organisms are classified into one of these three. Note that viruses are not in this list because they are not alive and do not necessarily share a common ancestry with each other, two major conditions necessary to fit into this classification system. (Figure 5.28 in the next section shows how the three domains are related.)

Archaeans are single-celled organisms that are distinct from bacteria and are very ancient. Archaean species thrive today in diverse habitats, from extreme conditions such as hydrothermal vents and hot springs, to the guts of mammals. Some of the beautiful colours of hot springs in places such as Yellowstone National Park are because of the presence of archaeans. The types of archaeans that prefer extreme conditions are called extremophiles and include thermophiles (heat-loving), methanophiles (methane-loving), and halophiles (salt-loving).

What do we do with viruses? How do we classify them? Viruses contain genetic information and yet they cannot reproduce outside a host cell; they do not feed, grow, or metabolize in the way that living organisms do, so they are considered to be non-living. For taxonomists, viruses are not classified as living things: they do not fall anywhere in the three domains. As a result, they are treated separately, and virologists have their own classification system.

Halocins are types of antibiotics made by halophile (salt-loving) archaeans. Just as penicillin was first discovered in a fungus, lots of pharmaceutical drugs come from naturally occurring compounds. Archaeans are currently being studied for the types of organic molecules they can produce, and some of them may hold the key to fighting diseases for which we do not yet have a cure.

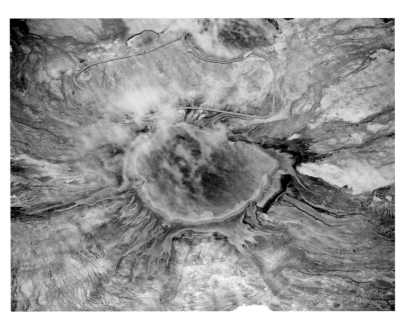

Grand Prismatic Thermal Springs in Yellowstone National Park. The bright colours around the edge of the hot water are caused by microbial colonies that include archaeans.

Eubacteria is the domain in which we find the bacteria you are most familiar with: the kind that makes your yogurt taste good, the kind that helps your intestines work properly, and also the kind that might give you an infection.

Eukaryote is the domain in which we find all other life besides Archaea and bacteria, from the microscopic single-celled yeast that helps bread to rise, to enormous organisms such as sequoia trees and blue whales. A eukaryote is recognizable by its membrane-bound nucleus and membrane-bound organelles.

Seven principal taxa

In order to classify the hundreds of thousands of different types of organisms on Earth, scientists have agreed to use a seven-level hierarchy of taxa. Each of the three domains is subdivided into these seven taxa:

- kingdom
- phylum
- class
- order
- family
- genus
- species.

Figure 5.17 This diagram is a very simplified way of showing the relationships between eight species from two phyla in one kingdom. It would be impossible to show the relationships of the hundreds of thousands of species in each of the kingdoms in this way. If this diagram was flipped upside down, can you see how it could be thought of as a tree? Also, remember that kingdoms can be classified under one of three domains.

The taxa that are higher up this list contain the most numbers of organisms, and the taxa at the bottom of the list contain the least number. For example, although there are hundreds of thousands of named animals in the Eukaryote kingdom (most of which are insects), there is only a single known species of humans on Earth today: *Homo sapiens*. So the higher taxa have very general characteristics encompassing many types of organisms, and the lower taxa have increasingly specific characteristics; the hierarchy narrows the categories down into smaller and smaller numbers of subcategories.

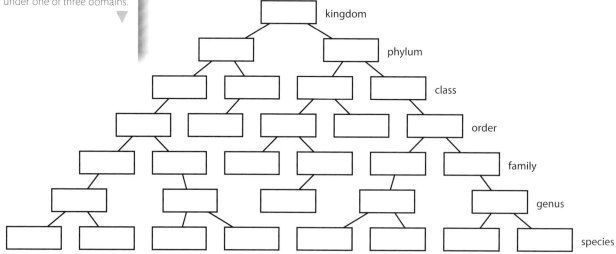

 To help remember the order of the taxa, a mnemonic (memory trick) is helpful. Make a sentence using the first letters of each level, such as 'King Philip Came Over For Good Soup'. The human brain is very poorly adapted for remembering lists of words but very highly adapted for remembering stories. Transforming lists into stories is a good example of a mnemonic.

Table 5.2 shows two examples of the full identification of two species according to the seven taxa we have just named.

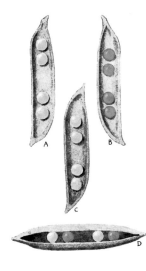

Taxa	Human	Garden pea
Kingdom	Animalia	Plantae
Phylum	Chordata	Angiospermophyta
Class	Mammalia	Dicotyledoneae
Order	Primate	Rosales
Family	Hominidae	Papilionaceae
Genus	*Homo*	*Pisum*
Species	*sapiens*	*sativum*

Table 5.2 The classification of two species

Figure 5.18 The garden pea, *Pisum sativum*, is the plant Gregor Mendel studied.

Other classifications

The system of kingdoms and taxa is used for identifying and naming organisms, but there are countless other ways to classify organisms. Here are some examples:

• by feeding habits – carnivore/herbivore
• by habitat – land dwelling/aquatic
• by daily activity – nocturnal/diurnal
• by risk – harmless/venomous
• by anatomy – vertebrates/invertebrates.

No single classification system is the 'right' way. Think of all the ways that the students in a class could be put into different groups: by eye colour, by shoe size, by birth date, by academic results, by favourite musical group, by alphabetical order, by length of fingernails, by what they had for breakfast! What is important for a system of classification is that it is clear, consistent, logical, easily implemented, and that there is a general consensus to apply it.

A common ancestral species

In biology, one of the objectives of classification is to represent how living (and extinct) organisms are connected. This means we are interested in natural classification, classifying organisms by their descent from a common ancestor. In Linnaeus' time, a century before Darwin and Mendel's work, the existence and function of DNA was not known, so classifications were based on observable characteristics. Today, it is preferable to use ancestry and genetics to classify organisms. The best way to establish a natural classification is to base it on DNA sequences. When the sequences are not available, the next best way is to look at derived characteristics, such as whether or not an organism can produce milk. There will be more about derived characteristics in Section 5.4.

CHALLENGE YOURSELF

3 Look up the following things to find out what their scientific names are:
 • your favourite animal
 • your favourite food
 • your favourite flower, tree, or house plant.

When genetic similarities are found, a genus can be established in which all similar species are placed. The members of this genus will have all evolved from a common ancestor, and this will be evident in the similarities between their gene sequences.

Without a universal classification system, each language, culture, or region may have a different name for an organism. For example, the pill bug and woodlouse sound like two different organisms but they are, in fact, the same one: *Armadillidium vulgare*. The common names do not reveal anything about a species' evolutionary links, but its scientific name does.

You may have come across this kind of invertebrate under rotting logs.

Reclassification

As noted before, Linnaean classification was limited to observable characteristics, and in Linnaeus's time little effort was made to classify organisms by their ancestry because nothing was known about the genetic connections between species. The consequence of this is that sometimes organisms were put in the same genus even though they are not in fact closely related to each other. With a better understanding of cell structure and metabolism, as well as the new techniques of gene sequencing developed over the past few decades, we now know that some organisms that were put into the same categories in the 1700s should not be together in the same genus or even the same order.

Today, many species have been reclassified. A good example is a group of flowers called asters that were all formerly in a genus called *Aster* that comprised hundreds of species distributed widely across geographical and temperature ranges at various altitudes in Europe, Asia, and the Americas. Many species of these plants are cultivated in gardens for their decorative flowers (an example is shown in the photo on page 261). In recent decades, taxonomists have split this group into species that can trace their ancestry to the Old World (Europe and Asia) and species that can trace their ancestry to the New World (North, Central, and South America).

Looking at the ancestry of the asters, revealed in part by the structure of the single-seeded fruit they make called an achene, it was decided that there was a significant enough difference between the species on the two sides of the Atlantic Ocean that reclassification was necessary. The new classification is a better reflection of which ones are more closely related to each other. Of the genera that were put into the New World group, one example is the blue wood aster, which has now been placed in the genus *Symphyotrichum*. Table 5.3 shows what the reclassification has done to the blue wood aster's scientific name.

Old classification	New classification
Aster cordifolius	*Symphyotrichum cordifolium*

Table 5.3 The classification of the blue wood aster

Blue wood aster.

One of the challenges to renaming organisms is that books and scientific journals, as well as gardening guides and museum herbarium collections, often still have the old scientific names. This means that, before using a scientific name, it is best to check that the name respects any recent reclassifications. Fortunately, with online databases and user-generated content in web-based encyclopaedias, names can be updated and notes can be left about the previous name, so that specialists doing research can usually find a species whether or not a new or an old name has been used. One such online database is the Integrated Taxonomic Information System (ITIS), which you can find in the hotlinks at the end of this section.

Another challenge is that, just because a group of taxonomists decides to make a change, it does not mean that everyone will agree with that change. In addition to resistance to breaking with tradition, or the insistence of some taxonomists to maintain stability in a name no matter what, there may be some scientists who disagree with the way new groups have been determined. Just because a committee

How are taxonomists classified? Answer: into lumpers and splitters. In taxonomy, there are two opposing philosophies concerning what to do when an organism does not fit well into existing categories: (1) broaden the definition of an existing category to include the new organism; or (2) invent a new category or subcategory. Specialists who take the first approach are referred to as lumpers, and those who take the second approach are referred to as splitters. As you can imagine, there can be lengthy discussions between the two groups. Generally speaking, lumpers focus on the similarities between organisms, while splitters focus on the differences between organisms.

of taxonomists insists that a certain difference in cell structure is a significant enough reason to change a classification, does not mean that everyone will embrace the decision. This is one of the reasons why, long after a decision has been made, it is still possible to see an older name in field guides, databases, scientific journals, and museum labels.

Natural classification

Natural classification uses ancestry to group organisms together, whereas artificial classifications use arbitrary characteristics, such as whether or not a plant or animal tastes good, or is useful to the textile industry, or whose name begins with the letter 'c'. You may laugh, but early classification systems were often based on listing the species by alphabetical order, the way a dictionary lists words.

Table 5.4 A summary of the differences between natural and artificial classification systems

Characteristics for natural classification systems	Characteristics for artificial classification systems
• Morphology • DNA • Diet • Habitat	• Alphabetical order • Human preference for taste or smell • Importance to industry • Monetary worth

The reasons for putting living organisms into groups according to a natural classification rather than an artificial one are numerous, and include:

• trying to make sense of the biosphere
• showing evolutionary links
• predicting characteristics shared by members of a group.

If you find a type of sea creature that you have never seen before, you should be able to find an identification key that was made by the experts who classified it. If you do a comprehensive search in the published literature of organisms that have already been identified and do not find a name for the organism, it is possible that you have discovered a new species. To put it into its appropriate category, you would find currently existing taxa that contain similar organisms. You would determine whether it had a backbone or not, if it had stinging cells or not, and so on, until you reached a family or genus that it fit into. Once you find that genus, you can look at the list of characteristics of the species in that genus and make predictions about your new species. You might be able to predict what it eats, how long it lives, whether or not it produces certain enzymes, or even certain characteristics about its cell structure or biochemistry.

In the other direction, if biologists look at characteristics common to all life forms, such as the basic information in DNA about fundamental processes such as cellular respiration and cell division, they can deduce what the common ancestor to all life was like. This organism, sometimes named LUCA for last universal common ancestor, or LUA for last universal ancestor, lived over 3.5 billion years ago and parts of its DNA code can be worked out by retracing and examining the ancestries of various forms of life.

Below, you will see some of the characteristics that scientists look for when classifying organisms. We will look at plants and animals, but be aware that there are other kingdoms not mentioned here.

Examples of plant phyla

Of the several phyla of plants, four represent many of the types of plants you are probably most familiar with.

- Bryophyta: the bryophyte phylum includes plants of very short stature, such as mosses.
- Filicinophyta: this phylum includes ferns and horsetails, among others.
- Coniferophyta: the conifer phylum includes cedar, juniper, fir, and pine trees, among others.
- Angiospermophyta: the angiosperm phylum includes all plants that make flowers and have seeds surrounded by a fruit.

Let's examine each of these phyla more closely.

Bryophyta

Bryophytes, such as the liverwort shown below, are referred to as non-vascular plants because they do not have true vascular transport tissue inside them, such as xylem tissue (which transports water and minerals up from the roots) or phloem tissue (which transports water and nutrients from the leaves towards the stem and roots).

Filicinophyta

Members of the Filicinophyta, on the other hand, are vascular plants, as are the other two phyla described in this section. Ferns are recognizable by the absence of flowers and by their triangular fronds made up of many smaller long thin leaves.

Coniferophyta

Conifers can be recognized by the fact that all of them produce woody stems and their leaves are in the form of needles or scales.

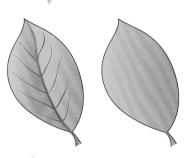

Figure 5.19 Vascular and non-vascular plants. Vascular plants have leaves with clearly visible veins because they have tubes for carrying liquids from one part of the plant to another. Non-vascular plants rely on diffusion and osmosis throughout the tissue rather than having specialized tubes. Their leaves tend to be very small.

Liverwort is an example of a bryophyte.

Trees that produce seed cones and have needle-like leaves are conifers.

This moss growing on the bark of a tree branch is also a bryophyte.

Examples from different plant phyla.

263

Angiospermophyta

The most obvious vegetative characteristic that allows angiosperms (i.e. members of the Angiospermophyta) to be identified quickly are their flowers and fruit. If the fruit has any seeds inside, the plant is an angiosperm.

The mosses, liverworts, and hornworts that make up the bryophytes do not produce flowers or seeds. Instead, they produce spores, which are microscopic reproductive structures. Bryophyte spores are transported by rainwater and ground humidity, which is one of the reasons why they are found most abundantly in damp habitats such as a forest floor. The same is true for the plants that are filicinophytes.

In contrast, all species of conifer use wind to help them reproduce by pollination. Most species of conifer produce seed cones with seed scales.

Although angiosperms also produce seeds, they do not produce cones and they are not always pollinated by wind. Many flowering plants rely on birds, insects, and sometimes mammals to transport their pollen from one flower to the next.

The sexual reproductive organs of angiosperms are their flowers. The fruit, which is the enlarged ovary of the plant, holds the seeds.

Examples of animal phyla

Of all the phyla of animals, we will consider seven here. Some of these you may be familiar with, but others you probably do not know much about. Only one of the categories of animals in these seven phyla has a backbone or vertebral column: they are called vertebrates. The other six categories are all invertebrates: they do not have a backbone.

- Porifera: this phylum consists of the sponges.
- Cnidaria: this phylum includes sea jellies (jellyfish) and coral polyps, among others.
- Platyhelminthes: this phylum is made up of flatworms.
- Annelida: this phylum is made up of segmented worms.
- Mollusca: this phylum contains snails, clams, and octopuses, among others.
- Arthropoda: this phylum includes insects, spiders, and crustaceans, among others.
- Chordata: these are the vertebrates, the animals that have a backbone.

Porifera

Sponges are marine animals that are sessile (i.e. they are stuck in place). They do not have mouths or digestive tracts. Rather, they feed by pumping water through their tissues to filter out food. They have no muscle or nerve tissue and no distinct internal organs.

A yellow tube sponge, one of the members of the phylum Porifera.

Cnidaria

Cnidarians are a diverse group, including corals, sea anemones, jellyfish (sea jellies), hydra, and floating colonies such as the Portuguese man-of-war. This diversity makes it difficult to give an overall description of common characteristics. However, one feature that unites cnidarians is that they all have stinging cells called nematocysts.

Some of these organisms are sessile, others are free-swimming, and some can be both depending on the period of their life cycle. To digest the food they catch in their tentacles, they have a gastric pouch with only one opening. Some of the free-floating species are carried by the current, but others are agile swimmers.

Platyhelminthes

Flatworms have only one body cavity: a gut with one opening for food to enter and waste to exit. They have no heart and no lungs. One of the most famous, or infamous, members of this phylum is the parasitic tapeworm that can infest the intestines of mammals, including humans. The reason for a flatworm's flat shape is that all the cells need to be close to the surface to be able to exchange gases by diffusion. Their bodies are not segmented (divided up into sections).

The common earthworm is an annelid.

Annelida

Annelids are the segmented worms, such as earthworms, leeches, and worms called polychaetes. Here, the word segmented refers to the fact that their bodies are divided up into sections separated by rings. Annelids have bristles on their bodies, although these are not always easily visible. Like the next two phyla, annelids have a gastric tract with a mouth at one end and an opening at the other end where wastes are released.

Mollusca

Most molluscs are aquatic, and include snails, clams, and octopuses. Many produce a shell reinforced with calcium. Like annelids, they have a one-way digestive system with both a mouth and an anus. But, unlike annelids, their bodies are not segmented.

Arthropoda

Arthropods have a hard exoskeleton made of chitin, segmented bodies, and limbs that can bend because they are jointed. Although the limbs are often used for walking, some are adapted for swimming, and others can form mouthparts.

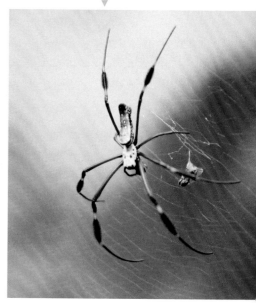

Spiders are arthropods.

Arthropods include insects, spiders, and scorpions, as well as crustaceans such as crabs and shrimps. They are true champions of diversity and adaptation because they have conquered most habitats worldwide; there are more than a million species of arthropod. They vary in size from the most minute mites, just over 100 μm long, to the Japanese giant spider crab, which is 4 m in length.

Chordata

The chordates are organisms that have a notochord at some point in their development. A notochord is a line of cartilage going down the back that provides support to the animal. It is always present at one stage in the development of a chordate organism, but can be absent from other stages. The vast majority of animals in this phylum have a bony backbone, such as birds, mammals, amphibians, reptiles, and fish, although some fish such as sharks have a cartilaginous spine instead of one made of bone. Unlike the six previous examples, these organisms are all called vertebrates. There are some exceptions to the generalization that all chordates have a backbone: sea squirts do not, for example, but are still classified in this phylum because they do develop a notochord.

When we say the word 'animal' to a child, he or she will probably think of animals with backbones, perhaps because many children's books feature vertebrates as the main characters. To a biologist, vertebrates are relatively rare; invertebrates, such as insects, are much more common on Earth.

The vertebrates

We will now explore the characteristics used to classify vertebrate organisms into the following five classes:

- fish
- amphibians
- reptiles
- birds
- mammals.

Fish

From goldfish to sharks, fish are a class of very diverse aquatic organisms that possess gills to absorb oxygen, and have skulls made of bone or cartilage. Great white sharks are well known for their jaws and teeth, and the vast majority of fish have these features, although they are not always visible. A small number of fish, such as lampreys, are jawless and use their mouths as suckers to stick onto a surface. Although fish can have limbs in the form of fins, none of the limbs have digits (fingers). Some marine mammals, such as whales, orcas, and dolphins, might resemble fish but are not, one reason being they have articulated bony fingers inside their fins.

A lamprey is a fish without a jaw. Instead, it uses its mouth as a sucker to hold on to rocks.

Amphibians

Amphibians include organisms such as frogs and salamanders; they start their lives in water. Their larval forms usually have gills to breathe underwater, but their adult forms develop lungs for breathing air. Most amphibians can also absorb oxygen through their skin. Most have four legs when they are adults, but there is a legless group called caecilians that resemble large worms or small snakes. They eat a wide variety of food, which they can chew with teeth. They might seem similar to reptiles, but their eggs do not have a membrane around the embryo. Like reptiles, however, amphibians cannot control their body temperature; they are called ectothermic (or, more informally, cold-blooded) and need to bask in the sunshine to warm up, and seek shade or water to cool off.

Reptiles

Organisms such as snakes, lizards, turtles, and alligators are classified as reptiles in part because they produce amniote eggs. Amniote eggs are characterized by having a membrane around the developing embryo to protect it, which is seen not only in reptiles with soft or hard-shelled eggs but also in birds and mammals. What sets reptiles apart from other animals is that they have scales on their body instead of feathers or fur. Like amphibians, reptiles are ectothermic; they cannot regulate their body temperature.

A tadpole is the larval stage of an amphibian such as this frog. In this photo, the young frog is almost ready to leave the water because its four limbs have developed.

This marine iguana needs to bask in the sun to warm up after a cold swim in the ocean. Notice the scales covering the body, and notice the pentadactyl forelimb.

Birds

All living species of birds are bipedal (have two legs) and possess wings, most of which are adapted for flight. All birds have feathers and lay eggs with hardened shells. Bird skeletons are often very lightweight, making them well-adapted for flight. Their low density is achieved by having hollow bones. Penguins are an example of a flightless bird, but their wings are well-adapted for swimming. Birds are also characterized by the fact that their jaws are in the form of beaks with no teeth, and they usually build nests for their young, albeit in a variety of places, such as in trees, on the ground, on cliff faces, and on urban structures. Their heart beat and breathing rates are relatively fast because they have a high rate of metabolism.

Mammals

Mammals include animals such as foxes, hippopotamuses, squirrels, and camels, and can be recognized by the fact that they have hair on their bodies and the females produce milk in specialized glands to feed their young. There are nearly 5500 species of known mammals in the world, most of which have four limbs adapted for life on land. Some mammals, such as whales and dolphins, are adapted for life in the water, and others, such as bats, are adapted for flight. Mammals are capable of thermoregulation: they maintain their body temperature at a fixed level.

Using a dichotomous key

When biologists encounter a species they do not recognize, they use a dichotomous key to establish which taxa it belongs to. If you have ever played a guessing game in which the rule is that you can only ask 'yes' or 'no' questions, then you already know how a dichotomous key works. Here are the basic principles.

1   Look at the first section of the key, which has a pair of sentences, (a) and (b), describing characteristics.
2   Next, look at the organism to see if the particular characteristic described in the first line (a) is present in the organism.
3   If the answer is yes, then go to the end of its line and find the number of the next pair of statements to look at, follow the number given and continue until the end. If the end of the line contains a name, it is the taxon for the organism.
4   If the answer is no, then go to the second statement just below it (b) and that one should be true, so go to the end of its line and find the number of the next pair of statements to look at. Follow the number given and continue until the end.

Keep going until you get to a name instead of a number: if you have answered each question correctly, that will be the name of the taxon your organism belongs to. Try identifying the organisms shown opposite using the key in the following example.

Worked example

Here is an example of a key for identifying the animal taxa listed in this chapter.

1   (a) No differentiated tissues, no symmetry or identifiable organs.. Porifera
   (b) Presence of differentiated tissues and organs 2
2   (a) Stinging cells present, can show radial symmetry....................... Cnidaria
   (b) No stinging cells 3
3   (a) Has two-way digestive tract and bilateral symmetry.................. Platyhelminthes
   (b) Has a one-way digestive tract (mouth and anus)......................... 4
4   (a) Does not possess a notochord at any time..................................... 5
   (b) Possesses a notochord at some stage.. 7
5   (a) Has an exoskeleton made of chitin .... Arthropoda
   (b) Does not have an exoskeleton made of chitin............................... 6
6   (a) Has a segmented body .... Annelida
   (b) Makes a shell reinforced with calcium.. Mollusca
7   (a) Four limbs present, with articulated digits.................................... 8
   (b) Limbs present, but they do not have digits .... Fish

8 (a) Does not produce an amnion... Amphibians
   (b) Can produce an amnion.. 9
9 (a) Presence of hair on the body, can make milk to feed young ...... Mammal
   (b) Absence of hair, cannot make milk 10
10 (a) Body covered with feathers... Bird
   (b) Body covered with scales .... Reptile

Use the key to find out which taxon each organism pictured below is in. Show how you did your work by writing the numbers and letters you followed.

1

2

3

4

CHALLENGE YOURSELF

4 Construct your own dichotomous key for use in identifying specimens. Because the example shown is for animal taxa in this chapter, try one for the plant taxa described in this chapter.

Campers and hikers can use a dichotomous key in a field guide to be sure that any mushrooms or plants they find are edible and not poisonous. They can also use a key to determine whether or not certain plants are endangered or protected species.

TOK In his classification of organisms, Linnaeus used physical characteristics and social behaviour to establish four groups of humans. Reading such descriptions today is shocking because, by modern standards, they have a racist nature. To what extent is it necessary to consider the social context of scientific work when evaluating ethical questions about research?

Solutions

1 1b →2b →3b →4a →5a = Arthropoda
2 1b →2a = Cnidaria
3 1b →2b →3b →4b →7a →8b →9b →10b = Reptile
4 1b →2b →3b →4a →5b →6b = Mollusca

Section summary

- The binomial nomenclature system is an internationally agreed upon classification system based on a natural classification of living organisms.
- Taxonomists establish scientific names, and organisms are placed into one of three domains (Archaea, Eubacteria, and Eukaryote) then into categories based on a hierarchy of taxa: kingdom, phylum, class, order, family, genus, and species.
- These taxa are arranged to show how organisms are related through common ancestry.
- Congresses are held regularly to debate new developments in scientific knowledge about ancestries, and sometimes old taxa need to be rearranged or renamed to comply with the new data.

To learn more about taxonomy and classification, go to the hotlinks site, search for the title or ISBN, and click on Chapter 5: Section 5.3.

• One benefit of using a natural classification (based on ancestry) is that predictions can be made about characteristics of newly discovered organisms. Artificial classifications (such as those based on names arranged in alphabetical order) do not have such benefits.

Exercises

9 List the three classification domains. Determine which domain each of the following organisms belongs to.

   (a) A single-celled organism that prefers very salty water.
   (b) Algae (hint: they have a nucleus).
   (c) Spider.
   (d) *Escherichia coli*.

10 Suggest one reason why viruses do not fit into the three-domain system.

11 Make a table with four columns headed Bryophyta, Filicinophyta, Coniferophyta, and Angiospermophyta. Make two rows labelled 'Physical characteristics' and 'Named examples'. Complete the eight empty cells of the table.

12 In the seven-taxa system, state the order that you belong to.

13 Using 10 different objects found in your school bag, design a dichotomous key.

NATURE OF SCIENCE

Falsification of theories with one theory being superseded by another: plant families have been reclassified as a result of evidence from cladistics.

5.4 Cladistics

Understandings:

● A clade is a group of organisms that have evolved from a common ancestor.
● Evidence for which species are part of a clade can be obtained from the base sequences of a gene or the corresponding amino acid sequence of a protein.
● Sequence differences accumulate gradually so there is a positive correlation between the number of differences between two species and the time since they diverged from a common ancestor.
● Traits can be analogous or homologous.
● Cladograms are tree diagrams that show the most probable sequence of divergence in clades.
● Evidence from cladistics has shown that classifications of some groups based on structure did not correspond with the evolutionary origins of a group or species.

Applications and skills:

● Application: Cladograms including humans and other primates.
● Application: Reclassification of the figwort family using evidence from cladistics.
● Skill: Analysis of cladograms to deduce evolutionary relationships.

Characteristics used for classification

Table 5.5 shows some types of characteristics that botanists and zoologists might study in order to help them decide how to classify an organism.

Table 5.5 Types of characteristics used for classifying organisms

Characteristic	Example/reason
Morphology	The shape of a plant's seed coat or the shape of a bird's bill
Anatomy	The number of petals on a flower or the type of digestive system in an invertebrate

Characteristic	Example/reason
Cytology	The structure of cells or their function
Phytochemistry	Special organic compounds that only plants can make, often to protect themselves from attack by insects
Chromosome number	Two species with the same chromosome number are more likely to be closely related than those with differing numbers
Molecular differences	Proteins and DNA sequences differ between one species and another

Classifying organisms using molecular differences is called molecular systematics. As technology is improved and becomes more affordable, more and more specialists are using methods involving protein sequences and DNA.

Clades

Cladistics is a system of classification that groups taxa together according to the characteristics that have evolved most recently. In this system, the concept of common descent is crucial to deciding into which groups to classify organisms. Cladistics is, therefore, an example of natural classification. To decide how close a common ancestor is, researchers look at how many primitive and derived traits the organisms share.

Primitive traits (also called plesiomorphic traits) are characteristics that have the same structure and function (e.g. leaves with vascular tissue to transport liquids around a plant) and that evolved early on in the history of the organisms being studied. Derived traits (also called apomorphic traits) are also characteristics that have the same structure and function but that have evolved more recently as modifications of a previous trait (e.g. flowers, which evolved more recently than leaves with vascular tissue, i.e. they are an adaptation of vascular leaves). By systematically comparing such characteristics, quantitative results show which organisms have a more recent split in the evolutionary past and which have a more distant split.

When a group can be split into two parts, one having certain derived traits that the other does not have, the groups form two separate clades. A clade is a monophyletic group. This means it is a group composed of the most recent common ancestor of the group and all its descendants. Although a clade can sometimes have just one species, usually it is made up of multiple species.

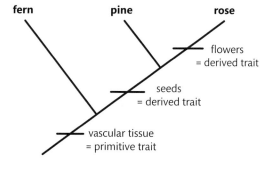

Figure 5.20 A simple cladogram showing three plants, all of which share one primitive trait (vascular tissue), two of which share the derived trait of seeds, and only one of which has the derived trait of possessing flowers. How cladograms are constructed will be covered later in this chapter.

Biochemical evidence of clades

Biochemical evidence, including DNA and protein structures, has brought new validity and confirmation to the idea of a common ancestor. For example, the fact that every known living organism on Earth uses DNA as its main source of genetic information is compelling evidence that all life on Earth has a common ancestor. As you saw in

Section 3.5 on genetic engineering, any gene from any organism can be mixed and matched with DNA from other organisms to generate a certain protein. Other than conceding that we all have a common ancestor, it would be difficult to explain how else this is true.

In addition, all the proteins found in living organisms use the same 20 amino acids to form their polypeptide chains. Again, this has been confirmed by the introduction of foreign genes using genetic engineering to get an organism to synthesize a protein that it never synthesized before.

Amino acids can have two possible orientations: left-handed and right-handed, depending on the way their atoms are attached together. The overwhelming majority of living organisms on Earth use left-handed amino acids to build their proteins, and only a small number of organisms (notably some bacteria) can use right-handed amino acids. For those who support the idea of the biochemical evolution of life, the most logical explanation for such chemical similarities is that they imply a common ancestry for all life forms that use left-handed amino acids to build their proteins.

Variations and phylogeny

Phylogeny is the study of the evolutionary past of a species. Species that are the most similar are most likely to be closely related, whereas those that show a higher degree of differences are considered less likely to be closely related. By comparing the similarities in the polypeptide sequences of certain proteins in different groups of animals, it is possible to trace their common ancestry. This has been done with the blood protein haemoglobin, with a mitochondrial protein called cytochrome *c*, and with chlorophyll, to name just three proteins.

With advances in DNA sequencing, the study of nucleic acid sequences in an organism's DNA, as well as its mitochondrial DNA, has been effective in establishing biochemical phylogeny. Changes in the DNA sequences of genes from one generation to the next are partly due to mutations, and the more differences there are between two species, the less closely related the species are.

Here is an imaginary example of a DNA sequence from four different organisms:

1   A A A A T T T T C C C C G G G G

2   A A A A T T T A C C C C G G G G

3   A A A A T T T A C C C G C G G G

4   A A C A T C T A C C A G C C T G

The differences have been highlighted in red. It should be clear that species 1 and 2 have the fewest differences between them, whereas species 1 and 4 have the most differences. As we have seen in Chapter 4, these differences can arise as a result of mutations. The second sequence shows only one difference with the first, but the fourth shows eight differences. The conclusion could be that species 1 and 2 are more closely related to each other than they are to species 3 or 4.

Figure 5.21 shows how these four imaginary species could be related.

Figure 5.21 A representation of the relationships between four species.

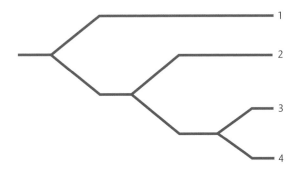

Often, such work by biochemists confirms what palaeontologists have hypothesized about the ancestries of the fossils they have studied. When one branch of science confirms the work of another branch, the findings have more credibility. In other cases, the biochemical evidence can be contradictory, which encourages scientists to reconsider their initial ideas.

The evolutionary clock

Differences in polypeptide sequences accumulate steadily and gradually over time, as mutations occur from generation to generation in a species. Consequently, the changes can be used as a kind of clock to estimate how far back in time two related species split from a common ancestor.

By comparing homologous molecules from two related species, it is possible to count the number of places along the molecules where there are differences. If the molecule is mitochondrial DNA, for example, we count the number of base pairs that do not match. Mitochondrial DNA is particularly interesting to study because, unlike DNA found in the cell's nucleus, it is not shuffled and mixed during meiosis or fertilization: it is passed on directly from mother to child without modification. This is why we can be sure that any modifications in mitochondrial DNA are due solely to mutations.

Imagine comparing certain DNA sequences from three species, A, B, and C. Between the DNA samples from species A and species C there are 83 differences. Between species A and species B there are only 26 differences. From these data, we can conclude that species B is more closely related to species A than species C is. There has been more time for DNA mutations to occur since the split between A and C than since the split between A and B.

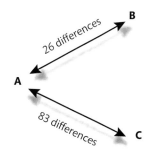

Figure 5.22 There are more genetic mutations between the DNA of A and C DNA than there are between the DNA of A and B. Therefore, species A is more closely related to species B than it is to species C.

One technique that has been successful in measuring such differences is DNA hybridization. The idea is simple: take one strand of DNA from species A and a homologous strand from species B and fuse them together. Where the base pairs connect, there is a match; where they are repelled and do not connect, there is a difference in the DNA sequence and therefore there is no match (see Figure 5.23).

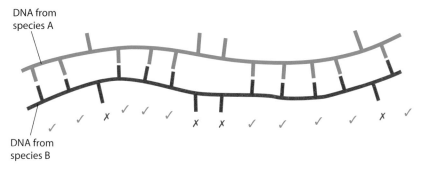

Figure 5.23 DNA hybridization between a strand of DNA from one species (in green) and another from a second species (in red). There are four places where a match does not occur.

We can take this further. If we see that 83 nucleotide differences is approximately three times more than 26 differences, we can hypothesize that the split between species A and species C happened about three times further back in the past than the split between the species A and B. This is the idea of using quantitative biochemical data as an evolutionary clock to estimate the time of the speciation events (see Figure 5.24).

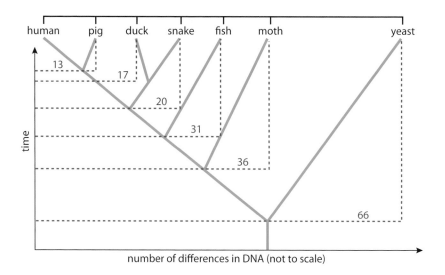

Figure 5.24 Biochemical differences (dotted red lines) can be used to see how far apart species are on a phylogenetic tree (in blue).

However, we need to be careful when using a word such as 'clock' in this context. Under no circumstances should we consider that the 'tick-tock' of the evolutionary clock, which is made up of mutations, is as constant as the ticking of a clock on the wall. Mutations can happen at varying rates. Consequently, all we have is an average, an estimation or a proportion, rather than an absolute time or date for speciation events. In an effort to double-check the timing of the evolutionary clock, biochemical data can be compared with morphological fossil evidence and radioisotope dating.

 Experts in various fields of study use this idea of accumulated change over time. For example, linguists look at changes in words and uses of vocabulary to trace the evolution of a language throughout the course of history. Some language experts can deduce when pigs were domesticated in a particular country just by looking at the names for 'pig' in the various languages in and around that country. Experts who study chain letters sent by the post or by email are interested in the number of modifications to the original letter over time. By comparing hundreds of versions of the same message, they can analyse what has been added or changed to see its evolution over time. With enough evidence, it is sometimes possible to deduce the origin and approximate date of the original letter in a chain, even if that letter was never found.

Analogous and homologous traits

In examining the traits of organisms in order to put them into their appropriate clades, thorough and systematic studies of their characteristics must be undertaken. Two types of characteristic that are considered are homologous characteristics and analogous characteristics.

As we saw earlier in this chapter, homologous characteristics are ones derived from the same part of a common ancestor. The five-fingered limbs found in such diverse animals as humans, whales, and bats are examples of homologous anatomical structures. The shape and number of the bones may vary, and the function may vary, but the general format is the same, and the conclusion is that the organisms that possess these limbs had a common ancestor.

Another example of a homologous characteristic is the presence of eyes. Such structures are seen in both vertebrates and invertebrates. Simple eyes found in molluscs such as the Nautilus function as pinhole cameras without a system of lenses, whereas highly evolved eyes like those of birds of prey use crystalline lenses, adjustable irises, and muscles to help focus on objects at different distances. Yet both types of eye have evolved from a common ancestor, because they all use one form or another of pigment cells and specialized nerve cells called photoreceptors that are light sensitive (see Chapter 7, Section A.3).

Homology is observed in DNA sequences as well. Certain combinations of base pairs coding for similar proteins can be found in diverse organisms. As with homologous anatomical features, these sequences are evidence of a common ancestry. The cytochrome *c* sequence studied in Section 3.1 is one example.

In contrast, analogous characteristics are those that may have the same function but they do not necessarily have the same structure and they are not derived from a common ancestor. Wings used for flying are an example: eagles, mosquitoes, bats, and extinct reptiles such as the pterosaurs all use (or used) wings to fly. Although these organisms are all classified in the animal kingdom, they are certainly not placed in the same clade simply because of their ability to fly with wings. There are many other characteristics that must be considered.

Another example of an analogous characteristic is fins in aquatic organisms. Both sharks and dolphins have pectoral fins that serve a very similar function: helping them to swim well. But sharks are fish whereas dolphins are aquatic mammals, and the two are classified differently in both the Linnaean system and in cladistics.

Table 5.6 A summary of the differences between analogous and homologous traits

	Homologous features	Analogous features
Form	Similar	Different
Function	Different	Similar
Examples	Pentadactyl limbs, eyes, certain DNA sequences	Insect wings versus bird wings, shark fins versus dolphin fins
Used as evidence of common ancestry	Yes	No

What do the sarcastic fringehead fish and the bald eagle have in common? Eyes: a homologous characteristic.

Cladograms

To represent the findings of cladistics in a visual way, a diagram called a cladogram is used. A cladogram showing bats, sharks, and dolphins, for example, would take into account their skeletal structures and other characteristics, such as the fact that bats and dolphins are mammals (see Figure 5.25). Thus, bats and dolphins are shown as more similar to each other than sharks are to either.

Figure 5.25 shows some key characteristics of a cladogram. For example, a node is the place where a speciation happened and where the common ancestor was found. The clade shown in yellow green is divided up into a sister group, a group showing the closest relatives, and an outgroup, which is a group that is less closely related to the

(!) To help you remember the difference between analogous and homologous, remember that these terms refer to anatomy (the flesh and blood) and that an analogy is used to compare very different things. The term 'homo' means same, so homologous refers to anatomically similar things.

others in the cladogram. Sharks are less closely related to bats and dolphins than bats and dolphins to each other. And yet, if we go back far enough, we will find another node showing that they do eventually have a common ancestor.

Figure 5.25 A cladogram showing three taxa organized into a clade, of which two are sister groups and one is an outgroup. Nodes show a common ancestor for the descendants that appear above them in this cladogram.

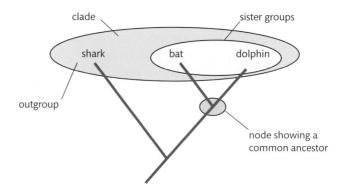

The essential idea behind cladograms constructed by studying biochemical differences is that an organism with the fewest modifications of a particular DNA sequence will be the most anciently evolved, and those with the most modifications (mutations) in the same DNA sequence will be the more recently evolved organisms. The former have nodes at the earliest splits of the cladogram, and the latter have nodes at the more recent splits.

Worked example

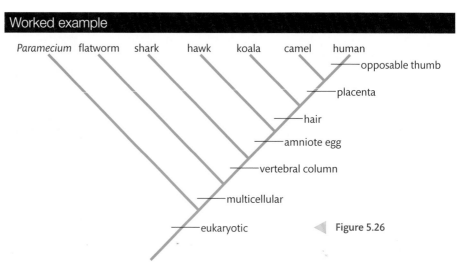

◀ **Figure 5.26**

1 What is the primitive characteristic in the cladogram shown in Figure 5.26?
2 Name the members of the mammal clade in this cladogram.
3 What is the outgroup when considering the clade of multicellular organisms?
4 Do shark eggs have a protective membrane (the amnios) around them?
5 Explain why there are no bacteria shown in this diagram.

Solutions

1 Being eukaryotic is the primitive characteristic shared by all.
2 Koala, camel, human.
3 The *Paramecium*.
4 No. Sharks are not amniotes.
5 Because the primitive characteristic requires the organisms to have a nucleus. If bacteria were to be added to this cladogram, a new primitive characteristic would need to be chosen.

Cladograms and classification

Cladistics attempts to find the most logical and most natural connections between organisms in order to reveal their evolutionary past. Cladistics is the study of clades, and cladograms are the diagrams that show the phylogeny of the clades being studied.

Every cladogram drawn is a working hypothesis. It is open for testing and for falsification. On the one hand, this makes cladistics scientific, but on the other hand, if it is going to be changing in the future as new evidence arises, it could be criticized for its lack of integrity.

Each time a derived characteristic is added to the list shared by organisms in a clade, the effect is similar to going up one level in the traditional hierarchy of the Linnaean classification scheme. For example, the presence of hair is part of what defines a mammal, so any species found after the line marked 'hair' should be in the class of mammals.

What about feathers? If an organism has feathers, is it automatically a bird? In traditional Linnaean classification, birds occupy a class of their own, but this is where cladistics comes up with a surprise. When preparing a cladogram, it becomes clear that birds share a significant number of derived characteristics with a group of dinosaurs called the theropods. This suggests that birds are an offshoot of dinosaurs rather than a separate class of their own.

Because birds are one of the most cherished and well-documented classes of organisms on Earth, this idea, when it was first suggested, was controversial to say the least. Some of the derived characteristics used to put birds and dinosaurs in the same clade are:

• a fused clavicle (the 'wishbone')
• flexible wrists
• hollow bones
• a characteristic egg shell
• the hip and leg structure, notably with backward-pointing knees.

By following the idea of parsimony, it is more likely that birds evolved from dinosaurs than from another common ancestor. This is where cladistics is clearer than the Linnaean system. In cladistics, the rules are always the same concerning shared derived characteristics and parsimony. In the Linnaean system, apart from the definition of species, which we have already seen is sometimes challenged, the other hierarchical groupings are not always clearly defined: what makes a class a class, or a phylum a phylum? Centuries after Linnaeus, we are still debating this question today.

Reclassification

From time to time, new evidence about a taxon requires a new classification. Either the taxon can be moved up or down the hierarchy (family to subfamily, for example), or from one family to another.

Plants commonly known as figworts used to be classified in the family Scrophulariaceae, and many of them have been used in herbal medicine. The name Scrophulariaceae, sometimes affectionately referred to by botanists as 'scrophs', comes from the time when plants were frequently named for the diseases they could be used to treat. The medical term 'scrofula' refers to an infection of the lymph nodes in the neck. Preparations made with figwort were given to patients who suffered from this infection, which was associated with tuberculosis.

Before the mid-1990s, the family Scrophulariaceae was characterized by morphological features such as how the flower petals were arranged in the bud before the flower opens. This feature is called aestivation, and botanists look for whether the flower petals overlap with each other or whether they are arranged in a spiral or not. Another characteristic that was used was the morphology of the nectaries, the parts of the flower that make nectar.

Since the mid-1990s, DNA analysis of the plants classified in this taxon have led botanists to rethink their classification. Analysis of zones of DNA markers such as the nuclear ribosomal internal transcribed spacer (ITS) region has revealed that the old classification system was not monophyletic, meaning the taxa did not share a most recent common ancestor. Rather, the old system was grouping together plants that belonged to separate branches, making it impossible to fit them into a cladogram.

The term used to describe species on separate branches is paraphyletic, so we now know that the old family Scrophulariaceae was paraphyletic. As an analogy, it would be similar to someone meeting your extended family for the first time and incorrectly assuming that your second cousins were your brothers and sisters, simply because you all had similar physical features. DNA testing would clearly show that second cousins have a more distant common ancestor than siblings do.

Plants that were in the Scrophulariaceae family have been given new families to belong to. One of the families that has incorporated species from the old classification is the family

The common foxglove, *Digitalis purpurea*, has been reclassified, so instead of being in the figwort family it is now in the plantain family.

Plataginaceae, and that is where we now find foxgloves. Foxgloves are now classified in a way that shows that they are more closely related to plantains; they are no longer considered to be figworts.

Moving the branches of the tree of life around and reclassifying a taxon in a new branch in this manner means changing the species' circumscription. Circumscription is the process of placing taxa where they clearly show monophyletic groups, allowing us to show that they all share a recent common ancestor.

Figure 5.27 An example of a modification of a species' circumscription. The clade that included species C, D, and E on the left was moved from the branch that included species A, and placed on the branch with species B instead, because C, D, and E show a common ancestry with species B. In the old cladogram on the left, B, C, D, and E are shown as being paraphyletic, whereas the new cladogram on the right is showing them as monophyletic.

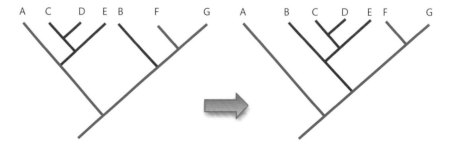

Every once in a while a new idea comes along and shakes the scientific community to the core. Reclassifying thousands of organisms by creating a new category of taxon would be a good example, and that is precisely what Carl Woese did in 1977. He proposed the domain Archaea.

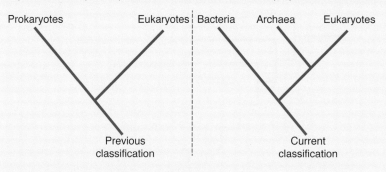

Figure 5.28 The classification of Archaea.

Influential scientists at the time, including Nobel laureate Salvador Lurid and eminent evolutionary biologist Ernst Mayr, opposed splitting the prokaryotes in this way. This is an illustration of how some scientists are conservative and prefer to keep things the way they are. What benefits does conservatism have in science?

NATURE OF SCIENCE

Notice how the reclassification of the foxglove is a good example of how scientists work. Observations were made initially based on morphology. The plant was classified into specific categories that included the family Scrophulariaceae, the figwort family. DNA sequencing was done on many species including foxgloves, and it was determined that some plants did not belong with the other figworts but instead belonged in the family Plantaginaceae along with the plantains. Studies were published in recognized botany journals and now foxgloves have a new family.

A certain amount of communication is needed in order to get everyone to use the new classification. Books on botany and websites on plant conservation, as well as university courses and online databases, must be updated, and the best ones make sure they are backwards compatible (making reference to the previous classification) and forwards compatible (incorporating the latest classification). Not everyone was happy about putting foxgloves with plantains, because visually the plants do not appear to have much in common. But nature is often counterintuitive. If things were obvious in nature, we wouldn't need science to understand it.

Worked example

1   Examine this cladogram of four genera of plants.

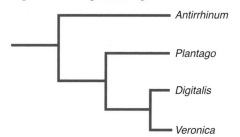

Figure 5.29

   (a) Name two sister taxa.
   (b) Name the outgroup in this cladogram.
   (c) Using a clearly marked label, indicate a node.
   (d) Which genus possesses characteristics that evolved more recently, *Digitalis* or *Plantago*?

Figure 5.30

2   Study the phylogenic tree below showing some primates and their chromosome numbers. Note that when there is great variety between one species and another within a taxon, a range of chromosome numbers is given.

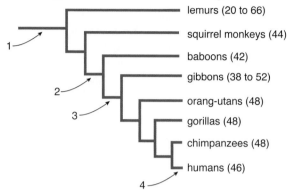

(a) Identify the numbered arrow that indicates a common ancestor for all the primates shown.

(b) Monkeys have tails whereas apes do not. Arrow number 3 shows the point when primates lost their tails. List the apes shown in the diagram.

(c) Identify the numbered arrow that indicates when bipedalism completely replaced walking on four legs.

(d) The great apes are the four primates shown that demonstrate the most recently developed derived traits. Identify which taxon in the diagram represents the lesser apes.

(e) All the great apes shown except one have the same number of chromosomes. Which species has a different number?

(f) Some evidence supports the idea that, in humans, two of our chromosomes fused together at some point in our evolution. What evidence is there in the cladogram to support this?

Solutions

1   (a) *Digitalis* and *Veronica*.

(b) *Antirrhinum*.

(c) Answers may vary: anywhere a horizontal line comes to a 'T' with a vertical line.

(d) *Digitalis* (it is the product of a more recent speciation).

2   (a) 1.

(b) Gibbons, orang-utans, gorillas, chimpanzees, humans.

(c) 4.

(d) Gibbons.

(e) Humans.

(f) All of our closest relatives in the great apes clade have 48 chromosomes whereas we have 46; this would suggest that, if one pair of chromosomes fused with another, we would have gone from 24 pairs to 23 pairs.

Section summary

• Cladistics is the study of clades, which are groups of organisms that have evolved from a common ancestor.

• By comparing similarities and differences between the DNA base sequences (or between amino acid sequences of a protein) of two species, the time since the two species diverged from a common ancestor can be estimated.

• Cladograms are tree diagrams that show such divergences, called species splits or speciation events, and they are drawn as nodes (where one line splits from another line).

• In addition to DNA sequences, physical characteristics such as analogous and homologous traits can be compared, but sometimes the groups formed by comparing structures do not match the clades formed by DNA sequences. Such instances may lead to considerable debate about into which taxon an organism should be placed.

Exercises

14 Distinguish between analogous and homologous structures.

15 Observe the three amino acid sequences below showing amino acids 100 to 116 in one of the polypeptides that makes up haemoglobin. Next to the human's sequence are two other species, A and B.

Amino acid	Human	Species A	Species B
100	PRO	PRO	PRO
101	GLU	GLU	GLU
102	ASN	ASN	ASN
103	PHE	PHE	PHE
104	ARG	LYS	ARG
105	LEU	LEU	LEU
106	LEU	LEU	LEU
107	GLY	GLY	GLY
108	ASN	ASN	ASN
109	VAL	VAL	VAL
110	LEU	LEU	LEU
111	VAL	VAL	ALA
112	CYS	CYS	LEU
113	VAL	VAL	VAL
114	LEU	LEU	VAL
115	ALA	ALA	ALA
116	HIS	HIS	ARG

(a) How many differences are there between the human sequence and the sequence of species A?

(b) How many differences are there between the human sequence and the sequence of species B?

(c) One of the sequences belongs to a horse and the other to a chimpanzee: which is species B more likely to be? Justify your answer.

Practice questions

1 Which of the following are used as evidence for evolution?

    I. Homologous structures.

    II. Selective breeding of domesticated animals.

    III. Overproduction of offspring.

  A I and II only.

  B I and III only.

  C II and III only.

  D I, II, and III.   *(Total 1 mark)*

2 Outline the process of adaptive radiation.   *(Total 3 marks)*

3 What is the mechanism of natural selection?

  A Any individuals in a population can be selected entirely by chance.

  B After a change in the environment a species will evolve adaptations to the new conditions.

  C If an adaptation to the environment is useful, an individual will develop it and pass it on to its offspring.

  D Variations amongst individuals of a population are selected by a changing environment.

    (Total 1 mark)

4 Antibiotic resistance in bacteria is an example of evolution in response to environmental change. Using another example, explain how an environmental change can lead to evolution.

    (Total 8 marks)

5 What are *Allium sativa* and *Allium cepa*?

  A Two different species of the same genus.

  B The same species of the same genus.

  C The same species but of a different genus.

  D Two different species of a different genus.   *(Total 1 mark)*

6 Which phylum does the plant below belong to?

  A Angiospermophyta.

  B Bryophyta.

  C Coniferophyta.

  D Filicinophyta.   *(Total 1 mark)*

7 The cladogram below shows the classification of species A to D. Deduce how similar species A is to species B, C, and D.

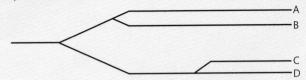

(Total 2 marks)

8 Using examples, distinguish between analogous characteristics and homologous characteristics.

(Total 4 marks)

9 Suggest two reasons for using cladograms for the classification of organisms.   *(Total 2 marks)*

10 Analyse the relationship between the organisms in the following cladogram.

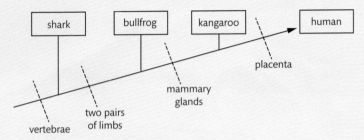

(Total 3 marks)

06 Human physiology

Essential ideas

6.1 The structure of the wall of the small intestine allows it to move, digest, and absorb food.

6.2 The blood system continuously transports substances to cells and simultaneously collects waste products.

6.3 The human body has structures and processes that resist the continuous threat of invasion by pathogens.

6.4 The lungs are actively ventilated to ensure that gas exchange can occur passively.

6.5 Neurones transmit the message, synapses modulate the message.

6.6 Hormones are used when signals need to be widely distributed.

The human body is composed of cells organized into tissues, tissues organized into organs, and organs organized into organ systems. The anatomy and physiology of the human body is so complex that researchers will be investigating it for many decades to come. In this chapter, you will learn about the physiology of some of the major organ systems of the body, and how those organ systems interact with each other. The science of anatomy is based on identifying structures and parts of structures. The focus of our study will be physiology, which is how the various organs and tissues within your body function. It is a fascinating story.

Artwork showing fertilization. Three sperm are shown, but only one will fertilize the ovum.

6.1 Digestion and absorption

NATURE OF SCIENCE

Use models as representations of the real world: dialysis tubing can be used to model absorption in the intestine.

Understandings:
- The contraction of circular and longitudinal muscle of the small intestine mixes the food with enzymes and moves it along the gut.
- The pancreas secretes enzymes into the lumen of the small intestine.
- Enzymes digest most macromolecules in food into monomers in the small intestine.
- Villi increase the surface area of epithelium over which absorption is carried out.
- Villi absorb monomers formed by digestion as well as mineral ions and vitamins.
- Different methods of membrane transport are required to absorb different nutrients.

Applications and skills:
- Application: Processes occurring in the small intestine that result in the digestion of starch and transport of the products of digestion to the liver.
- Application: Use of dialysis tubing to model absorption of digested food in the intestine.
- Skill: Production of an annotated diagram of the digestive system.
- Skill: Identification of tissue layers in transverse sections of the small intestine viewed with a microscope or in a micrograph.

Guidance
- *Students should know that amylase, lipase, and an endopeptidase are secreted by the pancreas. The name trypsin and the method used to activate it are not required.*
- *Students should know that starch, glycogen, lipids, and nucleic acids are digested into monomers, and that cellulose remains undigested.*
- *Tissue layers should include longitudinal and circular muscles, mucosa and epithelium.*

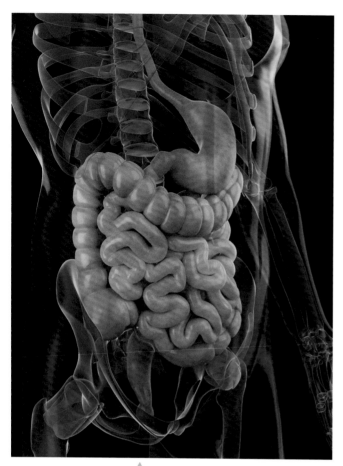

An artist's drawing of the ventral view of a healthy digestive system.

Digestion is an enzyme-facilitated chemical process

When you eat a snack or meal, a series of events is begun that leads to your body cells being provided with the nutrients that they need. Put very simply, the order of events is:

- ingestion – you eat the food
- digestion – a series of chemical reactions occurs, whereby the ingested food is converted into smaller and smaller molecular forms
- absorption – small molecular forms are absorbed through the cells of your digestive system and pass into nearby blood or lymphatic vessels
- transport – your circulatory system delivers the small molecular nutrients to your body cells.

Many of the foods we ingest have very large molecules that are too large to pass across any cell membrane. Yet to get into our bloodstream, molecules must pass through the cell membranes of our intestines and then through the cell membrane of a capillary vessel. Therefore any food that we eat must be chemically digested to a suitable size. Table 6.1 shows different types of molecules found in food and their molecular form before and after digestion.

Table 6.1 Food molecules

Molecule type	Molecular form ingested	Molecular form after digestion
Proteins	Proteins	Amino acids
Lipids	Triglycerides	Glycerol and fatty acids
Carbohydrates	Polysaccharides, disaccharides, monosaccharides	Monosaccharides
Nucleic acids	DNA, RNA	Nucleotides

When we digest food molecules, we hydrolyse them into their smallest components (as shown in the right-hand column of Table 6.1). The components can then be reassembled into larger molecules (macromolecules) that are useful to our bodies.

Role of enzymes during digestion

As food moves through your alimentary canal, many digestive enzymes are added to it along the way. Each digestive enzyme is specific for a specific food type. For example, lipase is an enzyme specific for lipid molecules, and amylase is specific for amylose (otherwise known as starch). As you may remember, enzymes are protein molecules that act as catalysts for reactions. As catalysts, the function of enzymes is to lower the activation energy of the reactions that they catalyse. This means that reactions taking place with an enzyme can occur with a lower input of energy than the same reaction

Humans are incapable of digesting cellulose, one of the most common organic substances on Earth. In fact very few living organisms are capable of digesting cellulose, because they can't produce the enzyme cellulase.

taking place without the presence of an enzyme. The input of energy is typically in the form of heat. Enzyme-catalysed reactions proceed at higher reaction rates at a lower temperature than the same reaction without an enzyme. The reactions of digestion are all very similar because they are all hydrolysis reactions.

Humans maintain a stable body temperature of 37°C. This temperature is warm enough to maintain a good molecular movement and, with the aid of enzymes, it provides enough activation energy for metabolic reactions to occur, including digestion.

The anatomy of the human digestive system

The human digestive system is fundamentally a long tube called the alimentary canal with two accessory organs (the pancreas and liver) that are connected by ducts into the canal. The alimentary canal begins with the mouth and ends with the anus. Any solids or liquids that you ingest are either, after digestion, absorbed into the bloodstream or, if not absorbed, eliminated as faeces.

The human digestive system shown in Figure 6.1 has been simplified so that you can use it as a basis for practising drawing and labelling the digestive system. The lungs are shown to give some perspective to the location of the thoracic cavity, which contains the heart and lungs, compared with the abdominal cavity, which contains all of the digestive structures shown apart from the mouth and oesophagus.

Make sure you practise the drawings that you will be expected to be able to produce in an exam. Adding labels to an existing diagram is relatively easy compared with starting from a blank piece of paper and producing an entire diagram with labels and/or annotated functions.

The alimentary canal is a muscular tube

Food does not make its one-way journey through the alimentary canal by gravity. Indeed, food material often has to move against gravity. So, what keeps food moving, and moving in the one direction? The answer is muscles, specifically smooth muscles. Smooth muscle is controlled by the autonomic nervous system (ANS), and you are not aware that your smooth muscle is contracting. The tube of the alimentary canal has two layers of smooth muscle, called circular and longitudinal. A simplified drawing of these two layers is shown in Figure 6.2. The contracting fibres of the inner, circular, muscles do indeed make a 'circle', as shown in this section, while the contracting fibres of the longitudinal muscles are positioned at right angles to the circular muscles. The muscle motion and food movement caused by the action of these two muscle layers is called peristalsis.

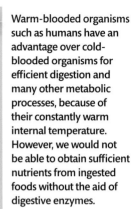

Warm-blooded organisms such as humans have an advantage over cold-blooded organisms for efficient digestion and many other metabolic processes, because of their constantly warm internal temperature. However, we would not be able to obtain sufficient nutrients from ingested foods without the aid of digestive enzymes.

Some digested molecules are absorbed into a system of your body called the lymphatic system. This is particularly true of fatty acids because of their non-polarity and relatively large molecular size.

Figure 6.1 The human digestive system.

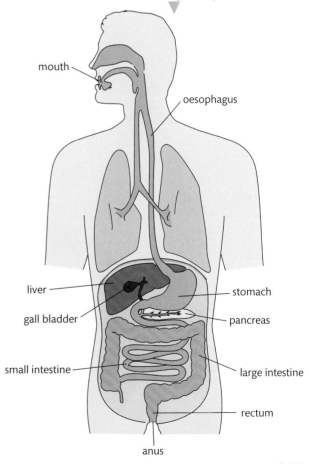

mouth

oesophagus

liver

gall bladder

small intestine

stomach

pancreas

large intestine

rectum

anus

287

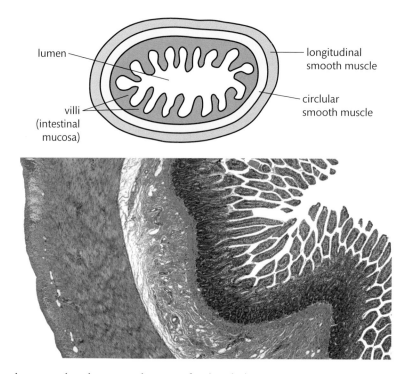

Figure 6.2 This simplified drawing shows a section of the small intestine showing the relative locations of the circular and longitudinal muscles. The same arrangement would also be found in the oesophagus, stomach, and large intestine. The only part of this sketch that is specific to the small intestine is the villi, used for absorption.

lumen — longitudinal smooth muscle

villi (intestinal mucosa) — circular smooth muscle

A light microscope photograph showing a small area of the small intestine. The white area in the upper right corner is the lumen (cavity) of the intestine, where unabsorbed food would be located. To the lower left of that are the villi, which are used for absorption. Further left are the circular and longitudinal muscle layers used for peristalsis.

A person who is hanging upside down can still swallow food and the food will travel 'up' to the stomach. This is because the food is moved by peristalsis, not by gravity.

Peristalsis is used in the stomach to mix food with digestive secretions, including a protein-digesting enzyme. This movement is called churning. In the rest of the alimentary canal, peristalsis causes a contraction just 'behind' the food mass and thus keeps it moving through the canal, as well as helping to mix the food with a variety of enzymes. The peristaltic movement is relatively fast within the oesophagus and slows dramatically in the intestines.

The role of the pancreas during digestion

The pancreas is a multipurpose organ. In addition to producing two important hormones (insulin and glucagon) involved in glucose metabolism, the pancreas produces three enzymes involved in digestion: lipase, amylase, and a protein-digesting enzyme known as an endopeptidase. Those three enzymes are part of a fluid known simply as pancreatic juice that is released into the first portion of the small intestine

Figure 6.3 Artwork showing the pancreas and pancreatic ducts leading to the lumen of the first section of the small intestine. The green tube shown is bringing bile from the liver (not shown) to be added to aid lipid digestion. The area at the top that is cut is where the stomach is located, and the lower area that is cut is where the very long small intestine continues.

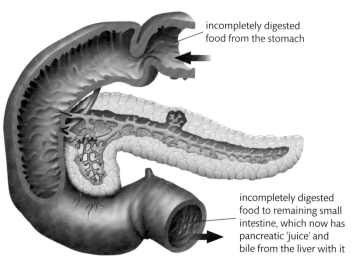

incompletely digested food from the stomach

incompletely digested food to remaining small intestine, which now has pancreatic 'juice' and bile from the liver with it

through a duct. Look closely at Figure 6.3 and you will see the pancreatic duct. The duct allows the three enzymes to enter the lumen (cavity) of the small intestine, where partially digested food from the stomach is being released.

Table 6.2 Digestive enzymes produced by the pancreas and secreted into the lumen of the small intestine

Enzyme	Substrate	Action
Lipase	Lipids (fats and oils)	Hydrolyses lipids into glycerol and fatty acids
Amylase	Starch	Hydrolyses starch into the disaccharide maltose. Another enzyme then hydrolyses maltose into glucose
Trypsin (an endopeptidase)	Proteins (polypeptides)	An endopeptidase that hydrolyses long polypeptides into smaller polypeptides. Further protein-digesting enzymes then hydrolyse the smaller polypeptides into amino acids

The role of the small intestine in digestion and absorption

As an example of what happens as ingested foods move through the small intestine, let's see how starch is digested and how its monomers are absorbed.

The chemical digestion of starch begins in the mouth, with the addition of saliva to the food. Saliva contains amylase, the enzyme that hydrolyses the starch polysaccharide into the disaccharide maltose. The hydrolytic activity of amylase ceases in the highly acidic environment of the stomach. Therefore, the starch remains largely undigested when the contents of the stomach are released into the small intestine.

As described earlier, the pancreas produces and secretes pancreatic juice, and sends that juice into the first section of the small intestine, which is called the duodenum. One of the components of pancreatic juice is amylase. The pH environment of the small intestine is neutral to slightly alkaline, which is the optimum pH for amylase. Thus the amylase molecules begin to catalyse the hydrolysis of starch to maltose. As peristalsis continues to move the food through the lumen of the small intestine, the hydrolytic reactions continue.

Within the small intestine there is another enzyme that completes the digestion of starch. The enzyme maltase catalyses the hydrolysis of maltose into two molecules of glucose. Maltase is produced by the cells of the inner lining of the small intestine, and typically remains bound into the plasma membranes of the epithelial cells that are in contact with the food material within the lumen.

Absorption of glucose into villi

The cells in the inner lining of the small intestine make up what is called the mucosa. The mucosa has many small folds or projections called villi (singular villus). Each villus is composed of many cells whose primary job is selectively absorbing molecules found in the lumen of the small intestine. The actual absorption occurs through cells in an epithelial layer that is in direct contact with the nutrients. The epithelial cells have tiny

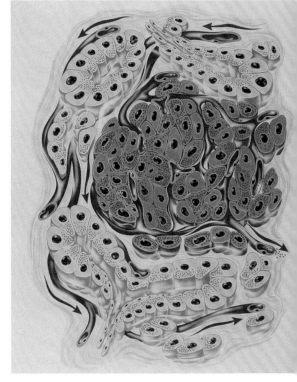

This illustration shows the cells that are involved in two major aspects of pancreatic function. The brightly coloured cells are endocrine (hormone-producing cells), which produce hormones that are then transported away by the bloodstream. The yellow-coloured cells are cells that produce digestive enzymes that are released into very small ducts (look closely at the lower left of the picture) that eventually join into the pancreatic duct that leads to the small intestine.

The hydrolytic enzyme lactase is being extracted commercially from certain yeasts, and is being used to hydrolyse the disaccharide lactose from milk and milk products. This is especially helpful for people who are lactose intolerant.

membrane projections called microvilli that extend into the lumen of the intestine. The villi and microvilli greatly increase the surface area for absorption within the small intestine, compared with a smooth-walled structure. The interior of each villus contains a capillary bed for nutrient absorption and transport of digested monomers by the bloodstream. In addition, there is a small vessel of the lymphatic system present, called a lacteal, that absorbs some of the nutrients. After passing through the epithelial cells of a villus, most monomers are absorbed into the inner capillary bed. However, some of the larger monomers, such as fatty acids, are absorbed first into a lacteal.

Here is a partial list of the substances absorbed through villi into the bloodstream or lymph fluid:

- water
- glucose (plus other monosaccharides)
- amino acids
- nucleotides
- glycerol
- fatty acids
- mineral ions
- vitamins.

A light microscope photograph showing a transverse section through several villi. Microvilli are too small to be seen at this magnification. The capillary bed inside each villus is clearly visible. The longitudinal and circular muscles of the wall of the intestine are also visible at the bottom of the photograph.

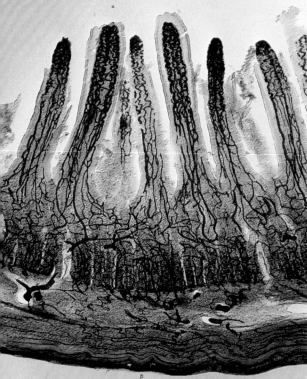

TOK Each country has its own laws concerning how food is labelled for consumers. Some countries require detailed lists of important information, such as fat content, fat type, calories per serving, etc., while other countries have no requirements at all. Do all the citizens of a country have a right to know the contents of the food that they are buying?

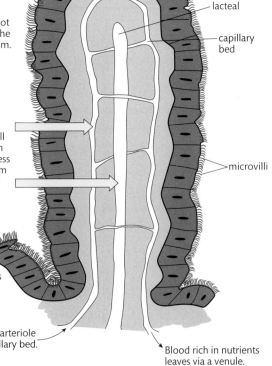

Undigested nutrients cannot pass through the villus epithelium.

lacteal

capillary bed

Digested nutrients in the lumen of the small intestine pass through the single-cell thickness of the villus epithelium to get to the capillary bed or lacteal.

microvilli

Figure 6.4 The structure of an intestinal villus. It is estimated that each square millimetre of small intestine contains approximately 10–40 villi. Thus the entire small intestine of a human contains millions of villi and even more microvilli.

The entire structure creates a tremendous surface area for absorption.

Blood from an arteriole enters the capillary bed.

Blood rich in nutrients leaves via a venule.

Transport mechanisms used by epithelial cells to absorb nutrients

A variety of mechanisms are used for nutrient molecules to cross the epithelial layer of the villi mucosa. Here is a summary of some of those transport mechanisms.

Passive mechanisms: no ATP used

- Simple diffusion: direct movement through the cell membrane following a concentration gradient. Examples: very small molecules and non-polar molecules, such as fatty acids, which dissolve through the biphospholipid layer of the membrane.
- Facilitated diffusion: movement through a cell membrane following a concentration gradient, but the molecule must travel through a protein channel because of its size and polarity. Examples: glucose and amino acids.

Active mechanisms: ATP expended

- Membrane pumps: molecules moved against their concentration gradient by certain proteins using ATP to 'pump' the molecule across the membrane. Examples: glucose, and amino acids under certain circumstances.
- Endocytosis (pinocytosis and phagocytosis): molecules are trapped in an invagination (infolding) of the membrane and pass through to the other side of the membrane as a vesicle. Example: some macromolecules that have not yet been fully digested.

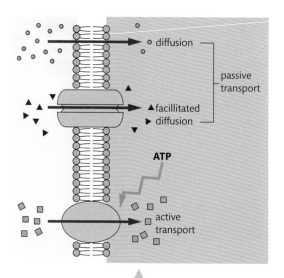

Figure 6.5 Schematic view of three of the more important mechanisms used by cells of the villi epithelium to absorb nutrients from the lumen of the intestine. The mechanism used depends on the size and polarity of the molecule being transported. Not shown is endocytosis, where a portion of the plasma membrane invaginates to take in many molecules at one time.

Section summary

- Food is moved along through the intestines by peristalsis. This movement is a result of the sequential contractions of circular and longitudinal muscles along the length of the intestines.
- The pancreas secretes three digestive enzymes (amylase, lipase, and an endopeptidase) into the lumen of the small intestine.
- Digestive enzymes are organic catalysts that hydrolyse (chemically digest) macromolecules into monomers in the intestines.
- Villi and microvilli greatly increase the internal surface area of the intestines for more efficient absorption of food monomers.
- Different nutrient monomers require different transport mechanisms for efficient absorption.

Exercises

1 A single sandwich is likely to contain carbohydrates, lipids, and proteins. From a biochemical viewpoint, what happens to each of these types of molecules upon digestion?

2 You ingest a glucose molecule within the starch of a breakfast cereal. List as many locations as you can that this single glucose molecule will visit from the time that it is in your mouth to the time it enters a muscle cell of your body.

3 What role does the pancreas play in the digestive process?

NATURE OF SCIENCE

Theories are regarded as uncertain: William Harvey overturned theories developed by the ancient Greek philosopher Galen on movement of blood in the body.

6.2 The blood system

Understandings:

- Arteries convey blood at high pressure from the ventricles to the tissues of the body.
- Arteries have muscle cells and elastic fibres in their walls.
- The muscle and elastic fibres assist in maintaining blood pressure between pump cycles.
- Blood flows through tissues in capillaries. Capillaries have permeable walls that allow exchange of materials between cells in the tissue and the blood in the capillary.
- Veins collect blood at low pressure from the tissues of the body and return it to the atria of the heart.
- Valves in veins and the heart ensure circulation of blood by preventing backflow.
- There is a separate circulation for the lungs.
- The heart beat is initiated by a group of specialized muscle cells in the right atrium called the sinoatrial node.
- The sinoatrial node acts as a pacemaker.
- The sinoatrial node sends out an electrical signal that stimulates contraction as it is propagated through the walls of the atria and then the walls of the ventricles.
- The heart rate can be increased or decreased by impulses brought to the heart through two nerves from the medulla of the brain.
- Epinephrine increases the heart rate to prepare for vigorous physical activity.

Applications and skills:

- Application: William Harvey's discovery of the circulation of the blood with the heart acting as the pump.
- Application: Pressure changes in the left atrium, left ventricle, and aorta during the cardiac cycle.
- Application: Causes and consequences of occlusion of the coronary arteries.
- Skill: Identification of blood vessels as arteries, capillaries, or veins from the structure of their walls.
- Skill: Recognition of the chambers and valves of the heart and the blood vessels connected to it in dissected hearts or in diagrams of heart structure.

Arteries, capillaries, and veins

Arteries are blood vessels taking blood away from the heart that has not yet reached a capillary. Veins are blood vessels that collect blood from capillaries and return it to the heart. Identifying a blood vessel as being an artery or a vein has nothing to do with whether the blood is oxygenated or deoxygenated. For example, blood leaving the right ventricle is flowing through pulmonary arteries, even though it needs to be re-oxygenated in the capillaries of the lung tissue. These blood vessels are pulmonary arteries because they are between the heart and the capillary bed. The newly oxygenated blood will be brought back to the heart by the pulmonary veins.

Arteries have a relatively thick, smooth, muscle layer that is used by the autonomic nervous system to change the inside diameter (lumen) of the blood vessels. In addition to smooth muscle, arteries have elastic fibres that help maintain the relatively high blood pressure achieved by the contractions of the ventricles. When blood is pumped into an artery, the elastic fibres are stretched and allow the blood vessel to accommodate the increased pressure. When the contraction is over, the elastic fibres provide another source of pressure as they return to their original position. This helps maintain the blood pressure between pump cycles. Remember that blood in arteries is at a high pressure because arteries are the vessels that are directly connected to the ventricles of the heart. When blood leaves an arteriole (the smallest of the arteries), it enters a capillary bed rather than a single capillary. A capillary bed is a network of capillaries that typically all drain into a single venule.

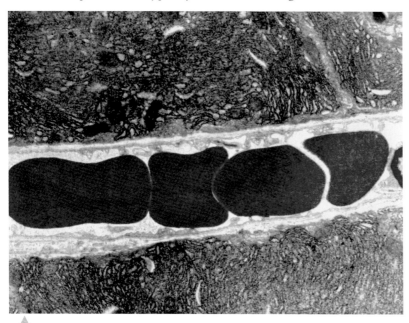

A false-colour transmission electron micrograph (TEM) of a capillary containing erythrocytes (red blood cells). Notice the thin 'wall' of the capillary, which is conducive to the movement of molecules in and out of the bloodstream.

When blood enters a capillary bed much of the blood pressure is lost. Blood cells make their way through capillaries one cell at a time. Chemical exchanges always occur through the single-cell thickness of capillaries, because the walls of arteries and veins are too thick to allow molecules in or out efficiently. Veins receive blood at a relatively low pressure from the capillary beds. Because this blood has lost a great deal of blood pressure, the blood flow through veins is slower than through arteries. To account for this, veins have thin walls and a larger internal diameter. Veins also have many internal passive 'one-way flow' valves that help keep the slow-moving blood travelling consistently towards the heart. Table 6.3 summarizes the three types of blood vessels.

Table 6.3 A comparison of arteries, capillaries, and veins

Artery	Capillary	Vein
Thick walled	Wall is 1 cell thick	Thin walled
No exchanges	All exchanges occur	No exchanges
No internal valves	No internal valves	Internal valves present
Internal pressure high	Internal pressure low	Internal pressure low

The heart, a double pump

The human heart is designed as a pair of side-by-side pumps. Each side of the heart has a collection chamber for the blood that moves in slowly from

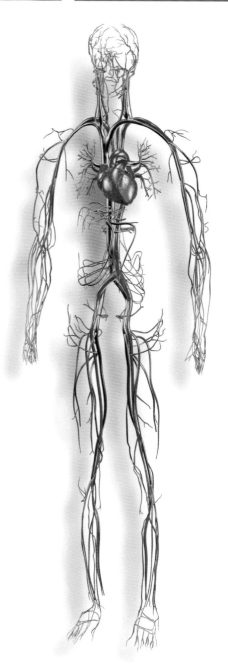

If all the tissue except blood vessels and heart were removed from a body, the shape of the body would still be visible.

 Fish have a two-chambered heart and amphibians have a three-chambered heart. Reptiles, birds, and mammals all have a four-chambered heart (although the ventricles of a reptile heart are only partially divided).

the veins. These thin-walled, muscular chambers are called atria. Each side also has a thick-walled muscular pump called a ventricle, which builds up enough pressure to send the blood out from the heart with a force we refer to as blood pressure. This double-sided pump works every minute of every day of your life. The blood that is pumped out from the heart typically makes a circuit through the following sequence of blood vessels:

- a large artery
- smaller artery branches
- an arteriole (the smallest type of artery)
- a capillary bed
- a venule (the smallest type of vein)
- larger veins
- a large vein, which takes the blood back to the heart to be pumped out once again.

The two sides of the heart form two major routes for blood to flow along (see Figure 6.6). The right side of the heart sends blood along a route that is called your pulmonary circulation. Along this route, the capillary beds are found in your lungs, where the blood picks up oxygen and releases carbon dioxide.

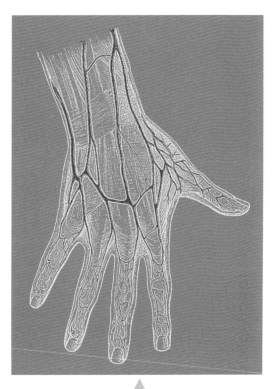

A drawing showing some of the larger blood vessels in the hand. Smaller vessels like capillaries cannot be seen without magnification.

The left side of the heart sends blood along a route that is called the systemic circulation. The artery that emerges from the heart at the beginning of this route is the aorta. Branches of the aorta carry blood to almost every organ and cell type in your body. Along this route, the capillary beds are found in your organs and tissues, where the blood picks up carbon dioxide and releases oxygen.

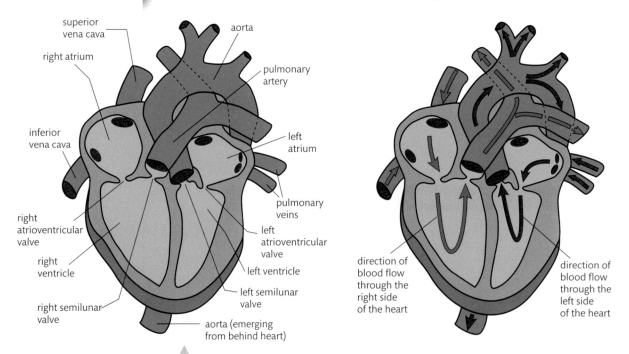

Figure 6.6 Human heart anatomy and blood flow. In the right diagram the blue arrows represent deoxygenated blood and the red arrows represent oxygenated blood.

Control of the heart rate

The majority of the tissue that makes up the heart is muscle. More specifically, it is cardiac muscle. Cardiac muscle spontaneously contracts and relaxes without any control by the nervous system. This is known as myogenic muscle contraction. However, the myogenic activity of the heart does need to be controlled, in order to make the timing of the contractions unified and useful.

Within the right atrium there is a mass of specialized tissue that has properties of both muscle and nervous system cells within its walls; this tissue is called the sinoatrial node (SA node). The SA node acts as the pacemaker for the heart by sending out an 'electrical' signal to initiate the contraction of both atria. For a person with a resting heart rate of 72 beats a minute, the signal from the SA node is sent out every 0.8 seconds. Also within the right atrium is another mass of specialized muscle tissue, known as the atrioventricular node (AV node). The AV node receives the signal from the SA node, delays for approximately 0.1 seconds, and then sends out another 'electrical' signal. This second signal goes to the thick muscular ventricles and results in their contraction. This explains why both atria, and then later both ventricles, contract in synchrony (see Figure 6.7).

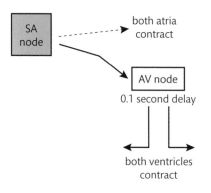

Figure 6.7 Myogenic control of the heart rate. The SA node acts as the pacemaker. The AV node relies on a signal from the SA node to send impulses to the ventricles. Notice the delay between the two events that allows the atria to contract, followed shortly after by the contraction of the ventricles.

During times of increased body activity, such as exercise, the heart rate needs to increase above the resting heart rate. This is because there is an increased demand for oxygen for cell respiration during periods of heavy exercise or activity. There is also a need to get rid of the increased levels of carbon dioxide that accumulate in the bloodstream. As exercise begins and carbon dioxide levels begin to rise, an area of your brainstem called the medulla chemically 'senses' the increase in carbon dioxide.

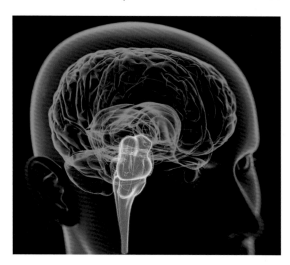

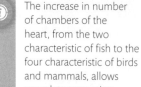

The increase in number of chambers of the heart, from the two characteristic of fish to the four characteristic of birds and mammals, allows complete separation of deoxygenated and oxygenated blood. In other words, the evolution of the four-chambered heart led to the separation of the pulmonary and systemic circulations.

As you continue your study of human physiology, look for instances where two or more systems of the body interact in order to accomplish an action. For example, during exercise, your heart rate cannot increase or return to its resting heart rate without the nervous system and the circulatory system interacting.

Much of the orange area of this computer artwork shows an area of the brainstem called the medulla (oblongata). Chemoreceptors in the medulla are sensitive to carbon dioxide changes in the blood as it passes through.

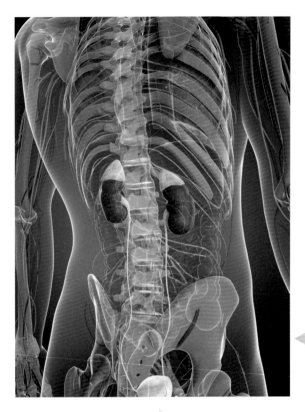

Computer artwork showing the two kidneys in a male. The lighter coloured tissue on the upper portion of each kidney is an adrenal gland. Like all endocrine glands, adrenal glands secrete their hormone (epinephrine) into the bloodstream for distribution to all parts of the body.

The medulla then sends a signal through a cranial nerve, called the cardiac nerve, to increase the heart rate to an appropriate level. This signal is sent to the SA node; it does not change the mechanism of how the heart beats, just the timing. After exercise, the level of carbon dioxide in the bloodstream begins to decrease and another signal is sent from the medulla. This time the signal is carried by a different cranial nerve, called the vagus nerve. Electrical signals from the vagus nerve result in the SA node once again adjusting the timing of the heart rate, so that the heart returns to its myogenic or resting heart rate.

The heart rate can also be influenced by chemicals. One of the most common is epinephrine (also called adrenaline). During periods of high stress or excitement, your adrenal glands secrete epinephrine into the bloodstream. Among other effects, epinephrine causes the SA node to 'fire' more frequently than it does at its resting heart rate, and thus the heart rate increases, sometimes dramatically so.

A (single) cardiac cycle is what most people think of as a 'heart beat'. A cardiac cycle is initiated by the SA node impulse and includes all the heart events that follow until another SA node signal begins a new cardiac cycle.

Changes in pressure within the heart chambers keep the blood moving

Heart valves open and close depending on the pressure of the blood on each side of the valve. The change in pressure also explains the movement of blood through and out of each chamber of the heart. Both the left and right sides of the heart work synchronously as a double pump. To understand the workings of the heart, it is only necessary to look at one side of the heart with the understanding that the other side has similar pressures and volumes of blood at the same time.

Let's examine the pressure and volume changes that occur on the left side of the heart. You do not have to memorize the pressure numbers given in the example, your focus should be on understanding how the given blood pressures result in the movement of blood and the opening and closing of the heart valves.

When both chambers are at rest

The term used for a chamber of the heart that is not contracting is diastole. The term used for a chamber of the heart that is contracting is systole. Thus the time period when both chambers are at rest can be described as both chambers undergoing diastole.

Figure 6.8 shows the left side of the heart with openings in the left atrium for entry of the pulmonary veins. The numbers inside each chamber or blood vessel represent the pressure measured in mm Hg. Heart valves open and close based on blood pressure differences on either side of any one valve. During this period of diastole for both chambers, the atrial pressure is just slightly higher than ventricular pressure, and this keeps the left atrioventricular valve open. Much of the blood that slowly returns to the left atrium via the pulmonary veins moves passively down to the left ventricle through this open valve. Notice also that the pressure in the aorta is much higher than in the left ventricle. This pressure difference keeps the left semilunar valve closed and prevents backflow into the ventricle.

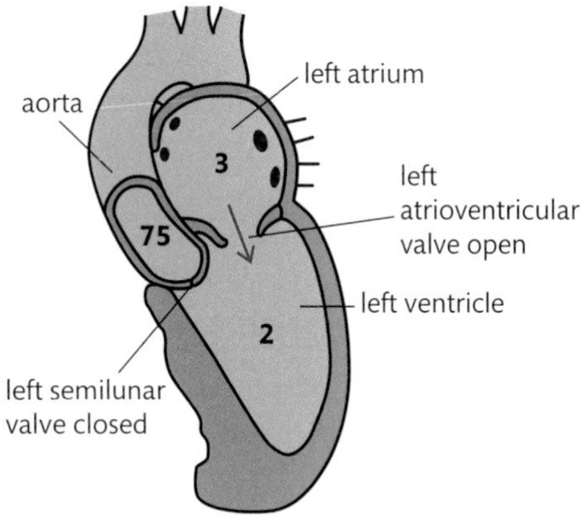

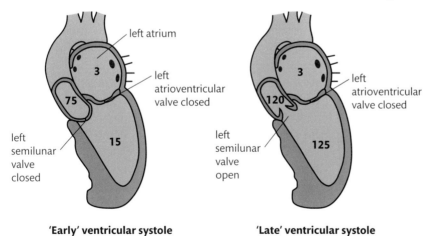

Figure 6.8 Blood pressure readings in mm Hg when both chambers are in diastole (rest). Notice that some blood is moving passively from the left atrium to the left ventricle.

The muscular walls of both atria are very thin, and the pressure exerted during atrial systole is very low. Conversely, the muscular walls of the ventricles are very thick, and the pressure exerted during ventricular systole is very high .

When the atria are in systole and the ventricles are in diastole

In Figure 6.9, the atrium is undergoing a systole (contraction). The pressure produced by this systole is not very high. The wall of each atrium is relatively thin muscle and is not capable of creating very much pressure. There is no need for great pressure because much of the volume of blood has already accumulated passively within the ventricle through the open atrioventricular valve. Any remaining blood in the atrium is moved to the ventricle by the systole.

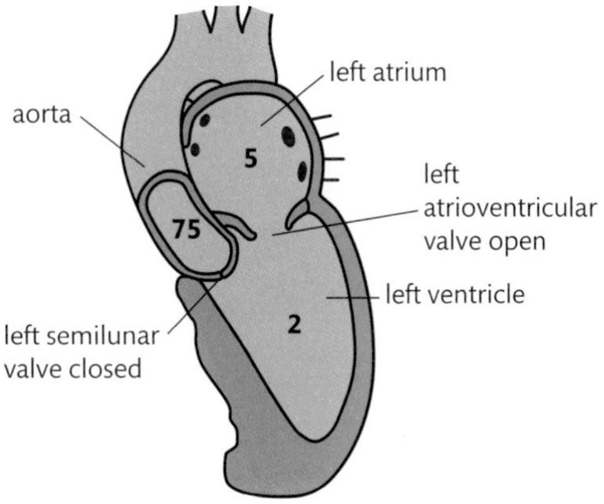

Figure 6.9 Typical blood pressure readings in mm Hg during atrial systole.

When the atria are in diastole and the ventricles are in systole

'Early' ventricular systole

'Late' ventricular systole

Figure 6.10 Blood pressure readings in mm Hg at early and late ventricular systole.

Figure 6.10 shows the blood pressures in early and late ventricular systole. As soon as ventricular systole begins, the pressure inside the ventricle increases to be greater than that in the atrium, so the atrioventricular valve closes to prevent backflow to the atrium (this creates the 'lub' sound that can be heard with a stethoscope). The pressure in the aorta is still far higher than in the ventricle, so the semilunar valve

Blood pressure is often measured in mm Hg, although the modern units for pressure are pascals (Pa) and kilopascals (kPa).

120 mm Hg = 16 kPa

80 mm Hg = 11 kPa

The mean population blood pressure varies widely from country to country. As a general rule, high blood pressure is positively correlated with the consumption of salt and obesity, and is negatively correlated with the consumption of fruits and vegetables.

An artery showing artherosclerosis. The dark area in the centre is the lumen, where blood flows. The light grey area surrounding the lumen is plaque. The lumen of this blood vessel is significantly smaller than it was at an earlier time in this person's life.

Illustration showing an occlusion (a clot caused by plaque build-up) in a coronary artery.

remains closed. There is a relatively large volume of blood in the ventricle during this time, and the ventricle is highly muscular. This combination of factors permits the ventricular pressure to build up considerably as systole continues. Finally, the pressure in the ventricle becomes greater than that in the aorta, and the semilunar valve opens, allowing the ventricle to pump the blood into the aorta. As the ventricle finishes its contraction, the pressure inside it once again drops below the pressure in the aorta, and the semilunar valve closes (this causes the 'dub' sound that can be heard with a stethoscope). Both chambers go back into diastole and the cardiac cycle repeats itself again, and again.

Build-up of plaque in arteries leads to atherosclerosis

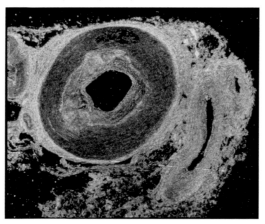

Atherosclerosis is a slow build-up of materials in the arteries that is collectively called plaque. Plaque is composed of lipids, cholesterol, cell debris, and calcium. The build-up of this material begins early in life and typically takes many, many years to become a serious problem. As arteries begin to build up plaque, they become harder and therefore less flexible. The inside lining of an artery is known as the endothelium. In a young person, the endothelium of each artery is smooth, with no plaque build-up. As the years progress, each person begins to deposit plaque. How much depends on a whole set of factors, with genetics and eating habits being of prime importance.

Occlusion in coronary arteries can lead to a heart attack

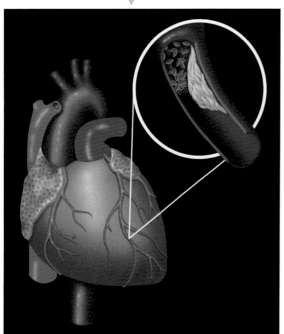

The heart has three major coronary arteries that supply the heart muscle with oxygen-rich blood. These arteries are branches direct from the aorta and carry blood that has recently been to the lungs. As you will recall, cardiac muscle never stops contracting, with alternating periods of systole and diastole occurring repeatedly throughout your life. Thus cardiac muscle is very oxygen-demanding. If any one of the three major coronary arteries, or one or more of their branches, is somehow blocked, some portion of the heart muscle is likely to be deprived of its oxygen supply. This is exactly what happens when atherosclerosis eventually leads to a partial or complete occlusion. The term occlusion describes the condition when plaque build-up has become so substantial that the blood vessel can no longer supply even a minimally healthy volume of blood to the tissue that it 'feeds'.

When a coronary artery or one of its main branches becomes blocked, it is known as a coronary thrombosis or an acute myocardial infarction, i.e. a heart attack.

Have you ever thought about how difficult it would be to convince everyone around you that something they and everyone else had been taught and firmly believed in was actually false? Especially something that has been believed for many centuries?

It would be an exceptionally difficult thing to do, and attempting to do this might mean you are considered to be a lunatic.

A man by the name of William Harvey made such an attempt after his experimental work showed how blood is circulated around the body. Prior to Harvey's experimental work, the authority on the movement of blood in the body was provided by the early Greeks (AD 100–200), including Pliny the Elder and Galen (of Pergamon). These Greeks postulated that blood was constantly being used up within the body, and they did not consider the closed circulation pattern we now know exists. Galen taught his students that there were two types of blood: 'nutritive blood' that was made by the liver, and 'vital blood' that was made by the heart and distributed through the arteries to carry the 'vital spirits'. Further, Galen taught his students that blood flowed from one ventricle of the heart to the other through tiny pores. In order to understand the context of Galen's teachings, you must imagine blood that is not flowing through blood vessels as we think of now, but rather seeping slowly from one location to another until the blood in the body is 'used up'. The latter was the thinking of virtually every person trained in medicine for more than 1300 years.

After years of animal dissections, live animal experimentation, and human cadaver dissections, William Harvey determined that the heart acts as a double pump (with systemic and pulmonary circulations), and that the blood is continuously circulated to/from the lungs and to/from the body. He was not able to see the capillaries that connected arteries to veins, but he postulated their existence. In 1628, Harvey published his work in a publication called *On the Movement of the Heart and Blood in Animals*. As you might imagine, at first many people did not believe Harvey's teachings. The nature of science sometimes dictates that good, new scientific knowledge takes time to become trusted.

Bloodletting was a common medical procedure that was based on Galen's theory of circulation. Bloodletting was a procedure whereby small cuts were made in order to drain blood from certain areas of the body. The thinking was that blood and other bodily 'humours' (fluids) needed to be in balance, and an illness was often attributed to these humours being out of balance. Bloodletting was believed to restore the healthy balance.

A leech, sometimes used for bloodletting procedures. A leech can increase its body size considerably after feeding on a blood meal.

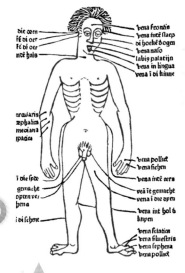

15th-century illustration of common bloodletting sites. The labelling is the original Latin. Bloodletting was sometimes done by making cuts and sometimes by the application of leeches.

Section summary

- Arteries carry blood away from the ventricles of the heart, and thus convey blood at high pressure to the tissues of the body.
- Arteries are able to change their lumen (internal diameter) because they have both smooth muscle and elastic fibres within their walls.
- Smooth muscle and elastic fibres within the walls of arteries help to maintain blood pressure in arteries between heart cycles.
- The only blood vessels that allow molecular exchanges with body tissues are capillaries.
- Veins collect low pressure blood from the capillaries in body tissues and return that blood to the heart atria.
- One-way low pressure blood flow in veins is assisted by internal valves within veins and the heart valves.
- The two sides of the heart provide a double circulation. The pulmonary circulation provides blood to be pumped to and from the lungs, and the systemic circulation provides blood to be pumped to and from the body tissues.
- A group of specialized muscle cells known as the sinoatrial node (SA node) initiates the heart beat in the right atrium, which sends out an electrical signal and thus acts as the pacemaker for the heart.

- This electrical signal from the SA node is propagated into the ventricles by the atrioventricular node (AV node)
- When body activity is increased, and the need for oxygen and carbon dioxide exchange is thus increased, the medulla oblongata can increase and later decrease the heart rate by control of two nerves running from the medulla to the SA node.
- The hormone epinephrine from the adrenal glands can also increase the heart rate.

Exercises

4 Identify all the heart chambers, valves, and blood vessels involved in one complete circuit of blood (only blood vessels immediately entering or exiting the heart need to be named). Name these in the order the blood passes through them, starting with the right atrium.

5 Before birth, a human foetus has a hole between the right atrium and left atrium. Work out how that changes the blood flow within the foetal circulation, and why foetal circulation has evolved such a pattern.

6 What causes heart valves to open and close?

NATURE OF SCIENCE

Risks associated with scientific research: Florey and Chain's tests on the safety of penicillin would not be compliant with current protocol on testing.

6.3 Defence against infectious disease

Understandings:

- The skin and mucous membranes form a primary defence against pathogens that cause infectious disease.
- Cuts in the skin are sealed by blood clotting.
- Clotting factors are released from platelets.
- The cascade results in the rapid conversion of fibrinogen to fibrin by thrombin.
- Ingestion of pathogens by phagocytic white blood cells gives non-specific immunity to diseases.
- Production of antibodies by lymphocytes in response to particular antigens gives specific immunity.
- Antibiotics block processes that occur in prokaryotic cells but not in eukaryotic cells.
- Viruses lack a metabolism and cannot therefore be treated with antibiotics. Some strains of bacteria have evolved with genes that confer resistance to antibiotics and some strains of bacteria have multiple resistance.

Applications and skills:

- Application: Causes and consequences of blood clot formation in coronary arteries.
- Application: Florey and Chain's experiments to test penicillin on bacterial infections in mice.
- Application: Effects of HIV on the immune system and methods of transmission.

Guidance
- Diagrams of skin are not required.
- Subgroups of phagocyte and lymphocyte are not required but students should be aware that some lymphocytes act as memory cells and can quickly reproduce to form a clone of plasma cells if a pathogen carrying a specific antigen is re-encountered.
- The effects of HIV on the immune system should be limited to a reduction in the number of active lymphocytes and a loss of the ability to produce antibodies, leading to the development of AIDS.

The world that we live in is literally infested with viruses and bacteria. Only a very, very small percentage of these are pathogenic to human beings; in fact, the vast majority of bacteria are very useful.

Primary defence is to keep pathogens out

Our bodies are exposed to many disease-causing agents. Any living organism or virus that is capable of causing a disease is called a pathogen. Pathogens include viruses, bacteria, protozoa, fungi, and worms of various types. Yet exposure to the vast majority of pathogens does not result in a disease. Primarily, this is because we are too well defended for most pathogens to enter our bodies and, if any do manage to enter, we have often previously developed immunity to that pathogen. For some pathogens, such as bacteria, there are chemicals called antibiotics that can work against the living bacterial cells but do not affect our body cells. Let's explore more about this interesting and important topic.

Skin and mucous membranes form a primary defence

The best way to stay healthy is to prevent pathogens from having the chance to cause disease. One way to do this is to try to stay away from sources of infection. This is why it is still common to isolate (or quarantine) people who have highly transmittable diseases. Obviously, it is not possible to isolate yourself from every possible source of infection. Therefore, the human body has some ingenious ways of making it difficult for pathogens to enter it and start an infection.

One of those ingenious ways is your skin. Think of your skin as having two primary layers. The underneath layer is called the dermis and is very much alive. It contains sweat glands, capillaries, sensory receptors, and dermal cells, which give structure and strength to the skin. The layer on top of this is called the epidermis. This epidermal layer is constantly being replaced as the underlying dermal cells die and are moved upwards. This layer of mainly dead cells forms a good barrier against most pathogens because it is not truly alive. As long as our skin remains intact, we are protected from most pathogens that can enter living tissues. This is why it is important to clean and cover cuts and abrasions of the skin when they do occur.

Pathogens can enter the body at a few points that are not covered by skin. These entry points are lined with tissue cells that form a mucous membrane. Cells of mucous membranes produce and secrete a lining of sticky mucus. This mucus can trap incoming pathogens and so prevent them from reaching cells that they could infect. Some mucous membrane tissue is lined with cilia. Cilia are hair-like extensions capable of a wave-like movement. This movement moves trapped pathogens up and out of mucous-lined tissues such as your trachea. Table 6.4 shows some common areas that have a mucous membrane.

False-colour scanning electron micrograph (SEM) of the mucous membrane lining of the trachea. The large white cells are called goblet cells and they secrete mucus. Hair-like cilia (in pink) are also visible.

Table 6.4 The locations of mucous membranes

Area with a mucous membrane	What it is and does
Trachea	The tube that carries air to and from the lungs
Nasal passages	Tubes that allow air to enter the nose and then the trachea
Urethra	A tube that carries urine from the bladder to the outside
Vagina	The reproductive tract leading from the uterus to the outside

According to an article published by the National Institute of Health (NIH), bacteria outnumber their human hosts by about 10 to 1 cells. In a typical human adult, bacteria would account for about 2% of his or her body mass.

301

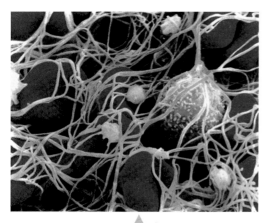

This false-colour SEM shows that small platelets (shown in pale green) have triggered the formation of insoluble fibrin protein fibres. Trapped in the fibrin are several red blood cells, platelets, and one white blood cell (shown in yellow).

Haemophilia is an inherited blood-clotting disorder. Haemophiliacs lack the ability to produce one of the chemicals needed for normal clotting.

Figure 6.11 Flowchart of the blood-clotting sequence. The sequence starts with a damaged blood vessel, and leads to a meshwork of fibrin that traps blood cells to form a clot. The image above shows blood cells trapped in fibres of fibrin.

Blood clotting minimizes the chances of infection and blood loss

When small blood vessels like capillaries, arterioles, and venules are broken, blood escapes from the closed circulatory system. Often the damaged blood vessels are in the skin, and so pathogens then have a way to gain entry into the body. Our bodies have evolved a set of responses to create a clot that 'seals' the damaged blood vessels, so preventing excessive blood loss and helping prevent pathogens from entering the body.

Circulating in the blood plasma are a variety of molecules called plasma proteins. These proteins serve many purposes, including some that are involved in clotting. Two of the clotting proteins are prothrombin and fibrinogen. These two molecules are always present in blood plasma, but remain inactive until 'called to action' by events associated with bleeding. Also circulating in the bloodstream are cell fragments known as platelets. Platelets form in the bone marrow, along with red blood cells (erythrocytes) and white blood cells (leucocytes), but do not remain as entire cells. Instead, one very large cell breaks down into many fragments, and each of the fragments becomes a platelet. Platelets do not have a nucleus and they have a relatively short cellular life span, of about 8–10 days.

Let's consider what happens when a small blood vessel is damaged (see Figure 6.11). The damaged cells of the blood vessel release chemicals that stimulate platelets to adhere to the damaged area. The damaged tissue and platelets release chemicals called clotting factors that convert prothrombin into thrombin. Thrombin is an active enzyme that catalyses the conversion of soluble fibrinogen into the relatively insoluble fibrin. The appropriately named fibrin is a fibrous protein that forms a mesh-like network that helps to stabilize the platelet plug. More and more cellular debris becomes trapped in the fibrin mesh, and soon a stable clot has formed, preventing both further blood loss and the entry of pathogens.

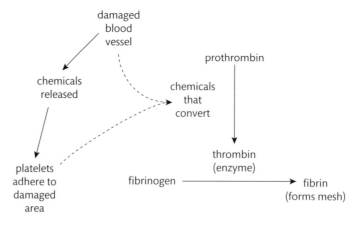

When pathogens get past skin and mucous membranes

When a pathogen, such as a pathogenic bacterial species, does enter the body, a series of events begins known as the immune response. If this is a first encounter with a particular pathogen, the response is known as a primary immune response. If it is a second (or third, etc.) encounter, the response is known as a secondary immune response. A primary immune response takes at least a week or more to be successful, and thus it is common to experience the symptoms associated with a disease while the immune system is working to reduce and finally eliminate the pathogen. A secondary immune response is both quicker and more intense, and thus symptoms are rarely experienced. The ability to accomplish a secondary immune response for a particular antigen is actually what we call being 'immune' to a disease.

Role of phagocytic white blood cells

White blood cells (leucocytes) are the cells in our bloodstream that help us fight off pathogens that enter our bodies, and also provide us with immunity for the many pathogens that we encounter more than once. One type of leucocyte that is involved very early on in the process of fighting off a pathogen is called a macrophage. Macrophages are large leucocytes that are able to change their cellular shape to surround an invading cell through the process of phagocytosis. Because macrophages can easily change their shape, they are able to squeeze their way in and out of small blood vessels. Therefore, it is not unusual for a macrophage to first encounter an invading cell outside the bloodstream.

When a macrophage meets a cell, it can recognize whether that cell is a natural part of the body and therefore 'self', or not part of the body and therefore 'not-self'. This recognition is based on the protein molecules that make up part of the surface of all cells and viruses. If the collection of proteins the macrophage encounters on a cell is determined to be 'self', then the cell is left alone. If the determination is 'not-self', the macrophage engulfs the cell by phagocytosis. Phagocytes typically contain many lysosome organelles, in order to digest chemically whatever has been engulfed. This type of response by the body is called non-specific, because the identity of the specific pathogen has not been determined, just the fact that it is something that is 'not-self' and therefore should be removed.

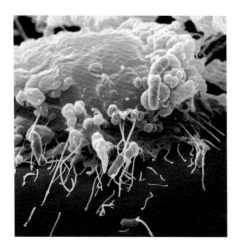

Antibodies produced by lymphocytes lead to specific immunity

Antibodies are protein molecules that are produced by the body in response to a specific type of pathogen. In other words, if you had a measles infection, you would produce one type of antibody, and if you contract a virus that gives you influenza (flu), you would produce another type of antibody. Each type of antibody is different because each type has been produced in response to a different pathogen. Each

Travel between far-reaching areas of our world has increased tremendously in the last century. With that increase in travel has come an associated increase in the rate of spread of global disease.

The role of macrophages in determining self versus not-self cells is called non-specific immunity, even though no real immunity is gained by the action of the macrophages.

False-colour SEM showing a macrophage (the large yellow cell) engulfing *Escherichia coli* bacteria (the small pink rods).

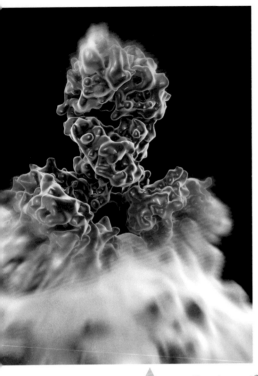

pathogen is made up of either cells with cell membranes or, in the case of a virus, a protein coat called a capsid. The cellular invaders, such as bacteria, have proteins that are embedded in their outer surface. In the language of the immune system, these foreign proteins are called antigens. You have just learned that 'not-self' proteins trigger an immune response. All of these 'not-self' proteins are antigens.

Each antibody is a protein that is Y-shaped. At the end of each of the forks of the Y is a binding site. The binding site is where an antibody attaches itself to an antigen. Because the antigen is a protein on the surface of a pathogen (such as a bacterium), the antibody thus becomes attached to the pathogen (see the artwork on the left).

The leucocytes that produce antibodies are a type of cell called plasma cells. Each of us has many different types of antibody-producing plasma cells and, as a general rule, each type of plasma cell can produce only one type of antibody. The problem is, each cell only produces a relatively small number of antibodies in comparison with the massive infection that may be present in the body. However, our continually evolving immune response has a way of producing many of the same type of plasma cells when they are needed. Here are the steps of a typical primary immune response.

Computer artwork showing an antibody attaching to a cell surface. One way antibodies function is to attach to and thus 'mark' a cell for destruction by certain types of leucocytes.

Artwork showing antibodies binding to a flu virus. Each antibody is uniquely designed to fit an antigen. This is part of your specific immunity, because of the specificity of the molecules involved in the 'match'.

1. A specific antigen type is identified (e.g. a particular cold virus).
2. A specific plasma cell is identified that can produce an antibody that will bind to the antigen (e.g. the proteins of the capsid coat of the cold virus).
3. The specific plasma cell type clones itself (divides repeatedly by mitosis) to increase rapidly the numbers of that type of plasma cell.
4. The newly formed 'army' of specific plasma cells begins antibody production.
5. The newly released antibodies circulate in the bloodstream and eventually find their antigen match (e.g. the proteins of the virus capsid).
6. Using various mechanisms, the antibodies help eliminate the pathogen.
7. Some of the cloned antibody-producing plasma cells remain in the bloodstream and provide immunity against a second infection by the same pathogen. These long-lived cells are called memory cells.
8. Memory plasma cells of this type respond quickly if the same antigen is encountered again (a secondary immune response).

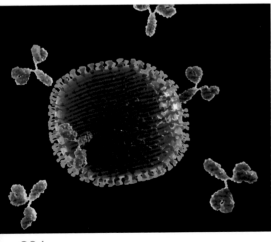

 Vaccines are weakened or non-pathogenic forms of pathogens that cause a primary immune response within your body. This leads to the production of the same memory lymphocytes as the actual disease does. Thus, following a vaccination, if you do encounter the actual pathogen, the memory cells will initiate a very quick secondary immune response. In most instances, the secondary immune response is so quick that symptoms associated with the pathogen do not have time to develop.

What is HIV and how does it affect the human immune system?

HIV is the abbreviation for a virus called human immunodeficiency virus. Just like any virus, HIV is very specific about which organisms and which cell types in an organism it infects. Unfortunately, the infected (host) cells in humans is one of the key lymphocyte cell types involved in the immune responses just described. A person infected with HIV will eventually experience a severe drop in his or her lymphocyte population, and will lose the ability to produce adequate antibodies. It typically takes many years after the initial infection by HIV before an infected person loses his or her specific immune response capability, but when it does happen the resulting immune disease is called AIDS or acquired immune deficiency syndrome.

When the symptoms of AIDS do begin, the infected person can no longer fight off pathogens as he or she could before, and a multitude of infections of various types begins. It is one or more of these secondary infections that most often takes the life of someone with AIDS. At the time of publication of this text, no effective treatment has been found to cure someone with an HIV infection. However, a variety of treatments have been found that are prolonging the time period between infection and the onset of symptoms of AIDS.

How is HIV transmitted?

The two most common ways that HIV is spread from person to person is by having unprotected sex with an infected person, and by using a hypodermic needle that has previously been used by someone who is HIV-positive (HIV$^+$). In addition, it is possible for an HIV$^+$ mother to infect her child during pregnancy, labour, delivery, or breastfeeding. In some countries, receiving a blood transfusion can spread HIV, but that is no longer a risk in countries where blood and blood products are routinely tested for contamination. Some medical treatments, such as injections for treating haemophilia, have been known to spread HIV when the injection was purified from human blood. In many areas of the world, these products are now produced by genetically engineered bacteria and have no risk of transmitting HIV.

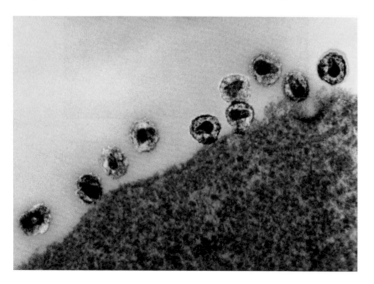

A false-colour TEM of HIV (small round objects) infecting a leucocyte.

TOK Do scientific researchers have a responsibility to communicate and collaborate freely with each other? Sometimes a competitive environment, striving to be the first to discover something, can get in the way of productive collaboration. An example was the limited collaboration between competing USA and French research teams in the early days of research on the pathogen that we now know as HIV.

The use of antibiotics to combat bacterial infections

Bacteria are prokaryotic cells. Humans and other animals are composed of eukaryotic cells. There are major structural and biochemical differences between prokaryotic and eukaryotic cells. For example, protein synthesis is similar in both types of cell,

305

but not exactly the same. Also, bacteria have a cell wall, a structure not characteristic of eukaryotic animal cells. Antibiotics are chemicals that take advantage of the differences between prokaryotic and eukaryotic cells, and selectively block some of the biochemistry needed by bacteria while having no effect on human or animal cells. There are many categories of antibiotics, depending on the biochemical pathway that is being targeted. One type of antibiotic may selectively block protein synthesis in bacteria, but have no effect on our cells' ability to manufacture proteins. Another type may inhibit the production of a new cell wall by bacteria, thus blocking their ability to grow and divide.

This also explains why antibiotics have no effect on viruses. Viruses make use of our own body cells' metabolism to create new viruses. Any chemical that could inhibit this would also be damaging to our own body cells. Thus antibiotics are chemicals with the ability to damage or kill prokaryotic cells, but not damage eukaryotic cells or their metabolism; because a virus has no metabolism of its own, antibiotics are not prescribed for any disease of viral origin.

NATURE OF SCIENCE

Alexander Fleming made the initial discovery of penicillin in 1928. However, Fleming became frustrated by his inability to isolate the chemical from the fungus that produced the antibiotic, and moved on to other work. About a decade later, Ernst Chain and Howard Florey picked up on Fleming's work and isolated a small amount of the penicillin compound. They injected eight mice with a deadly bacterial species and four of these mice were also injected with the newly isolated penicillin. The four mice that were not injected with penicillin all died within a day. The four mice that were injected with penicillin all lived for several days. Small-scale studies such as this would in fact have little credibility by the standards used today to judge the validity of experimental work.

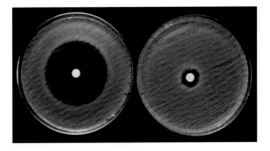

At the centre of each Petri dish is a tablet of penicillin. As you can see, growth of the strain of bacteria on the left is greatly inhibited by the penicillin that is diffusing outwards from the pellet. The strain of bacteria on the right is a strain that has developed a resistance to penicillin and its growth is not nearly as inhibited.

An unsolved dilemma: bacterial resistance to antibiotics

Remember that any one antibiotic is a specific chemical that selectively targets some aspect of prokaryotic cell biochemistry that is different from eukaryotes. Bacteria show genetic variation just like all other living organisms on Earth. Because bacterial population numbers can be incredibly large, and because bacteria can reproduce very quickly, the mathematical odds that within a bacterial population a genetic variant exists that is not affected by any one antibiotic is quite possible. That one (or a few) variant can then reproduce and repopulate a colony in a very short period of time with bacteria that are all resistant to the antibiotic. The surviving resistant bacteria would then be a new strain of bacteria.

The long-term use and overuse of antibiotics has now led to many pathogenic species of bacteria that have strains that are resistant to nearly all of the antibiotics in existence today.

Some strains of bacteria are even resistant to multiple antibiotics. *Staphylococcus aureus* is a bacterium that can be pathogenic, resulting in what many call a 'staph infection'. Some strains of *S. aureus* are referred to as MRSA (pronounced 'mersa'): these are strains of *S. aureus* that have developed a resistance to many types of antibiotics. MRSA infections are very difficult to treat and are becoming more and more frequent.

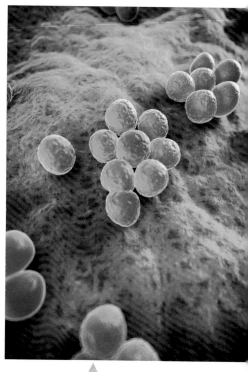

▲
Computer artwork showing MRSA bacteria (small blue spheres).

Section summary

- Most pathogens cannot gain entry into our living tissues because our skin and mucous membranes act as our primary (first) defence.
- When skin is cut, a blood clot forms when clotting factors are released from platelets, ultimately leading to a soluble blood-clotting protein (fibrinogen) being converted into an insoluble protein (fibrin).
- Some phagocytic white blood cells ingest any pathogens that are considered to be 'not-self', leading to a non-specific defence.
- Other white blood cells called B lymphocytes produce specific antibodies in response to a particular pathogen.
- Antibiotics are any chemicals that block a biochemically important pathway in prokaryotic cells (bacteria) but do not affect eukaryotic cell metabolism.
- Viruses are not affected by antibiotics because they lack their own metabolism.
- Some strains of pathogenic bacteria have evolved genes that give them resistance to certain antibiotics. A few strains have evolved to be resistant to multiple antibiotics.

Exercises

7 Why are some pathogenic viruses potentially lethal (e.g. HIV, *Ebola*), while others result in only fairly mild and temporary symptoms?

8 Distinguish between non-specific and specific immune responses.

9 What is a virus doing when it is not infecting a host cell?

10 In the very early years of research on the disease that we now know as AIDS, government funding for research was close to non-existent. Other than the fact that it was a fairly 'new' disease, can you think of one or more reasons why funding was so low?

6.4 Gas exchange

NATURE OF SCIENCE

Obtain evidence for theories: epidemiological studies have contributed to our understanding of the causes of lung cancer.

Understandings:

- Ventilation maintains concentration gradients of oxygen and carbon dioxide between air in alveoli and blood flowing in adjacent capillaries.
- Type I pneumocytes are extremely thin alveolar cells that are adapted to carry out gas exchange.
- Type II pneumocytes secrete a solution containing surfactant that creates a moist surface inside the alveoli to prevent the sides of the alveolus adhering to each other by reducing surface tension.
- Air is carried to the lungs in the trachea and bronchi, and then to the alveoli in bronchioles.
- Muscle contractions cause the pressure changes inside the thorax that force air in and out of the lungs to ventilate them.
- Different muscles are required for inspiration and expiration because muscles only do work when they contract.

Applications and skills:

- Application: Causes and consequences of lung cancer.
- Application: Causes and consequences of emphysema.
- Application: External and internal intercostal muscles, and diaphragm and abdominal muscles, as examples of antagonistic muscle action.
- Skill: Monitoring of ventilation in humans at rest and after mild and vigorous exercise.

Guidance

- *Ventilation can either be monitored by simple observation and simple apparatus, or by data logging with a spirometer or chest belt and pressure meter. Ventilation rate and tidal volume should be measured, but the terms vital capacity and residual volume are not expected.*
- *Students should be able to draw a diagram to show the structure of an alveolus and an adjacent capillary.*

Overview of the respiratory system

Our lungs act in concert with our heart and blood vessels to ensure that body cells are well supplied with oxygen and are able to give up carbon dioxide. Most people never seriously consider why we need oxygen, but everyone knows that we do. The process that requires oxygen (and gives off carbon dioxide) is aerobic cell respiration. In brief, this is a biochemical pathway in which the chemical bonds within a glucose molecule are broken down sequentially to release energy. Much of this energy is then stored as molecules of adenosine triphosphate (ATP). In aerobic organisms, the process requires oxygen molecules, and each of the six carbons of a glucose molecule is given off as a carbon dioxide molecule.

Throughout our lives we continuously repeat the process of filling our lungs with air and then expelling that air. This is called ventilation. Even though the air we breathe is inside our lungs for only a short period of time, it is long enough for diffusion of gases to occur. Within the lungs are a multitude of

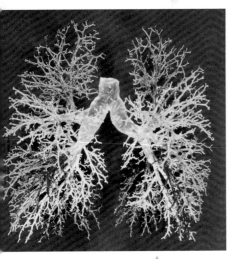

A resin cast image of airways in the lungs. The trachea divides into the right and left primary bronchi. Each primary bronchus continues to divide multiple times, leading to smaller and smaller bronchioles. You can see why the entire structure is sometimes called the 'bronchiole tree'.

Figure 6.12 Air can enter the trachea from either the mouth or nasal passages. The inhaled air passes through the larynx (the voicebox with vocal cords) and then down the trachea. The trachea branches many times into multiple bronchioles. Finally the air reaches the small air sacs (alveoli) surrounded by rich capillary beds.

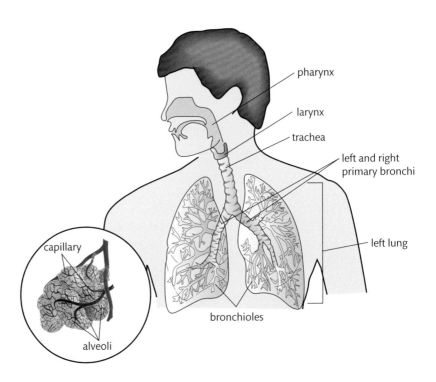

small spherical air sacs called alveoli. Oxygen in the alveoli typically diffuses into the bloodstream, and carbon dioxide from the bloodstream typically diffuses into the alveoli. Each breath in and out maintains the concentration gradients that encourage diffusion of oxygen into and carbon dioxide out of the nearby capillary beds that are adjacent to the many alveoli making up the bulk of lung tissue.

The mechanism of ventilation

We breathe in and out continuously all our lives. Each time we take a breath, a fairly complex series of events occurs that we do not even think about as it is happening. The

tissue that makes up our lungs is passive and not muscular, therefore the lungs themselves are incapable of purposeful movement. However, there are muscles surrounding the lungs, including the diaphragm, muscles of the abdomen, and the external and internal intercostal muscles (which surround your ribs).

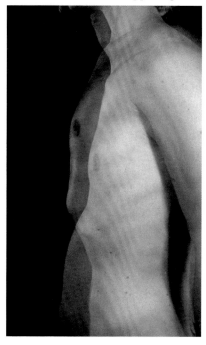

The mechanism of breathing is based on the inverse relationship between pressure and volume (see Figure 6.13). Put simply, an increase in volume will lead to a decrease in pressure, and vice versa. Whatever pressure does, volume will do the opposite. Your lungs are located within your thoracic cavity (or thorax). The thoracic cavity is closed to the outside air. Your lungs have only one opening to the outside air, and that is through your trachea (via your mouth and nasal passages). Thus we need to consider the two environments that affect each other: one is the closed environment of the thorax, and the other is the internal environment of the lungs.

CHALLENGE YOURSELF

3 Create a list of steps that trace a single erythrocyte that begins in the capillary bed adjacent to an alveolus. Name the major blood vessels and heart chambers that the erythrocyte goes through until it returns to another capillary bed in the lungs. Hint: You will need to take the cell through the remaining pulmonary circuit, into a systemic circuit starting with the aorta, and then eventually back through the first portion of another pulmonary circuit.

A double-exposure photograph showing the position of the chest during inspiration and expiration. Inspiration is occurring when the chest/rib cage is in the raised position.

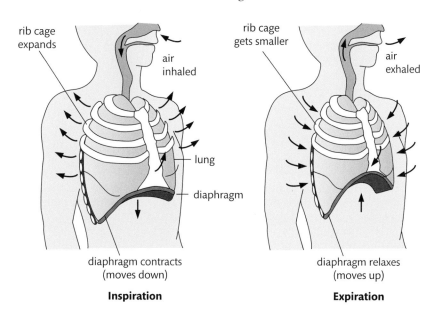

Figure 6.13 The mechanisms for inspiration and expiration (ventilation).

CHALLENGE YOURSELF

4   List the five steps (in order) necessary for expiration, with the following as your starting point.
    • The diaphragm relaxes and the internal intercostal muscles and a second set of abdominal muscles help to lower the rib cage. Collectively, these actions decrease the volume of the thoracic cavity.

Notice that different muscles are necessary for an inspiration versus an expiration. For example, the intercostal muscles are the muscles that are found between the ribs. There are two antagonistic sets of these muscles: external intercostals, which are used when breathing in, and the internal intercostals, which are used when breathing out.

Actions that lead to an inspiration (breathing in)

1   The diaphragm contracts, and at the same time the external intercostal muscles and one set of abdominal muscles help to raise the rib cage. Collectively, these actions increase the volume of the thoracic cavity.

2   Because the thoracic cavity has increased its volume, the pressure inside the cavity decreases. This leads to less pressure 'pushing on' the passive lung tissue.

3   The lung tissue increases its volume because there is less pressure exerted on it.

4   This leads to a decrease in pressure inside the lungs, also known as a partial vacuum.

5   Air comes in through your open mouth or nasal passages to counter the partial vacuum within the lungs, and fills the alveoli.

These steps are reversed for an expiration (breathing out).

All the steps become more frequent and exaggerated when you are exercising and thus breathing deeply. For example, the abdominal muscles and intercostal muscles achieve a greater initial thoracic volume. This leads to deeper breathing and thus more air moving into the lungs.

Monitoring ventilation in humans at rest and after mild and vigorous exercise
Safety alerts: Many schools and the IB animal experimentation policy require parent permission forms to be signed before any type of investigation of the pupils themselves is performed. If so, this must be completed well before the investigation begins.

Note: This investigation is best done as a whole class project with shared data sets.

This lab reinforces the concepts associated with changes in homeostatic mechanisms in the human body. Ventilation is the rate of breathing and is typically given as breaths min^{-1}. An increase in exercise predictably results in a greater use of oxygen and release of carbon dioxide to/from muscle tissue associated with the exercise.

Question
What is the correlation between ventilation rate and duration of exercise?

Hypothesis
Ventilation rate will be positively correlated with the increasing duration of a chosen exercise.

Planning steps necessary before beginning
Determine a safe exercise that can be accomplished by everyone that is happy to be a test subject. Typical examples might be walking up a flight of stairs or jumping jacks. Next, determine the maximum time duration that is both reasonable and safe for the exercise you have chosen. Hint: try to make it easy to subdivide your total duration time.

Summary of procedures
1   Choosing human subjects for experimentation is difficult as it is often not possible to account for comparable subjects based on criteria such as gender, age, body mass index (BMI) similarities, health, current level of activity (sports), and genetic background. You will probably have to make test groups from a very limited population of test subjects (e.g. your classmates). Try to set at least some limited criteria for test subjects. Try to make three to five test groups with as many test subjects in each group as possible. Five groups of five in each group would be ideal, but perhaps not realistic.

2   You will need baseline ventilation data for each individual test subject. Use a timer and count the number of breaths for a 20-second time period for each test subject. Record this as raw data and be sure to keep track of the identity of each person and his or her 20-second ventilation rate. The test subject can count his or her own breaths with someone else acting as a timer and recorder. An alternative is to use data-logging hardware and software that is designed to measure ventilation rate and perhaps tidal volume (the volume of air in a single breath).

3   Individually, have each test subject do one, and only one, of the exercise durations you predetermined. Very soon after each subject has finished, take a 20-second count of his or her number of breaths and record that data, again making sure to keep track of who it is

and the duration of his or her exercise. If the number of test subjects is very low, you may have to use one or more subjects for more than one exercise duration. If this is the case, make sure to allow as much recovery time between tests as possible.

Data-processing possibilities

- For each test subject, calculate a ventilation rate, expressed in breaths min^{-1}, for both the baseline and after-exercise raw data (the 20-second ventilation counts).

- For each test subject, calculate a percentage increase of ventilation rate, showing the increase after exercise compared with the baseline rate.

- Calculate the mean percentage increase for each group. Example: calculate the mean percentage increase for all the test subjects who did jumping jacks for 90 seconds.

- If your data set included at least five test subjects for each exercise duration, calculate the standard deviation of each of the means from the previous step.

Data-presentation possibilities

- Design and create a data table showing all the relevant raw data. Test subject numbers can be assigned instead of using names.

- Design and create a data table showing all the relevant processed data.

- Design and create a graph with exercise durations on the x-axis (with appropriate units) and mean percentage increases (% unit) on the y-axis.

- If the data set appears to be reasonably linear on your graph, draw a single best-fit line representing the overall data pattern.

- Add standard deviation error bars to each mean point plotted on your graph, and add a note to your graph that the error bars indicate standard deviation.

Gas exchange occurs in alveoli

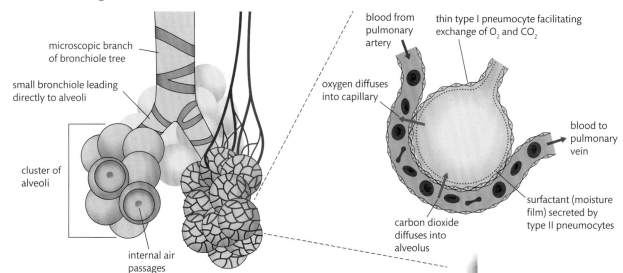

Figure 6.14 Microscopic view of a small area inside a human lung. Each cluster of alveoli is surrounded by a capillary bed for efficient gas exchange. The inset shows a sectioned drawing of a single alveolus and the structures that make gas exchange efficient.

When you take in air through your mouth or nasal passages:

• the air first enters your trachea

• then your right and left primary bronchi

• then smaller and smaller branches of the bronchi

• then very small branches called bronchioles

• then, finally, the air enters the small air sacs in the lungs called alveoli.

Alveoli in the lungs are found as clusters at the ends of the smallest bronchioles. In appearance they are very similar to a bunch of grapes. There are approximately 300 million alveoli in each of your lungs. Each cluster of alveoli has one or more surrounding capillary bed(s).

The blood entering these capillary beds comes from the right ventricle via the pulmonary arteries. As you will recall, blood within the pulmonary arteries is relatively low in oxygen and high in carbon dioxide. While this blood is in the capillary bed surrounding a cluster of alveoli, oxygen diffuses from the air in each alveolus through the membranes, which is only through two cells. The first of these is the single cell making up the structure of the alveolus, and the second is the single cell making up the wall of the capillary. Carbon dioxide diffuses in the opposite direction through the same two cells. As long as a person continues breathing, and refreshing the gases within the alveoli, the concentration gradients of these two gases will ensure diffusion of each gas in the direction that the body needs for healthy gas exchange.

Figure 6.15 Relationship between ventilation, gas exchange, and cell respiration.

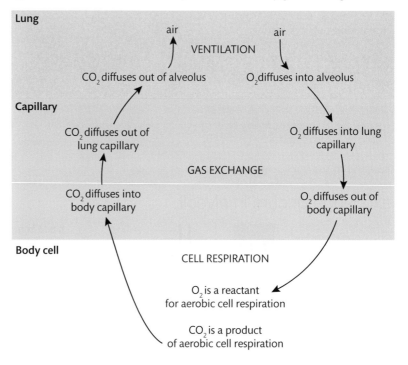

Alveoli are composed of specialized cells called pneumocytes

An alveolus is an evolutionary marvel designed for efficient gas exchange. As mentioned above, one of the design features of an alveolus is that it is composed of a single layer of cells, to facilitate oxygen and carbon dioxide diffusion. This single cell layer is composed of two different types of cells called pneumocytes.

Type I pneumocytes

This type of alveolar cell is very thin but has a very large membrane surface area, making it well designed for diffusion. If damaged, these cells are incapable of mitosis for replacement.

Type II pneumocytes

This type of alveolar cell is cuboidal in shape and thus has relatively little membrane surface area. These cells produce and secrete a solution that acts as a surfactant. This reduces the surface tension of the moist inner surface of alveoli, and prevents the sides of the alveoli from sticking to each other. Type II pneumocytes are capable of mitosis for replacement of both types of alveolar cells if they are damaged.

Causes and consequences of emphysema

Emphysema is a disease whereby the alveoli in the lungs are progressively destroyed. The leading cause of emphysema is smoking. Emphysema is one of the diseases collectively known by the acronym COPD (chronic obstructive pulmonary disease). Emphysema is a chronic, slowly progressive disease that turns healthy alveoli into large, irregularly shaped structures with gaping holes. This reduces the surface area for gas exchange, and so less oxygen reaches the bloodstream. This explains the symptom described as 'shortness of breath'. At first, shortness of breath only occurs when the afflicted person does strenuous activity, but over time the inability to get sufficient gas exchange becomes constant.

The diagnosis of emphysema is often delayed because the symptoms develop slowly. People often associate the symptoms of emphysema with natural ageing, and people can initially find ways to compensate for their breathing problems.

Although long-term tobacco smoking is the leading cause of emphysema, there are other causes, including long-term exposure to the following:

- marijuana smoke
- fumes from manufacturing plants
- coal dust
- air pollution.

There is no cure for emphysema, but the progression of the disease can be slowed drastically with the cessation of smoking or exposure to other risk factors. To prevent emphysema, it is common sense not to even begin smoking, and to wear a protective mask when working around dust or chemical fumes.

Light microscope photograph of a section of lung taken from a diseased patient with emphysema. Notice the large gaping holes where healthy alveoli once were.

A better understanding of the causes of emphysema and lung cancer has led to massive campaigns to educate people about the dangers of smoking. In areas of the world where information concerning the dangers of smoking have been regularly and widely circulated, the percentage of people who smoke has declined.

Causes and consequences of lung cancer

Lung cancer is a cancerous growth that begins in the lungs. It is a cancer that is prone to spreading, a process called metastasizing. The brain, bones, liver, and adrenal glands are likely targets for lung cancer that has metastasized. The cancerous growth in the lungs takes over areas of healthy tissue that once provided a combination of bronchioles and alveoli. The larger the growth, the more the lung tissue becomes dysfunctional. Lung cancer can also result in internal bleeding in the lungs.

Lung cancer is caused by one or more carcinogen (a substance that is known to cause cancer) that enters the lung tissue and mutates cells into a cancerous growth. Sometimes the body is able to eliminate the early cancerous growth, but not always. More often than not, the carcinogen enters the lungs in cigarette smoke, although other fumes and substances have been known to be the source of the carcinogen.

The best treatment of lung cancer is achieved when the disease is diagnosed early in its progression. Lung cancer has a very high mortality rate.

Asbestos, once commonly used in building insulation products, is another carcinogen that can result in lung cancer. Many companies specialize in the safe removal of asbestos insulation from older buildings.

Recent data supports a direct correlation between those countries and cultures that have shown a decrease in the number of people who smoke and a corresponding decrease in the incidence of lung cancer. Conversely, those areas of the world that are showing an increase in the number of people smoking are showing an increase in the incidence of lung cancer.

Section summary

- Ventilation is the act of breathing, an inspiration followed by an expiration. Ventilation continually maintains appropriate levels of oxygen and carbon dioxide in the lungs.
- Microscopic air sacs in the lungs, called alveoli, exchange oxygen and carbon dioxide with nearby capillary beds, in order to oxygenate the blood and to remove excess carbon dioxide.
- Alveoli are made up of two types of cells called pneumocytes.
  - Type 1 pneumocytes are the most numerous, and are thin to help carry out gas exchange.
  - Type 2 pneumocytes secrete a solution containing surfactant. This solution reduces the surface tension between nearby cells and thus prevents cells from adhering to each other.
- The trachea carries air to both lungs, and branches into two bronchi (one for each lung). Further subdivisions of the bronchi lead to small bronchioles and finally clusters of alveoli.
- The lungs are a passive tissue incapable of providing the movements associated with ventilation. Instead, muscle contractions from the diaphragm, intercostal muscles, and abdominal muscles lead to volume and pressure changes inside the thoracic cavity, which lead to ventilation.
- One set of these muscles contracts for an inspiration and another (antagonistic) set contracts for an expiration.

Exercises

11 Stopping smoking seems like such an easy, simple thing for people to do. Why do you think more people are not successful at stopping?

12 How are alveoli well adapted for efficient gas exchange?

13 Why are there two sets of muscles involved in ventilation (breathing)?

6.5 Neurones and synapses

Understandings:
- Neurones transmit electrical impulses.
- The myelination of nerve fibres allows for saltatory conduction.
- Neurones pump sodium and potassium ions across their membranes to generate a resting potential.
- An action potential consists of depolarization and repolarization of the neurone.
- Nerve impulses are action potentials propagated along the axons of neurones.
- Propagation of nerve impulses is the result of local currents that cause each successive part of the axon to reach the threshold potential.
- Synapses are junctions between neurones and between neurones and receptor or effector cells.
- When presynaptic neurones are depolarized they release a neurotransmitter into the synapse.
- A nerve impulse is only initiated if the threshold potential is reached.

Applications and skills:

- Application: Secretion and reabsorption of acetylcholine by neurones at synapses.
- Application: Blocking of synaptic transmission at cholinergic synapses in insects by binding of neonicotinoid pesticides to acetylcholine receptors.
- Skill: Analysis of oscilloscope traces showing resting potentials and action potentials.

Guidance

- *The details of structure of different types of neurones are not needed.*
- *Only chemical synapses are required, not electrical, and they can simply be referred to as synapses.*

The organization of the human nervous system

The brain and spinal cord comprise the central nervous system (CNS). These two structures receive sensory information from various receptors, and then interpret and process that sensory information. If a response is needed, some portion of the brain or spinal cord initiates a response that is called a motor response.

The cells that carry this information are called neurones. Sensory neurones bring information in to the CNS, and motor neurones carry response information to muscles.

Together, sensory neurones and motor neurones make up the peripheral nerves. A neurone is an individual cell that carries electrical impulses from one point in the body to another, and does so very quickly. When many individual neurones group together into a single structure, that structure is called a nerve. Think of a nerve as being like a telephone cable: a protective sheath surrounding many individual wires. Each wire within that cable is like a neurone. The connection between the CNS and your body is made by two sets of nerves.

- Spinal nerves emerge directly from the spinal cord. They are mixed nerves, as some of the neurones within them are sensory and some are motor. There are 31 pairs of spinal nerves.
- Cranial nerves emerge from an area of the brain known as the brainstem. One well known example is the optic nerve pair, which carries visual information from the retina of the eyes to the brain. There are 12 pairs of cranial nerves.

The central nervous system (CNS) consists of the brain and spinal cord. The peripheral nervous system (PNS) is made up of the nerves and branches that enter and leave the spinal cord and brainstem.

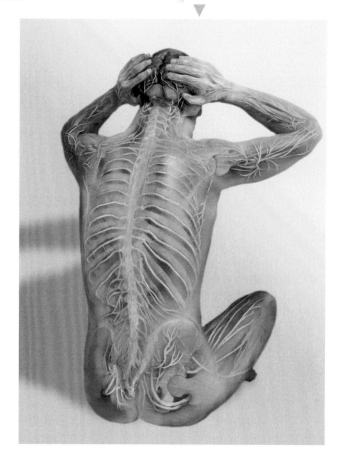

Neurones

The cells that have been evolutionarily designed to transmit electrical impulses are called neurones. Neurones can be unusually long. In the human body, there are neurones that extend from the lower portion of the spinal cord all the way to the big toe: single cells that extend a distance of about 1 metre! Of course, not all neurones are that long; in fact, some neurones are quite short.

The three main subparts of a single neurone are its dendrites, cell body, and axon. At the end of the axon are synaptic terminal buttons, which release chemicals called neurotransmitters that continue the impulse chemically to the next neurone(s) or

 Blue whales have some neurones that are approximately 25 m in length.

possibly a muscle. An impulse is always carried from the dendrite end of a neurone along the membrane of the cell body down the axon, and results in a release of a neurotransmitter. The impulse does not travel in the opposite direction because neurotransmitter molecules cannot be released from the dendrite end of neurones, and the 'message' would simply stop at that point.

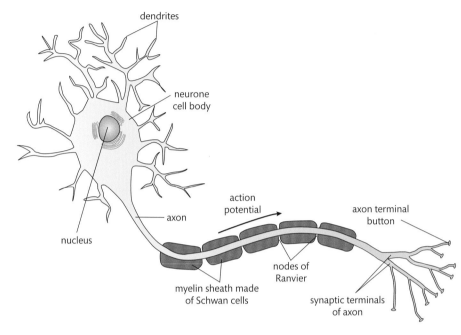

Figure 6.16 The structure of an individual neurone. The function of the myelin sheath and nodes of Ranvier are described on pages 319–320.

Light microscope photograph of a section of a nerve. The very large circle is the entire nerve, and each small circle within it is one of the axons of a neurone contained within that nerve. ▼

What is a nerve impulse?

People often equate a nerve impulse to electricity. In some ways this is accurate, as a nerve impulse can be measured in the same way as electricity. For example, an action potential (or impulse) has a voltage, although the typical unit for this voltage is millivolts. In other ways, however, electricity and action potentials are very different. True electricity is a flow of electrons down a conductor; this is not the nature of an action potential. Let's look at what a nerve impulse actually is.

The term 'nerve impulse' is very misleading because a nerve does not carry an impulse; the individual neurones within the nerve are each capable of carrying the impulse. As axons of neurones are typically quite long, it is convenient to think of the conductor of a neurone impulse as the axon. The axons of neurones in some organisms (including humans) that have a very highly developed nervous system, have surrounding membranous structures collectively called the myelin sheath. The myelin sheath greatly increases the rate at which an action potential passes down an axon. In order to study the nature of an action potential, it is best to study an axon that does not have a myelin sheath, otherwise known as a non-myelinated neurone.

Resting potential: not currently sending an impulse

Let's look first at what an axon of a neurone is like when it is not sending an impulse. The time period during which an area of a neurone is ready to send an action potential, but is not actually sending one, is called the resting potential, and this area of the neurone is said to be polarized. The resting potential is created by the active transport of sodium ions (Na^+) and potassium ions (K^+) in two different directions. The vast majority of the sodium ions are actively transported out of the axon cell into the intercellular fluid, and the majority of the potassium ions are transported into the cytoplasm. This active transport of sodium and potassium in opposite directions is an active transport mechanism called the sodium–potassium (Na/K) pump. The Na/K pump works by transporting three sodium ions 'out' for every two potassium ions 'in'. In addition, there are negatively charged organic ions permanently located in the cytoplasm of the axon. The net result of the position of the charged ions leads to a net positive charge outside the axon membrane (positive in relation to the inside) and a net negative charge inside the axon membrane (see Figure 6.17).

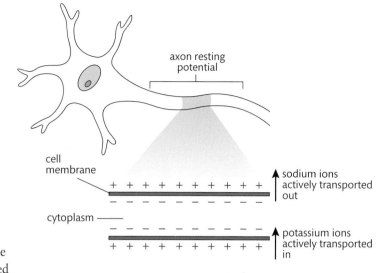

Depolarization: sending an impulse

An action potential is often described as a self-propagating wave of ion movements in and out of the neurone membrane. The movement of the ions is not along the length of the axon, but instead consists of ions diffusing from outside the axon to the inside, and from inside the axon to the outside. The resting potential requires active transport (the Na/K pump) to set up a concentration gradient of both sodium and potassium ions. As sodium ions are actively transported to the outside of the membrane, they diffuse in when a channel opens. This diffusion of sodium ions is the 'impulse' or action potential, and results in the inside of the axon becoming temporarily positive in relation to the outside. It is a nearly instantaneous event that occurs in one area of an axon, and is also called a depolarization. This depolarized area of the axon then initiates the next area of the axon to open up the channels for sodium, and thus the action potential continues down the axon. This is the self-propagating part of an action potential; once you start an impulse at the dendrite end of a neurone, that action potential will self-propagate to the axon end of the cell, where the synaptic terminals are located.

Each action potential must reach a minimum threshold in order to be self-propagated. This begins at the first receptor neurone that began the chain of events. A receptor neurone is a neurone that is modified to begin the sequence of events by transducing (converting) a physical stimulus of some kind into the first action potential. For example, some of the cells that make up the retina of your eyes are receptor cells. Each type of retinal cell has a minimum physical stimulus magnitude that is required in order to begin the impulse. For some retinal cells this is a minimum intensity of light. If that minimum intensity is not reached, no action potential begins. If the minimum is reached, an action potential is initiated and begins to self-propagate. There is no such thing as a strong impulse or a weak impulse: if the minimum threshold for that type of receptor is reached, an impulse begins. When a nerve impulse is being self-propagated along a neurone, that is happening because each successive area of the neurone membrane has reached its threshold and is causing the next area of the membrane to also reach its threshold.

Typically we are not aware of single impulses that reach our brain. If we sense a small amount of pressure on some area of our skin, it is because a few pressure receptors in that area have reached their threshold. If we feel a greater pressure, it is because the pressure has caused even more receptors in that area to reach their minimum threshold.

Nerve impulses are action potentials propagated along the axons of neurones.

317

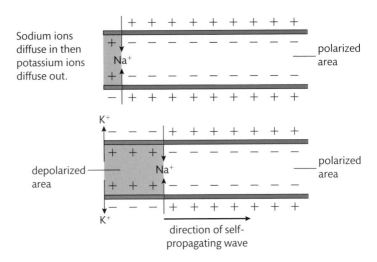

Figure 6.18 A neurone axon during and shortly after a depolarization.

Sodium ions diffuse in then potassium ions diffuse out.

polarized area

K⁺

depolarized area

Na⁺

polarized area

K⁺

direction of self-propagating wave

Repolarization: return to the resting potential

Neurones do not send just one action potential; one neurone may send dozens of action potentials in a very short period of time. When one area of an axon has opened a channel to allow sodium ions to diffuse in, that area cannot send another action potential until ions have been restored to the positions characteristic of the resting potential. Diffusion cannot do this, thus active transport is required to pump ions to their resting potential positions.

If you recall from earlier, a depolarization is when sodium ions diffuse through the axon membrane from outside to inside. This means that, for a very short period of time, both sodium ions and potassium ions are inside together (this is why the inside of the membrane becomes positive relative to the outside). You may also recall that the active transport mechanism that resulted in the resting potential positions of sodium and potassium was the Na/K pump. This pump only works by moving sodium in one direction and potassium in the other direction across the membrane. Thus, immediately following an action potential (depolarization), membrane proteins open to potassium ions and allow them to diffuse out of the axon. This is the first step of repolarization because it separates many of the sodium and potassium ions on different sides of the membrane. The problem is that these two ions are on the opposite side of the membrane in relation to where they need to be for the resting potential. The good news is that they are now in a position that allows the Na/K pump to once again begin actively transporting them across the membrane at the ratio characteristic of this pump (three sodium ions pumped out for every two potassium ions pumped in). This entire series of events, beginning with potassium ions diffusing out of the localized area of the membrane, is called repolarization. All of this is necessary for that local area of the membrane to be ready to send another impulse.

Figure 6.19 Return to the resting potential.

After sodium ions and potassium ions diffuse, both are actively transported back to their resting potential locations.

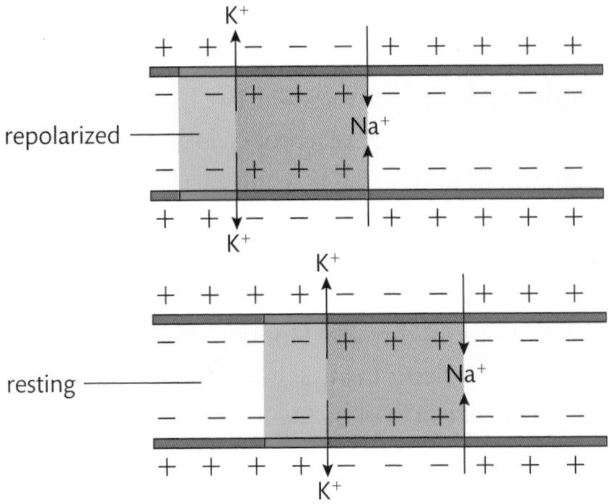

K⁺

repolarized

Na⁺

K⁺

K⁺

resting

Na⁺

K⁺

Saltatory conduction by neurones that have a myelin sheath

Many neurones of an organism with an advanced nervous system have axons with a myelin sheath; they are said to be myelinated. As an axon is like a long fibre, these axons are sometimes referred to as myelinated fibres. The myelin sheath is actually a series of cells, called Schwann cells, that have each wrapped themselves around the axon multiple times, creating multiple layers of the same cell membrane. The Schwann cells are spaced evenly along any one axon, with small gaps between them; these gaps are called nodes of Ranvier.

Saltatory conduction is the term used to describe the phenomenon whereby an action potential of myelinated axons skips from one node of Ranvier to the next as the impulse progresses along the axon towards the synaptic terminals. In other words, the action potential does not have to undergo the time-consuming and energy-expensive ion movements in the area of the membrane underneath the myelin material. The reason for this is that the myelin sheath acts as an insulator, preventing charge leakage through the membrane. The cytoplasm within the axon is electrically conductive, which allows the electrical potential to skip from one node of Ranvier to the next. The advantage of this is two-fold.

The term saltatory comes from the Latin word 'saltare', which means to hop or leap.

Illustration showing neurones with myelinated axons and nodes of Ranvier.

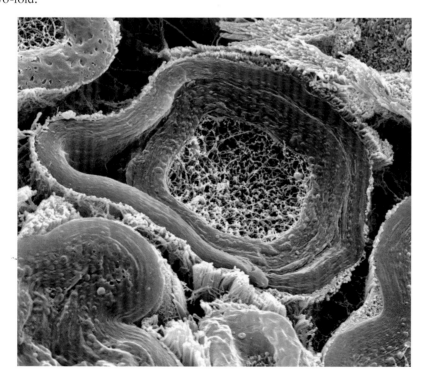

A false-colour SEM of a sectioned neurone with a myelin sheath. The axon is the centre beige area, and the myelin sheath is the surrounding yellow and green area.

- The impulse travels much faster compared with an impulse in non-myelinated fibres, because the in/out ion movements characteristic of an impulse take time, and saltatory conduction allows areas of the membrane to be skipped. This is very important for the efficient neural processing characteristic of organisms with a high functioning nervous system.
- Less energy in the form of ATP is expended for the transmission of impulses, as the only locations where the Na/K pump needs to re-establish resting potentials is at the nodes of Ranvier.

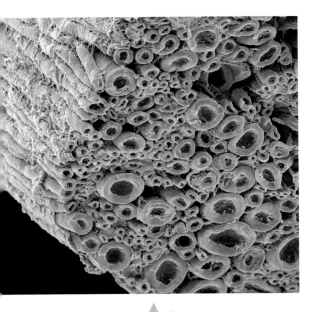

A false-colour SEM of a nerve (bundle of neurones) with myelin sheaths. The blue colour shows the axons, and the surrounding yellow is the myelin sheath of each axon.

Figure 6.20 A graph showing the voltage changes across the membrane of an axon for three nerve impulses. Some of the important events are labelled on one of these impulses.

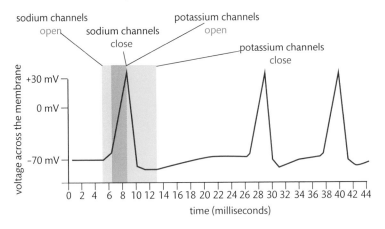

CHALLENGE YOURSELF

5   Use Figure 6.20, showing the change in voltage for a neurone sending impulses down its axon, to answer the following questions.
  (a) If each spike on this graph shows an impulse somewhere in the middle of an axon, what event must have just occurred in the area of the axon just preceding this one?
  (b) If the axon shown is myelinated, where along the axon did these voltage changes occur?
  (c) If this graph shows an impulse somewhere in the middle of an axon, and this is a myelinated fibre, what area of the axon will next undergo an action potential?
  (d) Where along the x-axis of the graph would the sodium–potassium pump be beginning to work to re-establish a resting potential?
  (e) What do you think would happen if discrete sensory information from a receptor was being received repeatedly at a rate faster than about 5 milliseconds apart?

Synapses: chemical communication between neurones

When one neurone communicates with another, the communication is chemical and occurs where two (or more) neurones adjoin each other in an area called a synapse. The two neurones always align with each other so that the axon's synaptic terminals of one neurone adjoin the dendrites of another neurone. The chemical, called a neurotransmitter, is always released from the synaptic terminal buttons of the first neurone, and typically results in a continuation of the impulse when the neurotransmitter is received by the dendrites of the second neurone. The neurone that releases the neurotransmitter is called the presynaptic neurone, and the receiving neurone is called the postsynaptic neurone.

At the distal end of axons, as part of the synaptic terminals, are swollen membranous areas called terminal buttons. Within these terminal buttons are many small vesicles filled with the chemical neurotransmitter. There are many examples of neurotransmitters; a very common example in humans is acetylcholine.

When an action potential reaches the area of the terminal buttons, it initiates the following sequence of events (see Figure 6.21).

1   Action potential results in calcium ions (Ca^{2+}) diffusing into the terminal buttons.
2   Vesicles containing the neurotransmitter fuse with the plasma membrane and release the neurotransmitter.
3   The neurotransmitter diffuses across the synaptic gap (or cleft) from the presynaptic neurone to the postsynaptic neurone.
4   The neurotransmitter binds with a receptor protein on the postsynaptic neurone membrane.
5   This binding results in an ion channel opening and sodium ions diffusing in through this channel.
6   This initiates the action potential to begin moving down the postsynaptic neurone because it is now depolarized (the action potential is now self-propagating).
7   The neurotransmitter is degraded (broken into two or more fragments) by a specific enzyme(s) and neurotransmitter is released from the receptor protein.
8   The ion channel closes to sodium ions.
9   Neurotransmitter fragments diffuse back across the synaptic gap to be reassembled in the terminal buttons of the presynaptic neurone (often called reuptake).

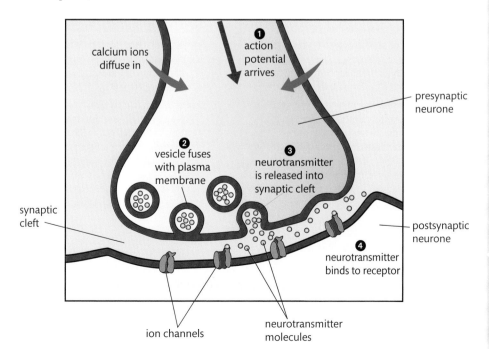

Figure 6.21 The mechanism of synaptic transmission.

Many mental disorders are associated with imbalances of certain neurotransmitters within the brain. There are approximately 50 different neurotransmitters that have been identified as active in the human brain. An imbalance of just one can result in conditions such as schizophrenia or severe depression. A large number of pharmaceuticals have been developed to treat these conditions based on our knowledge of how synapses and neurotransmitters work.

Synapses can also occur where a motor neurone adjoins muscle tissue. This type of synapse is called a motor end plate or neuromuscular junction. The mechanism for this type of synapse is almost the same as a neurone–neurone synapse, although the end result leads to the muscle undergoing a contraction. Another place for a synapse is between a receptor neurone (cell) of the nervous system and the first sensory neurone.

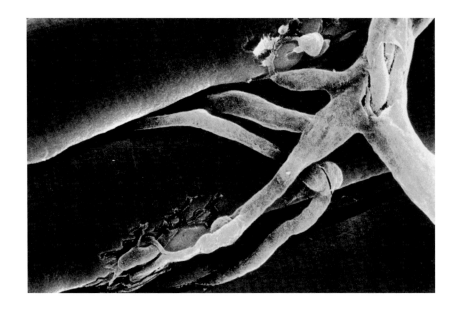

Synapses can be between a receptor and first sensory neurone, or between two neurones, or between a motor neurone and muscle. This false-colour SEM shows a synapse between a neurone (green) and a muscle fibre (red).

Early studies of neonicotinoid pesticides suggested that they were relatively safe from an ecological viewpoint. More recent studies are showing some possible links to the 'colony collapse syndrome' being experienced by honeybee colonies. Each country must consider the mounting evidence, but chemicals in our environment have ways of crossing international borders through water, air, and many other means. If neonicotinoids are shown to cause damage to honeybee colonies, an international effort to curtail or stop their use will be necessary.

A new class of insecticides based on blocking synaptic transmission

Neonicotinoid insecticides are a relatively new class of insecticide that are chemically similar to nicotine. This type of insecticide works by binding to postsynaptic receptors that normally accept the neurotransmitter acetylcholine. When acetylcholine binds to the receptor protein, the result is the normal continuation of the action potential along the postsynaptic neurone. When neonicotinoid molecules bind to the same receptor proteins, the action potential is not propagated. In addition, the neonicotinoid molecules are not broken down by the enzyme acteylcholinesterase and thus the receptor becomes permanently blocked. This leads to a paralysis of the affected insect, and eventually death.

NATURE OF SCIENCE

The fields of psychology, chemistry, biology, and medicine all combine to contribute to our knowledge of memory and learning. One of the many complications for research on memory and learning is the sheer complexity of the human brain. Often, complex biological systems are best studied by using simpler 'models' that represent the more complex activity.

Biologists often use invertebrates that have a simpler nervous system compared with humans and other vertebrates. One interesting invertebrate is a sea snail called *Aplysia*. This marine snail can be stimulated to retract its siphon when it is touched, as part of its defence mechanism. The snail can learn from experience, and can keep its siphon protected for a longer period of time after being given a chance to learn. In addition, repeated touching of the siphon leads to a greater number of synapses between neurones in the very simple brain of *Aplysia*. This can be observed and documented because *Aplysia* has very few, but very large, neurones that can be easily seen. Use the hotlinks at the end of this section to see a video of *Aplysia* and this research.

Section summary

• Neurones are cells well adapted for carrying electrical impulses from one neurone to the next or from a neurone to a muscle.

• Saltatory conduction is the term that describes how a neurone with a myelin sheath is able to skip the electrical signal (impulse) from one node of Ranvier to the next node of Ranvier. Nodes of Ranvier are areas of exposed axon between adjoining Schwann cells making up the myelin sheath.

- The Na/K pump is the active transport mechanism that generates the ion gradients known as a resting potential. Resting potential is when an axon of a neurone is not sending an impulse.

- A nerve impulse consists of action potentials propagated along the membrane of a neurone from dendrites to cell body and finally along an axon.

- The neurone membrane undergoes a depolarization followed by a repolarization during the transmission of an impulse.

- Propagation of an impulse is the result of a membrane reaching a threshold level of potential in order to initiate a depolarization.

- A presynaptic neurone releases a chemical known as a neurotransmitter in order to continue the impulse to a postsynaptic neurone or effector cells (muscle tissue).

Exercises

14 Explain the advantage that myelinated neurones have over non-myelinated neurones.

15 Individual neurones do not send action potentials with different 'strengths'. An action potential is either propagated (sent) or it is not. What is the term that describes the minimum electric potential necessary to propagate an impulse?

16 Arrange these events in the correct sequence to represent synaptic transmission.

  (a) Binding of neurotransmitter to receptor protein on postsynaptic neurone.
  (b) Enzyme degrades neurotransmitter.
  (c) Ca^{2+} ions enter synaptic (terminal) buttons.
  (d) Reuptake of neurotransmitter fragments.
  (e) Neurotransmitter diffuses across synaptic gap.
  (f) Na^+ ions diffuse into postsynaptic neurone channels.

To learn more about *Aplysia*, go to the hotlinks site, search for the title or ISBN, and click on Chapter 6: Section 6.5.

6.6 Hormones, homeostasis, and reproduction

Understandings:

- Insulin and glucagon are secreted by β and α cells of the pancreas, respectively, to control blood glucose concentration.
- Thyroxin is secreted by the thyroid gland to regulate the metabolic rate and help control body temperature.
- Leptin is secreted by cells in adipose tissue and acts on the hypothalamus of the brain to inhibit appetite.
- Melatonin is secreted by the pineal gland to control circadian rhythms.
- A gene on the Y chromosome causes embryonic gonads to develop as testes and secrete testosterone.
- Testosterone causes prenatal development of male genitalia and both sperm production and development of male secondary sexual characteristics during puberty.
- Oestrogen and progesterone cause prenatal development of female reproductive organs and female secondary sexual characteristics during puberty.
- The menstrual cycle is controlled by negative and positive feedback mechanisms involving ovarian and pituitary hormones.

NATURE OF SCIENCE

Developments in scientific research follow improvements in apparatus: William Harvey was hampered in his observational research into reproduction by lack of equipment. The microscope was invented 17 years after his death.

Applications and skills:

- Application: Causes and treatment of type I and type II diabetes.
- Application: Testing of leptin on patients with clinical obesity and reasons for the failure to control the disease.
- Application: Causes of jet lag and use of melatonin to alleviate it.
- Application: The use in IVF of drugs to suspend the normal secretion of hormones, followed by the use of artificial doses of hormones to induce superovulation and establish a pregnancy.
- Application: William Harvey's investigation of sexual reproduction in deer.
- Skill: Annotate diagrams of the male and female reproductive system to show names of structures and their functions.

Guidance

- *The roles of FSH, LH, oestrogen, and progesterone in the menstrual cycle are expected.*
- *William Harvey failed to solve the mystery of sexual reproduction because effective microscopes were not available when he was working, so fusion of gametes and subsequent embryo development remained undiscovered.*

There are two main categories of glands. Exocrine glands are those that produce a secretion (enzyme, saliva, etc.) that is carried to a nearby, specific, location via a duct. Endocrine glands always produce one or more hormones, and these hormones are always secreted into the blood for distribution throughout the body.

Homeostasis

The human body typically stays within certain limits for many physiological variables. This is referred to as homeostasis. Here are some representative physiological variables:

- blood pH
- blood carbon dioxide concentration
- blood glucose concentration
- body temperature
- water balance within tissues.

Each of these variables has an expected value or set point that is considered to be normal for homeostasis. For example, you often hear that our internal body temperature is 37°C (98.6°F). However, there is an inevitable fluctuation around this exact temperature, depending on what a person has been doing, for example exercising or being out in very cold weather.

Figure 6.22 Some of the more common endocrine glands within the human body. Each of these glands produces one or more hormones that are secreted into the bloodstream and are carried to target tissues within the body. Target tissues are those cells that are influenced by any one hormone.

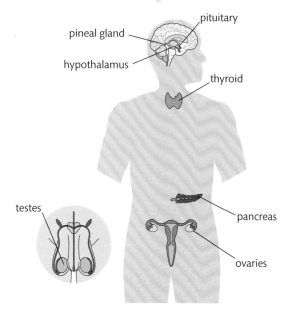

pituitary

pineal gland

hypothalamus

thyroid

testes

pancreas

ovaries

The physiological processes that bring a value back towards a set point are called negative feedback mechanisms. Think of negative feedback control as working like a thermostat. The thermostat triggers one set of actions that is required when a value rises above its set point, and another set of actions when a value falls below its set point. Thus negative feedback functions to keep a value within the narrow range that is considered normal for homeostasis.

The nervous and endocrine systems work cooperatively in order to ensure homeostasis. Many of the homeostatic mechanisms initiated by your nervous system are under the control of your autonomic nervous system. The endocrine system consists of numerous glands that produce a wide variety of hormones. Each hormone is transported by the bloodstream from the gland where it is produced to the specific cell types in the body that are influenced by that particular hormone.

Selected hormones and their functions

Each hormone has a specific gland that produces and secretes the hormone into nearby capillary beds for distribution to body cells. Not all body cells are influenced by any one hormone: those cells that are influenced by a hormone are called the target tissue(s) of the hormone. Some hormones (e.g. leptin) have very specific and limited target tissues, while others (e.g. insulin) have a broad range of target tissues.

Thyroxin

The gland that produces and secretes thyroxin is a 'butterfly'-shaped gland located in your neck called the thyroid gland. Thyroxin is created from an amino acid and iodine, and exists in two forms, one called T4 and the other called T3. The numbers indicate the number of iodine atoms within the structure. Both T3 and T4 enter the target cells (almost all cells in the body), where the T4 form is typically converted to the T3 form. The T3 form enters the nucleus of the cell and acts as a transcription regulator, leading to an increase in messenger (m)RNA and thus a resultant increase in proteins. Ultimately these proteins lead to an increase in the metabolism of the cell. Thus a cell under the influence of thyroxin will have a greater need for oxygen and other indicators of an increased metabolic rate. Someone who secretes too much thyroxin is said to have hyperthyroidism, and someone who secretes too little is said to have hypothryroidism. Both conditions can have serious symptoms.

In addition to increasing the metabolic rate, thyroxin helps to regulate internal body temperature. An increase in metabolic rate produces more heat from the increased chemical reactions that are occurring. Therefore an increase in thyroxin will lead to an increase in body temperature, and vice versa.

Leptin

Leptin is a hormone that is produced by adipose (fat) tissue in the body. The more fat stored in the body, the more leptin is produced and secreted into the bloodstream. Leptin's target cells are in the hypothalamus of the brainstem. Under ideal circumstances, leptin has the effect of lowering your appetite. Evolutionarily, the logic is simple: if someone has enough fat reserves, that person does not need to eat as much anymore. Unfortunately that simple logic doesn't always hold true, as evidenced by the very large incidence of obesity in modern society today. People who are obese are known to have a greater level of leptin circulating in their bloodstream. Researchers are working on why they appear to have become 'desensitized' to this high level of the appetite-controlling hormone. Some researchers have suggested that the function of leptin is related to increasing appetite when fat reserves are low, but not as an appetite suppressant when fat reserves are high.

Melatonin

Deep within your brain is a very small gland called the pineal gland. Many animals use their pineal gland to help regulate their daily 24-hour cycle of activity, called the circadian rhythm. The hormone produced and secreted from the pineal gland is called melatonin. The pineal gland produces very little melatonin during the daytime, and is at peak production after dark, with maximum production occurring between 2 a.m. and 4 a.m. The natural circadian rhythm is altered when a person alters his or her period of exposure to light over a short period of time, especially when coupled with a

As mentioned, the synthesis of thyroxin requires iodine. People whose diets are deficient in iodine can develop hypothyroidism. Over time, with a deficiency of iodine, the thyroid gland tries to compensate by growing larger, and becomes markedly visible as it swells in size. An enlarged thyroid growth is called a goitre. Iodine deficiency has in fact become very rare in modern humans because most table salt has iodine added to it, thus it is sold as 'iodized salt'.

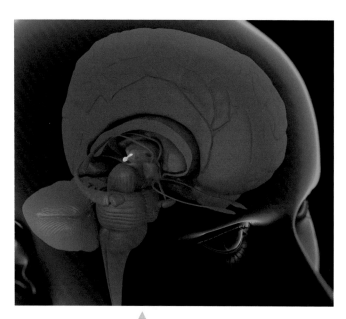

The pineal gland highlighted in a sectioned view of the human brain. The right cerebrum and a portion of the brainstem has been removed in order to show the location of this small gland associated with sleep/wake cycles.

disruption of their normal sleep schedule. This is what is typically called 'jet lag', produced when a person travels through several time zones in a short period of time. Similar disorientation symptoms can be felt by people who work temporary night shifts or have other irregular time patterns of sleep versus being awake. Many people report a decline in the disorienting effects of jet lag by taking melatonin pills until their own circadian rhythm has naturally reset.

Insulin and glucagon help regulate glucose levels

Insulin and glucagon are hormones that are both produced and secreted by the pancreas. In addition, they are both involved in the regulation of blood glucose levels. Cells rely on glucose for the process of cell respiration. Cells never stop cell respiration and thus are constantly lowering the concentration of glucose in the blood. Many people eat three or more times a day, including foods containing glucose, or carbohydrates that are chemically digested to glucose. This glucose is absorbed into the bloodstream in the capillary beds of the villi of the small intestine, and thus increases the blood glucose level. So one factor that causes our blood glucose levels to fluctuate is simply that our blood does not receive constant levels of glucose. The increase and decrease in blood glucose levels goes on 24 hours a day, every day of your life. However, even though blood glucose is expected to fluctuate slightly above and below the homeostatic normal level, it must be maintained reasonably close to the body's set point for blood glucose level, and negative feedback mechanisms ensure this.

In the intestinal villi, the glucose travels through a multitude of capillaries, small venules, and veins into the hepatic portal vein, which takes the blood to the liver. The glucose concentration in the hepatic portal vein varies depending on the time of your last meal and the glucose content of the food you ate. The hepatic portal vein is the only major blood vessel in the body in which blood levels fluctuate to a large degree. All other blood vessels receive blood after it has been processed by liver cells called hepatocytes. Hepatocytes are triggered into action by the two pancreatic hormones, insulin and glucagon. These two pancreatic hormones are antagonistic: they have opposite effects on blood glucose concentration.

What happens when blood glucose begins to rise above the set point?

In the pancreas there are cells known as β (beta) cells that produce the hormone insulin. Insulin is then secreted into the bloodstream and, because all body cells communicate chemically with blood, all cells are exposed to insulin. Insulin's effect on body cells is to open protein channels in their plasma membranes. These channels allow glucose to diffuse into the cell by the process known as facilitated diffusion.

There is another important effect attributed to insulin. When blood that is relatively high in glucose enters the liver by the hepatic portal vein, insulin stimulates the hepatocytes to take in the glucose (a monosaccharide) and convert it to glycogen (a polysaccharide). The glycogen is then stored as granules in the cytoplasm of the hepatocytes. The same effect occurs in muscles (see the adjacent TEM).

The two effects of insulin both have the same ultimate result, which is to lower the glucose concentration in the blood or, to put it more simply, to reduce blood glucose.

What happens when blood glucose begins to fall below the set point?

The blood glucose level typically begins to drop below the set point when someone has not eaten for many hours or exercises vigorously for a long time. In either situation, the body needs to use the glycogen made and stored by the liver (and muscle cells). Under these circumstances, α (alpha) cells of the pancreas begin to produce and secrete the hormone glucagon. The glucagon circulates in the bloodstream and stimulates hydrolysis of the granules of glycogen stored in hepatocytes and muscle cells; the hydrolysis produces the monosaccharide glucose. This glucose then enters the bloodstream. The ultimate effect is to increase the glucose concentration in the blood or, to put it more simply, to increase blood glucose (see Figure 6.23).

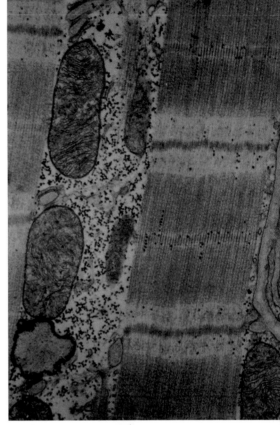

TEM of a cardiac muscle cell. Granules of glycogen can be seen as small black dots. Glucose is stored as glycogen in liver and muscle cells, and later can be reconverted back to glucose. Two mitochondria (ellipses) can be seen on the left.

An endocrinologist is a physician who specializes in disorders associated with one or more hormones that are either under-produced (hyposecretion) or over-produced (hypersecretion). Hormone therapy is a branch of medicine that attempts to correct resulting disorders. Common examples are insulin for diabetes, melatonin for sleep disorders, and reproductive hormones following female menopause.

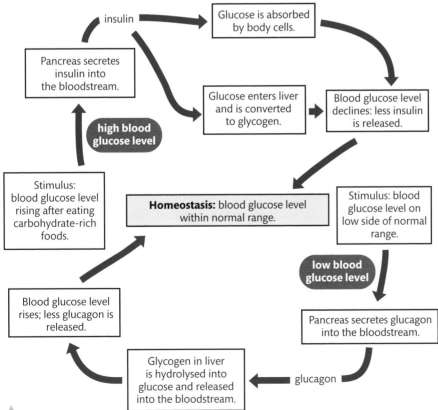

Figure 6.23 Negative feedback control of blood glucose level.

Diabetes

Diabetes is a disease characterized by hyperglycaemia (high blood glucose). Type I is typically caused when the β cells of the pancreas do not produce sufficient insulin; type II diabetes is caused by body cell receptors that do not respond properly to insulin. You will recall that the hormone insulin should result in increased facilitated diffusion of glucose (through channels) into almost all body cells. This diffusion into body cells lowers the amount of glucose in the bloodstream. People who have untreated diabetes have sufficient glucose in their blood, but not in their body cells where it is needed.

Type I diabetes is controlled by the injection of insulin at appropriate times. Type II diabetes is controlled by diet. Uncontrolled diabetes of either type can lead to many serious effects, including:

- damage to the retina, leading to blindness
- kidney failure
- nerve damage
- increased risk of cardiovascular disease
- poor wound healing (and possibly gangrene, thus making amputation necessary).

Type I diabetes is an autoimmune disease. The body's own immune system attacks and destroys the β cells of the pancreas so that little or no insulin is produced by individuals with type I diabetes. Less than 10% of diabetics have this type of the disease. Type I diabetes most often develops in children or young adults, but can develop in people of any age.

The top three countries for the number of people with diabetes are: (1) China (more than 90 million); (2) India (more than 60 million); (3) USA (more than 23 million).

Type II diabetes is the result of body cells no longer responding to insulin as they once did. This is known as insulin resistance. Initially, the pancreas continues to produce a normal amount of insulin, but this level may decrease after a period of time. Type II diabetes is the most common form of diabetes; approximately 90% of diabetics have this type. Type II diabetes is often associated with genetic history, obesity, lack of exercise, and advanced age, and is more common in certain ethnic groups.

Human reproduction

Despite all of the cultural 'trappings' that societies incorporate into the process of human reproduction, it is basically a male gamete (sperm) fertilizing a female gamete (egg or ovum). This cellular union ensures that half of the genetic makeup of the resulting zygote is derived from each parent. Thus, like all forms of sexual reproduction, reproduction in humans serves the bigger purpose of ensuring genetic variation in the species. In both sexes, hormones play a key role in both the development of sexual dimorphism (different body forms of males and females) and the regulation of sexual physiology.

For example, in males the hormone testosterone:

- determines the development of male genitalia during embryonic development
- ensures the development of secondary sex characteristics during puberty
- ensures sperm production as well as maintains sex drive following puberty.

The structures of the male and female reproductive systems are adapted for the production and release of the gametes. In addition, the female reproductive system ensures a suitable location for fertilization and provides an environment for the growth of the embryo/foetus until birth.

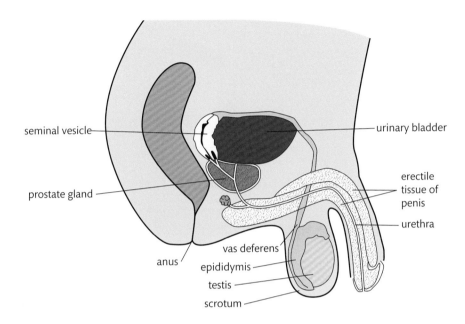

Figure 6.24 Male reproductive system (plus bladder).

Table 6.5 The male reproductive anatomy and function

Male structure	Function(s)
Testis	The male gonads: the sperm are produced here in small tubes called seminiferous tubules
Epididymis	The area where sperm are received, become mature, and are capable of swimming motion via movement of their flagella
Scrotum	Sacs that hold the testes outside the body cavity so that sperm production and maturation can occur at a temperature cooler than body temperature
Vas deferens	A muscular tube that carries mature sperm from the epididymis to the urethra during an ejaculation
Seminal vesicles	Small glands that produce and add seminal fluid to the semen
Prostate gland	A gland that produces much of the seminal fluid, including carbohydrates for the sperm
Penis	An organ that becomes erect as a result of blood engorgement in order to facilitate ejaculation
Urethra	After all the glands have added fluids, this is the tube via which the semen leaves the penis

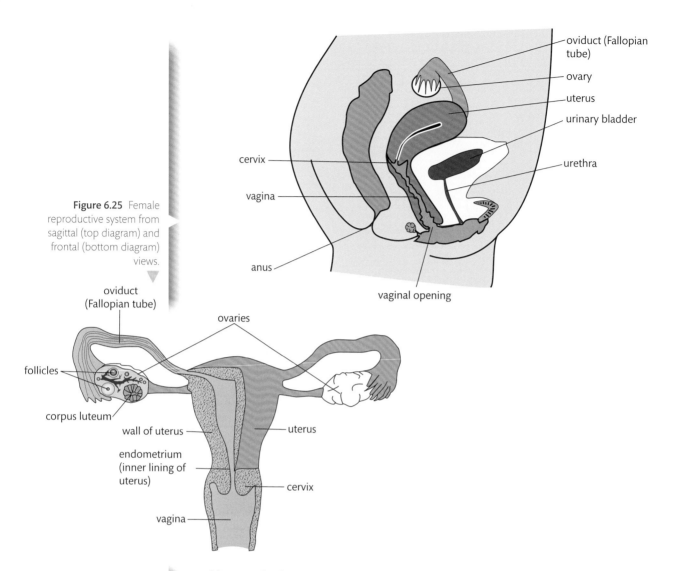

Figure 6.25 Female reproductive system from sagittal (top diagram) and frontal (bottom diagram) views.

Table 6.6 The female reproductive anatomy and function

Female structure	Function(s)
Ovaries	Organs that produce and secrete oestrogen. They also produce and release the ovum (in the form of secondary oocytes). The area where ovulation occurs grows into the corpus luteum, which temporarily produces the hormone progesterone
Fallopian tubes (oviducts)	Ducts that carry the ovum (or early embryo) to the uterus
Uterus	A muscular structure where the early embryo implants and develops if a pregnancy occurs
Endometrium	The highly vascular inner lining of the uterus
Cervix	The lower portion of the uterus, which has an opening to the vagina that allows the sperm to enter for fertilization and provides a pathway for childbirth
Vagina	A muscular tube that leads from the external genitals to the cervix; semen is ejaculated here during sexual intercourse

How does a person become male or female?

You will learn (or have already learnt) that the genetics of becoming male or female depends on whether you inherit an X or a Y chromosome from your father. Because your mother has two X chromosomes, an ovum can only contain an X chromosome. One half of all sperm cells contains an X and one half contains a Y chromosome. If a sperm cell containing an X chromosome fertilizes an ovum, a female is produced. Conversely, if a sperm cell containing a Y chromosome fertilizes an ovum, a male is produced.

So, what happens as a result of the XX or XY combinations? The answer lies in the hormones that are produced by each embryo. Embryos of both sexes are virtually identical until about the eighth week following fertilization. Alleles that interact on both of the X chromosomes of female embryos then result in relatively high oestrogen and progesterone production, resulting in the prenatal development of female reproductive structures. Genes located on the single Y chromosome are

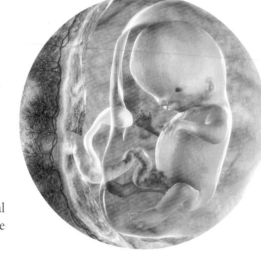

responsible for early testes development and relatively high testosterone production, resulting in male reproductive structures during subsequent foetal development. It is interesting to note that the male and female reproductive structures have common origins in the pre-8-week-old embryo. In other words, the same embryonic tissue that becomes the ovaries gives rise to the testes, the same embryonic tissue that gives rise to the clitoris gives rise to portions of the penis, etc. Another way of expressing this is to say that some female and male reproductive structures are homologous.

It was once assumed that embryos that produced testosterone changed from the 'default' sex of female to male. There is now evidence that each sex requires the influence of specific hormones in order to follow its pathway.

Illustration of a human 8-week-old embryo. The development of internal and external structures characteristic of the sex of the embryo begin about this time. A portion of the placenta is shown on the left, with the umbilical blood vessels within the umbilical cord stretching from the placenta to the embryo.

TOK

How much influence should a government have on family planning? A good example of government influence is the One Child Policy of the People's Republic of China. Some, but not all, couples are fined for having more than one child. The policy has had reasonable success as a population control measure, but is resulting in a disproportionately high percentage of males in certain areas of China.

Leydig cells in each testis produce testosterone. Leydig cells are found between the small tubules (seminiferous tubules) that produce spermatozoa (sperm cells). Two seminiferous tubules are shown in cross-section on the upper and left parts of the figure, with Leydig cells in between. Inside the seminiferous tubules you can see developing spermatozoa with flagella surrounded by cells in various stages of meiosis.

Although males typically experience a lower sperm count as they age, fertility has been documented in men as old as 94 years.

NATURE OF SCIENCE

In Section 6.2 you learnt about the work of William Harvey and how he provided the first valid explanation of how blood circulates in the body. William Harvey was also responsible for much of the early knowledge of a branch of biology that we now call embryology. Embryology is the study of the early development of embryos from fertilized egg to birth. William Harvey's insights were considerable, but lacked information about the earliest embryonic development stages. This was because William Harvey carried out his studies before the microscope had been invented. William Harvey died 17 years before the invention of the microscope.

Role of sex hormones during puberty

When females and males reach puberty, the same hormones that first determined their physical sex are produced and secreted in higher amounts. The increased production of hormones at this time results in the secondary sex characteristics (the attributes that are characteristic of a sex that only appear at puberty).

The secondary sex characteristics of females that arise as a result of increased oestrogen and progesterone production at puberty are:

• enlargement of breasts
• growth of pubic and underarm hair
• widening of hips.

The secondary sex characteristics of males that arise as a result of increased testosterone production at puberty are:

• growth of facial, underarm, chest, and pubic hair
• enlargement of the larynx and associated deepening of the voice
• increased muscle mass
• enlargement of the penis.

The menstrual cycle

Starting at puberty, human females begin a hormonal cycle known as the menstrual cycle. Each cycle lasts, on average, 28 days. The purpose of the menstrual cycle is to time the release of an egg or ovum (ovulation) for possible fertilization and later implantation into the inner lining of the uterus. This implantation must occur when the uterine inner lining (the endometrium) is rich with blood vessels (i.e. highly vascular). The highly vascular endometrium is not maintained if there is no implantation. The breakdown of the blood vessels of the endometrium leads to the menstrual bleeding (menstruation) of a typical cycle. This menstruation is a sign that no pregnancy has occurred.

Figure 6.26 Hormonal summary of the menstrual cycle.

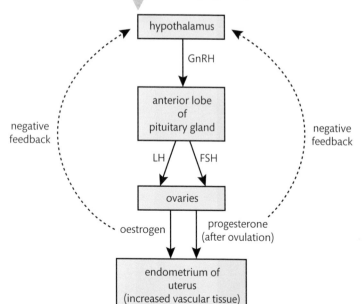

Hormones from the hypothalamus and pituitary gland

A part of a female's brainstem known as the hypothalamus is the regulatory centre of the menstrual cycle. The hypothalamus produces a hormone known as gonadotropin-releasing hormone (GnRH). The target tissue of GnRH is the nearby pituitary gland, and it results in the anterior pituitary producing and secreting two hormones into the bloodstream. These two hormones are follicle-stimulating hormone (FSH) and luteinizing hormone (LH). The target tissues for these two hormones are the ovaries.

The effects of FSH and LH on the ovaries

The hormones FSH and LH have several effects on the ovaries. One of these effects is to increase the production and secretion of another reproductive hormone by the follicle cells of the ovary. This hormone is oestrogen. Like all hormones, oestrogen enters the bloodstream. Its target tissue is the endometrium of the uterus. One effect of oestrogen is an increase in the density of blood vessels of the endometrium, that is, as stated earlier, the endometrium becomes highly vascular. Another effect of oestrogen is to stimulate the pituitary gland to release more FSH and LH. This is the positive feedback loop of the menstrual cycle, specifically these two sets of hormones increasing because of the increase of the other(s).

Another effect of FSH and LH is the production of structures within the ovaries known as Graafian follicles. Within the ovaries are cells known as follicle cells, and the true reproductive cells that are at a stage of development called oocytes. Under the chemical stimulation of FSH and LH, the somewhat randomly arranged follicle cells and oocytes take on a cellular arrangement known as a Graafian follicle.

A spike in the level of FSH and LH leads to ovulation (the release of the oocyte from the Graafian follicle). The oocyte is accompanied by the inner ring of follicle cells of the Graafian follicle. This entire structure is known as a follicle, and typically enters the Fallopian tube soon after ovulation. The outer ring of follicle cells remains within the ovary. These follicle cells begin to produce and secrete another hormone, progesterone. The cells of this outer ring begin to divide and fill in the 'wound' area left by ovulation, and

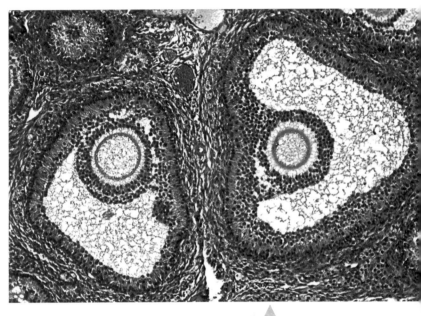

A light micrograph showing a human ovary section. Two Graafian follicles are visible, with an oocyte at the centre of each (two inner circles).

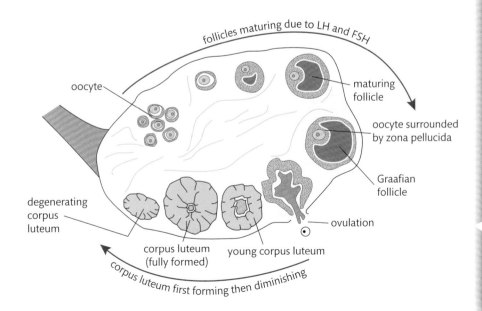

Figure 6.27 Ovary events during a single menstrual cycle. Twenty-eight days of ovarian events are being shown with a single ovary as if in time lapse.

333

this forms a glandular structure known as the corpus luteum. The corpus luteum will be hormonally active (producing progesterone) for only 10–12 days after ovulation. Progesterone is a hormone that maintains the thickened, highly vascular endometrium. As long as progesterone continues to be produced, the endometrium will not break down and an embryo will still be able to implant. In addition, the high levels of both oestrogen and progesterone at the same time provide a negative feedback signal to the hypothalamus. The hypothalamus does not produce GnRH when the oestrogen and progesterone levels are high, so FSH and LH remain at levels that are not conducive to the production of another Graafian follicle during this time.

Assuming there is no pregnancy, the corpus luteum begins to break down after 10–12 days, and this leads to a decline in both progesterone and oestrogen levels. As both of these hormone levels fall, the highly vascular endometrium can no longer be maintained. The capillaries and small blood vessels begin to rupture and menstruation begins. The drop in progesterone and oestrogen also signals the hypothalamus to begin secreting GnRH, and thus another menstrual cycle begins. Because the menstrual cycle is a cycle, there is no true beginning or ending point. The first day of menstruation is designated as the first day of the menstrual cycle simply because this is an event that can be easily discerned (see Figure 6.28).

Figure 6.28 Events occurring during a 28-day menstrual cycle. Note that these events are all aligned on the same time scale. Ovulation and possible fertilization occur near the middle of the cycle.

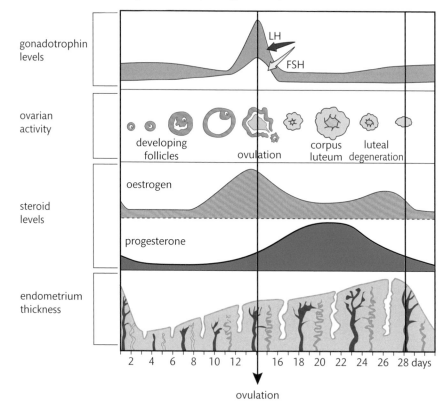

In vitro fertilization (IVF)

Natural fertilization typically occurs in one of a female's Fallopian tubes 24–48 hours after ovulation. The resulting zygote begins to divide by mitosis, and takes several more days to travel down the Fallopian tube to the endometrium of the uterus. When the embryo reaches the endometrium, it has already divided mitotically many times and is a ball of about 100 cells. The embryo, called a blastocyst at this stage, will then implant in the highly vascular tissue of the endometrium.

Some couples are unable to bear children. There is a wide variety of possible reasons for infertility, including:

• males with low sperm counts
• males with impotence (failure to achieve or maintain an erection)
• females who cannot ovulate normally
• females with blocked Fallopian tubes.

Reproductive technologies have been developed to help overcome these situations. One of the most common of these new technologies is *in vitro* fertilization (IVF).

Hormone therapy

As part of the IVF procedure, a woman must have eggs 'harvested' from her ovaries. In order to ensure the proper timing for this, and to maximize the number of available ova, the woman undergoes about a month of hormone therapy. During the first 2 weeks she injects a drug (or uses a nasal spray of the drug) that suspends her own natural hormones associated with her menstrual cycle. Then for the next 12 days or so she takes hormone injections that include FSH. This ensures that she will produce many Graafian follicles in each ovary and provide many potential ova (oocytes) for harvesting. The production of many more eggs than is typical of a normal menstrual cycle is called superovulation.

When the time is right, several eggs (oocytes) are then harvested surgically. To obtain the sperm cells that are needed for fertilization, the man ejaculates into a container. Harvested eggs are mixed with the sperm cells in separate culture dishes. Microscopic observation reveals which ova are fertilized, and whether the early development appears normal and healthy. Between one and three healthy embryos are later introduced into the woman's uterus for implantation. Any healthy embryos from the culturing phase that are not implanted can be frozen and used later if another implantation procedure is needed.

TOK Screening the embryos used in IVF for certain genetic conditions is becoming a common practice. Screening for desirable traits is possible, and may soon become a routine part of the IVF procedures offered by medical clinics. How much will the course of human evolution be effected by such screening practices?

NATURE OF SCIENCE

Always consider the source! If you do a web search for IVF, many of the sites you will encounter will be from private clinics that offer IVF as a paid service. This doesn't mean the information on those sites is incorrect, but it does mean you need to consider the possible bias behind the information.

Section summary

• The level of glucose dissolved in the bloodstream is known as the blood glucose concentration. Blood glucose needs to remain within a fairly narrow range. A pair of hormones (insulin and glucagon) is secreted from the pancreas to help maintain glucose within this normal homeostatic range.
• The thyroid gland secretes a hormone known as thyroxin that regulates metabolic rate and helps maintain body temperature.
• Appetite is controlled by a hormone (leptin) secreted by cells in adipose (fat) tissue.
• A small gland within the brain known as the pineal gland secretes melatonin to help control our 24-hour cycle known as the circadian rhythm.
• An embryonic male has a gene on the Y chromosome that causes the development of testes and subsequent secretion of testosterone.

To learn more about this chapter, go to the hotlinks site, search for the title or ISBN, and click on Chapter 6.

- Testosterone leads to embryonic development of male sex organs (genitalia) and post-puberty production of sperm and male secondary sex characteristics.
- An embryonic female produces oestrogen and progesterone, leading to prenatal female reproductive organs and post-puberty secondary female sex characteristics.
- The female menstrual cycle leads to ovulation and preparation of the uterus for possible implantation. This cycle is controlled by feedback mechanisms involving pituitary and ovary hormones.

Exercises

17 If possible, without looking back though this chapter, give a very brief description of the function of each of these hormones: insulin, glucagon, thyroxin, leptin, and melatonin.

18 What is an example of a positive feedback loop in the menstrual cycle?

19 What is an example of a negative feedback loop in the menstrual cycle?

Practice questions

1 The first figure shows a cross-section through the small intestine, and the second figure shows an enlarged longitudinal section through a single villus.

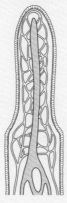

Using these diagrams, outline **three** ways in which the structure of the small intestine is related to its function of absorbing food.

(Total 3 marks)

2 Draw a diagram of the human digestive system.

(Total 4 marks)

3 Explain the relationship between the structure and function of arteries, veins, and capillaries.

(Total 9 marks)

4 What are the structures labelled I and II on the diagram of the heart?

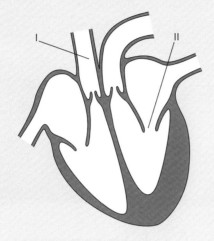

A I is the pulmonary artery and II is the atrioventricular valve.

B I is the pulmonary vein and II is the atrioventricular valve.

C I is the pulmonary artery and II is the semilunar valve.

D I is the pulmonary vein and II is the semilunar valve.

(Total 1 mark)

5 Explain why antibiotics are effective against bacteria but not viruses.

(Total 3 marks)

6 A blood clot contains a network of protein. What is the protein?

A Fibrin

B Fibrinogen

C Haemoglobin

D Thrombin

(Total 1 mark)

7 What happens during inhalation?

A Both the external intercostal muscles and the diaphragm contract.

B The internal intercostal muscles contract and the diaphragm relaxes.

C The external intercostal muscles relax and the diaphragm contracts.

D Both the internal intercostal muscles and the diaphragm relax.

(Total 1 mark)

8 Describe the principles of synaptic transmission in the nervous system.

(Total 6 marks)

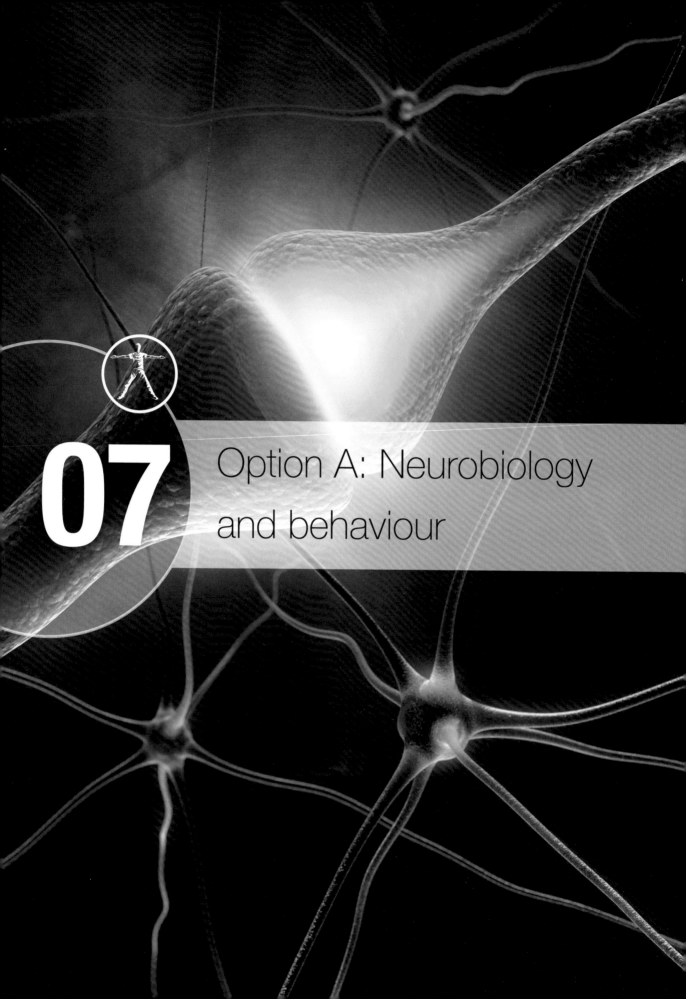

07

Option A: Neurobiology and behaviour

Essential ideas

A.1 Modification of neurones starts in the earliest stages of embryogenesis and continues to the final years of life.

A.2 The parts of the brain specialize in different functions.

A.3 Living organisms are able to detect changes in the environment.

Active neurones in the brain are communicating using chemical messaging.

Do video games have a long-term effect on brain functioning? Does learning a second language make your brain more efficient? Scientists, using both animal models and new technologies, are now discovering the answers to these questions. For example, Yang Wang, a radiologist from the School of Medicine in Indiana, is using functional magnetic resonance imaging (fMRI) to study the brains of young adults watching violent video games. Technology has also given us the ability to collect data on how neurones migrate in the developing brain and communicate with each other. We now know that the brain is plastic throughout our lives. It keeps on being moulded through new experiences, like learning a new language. Research on how drugs affect the brain has allowed medications to be developed that improve the lives of people with biochemical imbalances. Animal models have helped us understand the problem of addiction.

The study of neurogenesis in the embryonic brain has provided us with data showing that neurones are producing and responding to chemical messages. Nerve cells communicate with each other using molecules. As the immature nerve cells migrate to their final home and the brain matures, millions of connections are formed and then lost. Those connections that are reinforced by experience remain as learning and memory.

A.1 Neural development

NATURE OF SCIENCE

Use models as representations of the real world: developmental neuroscience uses a variety of animal models.

Understandings:

- The neural tube of embryonic chordates is formed by infolding of ectoderm followed by elongation of the tube.
- Neurones are initially produced by differentiation in the neural tube.
- Immature neurones migrate to a final location.
- An axon grows from each immature neurone in response to chemical stimuli.
- Some axons extend beyond the neural tube to reach other parts of the body.
- A developing neurone forms multiple synapses.
- Synapses that are not used do not persist.
- Neural pruning involves the loss of unused neurones.
- The plasticity of the nervous system allows it to change with experience.

Applications and skills:

- Application: Incomplete closure of the embryonic neural tube can cause *spina bifida*.
- Application: Events such as strokes may promote reorganization of brain function.
- Skill: Annotation of a diagram of embryonic tissues in *Xenopus*, used as an animal model, during neurulation.

Guidance

- *Terminology relating to embryonic brain areas or nervous system divisions is not required.*

Neural tube formation

Have you ever wondered how all the organs in our body form from just one fertilized egg? The study of this development, from a fertilized egg to a fully formed organism, is called embryogenesis. Scientists have come to understand the processes of embryogenesis by studying various animal models. Because the ultimate goal is to understand embryogenesis in humans, animals in the same phylum with similar developmental patterns have been studied. Humans belong to the phylum Chordata (chordates) and are in the subphylum Vertebrata (vertebrates). Vertebrates, which include fish, amphibians, reptiles, birds, and mammals, are all therefore considered as possible animal models. A frog is an animal that has been studied extensively because it is (or was) readily available and can be collected from local ponds by scientists. During the earliest part of the 20th century, chicks were added to the study of embryogenesis. Birds are warm-blooded vertebrates, and fertile chick eggs are available all over the world for scientists to use, with very little expense involved. Historically, scientists moved away from the study of 'lower' chordates such as frogs to the study of 'higher' chordates such as chicks, with the aim of understanding normal and abnormal embryogenesis.

One of the benefits of these studies of embryogenesis is that it enabled scientists to learn the key principles of neural development. Using the frog embryo as an example, we can see how the nervous system of an embryonic chordate develops.

After fertilization, cells of the frog embryo develop into three distinct tissue layers: the outermost layer (ectoderm), which will become the brain and nervous system of the adult frog; the inner layer (endoderm), which forms the lining of the gut and the lining of other organs; and the middle layer (mesoderm), which develops into the skeletal, reproductive, circulatory, excretory, and muscular system of the adult frog. A cavity in the centre of the frog (*Xenopus*) embryo is a primitive gut called the archenteron.

Table 7.1 The names of the three embryonic tissue layers of *Xenopus* (a frog)

Ecto (outer)	Derm (skin)
Meso (middle)	Derm (skin)
Endo (inner)	Derm (skin)

From these layers, one of the first organs to develop is the neural tube, which will eventually become the brain and spinal cord of the frog. In embryos, the presence of one tissue that is developing causes the development of another tissue. In this case, the presence of the notochord, a mesodermal tissue, causes the ectoderm to develop into a neural plate. As embryogenesis continues, the neural plate folds in, closes, and becomes the neural tube. The neural tube then elongates and becomes the brain and spinal cord of the frog.

Here is a picture of the embryonic tissues of *Xenopus* (a species of frog).

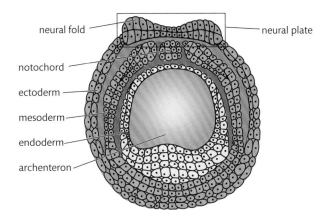

neural fold — neural plate
notochord
ectoderm
mesoderm
endoderm
archenteron

Figure 7.1 Embryonic tissues in *Xenopus*. Campbell and Reece 1999

··

CHALLENGE YOURSELF

1 Redraw the picture of the embryonic tissues of *Xenopus* and label it without looking at Figure 7.1. Annotate the figure you have drawn. To annotate you must describe the fate of each part as it develops into the adult *Xenopus* frog. Annotate using a table of your own design.

··

NATURE OF SCIENCE

What are model organisms? Model organisms are organisms that are easy to study, and are used widely by scientists studying in a similar field. The following table will give you an idea of what organisms provide good models for particular studies, and why.

Table 7.2 Examples of model organisms

Field of study	Characteristics needed for the model/why the species provides a good model	Suitable species
Genetics	Large numbers and short generation times	Fruit fly Baker's yeast Nematode worm
Developmental biology	Robust embryos that are easily manipulated	Chicken African clawed frog (*Xenopus*)
Genomic studies, such as genes that cause diseases	60% of human genetic diseases studied have a counterpart in the fruit fly and nematode	Fruit fly Nematode
Comparative genomics	The mouse genome is similarly organized to the human genome	Mouse

To learn more about model organisms, go to the hotlinks site, search for the title or ISBN, and click on Chapter 7: Section A.1.

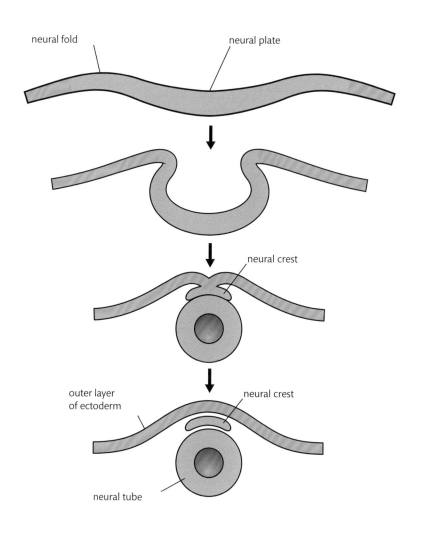

Figure 7.2 Formation of the neural tube from the neural plate. Campbell and Reece 1999

Spina bifida

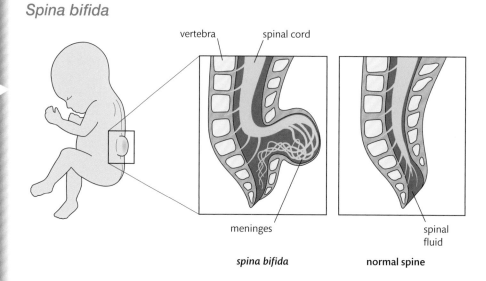

Figure 7.3 *Spina bifida* is caused by incomplete closing of the neural tube. http://babygilbertfund.com/

The closure of the neural tube does not take place simultaneously all along the body of the embryo. The area where the brain forms is well advanced compared with the caudal (tail) area. Closure of the neural tube in the tail area occurs more slowly and may not even completely close during embryonic development. This failure to close the human posterior (caudal) neural tube at day 27 of development results in the condition of *spina bifida*. How severe this is depends on how much of the spinal cord remains exposed.

Neurogenesis and migration of neurones

The neurones of the central nervous system (CNS) in the developing vertebrate embryo originate in the neural tube. Neuroblasts are immature neurones that are the precursor cells of neurones. The process of differentiation from neuroblast to neurone is called neurogenesis. As soon as the neural tube begins to transform into specific brain parts, two major families of cells begin to differentiate. These two types of cells are neurones and glial cells. Neurones carry messages, while glial cells do not carry messages. Ninety per cent of brain cells are glial and have many functions. One important function is physical and nutritional support of the neurone. Most of the new neurones in the human cortex are formed between the fifth week and the fifth month of development.

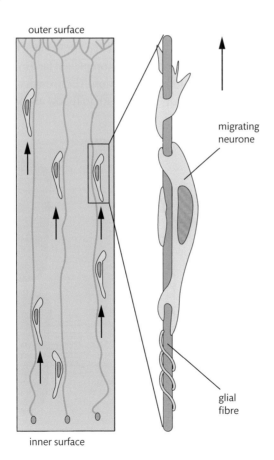

Glial cells provide a scaffolding network along which the immature neurones migrate. Along this scaffolding of the glial cells, immature nerve cells can migrate to their final location, mature, and send out their axons and dendrites.

Closure of the human neural tube seems to be controlled by a combination of genetic and environmental factors. Certain genes have been found to control the formation of the mammalian neural tube, but dietary factors also seem to be critical. The US health service recommends that women take supplemental folic acid during pregnancy to prevent neural tube defects. One estimate suggests that using vitamin B_{12} as a supplement can prevent 50% of neural tube defects.

Helen Cooper and her team at the Queensland Brain Institute have identified signalling molecules that may be used to promote the birth of new neurones, which will then migrate to damaged regions of the brain. This could be a major step forward in achieving functional recovery in a damaged brain.

Figure 7.4 Scaffolding glial cells allow neurones to reach their final destination.

Neuroblasts are cells in the embryo that will become neurones.

Two cell types formed by neurogenesis are neurones, which carry messages around the brain, and glial (glue) cells, which provide the support and the nutrition for the neurones.

'Glia' means glue in Greek. The word neurogenesis comes from 'neuro' meaning nerve cell and 'genesis' meaning beginning.

Axons of the neurone contact a favourable surface.

Axons grow 1 mm per day.

Axons respond to chemical messages from the target cell.

Axons form synapses with the target cell.

The signal molecule from the target cell is called CAM.

The growth cone of the axon has CAM-specific receptors. (A mnemonic device is: Can the Axon Make it to the right target using its receptors).

The target cell also secretes chemoattractive or chemorepellent factors.

The axon will grow towards the target cell if the message is chemoattractive.

Can you draw a labelled cartoon to help you remember the steps of axon growth?

Neuroblasts differentiate into neurones. Neurones grow towards their target cells. The target cells give chemical signals, e.g. CAM, to the neurone.

Axon growth

As the neurone grows, it will send out one long axon moving towards a distant area. At the tip of the axon is a growth cone, which directs the axon. In cell cultures it is possible to watch axons grow. When an axon contacts an unfavourable surface it contracts, but with a favourable surface it persists. An axon can move forward at about 1 mm a day.

When neurones have reached their final location, synaptic connections must be made with their target cells. These target cells produce chemical messages that the neurone responds to. The signal molecule from the target cell can be secreted into the extracellular environment or carried on the target cell's surface. The neurone responds to the chemical messages by forming synapses with the target cell.

Certain molecules from the target cell can act as signals to the growth cone. One type of signal molecule is called a cell adhesion molecule (CAM). CAMs are located on the surface of cells in the growth environment of the axon. The growth cone of the axon has a receptor called a CAM-specific receptor, so that when a CAM and its receptor recognize each other, chemical messaging takes place within the neurone. This results in the activation of enzymes within the neurone that contribute to the elongation of the axon.

Some receptors on a growth cone can also pick up the signal of molecules secreted by the target cell that diffuse into the extracellular environment. These are called chemotrophic factors. These factors can be attractive or repellent. Chemoattractive factors attract the axon to grow towards it. Chemorepellent factors repel the axon, so that the axon will elongate in a different direction. The growth cone responds to the various chemical stimuli that show it what path to follow and what connections to make.

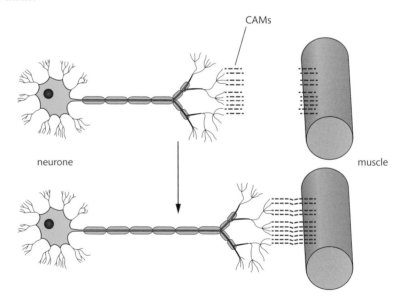

Figure 7.5 Signal molecules called CAMs attract the axons to their target muscle cells.

Some axons extend beyond the neural tube

Some neurones, for example mammalian motor neurones, have to send their axons out of the area of the neural tube and travel much further in their journey towards other target cells. This gives the mammal the ability to control voluntary muscular movement. The motor neurones must extend their axons out of the CNS (the brain and spinal cord) in order to form these circuits. Newly developed motor neurones, which extend axons from the spinal cord, are some of the longest neurones in the body. During embryogenesis, these cells follow the same pathways to synapse with muscle targets as other neurones located within the CNS. The muscles that need to attract the axons will produce CAMs. The CAM receptor in the axon will activate enzymes to cause the growth cone of the axon to grow towards the muscle.

Multiple synapses

A huge number of synapses are formed during early brain development. Imagine if you could not remember your password and were desperate to download a movie. You would try all of the passwords you have ever used until one of them worked perfectly. A developing neurone does the same sort of thing, trying out all the possible connections to see which is the best fit. A single nerve cell can make a myriad of connections with its neighbouring nerve cells at the many points of branching that radiate from the main cell body. Not every cell will be the best partner. The job of the neurone is to find the best fit. In other words, only those synapses that have a function will survive, and the rest will gradually weaken until they disappear. Just think how easy it is to forget a password that you never use.

The neurones of the brain try to form a synapse with any nearby target cell, and then attempt to test out the connection. Will the connection work? Many do not, and those connections are eliminated. When the connections are between functionally compatible neurones, the result is a strengthening of communication.

Neuroscientist Z. Josh Huang, at Cold Springs Harbor Laboratory, in an article published in the *Journal of Neuroscience*, described the behaviour of neurones making tentative connections with almost every available partner. Lots of partners are tried, and eventually one is found that is compatible. Huang goes on to state that one mechanism at work during these rapid connections is controlled by a type of neural adhesion molecule that is recruited to the site of the connection. This adhesion molecule is also a type of CAM, called immunoglobulin CAM (IgCAM), and it acts like a lock and key. CAMs form a physical but reversible glue-like bond between the tentative projection of one cell's axon and the receiving structure on a neighbouring cell. Eventually, many of these connections are lost because it turns out they are not with the right partner cell.

Some synapses do not persist

Just as you would not use any passwords that do not work, the neurone will not keep any synapses that do not work. Most of our information about how the growth cones of an axon find their way to the target cell comes from the study of neurones that have travelled to a muscle from the spinal cord. Where they connect is called the neuromuscular junction. The axons form synapses that compete for the ability to innervate a muscle fibre. Specific molecules from the neurones and muscles facilitate these connections. The strongest connection will survive, and the rest are eliminated.

A muscle fibre is the site of a heated competition, with multiple synapses trying to win. Eventually, the connection made will be the best one between one motor neurone and the muscle fibre. As development proceeds, the other synapses are eliminated. Finally, the strength of the remaining synapse is increased. This is how the circuitry of the nervous system is formed.

Even new muscle cells in the embryo are producing CAM, attempting to attract a growing neurone from the spinal cord.

The growth cone in the axon will respond by growing towards the muscle cell.

An axon that begins in the spinal cord and innervates a muscle in the foot can be as long as 1 m (3 feet).

The word synapse is 113 years old. It was first coined in a textbook of physiology written in 1897. The author, Michael Foster, derived the word from the Greek words 'syn' and 'haptein', which mean together and clasp, respectively.

345

Neural pruning

Pruning results in the overall number of neurones being reduced. When an infant is 2 or 3 years old, he or she has 15 000 synapses per neurone. This is twice as many as in an adult brain. Neural pruning eliminates axons that are not being used. The purpose of neural pruning seems to be to remove the simpler connections made in childhood and replace them with the more complex wiring made in adulthood. As we have seen with other descriptions of neurone activity, pruning seems to follow the 'use it or lose it' principle. Synapses that are rarely used are eliminated, and those with strong connections are maintained. The removal of unneeded connections leads to improvement in brain efficiency.

Scientists supported by the National Institutes of Health in the USA have been studying pruning using the mouse as a model organism. They have discovered that cells called microglia, a type of glial cell, can prune unused synapses. This precise elimination of synapses that are unused and the strengthening of the more active synapses is a key part of normal brain development. Researchers hypothesize that microglia select a synapse for removal based on the inactivity of the synapse.

Worked example

What is neural pruning and why is it important?

Solution

The neurones of the brain try to form a synapse with any nearby target cell and then attempt to test out the connection. Will the connection work? Many do not and the connection is eliminated. This is neural pruning. When the connections are between functionally compatible neurones, the result is a strengthening of communication.

The purpose seems to be removal of the simpler connections of childhood and replacement by more complex wiring present in adulthood.

The plasticity of the nervous system

Brain plasticity is the concept, now widely accepted, that the brain has the ability to change and adapt as a result of experience. Until 1960, researchers believed that only the brain of an infant or child could change, and that by adulthood the brain was unchangeable. Modern research has demonstrated that the adult brain does have plasticity. It can rewire itself after suffering massive strokes. Today we understand that the brain can create new neurones and new pathways. Scientists have shown that plasticity can vary with age, and that it is influenced by both environment and heredity. Thus we now know that the brain and nervous system are not static as previously thought.

The brain exhibits two types of plasticity: functional and structural. Functional plasticity is the ability of the brain to move functions from a damaged area to an undamaged area. Structural plasticity refers to the fact that the brain can actually change its physical structure as a result of learning.

An example of a functional shift can be illustrated by studying a tennis player who has suffered a stroke and has a paralysed left arm. During his rehabilitation, his good arm and hand are immobilized by the physical therapist, so that he can't use them.

If a young child is deprived of stimulation, certain neurone pathways and synapses may be discarded. This is neural pruning. Synapses that are highly active will be preserved, while those that are underactive will be pruned. As we have seen, a 2–3-year-old child has the most synapses. Early childhood is the best time to learn language skills, when the excess synapses provide the raw material for the language experience to act on. Research into bilingualism suggests that exposure to more than one language is an excellent means of cognitive strengthening when young.

To learn more about brain plasticity, go to the hotlinks site, search for the title or ISBN, and click on Chapter 7: Section A.1.

The tennis player is then given the task of cleaning tables. At first the task is impossible for him, but slowly his bad arm begins to remember how to move, and eventually he is back playing tennis. The functions in the brain areas that were killed by the stroke are transferred to healthy regions. New connections are formed between the intact neurones; these neurones are stimulated by activity.

An example of a structural shift in the brain is has been shown in a study of London taxi drivers by McGill University scientists. By observing London taxi drivers using magnetic resonance imaging (MRI) techniques to obtain images of their brains, the scientists discovered that experienced drivers have a larger hippocampus area in their brain than other drivers. This seems to be because their job needs their brain to store large amounts of information and to have good spatial understanding. London taxi drivers have to pass an extensive test on 320 standard routes throughout the city before they can start working. Most drivers prepare for the test over 34 months by practising the routes on a moped. MRIs have shown a structural change in the hippocampus of these taxi drivers, which increases with the length of time a driver has been doing the routes.

Worked example

What is adult brain plasticity? What is the difference between structural and functional plasticity?

Solution

- The adult brain can change and adapt as a result of experience.
- The adult brain can rewire after a massive stroke.
- Functional plasticity is the ability to move functions from a damaged area to an undamaged area.
- Structural plasticity means that the brain can actually change its physical structure as a result of learning.

Stroke may promote reorganization of brain function

Neuroimaging studies on stroke patients suggest that functional and structural reorganization of the brain takes place during recovery. This includes axon sprouting (new connections between axons), post-stroke neurogenesis (migration of new neurones to the site of the injury), differentiation of immature glial cells, and new associations with neurones and blood vessels.

Does the brain do this all by itself, or do we have some input into how this reorganization takes place? We know that after a stroke there are both chemical and physical changes in the pathways. What can be done to promote recovery?

In animal models with primates, it has been shown that improvement can be made with intervention. After a stroke resulting in weak hand movement in monkeys, the monkeys that did exercises with food rewards improved more rapidly than those that did not exercise. The part of the brain that improved shoulder movement took over the movement of the hand. The brain had reorganized itself in those monkeys that had received therapy.

In addition to animal models, new technologies have increased our knowledge of how the brain recovers from a stroke. Functional magnetic resonance imaging (fMRI), positron emission tomography (PET), brain mapping (magnetoencephalography, MEG) and other technologies have unravelled the many brain changes that take place in response to rehabilitation strategies and drugs. A common condition that results from a stroke is partial or complete loss of language function, called post-stroke aphasia (PSA). It had been estimated previously that the window for improvement of PSA was the first year following the stroke. Results of modern brain imaging studies have demonstrated that the recovery of language function can occur well beyond this period. These brain imaging and mapping techniques help clinicians and researchers design better strategies to enhance recovery.

Worked example

Can you remember? Write the correct term to describe each of the following statements.

1 An animal model used in the study of neurulation.
2 Can result in both structural and functional reorganization of the brain.
3 The ability of the brain to move from a damaged to an undamaged area.
4 The ability of the brain to change its physical structure.
5 Elimination of axons not being used.
6 The brain can rewire after a stroke.
7 Incomplete closure of the neural tube.

Solutions

1 *Xenopus.*
2 Stroke.
3 Functional shift.
4 Structural shift.
5 Neural pruning.
6 Plasticity.
7 *Spina bifida.*

Two Mayo Clinic scientists have worked as a team to address the problem of regeneration of nerve tissue in spinal cord injury patients. Anthony J. Windebank, a neurologist, has implanted stem cells into damaged nerve tissue. He manipulated the stem cells so that they would promote nerve regeneration. The stem cells delivered the neural growth factors needed for nerve regeneration, but something else was needed for the spinal cord injury to be repaired. In order for the axons to find and connect with an appropriate target cell, a scaffold was needed. Michael J. Yaszemski, a biomedical engineer, was able to create such scaffolding. He designed tubing that acts as a synthetic, biodegradable scaffold. This scaffold can connect severed axons. Working together, these two scientists have pioneered a technique to insert stem cells into scaffold implants in injured spinal cords in animals. Eventually, this work will proceed to human trials.

Section summary

- Neurogenesis is the development of the brain and spinal cord from the ectoderm of an embryo. The ectoderm folds into the neural tube. Nerve cells (neurones) are formed by differentiation from the neural tube.
- Neurones grow towards target cells. Neurones respond to chemical messages produced by the target cells. The chemical messages are called CAM.

TOK

Gregoire Courtine, who works at the Brain Mind Institute in Switzerland, has decided to switch the paradigm for those who have spinal cord damage and paraplegia. The switch is to change the view of the patient from a 'non-functioning person' to a 'person who is in a dormant state'. He describes his idea by imagining an injured patient as a car with all the parts (muscle, bone, etc.) present but the engine turned off. His goal is to produce a pharmaceutical cocktail to prepare the nerves for stimulation. Next he will surgically implant a mechanical object that will communicate between the brain and the spinal cord. Eventually the person will be able to move and walk again. He has called his research programme the 'rewalk' programme. How is this a new paradigm of how paraplegics are viewed?

To learn more about work with spinal cord injuries and see the work of Professor Courtine, go to the hotlinks site, search for the title or ISBN, and click on Chapter 7: Section A.1.

- During brain development a large number of synapses are formed between neurones. Only the strongest synapses are used and strengthened and the rest are eliminated. Elimination of some connections is called neural pruning.
- Modern research has shown that brains of all ages have plasticity. Functional plasticity is the ability of the brain to move functions from a damaged area to an undamaged area. Structural plasticity means that the brain can change its physical structure as a result of learning.

Always include examples in answers to compare and contrast questions. Remember that compare and contrast means to give similarities and differences between two or more items, referring to both of them throughout.

Exercises

1 Describe *spina bifida*.
2 Outline the differentiation and migration of immature neurones.
3 Explain neural pruning.
4 Compare and contrast functional and structural plasticity of the brain.

A.2 The human brain

NATURE OF SCIENCE

Use models as representations of the real world: the sensory homunculus and motor homunculus are models of the relative space human body parts occupy on the somatosensory cortex and the motor cortex.

Understandings:

- The anterior part of the neural tube expands to form the brain.
- Different parts of the brain have specific roles.
- The autonomic nervous system controls involuntary processes in the body using centres located mainly in the brainstem.
- The cerebral cortex forms a larger portion of the brain and is more highly developed in humans than other animals.
- The human cerebral cortex has become enlarged principally by an increase in total area with extensive folding to accommodate it within the cranium.
- The cerebral hemispheres are responsible for higher order functions.
- The left cerebral hemisphere receives sensory input from sensory receptors in the right side of the body and the right side of the visual field in both eyes, and vice versa for the right hemisphere.
- The left cerebral hemisphere controls muscle contraction in the right side of the body, and vice versa for the right hemisphere.
- Brain metabolism requires large energy inputs.

Applications and skills:

- Application: Visual cortex, Broca's area, nucleus accumbens as areas of the brain with specific functions.
- Application: Swallowing, breathing, and heart rate as examples of activities coordinated by the medulla.
- Application: Use of the pupil reflex to evaluate brain damage.
- Application: Use of animal experiments, autopsy, lesions, and fMRI to identify the role of different brain parts.
- Skill: Identification of parts of the brain in a photograph, diagram, or scan of the brain.
- Skill: Analysis of correlations between body size and brain size in different animals.

Guidance
- *Image of the brain should include the medulla oblongata, cerebellum, hypothalamus, pituitary gland, and cerebral hemispheres.*
- *Although specific functions can be attributed to certain areas, brain imagery shows that some activities are spread in many areas, and that the brain can even reorganize itself following a disturbance such as a stroke.*

The neural tube expands to form the brain

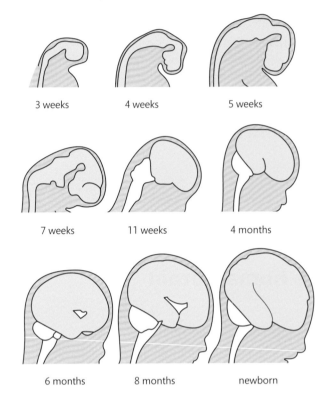

3 weeks 4 weeks 5 weeks

7 weeks 11 weeks 4 months

6 months 8 months newborn

Figure 7.6 The neural tube expands to form the brain.

From the study of neurogenesis in Section A.1, you should now be familiar with the neural tube and how it is formed. To form the brain, nerve cells migrate to the outer edge of the neural tube and cause the walls to thicken. Eventually, the neural tube develops into the entire central nervous system: the brain and the spinal cord. The anterior end of the neural tube (forebrain) expands dramatically into the cerebral hemispheres. The posterior end of the neural tube develops into the other brain parts and the spinal cord. Neural development is one of the first systems to begin developing and one of the last systems to finish developing before birth. Brain development is one of the most complex systems in the embryo.

Researchers from the University of Texas Health Science Center in San Antonio have reported that eating less during early pregnancy impairs foetal brain development in a non-human primate model.

Different parts of the brain have specific roles

The brain is the most complex organ in the body. This jelly-like group of tissues, weighing 1.4 kg, produces our thoughts, feelings, actions, and memories. It contains an amazing 100 billion neurones, with thousands of synapses making the amount of connectivity literally mind-boggling. New connections are formed every day of our lives. These new connections store memories, learning, and personality traits. Some connections are lost and others are gained. No two brains are identical, and your brain continues to change throughout your life.

The brain regulates and monitors unconscious body processes such as blood pressure, heart rate, and breathing. It receives a flood of messages from the senses, and responds by controlling balance, muscle coordination, and most voluntary movement. Other parts of the brain deal with speech, emotions, and problem solving. Your brain allows you to think and dream.

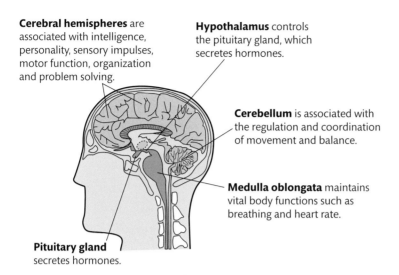

Cerebral hemispheres are associated with intelligence, personality, sensory impulses, motor function, organization and problem solving.

Hypothalamus controls the pituitary gland, which secretes hormones.

Cerebellum is associated with the regulation and coordination of movement and balance.

Medulla oblongata maintains vital body functions such as breathing and heart rate.

Pituitary gland secretes hormones.

Figure 7.7 Parts of the human brain.

The following bullet points would be suitable text for annotating a diagram of the brain.

- Cerebral hemispheres act as the integrating centre for higher complex functions such as learning, memory, and emotions.
- The hypothalamus maintains homeostasis, coordinating the nervous and the endocrine systems. It synthesizes hormones which are stored in the posterior pituitary and releases factors regulating the anterior pituitary.
- The cerebellum is often called 'the little brain' because it has two hemispheres and a highly folded surface. It coordinates unconscious functions, such as movement and balance.
- The medulla oblongata controls automatic and homeostatic activities, such as swallowing, digestion, vomiting, breathing, and heart activity.
- The pituitary gland has two lobes, the posterior lobe and the anterior lobe. Both are controlled by the hypothalamus, and both produce and secrete hormones regulating many body functions.

Role of the medulla

The medulla oblongata contains a 'swallowing centre' that coordinates the muscles of the mouth, pharynx (throat), and larynx (Adam's apple), so that a bolus of food will move down the oesophagus to your stomach during swallowing, and not down your windpipe (trachea).

The medulla oblongata controls breathing by monitoring the level of carbon dioxide in the blood. If there is an increase in carbon dioxide (meaning low oxygen), the rate and depth of breathing are increased so that more oxygen is take in.

The medulla oblongata is also the cardiovascular centre for the body. The heart rate will slow down if it is activated by the cardioinhibitory centre or speed up if it is activated by the cardioaccelerator centre. When you first begin to exercise, the cardioinhibitory centre stops causing an increase in heart rate. During more strenuous exercise, the heart rate increases by direct stimulation of the cardioacclerator centre.

CHALLENGE YOURSELF

2 Study Figure 7.7, then try to draw a picture of the brain without looking at it.
   - After you have drawn the picture, put on the labels.
   - Every label must have a line leading exactly to the part it is referring to.
   - Use straight lines and a ruler. Never use arrowheads when labelling. Only use arrows when you are writing about a process such as photosynthesis.
   - Next annotate the diagram. Annotate means to write the function of each labelled part.

Table 7.3 The role of the medulla

Swallowing	Coordinates muscles of mouth, throat, and larynx
Breathing	Monitors carbon dioxide in the blood. If carbon dioxide is high, your breathing will increase
Heart rate	Speeds up or decreases the rate in response to the autonomic nervous system (see Figure 7.11)

Identifying the role of different brain parts

The study of the complex information processing system that includes the brain and the nervous system is called neuroscience or neurobiology. New technology has provided us with valuable insights into the functions of our brains. Animal experimentation has allowed us to see exactly what causes some of our behaviour. Brain injuries have been studied to show what occurs when parts of the brain are damaged. Brain scans using fMRI have revealed the effects of addictive drugs on the brain. There are published studies of how pain is perceived, and how endorphins act as painkillers.

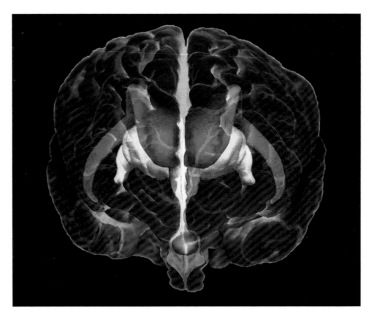

Brain lesions

One method of studying the brain is to look at people who have had injuries to particular areas of their brain. Lesions in identifiable areas of the brain tell us indirectly about the function of those parts of the brain. Some lesions that have been studied were in either the right or the left half of the brain, and have provided us with information about the differences between the two halves.

The brain is divided into the left and the right hemispheres. These hemispheres are connected by a thick band of axons called the corpus callosum. The two hemispheres do not have exactly the same functions.

The left hemisphere contains areas important for all forms of communication. Left-hemisphere damage can result from a stroke (broken or blocked blood vessels in the

TOK

New technology to study the human brain has been advancing at a rapid rate. Does this new knowledge of the human brain have intrinsic value or is it a double-edged sword that can be used for good and bad? Just as nuclear physics might be used to develop cheap sources of energy or to make bombs, could human brain research have both good and bad consequences? What are some of the potential benefits of new technology that has been developed to study the human brain? What are some of the potential hazards?

This is a coloured composite three-dimensional functional magnetic resonance imaging (fMRI) and computed tomography (CT) scan of the human brain, seen from the front. The ventricles (pink) circulate the cerebrospinal fluid, which cushions the brain. Beneath the ventricles lie the thalami (orange), and the hypothalamus (green, centre), which controls emotion and body temperature, and releases chemicals that regulate hormone release from the pituitary gland (the round green body at the lower edge).

brain). After left-hemisphere damage, patients may have difficulty speaking or doing complicated movements with their hands or arms. Deaf people who have had left-hemisphere damage may no longer be able to use sign language to communicate.

The right hemisphere is not involved in communication, although it does help us to understand words. It specializes in receiving and analysing the information that comes from all of our senses. When people have lesions in the right hemisphere, they have problems identifying faces and locating an object correctly in space. Such a patient might not be able to identify melodies, for example. The right hemisphere helps us understand what we hear and what we see.

Early experiments with brain lesions were done in the mid-1800s with people who had particular injuries. Two neurologists observed that people who had injuries on the left side of the brain had speech and language problems. People who had injuries in the same areas but on the right side of the brain had no language problems. The two areas of the brain important for language are named after these scientists: Pierre Paul Broca and Cark Wernicke. Injury to the Broca's area interferes with the ability to vocalize words; injury to the Wernicke's area affects the ability to put words into sentences. Both areas are on the left side of the brain.

Another series of experiments was carried out in the 1960s. Scientists trying to find out about brain functions became interested in studying a group of patients who had undergone surgery to sever their corpus callosum to relieve symptoms of epilepsy. Experiments were devised to determine how splitting the brain affected these patients. Researchers already knew that input from the right visual field is received by the left hemisphere, and input from the left visual field is received by the right hemisphere.

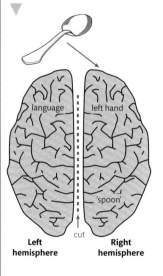

Figure 7.8 The split-brain experiment with a spoon.

The scientists projected a picture of a spoon onto the right side of a card with a dot in the middle. If a split-brain person is sitting down looking at the dot and a picture of the spoon is flashed up, the visual information about the spoon crosses the optic chiasma and ends up on the left hemisphere. The person has no trouble identifying the spoon and says 'spoon'. (The language centre is in the left hemisphere.)

If the spoon is projected on the left side of the dot, the information goes to the right side of the brain, where there is no language ability (see Figure 7.8). In this case the person will say that he or she has seen nothing. Then the scientists asked the same person to pick up a spoon with his or her left hand. The subject correctly picks up the spoon. The verbal information travels to the right hemisphere, which understands what a 'spoon' is even if the word 'spoon' cannot be verbalized. If that person is then asked what is in his or her hand, he or she will not be able to say 'it is a spoon'. The right hemisphere has little language ability.

Functional magnetic resonance imaging (fMRI)

Functional magnetic resonance imaging (fMRI) uses radio waves and a strong magnetic field, not X-rays. This instrument enables scientists to see the blood flow in the brain as it is occurring. Researchers make movies of what is going on in the brain as a subject performs tasks or is exposed to various stimuli. This method can produce a new image every second. It can determine with some precision when regions of the brain become active and how long they remain active. This means it is possible to determine whether brain activity occurs in the same region or different regions at the same time as a patient responds to experimental conditions. A different tool called a positron emission tomography (PET) scanner is slower but has the advantage of being able to identify the areas of the brain activated by neurotransmitters and drugs. An fMRI is used by doctors to determine:

- a plan for surgery
- treatment for a stroke
- placement of radiation therapy for a brain tumour
- the effects of degenerative brain diseases such as Alzheimer's
- the diagnosis of how a diseased or injured brain is working.

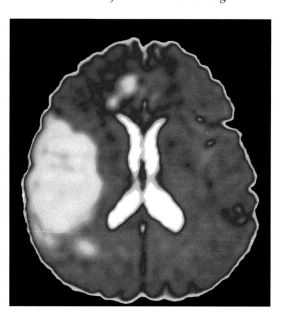

fMRI scan of the brain of a patient after a stroke. The large area of yellow is a result of lack of blood flow to that area of the brain. The blockage of blood flow may be due to a blood clot. Strokes can cause the hemisphere in which they are located to lose function.

Animal experiments

One type of relevant animal experimentation is to expose animal models to addictive substances in controlled situations. Animal models respond in similar ways to humans when addicted. Addicted animals:

- want more and more of the substance
- spend lots of time and energy getting the substance
- keep taking the substance despite adverse conditions
- have withdrawal symptoms upon withdrawal of the substance
- go back to the substance when stressed
- go back to the substance with another exposure to that substance.

To test whether a chemical meets the criteria for an addictive substance, a controlled self-administration experiment is designed and the response of the animal is recorded to see whether it fits the above model for addiction (see Figure 7.9).

1   An animal is trained to press a lever to get a reward.
2   The animal is given an injection of an addictive substance as it pushes the lever.
3   The lever will automatically give the injection if it is pushed by the animal (self-administration).
4   In order for this to be a controlled experiment, two levers must be available, one that gives the substance and one that does not (we want to be sure the animal is not just pushing the lever randomly).

5   If the substance is 'reinforcing', the animal will seek to repeat the experience by pushing that lever much more frequently. This would support the hypothesis that the substance is addictive.

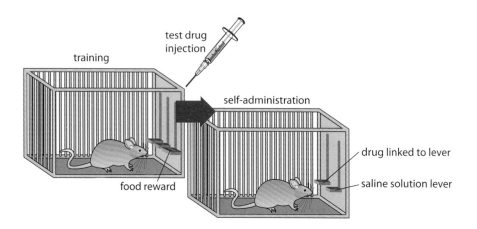

Figure 7.9 A self-administration experiment.

Researchers have recently used a self-administration experiment to support the hypothesis that acetaldehyde, which is a component of tobacco smoke, increases the addiction of adolescents to tobacco (see Figure 7.10).

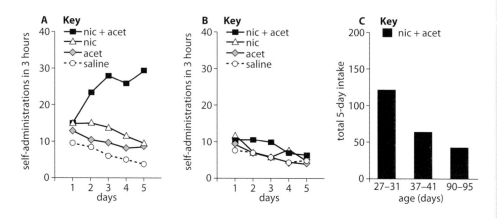

Figure 7.10 Adolescent rat experiments with nicotine and acetaldehyde.
A Adolescent rats (27 days old) self-administered nicotine combined with acetaldehyde with increasing frequency over 5 days, but did not with nicotine alone, acetaldehyde alone, or saline.
B Adult rats (90 days old) did not demonstrate any preference.
C The total 5-day intake of nicotine plus acetaldehyde was greatest for the youngest group of animals. This suggests that vulnerability to tobacco addiction decreases with age.

Animal experiments can shed light on the way that drugs promote abuse and addiction. Yet animal experiments can never replicate the complete picture of human interactions with drugs. Social factors are not considered in these experiments. Thus the results need to be interpreted with caution. Recent advances in technology have enabled researchers to use fMRI to answer questions that previously required an animal model.

A report released by the World Health Organization (WHO) claims that neurological disorders, such as Alzheimer's disease, epilepsy, stroke, headache, Parkinson's disease, and multiple sclerosis, affect 1 billion people worldwide.

According to Karl Popper, science is based on a series of theories. Scientific beliefs change over time, and it can be argued that a newer theory is closer to the truth than a previous theory. With enough evidence, there may be a paradigm shift as a new theory has more evidence to support it. Currently, the prevailing theory about the cause of Alzheimer's disease is that amyloid plaque accumulates on neurones. Alzheimer's disease results in extreme memory loss and affects millions of people worldwide. New research by Ben Barnes, published in the *Journal of Neuroscience* in 2013, is counter to the prevailing theory about Alzheimer's disease. The problem may not be the accumulation of plaque but an accumulation of a protein called C1q, which builds up on the synapse. Will there be a paradigm shift regarding the cause of Alzheimer's disease?

Autopsy

Autopsy can also be used to determine what brain parts are involved in certain functions. Paul Broca was a French surgeon who discovered the area of the brain involved in language. He autopsied the brain of a deceased patient who had a strange language disorder. The man was able to understand spoken language and could move his mouth and tongue, so he did not have motor impairment. However, he could not express his thoughts by writing or speaking. Following an autopsy of the man's brain, a lesion was discovered in the left inferior frontal cortex located in the left cerebral hemisphere. After studying the brains of eight other patients with similar disorders and finding the same lesions, Broca described this area of the brain in the left hemisphere as the language centre. This specific area in the left hemisphere is now called Broca's area and was the first area of the brain to be associated with a specific function.

Table 7.4 Methods for identifying the roles of different parts of the brain

Method	Results that can be determined
fMRI	Blood flow in the brain to determine whether a patient has had a stroke (blockage of blood flow) Brain tumour Effects of Alzheimer's disease
Brain lesion	Activities that reside in each hemisphere: left is for communication right is for analysis
Autopsy	Learning what areas of the brain control certain functions, e.g. a man who could not express his thoughts in writing and speaking had a lesion in the left cerebral hemisphere
Animal experimentation	Effect of drugs on the animal brain Addiction in the animal

The autonomic nervous system has two divisions

The brain is part of the central nervous system (CNS). The other part of the nervous system is the peripheral nervous system (PNS). The peripheral nervous system is considered to have two parts, the somatic system and the autonomic system (ANS). The somatic system takes sensory information from sensory receptors to the CNS and then sends back motor commands from the CNS to the muscles. The pain reflex arc is part of this system.

The ANS of the PNS is involuntary and regulates the activities of glands, smooth muscle, and the heart. Within the brain the ANS is located in the medulla oblongata. There are also two divisions to the ANS: the sympathetic system and the parasympathetic system.

CNS:

• brain

• spinal cord.

PNS:

• somatic (voluntary), information is received by the senses and messages sent to the skeletal muscles

• autonomic (involuntary), controls cardiac muscle of the heart, smooth muscle, and glands, consisting of two systems that are antagonistic

  • the sympathetic system

  • the parasympathetic system.

Table 7.5 The two PNS systems

Sympathetic system	Parasympathetic system
Important in an emergency	Important in returning to normal
Response is 'fight or flight'	Response is to relax
Neurotransmitter is noradrenaline	Neurotransmitter is acetylcholine
Excitatory	Inhibitory

As you can see, the sympathetic and the parasympathetic systems are antagonistic (see Figure 7.11). The sympathetic system is associated with 'fight or flight'. If you are facing an emergency, you need a quick supply of glucose and oxygen. The sympathetic system increases both the heart rate and the stroke volume (the amount of blood pumped by the left ventricle in each contraction) of the heart. It dilates the bronchi to give you more oxygen. It also dilates the pupil of the eye by making the radial muscles of the iris contract. Digestion is not necessary in an emergency, so the flow of blood to the gut is restricted by contraction of the smooth muscle of the blood vessels carrying blood to the digestive system (causing the diameter of the blood vessels to narrow).

If you are not in an emergency situation and are in a relaxed state, the parasympathetic system takes over. Parasympathetic nerves return the system to normal. The pupil of your eye constricts (gets smaller) to protect the retina, caused by contraction of the circular muscles of the iris. The heart rate slows and stroke volume is reduced. Blood flow returns to the digestive system. The smooth muscles of the blood vessels relax and the diameter of the blood vessels becomes wider.

To remember these confusing systems try to make sense of the terms. Peripheral is what is on the outside of the brain and the spinal cord. Somatic has to do with the body, and you know skeletal muscles are voluntary. Autonomic is similar to 'automatic', so you can remember that these functions are not voluntary. Sympathetic is when you are in 'sympathy' with your fear of a lion chasing you. Whereas with the parasympathetic system you are like a 'parrot' sitting up in a tree completely relaxed, because the lion is down on the ground.

If you can take the complex terms of biology and relate them to something else, you will find it easier to remember them.

Figure 7.11 Effects of the autonomic nervous system.

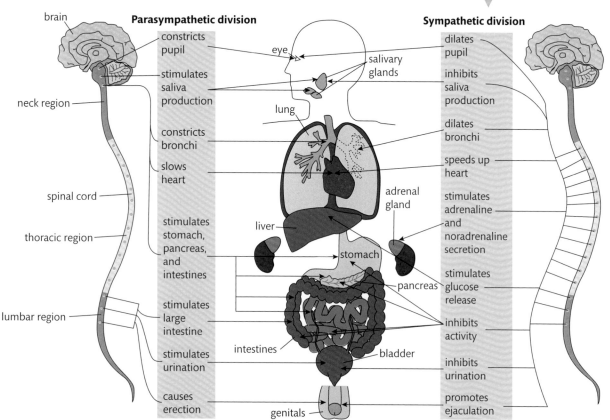

357

Make up a story to help you remember the different systems correctly. For example, you would be in 'flight' mode if you were running away from a lion. Your body would be in 'sympathy' with you (sympathetic system). Look at Figure 7.11. Your heart would be racing and your pupils dilated, but the blood flow to your stomach and intestines would be stopped. (You do not need to digest your food as you are running away from a lion.)

However, if you reach the high branches of a tree and are safe, the parasympathetic system would kick in. Look at Figure 7.11 again. Your heart would slow, your bronchi would constrict, and so would your pupils. You do not need to be in 'flight' mode any more.

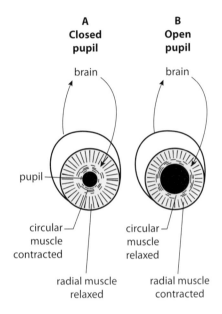

Figure 7.12 The pupil reflex.

The pupil reflex

In order to see the pupil reflex, ask someone to close their eyes and then suddenly open them (see Figure 7.12). You will see the pupil close in response to the sudden input of light as the eyes open. This is as much a reflex as the pain reflex. However, instead of having its connection in the spinal cord, as with the pain reflex, this is a cranial reflex. The sensory and motor neurones connect in the brain rather than the spinal cord.

In the eye, the iris surrounds the opening over the lens that we call the pupil. The iris contains two sets of smooth muscle to open and close the pupil like the aperture on a camera. The pupil closes as a result of a parasympathetic response caused by acetylcholine. If you go to an eye doctor, he or she may dilate your pupils by using a drug called atropine. Atropine stops the action of the neurotransmitter, acetylcholine. Constriction of the pupil happens because of a motor neurone causing the circular muscle to contract and so the radial muscle relaxes.

The pathway of the pupil reflex is shown in Figure 7.13 and described below.

- The optic nerve receives the messages from the retina at the back of the eye. The retina contains photoreceptors that receive the stimulus of light. Photoreceptors synapse with the bipolar neurones and then with the ganglion cells. Nerve fibres of the ganglion cells become the optic nerve.
- The optic nerve connects with the pretectal nucleus of the brainstem (the rectangle in Figure 7.13).
- From the pretectal nucleus, a message is sent to the Edinger–Westphal nucleus (the triangle in Figure 7.13), the axons of which run along the oculomotor nerves back to the eye.
- Oculomotor nerves synapse on the ciliary ganglion (the small circle in Figure 7.13)
- The axons of the ciliary ganglion stimulate the circular muscle of the iris, so it contracts.

Brain death

As a result of recent advances in the treatment of patients, it is possible to artificially maintain the body without the impulses that normally come from the brain. The brainstem controls heart rate, breathing rate, and blood flow to the digestive system. The brain also controls body temperature, blood pressure, and fluid retention. All of these functions can be controlled for a patient without a functioning brain.

You may have heard news reports about patients who are living on life support systems but their brain shows no electrical activity. In some of these cases, family

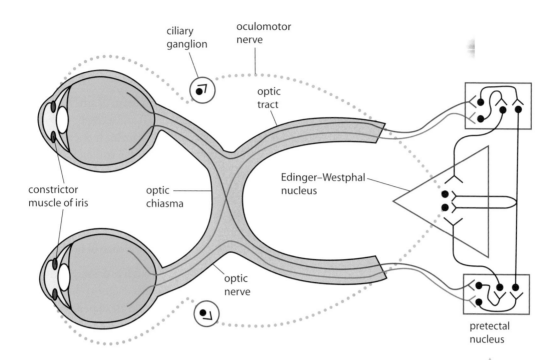

ciliary ganglion

oculomotor nerve

optic tract

constrictor muscle of iris

optic chiasma

Edinger–Westphal nucleus

optic nerve

pretectal nucleus

Figure 7.13 Parasympathetic pathways in the pupil reflex.

members may wish to keep the patient on life support because they do not believe that the person is dead. Other family members may believe that the person is dead, because the patient is 'brain dead'. What exactly does brain death mean?

The legal description of brain death is 'that time when a physician(s) has determined that the brain and brainstem have irreversibly lost all neurological function'. But people may still wonder if the patient could be in a coma. Patients in a coma have neurological signs that can be measured. These signs are based on responses to external stimuli. When examining for brain death, a physician must first perform a toxicology test to make sure that the patient is not under the influence of drugs that would slow down neurological reflexes. A diagnosis of brain death includes the following.

• Movement of extremities: if arms and legs are raised and let fall, there must be no other movement or hesitation in the fall.
• Eye movement: eyes must remain fixed, showing a lack of brain-to-motor-nerve reflex (as the head is turned there is no rolling motion of the eyes).
• Corneal reflex: this must be absent (when a cotton swab is dragged over the cornea, the eye does not blink).
• Pupil reflex: this must be absent (pupils do not constrict in response to a very bright light shone into both eyes).
• Gag reflex: this must be absent (the insertion of a small tube into the throat of a comatose patient will cause a gag reflex).
• Respiration (breathing) response: this must be absent (if the patient is removed from a ventilator, he or she does not breathe).

Following assessment by one or more physicians, a patient who shows none of these functions can be pronounced 'brain dead'. If the patient is missing all of the reflex responses and pupil responses, the evidence is clear that the brain will not recover.

However, in a brain-dead person there can still be spinal reflexes. The knee jerk response can still be functional. You may recall that the spinal reflexes do not involve the brain. In some brain-dead patients, a short reflex motion can still be exhibited if the hand or foot is touched in a certain manner.

Many doctors order further tests in order to confirm brain death. Two tests commonly used are the electroencephalogram (EEG) and a cerebral blood flow (CBF) study. The EEG measures brain activity in microvolts. It is a very sensitive test. Some electrical activity will be shown on an EEG if a patient is in a deep coma. The lack of activity in a brain-dead patient is called electrocerebral silence (see Figure 7.14).

To measure blood flow to the brain, a radioactive isotope is injected into the bloodstream. A radioactive counter is then placed over the head for about 30 minutes. If no activity is detected, this is conclusive evidence of brain death.

As you can see, the diagnosis of brain death is a very thorough process. At the end of the testing, there can be no doubt about the result. Once this diagnosis has been made, the patient may still be maintained on a ventilator, but a brain-dead person will not recover brain function.

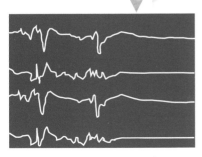

Figure 7.14 EEG showing activity followed by electrocerebral silence.

To learn more about reflexes, go to the hotlinks site, search for the title or ISBN, and click on Chapter 7: Section A.2.

Figure 7.15 More intelligent animals have more highly developed cortical surfaces. https://faculty.washington.edu/chudler/brainsize.html

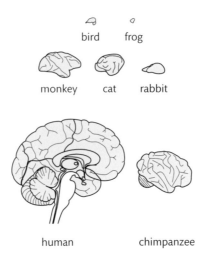

The cerebral cortex

The cerebrum develops from the front part of the neural tube. It is the largest part of the mature brain. As we have seen, the cerebrum consists of two divisions, the left and right cerebral hemispheres. The cerebral hemispheres are covered by a thin layer of grey matter (cells with no myelin sheath around them) called the cerebral cortex. This layer is less than 5 mm thick but contains 75% of the body's neurones. The cortex is where you perform tasks such as:

• reasoning
• language
• complex thought
• visual processing
• motor movement
• remembering
• speech.

The human brain is larger in proportion to its body size than brains of other animals. Orcas (killer whales) may have larger brains by actual volume, but when brain size is compared using a formula that takes body size into account, the human brain is three times as large as that of a chimpanzee and more than twice as large as that of an orca. The expansion of the human brain has come from the growth of the cerebral cortex.

The correlation between body size and brain size

The weight of the brain compared with the weight of the body is called the E:S ratio, where E stands for brain weight and S stands for body weight. Table 7.6 shows the E:S ratio for various species. You can see that humans and mice have the same E:S ratio, while the E:S for small birds is larger than that for humans. Should we therefore conclude that small birds, whose brains are comparatively larger in relation to their size compared with larger animals, are more intelligent than humans? You can see that the brain weight of a vertebrate does not appear to increase linearly with body weight. However, the trend seems to be that the larger an animal gets, the smaller its brain to body ratio. Small mice have a relatively large brain. Large elephants have a relatively small brain.

To improve on the simple ratio method, an equation was developed where E = weight of the brain, S = weight of the body, C = a constant, and r = an exponential constant. Using the formula E = CSr, we can establish the relative capacity of brains of different species with different body weights.

When a value of C can be established for each species, then we can find the EQ or encephalization quotient: EQ = C/average mammalian value. For example, if the EQ of a certain species is 3.0 then the species has a value of C three times as high as a mammal of comparable weight with average encephalization (the ratio between actual brain size and predicted brain mass for an animal of a given size).

Look at the chart of EQ quotients (Table 7.7). A dolphin has an EQ of 5.31, which shows that it is twice as encephalized as a chimpanzee, which has an EQ of only 2.49.

Table 7.6 E:S correlation between the weight of the brain and the weight of the body for different animals
http://en.wikipedia.org/wiki/Brain-to-body_mass_ratio

Species	Simple brain-to-body ratio (E:S)
Small ants	1:7
Small birds	1:14
Human	1:40
Mouse	1:40
Cat	1:110
Dog	1:125
Squirrel	1:15
Frog	1:172
Lion	1:550
Elephant	1:560
Horse	1:600
Shark	1:2496
Hippopotamus	1:2789

Table 7.7 Encephalization quotient (EQ) data
http://serendip.brynmawr.edu/bb/kinser/Int3.html

Species	EQ	Species	EQ
Man	7.44	Cat	1.00
Dolphin	5.31	Horse	0.86
Chimpanzee	2.49	Sheep	0.81
Rhesus monkey	2.09	Mouse	0.50
Elephant	1.87	Rat	0.40
Whale	1.76	Rabbit	0.40
Dog	1.17		

CHALLENGE YOURSELF

We can agree that if the brain weight is large relative to the body (EQ), the animals may be able to accomplish more complex tasks. However, other factors may also be involved. See if you can answer the following questions using the EQ values shown in Table 7.7.

3 Can you see which four animals have diets of meat or fish?

4 Suggest why this diet is beneficial to the species.

5 Which three animals have a plant and insect diet?

6 Why is this diet not as beneficial to a species?

7 Can you think of any animal behaviour that would place a species high on the encephalization scale?

8 Why are rat and rabbit at the bottom in comparison with the other species?

9 Can you guess the name of an invertebrate animal that has a high EQ?

The enlargement of the cerebral cortex

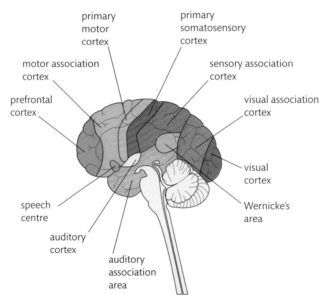

Figure 7.16 Functional divisions of the cerebral cortex. https://faculty.washington.edu/chudler/functional.html

Greater cognitive ability and more advanced behaviour are associated with an increase in size of the cerebral cortex. When we compare human brains with those of other animals, the biggest difference appears to be in the surface area of the cerebral hemispheres. In a mouse, for example, the surface of the cerebral cortex is smooth, while in a dog it is very convoluted. When we study monkeys and apes, even more folds are found in their cortex. In order for the brain to fit into a skull that is actually in proportion to the body, the brain has to fold in on itself. An increased surface area is needed for more complex behaviours, but it still has to fit into the limited space of a skull. One way to have more working surface is to add folds to the surface. If you scrunch up a sheet of A4 paper, it has the same surface area but can take up less space than a flat piece of A4 paper. As species evolved to be able to do more complex behaviours, they had to develop more working area for their brain. The more folding, the more surface area there can be. In this way a larger surface area of cerebral cortex can be contained in a limited space.

A 6-month-old foetus has a completely smooth cerebral cortex. By birth its brain has become the walnut-like structure we would expect to see. The folding of the cerebral cortex during development of the human embryo takes place during the last 3 months of development.

Functions of the cerebral cortex

The extensive folding of the cerebral cortex and the large numbers of neurones present in the cortex are evidence of the importance of this brain part. The higher order functions performed by the cerebral cortex are shown in Table 7.8.

Table 7.8 Functional areas of the cerebral cortex

Part	Function
Prefrontal cortex	Organizes thoughts, solves problems, and formats strategies
Motor association cortex	Coordinates movement
Primary motor cortex	Plans and executes movements
Primary somatosensory cortex	Processes information related to touch
Sensory association cortex	Processes sensory information of perceptions or multisensory information
Visual association area	Processes visual information
Visual cortex	Recognizes visual stimuli
Wernicke's area	Understands written and spoken language
Auditory association area	Processes auditory information
Auditory cortex	Detects sound quality such as loudness or tone
Broca's area	Produces speech and language

The visual cortex, Broca's area, and nucleus accumbens

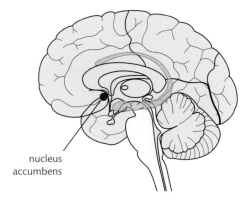

nucleus accumbens

Figure 7.17 Nucleus accumbens is associated with the rewards circuit in the brain.

Broca's area is one of two parts of the cerebral cortex linked to speech and language (the other is Wernicke's area). Broca's area is labelled 'speech centre' in Figure 7.16. When a patient has a brain injury causing lack of language production, it is called Broca's aphasia. Paul Broca discovered the language function of this area.

The nucleus accumbens (see Figure 7.17) is associated with the reward circuit in the brain. It responds chiefly to two neurotransmitters: dopamine and serotonin. Dopamine promotes desire, while serotonin inhibits desire. The activation of dopamine in the nucleus accumbens is associated with the anticipation of a reward. Drugs such as cocaine and nicotine also increase dopamine production in the nucleus accumbens. The reward of increased dopamine can result in addiction.

The visual cortex is the part of the brain that receives information from the cells in the retina of the eye. The visual cortex (see Figure 7.16) is one of many brain centres that cooperate to produce vision.

The left cerebral hemisphere receives sensory information from the right side of the body, and vice versa

The cerebral cortex is the thin layer on the surface of the left and right cerebral hemispheres and is responsible for all higher order functions. The cerebral cortex is made up of unmyelinated neurones and is called grey matter. The two cerebral hemispheres are connected by a thick band of tissue called the corpus callosum, through which communication takes place between the right and left sides of the brain. The corpus callosum is made up of myelinated neurones and is called white matter. Each cerebral hemisphere is responsible for one half of the body. The left cerebral hemisphere receives sensory input from sensory receptors on the right side of the body and the right side of the visual field in both eyes, and vice versa for the right hemisphere.

Each side of the cortex is divided into further sections depending on the activity that it performs. For example, look at Figure 7.16 and you can see the primary somatosensory cortex and the motor cortex. The primary somatosensory cortex is the main area for receiving the sense of touch. Sensory input from the right hand is sent to the left primary somatosensory cortex, and vice versa.

The neural pathways for vision travel to the primary visual cortex. As you might expect, the right side of the brain receives information from the left visual field, and the left side of the brain receives information from the

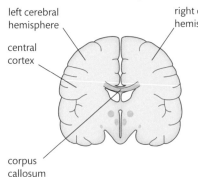

Figure 7.18 The corpus callosum connects the two cerebral hemispheres.

left cerebral hemisphere

central cortex

right cerebral hemisphere

corpus callosum

NATURE OF SCIENCE

Look at the diagram of a cross-sectional map of the primary somatosensory cortex (Figure 7.19).

The relative space that the human body parts occupy in the sensory cortex can be illustrated by a 'cartoon-like' homunculus (man). In this picture you can see the homunculus, a distorted model that reflects the relative space that human body parts occupy in each cortex. Notice that the head occupies a large area but the hips and legs only occupy a small area. Sensory information from the head is much more important and has more brain space available to it than sensory information from for hip or leg. What seems to be more important in the motor cortex, the head or the knee?

Figure 7.19 This homunculus cartoon shows the relative importance of areas of the body in the primary motor cortex and the primary somatosensory cortex.

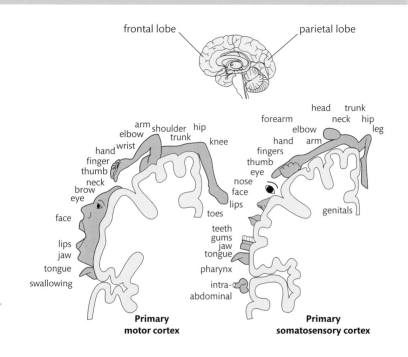

frontal lobe

parietal lobe

Primary motor cortex

Primary somatosensory cortex

right visual field. Looking at Figure 7.20, you can see that the optic nerves from the left field, shown in blue, can cross over at the optic chiasm so that the information from left field of view is received by right side of the brain, and vice versa.

Practise drawing diagrams of the neural pathway for vision until you understand it thoroughly.

The left cerebral hemisphere controls muscle contraction in the right side of the body, and vice versa

Now let's look at the motor cortex. The motor cortex controls voluntary movements. As you can guess, the motor cortex in the right cerebral hemisphere controls movement on the left side of the body, and vice versa. This can be very obvious in patients who have had a stroke.

When a person has a stroke, it is localized and often occurs in either the left or right cerebral hemisphere. A stroke is caused by a blocked or ruptured blood vessel. This interrupts oxygen flow to the brain cells. If a motor area of the cerebral hemisphere on the left side of the brain is affected, then paralysis will be seen in the right arm and right leg. The location of the paralysis tells the doctor which side of the brain has been injured as a result of loss of oxygen. Fortunately, because the brain has plasticity, other parts of the brain may take over during rehabilitation and facilitate the return of full motion.

Brain metabolism requires large energy inputs

Neurones have a high energy need because they are always in a state of high metabolic activity. As you will recall, metabolism consists of all the chemical activities performed by a cell. Neurones perform many tasks that are similar to other cells, such as repairing or rebuilding their structural components. However, the chemical signals that are responsible for the communication between neurones consume half of all the energy used by the brain. This is why a brain cell needs twice the amount of energy as any other cell in a body.

Glucose is the primary energy source that fuels the metabolism of neurones in the human brain. Neurones cannot store glucose, so the blood must deliver a constant supply. Because of its high rate of metabolism, glucose is used up rapidly by neurones during mental activity. In an experiment on rats, scientists at the University of Illinois College of Medicine found that young rats have a good supply of glucose to the area of the brain involved in learning and memory, while older rats to do not have such a good supply. The supply of glucose for older rats runs out much more quickly. When glucose runs out, the behaviour of the older rats indicates that there is a large deficit in learning.

Blood sugar (glucose) is supplied by the food that you eat. High-quality carbohydrates, such as fruits, vegetables, legumes, grains, and dairy, are the best source of glucose. These foods provide the brain with a supply of glucose that lasts for hours. Food such as sugar snacks and drinks provide glucose quickly, but the supply does not last as long and can result in low brain activity. It has been seen in animal models that sustained levels of glucose in the brain are beneficial for learning.

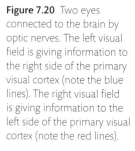

left visual field — right visual field

left eye — right eye

optic nerve

optic chiasm

lateral geniculate nucleus

primary visual cortex

Figure 7.20 Two eyes connected to the brain by optic nerves. The left visual field is giving information to the right side of the primary visual cortex (note the blue lines). The right visual field is giving information to the left side of the primary visual cortex (note the red lines).

The hand area of the primary motor cortex is known to be larger among professional pianists than among amateur pianists. Peter L. Strick, from the Department of Neurobiology, Pitt School of Medicine, suggests that this indicates that extensive practice induces changes in the primary motor cortex.

Worked example

Why is it better to eat an apple, rather than candy, when you are studying for a test?

Solution

Sugary snacks can give you quick glucose, but you need some more long-lasting brain energy when studying for a test. The candy will give you quick energy, but soon after you might get really sleepy. That would be the 'sugar' low that can occur after a 'sugar' high. The apple contains sugars but it must be digested, and its sugars are absorbed more slowly into the blood.

Angelman's syndrome is diagnosed from well-recognized abnormal patterns on an electroencephalogram (EEG). Symptoms include developmental delay of 6–12 months in babies, in addition to facial abnormalities and seizures. Angelman's syndrome is a genetically inherited disorder that primarily affects the nervous system.

Section summary

- Different parts of the human brain have different functions. The brain regulates unconscious activities such as heart rate, blood pressure, breathing, balance, muscle coordination, and voluntary movement. It also deals with emotion, speech, and problem solving, as well as allowing you to think and dream.
- Scientists have learned about the function of the parts of the brain by using brain scans such as functional magnetic resonance imaging (fMRI), by studying brain injuries, by animal experimentation, and by performing autopsies.
- Divisions of the nervous system include the central nervous system (CNS, the brain and spinal cord) and the peripheral nervous system (PNS).
- The two parts of the PNS are the sympathetic system and the parasympathetic system. The sympathetic system responds to an emergency and the parasympathetic system returns the system to normal. The pupil reflex is an example of how these two systems work. The pupil dilates in an emergency and constricts as the system returns to normal.
- Brain death is when the brain and brainstem have irreversibly lost all neurological function.
- The human brain is larger in proportion to its body than the brains of other animals. The measurement that shows the relationship of brain size to body size is the encephalization quotient.
- When comparing the brain to body relationship, the biggest difference is the large size of the human cerebral cortex. Extensive folding of the cerebral cortex allows a large number of neurones to be present.
- Certain areas of the cerebral hemisphere have specific functions. The cerebral hemisphere is the area of integration for complex functions such as learning, memory, and emotions.

Exercises

5 Draw and annotate a diagram of the human brain.

6 Describe how an fMRI is used to identify the role of different brain parts.

7 State the specific function of each of the following: Broca's area; nucleus accumbens; visual cortex.

8 Explain how folding has allowed the cerebral cortex to become more highly developed in humans than in other animals.

9 Explain why brain metabolism requires a large input of energy.

A.3 Perception of stimuli

Understandings:

- Receptors detect changes in the environment.
- Rods and cones are photoreceptors located in the retina.
- Rods and cones differ in their sensitivities to light intensities and wavelengths.
- Bipolar cells send the impulses from the rods and cones to ganglion cells.
- Ganglion cells send messages to the brain via the optic nerve.
- The information from the right field of vision from both eyes is sent to the left part of the visual cortex and vice versa.
- Structures in the middle ear transmit and amplify sound.
- Sensory hairs of the cochlea detect sounds of specific wavelengths.
- Impulses caused by sound perception are transmitted to the brain via the auditory nerve.
- Hairs in the semicircular canals detect movement of the head.

Applications and skills:

- Application: Red–green colour blindness as a variant of normal trichromatic vision.
- Application: Detection of chemicals in the air by the many different olfactory receptors.
- Application: Use of cochlear implants by deaf patients.
- Skill: Labelling a diagram of the structure of the human eye.
- Skill: Annotation of a diagram of the retina to show the cell types and the direction in which light moves.
- Skill: Labelling a diagram of the structure of the human ear.

Guidance

- *Humans' sensory receptors should include mechanoreceptors, chemoreceptors, thermoreceptors, and photoreceptors.*
- *Diagram of human eye should include the sclera, cornea, conjunctiva, eyelid, choroid, aqueous humour, pupil, lens, iris, vitreous humour, retina, fovea, optic nerve, and blind spot.*
- *Diagram of retina should include rod and cone cells, biopolar neurones, and ganglion cells.*
- *Diagram of ear should include pinna, eardrum, bones of the middle ear, oval window, round window, semicircular canals, auditory nerve, and cochlea.*

Sensory receptors and diversity of stimuli

Certain foods can make you feel comforted. Seeing a familiar face in a crowd can make you feel at ease. Listening to your favourite music can make you feel happy. We have learned to link certain tastes, sights, and sounds with emotions. Sensory cells send messages to certain parts of the brain that control emotion and memory.

Taste and sound are not just for pleasure. They also protect us. We remember the taste of mouldy food. We move out of the way when we hear a car coming. Many lives have been saved by smelling smoke.

Sense organs are the windows to the brain. They keep the brain aware of what is going on in the outside world. When stimulated, the sense organs send a message to the central nervous system. The nerve impulses arriving at the brain result in sensation. We actually see, smell, taste, and feel with our brain rather than our sense organs.

NATURE OF SCIENCE

Understanding of the underlying science is the basis for technological developments: the discovery that electrical stimulation in the auditory system can create a perception of sound resulted in the development of electrical hearing aids and ultimately cochlear implants.

We link certain tastes to emotion and memory. Some foods make us remember our childhood.

Receptors detect changes in the environment

Mechanoreceptors

Mechanoreceptors are stimulated by a mechanical force or some type of pressure. The sense of touch is caused by pressure receptors that are sensitive to strong or light pressure. In our arteries, pressure receptors can detect a change in blood pressure. In our lungs, stretch receptors respond to the degree of lung inflation. We can tell the position of our arms and legs by the use of proprioceptors found in muscle fibres, tendons, joints, and ligaments. These receptors help us maintain posture and balance. In our inner ear, there are pressure receptors sensitive to the waves of fluid moving over them. This gives us information about our equilibrium.

Chemoreceptors

Chemoreceptors respond to chemical substances. Using this type of receptor, we can taste and smell. They also give us information about our internal body environment. Chemoreceptors in some blood vessels monitor pH changes. Changes in pH signal the body to adjust the breathing rate. Pain receptors are a type of chemoreceptor that respond to chemicals released by damaged tissues. Pain protects us from danger. The pain reflex makes us pull away, for example, from a hot object. Olfactory receptors respond to smell.

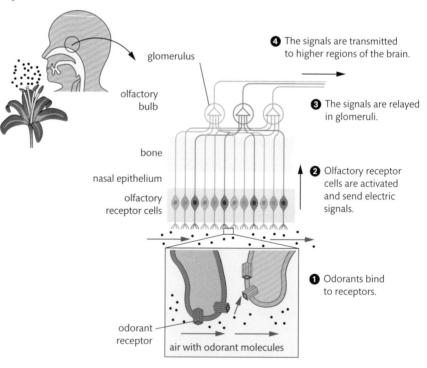

Figure 7.21 How receptors function in the olfactory system.

How does smell work? Everything you can smell, like bread baking, onions, coffee, anything good or bad, is releasing volatile molecules that diffuse into the air. These molecules then reach the olfactory receptors in your nose: 10 000 different smells can be detected by these receptors in humans.

At the top of your nasal passage is a patch of specialized neurones that contain the olfactory receptors. A given molecule may stimulate more than one receptor. The combination of several receptors is registered by the brain as a certain smell. Scientists have hypothesized that each of our hundreds of olfactory receptors is encoded for by a specific gene. Each specific gene recognizes a different smell. If your DNA does not have a certain gene, you may be unable to smell a certain smell. For example, some people cannot smell digested asparagus but others can.

Chemoreceptors are very important in the entire animal kingdom. Chemoreception is the oldest and most universal sense. It probably guides the behaviour of animals more than any other sense. For example, it allows bees to have social organization regulated by chemical molecules called pheromones. Vertebrates also respond to pheromones. Sex pheromones in vertebrates are chemicals that help individuals of the same species find each other and mate. Some animals find their prey by tracking chemicals released by the prey into the environment. For example, when a blue crab is hunting a clam, it finds the clam by following the chemical released into the river by the clam.

Thermoreceptors

Thermoreceptors respond to a change in temperature. Warmth receptors respond when the temperature rises; cold receptors respond when the temperature drops. Human thermoreceptors are located in the skin.

Photoreceptors

Photoreceptors respond to light energy; they are found in our eyes. Our eyes are sensitive to light and give us vision. Rod cells in our eyes respond to dim light, resulting in black and white vision; cone cells respond to bright light, giving us colour vision.

Table 7.9 A summary of major sensory receptors

Sensory receptor type	Example/location	Function
Mechanoreceptors	Arteries, lungs, tips of fingers	Generate nerve impulses when stimulated, may indicate touch, pressure, stretch, balance
Chemoreceptors	Nose, mouth, blood vessels	Respond to chemicals in solution, e.g. taste, smell, and blood chemistry
Thermoreceptors	Skin, lining of mouth	Detect hot and cold temperatures
Photoreceptors	Retina of the eyes (rods and cones)	Respond to light energy

The structure and function of the human eye

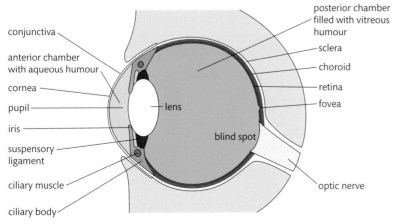

Figure 7.22 The human eye.

369

CHALLENGE YOURSELF

10 Many pictures are available online that you can use to practise labelling the parts of the eye. Print out a picture with missing labels and practise labelling the eye until you are sure you have learned all the parts perfectly. Use the hotlinks at the end of this section to find a diagram you can label as an interactive task. Next learn the function by covering up one side of Table 7.10 with a piece of paper and trying to recreate it.

Figure 7.23 Structure of the retina.

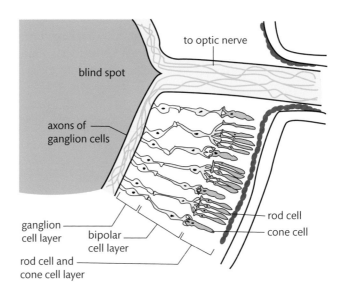

Figure 7.24 Structure and function of the retina.

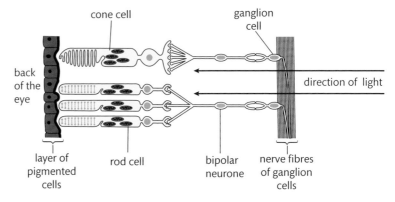

Table 7.10 summarizes the functions of the various parts of the eye.

Table 7.10 The functions of various parts of the eye

Part	Function
Iris	Regulates the size of the pupil
Pupil	Admits light
Retina	Contains receptors for vision
Aqueous humour	Transmits light rays and supports the eyeball
Vitreous humour	Transmits light rays and supports the eyeball
Rods	Allow black and white vision in dim light

Part	Function
Cones	Allow colour vision in bright light
Fovea	An area of densely packed cone cells where vision is most acute
Lens	Focuses the light rays
Sclera	Protects and supports the eyeball
Cornea	Focusing begins here
Choroid	Absorbs stray light
Conjunctiva	Covers the sclera and cornea and keeps the eye moist
Optic nerve	Transmits impulses to the brain
Eye lid	Protects the eye

The retina

Vision begins when light enters the eye and is focused on the photoreceptor cells of the retina (see Figure 7.23). The photoreceptor cells are the rods and the cones. Notice in Figure 7.24 that both the rods and cones synapse with their own bipolar neurones. Each bipolar neurone synapses with a ganglion cell. The axons of the ganglion cells make up the optic nerve, which carries the message of vision to the brain.

The following bullet points would be suitable for annotating a diagram of the retina.

- Rod cells are photoreceptor cells that are very sensitive to light. They receive the stimulus of light, even very dim light, and synapse with a bipolar neurone.
- Cone cells are photoreceptor cells that are activated by bright light. They receive the stimulus of bright light and synapse with a bipolar neurone.
- Bipolar neurones are cells in the retina that carry impulses from a rod or a cone cell to a ganglion cell of the optic nerve. They are called bipolar because they each have two processes extending from the cell body.
- Ganglion cells synapse with the bipolar neurones and send the impulses to the brain via the optic nerve.

Rods and cones

Table 7.11 provides a comparison of rods and cones.

Table 7.11 Rods and cones

Rods	Cones
These cells are more sensitive to light and function well in dim light	These cells are less sensitive to light and function well in bright light
Only one type of rod is found in the retina. It can absorb all wavelengths of visible light	Three types of cone are found in the retina. One type is sensitive to red light, one type to blue light, and one type to green light
The impulses from a group of rod cells pass to a single nerve fibre in the optic nerve (see Figure 7.24)	The impulse from a single cone cell passes to a single nerve fibre in the optic nerve (see Figure 7.24)

CHALLENGE YOURSELF

11 The next challenge is to learn the parts of the retina using Figure 7.24. The best way to learn this picture is to draw it and label the parts. Be accurate. Notice that the cone cell has only one part, while the rod cell has three. Make sure you understand where the back of the eye is, and the direction from which the light is coming. You can use Figures 7.23 and 7.24 so that you can really understand what is happening. To test yourself another way, try to explain the retina to someone else using the picture.

The steps of the vision pathway in the retina are as follows.

- Rods and cones receive the light stimulus.
- Rods and cones synapse with a bipolar neurone.
- The bipolar neurone carries the impulse to the ganglion cell.
- The ganglion cell is located in the optic nerve.
- The optic nerve carries the impulse to the brain.

Red–green colour blindness

Normal vision uses the three classes of cones, red, green, and blue, and is called trichromatic vision. Some individuals are dichromatic and have red–green colour vision defects; dichromatic vision is a variant of trichromatic vision. Red–green defects are inherited as a sex-linked trait: sons can inherit the defect from their mother. It is very rare for females to have this trait. Dichromatic vision can be caused by the presence of blue and green cones with no functional red cones (red-blindness), or by the presence of blue and red cones with no green cones (green-blindness). Dichromats see the world differently depending on the variation they have inherited. Many websites have tests for colour blindness.

To complete a test for colour blindness, go to the hotlinks site, search for the title or ISBN, and click on Chapter 7: Section A.3.

Information from the right field of vision from both eyes is sent to the left part of the visual cortex, and vice versa

Review the information in Section A.2 on the human brain and the visual cortex.

The structure of the ear

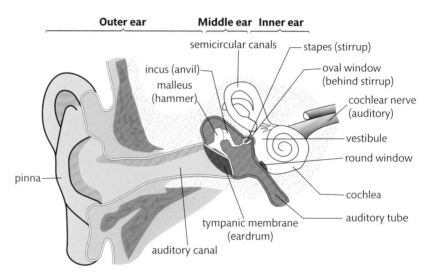

Figure 7.25 Anatomy of the human ear.

How sound is perceived by the ear

Sound waves are successive vibrations of air molecules caught by the outer ear. When they travel down the auditory canal, they cause the eardrum (tympanic membrane) to move back and forth slightly.

Structures in the middle ear transmit and amplify sound

• The bones of the middle ear, the malleus, incus, and stapes, receive vibrations from the tympanic membrane and multiply them approximately 20 times.
• The stapes strikes the oval window, causing it to vibrate.
• This vibration is passed to the fluid in the cochlea.
• The fluid in the cochlea causes special cells, called hair cells, to vibrate.
• The hair cells, which are mechanoreceptors, release a chemical neurotransmitter across a synapse to the sensory neurone of the auditory nerve.
• Vibrations are transformed into nerve impulses.

- The chemical message stimulates the sensory neurone.
- Impulses caused by sound perception are transmitted to the brain by the auditory nerve.
- The round window releases pressure so fluid in the cochlea can vibrate.

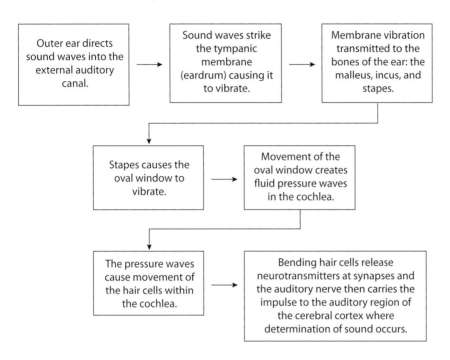

Figure 7.26 The physiology of hearing.

CHALLENGE YOURSELF

12 Here is another opportunity to learn the parts of one of your receptors, the ear. Again find a picture online, print it out, and label it. Label the parts from memory and then begin to learn the bullet points given above in order. Do you have a younger brother or sister who might be fascinated by you telling them the story of how we hear?

Sensory hairs of the cochlea detect sounds of specific length

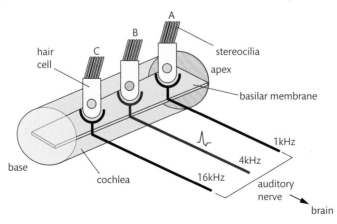

Figure 7.27 The stereocilia in the cochlea detect sounds of a specific wavelength. Hz measures the frequency of those sound waves. Hz is the SI symbol for hertz. A kHz is 1000 cycles per second of waves. Human hearing range is between 20 and 20 000 Hz.

The hair cells of the cochlea have stereocilia that stick out of the hair cells and detect sounds of a specific wavelength. As the stereocilia on the hair cells bend back and

According to the *American Journal of Industrialized Medicine*, excessive noise is a global occupational health hazard resulting in noise-induced hearing loss (NIHL). Adult-onset hearing loss is the 15th most serious world heath problem.

The cochlea has more than 32 000 hair cells.

forth, an internal change in the hair cell itself is created. This change produces an electrical impulse that is carried to the auditory nerve.

Short, high-frequency waves produce high-pitched sounds, while long, low-frequency waves produce low-pitched sounds. The sound, which is sensed by the brain, is processed in the auditory area of the cerebral cortex. Hearing varies between people and changes with age. Hearing can also be affected by high-frequency noise. Listening to high-frequency sound for too long can damage the hair cells in the cochlea, and cochlear hair cells do not grow back. That is why many musicians wear protective ear devices when playing in concerts.

Here are some suggestions from a health professional on how to prevent hearing loss in teenagers.

You can enjoy listening to music yet avoiding harmful listening habits that can lead to permanent hearing loss, by following these steps.

- Switch to headphones: headphones isolate the background noise, so that you can hear the music with less increase in volume.
- Anything higher than 85 dB can cause damage.
- Listening for extended periods of time can impair hearing. Take breaks.
- Try the 60/60 rule: never turn your volume past 60% and only insert earphones for a maximum of 60 minutes per day.

Hair cells in the semicircular canals detect movement of the head

We have three semicircular canals in each inner ear. These semicircular canals control our equilibrium, and give our brain a three-dimensional report of our position. The canals contain fluid and hair cells. Movement of the fluid over the hair cells detects rotational movement of the head. The hair cells are sensory receptors that send messages to the vestibular nerve. This information, which is relayed to the brain, tells us our position. Are we upside down or falling backwards? We can maintain our balance in precarious positions because of the accuracy of the hair cells in the semicircular canals of our ears.

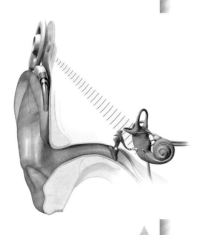

Cochlear implant.

Use of cochlear implants in deaf patients

Cochlear implants are a product of medical technology that has improved the lives of people with severe to profound hearing loss when a hearing aid is not a solution. Cochlear implants convert sound into electrical signals that are sent directly to the brain. A cochlear implant works in the following manner.

- An external processor is worn behind the ear or attached to the hair.
- The microphone in the external processor picks up the sound signal.
- The external processor digitizes the sound and transfers the electrical signal to the implant, which has been surgically placed in the cochlea.
- The implant acts like a miniature computer, deciphering the digitized sound and transferring it into electrical signals.
- The auditory nerve picks up the electrical signals and sends a message to the brain.
- The brain interprets the signals as sound.

Animal horns were the first hearing aid, used in the 13th century. Technology has developed many improvements over the years. In 1878, Francis Blake and David Edward Hughes discovered that carbon transmitters could amplify sound, which was a big advance over the horn! In 1920, the vacuum tube was invented. The Radioear was the name of one of the hearing aids that used a vacuum tube. In 1950, Bell Laboratories invented the transistor battery, which was small and a big improvement over the vacuum tube. Since 1967 the digital hearing aid has been the main type of hearing device. It is small and convenient to wear. However, we know that, using technology, scientists will develop future improvements to help those with hearing loss.

The following might be an interesting experiment to try with a class of students. Can most people identify the smells correctly? Is there a significant difference in males and females of the same age?

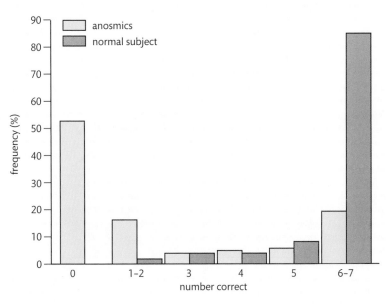

Figure 7.28 Anosmia. Purves et al. 2001

Anosmia is the inability to identify common smells. When subjects are presented with seven common smells (a test frequently used by neurologists), the vast majority of 'normal' individuals can identify all seven smells correctly. The smells used for the graph shown were baby powder, chocolate, cinnamon, coffee, mothballs, peanut butter, and soap. Some people, however, have difficulty identifying even these common smells. When individuals already identified as anosmics were presented with these seven smells, only a few could identify all of them (less than 15%), and more than half could not identify any of them.

Section summary

- Our receptors, mechanoreceptors, chemoreceptors, thermoreceptors, and photoreceptors detect changes in our environment.
- Each part of the eye has an important function. The sense of vision is carried through the optic nerve to the brain.
- The retina contains two types of photoreceptor cells. They are the rods, which are more sensitive to light and function well in dim light, and the cones, which function in bright light.
- The three classes of cones are red, green, and blue. A red–green defect of the cone cells can be inherited as a genetic trait and is usually passed from mother to son.

To learn more about sensory organs and colour blindness, go to the hotlinks site, search for the title or ISBN, and click on Chapter 7: Section A.3.

CHALLENGE YOURSELF

Look at Figure 7.29 and answer the following questions.

13 What % of smells can people between the ages of 20 and 40 identify? Give a range.

14 What % of smells can people between the ages of 50 and 70 identify? Give a range.

15 What name do we give to data that fall far above or far below the line of best fit?

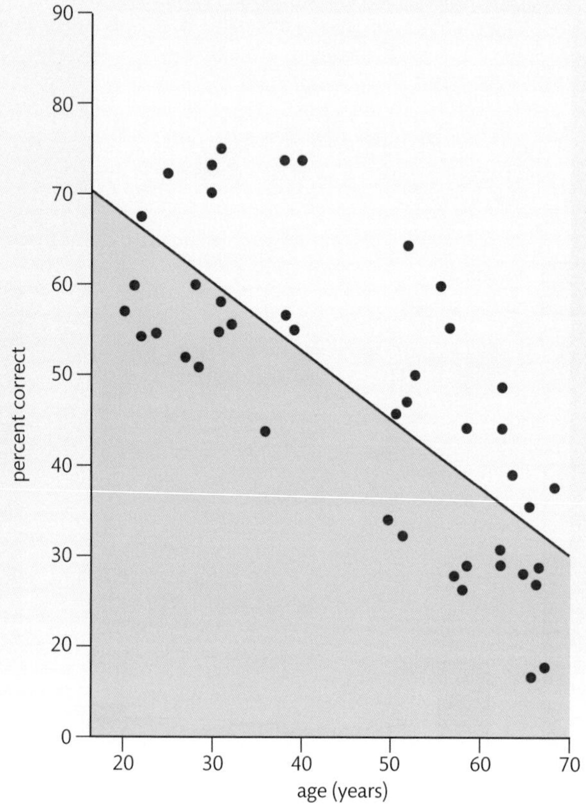

Figure 7.29 Normal decline in olfactory sensitivity with age. Purves et al. 2001

- Rods and cones synapse with bipolar neurones, which then synapse with ganglion cells. Ganglion cells send the impulses to the brain via the optic nerve.
- Information from the right field of vision from both eyes is sent to the left part of the visual cortex of the brain, and vice versa.
- The ear is used in both hearing and balance. Each part of the ear has an important function. Working together, the parts of the ear bring the sense of hearing via the auditory nerve to the brain.
- Medical technology can replace some parts of the human ear that are not functioning. For example, cochlear implants convert sound into electrical signals that travel to the brain.

To learn more about the evolutionary link between an animal's movement and its inner ear, go to the hotlinks site, search for the title or ISBN, and click on Chapter 7: Section A.3.

10 Label a diagram of the retina and show the direction in which the light moves.

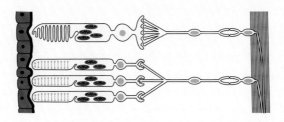

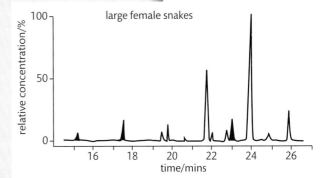

Figure 7.30 The structure of the retina.

11 Compare and contrast rods and cones.

12 Describe red–green colour blindness.

13 Outline the use of cochlear implants in deaf patients.

14 Explain how sound is perceived by the ear.

Practice questions

1 In many vertebrate species, individuals of one or both sexes select for some features among potential mates in an effort to optimize their reproductive success. Sex pheromones are chemicals that help in chemical communication between individuals of the same species. The male red-garter snake, *Thamnophis sirtalis*, displays a courtship preference for larger female snakes. Researchers tested the hypothesis that males could distinguish among females of varying size by the composition of the skin lipids that act as pheromones.

Skin lipid samples were collected from small females (46.2 ± 2.7 cm in length) and large females (63 ± 2.6 cm in length). The samples were analysed by gas chromatography and the relative concentrations of saturated and unsaturated lipids were determined. The graphs show the time profiles when different lipids emerged from the gas chromatography column.

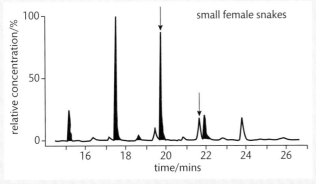

LeMaster and Mason 2002

LeMaster and Mason 2002

The shaded peaks represent saturated lipids and the unshaded peaks represent unsaturated lipids.

(a) Using the graph for large female snakes, state the relative concentration of the unsaturated lipid corresponding to the peak at 26 minutes. (1)

(b) Using the graph for small snakes, calculate the ratio of unsaturated to saturated lipids indicated by the arrows (1)

(c) Compare the pheromone profile of large female snakes with the profile of small female snakes. (2)

(d) (i) Suggest an experiment to test the hypothesis that the male red-garter snake could discriminate between larger and smaller female snakes (2)

(ii) Suggest an advantage for male snakes selecting larger females. (1)

(Total 7 marks)

2 Discuss the use of the pupil reflex for indication of brain death.

(Total 2 marks)

3 Compare the roles of the parasympathetic and sympathetic nervous systems.

(Total 4 marks)

4 Queen honey bees produce pheromones (chemicals) that modulate many aspects of worker bee physiology and behaviour. This is critical for colony social organization. During the first 24 days, worker bees, *Apis millifera*, go through a series of occupational specializations controlled by the pheromones of the queen. The diagram below is a record of the first 24 days in the life of one worker bee. Adding the heights of the bars for a particular day gives 100% of the activity for that day.

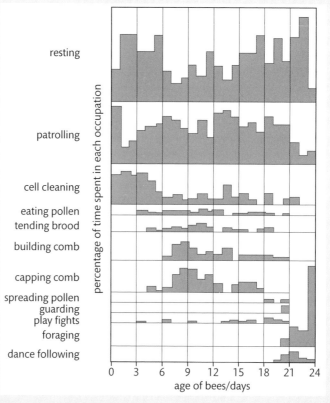

Gould 1992

(a) (i) Determine the percentage of time the bee spent on cleaning on day 1. (1)

(ii) Calculate the ratio of time spent foraging to the time spent patrolling on day 24. (1)

(b) Identify the two most common activities of the bee over the 24 days. (1)

(c) Other than resting and patrolling, describe the changes in the bee's activities over the 24 days. (3)

(d) Suggest why patrolling is a social behaviour. (1)

(Total 7 marks)

5 Blue crabs, *Callinectus sapidus*, hunt clams in river streams. In response to being attacked the clams release chemicals. The hunting behaviour of the blue crabs was studied by recording their movements after the release of the chemical, which was visualized by adding a dye (noted by shading in the figure below). The behaviour was studied and recorded under three different water velocities (expressed in cm s^{-1}).

Each graph below shows the movement of a single crab recorded at 1 s intervals, as it moves upstream towards the source of the chemical.

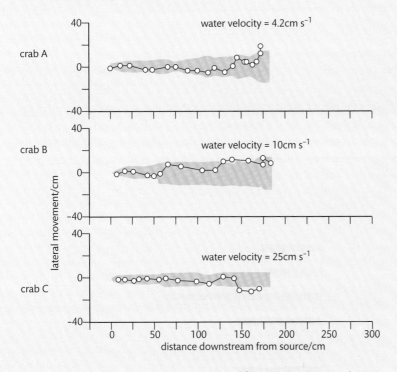

Adapted from Zimmer-Faust et al. 1995

(a) Identify which crab shows the greatest lateral movement. (1)

(b) Calculate the greatest speed of crab movement at 150 cm from the source of the chemical. (1)

(c) Compare the effect of water velocity on the hunting behaviour of blue crabs. (2)

(d) Discuss two other factors that could influence the outcome of this experiment. (2)

(Total 6 marks)

6 **(a)** Label the diagram of the human eye shown below. (2)

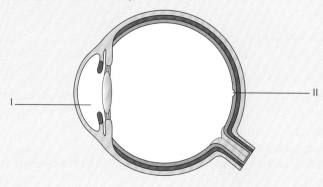

I

II

Jones and Jones 1997

(b) State **one** effect of the parasympathetic nervous system. (1)

(*Total 3 marks*)

7 In the bee *Centris pallida*, the male performs one of two mating behaviours known as patrolling or hovering. Insect pheromone (chemical) signalling controls mating behaviour. Patrolling bees search close to the ground, waiting to mate with virgin females as soon as they mature and emerge from their burrows. When a female emerges, the patrolling males spend so much time fighting among themselves that often none of them mate with the female so it flies to a tree to feed. The hovering bees fly higher than the patrolling bees, or fly around the trees. When a hovering bee sees a female he pursues her and tries to mate with her.

Scientists caught 100 hovering bees, 250 patrolling bees, and 150 mating bees and measured the width of the head of each bee.

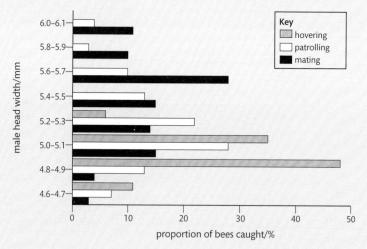

Chapman and Reiss 1999

(a) Identify the largest head width range found in the sample of hovering bees. (1)

(b) Calculate the number of mating bees with head width from 5.8 to 5.9 mm. (1)

(c) Deduce the relationship between head width and mating success. (2)

(d) Suggest why bees with small heads tend to hover rather than patrol. (1)

(*Total 5 marks*)

8 Evidence suggests that the behaviour of bees is often a response to odours. Scientists placed bees 200 cm away from an attractive odour source. An experimental group of bees had previous exposure to the odour, a control group had no previous exposure. Both the percentage of bees flying towards (orientated flight) and the percentage circling the odour source were measured.

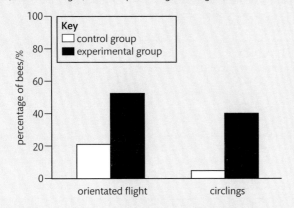

Adapted from Chaffiol et al. 2005

(a) Calculate the percentage increase in orientated flight between the control group and the experimental group. (1)

(b) Describe the effect of previous exposure to the odour on the flight of bees. (2)

(c) Outline the type of behaviour that the experimental group demonstrates. (1)

(d) Discuss the implications of this study for the survival of bees. (3)

(Total 7 marks)

9 **(a)** Label the diagram of the retina below. (2)

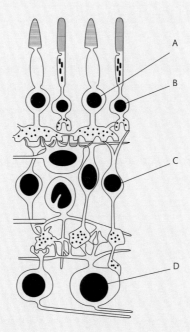

Adapted from Dowling and Boycott 1966
© 1966, The Royal Society. By permission of the Royal Society.

(b) Draw an arrow on the diagram above to indicate the direction in which light is moving. (1)

(c) Compare the functions of rod and cone cells. (3)

(Total 6 marks)

08

Option B: Biotechnology and bioinformatics

Essential ideas

| **B.1** | Microorganisms can be used and modified to perform industrial processes. |

| **B.2** | Crops can be modified to increase yields and to obtain novel products. |

| **B.3** | Biotechnology can be used in the prevention and mitigation of contamination from industrial, agricultural, and municipal wastes. |

Nucleotides of the human genome.

Biotechnology has been used for centuries to bake bread, make cheese, and brew alcoholic beverages. However, recent developments in biotechnology have given the term a new meaning. Modern biotechnology has captured the attention of everyone. Modern biotechnology offers us the chance to make dramatic improvements in industry, agriculture, medicine, and environmental science. Bioinformatics is the workhorse of biotechnology, and includes processes such as data mining and managing databases of biological information.

Because microorganisms are so metabolically diverse and have a fast growth rate, they can be invaluable to us. With genetic engineering we have accomplished mass production of penicillin, a key antibiotic; mass production of citric acid, one of the most widely used food-flavouring agents; and the production of biogas, which could be a main energy source of the future.

You may have heard of GMOs (genetically modified organisms). Genetic modification has created soybeans that are resistant to herbicides. When the herbicides are applied to kill the weeds, the soybeans are not affected. Genes for making vaccines have been put into plants, which can solve the problems of cost and global shortages of vaccines. Large databases have been developed to help find the genes necessary for these genetic modifications. The long-term impact of these new processes is unknown. Have these new discoveries been properly scrutinized?

Diverse metabolic processes can be used to help us clean up our polluted planet. Some bacteria are used to break down oil spills, remove benzene from polluted waters, and eliminate toxic mercury. The recent discovery of groups of organisms called biofilms could be very important for these types of processes.

B.1 Microbiology: organisms in industry

Understandings:

- Microorganisms are metabolically diverse.
- Microorganisms are used in industry because they are small and have a fast growth rate.
- Pathway engineering optimizes genetic and regulatory processes within microorganisms.
- Pathway engineering is used industrially to produce metabolites of interest.
- Fermenters allow large-scale production of metabolites by microorganisms.
- Fermentation is carried out by batch or continuous culture.
- Microorganisms in fermenters become limited by their own waste products.
- Probes are used to monitor conditions within fermenters.
- Conditions are maintained at optimal levels for the growth of the microorganisms being cultured.

383

Applications and skills:

- Application: Deep-tank batch fermentation in the mass production of penicillin.
- Application: Production of citric acid in a continuous fermenter by *Aspergillus niger* and its use as a preservative and flavouring.
- Application: Biogas is produced by bacteria and archaeans from organic matter in fermenters.
- Skill: Gram staining of Gram-positive and Gram-negative bacteria.
- Skill: Experiments showing zone of inhibition of bacterial growth by bactericides in sterile bacterial cultures.
- Skill: Production of biogas in a small-scale fermenter.

Microorganisms in industry

There are three main reasons why microorganisms are used in industry.

1   They are small. Microorganisms such as yeast and bacteria are single-celled organisms.

2   They have a fast growth rate. For example, bacteria reproduce by binary fission (splitting) and can reproduce in 30 minutes. If you start with 100 cells at time 0, how many cells will you have in 30 minutes? In 60 minutes? In 90 minutes? The answers: 200, 400, and 800, respectively.

3   They are metabolically diverse. This means that they have diverse sources of carbon, which they use to build other molecules. Some microorganisms use larger organic molecules such as glucose, $C_6H_{12}O_6$, for a carbon source. Others use molecules as small as methane, CH_4. They also use diverse sources of energy. Some microorganisms use sunlight and others use the energy held in the chemical bonds of molecules.

Microorganisms can be classified into four nutritional groups based on their type of metabolism.

- Photoautotrophic organisms use sunlight for energy, and carbon dioxide (CO_2) as their carbon source. Examples include algae.

- Photoheterotroph organisms use sunlight for energy, and carbon from organic compounds as their carbon source. Examples include purple bacteria.

Bacterial colonies growing on nutrient agar in a Petri dish.

- Chemoautotroph organisms use inorganic compounds for energy, and carbon dioxide as their carbon source. Examples include sulfur bacteria that use hydrogen sulfide (H_2S) for energy.
- Chemoheterotroph organisms use preformed organic compounds as their energy source and as their carbon source. Examples include fungi, protozoa, and bacteria.

CHALLENGE YOURSELF

1   Fill in Table 8.1 as you read about the metabolic diversity of microorganisms.

Table 8.1 Examples of different types of metabolism of microorganisms

Type of metabolism	Energy source	Carbon source	Example

'Auto' means self and 'troph' means feeder, so an autotroph is a self-feeder. An alga makes its own glucose through the process of photosynthesis. 'Hetero' means other. Bacteria must decompose other organisms or products of organisms in order to get their food.

Products made by microorganisms

What are some of the products made from microorganisms? See how many you can think of before you look at the lists of examples below.

Foods:

- bread
- cheese
- yogurt
- wine
- beer
- soy sauce
- many more.

Commodities:

- food additives such as amino acids and vitamins
- solvents such as alcohol and acetone
- biofuels such as ethanol and methane.

Chemicals:

- pharmaceuticals such as antibiotics and steroid hormones
- biochemicals such as enzymes and proteins.

In the making of yogurt, lactose sugar in the milk is broken down by the lactase enzyme of the bacteria fermenting the milk.

Pathway engineering

Remember the enzymatic pathways you studied which are necessary for cell respiration and photosynthesis? Using pathway engineering, scientists attempt to introduce new genes to adjust these pathways. Pathway or metabolic engineering is the practice of optimizing genetic and regulatory processes within microorganisms for our use. The point of controlling the genes of a microorganism and regulating its biochemical pathways is to increase the production of a substance that we want by that cell.

Here is an example of pathway engineering.

- A bacteria such as *Escherichia coli* has a biochemical pathway that it uses to make a short-chain (2-carbon) alcohol.
- We introduce new genes into the *E. coli* bacteria that change the genes and modify the way the pathway works. In other words, we regulate the pathway by changing the genes that control the pathway.
- The product of the pathway is now a long-chain (5-carbon) alcohol made by the *E. coli*. The pathway has been engineered.

> *E. coli* makes a short-chain alcohol C–C (not much energy stored in these few chemical bonds)

$\rightarrow$ new gene added

> *E. coli* makes a long-chain alcohol C–C–C–C–C
>
> (this long chain obviously has more bonds, so more energy is trapped in it that can be used as fuel)

Such an engineered pathway was first achieved at UCLA at the Henry Samueli School of Engineering and Applied Science. But why do we want to make longer chain alcohols? Longer chain molecules are of interest to us because they contain more energy, and are important in the production of gasoline and jet fuel.

Metabolites of interest

The alcohol produced by *E. coli* in the example above is called a metabolite. A metabolite is a product of a biochemical pathway. Enzymes regulate these pathways and genes control the enzymes. Thus we have seen with *E. coli* that a change in genes can affect the pathway and produce a desired product, the metabolite of interest. This can be done without interfering with the normal bacterial growth and reproduction. Industrial microbiology attempts to modify the existing pathways of microorganisms so that they can be efficient factories for particular compounds (the metabolites of interest). Pathway engineering has been very successful using bacteria and yeast because:

- these organisms have a high yield compared with plants
- these organisms have a fast growth rate
- the desired product can be easily purified
- the carbon sources needed (glucose or glycerol) are simple and inexpensive.

The beneficial outcomes of the technique of pathway engineering, which was only developed in the 1990s, include:

- sustainable processes for the production of fuel and chemicals from renewable sources
- drugs to treat diseases
- increased production of antibiotics and supplements
- processes to help clean up the environment.

Successful pathways

The French company Sanofi has begun brewing baker's yeast to make malaria drugs on an industrial scale. It will produce 70 million doses a year. This breakthrough was published in the journal *Nature* in April 2013. The drug is called artemisinin.

Amyris is the biotech start-up company that initially engineered the pathway to produce artemisinin. Before that, the drug could only be obtained from sweet wormwood plants. The costs of obtaining it from the plants are high and production is unstable. Three enzymes were isolated and taken from the sweet wormwood plant and introduced into a pathway in baker's yeast. The pathway-engineered process will take about 3 months to produce the metabolite of interest, compared with the 15 months for the plant-based method. The pharmaceutical company Sanofi has pledged to sell the drug without profit.

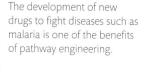

The development of new drugs to fight diseases such as malaria is one of the benefits of pathway engineering.

Figure 8.1 The pathway to artemisinic acid.

Figure 8.1 shows the pathway to artemisinic acid, which will be chemically converted into the malaria drug artemisinin. The enzymes are obtained from the sweet wormwood plant.

> Malaria affects millions of people and kills 650 000 a year. Most victims are children.

> Malaria is one of the oldest diseases known to humans. In the 4th century BC malaria devastated the populations of the Greek city states.

Worked example

1 What is a metabolite?
2 Name an organism whose 'pathway' was engineered.
3 What metabolite was made as a result of pathway engineering?
4 Name a second organism.
5 What metabolite was made as a result of pathway engineering of this organism?

Solutions

1 A product of a biochemical pathway.
2 *E. coli.*
3 Long-chain alcohol.
4 Yeast.
5 Artemisinic acid.

Researchers at MIT and Tufts University have engineered a metabolic pathway of the bacteria *E. coli*. They have enabled it to produce a large quantity of a precursor molecule to the important anticancer drug Taxol. Taxol is a powerful inhibitor of cell division that is used to treat ovarian, lung, and breast cancer. This drug was initially isolated from the Pacific yew tree, *Taxus brevifolia*. Two to four trees are needed to produce enough drug to treat one patient. Drug companies anticipate that using *E. coli* will significantly lower the cost of the drug.

Half of all prescription drugs are from rainforest plants or marine sponges. Sweet wormwood comes from the forests of China. However, rampant deforestation is decimating China's forests: 80% have already been lost.

Fermentation

NATURE OF SCIENCE

The discovery of a bacteria that causes stomach ulcers was the result of serendipity. The researchers who hypothesized that it was not acid but bacteria that caused ulcers could not get the bacteria to grow. Without evidence, there was no support for their hypothesis. By accident they left the bacteria in a culture dish for 4 days over a holiday weekend. When they returned the bacteria had grown. In 1950, J. Robin Warren and Barry Marshall won the Nobel Prize for this discovery. Antibiotics can often be used to cure ulcers instead of surgery.

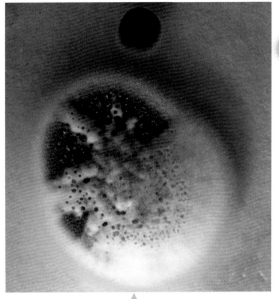

A colony of *Penicillium* mould growing in a Petri dish of nutrient agar. Notice the shiny yellow bacterial colonies in the lower right corner. The mould may just grow over the top of the bacteria and kill the colonies.

In 1928, Alexander Flemming, a Scottish biologist, noticed that *Penicillium notatum*, a mould, had killed staphylococcus bacteria in a culture dish. It was then discovered that penicillin has an active ingredient that inhibits the synthesis of cell walls of bacteria, so preventing them from reproducing. That initial serendipitous discovery let to the development of penicillin as an antibiotic. Penicillin was used to treat the thousands of wounded during World War II, thus saving many lives.

As it is possible to come up with many hypotheses to fit a given set of observations, how did Alexander Flemming in 1928 prove that it was the mould that had killed the staphylococcus bacteria in the culture dish, and not something else?

Industrial microbiology is now growing microorganisms on a large scale to produce valuable products such as penicillin commercially. This process is referred to as fermentation. Currently, antibiotics are the most important product of fermentation.

Figure 8.2 A fermenter. http://www.htl-innovativ.at/index.php?lang=eng&modul=detail&id=178

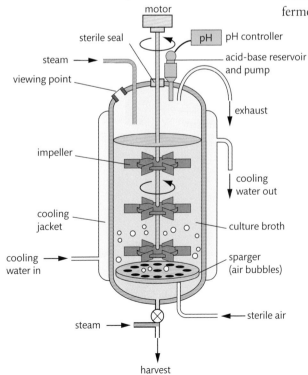

Large-scale production of metabolites

The need for penicillin means that there is a demand for large-scale production. Fermenters have been developed that are large-scale vats that can be controlled so that fermentation can take place in an optimal environment. Fermenters have:

- a size that fits the need for optimum production of the desired metabolite, e.g. penicillin
- a means of mechanical agitation or air bubbles for mixing the microorganism with the substrate materials
- devices to maintain the optimum temperature
- probes to monitor the environment for optimum industrial production
- processes for avoiding contamination.

Eventually, the end product can be turned into crystals, packaged, and sold.

Probes

Sterile probes are commonly used to monitor the following conditions in large-scale fermenters:

- oxygen concentrations
- carbon dioxide concentrations
- pH levels
- temperature
- pressure
- stirrer speed.

An imbalance in the any of above could have a harmful effect on the growth of the microorganism that is producing the metabolite of interest.

Batches

A batch is the volume of nutrients and other materials (substrate) added to a fermenter. Two types of batches are:

1. fed-batch, where the nutrient and substrate are added a little at a time
2. continuous-batch, where the substrate is added continuously and an equal amount of fermented medium is continuously removed.

Deep-tank fermentation of penicillin

The current type of mould that is used to produce penicillin industrially is *Penicillium chrysogenum*. This mould gets its energy to reproduce and grow from glucose. This occurs in a liquid medium in flasks outside the batch fermenter, and produces pyruvic acid as the primary metabolite. We do not want to collect this metabolite, but its production is unavoidable because it is a product of the mould breaking down glucose to get energy. When the biomass of *Penicillium* has reached a sufficient level, it is placed in the batch fermenter (see Figure 8.3).

The batch fermenter is missing glucose, which will starve the *Penicillium*. Why do we want this mould to starve? It is in fact when *Penicillium* mould is starving that it makes penicillin! Penicillin is a secondary metabolite produced in times of stress by the *Penicillium* mould: it is a defence mechanism against other organisms in its environment. Secondary metabolites are metabolites produced by a microorganism that are not used for energy. We need to duplicate the starvation mode for the mould so that it will make large quantities of penicillin.

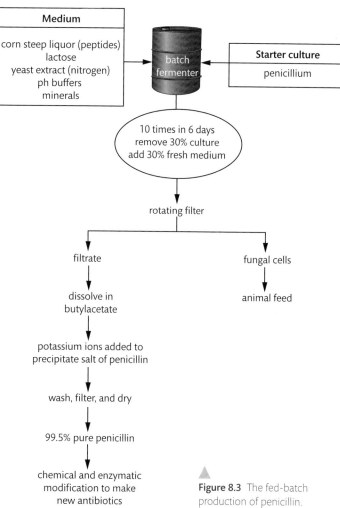

Figure 8.3 The fed-batch production of penicillin.

This is *Penicillium* again, growing in a Petri dish. Remember that when the mould is starving it makes penicillin. In batch fermentation, the starvation mode needs to be duplicated so that the mould will make large quantities of penicillin.

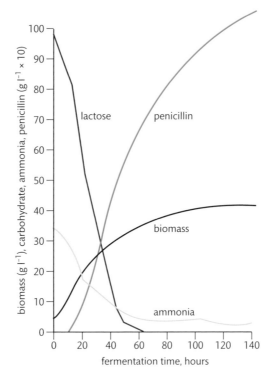

Figure 8.4 Penicillin fermentation using *Penicillium chrysogenum* during secondary metabolism. The production of penicillin increases as the biomass of the mould levels off (the stationary phase).

The following substances are put into the deep-tank fermenter to produce penicillin:

- lactose
- yeast extract
- corn steep liquor
- buffers
- minerals.

Using lactose in the medium of the batch fermenter will begin to starve the *Penicillium*. Notice on the graph that, as the lactose is broken down, the penicillin is produced. Yeast extract is a source of nitrogen; corn steep liquor provides peptides; buffers resist pH changes; and minerals are needed by the mould for nutrients.

Also notice on the graph that the biomass of the mould is levelling off while the penicillin production is increasing. The stage of bacterial growth when penicillin is produced is called the stationary phase. The bacteria is hardly reproducing at all, but making large quantities of penicillin. Why?

The mould is in a stressful situation because of the lack of a sugar and carbon source. It responds by making penicillin to defend itself against other organisms that might be present and competing with it for the lactose.

Optimal conditions in the fermenter

Optimal conditions in a deep-tank fermenter are maintained by:

- a fed-batch method, which is ideal to keep *Penicillium* producing penicillin
- probes, which measure the pH, temperature, and oxygen levels
- oxygen, which is added by the sparger (see Figure 8.2) because *Penicillium* is an aerobic organism and needs an oxygen supply for fermentation
- a cooling jacket, which reduces the heat given off by metabolism
- NaOH, to maintain the correct pH of 6.5.

Fermenters are limited by their own waste products

When penicillin builds up in the fermenter, the excess penicillin inhibits an enzyme in the penicillin-producing pathway, so production stops. Thus the penicillin product must be removed efficiently for the system to continue. The volume in the fermenter must remain constant, so more material is added in a fed-batch manner as the product is removed.

Aspergillus is a common species of mould found all over the world in many different climates. This mould grows on carbon-rich substrates such as glucose and starch

Continuous-batch fermentation of citric acid

Another product that is very commonly used and made by a mould is citric acid. It is not an antibiotic but a food additive. Look at a can of tomatoes in your food cupboard and you will probably see citric acid on the label. You might also see citric acid on the ingredient lists of powdered drinks, jars of jam, jars of maraschino cherries, or sundried tomatoes, and many other foods. Citric acid is one of the most important industrial microbial products: 550 000 tonnes of citric acid are made every year by the simple mould *Aspergillus niger*.

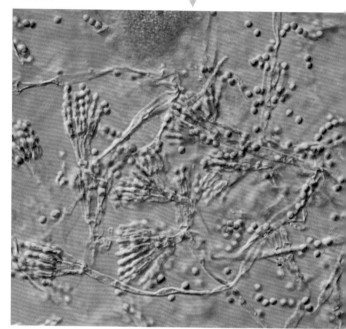

Uses of citric acid

Before the production of citric acid by fermentation, it was obtained from the juice of citrus fruit. When World War I interfered with the harvesting of the Italian lemon crop, natural citric acid became a rarity. In 1917 an American food chemist discovered that *A. niger* could efficiently produce citric acid. Industrial production was started 2 years later. Citric acid is a flavour enhancer, maintains the pH of a food product, and can be used as a preservative. Most industrially produced citric acid is made using *A. niger* with molasses as the substrate, i.e. as the carbon and sugar source.

In this molecular model of citric acid carbon is shown in black, hydrogen in white and oxygen in red.

Production of citric acid

Researchers have found that continuous-batch fermentation for 50 days using molasses as a substrate gives an 85% yield of citric acid, whereas fed-batch fermentation only yields 65% of citric acid.

Continuous-batch fermentation is an open system where equivalent amounts of a sterile nutrient solution such as molasses are added to the fermenter. An equal amount of solution containing the metabolite of interest is withdrawn. Thus the total amount remains the same. This maintains a steady-state in the fermenter, where the loss of mould cells is balanced by the growth of new mould cells.

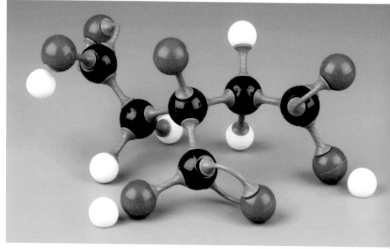

CHALLENGE YOURSELF

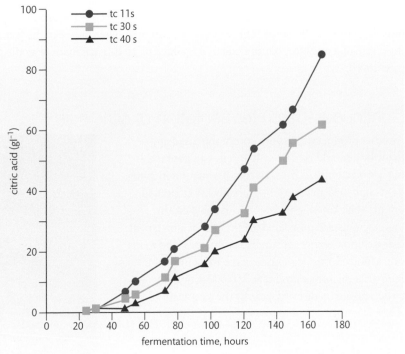

Figure 8.5 The effect of agitation: the relationship between circulation time (tc) and citric acid production by *A. niger* in a tubular loop bioreactor. Papagianni 2007

2 Look at Figure 8.5. Compare and contrast the results of agitation time on citric acid production at 11 seconds, 30 seconds, and 40 seconds.

3 What conclusion can you draw from this graph?

4 Formulate a hypothesis as to why this is occurring.

Worked example

1 What is the purpose of fermentation in industry?

2 How are conditions monitored?

3 Name four conditions that are monitored.

4 Name the two types of 'batches'.

5 Name one mould used in industrial fermentation.

6 What metabolite does it produce?

7 Name another mould used in industrial fermentation.

8 What metabolite does it produce?

Solutions

1 To make metabolites on a large scale.

2 Using probes.

3 pH, temperature, concentration of carbon dioxide, and of oxygen.

4 Fed and continuous. Fed is where the nutrient and substrate are added a little at a time. Continuous batch is where substrate is continuously added and an equal amount of fermented medium is continuously removed.

5 *Penicillium chrysogenum.*

6 Penicillin.

7 *Aspergillus niger.*

8 Citric acid.

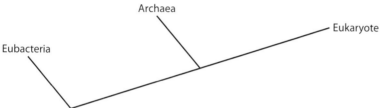

Biogas production by archaeans and bacteria

One of the renewable energy sources of the future may be biogas. In the UK it is projected that 17% of vehicle fuel has the potential to be replaced by compressed biogas. Biogas can be used for heating and cooking as well as running engines. Where does biogas come from and how do we get it? Not surprisingly, it is one more product that can be produced by microorganisms.

Classification of archaeans

Carl Woese was studying microorganisms when he realized that scientists were making mistakes in their classification of living things. Thanks to new technology, Woese and his colleagues noticed a large difference in the ribosomal (r)RNA of a group previously considered to be prokaryotes. Based on this, Woese and his colleagues suggested a classification level called a domain. According to this system, there are three domains of all living things: Archaea, Eubacteria (prokaryotes), and Eukaryote (eukaroytes).

Archaea

Eukaryote

Eubacteria

Figure 8.6 The three domains for classifying living organisms.

- Eubacteria: 'true' bacteria, prokaryotes with no organized nucleus and no membrane-bound organelles. An example is *Escherichia coli*, which is commonly found in animal waste products.
- Archaea: archaeabacteria or 'ancient' bacteria are also prokaryotes. Most groups live in extreme environments. An example is the sulfur bacteria that inhabits the hot springs of Yellowstone National Park in the USA.
- Eukaryote: single-celled and multicellular organisms that all have their DNA contained in a nucleus. The kingdoms of plants, animals, protists, and fungi belong here.

Biogas fermenter

Both prokaryotes and archaeans work in a fermenter when biogas is produced. In the fermenter, the enzymes of the prokaryotes and archaeans break down biodegradable materials such as plant products by anaerobic digestion (digestion without oxygen). The materials produced are simple molecules, one of which is biogas. Biogas is made of:

- 50–75% methane
- 25–45% carbon dioxide
- 0–10% nitrogen
- 0–3% hydrogen sulfide
- 2–7% water.

In a biogas fermenter the following process takes place, in this sequence, in the absence of oxygen:

1 liquefaction, the hydrolysis (splitting) of long-chain organic compounds

2 acidification, resulting in short-chain fatty acids, plus hydrogen and carbon dioxide

Large biogas fermenters: the advantage of biogas over wind and solar is that it is always available. Biogas can be stored and accumulated.

Using a small-scale biogas digester such as this one in India, farmers can trap methane instead of letting it escape from rotting manure into the environment. Methane from farms is a significant greenhouse gas.

3 acetic acid formation, resulting in acetic acid, plus hydrogen and carbon dioxide

4 methane formation (methanogenesis), the action of archaean bacteria on the products to produce methane.

Each of the four stages requires specific bacteria. In the fourth stage, the microorganism required to produce the biogas (methane) is an archaean. Other factors must be kept constant:

• there must be no free oxygen (the bacteria in the fermenter are anaerobic)
• the temperature must be about 35°C
• the pH must not be too acidic because methane-producing bacteria are sensitive to acid.

Sometimes small farms use biogas fermenters. The biogas produced can be used to run electrical machinery, which reduces a farmer's costs. A high-quality fertilizer without weeds or odour is a by-product that can be used instead of manure, and pollution caused by water run-off containing animal waste is reduced. Globally, methane emission is lowered with the use of biogas. Methane is a greenhouse gas that contributes to global warming.

Gram staining

In order to help identify different groups of bacteria, staining techniques are used. Bacteria can be divided into two groups based on the structure of their cell wall; the Gram stain differentiates between the two types. Gram-positive bacteria have a simple cell wall and Gram-negative bacteria have a cell wall that is more complex (see Figure 8.7). They differ in the amount of peptidoglycan present. Peptidoglycan is an important material for bacteria. It consists of sugars joined to polypeptides, and acts like a giant molecular network protecting the cell. Gram-positive bacteria have large amounts of peptidoglycan and Gram-negative bacteria have a small amount. Only Gram-negative bacteria have an outer membrane with attached lipopolysaccharide molecules. Lipopolysaccharides are carbohydrates bonded to lipids. These molecules are usually toxic to a host. The outer membrane protects against the host defences. The outer membrane also protects the Gram-negative bacteria from antibiotics.

Can you see why an antibiotic like penicillin works more effectively against Gram-positive bacteria? The Gram-positive bacteria have no outer membrane to protect them from an antibiotic.

Table 8.2 compares the cell walls of Gram-positive and Gram-negative bacteria.

Table 8.2 Gram-positive and Gram-negative bacteria

	Gram-positive bacteria	Gram-negative bacteria
Cell wall structure	Simple	Complex
Amount of peptidoglycan	Large amount	Small amount
Peptidoglycan placement	In outer layer of bacteria	Covered by outer membrane
Outer membrane	Absent	Present with lipopolysaccharides attached

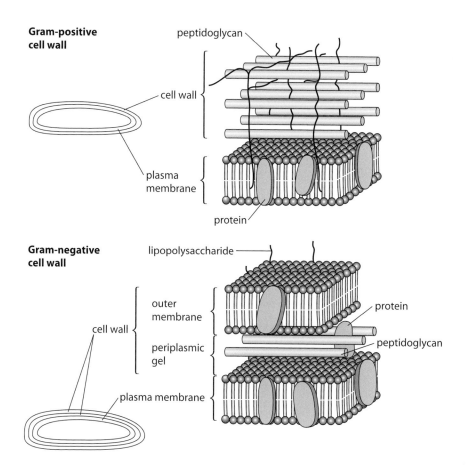

Figure 8.7 Diagram of the cell wall structure of bacteria.

Worked example

If you were sick with a bacterial infection, would you prefer it to be a Gram-negative bacterium or a Gram-positive bacterium that was infecting you? Why?

Solution

Gram positive. Gram-positive bacteria can be destroyed by antibiotics because they do not have an outer membrane to protect them.

Worked example

Look again at Figure 8.7. To help you remember the structure of the cell wall of Gram-negative bacteria and Gram-positive bacteria, can you think of two different types of cookie/biscuit that imitate the cell wall structure of each?

Solution

Gram-negative bacteria are like a cookie or biscuit with cream or frosting/icing between two outside pieces. The frosting or icing in the centre is the peptidoglycan. Gram-positive bacteria are like a cookie or biscuit with frosting or icing only on the top. Again, the frosting/icing is the peptidoglycan. Remember that Gram-positive bacteria are not resistant to antibiotics because they do not have an outer membrane (a top layer of cookie/biscuit above the frosting/icing).

 Memory tip: it is positive to be infected by a Gram-positive bacterium.

Gram-stain technique

Safety alerts: Follow standard safety protocols for bacterial work.

Gram-positive bacteria retain the primary dye and Gram-negative bacteria are easily decolourized.

- Add bacteria to a glass slide and fix on the slide with heat.
- Apply crystal violet stain.
- Flood with iodine.
- Rinse off iodine.
- Decolorize with alcohol.
- Counterstain with safranin.

Gram-positive bacteria will stain violet and Gram-negative will stain pink.

Production of biogas in a small-scale fermenter

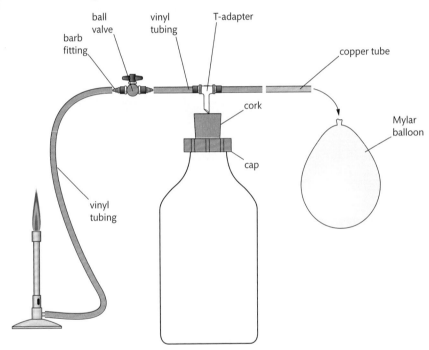

Figure 8.8 Production of biogas in a small-scale fermenter.

When a slurry of organic material and water is added to the fermenter, eventually methane will be produced. The methane can be collected in the Mylar balloon. To test whether it is methane, attach the burner and squeeze the balloon. If the burner lights it is methane gas rather than just carbon dioxide.

Biogas may be directly combustible and used in boilers, turbines, or fuel cells. It can be used for heating water, producing steam, or for space heating. Biogas can be used in all applications designed for natural gas.

Section summary

- Microorganisms are very useful in industrial processes because they are small, have a fast growth rate, and are metabolically diverse. Their metabolic diversity allows them to use different sources of energy, such as sunlight, organic molecules, and inorganic molecules.
- Many different foods, such as yogurt, chemicals, such as antibiotics, and commodities, such as biofuels, are made industrially using microorganisms.
- Metabolic engineers try to modify the metabolism of microorganisms by engineering their biochemical pathways in order to make metabolites for our use. One such metabolite is penicillin.

- Large-scale production of metabolites is done commercially in fermenters.
- Penicillin is a metabolite made in a large-scale fermenter by the *Penicillium* mould.
- Optimum conditions are maintained in fermenters with the use of probes, an oxygen supply, and both temperature and pH control mechanisms.
- Citric acid is another important industrial metabolite, made by the mould *Aspergillus niger*.
- Biogas is made by fermentation of biodegradable materials such as plant products. This process takes place in the absence of oxygen (anaerobically) by the action of several specific types of bacteria.
- Bacteria can be divided into two types based on a stain called the Gram stain. Gram-negative bacteria have an outer membrane, which protects them from antibiotics and host defenses. Gram-positive bacteria do not have an outer membrane and so are susceptible to antibiotics.

Exercises

1 Describe pathway engineering.

2 Compare and contrast batch and continuous culture.

3 Compare and contrast Gram-negative and Gram-positive bacteria.

4 List four reasons why pathway engineering of bacteria and yeast has been very successful.

B.2 Biotechnology in agriculture

NATURE OF SCIENCE

Assessing risks and benefits associated with scientific research: scientists need to evaluate the potential of herbicide resistance genes escaping into the wild population.

Understandings:

- Transgenic organisms produce proteins that were not previously part of their species' proteome.
- Genetic modification can be used to overcome environmental resistance to increase crop yields.
- Genetically modified crop plants can be used to produce novel products.
- Bioinformatics plays a role in identifying target genes.
- The target gene is linked to other sequences that control its expression.
- An open reading frame is a significant length of DNA from a start codon to a stop codon.
- Marker genes are used to indicate successful uptake.
- Recombinant DNA must be inserted into the plant cell and taken up by its chromosome or chloroplast DNA.
- Recombinant DNA can be introduced into whole plants, leaf discs, or protoplasts.
- Recombinant DNA can be introduced by direct physical and chemical methods, or indirectly by vectors.

Applications and skills:

- Application: Use of tumour-inducing (Ti) plasmid of *Agrobacterium tumefaciens* to introduce glyphosate resistance into soybean crops.
- Application: Genetic modification of tobacco mosaic virus to allow bulk production of hepatitis B vaccine in tobacco plants.
- Application: Production of Amflora potato (*Solanum tuberosum*) for paper and adhesive industries.
- Skill: Evaluation of data on environmental impact of glyphosate-tolerant soybeans.
- Skill: Identification of an open reading frame (ORF).

Guidance

- A significant length of DNA for an open reading frame contains sufficient nucleotides to code for a polypeptide chain.
- Limit the chemical methods of introducing genes into plants to calcium chloride and liposomes.
- Limit the physical methods of introducing genes into plants to electroporation, microinjection, and biolistics (gunshot).
- Limit vectors to Agrobacterium tumefaciens *and tobacco mosaic virus.*

Genetic modification of crops

You may have already heard of genetically modified (GM) crops. A GM plant has been modified with the introduction of a gene that does not normally occur in that species. When genes are expressed, the result is a protein or series of proteins. GM plants have been given new genes so that new proteins are made.

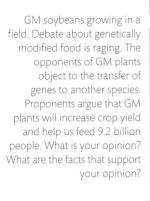
GM soybeans growing in a field. Debate about genetically modified food is raging. The opponents of GM plants object to the transfer of genes to another species. Proponents argue that GM plants will increase crop yield and help us feed 9.2 billion people. What is your opinion? What are the facts that support your opinion?

A new proteome

A proteome is the set of proteins expressed by the genome (all the genes) of a species. For example, soybeans have certain genes that express proteins that give the soybean specific traits. Proteins can be enzymes or structural molecules that cause physical characteristics (e.g. colour and leaf shape). When a new gene is introduced into a species, that new gene is called a transgene. Transgenic organisms produce proteins that were not previously part of their species' proteome. For example, a gene can be introduced to make soybeans resistant to the herbicide glyphosate. When glyphosate is sprayed onto weeds, the transgenic soybean is not harmed because it is resistant to it. The weeds are killed and the soybean crop benefits. The transgenic soybeans are an example of a genetically modified organism (GMO).

Worked example

Provide the terms that describe the following statement, or answers to the questions.

1 All of the genes of a certain species.
2 A set of proteins expressed by the genome of a species.
3 A new gene introduced into a crop.
4 An organism that produces proteins not previously part of the proteome of that species.
5 A gene introduced into soybeans.
6 A spray for weeds.
7 Desired benefits for soybean crops.
8 A GMO plant.

Solutions

1 Genome.

2 Proteome.

3 Transgene.

4 Transgenic.

5 Glyphosate resistance.

6 Glyphosate.

7 Soybean grows well because the weeds have been killed.

8 GMO soybean.

Increasing crop yield

Why do we need biotechnology to help increase crop yields? By 2050 the world population will have increased to 9.2 billion, a 4-fold increase in 100 years, making food production a huge social issue. In the 1800s Thomas Malthus famously predicted that our food demand would outstrip our food supply. We are facing that situation now. However, new technologies using recombinant DNA to produce transgenic crops may be able to increase the yield of some of the basic crops. In 2007, 12 million farmers in 23 countries were growing GM crops.

Environmental resistance

The goal of GM crops is to overcome environmental resistance to increase crop yields. Environmental resistance consists of limiting factors in the environment which keep populations from reaching their maximum growth potential. Introducing a new gene can enhance the capacity of a crop plant to overcome the limitations of their environment. Some examples of limitations to crop yield and how they have been overcome are as follows.

- Insects: GM plants resistant to insects give a higher yield; examples of such GM crop plants include tobacco, tomato, potato, cotton, maize, sugar cane, and rice.
- Viral disease: 20 plant species are resistant to 30 viral diseases, preventing huge crop losses; for example, papaya has been given a gene that helps it resist the ring spot virus.
- Weeds: when a herbicide is sprayed to kill weeds, herbicide-resistant plants are not harmed and so the crop is not affected; for example, the crop yield of GM soybeans is higher.
- Drought: drought resistance can help prevent crop damage; for example, rice has been engineered so that it is protected against prolonged drought.

GM plants can overcome the factors that limit crop yields.

Novel products from GM plants

Novel products from GM plants include vitamins, pharmaceuticals, enzymes, and vaccines. Below are specific examples of the outcomes of genetic modification. As you will see, the introduction of new genes into crop plants can be done by physical methods, chemical methods, or by using a microorganism as a vector. Two microorganisms that are commonly used are a bacterium, *Agrobacterium tumefaciens*, and a virus, the tobacco mosaic virus, TMV.

In the 1800s, Thomas Malthus predicted that food demand would outstrip food supply.

By 2007, Spain was producing 50% of GM crops. Spain is the major European producer of maize genetically modified with a pesticide gene that kills insects that attack it. China is increasingly producing cotton with the same pesticide gene: currently 66% of its cotton crop has this gene.

Fifteen per cent of post-harvest food crops in developing countries is lost to insects.

Glyphosate resistance in soybean plants

Using less pesticide and herbicide is a goal. It was recognized in the 1950s that herbicides and pesticides harm many other organisms in an ecosystem as well as the targets. The development of herbicide-resistant soybeans has been developed as a response to this concern. Using a bacterium that naturally infects plants as a vector, a herbicide-resistant gene has been introduced into soybeans, *Glycine max*.

Figure 8.9 *Agrobacterium* is used to introduce glyphosate resistance into soybeans, *Glycine max*.

Agrobacterium tumefaciens + DNA

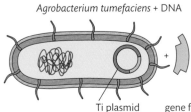

Ti plasmid

gene for glyphosate resistance is inserted into the plasmid

1 Tissue from a normal soybean is grown in culture medium.

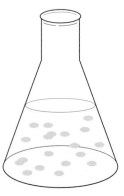

2 *Agrobacterium* introduces the new gene into the soybean cells growing in the liquid culture.

3 Each cell in the culture is grown into an entire plant, which contains the glyphosate-resistant gene.

Agrobacterium tumefaciens (agrobacter) is a pathogenic (disease-causing) bacterium that attacks plants. It can be engineered to be non-pathogenic but still have the ability to insert DNA into a plant. Agrobacter contains a circular piece of DNA called a plasmid that can enter a plant cell and insert genes into its chromosome. Scientists have developed methods to engineer this plasmid, called a Ti plasmid (tumour-inducing plasmid), and make it a vector for carrying genes of interest into plants. The plants express the gene by making a protein that is the desired product. In the case of soybeans, the protein is an enzyme that allows the plant to use an alternative pathway that causes resistance to the herbicide glyphosate. We call the soybeans glyphosate-tolerant soybeans. The common name for glyphosate is Roundup. Plants that contain this herbicide are called 'round-up ready'. Fields can be sprayed with glyphosate and the weeds are killed but the soybeans are not affected. Glyphosate is a broad-spectrum herbicide that travels in the phloem of the plant and is readily translocated to roots, stems, and leaves. It inhibits an enzyme, EPSPS, that is necessary for making essential amino acids. Without these essential amino acids, a plant cannot synthesize the proteins needed for growth.

Soybeans are a very valuable crop. An enormous amount of protein is produced per acre by soybeans. Soybean products include tofu, soymilk, and soy sauce.

Hepatitis B vaccine production from tobacco plants

Hepatitis B is an infectious disease of the liver caused by the hepatitis B virus. The disease has caused epidemics in many parts of the world. Vaccines for this disease have been routinely used since the 1980s. For years this vaccine has been made from yeast, but it is not cheap and has to be refrigerated. Most developing countries cannot afford it.

Hepatitis B is a vaccine that can be made by tobacco plants in bulk. A gene that makes an antibody to hepatitis B is inserted into a modified version of the tobacco mosaic virus (TMV). TMV is a retrovirus that has the capacity to cause disease in tobacco plants. As the virus is scratched on to the leaves of the tobacco plant, the plant becomes infected with the gene-carrying virus. The virus transfers the gene to the plant cells, and the result is the generation of antibodies. After a few days, leaves can be cut and fed to mice. The mice serum is then collected which provides a vaccine. Tobacco plants have plenty of biomass, so it is easy to see how bulk vaccines can be made.

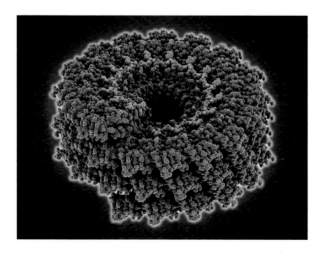

A computer model showing the molecular structure of the tobacco mosaic virus (TMV). This virus is made of RNA (green) and a protein coat (pink).

401

The Amflora potato

Just recently, for the first time since 1998, a GM crop has been approved to be grown in a European Union (EU) country. BASF Plant Science has developed a genetically modified potato, *Solanum tuberosum*, plant that is not to be consumed as a food product but to be used by industry. In order to be approved, various safeguards have been put in place to prevent this potato from mixing with conventional potato plants. Many rules and regulations must be followed about where the crop is grown, who grows it, and how it is shipped to a factory.

Amflora is a genetically optimized potato that produces only one starch component and is used for technical applications.

The potato is called the Amflora potato, and it is a breakthrough in production of amylopectin, a type of starch made by potatoes. Normally, potatoes produce 20% amylose and 80% amylopectin. The Amflora potato produces 100% amylopectin, which is a desirable product for industry. The gene in this potato that produces the 20% amylose has been turned off. Amflora starch is beneficial to the paper and adhesive industry. It gives printer paper a glossier look and makes concrete stick better to walls.

Despite regulatory approval by the EU, on 16 January 2012 BASF announced that it is pulling its genetic engineering division out of Europe and stopping production of its GM Amflora potato for the European market. The reason cited was lack of acceptance of this technology by consumers, farmers, and politicians.

NATURE OF SCIENCE

Scientists must assess the risks and benefits associated with scientific research. Genetic modification of crops has many risks to be considered:

* the potential for herbicide-resistance genes to escape into the wild population
* unintended harm to other organisms, such as insect pollinators and amphibians
* reduced effectiveness of herbicides
* possible human health risks, for example some studies have found glyphosate in human urine.

Have there been allergic reactions to the new gene put into a plant?

NATURE OF SCIENCE

Are the risks worth it? Use the hotlinks at the end of this section to watch a movie called GMO/OMG that premiered in New York City in September 2013.

CHALLENGE YOURSELF

Adoption rates of GR (glyphosate-resistant) soybeans and cotton in the USA are shown in Figure 8.10. This bar chart shows the percentage of crop adoption over a 10-year period. Look at the bar chart and answer the following questions.

5 Compare and contrast the data regarding the two plant species.

6 Suggest a reason that might explain the differences.

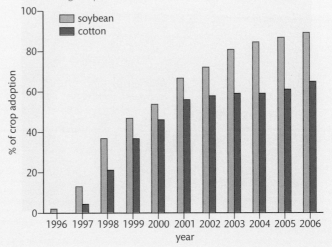

Figure 8.10 The percentage of soybean and cotton crop adoption over 10 years. Duke and Cerdeira 2007, Fig. 1

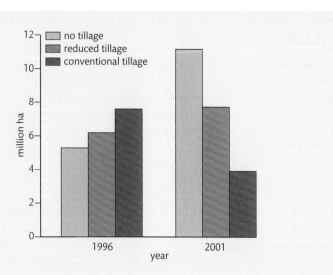

Topsoil loss caused by tillage (the preparation of soil by mechanical agitation, such as digging, stirring, and overturning) is the most destructive effect of crops planted in rows. Tillage contributes to soil erosion by water and wind, soil moisture loss, and air pollution from dust. Glyphosate-resistant plants reduce tillage. Reduction in tillage improves soil structure, and results in reduced run-off and less pollution of rivers and streams.

Look at Figure 8.11 and answer the following questions.

7 Compare and contrast tillage results from 1996 and 2001.

8 Suggest a reason for these numbers.

9 Explain the environmental impact of these numbers.

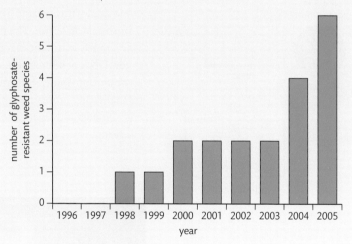

Based on data from 'Facts About Glyphosate-Resistant Weeds', Purdue Extension, www.ces.purdue.edu/extmedia/GWC/GWC-1.pdf.

10 Describe the resistance seen in weed species in the USA to glyphosate.

11 Using the knowledge you have gained about how organisms change over time, describe how this may have occurred.

12 Compare and contrast resistance of weed species from 1996 to 2005.

13 Do some research and find one solution that scientists might suggest in solving this problem. Give one answer, although there may be many.

Figure 8.11 Soybean tillage methods by hectares farmed in the USA in 1996 and 2001. Duke and Cerdeira 2007, Fig. 2

Figure 8.12 Glyphosate-resistant weed species in the USA.

 The word 'compare' in a question means you need to write down the similarities and contrast the differences between two or more things.

 TOK Discuss the view of Karl Popper that, for science to progress, scientists must question and criticize the current state of scientific knowledge.

Physical methods as a direct means of inserting genes into plants

In order to produce GM plants, methods had to be developed to deliver the transgene without damaging the plant cell. After introducing the gene, the plant cell must be able to reproduce an entire plant. The three methods used currently are: electroporation, microinjection, and biolistics. Just as one screwdriver does not work for all DIY jobs, molecular biologists have several tools to choose from as they try to transfer genes into a plant.

Electroporation

Electroporation makes pores in the cell membrane using electrical impulses. The cell membrane of a plant cell is surrounded by a cell wall that, as you will remember, is made of cellulose. The cell wall gives the cell shape. The cell wall is removed to expose the protoplast, a plant cell that has had its cell wall removed. When short high-voltage electrical impulses are applied to a suspension of protoplasts, small microscopic pores are created in the cell membrane, enabling DNA to enter the cell and nucleus. In this way, transgenes can be embedded in a plant cell.

Figure 8.13 Biolistics (gunshot).

Biolistics

As you can see from Figure 8.13, with biolistics DNA is coated onto microparticles of gold or tungsten and fired with an explosive charge from a particle gun. The plant cells are transformed, meaning that the new DNA of interest is added to the chromosome of the plant cell. Finally, the transformed plant cell acclimates and regenerates into a plant.

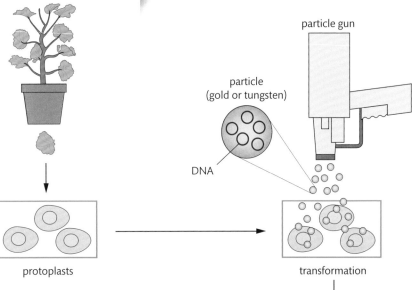
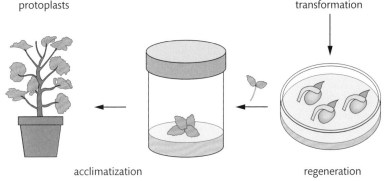

particle gun

particle (gold or tungsten)

DNA

protoplasts

transformation

acclimatization

regeneration

A gene gun or biolistic particle delivery system is a device for injecting cells with genetic information.

Microinjection

As the term suggests, with microinjection the DNA is injected into a protoplast with a microneedle. This method is very labour intensive because it is done one protoplast at a time. A whole plant is then grown from each protoplast.

Table 8.3 Physical means of introducing genes into plants are direct methods

Electroporation	Remove the cell wall to expose the protoplast Use short high-voltage impulses to make pores in the cell membrane DNA can enter through the pores
Biolistics	DNA is coated on a gold particle This is fired from a high-energy particle gun and enters the cell through the cell wall
Microinjections	DNA is injected directly into the protoplast with a microneedle

Electroporation and microinjection use protoplasts, which are plant cells without the cell wall. Biolistics coats particles with DNA and fires them right through the cell wall.

Chemical methods as a direct means of inserting genes into plants

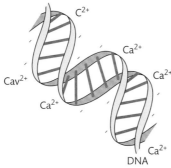

Calcium phosphate

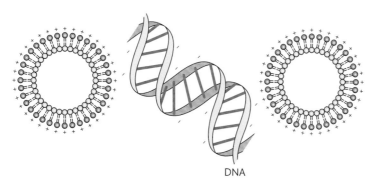

Artificial liposomes

Figure 8.14 Transfection: DNA transfer in to a eukaryotic cell. Calcium binds with DNA for easy transfer into a cell; a liposome can also be used to carry DNA into a cell.

There are two chemical methods for inserting new DNA into plant cells.

The first method uses transfection. Transfection means to 'infect with a new DNA molecule'. With this procedure, calcium chloride and a buffered saline solution containing phosphate ions are added to the DNA. The calcium and phosphate ions bind with the DNA. Cells then take up the DNA by endocytosis or phagocytosis. This method is successful because the calcium phosphate coats the negatively charged DNA and neutralizes it. This allows the DNA to cross the cell membrane.

The second method uses liposomes. Liposomes are artificially prepared sacs of lipid molecules that have an aqueous interior. DNA can be put into the aqueous centre of the liposome. Next, the liposome is fused with the lipid bilayer membrane of a cell and the DNA is transferred into the cell. This very efficient transfer is called 'lipofection'.

Table 8.4 Chemical means of inserting genes into plants are direct methods

Transfection	Calcium phosphate coats DNA Neutralized DNA can cross the cell membrane
Liposomes	Liposomes can fuse with DNA DNA plus liposomes are taken up by endocytosis by the cell

Vectors as an indirect means of inserting genes into plants

Vectors are carriers of genes. We have just learned about two common vectors that are used to indirectly transfer genes to plants.

1 *Agrobacterium tumefaciens* is a bacterium that can be used to introduce genes into many different plants. It carries the gene to make the new product in its plasmid. When it infects the cells of the plant, those cells take up the plasmid and carry the genes to the chromosome in the nucleus or to the DNA in the chloroplast.

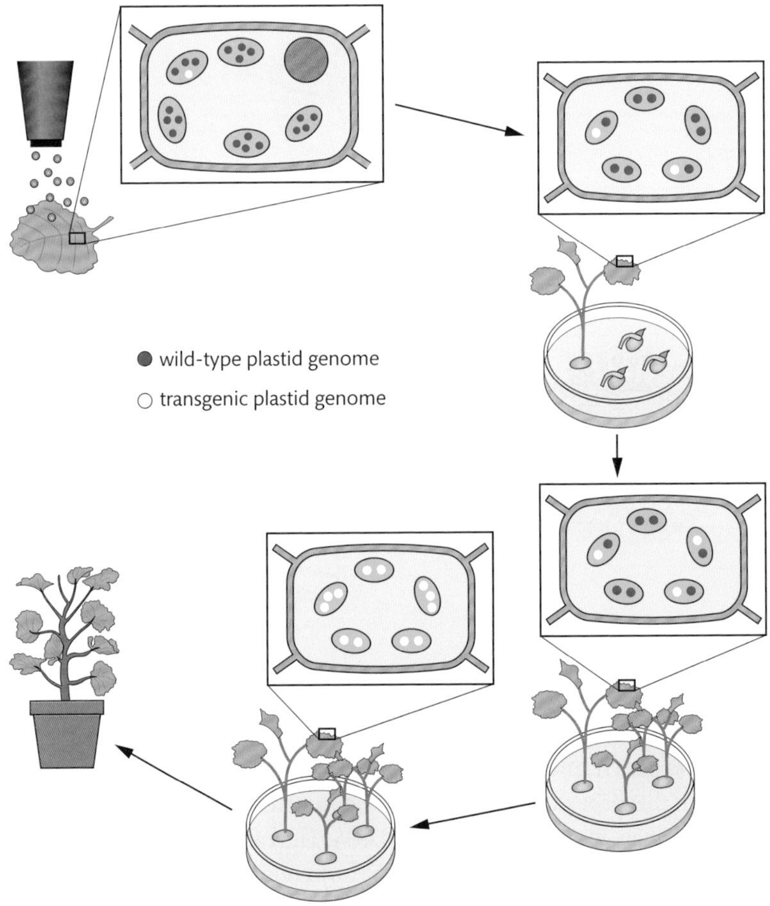

Figure 8.15 Recombinant DNA plasmids are injected into the chloroplast of the plant cell. The new DNA will be integrated into the chloroplast DNA (plastid genome).

● wild-type plastid genome

○ transgenic plastid genome

2   Tobacco mosaic virus is a pathogen. It is used with *A. tumefaciens* to carry the genes for hepatitis antigen into tobacco plants. Bulk vaccines can then be made from the tobacco plants.

Table 8.5 Vectors insert genes into plants indirectly

Agrobacter	A new gene is put into the plasmid of the bacterium The bacterium infects the plant and carries in the new gene
Tobacco mosaic virus	Helps agrobacter carry a new gene into tobacco plants The tobacco plants can now make a vaccine against hepatitis

Identifying a target gene using bioinformatics

Bioinformatics combines computer science and information technology in an attempt to understand biological processes. It has been used to sequence whole genomes. You have heard of the Human Genome Project. That project has sequenced the whole human genome using information technology and computers. The genomes of many bacteria, plants, fruit flies, worms, etc., have been sequenced.

Imagine that you want to retrieve the DNA sequence of a target gene, for example the gene that makes soybeans resistant to glyphosate. Sounds tricky, doesn't it? It was very tricky before the databases used in bioinformatics were constructed. Now you can go to a database such as GenBank and find the gene you are looking for.

Using an open reading frame

The gene you are looking for in the database will be an open reading frame (ORF). An ORF is a length of DNA that has a start code of ATG and does not exhibit any of the stop codes (TAA, TAG, TGA). An ORF must have sufficient nucleotides to code for a polypeptide chain or a series of amino acids making up a protein. Usually about 300 nucleotides separate the start code from the stop code. When a scientist is looking for a protein and has the DNA sequence, he or she can go to the National Center for Biotechnology Information (NCBI), a public site, and use the ORF finder to find the protein-coding region for the target DNA sequence. This is called ORFing!

Worked example

1   Explain ORF.

2   How many nucleotides usually make up an ORF?

3   What is ORFing?

Solutions

1   An ORF is a length of DNA that has a start code of ATG and does not exhibit any of the stop codes (TAA,TAG, TGA).

2   300.

3   When a scientist is looking for a protein and has the DNA sequence, he or she can go to the National Center for Biotechnology Information, a public site, and use the ORF finder to find the protein-coding region for that DNA sequence. This is called ORFing.

GMOs are involved in controversy in different countries regarding whether 'GMO' should be put on food labels. Are GMOs labelled in your country? Why or why not?

To learn more about bioinformatics and GenBank, go to the hotlinks site, search for the title or ISBN, and click on Chapter 8: Section B.2.

CHALLENGE YOURSELF

14 In this example two of the three possible reading frames are open. Which one is not open?
(a) ...G CTC AAA ATG GGT CC...
(b) ...AA ATC TGA AGT GAT CC...
(c) ATC ATT AAT TTT TGC C...

Because it is so important to remember that ATG has to be at the beginning of an ORF, and if it is in the middle it is not an ORF, use this mnemonic to remember it: A = All, T = That, G = Goes. It is always good to use mnemonic devices to remember obtuse facts!

Linking the target gene to other sequences that control its expression

When a scientist is working with DNA that is to be transferred into a vector like agrobacter, the gene must undergo several modifications in order to be effective. The following diagram (Figure 8.16) is a representation of a transgene, an artificially designed construct, containing the necessary components for integration into a plasmid and production of a protein.

Figure 8.16 Representation of a transgene.

| marker gene | promoter | transgene | termination sequence |

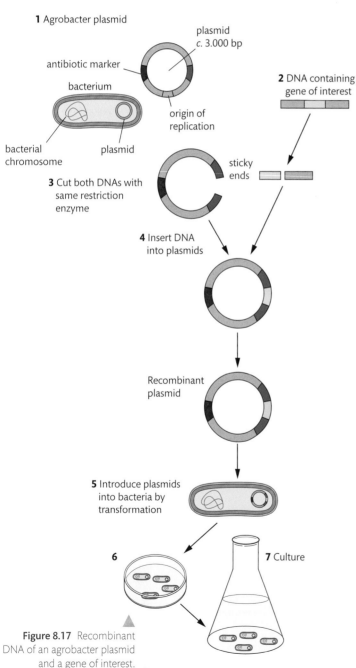

1 Agrobacter plasmid

plasmid
c. 3.000 bp

antibiotic marker

bacterium

bacterial chromosome

plasmid

origin of replication

2 DNA containing gene of interest

3 Cut both DNAs with same restriction enzyme

sticky ends

4 Insert DNA into plasmids

Recombinant plasmid

5 Introduce plasmids into bacteria by transformation

6

7 Culture

Figure 8.17 Recombinant DNA of an agrobacter plasmid and a gene of interest.

- A promoter gene must be present in order for a gene to be translated into the protein product.
- The transgene is the target gene (for example the gene for resistance to glyphosate).
- A termination sequence signals the end of the gene sequence.
- A marker gene tells the scientist if the construct has been successfully taken up by bacterial plasmids that will carry it to the plant.

Inserting recombinant DNA into the plant cell

The following describes how you would put a gene of interest (in this case glyphosate resistance) into the plasmid of a vector (in this case agrobacter).

1   Engineer the plasmid DNA from the bacterium (agrobacter) by adding a marker gene. The marker gene will give antibiotic resistance that will be necessary in a later step. (Notice the bacterium has its own circular chromosome and the plasmid DNA. Only the plasmid DNA is used.)

2   Obtain the DNA of the gene of interest from another organism.

3   Cut both DNAs with the same 'molecular scissors', which are called restriction enzymes. Doing this gives them the ability to stick together and attach.

4 The sticky ends attach and the target gene is placed in the plasmid.

5 Introduce the recombinant DNA (the target gene from another organism + plasmid DNA) back into the bacteria.

6 Spread the cells on nutrient medium containing an antibiotic. Will the cells grow if they do not have the plasmid? No, they will not grow. The antibiotic will kill them. But if they have the plasmid they will be resistant to the antibiotic, so you can tell if the plasmid has been taken up by the cells.

7 Grow the cells with the plasmid in a culture vessel.

Worked example

1 What are the three things attached to the transgene (target gene) in the plasmid?

2 All four DNA pieces connected together are put into a plasmid of agrobacter. Some agrobacter is spread on a dish of nutrient media with an antibiotic in it. Will the bacteria grow on the nutrient media?

3 Why?

4 Now the agrobacter can infect the soybeans plants and carry the gene we are interested in. What is that gene?

Solutions

1 Marker, promoter (promotes the activity of the gene), termination sequence (has a stop code).

2 Yes.

3 It has the marker gene for antibiotic resistance.

4 It is the gene for glyphosate resistance.

Methods of inserting recombinant DNA into plants

Recombinant DNA can be introduced into whole plants, leaf discs, or protoplasts. After inserting the DNA, the plant will be genetically modified. Genetic modification can be used to increase crop yields or produce novel products. The following are descriptions of each method.

• Leaf discs. For example, discs removed from tobacco plants are incubated with the genetically engineered agrobacter for 24 hours. Eventually the plant cells will acquire the DNA from the bacteria.

• Whole plants. Submerge the plant in a bacterial solution containing the modified plasmid. Apply a vacuum to help force the bacterial solution into the air spaces between the plant cells. Agrobacter will move the plasmid into many of the cells of the plant.

• Protoplasts. By microinjection or biolistics (see above).

Section summary

• A genetically modified plant (a GM crop) has been modified by the introduction of a gene that does not normally occur in that species. The new gene is called a transgene. Glyphosate-resistant soybeans are an example of GM plants.

• The goal of GM plants is to increase crop yield and overcome environmental factors (weeds or insects) that prevent higher crop yields.

If the cells have been transformed by the new plasmid, they will grow on the antibiotic media. The new plasmid makes the cells resistant to the antibiotic. The gene of interest is also in the plasmid.

Glyphosate-resistant crops (GRCs) have both risk and benefits. The benefits include a reduced need for the use of fossil fuel for tillage and a much lower use of other more toxic herbicides that affect our soil and water. However, there is a risk that GRCs might directly alter food safety. Much controversy about GRCs exists in the world community.

To find out more about GMO, GenBank, and NCBI, go to the hotlinks site, search for the title or ISBN, and click on Chapter 8: Section B.2.

- Plants can be engineered to produce new products by the introduction of new genes. Tobacco plants can be engineered to produce the hepatitis B vaccine. Amflora potatoes were engineered to produce a new type of starch important to the paper industry.
- Physical methods of inserting genes into plants include electroporation, biolistics, and microinjection.
- Chemical methods of inserting genes into plants include transfection and the use of liposomes.
- Bacteria such as *Agrobacterium tumefaciens* can also be used to introduce genes into plants. The bacteria act as vectors carrying the new gene as they infect the plant.
- Computer science helps scientists target a gene of interest. Scientists use a database and find the gene of interest in an open reading frame (ORF). The ORF must have sufficient nucleotides to code for a polypeptide chain long enough to make up a protein.
- When a gene is identified, it can be transferred into a vector, such as *Agrobacterium tumefaciens*, and introduced into a whole plant, a leaf disc of a plant, or a protoplast of a plant.

Exercises

5 Describe three physical methods of introducing recombinant DNA into plants.

6 Describe glyphosate resistance in soybeans.

NATURE OF SCIENCE

Developments in scientific research follow improvements in apparatus: using tools such as the laser scanning microscope has led researchers to deeper understanding of the structure of biofilms.

B.3 Environmental protection

Understandings:

- Responses to pollution incidents can involve bioremediation combined with physical and chemical procedures.
- Microorganisms are used in bioremediation.
- Some pollutants are metabolized by microorganisms.
- Cooperative aggregates of microorganisms can form biofilms.
- Biofilms possess emergent properties.
- Microorganisms growing in a biofilm are highly resistant to antimicrobial agents.
- Microorganisms in biofilms cooperate through quorum sensing.
- Bacteriophages are used in the disinfection of water systems.

Applications and skills:

- Application: Degradation of benzene by halophilic bacteria such as *Marinobacter*.
- Application: Degradation of oil by *Pseudomonas*.
- Application: Conversion by *Pseudomonas* of methyl mercury into elemental mercury.
- Application: Use of biofilms in trickle filter beds for sewage treatment.
- Skill: Evaluation of data or media reports on environmental problems caused by biofilms.

  Guidance
  - *Examples of environmental problems caused by biofilms could include clogging and corrosion of pipes, transfer of microorganisms in ballast water, or contamination of surfaces in food production.*

Responses to pollution incidents

You may have read about the BP oil spill off the Gulf Coast of the USA in 2010. The oil gushed out of the Deepwater Horizon oil rig under the Gulf waters for days. The result was devastation of both the ecology and the economics of that area for months. It is still not clear what the full ramifications of the spill are to the fishing, shrimping, and crabbing industries in the area, all of which are very important to the Gulf states. Many different techniques were used as an attempt to clean up this environment.

Whether it be on the coast of Spain, Australia, or the USA, what response methods are used to clean up oil spills in the marine environment? Currently, there are three types of methods: physical, chemical, and bioremediation.

Fire boats battle blazing remnants of the Deepwater Horizon rig the day after it exploded in April 2010.

Physical methods used to clean up oceanic habitats include:

• booms, which collect the oil
• skimmers, which skim the oil off the top of the water
• adsorbent materials, which soak up the oil and are then collected and removed.

Physical methods used to clean up shore habitats include:

• pressure washing
• raking
• bulldozing.

Chemical methods used to clean up habitats include:

• dispersing agents, which act like soap and break up the large oil molecules into small droplets
• gelling agents, which are chemicals that react with oil to form solids.

Bioremediation agents are microorganisms that are added to the environment to speed up the rate at which natural biodegradation will occur. Fertilizer is added as a source of nitrogen and phosphate for the microorganisms to increase their activity.

Bioremediation

Bioremediation is the process of using an organism's metabolism to break down pollutants. (Check back to Section B.1 to review the different metabolic strategies of microorganisms.) The result is that environmentally undesirable properties of a substance disappear. Many microorganisms can be used to decontaminate an area, because they have the right enzymes to break down the long chains of hydrocarbon molecules that are found in organic pollutants. The products produced after the breakdown are environmentally neutral.

TOK Some people think there has been a paradigm shift over the last 50 years regarding waste disposal. In the 1950s it was common to dump wastes into rivers and streams or into the soil. Sometimes people changed the oil in their car and just dumped the oil on the ground. Boaters dumped their waste in the water. Industry used lakes and rivers to get rid of their waste. If you agree that a paradigm shift has occurred, what has caused it? Explain.

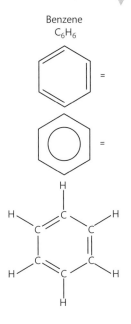

Figure 8.18 The structure of benzene.

Benzene
C_6H_6

Bioremediation of benzene by *Marinobacter*

An example of bioremediation of a hydrocarbon pollutant is the action of *Marinobacter* on benzene. During oil exploration, by-products of the extraction process are very salty water, called brine, and benzene. Brine is also referred to as produced water. As most microorganisms cannot live in high salt concentrations, bioremediation of the by-products of benzene can only be accomplished by a salt-tolerant species (a halophile, meaning salt-loving). Benzene is extremely undesirable in the environment because it is very stable (and so long lasting) and a known carcinogen. However, when *Marinobacter* breaks down benzene the product is simply carbon dioxide.

In an experiment using *Marinobacter*, published in the *Journal of Applied and Environmental Microbiology* in September 2003, it was shown, by using genetic analysis, that the bacteria *Marinobacter* was the dominant member of a culture mix that degraded benzene consistently over a 2.5-week period at room temperature in brine conditions (see Figure 8.19). After 4 weeks all of the products of benzene degradation had been converted to carbon dioxide.

Bioremediation of oil by *Pseudomonas*

Oily waste water poses a hazard for both marine and terrestrial ecosystems. Physical and chemical clean ups do not degrade the oil satisfactorily. Biodegradation is the preferred method for degrading oil, resulting in compounds that do not damage the ecosystems.

In August 2005 an article was published in the *Journal of Zhejiang University Science* demonstrating that *Pseudomonas aeruginosa* can biodegrade crude oil if another molecule is present. That other molecule is rhamnolipid, which is an effective emulsifier (surfactant) and creates much more surface area upon which the microorganism can act. The process works even better if a second molecule is present; that molecule is glycerol. It is hypothesized that glycerol gives *Pseudomonas* extra nutrients. In the experiment published in the article, using both glycerol and rhamnolipid, 58% of the crude oil was degraded.

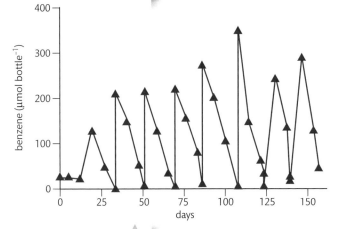

Figure 8.19 Repeated use of benzene (▲) as the sole carbon and energy source in the presence of 2.5 M NaCl by microorganisms. The cultures were maintained in 1-l capacity bottles at room temperature. After an initial lag period, the bacteria degraded 200–300 μmol of added benzene bottle⁻¹ consistently in 2.5 weeks. The results for only one bottle are shown; duplicate enrichments behaved similarly. Nicholson and Fathepure 2004

CHALLENGE YOURSELF

In another experiment, *Pseudomonas* was used to degrade car oil left in soil. Look at Figure 8.20. Notice that various combinations were attempted. For example, *Pseudomonas* + glycerol means that glycerol (just like the experiment above) had been added to the *Pseudomonas*.

Look at the graph and answer the following questions.

15 Compare and contrast the *Pseudomonas* and the *Pseudomonas* + glycerol treatment.

16 Based on these data, what are the two best additives that allow *Pseudomonas* to be the most effective at oil degradation?

17 What do these additives provide the bacteria with?

18 What did the surfactant do to facilitate oil degradation?

19 After the *Exon Valdez* oil spill in Alaska, scientists dumped a lot of phosphates and nitrates (inorganic fertilizer) on one of the beaches and the oil was quickly cleaned up by naturally occurring *Pseudomonas*. Can you explain why?

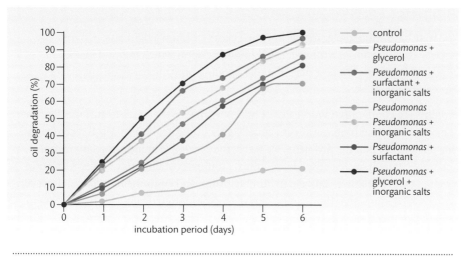

To learn more about using bacteria to clean up oil spills, go to the hotlinks site, search for the title or ISBN, and click on Chapter 8: Section B.3.

Figure 8.20 The effect of various nutrients on the degradation of car oil left in soil by the bacteria *Pseudomonas*. Sathiya Moorthi et al. 2008, Fig. 1

Pseudomonas also cleans up mercury pollution

Mercury from substances such as discarded paint and fluorescent bulbs pollutes our environment. Mercury can leach into the soil and water from the places where mercury-containing products have been dumped. Another bacteria, *Desulfovibrio desulfuricans*, makes the mercury more dangerous. This bacterium adds a methyl group to mercury, converting it into highly toxic methyl mercury. This toxic methyl mercury attaches to plankton that is then eaten by small fish that are then eaten by larger fish. The methyl mercury builds up in the bodies of fish in a process called biological magnification. Human mercury poisoning has been attributed to ingestion of methyl mercury.

Pseudomonas comes to the rescue again. It first converts the methyl mercury to mercuric ions, and then changes the mercuric ions to the relatively harmless form of elemental mercury.

$$CH_4Hg \rightarrow CH_4 + Hg^{2+}$$

methyl   methane   mercuric
mercury   ion

$$Hg^{2+} + 2H \rightarrow Hg + 2H^+$$

mercuric   hydrogen   elemental   hydrogen
ion   atoms   mercury   ions

Figure 8.21 Formulas for the bioremediation of mercury.

Table 8.6 Bacteria used in bioremediation

Marinobacter	Halophilic or salt loving By-products of oil exploration are very salty water and benzene Degrades benzene, a known carcinogen, into non-toxic products
Pseudomonas	Degrades oil Physical and chemical clean up alone gives poor results The molecules of glycerol and rhamnolipid help with the oil break down
Pseudomonas	Cleans up mercury pollution Mercury pollution comes from paint and fluorescent bulbs Methyl mercury can build up in the bodies of fish by biological magnification Changes toxic methyl mercury into harmless elemental mercury

Very few countries have sufficient resources for combating oil spills and other pollution incidents on their own. Norway therefore cooperates closely with other nations on mutual assistance in the Copenhagen Agreement. Denmark, Iceland, Finland, Sweden, and Norway are all parties in this.

413

Laser scanning microscopy images enable quantitative study of biofilm structure. A software suite of image-processing tools for full automation of biofilm morphology quantification has been developed. The software toolbox is implemented on a web server and a user-friendly interface has been developed to facilitate image submission, storage, and sharing. These strategies have enabled researchers to have a deeper understanding of biofilms.

Have you ever heard of desert varnish rocks? Sometimes a whole mountain range is coloured red because of the red stain of biofilms. Scraping off the stain is how petroglyphs (carvings or inscriptions on rocks) were left on cave walls. The stain is a desert biofilm.

As many as 300 different species of bacteria can inhabit dental plaque.

Emergent properties are based on the idea that the whole is greater than the sum of its parts. Does a reductionist's view of science negate the concept of emergent properties?

Biofilms

You may have studied paradigms in your Theory of Knowledge class. A paradigm is a way thinking about a topic: it is a framework upon which to build ideas. The concept of biofilms is a new way of understanding how microorganisms exist in our environment.

Biofilms are cooperative aggregates of microorganisms that stick to surfaces like glue. We now know that biofilms affect virtually everything around us. Until recently no-one recognized that the problems we were trying to solve in industry, environment, and public health, were caused by biofilms. Biofilms cost billions of dollars a year in product contamination, damage to human health, and equipment damage. However, we have also found that they can be part of the solution to dealing with pollution in our environment, such as treating sewage, industrial waste, and contaminated soil. The research has just begun on this new paradigm of biofilms in our environment.

Cooperative aggregates

Working in teams is always a great idea, and it seems that microorganisms have figured that out. The success of biofilms is due to the following facts.

- They are cooperative aggregates of microorganisms.
- The microorganisms can include many different types united together, such as fungi, bacteria, and algae.
- They hold themselves together by secreting extracellular polymeric substances (EPS) that stick to surfaces like glue.
- They can develop in a short time, even in hours.

Some examples of biofilms you would recognize are plaque on your teeth, which your dentist has to remove, and slimy waste that blocks kitchen drains. Even a persistent infection of a cut in your skin can be because of a biofilm.

Emergent properties

Emergent can be defined as novel and coherent structures, properties, and patterns arising during the self-organization of a complex system. In a biofilm, the properties of the biofilm community are greater than the properties of the individual components. The emergent properties of biofilms include:

- complex architecture
- quorum sensing
- resistance to antimicrobials.

Complex architecture

Put a clean glass slide in a pond and almost immediately a film will begin to form on the slide. The same thing happens with a tooth that has just been cleaned perfectly by the dentist. This is called a conditioning film, and it occurs in seconds as microorganisms attach to barren substrates. Videos show that certain bacteria do a little wiggle dance that helps the aggregates of cells form. As the cells join together in colonies, a more stable attachment is formed and they begin to produce EPS. Industry has invested a lot of time and money to create surfaces resistant to these attachments. It would save huge amounts of money if oil pipelines, dental drills, and medical catheters, to mention just a few items, had improved surfaces.

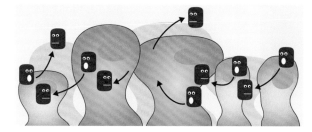

Quorum sensing

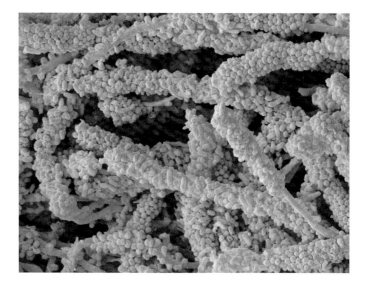

Electron micrograph of microroganisms on teeth forming a biofilm (plaque). Accumulation of plaque can cause dental disease in the teeth and gums as a result of the high concentration of metabolites produced by the biofilm.

Quorum sensing is an emergent property. Quorum sensing is the ability of microorganisms in a biofilm to cooperate with each other. Scientists have used a molecular tool called green fluorescent protein that they attach to bacterial genes to mark which genes are acting. Using the glow of the green fluorescent protein, they have discovered that when bacteria irreversibly attach to a substrate, a gene begins to make more EPS in all the bacteria. In other words, the genes make more sticky glue to adhere the bacteria even more strongly to the substrate. They seem to be able to 'talk' to each other in order to make more EPS.

Ants and honeybees use quorum sensing to make decisions about new nest sites.

As the colonies of bacteria become more dense, they can coordinate the expression of their genes in response to the density of their population. They accomplish this in the following manner.

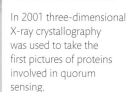

NATURE OF SCIENCE

In 2001 three-dimensional X-ray crystallography was used to take the first pictures of proteins involved in quorum sensing.

- The first few bacteria make signalling molecules called inducers.
- Other bacteria have receptors that receive the signal of the inducer. The bacteria that received the first message then make even more inducer.
- Soon the quantity of inducer in the population is high. This stimulates the bacteria in the population to transcribe their genes all at the same time.
- A very strong biofilm of cells and matrix is made as a response of all the cells working together.

Lung infections can be caused by *Pseudomonas aeruginosa*. This bacteria uses quorum sensing to cooperate and form biofilms in the lungs. It can grow without harming the host, but when it reaches a certain population size it becomes aggressive and the biofilm becomes resistant to the immune system of the host.

A colour SEM of a *Staphylococcus aureus* biofilm found on the microscopic fibres of a wound dressing.

Resistance to antimicrobial agents

Biofilms are very resistant to antimicrobial agents. The fact that biofilms are implicated in human disease is of great concern to the medical community. For example, *P. aeruginosa*, which can cause infections in patients with cystic fibrosis, can exist as a biofilm. When *P. aeruginosa* has grown to a biofilm state, it is between 10 and 1000 times more resistant to antimicrobials. Biofilms can grow on implants such as hip replacements and catheters. Because of the biofilm's increased resistance to antimicrobials, the hip or catheter must be replaced, causing trauma to the patient and increased medical costs.

Research is being done to try to determine what makes biofilms resistant to antimicrobials. It may be because the polysaccharide matrix in which they live protects them, or because the biofilm is such a mix of organisms many resistant strategies have been developed. Many hypotheses have been formulated and work on this is ongoing.

Worked example

1 List the characteristics of biofilms.
2 What are the three properties of a biofilm? Explain each property.
3 Give examples of biofilms.

Solutions

1 • Cooperative aggregates of microorganisms.
   • Many different types united together, such as fungi, bacteria, and algae.
   • Hold themselves together by secreting extracellular polymeric substances (EPS) that stick to surfaces like glue.
   • Can develop in a short time, even in hours.

2

Complex architecture	Join together in colonies Produce EPS or glue Attach to surfaces
Quorum sensing	Cell to cell communication Coordinate the expression of genes so that more EPS is made Make signalling molecules called inducers that signal all the bacteria to transcribe their genes at the same time
Resistance to antimicrobials	Are 10–1000 times more resistant to antimicrobials

3 Can grow on implants, such as new hip joints, or oil pipelines, or in dental drills, or as plaque on your teeth, to mention just a few.

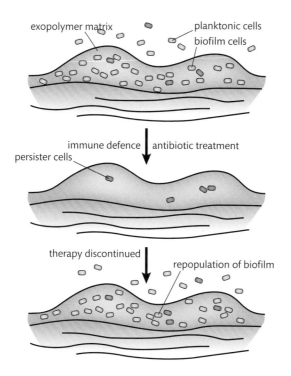

exopolymer matrix — planktonic cells — biofilm cells

immune defence | antibiotic treatment

persister cells

therapy discontinued

repopulation of biofilm

Figure 8.23 Model of biofilm resistance to antibiotics. Initially the antibiotic kills the biofilm cells (green). The immune system kills some persisters (pink). After the antibiotic treatment is reduced, the persisters repopulate the biofilm.
Biofilm drug resistance: Persister cells, dormancy and infectious disease *Nature Reviews Microbiology*, 5, January, pp. 48-56, Fig. 4 (Kim Lewis 2007), Copyright 2007. Reprinted by permission from Macmillan Publishers Ltd.

Biofilms and trickle filter beds

A trickle filter is a biofilm of aerobic bacteria attached to the surface of filter media. Waste water trickles over the filter media and the attached aerobic bacteria oxidize the organic matter in the waste. The media used currently are plastic particles with high surface areas.

- The biofilm of aerobic bacteria covers each plastic particle.
- Oxygen is dissolved in the water of the filter bed and is made available to the biofilm by diffusion from the water.
- The waste water is applied with a rotary arm that causes the waste water to trickle over the media intermittently.
- The end product of this breakdown by the aerobic bacteria biofilm is carbon dioxide.
- Carbon dioxide diffuses out of the biofilm into the flowing liquid.
- Treated waste water is collected through an underwater drainage system.

This is a trickling filter system at a sewage plant in Yorkshire, England. Have you visited the waste treatment plant in your community?

Figure 8.24 The process of trickle filtering.
http://scetcivil.weebly.com/uploads/5/3/9/5/5395830/m18_l26-trickling_filter.pdf

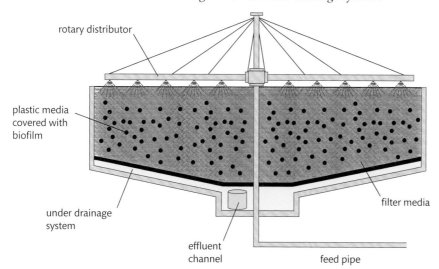

rotary distributor

plastic media covered with biofilm

under drainage system

effluent channel

feed pipe

filter media

417

1 At source port

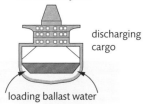

discharging cargo

loading ballast water

2 During voyage

cargo hold empty

ballast tanks full

3 At destination port

loading cargo

discharging ballast water

4 During voyage

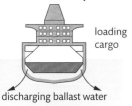

cargo hold full

ballast tanks empty

Figure 8.25 Cross-section of ships showing ballast tanks and the ballast water cycle.

Figure 8.26 Distribution of temperature differences between undischarged ballast water and pier-side water for 32 vessels arriving at the Port of Hampton Roads. Values greater than 0 indicate the ballast water was warmer than the pier-side water. Green bars represent vessels with exchanged ballast water; yellow bars represent unexchanged water. When both exchanged and unexchanged vessels have the same temperature difference, they are stacked. The sum of all the bar values is 100. Drake et al. 2007, p. 339, Fig. 1

CHALLENGE YOURSELF

Ship ballast water is a prominent vector of aquatic invasive species, which includes microorganisms, to coastal regions. Within a given ship, part of the microorganism population is biofilms formed on the internal surfaces of the ballast water tanks. The reasons for concern about this issue are that:

- microorganisms are much more abundant than macroorganisms (larger organisms)
- microorganisms are transferred by ship in much greater numbers than larger organisms
- once released, microorganisms, because of their small size, can easily become an invasive species
- their small size facilitates their rapid dispersal
- pathogenic bacteria, viruses, and microalga can have devastating effects on the economics of an area and the balance of the ecosystem
- microorganisms in biofilms are extremely resistant to chemical disinfectants
- field sampling has shown that 10% of ballast water tank surfaces are covered with biofilms.

A question posed by one study was as follows. Once the organisms are moved to a new location, the success of their invasion is a function of their ability to survive and reproduce. Would a temperature difference in the new water be a factor that could interfere with this ability to survive? The difference in temperature between the ballast waters and the receiving water was calculated (see Figure 8.26). Then assumptions about bacterial tolerance to temperature differences were applied.

- Tolerance: the temperature tolerance of bacteria is usually a range of 30°C. They can tolerate discharge into water that is ±15°C that of the ballast water.
- Optimality: if bacteria have an optimum range of 10°C, and if they inhabit ballast water at the midpoint of their optimal range, then their optimum growth will occur at ±5°C.

Using Figure 8.26, answer the following questions.

20 If microorganisms tolerate a water temperature ±15°C that of ballast water, then what percentage of microorganisms sampled could tolerate that new environment?

21 If the microorganisms grow at the optimum temperature, what percentage of microorganisms encountered optimal temperatures?

22 Because of the temperature differences between the ballast water and the ocean water, is temperature a limiting factor preventing the survival of bacteria discharged from ballast water? Explain.

23 Name two other environmental factors that could affect the microorganisms that are released from ballast water and that could also be studied.

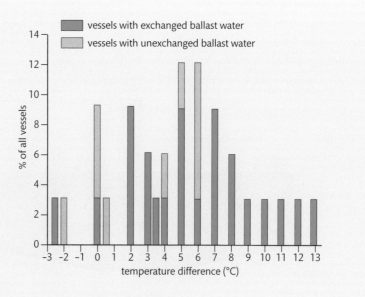

418

Bacteriophages and the disinfection of water systems

Bacteriophages are viruses found in human waste products. They are widely used for water quality assessment. Bacteriophages are organisms that are rapidly grown and easily detected. Thus they are a perfect indicator organism for the presence of human or animal waste products in water. Other viruses present in human waste are not so easy to culture and grow. Bacteriophages are helpful in assessing the resistance of viruses to the waste water disinfectant process. Studies worldwide support the value of using bacteriophages as a tool for monitoring the efficiency of waste water treatment and the disinfection process with regard to animal and human viruses.

Biofilms clean polluted waterways

Can biofilms help us clean small polluted bodies of water? Researchers have shown that this can work. To begin with, layers of mesh topped with soil and plants called rafts are created. Eventually, the roots of the plants will grow into the water below. Bacteria will then colonize the rafts and form sticky sheets of biofilm that coat the matrix and the roots of the plants. Biofilm bacteria use the excess nitrogen and phosphates that are polluting the water for nutrients. They work in concert with the plant roots, which also absorb nitrogen and phosphates. The sticky biofilms also bond with other pollutants, such as suspended solids, copper, lead, and zinc, removing them from the water. A good example of how this works can be seen in the study of Fish Fry Lake near Billings, Montana, USA. Five years ago this lake was dying. As of September 2012, the algal bloom has gone, the oxygen levels are up, and a community of fish has made a resurgence. This is all due to the rafts of floating islands of plants and biofilm, which have reduced the nitrogen concentration by 95% and the phosphate concentration by 40%. Levels of dissolved oxygen, which are so important to fish, are 60 times

greater than they were at the beginning of this project. Hopefully, new research using biofilms can help bring back some of our polluted waterways.

Biofilms may be good to use for crude oil degradation. In the second half of the 20th century oil spillage and pollution in the marine environment was a huge problem. In January 2013 researchers in India found that biofilms of *Pseudomonas* bacteria were able to degrade crude oil in a marine environment. In fact, these bacteria grew larger biomasses as they degraded the oil compared with the same bacteria living on glucose.

Rafts of floating islands of plants and their biofilms can reduce the levels of pollutants in small bodies of water.

The use of biofilm as an adsorbent of pollutant ions is one of the new technologies for treatment of contaminated water. An understanding of the properties of biofilms has allowed scientists to see their benefit in water clean-up efforts. In a study presented at a conference at Kyoto University in Japan, natural biofilms from the surface of stones were used to adsorb lithium ions and remove them from a lake.

Section summary

- Bioremediation uses the metabolism of a microorganism to break down pollutants until they are environmentally neutral. *Marinobacter* acts on benzene. *Pseudomonas* breaks down oil and detoxifies mercury.
- Biofilms are cooperative aggregates of microorganisms that stick like glue to surfaces. Both industry and health services have spent billions creating surfaces resistant to the attachment of destructive biofilms.
- Biofilm organisms communicate through quorum sensing. This allows them to build a polysaccharide matrix that surrounds them and protects them from antimicrobials.
- In Yorkshire in the UK, scientists have put biofilms to good use and have begun to clean waste water by running it over a trickle filter system covered with a biofilm of aerobic bacteria.
- Bacteriophages are indicator organisms for the presence of human or animal waste products in water.

Exercises

7 Briefly describe the emergent properties of biofilms.

8 List some pollutants metabolized by microorganisms.

9 Describe the use of biofilms in a trickle bed filter.

Practice questions

1 Release of sewage in marine waters is a common practice but it can cause water contamination with pathogens. A series of experiments was conducted to compare inactivation rates of two different groups of microbes with different sunlight exposures. One group was faecal coliform bacteria and the other was coliphage viruses. Experiments were conducted outdoors using 300-litre mixtures of sewage–seawater in open-top tanks.

A 2-day experiment was carried out with untreated sewage added to seawater. Both days were sunny with no clouds. The figure below shows the inactivation of the microbes in seawater as a function of the cumulative amount of sunlight and time. The survival curves of the two microbes are plotted against sunlight exposure (lower x-axis) during daylight periods and against time during the overnight period (upper x-axis). The y-axis gives counts of bacteria and viruses per 100 ml.

(a) Identify the time at which faecal coliform bacteria counts fell below 1 unit per 100 ml. (1)

(b) Deduce, using the data in the graph, the effect of sunlight on

   (i) faecal coliform bacteria (2)

   (ii) coliphage viruses. (2)

(c) For an accidental sewage spill, suggest, giving a reason, which of the two microbes may be most useful as a faecal indicator 2 days after the spill. (1)

(Total 6 marks)

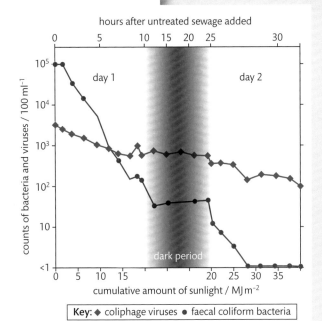

Key: ◆ coliphage viruses ● faecal coliform bacteria

Adapted from Sinton 1999

2 Waste water from factories producing polyester fibres contains high concentrations of the chemical terephthalate. Removal of this compound can be achieved by certain bacteria. The graph below shows the relationship between breakdown of terephthalate and conversion into methane by these bacteria in an experimental reactor.

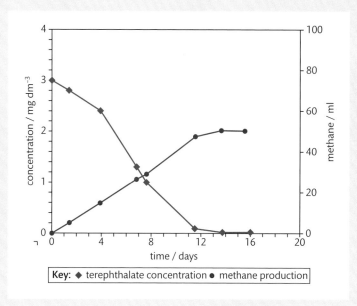

Adapted from Wu et al. 2001

(a) The reactor has a volume of 12 l. Calculate the initial amount of terephthalate in the reactor. (1)

(b) Describe the relationship between terephthalate concentration and methane production. (2)

(c) Suggest which bacteria can be used for the degradation of terephthalate. (1)

(d) Evaluate the efficiency of the terephthalate breakdown into methane. (2)

(Total 6 marks)

3 Outline some environmental resistance factors that crop plants can be genetically modified to overcome.

(Total 4 marks)

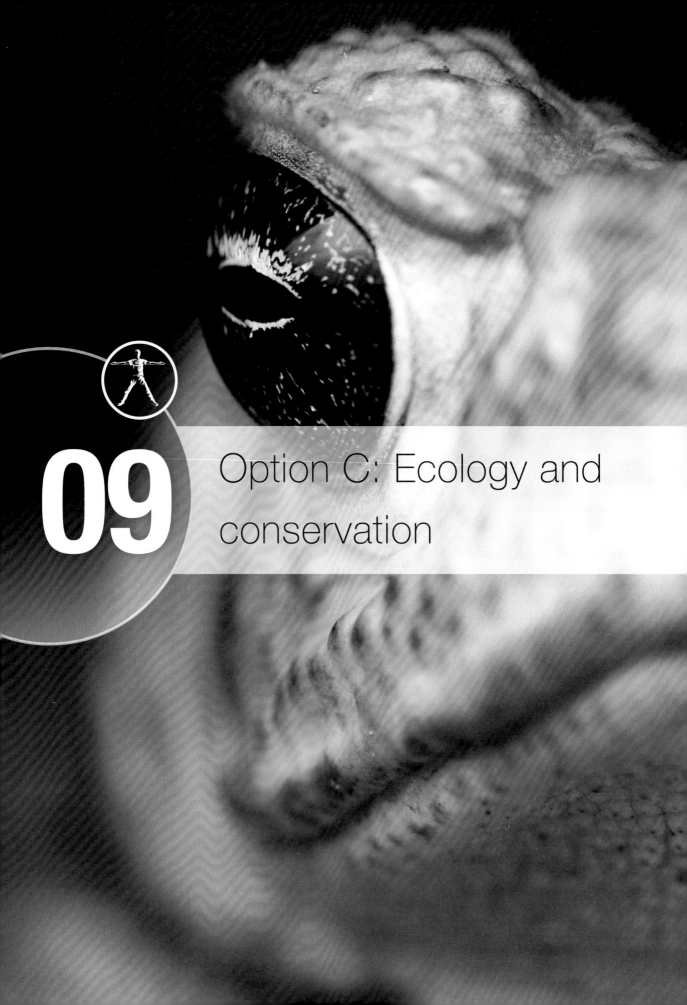

09

Option C: Ecology and conservation

Essential ideas

C.1	Community structure is an emergent property of an ecosystem.
C.2	Changes in community structure affect and are affected by organisms.
C.3	Human activities impact on ecosystem function.
C.4	Entire communities need to be conserved in order to preserve biodiversity.

The cane toad, *Rhinella marina*. The cane toad was brought to Australia in the 1930s in an unsuccessful attempt to control the population of beetles that were eating the sugar cane crop.

A community is a group of populations living together and interacting with each other in an area. The community might be named by an environmental feature, for example a sand dune community or pond community. Other communities might be named after the dominant plant species, such as an oak community or a redwood forest community.

The distribution of organisms in communities is affected by both abiotic (non-living) and biotic (living) features. We are interested in studying all these factors to determine what may affect a certain population of organisms. For example, does the fact that cars drive up to the beach with their lights on affect sea turtle reproduction at that beach? Is the rabbit population in a forest decreasing because of an increase in the fox population?

The study of populations tells us about the factors that affect all the living things around us. It can be used to predict what might happen to, for example, populations of fish in the marine environment if we continue to overfish. The population growth model of a simple organism like yeast can show us a typical pattern that can be applied to other populations. If we want to know how many animals are in a population, we can estimate the population size by using the technique of capture–mark–release–recapture.

Biodiversity is nature's 'backup': it is the reserve needed to survive a disaster. A disaster could wipe out the majority of organisms, but leave the few that are the best adapted. In order to know how much biodiversity exists in an ecosystem, we must be able to measure it. The Simpson's index of biodiversity is one method of measuring diversity.

C.1 Species and communities

Understandings:

- The distribution of species is affected by limiting factors.
- Community structure can be strongly affected by keystone species.
- Each species plays a unique role within a community because of the unique combination of its spatial habitat and interactions with other species.
- Interactions between species in a community can be classified according to their effect.
- Two species cannot survive indefinitely in the same habitat if their niches are identical.

Applications and skills:

- Application: Distribution of one animal and one plant species to illustrate limits of tolerance and zones of stress.
- Application: Local examples to illustrate the range of ways in which species can interact within a community.
- Application: The symbiotic relationship between zooxanthellae and reef-building coral reef species.
- Skill: Analysis of a data set that illustrates the distinction between fundamental and realized niche.
- Skill: Use of a transect to correlate the distribution of plant and animal species with an abiotic variable.

Limiting factors affect the distribution of species in a community

Why do you live where you live? Is it because it's near public transport? Is it where your family has always lived? Is it because of its proximity to a school? Some factors limit where we choose to live. Other organisms have factors that limit where they live because of necessity, not choice. The distribution of a species depends on these factors, which are both abiotic (non-living) and biotic (living).

Abiotic factors include:

- light, for example day length and intensity
- atmosphere, for example the amount of CO_2, O_2, or N_2 in the atmosphere
- water availability
- temperature
- salinity of soil or water
- soil conditions, for example pH, aeration, soil composition (loam, clay, or coarse soil), soil components such as the amount of humus, sand, or rock.

Biotic factors include:

- living organisms in the ecosystem
- inter-relationships of organisms, such as symbiosis, parasitism, or predator–prey relationships, and competition for resources of food, water, and mates.

Use a mnemonic device to remember the list of abiotic and biotic factors: LAWs To Save Soil help us Live In the world.

The distribution of species depends on their tolerance of limiting factors

Figure 9.1 The law of tolerance states that distribution of species in an ecosystem is determined by the limits of physical and chemical factors that can be tolerated.

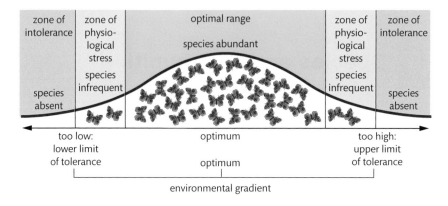

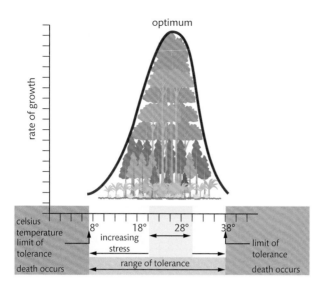

Figure 9.2 For every factor influencing growth, reproduction, and survival, there is an optimum level. Above and below the optimum, there is increasing stress, until survival becomes impossible at the limits of tolerance. http://apesnature. homestead.com/chapter2.html

The limits of tolerance and stress for organisms in an ecosystem have been described by an ecologist called Victor Shelford. Shelford's law of tolerance states that the levels of one or more chemical or physical factors determine the abundance and distribution of a species in an ecosystem. When the factors fall below or rise above the levels tolerated by the species, that species will cease to exist in that ecosystem.

NATURE OF SCIENCE

Hypothetical curves illustrating zones of stress and tolerance can help us understand what is occurring in the real world.

Limits of tolerance and zones of stress: an animal example

Kangaroos in Australia are a good example of how climate can be a limiting factor in the distribution of species. This can be seen in Figure 9.3.

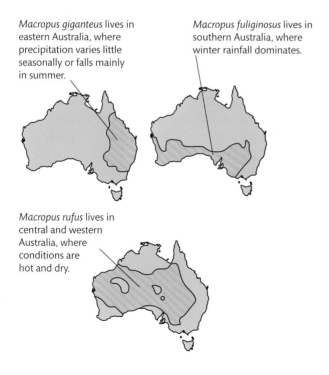

Macropus giganteus lives in eastern Australia, where precipitation varies little seasonally or falls mainly in summer.

Macropus fuliginosus lives in southern Australia, where winter rainfall dominates.

Macropus rufus lives in central and western Australia, where conditions are hot and dry.

Figure 9.3 Climate and distribution of three different kangaroo species.

This distribution of kangaroos in Australia has been stable for over a century. The red kangaroo, *Macropus rufus*, lives in the arid and semi-arid interior of Australia. The distribution of the red kangaroo reflects the interaction of the mean annual temperature and the mean annual precipitation. Look at the graphs in Figure 9.4.

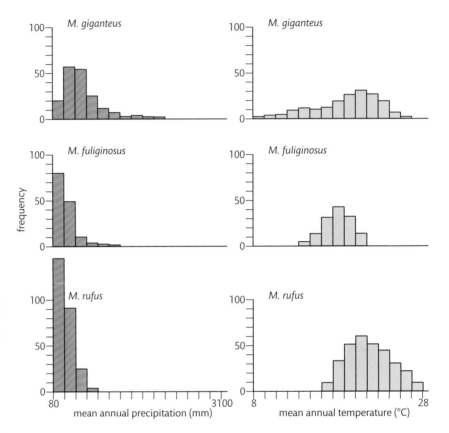

Figure 9.4 Three species of kangaroo have different limits of tolerance to precipitation and temperature. Caughley et al. 1987

You can see from the graphs that the red kangaroo is tolerant of much lower mean precipitation and higher mean temperatures than the other two species. This affects its distribution and its success in the difficult, arid, and hot interior of Australia, which is dominated by desert and savannah. Red kangaroos can live where the mean annual rainfall can be as low as 80 mm and the temperature can be as high as 40°C. This species of kangaroo possesses certain adaptations that increase its tolerance to extremes of high temperature and low moisture. For example, the lighter fur colour of the red kangaroo reflects sunlight better than the dark fur of the other kangaroo species. The nasal openings of the red kangaroo are larger than the other kangaroos, which increases its evaporative cooling ability. The kidneys of the red kangaroo conserve water by producing more concentrated urine. These reasons explain the limits of tolerance of the red kangaroo and how they differ from the other kangaroos in Australia.

You may notice on maps of the distribution of kangaroos in Australia that no kangaroos live in the north. Research has determined that the north is probably too hot for the eastern grey kangaroo, *Macropus giganteus*, too dry in winter for the western grey kangaroo, *Macropus fuliginosus*, and too wet for the red kangaroo. This supports the idea that the dry and hot limits of the distribution of the red kangaroo represent the levels to which it is well adapted.

Limits of tolerance and zones of stress: a plant example

A genus of plant along the coast of California, USA, shows a distribution pattern based on its level of tolerance to extreme environmental conditions. The plant is a shrub in the genus *Encelia*.

Encelia frutescens

Encelia frutescens is a species of flowering plant in the daisy family known by the common names button brittlebush and bush encelia.

Scientific classification	
Kingdom:	Plantae
Phylum:	Angiospermophyta
	Eudicots
	Asterids
Order:	Asterales
Family:	Asteraceae
Genus:	*Encelia*
Species:	*E. frutescens*
Binomial name	
Encelia frutescens	

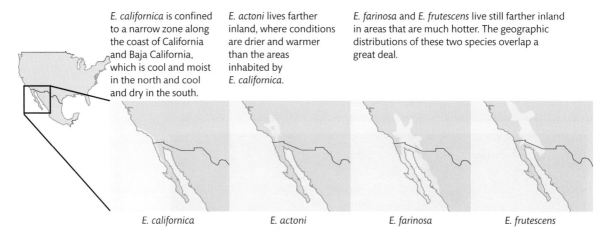

E. californica is confined to a narrow zone along the coast of California and Baja California, which is cool and moist in the north and cool and dry in the south.

E. actoni lives farther inland, where conditions are drier and warmer than the areas inhabited by E. californica.

E. farinosa and E. frutescens live still farther inland in areas that are much hotter. The geographic distributions of these two species overlap a great deal.

E. californica   E. actoni   E. farinosa   E. frutescens

Figure 9.5 The distribution of four *Encelia* species.

Look at Figure 9.5, which shows the distribution of four *Encelia* species. The species we will be looking at is *E. frutescens*, the button brittlebush. It lives in the hottest and driest area on the coast. Rainfall can vary there from 100 mm to 400 mm yr^{-1}, and, compared with the other coastal areas pictured, the temperature range of *E. frutescens* is very hot, from 35 to 40°C. When we study the physiology of *E. frutescens*, we can see that is has adaptations that have enabled it to live in this extreme range of heat and dryness. It does not overheat because it has leaves that transpire at a high rate and are cooled by evaporation as a result. You might wonder how it gets enough water to cool its leaves by evaporation in one of the hottest and driest deserts in the world: notice that its microenvironment is limited to streambeds and desert washes (see Figure 9.6). Along these beds, run-off water soaks into the soil, increasing the ability of the deep roots of *E. frutescens* to reach moisture. The limiting factor is in fact the availability of water in the streambeds and desert washes that it can access with its long root system. Because it has leaves that are not protected with hairs, it cannot survive dryness. Its nearest neighbour, *E. farinosa*, has pubescent leaves, which are leaves that are covered with hundreds of small hairs. These hairs allow *E. farinosa* to live on slopes in shallow soils that contain limited water. The hairs trap water so that its transpiration is limited, and they provide protection from the wind that would otherwise dry out the surface of the plant. *E. frutescens* cannot survive on the slopes with less water because it has no surface hairs on its leaves and needs water to replace the water lost by transpiration.

Figure 9.6 Temperature regulation and distribution. Molles 2010, p. 207, Fig. 9.7

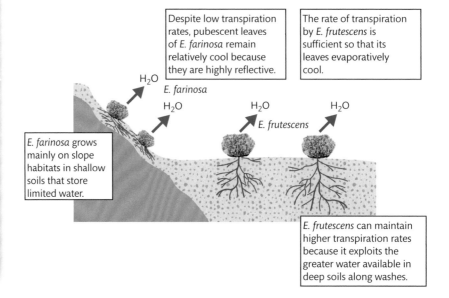

Despite low transpiration rates, pubescent leaves of *E. farinosa* remain relatively cool because they are highly reflective.

The rate of transpiration by *E. frutescens* is sufficient so that its leaves evaporatively cool.

H_2O
E. farinosa
H_2O
H_2O
E. frutescens
H_2O

E. farinosa grows mainly on slope habitats in shallow soils that store limited water.

E. frutescens can maintain higher transpiration rates because it exploits the greater water available in deep soils along washes.

Flowers can be mistaken for buds until you look closely.

TOK Random samples are taken to study the numbers of plants in a certain area. Are data obtained from random samples justified?

The geographical range of *E. frutescens* is regulated by both temperature and moisture.

Table 9.1 The distribution of one animal and one plant species

Organism/adaptation	Distribution	Zone of tolerance and stress
Macropus rufus, red kangaroo		
Has nasal openings that are larger than other kangaroos for good cooling ability Kidney acts to conserve water	Difficult arid and hot area in the interior of Australia Dominated by desert and savannah Temperature as high as 40°C Annual rainfall as low as 80 mm	Tolerates much lower mean precipitation and higher temperatures that other species of kangaroo Not able to live in the northern area of Australia because it is too wet
Encelia frutescens, button brittlebush		
Leaves transpire at a high rate for evaporative cooling of the plant, which prevents overheating	Hot dry areas on the coast of California Temperature range of 35–40°C In areas of extreme heat and dryness	Must live where there are streambeds and desert washes Its deep roots can reach moisture so that evaporative cooling can take place

Keystone species

A keystone species is one that is not necessarily abundant but exhibits a strong control over the structure of a community. How do we determine which organism is the keystone species?

A good method to determine whether an organism is a keystone species is to perform a removal experiment. Ecologist Robert Paine first attempted this method. He was studying an intertidal area of western North America. When Paine removed the sea star, *Pisaster ochraceous*, manually from the intertidal area, a mussel, *Mytilus californianus*, was able to take over the rocky area and exclude algae and other invertebrates from that zone (see Figure 9.7). The mussel simply took over the space available when there was no sea star to keep it in check. It was evident that it was the sea star that limited the number of mussels that could reproduce and attach to the rocks. Paine collected data that showed that, when sea stars were present, 15–20 different species of invertebrates and algae were present. Without the sea star, the diversity rapidly declined to five species. This supported the hypothesis that the sea star was the keystone species. When it was present, it had control over the diversity of the community. When it was absent, the diversity was lost.

Worked example

1 What is one method used to determine whether an organism is a keystone species?
2 Give an example.

Solutions

1 A good method to determine whether an organism is a keystone species is to perform a removal experiment.
2 When scientists manually removed the sea star, *Pisaster ochraceous*, from the intertidal area, a mussel, *Mytilus californianus*, was able to take over the rocky area and exclude algae and other invertebrates from that zone.

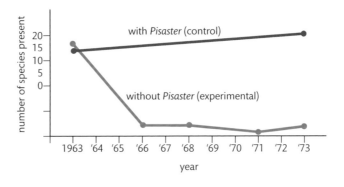

Figure 9.7 Testing a keystone species hypothesis. The effect of removing the sea star, *Pisaster ochraceous*, manually from an intertidal area over a 10-year period. Campbell and Reece 2002, Fig. 53.14

CHALLENGE YOURSELF

Look at Figure 9.8.

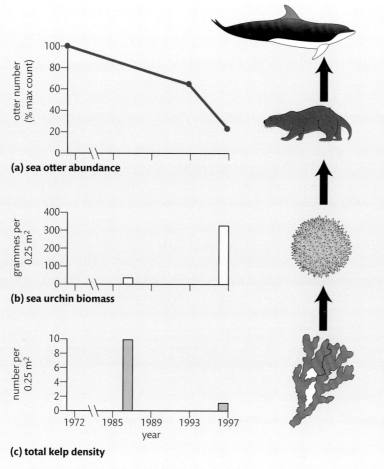

(a) sea otter abundance

(b) sea urchin biomass

(c) total kelp density

Figure 9.8 A food chain in the North Pacific of kelp–sea urchin–sea otter–orca. Adapted from Campbell and Reece 2002, Fig. 53.15

1 Look at the food chain shown at the sides of the graphs. Which organism would you hypothesize is the keystone species?

2 Use the graphs and explain why the data support your hypothesis.

3 The imbalance over 20 years is probably caused by the decline in seals and sea lions, which are also food for orca. Can you think of a reason for the decline in seals and sea lions?

Each species plays a unique role within a community

The unique role that a species plays in the community is called its niche. A famous ecologist, Eugene Odum, once said 'If an organism's habitat is its address, the niche is the habitat plus its occupation.' We could put it another way and say that the concept of niche includes where the organism lives (its spatial habitat), what and how it eats (its feeding activities), and its interactions with other species.

Spatial habitat

Every type of organism has a unique space in the ecosystem. The area inhabited by any particular organism is its spatial habitat. The ecosystem is changed by the presence of the organism. For example, leopard frogs, *Rana pipiens*, live in the ponds of Indiana (USA) dunes. They burrow in the mud in between the grasses on the edge of the pond.

Feeding activities

The feeding activities of an organism affect the ecosystem by keeping other populations in check. For example, the leopard frogs in the Indiana dunes eat the aquatic larvae of mosquitoes, dragonflies, and black flies. The presence of the leopard frog helps keep the populations of these insects in check.

Interactions with other species

The interactions of an organism with other species living in its ecosystem include competition, herbivory, predation, parasitism, and mutualism. The organism may be in competition with another organism for the food supply. It may itself be the prey for a larger predator. It may harbour parasites in its intestines. These complicated interactions are difficult to uncover, but they indicate the importance of the organism in the ecosystem. The predator of the green frog is the blue heron. Without the green frog in the sand dune ecosystem, the heron would have a significantly reduced food supply. Frogs are homes for flatworm parasites that live in their intestines. Without doubt there are many other relationships between the green frog and other species.

One of the jobs of an ecologist is to collect data on the niches of particular organisms in an ecosystem. If an organism is in danger of becoming extinct in an ecosystem, it is necessary to understand as many of its interactions as possible in an attempt to determine the cause of its extinction. What follows now are some explanations and examples of interactions between species.

Worked example

Describe the niche of a lion in Africa, or some other animal of your choice that you can research on the internet.

Solution

- Spatial habitat: savannah in Africa.
- Feeding activity: the lion is a secondary consumer; it eats giraffes, zebra, warthogs, and antelopes. It is the largest predator of the savannah. It hunts in the open country during the day and in vegetation at night. It also eats birds, rodents, and some reptiles.
- Interactions with other species: the lion marks its territory by roaring, urinating, and patrolling. It defends its territory and its pride (females). Leopards and hyenas prey on lion cubs.

Competition

When two species rely on the same limited resource, one species will be better adapted than the other to benefit from the resource.

- Example 1: In the USA, coyotes, *Canis latrans*, and red foxes, *Vulpes vulpes*, are both predators that eat small rodents and birds. Coyotes inhabit grassland communities in the USA, while the red fox prefers the edges of forests and meadows. Because more farmland has been created and more forests removed, the habitat of the red fox is disappearing and is overlapping with that of the coyote in the grasslands. The two species are competing for a smaller food

The habitat of the red fox is disappearing.

supply and it is possible that one will become extinct in that habitat.

- Example 2: In the coastal dunes of the UK, the natterjack toad, *Epidalea calamita*, is facing tough competition from the common toad, *Bufo bufo*. Disturbance of the dune area is limiting the habitat available to both toads.

Herbivory

A herbivore is a primary consumer (plant eater) that feeds on a producer (plant). The growth of the producer is critical to the well-being of the primary consumer. This is an interaction between plants and animals.

- Example 1: Rabbits, *Oryctolagus cuniculus*, eat marram grass in a sand dune ecosystem.
- Example 2: The monarch butterfly, *Asclepias syriaca*, larvae eat the leaves of the milkweed plant.

Predation

A predator is a consumer (animal) eating another consumer (animal). One consumer is the predator and another is the prey. The number of prey affects the number of predators and vice versa.

- Example 1: The Canadian lynx, *Lynx canadensis*, and the arctic hare, *Lepus arcticus*, form a classic example of predator–prey interaction. The lynx preys on the hare. Changes in the numbers of the lynx population are followed by changes in the numbers of the hare population.
- Example 2: The blue heron, *Ardea herodias*, is a predator on frogs in the ponds of American sand dune ecosystems.

Parasitism

A parasite is an organism that lives on or in a host and depends on the host for food for at least part of its life cycle. The host can be harmed by the parasite.

- Example 1: *Plasmodium* is a parasite that causes malaria in humans. It reproduces in the human liver and red blood cells. Part of the life cycle of the *Plasmodium* takes place in the body of the *Anopheles* mosquito. The mosquito is the vector that transmits the malaria parasite from one human to another.
- Example 2: Leeches, *Hirudo medicinalis*, are parasites that live in ponds. Their hosts are humans and other mammals. Leeches puncture the skin of a host and secrete an enzyme into the wound to prevent clotting. Leeches can ingest several times their weight in blood.

Canadian lynx walking through deep snow tracking an Arctic hare.

Mutualism

Two species living together where both organisms benefit from the relationship is termed mutualism.

- Example 1: Lichen is a mutualistic relationship between algae and fungi. The algae, *Trebouxia*, photosynthesize and make carbohydrates (food) that the fungi can use. The fungi, mainly *Ascomycota* species, absorb mineral ions needed and used by the algae.

- Example 2: *Rhizobium* is a nitrogen-fixing bacterium that lives in the roots of leguminous plants such as beans and peas. *Rhizobium* fixes nitrogen (transforms atmospheric nitrogen into a form that is useable by plants), which the plant can then use to make proteins. The plant makes carbohydrates (during photosynthesis), which can be used as food by the *Rhizobium*.

- Example 3: Clownfish, *Amphiprion ocellaris*, and sea anemones, *Anemonia sulcata*, live together for mutual benefit. Clownfish are small brightly coloured fish that live within the area of the tentacles of the poisonous sea anemone. The clownfish is covered with mucus that protects it from the sting of the sea anemone. Clownfish lure other fish to the waiting tentacles of the sea anemone. After the sea anemone kills the fish, the clownfish and the sea anemone both eat the remains. The clownfish also nibble off the remains of dead sea anemone tentacles.

Cavernous star coral, *Montastraea cavernosa*. The greenish colour on the coral is zooxanthellae algae.

- Example 4: Zooxanthellae are single-celled algae that live in the tissue of reef-building coral. The coral provides the compounds and the environment for photosynthesis for zooxanthellae. In turn, the algae provide food for the coral. The algae give the coral a boost of nutrients so that it can secrete the skeleton of calcium carbonate that it needs to build the reef. This is a highly efficient exchange of nutrients in a nutrient-poor environment. This relationship of mutual benefit is called mutualism or symbiosis, living together for mutual benefit.

The relationship between zooanthellae and coral is a type of symbiosis. The coral and algae live together. 'Bio' is the Greek word for living, and 'sym' is the Greek word for together.

Worked example

Describe the species interaction of each of the following pairs of organisms.

1. Lynx and hare.
2. Coyote and red fox.
3. Legume and bacteria.
4. Natterjack toad and common toad.
5. Monarch butterfly larva and milkweed.
6. Clownfish and sea anemone.
7. Blue heron and frog.
8. *Plasmodium* and human.

Solutions

1. The lynx is the predator and the hare is the prey. If the number of prey decreases, the population of predators will decrease because there is less food to eat. If the population of prey increases, predators will have more food and will be able to produce more offspring, and so their numbers will also increase.

2. These animals are in competition for the same limited resources. It is possible that one animal will become extinct in that ecosystem.

3. Mutualism exists here because both species benefit. The legume (bean or pea plant) makes carbohydrates that the bacteria use; the bacteria fix free nitrogen gas from air that then provides the plant with nitrogen (fertilizer).

4. These animals are in competition. There is only a small amount of habitat left in Britain and they must share it. One of them may become extinct in that ecosystem.

5. The butterfly lays its eggs on the milkweed plant and the caterpillar eats the leaves of the milkweed. This is herbivory.

6. This is mutualism. They live together for mutual benefit. Clownfish lure other fish to the anemone and the clownfish eats the leftovers from the anemone.

7. The blue heron predates the frog. If the frog population decreases, the blue heron population will also decrease.

8. In parasitism, the parasite is helped and the host is harmed. *Plasmodium* can reproduce in the red blood cells of humans, so it benefits. Humans are harmed by the disease that the parasite causes.

CHALLENGE YOURSELF

4 What interactions between species have you learned about in this section? List four or five types of interactions and give examples of each.

Competitive exclusion

You will recall that the red fox and coyote may now be in competition with each other for resources. They seem to both hunt for their food in the same areas, and the food supply may be dwindling as a result of the forests and grasslands being turned into farmland. If the fox and the coyote do begin to occupy the same niche in the ecosystem, the principle of competitive exclusion can be used to predict the end result.

The principle of competitive exclusion states that no two species in a community can occupy the same niche.

In 1934, the competitive exclusion principle was demonstrated by a Russian ecologist, G. F. Gause. He performed a laboratory experiment with two different species of *Paramecium*: *P. aurelia* and *P. caudatum* (see Figure 9.9). His experiments showed the effects of interspecific competition between two closely related organisms. When each species was grown in a separate culture, with the addition of bacteria for food, they did equally well. When the two were cultured together, with a constant food supply, *P. caudatum* died out and *P. aurelia* survived. *P. aurelia* out-competed *P. caudatum*. The experiment supported the Gausian hypothesis of competitive exclusion. When two species have a similar need for the same resources, one will be excluded. One species will die out in that ecosystem and the other will survive. *P. aurelia* must have had a slight advantage that allowed it to out-compete *P. caudatum*.

Figure 9.9 Competitive exclusion.

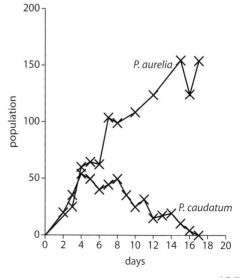

List five facts that show your understanding of the principle of competitive exclusion.

Solution

- Two species cannot coexist in the same community if the niches are identical.
- When resources are limited, only one of the species will survive in competition for the same niche.
- Gause did an experiment with two species of *Paramecium* to demonstrate this.
- One species of *Paramecium* (*P. caudatum*) died out and the other species (*P. aurelia*) survived.
- *P. caudatum* and *P. aurelia* were in the same community and had an identical niche. That is why they could not coexist and one of them eliminated the other.

Fundamental niche versus realized niche

The red fox's habitat in the USA is the forest edge. Its food consists of small mammals, amphibians, and insects. It interacts with other species, such as the mosquitoes that suck its blood and scavengers that eat its leftovers. This is the fundamental niche of the red fox. The fundamental niche is the complete range of biological and physical conditions under which an organism can live.

What has happened to the red fox's fundamental niche? The forest edge has been turned into farmland in many places. Some of the species eaten by the red fox have disappeared. The red fox must survive in a narrower range of environmental conditions. Now there is direct competition from the coyote, whose niche has also been changed. This new and narrower niche is called the realized niche.

The fundamental niche of a species is the potential mode of existence, given the adaptations of the species.

The realized niche of a species is the actual mode of existence, which results from its adaptations and competition with other species.

Worked example

1   Make a comparison between the fundamental niche and realized niche.
2   Would a scientist attempt to measure the realized niche in a laboratory or in the field?

Solutions

1

Fundamental niche	Realized niche
Potential mode of existence	Actual mode of existence
The organism uses its adaptations with no competition from other species	The organism uses its adaptations but is in competition with other species

2   To measure the realized niche, measurements would have to be taken in the environment where the animal actually lives (in the field). In this environment, all of the competitors will be interacting with the animal so that the realized niche can be determined. If a scientist wanted to see what the animal's potential or fundamental niche really is, the measurement could take place in a laboratory, where there is no competition occurring and the animal can reach its full potential without interference.

CHALLENGE YOURSELF

Paramecium caudatum is a single-celled organism that lives in fresh water. In an experiment researchers allowed *P. caudatum* to grow for 28 days in order to determine its normal growth curve. Every 7 days, ten random samples were collected from the population. The data recorded are shown in Table 9.2

Table 9.2 Random samples of the population density (number per mm³, ±5 organisms) of a culture of *P. caudatum* taken over 28 days

Sample number	Day 7	Day 14	Day 21	Day 28
1	143	200	300	390
2	155	205	315	360
3	165	185	295	375
4	135	235	350	365
5	143	195	295	410
6	145	265	320	370
7	165	265	340	380
8	175	195	370	390
9	105	215	325	390
10	169	290	340	320
Mean				

Paramecium caudatum, seen under a light microscope.

5   Calculate the means of the data and graph them.

6   Will this give you a picture of the fundamental or realized niche? Give your hypothesis as to what the results will show.

A second experiment was performed where *P. caudatum* was placed in a culture with another species of *Paramecium*. The researchers wanted to know, when the two species are competing for resources, what will be the result?

Tables 9.3 and 9.4 show the data that were collected over 28 days.

 Make sure to label all parts of a graph: the title, x-axis, y-axis, units, and uncertainties.

Table 9.3 Random samples of the population density (number per mm³, ±5 organisms) of *P. caudatum* taken over 28 days

Sample number	Day 7	Day 14	Day 21	Day 28
1	169	290	340	300
2	105	215	325	315
3	175	195	370	295
4	165	265	340	350
5	145	265	320	295
6	143	195	295	320
7	135	235	350	340
8	165	185	295	370
9	155	205	315	325
10	143	200	300	340
Mean	150	225	325	325

(The means have been calculated for you.)

Table 9.4 Random samples of the population density (number per mm³, ±5 organisms) of *P. bursaria* taken over 28 days

Sample number	Day 7	Day 14	Day 21	Day 28
1	75	160	210	160
2	85	150	190	190
3	65	150	190	250
4	75	140	220	180
5	85	140	230	180
6	65	130	180	230
7	75	170	180	220
8	95	170	250	190
9	70	130	190	190
10	60	160	160	210
Mean	75	150	200	200

7 Graph the data from this experiment.

8 Is this graph showing the fundamental or realized niche of *P. caudatum*? Explain your answer.

Use of a transect to correlate the distribution of a plant with an abiotic variable

Marram grass.

A transect is a method of sampling a population of plants or animals along a longitudinal section of an ecosystem. The observer moves along a fixed path to count the occurrences of the plant or animal along the path. It is much more accurate to use this type of transect with plants, because they do not move. Line transects are used to illustrate a particular gradient of an abiotic factor, such as sunlight or soil moisture, that is present in the ecosystem.

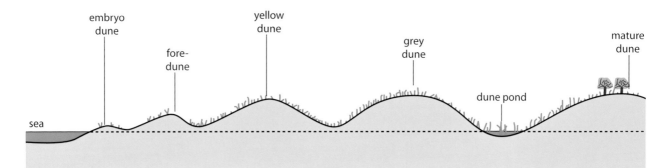

An example can be seen in Figure 9.10, showing the transect of a coastal dune. Let's look at the distribution of marram grass in the coastal dune ecosystem and how it is affected by the abiotic factor of soil pH.

Figure 9.10 Transect of a coastal sand dune.

If you were asked to do a transect, you would do the following.

• At right angles to the sea, lay a tape in a line all the way up the dunes.
• Every 10 or 20 m along the tape, mark out a quadrat (a square of a certain size).
• Identify and count the tufts of marram grass in the quadrat.
• Take several samples of the soil in each quadrat and use a soil test kit to determine the pH of the soil.
• Record all the data in a table.
• Turn it in to a diagram of your choice.

You can now determine the pattern of distribution of marram grass from the youngest dune to the oldest dune and see if it correlates with changes in the soil pH.

Transect information can be very useful when making decisions about ecosystems that are important to us. Here is an example of how transects can be important in an ecosystem. In this example, an experiment was performed to determine whether artificial light would affect the foraging behaviour of salamanders in an ecosystem.

Transects were established in forested areas at the Mountain Lake Biological Station in Virginia, USA. Half of the transects were lit by strings of white minilamps placed within the transects. The other half were not lit. The researchers walked each transect at night in order and counted the number of salamanders. There were significantly more active salamanders in the dark transects than in the light ones. The salamanders in the dark transects were foraging for food. The salamanders in artificial light were not foraging. This experiment shows how the use of artificial light to illuminate a campsite or even a research station can affect some organisms negatively.

Section summary

• Both biotic and abiotic factors limit the distribution of species in a community. The distribution of organisms depends on their tolerance of limiting factors. For example, the red kangaroo can live in the dry and hot conditions of the interior of Australia but cannot live in the north of the country because it is too wet.

• A keystone species exhibits strong control over a community but is not necessarily the most abundant species. The presence of the keystone species maintains the diversity of the community. For example, without the sea star in an intertidal community the number of species present declines.

• The niche is the unique role that each species plays in a community. The spatial habitat it occupies, its feeding activities, and its interaction with other species, all comprise the niche of an organism in a community. When ecologists study the niche of an organism, they can determine the significance of the organism to the diversity of the community.

- Species interactions in a community include competition, herbivory, predation, parasitism, and mutualism.

- The competitive exclusion principle states that no two species in a community can occupy exactly the same niche. With limited food supply, competition will occur and one species will outcompete the other. This can be demonstrated with an experiment using two species of *Paramecium*.

- The fundamental niche is the complete range of physical and biological conditions under which an organism could live. The realized niche is the conditions under which the organism actually lives in a certain community.

- The transect method can be used to sample a population of plants in a community. A transect shows the distribution of a particular plant. For example, a transect can show the distribution of marram grass in a sand dune community.

To learn more about sampling in fieldwork, and about using transects, go to the hotlinks site, search for the title or ISBN, and click on Chapter 9: Section C.1

Exercises

1 Describe a method to determine whether an organism is a keystone species in an ecosystem.
2 Design an experiment using a transect to correlate the distribution of a plant with an abiotic factor.
3 Outline an example of symbiosis.

NATURE OF SCIENCE

Use models as representations of the real world: pyramids of energy model the energy flow through ecosystems.

C.2 Communities and ecosystems

Understandings:
- Most species occupy different trophic levels in multiple food chains.
- A food web shows all the possible food chains in a community.
- The percentage of ingested energy converted to biomass is dependent on the respiration rate.
- The type of stable ecosystem that will emerge in an area is predictable based on climate.
- In closed ecosystems energy but not matter is exchanged with the surroundings.
- Disturbance influences the structure and rate of change within ecosystems.

Applications and skills:
- Application: Conversion ratio in sustainable food production practices.
- Application: Consideration of one example of how humans interfere with nutrient cycling.
- Skill: Comparison of pyramids of energy from different ecosystems.
- Skill: Analysis of a climograph showing the relationship between temperature, rainfall, and the type of ecosystem.
- Skill: Construction of Gersmehl diagrams to show the inter-relationships between nutrient stores and flows between taiga, desert, and tropical rainforest.
- Skill: Analysis of data showing primary succession.
- Skill: Investigation into the effect of an environmental disturbance on an ecosystem.

Guidance
- *Examples of aspects to investigate in the ecosystem could be species diversity, nutrient cycling, water movement, erosion, leaf area index, among others.*

Energy flow through the ecosystem

What do you think is the direction of energy flow for any ecosystem? If you constructed a food chain like this one, then you know.

$$grass \rightarrow cow \rightarrow human$$

Plants are at the bottom of the food chain. They contain the highest amount of energy, which they obtain from sunlight. The source of energy for most ecosystems is the Sun. A few food chains are supported by bacteria that can trap chemical energy.

Only 5–20% of the Sun's energy that is trapped by plants is transferred to the primary consumers eating the plants. Why is this? Because 80–95% of the energy is lost as heat or used for maintenance by the plant. Energy is lost as heat as it moves from producer (e.g. grass) to primary consumer (e.g. a cow) to secondary consumer (e.g. a human).

This is the same reason why the fuel we put in a car is only partially used to run the car. A large percentage of the energy provided by the fuel is lost as heat. This is why there is a fan in the engine of a car. A law of physics called the second law of thermodynamics states that, when energy is transferred, a proportion of it is lost as heat energy. This law applies equally to cars and ecosystems.

Where is the energy from the Sun actually kept in the plant? Plants produce glucose during photosynthesis. Plants also break down the glucose molecules and use the energy released for maintenance activities. The breakdown is called respiration. Maintenance activities that need energy are growth, repair, and reproduction. When the glucose is used as fuel for these activities, some of the energy is lost. Some of the energy moves through the ecosystem as excretion. Some energy is left in undigested food and is passed on to decomposers. When an organism dies, its body is decomposed and the energy transferred to decomposers.

Gross production, net production, and biomass

Pyramids of energy show how much energy is left at each trophic level (see Figure 9.11). Each block in the pyramid represents a trophic level (producers, primary consumers, secondary consumers, tertiary consumers). The width of the block indicates how much energy it contains. At each level, the blocks get narrower, and the block at the top is very narrow. The number at each level represents the amount of energy at each level. Can you see that only 10% of the energy from one trophic level is transferred to the next level? This diagram represents the ideal situation. In an actual ecosystem, the percentage transfer from one level to the next depends on many factors and may vary between 5% and 20%. In animal husbandry (farming), the transfer value is often higher than 10%. However, the loss of energy between producer and consumer explains why a kilogramme of beef is more expensive than a kilogramme of corn.

Figure 9.11 A pyramid of energy (not drawn to scale).

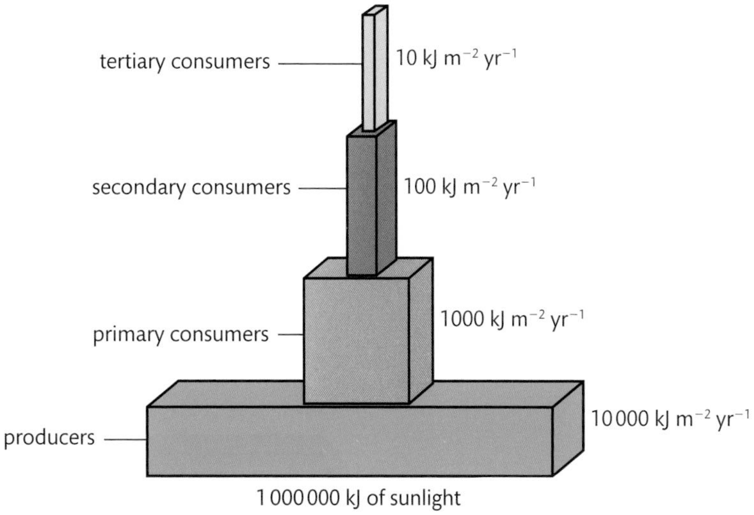

tertiary consumers — 10 kJ m^{-2} yr^{-1}

secondary consumers — 100 kJ m^{-2} yr^{-1}

primary consumers — 1000 kJ m^{-2} yr^{-1}

producers — 10 000 kJ m^{-2} yr^{-1}

1 000 000 kJ of sunlight

Doing practice calculations like this will help you understand how this works.

Figure 9.12 is a pyramid of energy with greater detail than the idealized pyramid shown in Figure 9.11. First, look at the simpler view at the bottom of the figure. The gross production of the producers is 20 810 kilojoules per metre squared per year (kJ m^{-2} yr^{-1}). Can you calculate what percentage of energy moved up to the herbivores?

Figure 9.12 A pyramid of energy for the ecosystem in Silver Springs, Florida, USA, measured in kJ m^{-2} yr^{-1}.

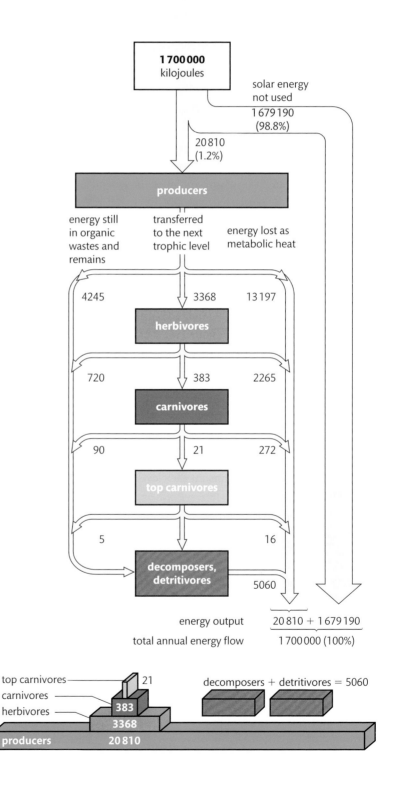

1   Using Figure 9.12, what percentage of the energy of the herbivores is moved up to the carnivores in this energy pyramid?

2   What percentage of the energy of the producers is eventually transferred to the top carnivores?

Solutions

1   Divide the energy of the carnivores (383 kJ m^{-2} yr^{-1}) by the energy of the herbivores (3368 kJ m^{-2} yr^{-1}).

$$\frac{383}{3368}$$

= 0.11.

Multiply by 100 to get 11%.

2   Divide the energy of the top carnivores (21 kJ m^{-2} yr^{-1}) by the energy of the producers (20 810 kJ m^{-2} yr^{-1}).

$$\frac{21}{20\ 810}$$

= 0.001.

Multiply by 100 to get 0.1%.

About 16% of the energy moved up to herbivores. Now look at the detailed energy flowchart at the top half of Figure 9.12. Notice that 1 700 000 kJ of energy are input from the Sun and that only 1.2% of the Sun's energy was captured by the producers. The producers have a gross production of 20 810 kJ m^{-2} yr^{-1}. Gross production is the energy that they have available. Notice that some of that energy is lost as metabolic heat and net system loss (heat, respiration, and maintenance). Look on the other side of the figure, and you will see how much is transferred to 'organic wastes and remains'. This energy eventually flows through decomposers, like mould and bacteria in the soil, and detritivores, like earthworms. Calculate the percentage of energy that is lost as respiration (metabolic heat) as it moves to herbivores.

The answer is 63%. About 16% was transferred to herbivores and the rest was transferred to decomposers and detritivores. The energy reaching the carnivores is 11.4%, and only 5.5% flows up to the top carnivores. Look at the bottom of the energy flow diagram and you will see that eventually all the energy that flows through the ecosystem is lost as metabolic heat.

However, within the specific time period covered by a diagram such as Figure 9.12, organisms are storing some of energy. For example, a young forest accumulates organic matter as the tree grows. The slow rate of decay in a peat bog causes peat to build up. Some energy-flow diagrams include a cube to represent storage.

Worked example

1 Still using Figure 9.12, what percentage of the energy of the producers is lost as metabolic heat and net export from this ecosystem as the energy is transferred to the herbivores?
2 What percentage of the energy of the producers is in organic waste and remains?
3 We have already calculated percentages for the three paths of energy. List the percentage of energy that is:

- lost as metabolic heat
- transferred to herbivores
- left in organic waste.

Solutions

1 Divide the energy that is lost by the energy of the producers to find the percentage that is lost.

$$\frac{13\,197}{20\,810}$$

$= 0.63.$

$0.63 \times 100 = 63\%.$

2 Divide the energy of the organic waste (4245) by the energy of the producers (20 180) to find the percentage still in organic waste and remains.

$$\frac{4245}{20\,180}$$

$= 0.2039.$

Round this up to 0.21; $0.21 \times 100 = 21\%$.

3 Percentage of energy:
- lost as metabolic heat = 63%
- transferred to herbivores = 16%
- left in organic waste = 21%.

Notice that, at the end of the flowchart, the energy output is the same as the energy input. The energy flows through the ecosystem and eventually is lost. However, it is interesting to note that some ecosystems store the energy for a very long period of time before losing it. A young forest keeps the energy in the trees as they grow and the trees do not lose that energy until they eventually die and decompose, which may take hundreds of years.

Now that you understand energy pyramids, we can define some important terms.

- Gross production is the total amount of energy trapped in the organic matter produced by plants per area per time in kilojoules, measured as kilojoules per metre squared per year ($kJ\,m^{-2}\,yr^{-1}$).
- Net production is the gross production minus the energy lost through respiration, also measured as ($kJ\,m^{-2}\,yr^{-1}$).
- Biomass is the dry weight of an organism, measured in grammes per metre squared per year ($g\,m^{-2}\,yr^{-1}$).

1   The term 'net production' means all of the energy directly transferred to the next trophic level. What is the net production in this example (Figure 9.12)?

2   The term 'respiration' is used to describe all of the energy not transferred directly to herbivores. What is the percentage of the energy lost to respiration?

Solutions

1   The net production is 16%, because 16% of the energy was transferred to the herbivores.

2   63% + 21% = 84% lost to respiration.

In terms of an ecosystem, biomass is the dry weight of all the organisms at a certain tier of an ecosystem. The reason why we use dry weight is that the actual weight of the organisms includes a large amount of water. Water needs to be removed and the dry weight measured.

Calculating gross production and net production

In order to calculate the values of gross production and net production, we use the equation:

$$\text{gross production} - \text{respiration} = \text{net production}$$

So, if:

$$\text{gross production} = 809 \text{ kJ m}^{-2} \text{ yr}^{-1}$$

and:

$$\text{respiration} = 729 \text{ kJ m}^{-2} \text{ yr}^{-1}$$

then:

$$\text{net production} = 80 \text{ kJ m}^{-2} \text{ yr}^{-1}$$

Constructing a pyramid of energy

Using the data below, construct a pyramid of energy without looking back at Figure 9.12.

Trophic level	Energy flow ($\text{kJ m}^{-2} \text{ yr}^{-1}$)
Producers	20 810
Primary consumers	3368
Secondary consumers	383
Tertiary consumers	21

After you have drawn the pyramid, check Figure 9.12 to see if yours is correct. Have you drawn each block in proportion to the numbers? Have you placed the correct labels at each trophic level? Have you remembered a title for your pyramid?

Draw an energy pyramid that represents these data:

Trophic level	Energy flow/kJ m^{-2} yr^{-1}
Producers	36 381
Primary consumers	595
Secondary consumers	47

Solution

Your pyramid should look like this.

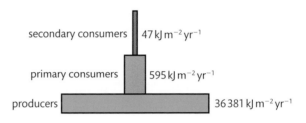

Pyramids of biomass

Pyramids of biomass are similar in shape to pyramids of energy. The higher trophic levels have a lower total biomass per unit area of ecosystem (see Figure 9.13). Biomass is lost during respiration at each trophic level. When glucose is broken down for energy, it is converted into carbon dioxide gas and water. Carbon dioxide and water are excreted and the biomass of glucose is lost. Each successive level of the ecosystem loses more and more biomass. The energy per gramme of food does not decrease, but the total biomass of food is less at each trophic level. Notice in Figure 9.13 how little biomass is present in tertiary consumers compared with producers. It is very similar to what we saw when we looked at the pyramid of energy.

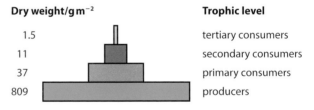

Figure 9.13 Pyramid of biomass.

A pyramid of numbers also has a similar shape as the pyramid of energy. Only a small amount of energy can flow all the way up to the highest trophic level. The total biomass of food available at the top trophic levels is also small. As the top predators, such as a shark or a lion, must be large enough to overwhelm their prey, there can be only relatively few of them.

Give three reasons for low biomass and low numbers of organisms at higher tropic levels.

Solution

- Biomass is lost at each trophic level through respiration as glucose is broken down into carbon dioxide and water. Carbon dioxide and water are excreted.
- Because the top predators must be large enough to overwhelm their prey, there can be only relatively few of them. The total biomass of the top predators such as eagles is much less that the total biomass of all the insects in the ecosystem.
- Energy loss at each level does not allow many organisms to exist at the top tropic level. This results in low biomass and low numbers at the top.

Difficulties of classifying organisms into trophic levels

In order to understand the relationships of an ecosystem completely, something more than food chains and pyramids needs to be constructed. A food web gives a true but complicated picture of what is being eaten in an ecosystem (see Figure 9.14). Can you see the following difficulties when you look at the food web in Figure 9.14?

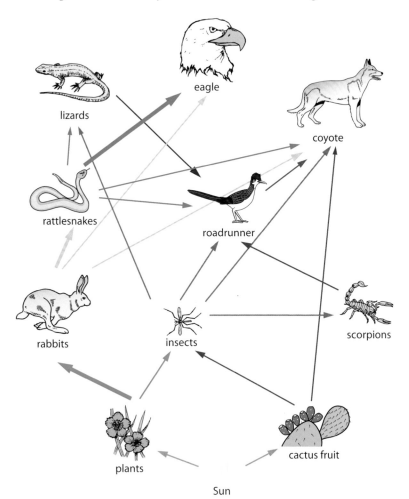

eagle

lizards

coyote

rattlesnakes

roadrunner

rabbits

insects

scorpions

plants

cactus fruit

Sun

Figure 9.14 A desert food web.

- An eagle is a tertiary consumer when eating rattlesnakes, but a secondary consumer when eating rabbits.
- A coyote is a primary consumer when it eats the fruit of a cactus, but a tertiary consumer when it eats a rattlesnake.
- A lizard is a tertiary consumer when it eats rattlesnake eggs, but a secondary consumer when it eats insects.

Another difficulty is where to put omnivores. For example, the following omnivores are difficult to classify into one trophic level.

- Grizzly bears eat plants, insects, and some mammals. Which food is eaten depends on the season, the temperature, and the bear's ability to forage for food. Are they primary consumers, secondary consumers, or tertiary consumers?
- Raccoons eat mice, bird eggs, fish, frogs, nuts, and fruits. The food most dominant in the diet might depend on the season or competition from other animals. Is the raccoon mainly a primary consumer or a secondary consumer?
- Chimpanzees eat both fruit and termites. Is the chimpanzee mainly a primary consumer?

TOK

Raymond Lindeman was an ecologist who formulated a new paradigm of energy flow through ecosystems. In addition to grouping organisms into primary producers, primary consumers, etc., he was the first scientist to measure trophic efficiency. Trophic efficiency is the production of one trophic level that is transferred to the next trophic level. This concept, first formulated in 1942, remains influential today.

Worked example

List two difficulties in classifying organisms into trophic levels.

Solution

- An organism might be classified as a secondary or tertiary consumer depending on what it is eating. For example, an eagle is a tertiary consumer when eating a rattlesnake but a secondary consumer when eating a rabbit.
- Omnivores eat organisms from all levels of the food chain. For example, a grizzly bear eats plants, insects, and some mammals

Comparing pyramids of energy

Table 9.5 A comparison of Cedar Bog and Lake Mendota, Wisconsin, USA

| Trophic level | Cedar Bog | | Lake Mendota | |
	Productivity (cal cm^{-2} yr^{-1})	Efficiency (%)	Productivity (cal cm^{-2} yr^{-1})	Efficiency (%)
Solar radiation	119.000		119.000	
Plants	111	0.1	480	0.4
Herbivores	14.8	13.3	41.6	8.7
Carnivores	3.1	22.3	2.3	5.5
Higher carnivores			0.3	13.0

CHALLENGE YOURSELF

9 Referring to Table 9.5, what percentage of energy is passed on to the next trophic level from the plants of Cedar Bog to the herbivores of Cedar Bog?

10 What percentage of energy is passed on to the next trophic level from the plants of Lake Mendota to the herbivores of Lake Mendota?

When comparing the energy pyramids of two different ecosystems you will notice that the difference is in their efficiency. Look at Table 9.5 comparing the two lakes and you will see the transfer of energy at each trophic level. Notice that typically the organisms at higher and higher trophic levels are increasingly more efficient. Only a small percentage of the Sun's energy that plants absorb is available for transfer to the herbivores. Plants use up the energy through high assimilation and growth. Herbivores are slightly more efficient and carnivores are even more efficient. Cedar Bog has three trophic levels, while Lake Mendota has four. Five trophic levels are the limit for most systems. Lake Mendota can sustain another trophic level because it has a significantly larger biomass than Cedar Bog.

Here are two pyramids representing what we have just seen in Table 9.5.

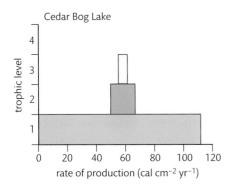 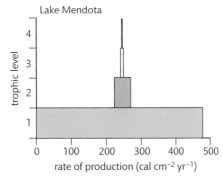

Figure 9.15 Annual production by trophic level in two lakes.
Molles, Jr. 2010, Fig. 18.16

Conversion ratio in sustainable food production

The feed conversion ratio (FCR) is a measure of the efficiency of an animal's ability to convert feed mass into increased body mass. It is expressed as a ratio:

$$\frac{\text{mass of food eaten}}{\text{body mass gain}} \qquad \text{For example:} \qquad \frac{8 \text{ kg of food}}{1 \text{ kg of weight gain}} = 8$$

Table 9.6 shows some estimates for farmed animals.

Table 9.6 Animal FCR

Animal	FCR
Cattle	5–8
Sheep	4–5
Pork	3
Poultry	2
Carnivorous fish (salmon)	2
Herbivorous fish (tilapia)	1.2–1.6

Animals with low FCR can be seen to be efficient users of food. The FCR shows us how much energy is being lost during the transfer from plant to animals, as we have seen with energy pyramids.

Can sustainable agriculture methods improve the FCR? The principles of sustainable agriculture are:

- maintenance of food safety
- improving the environment

- using resources efficiently
- improving the lives of families and society as a whole.

One practical example of sustainable food production is fish farming. Notice from Table 9.6 that fish have a very low FCR. Fish farmers are attempting to lower the FCR to 1. This would mean that the amount of feed given to the fish would be changed into 'fish mass' equal to the mass of feed. Therefore nothing would be lost and everything is gained, so long as other resources are not wasted.

Worked example

Why lower the FCR to 1 for fish?

Solution

This would mean that the amount of feed given to the fish is changed into 'fish mass' equal to the mass of the feed. Thus, nothing is lost and everything is gained as long as the other resources are not wasted.

A fish farm, Corfu, Greece.

> Warm-blooded animals (homeotherms) are less efficient at converting food to biomass than cold-blooded animals (poikilotherms). So you can see why a fish is more efficient than a cow.

> The World Health Organization recently reported that more than 3 billion people are undernourished. This is the largest number and proportion of malnourished people ever recorded in history. The food shortage and malnourishment problem is primarily related to rapid population growth in the world plus a declining per capita availability of land, water, and energy resources.

Change in ecosystems over time by primary and secondary succession

Ecological succession is the change in the abiotic (non-living) and biotic (living) factors in an ecosystem over time. It is the reason why some species gradually replace other species in one particular area.

Primary succession

Primary succession begins when plants begin growing on a previously barren and lifeless area. Let's consider a newly created volcanic island. The plants that first colonize it are able to exist where temperature changes are extreme and there is little or no soil. The first colonizers are usually lichens. They are pioneer plants that can decompose thin layers of rock. As they die and decompose, a thin layer of soil is formed. This is just enough for some moss to get a foothold. This is the start of primary succession. Eventually, there will be enough soil for other seeds to germinate. Coconuts may be washed ashore and begin to germinate. Coconut palm trees will grow. Animals may swim, fly, or be carried on floating vegetation from other islands and populate the new island.

Secondary succession

In secondary succession, a new group of organisms takes over following a natural or artificial upheaval of the primary succession. Secondary succession is much faster than primary succession because soil is already present and there may be existing seeds and roots present. Recolonization of an area after a forest fire is an example of secondary succession.

Table 9.7 summarizes the differences between primary and secondary succession.

Table 9.7 Primary and secondary succession

Primary succession	Secondary succession
Begins with no life	Follows a disturbance of primary succession
No soil	Soil is present
New area, e.g. a volcanic island	Old area, e.g. following a forest fire
Lichen and mosses begin to grow on volcanic rocks	Seeds and roots are already present
Biomass low	Biomass higher
Low production*	Higher production*

* Production is the increase in biomass or energy m^{-2} yr^{-1}. When production is low, it is because there are only a few plants; higher production occurs when many plants are present.

Species diversity and production in a primary succession

Coastal sand dunes are excellent examples of primary succession that are both interesting to walk through and have been studied extensively. If you do not live near the coast, use the hotlinks at the end of this section to find some resources. If you do live near the coast, you may find it more interesting to walk in the dunes after you have learned about the animals and plants that live there. Dunes are areas that need public support in order to be preserved as natural habitats.

Foredune

Primary succession starts on the foredune, where there is no soil, only sand. Lyme grass, *Leymus arenarius*, and marram grass, *Ammophila arenaria*, are pioneer plants on a new dune. Lyme grass is the more salt tolerant of the two species. It is generally fast growing and its roots help bind the sand and stabilize the dune. Marram grass has long underground roots that also spread sideways. It can spread 3 m yr^{-1}. Marram grass also has a special adaptation for life on a foredune: it has a growth spurt when covered with sand. There is little diversity of plant life on the foredune.

Yellow dune

At the yellow dune stage, the dune is developing a thin layer of soil from years of marram grass plants living and dying there. It has now been invaded by other plants with roots that are even better at binding the sand. These plants are sand sedge and sand bindweed. Rabbits may be common in this dune, and their droppings add nutrients to the soil. In the summer, fast-growing plants like dandelions and thistles grow here. Humus (organic matter in the soil) begins to build up as the original pioneer plants die and decay. Notice that, at this stage, the community is more complicated. More species are present and soil is beginning to form.

Grey dune

The grey dune stage has developed a layer of humus from years of plants dying and decomposing. Humus holds water. This dune is much farther inland and sand is not deposited here. Eventually, thick shrubs will grow on this dune.

Mature dune

The final stage in dune succession is the mature dune, which can support a forest. At the Indiana dunes, the mature dune has an oak–hickory forest. Hundreds of species of wild flowers are protected by the shade of the trees. Mosses and ferns grow on the forest floor. The humus is thick as a result of 200 years of plants dying and decaying. The moisture content of the soil is high because of the high amount of humus. The forest is full of insects, birds, and mammals. The temperature is 10% cooler on the mature dune than on the foredune. Lack of wind and blowing sand makes this a comfortable place for both animals and plants.

During the development of the primary succession on sand dunes, you can see that the following changes have occurred:

- few species to many species
- pioneer species to species that compete with others for nutrients
- little diversity to high diversity, the mature forest is home to hundreds of different species
- simple relationships to more complex relationships of mutualism, competition, and predation
- more and more biomass at each stage of the succession.

A stable ecosystem will emerge based on climate

Ecological succession will occur until finally it develops enough complexity to become a stable community. The type of stable community that will emerge in an area is predicted by climate. This predicted ecosystem is called the climax community. When a climax community is extensive and well developed, it is called a biome. For example, at the Indiana dunes, the climax community is a temperate forest. This is because of the mean annual precipitation levels and mean annual temperatures that are common in the area of the Indiana dunes. Figure 9.10 shows the succession along a dune profile.

As Britain has a similar mean annual precipitation and mean annual temperature to the Indiana dunes, the climax community of coastal sand dune succession is also a temperate forest. It is also formed in a similar fashion. Primary succession occurs along the coast as lyme grass and marram grass, which are the pioneer species, bind the sand in place. The youngest dune with these species is always closest to the shore. The woodland climax community is always the furthest from the shore, just as it is in the USA (see Figure 9.10).

Sand dunes in the Outer Hebrides, UK

Marram grass
▼

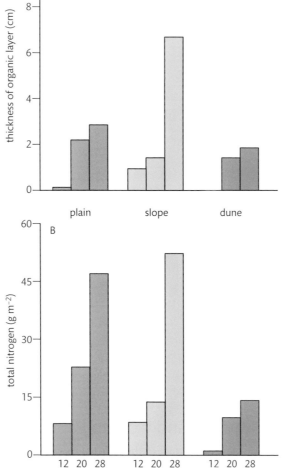

Analysis of data showing primary succession

In order to study primary succession, one group of researchers built a sand dike to model what would happen during 28 years of primary succession on a sand dune. See Figure 9.16.

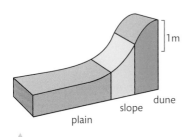

Figure 9.16 Sand dike study model showing plains, slope, and dune.
Adapted from Olff et al. 1993, Fig. 1

The dike consisted of plains, slope, and dune. Over 28 years data were collected that are shown in these graphs.

Figure 9.17 Primary succession as seen in the plain, slope, and dune dike.
A Growth in thickness over 28 years on the sand dike model.
B Total amount of nitrogen in the organic layers over 28 years in three different areas on the sand dike model.
Olff et al. 1993, Fig. 10.

453

CHALLENGE YOURSELF

11 Using Figure 9.17, compare and contrast the thickness of the organic layer of each area over time.

12 Using Figure 9.17, describe the difference in total nitrogen among the three areas.

Figure 9.18 Reconstruction of total biomass **A**, above-ground biomass **B**, and below-ground biomass **C** of different plant species in plain, slope, and dune at three stages of primary succession. Totals with the same letter within each subfigure were not significantly different. Olff et al. 1993, Fig. 6

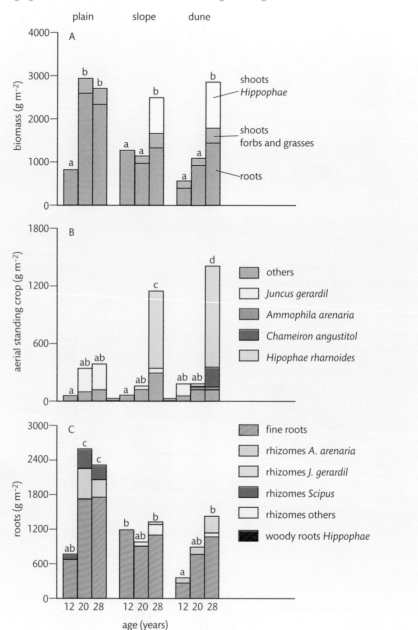

13 Using Figure 9.18, describe the changes in biomass over the 28 years.

14 Using Figure 9.18, compare the changes in aerial standing crop for the slope and the dune.

15 Using Figure 9.18, which area had the largest increase in root mass? What environmental factor could have caused this?

Biosphere and biomes

If you view the surface of the Earth in a satellite picture, you can see large swathes of land covered with trees, other areas covered with ice, and other areas with nothing that can be seen. The living part of the Earth that you can see is called the biosphere. The biosphere comprises all the parts of the Earth where organisms live. Some organisms live in the Earth's crust and some live in the atmosphere. Anywhere that organisms live is considered to be part of the biosphere.

Biomes are divisions of the biosphere. Each biome is a part of the biosphere and is defined by its vegetation and community structure.

Distribution of biomes

Biomes occur because of global weather patterns and topography (see Figure 9.19). Certain species are found in one type of biome and not in others.

Figure 9.19 The distribution of some biomes by altitude and latitude.

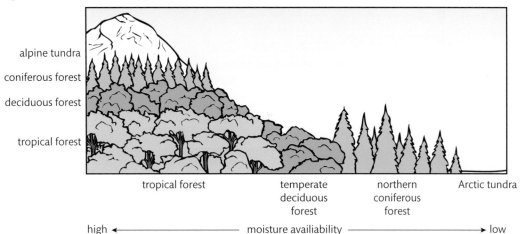

A climograph plots the temperature and rainfall in a particular region. In Figure 9.20, you can see that the mean annual precipitation (rainfall) is similar for a coniferous forest and a temperate forest, but the temperature is different. The mean annual temperature is colder for the coniferous forest. Compare the mean annual precipitation for grasslands and tropical forests. You can see that precipitation in the tropical forest is much higher. Rainfall and temperature affect the distribution of biomes.

The following combinations of temperature, rainfall, and elevation determine the biomes in North America.

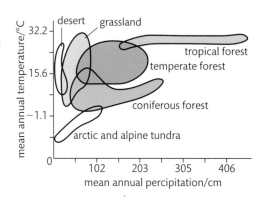

Figure 9.20 A climograph.

Tundra

High elevations with low temperatures and low precipitation are the conditions that result in tundra. Plants and animals that live in the tundra are adapted to a cold and dry environment.

Coniferous forest

High elevations with less cold temperatures and slightly more rainfall are the conditions that result in coniferous forest. Because the ground freezes during some months of the year, coniferous (cone-bearing) trees are well adapted for conserving water when it is frozen. Animals have heavy coats of fur in the winter and lose some of the fur in the summer.

Temperate forest

At lower elevations, where temperatures are warmer and more water is available, the conditions produce temperate forest. Plants and animals in these forests must be adapted for a wide range of conditions: warm in the summer with lots of water, and cool in the winter when water may be unavailable because it is frozen. Many trees in this forest will lose their leaves in the winter to reduce water loss.

Desert

At low elevations with warm temperatures and little precipitation, the conditions produce desert. Desert animals and plants have very specific adaptations that enable them to survive in this extremely hot and dry biome. A desert kangaroo rat has a specialized kidney for recycling water in its body. Cacti have spines instead of wide leaves to reduce water loss.

Tropical forest

At low elevations with warm temperatures and very high moisture, the conditions result in tropical forest. This forest is extremely productive, with high primary productivity as a result of the combination of high temperatures and high rainfall.

Table 9.8 Characteristics of the seven major biomes

Biome	Temperature	Moisture	Characteristics of vegetation
Desert	Mostly very hot with soil temperatures above 60°C (140°F) in the daytime	Low precipitation: less than 30 cm per year	Cacti and shrubs with water storage tissues, thick cuticles and other adaptations to reduce water loss
Grassland	Cold temperatures in winter and hot in summer	Seasonal drought is common with occasional fires, medium amount of moisture	Prairie grasses that hold the soil with their long roots; occasional fire prevents trees and shrubs from invading the grasslands
Shrubland (chaparral, matorral, maquis and garigue, dry heatherlands, fynbos)	Mild temperatures in winter and long, hot summers	Rainy winters and dry summers	Dry woody shrubs are killed by periodic fires. Shrubs store food in fire-resistant roots. They re-grow quickly and produce seed that germinates only after a fire
Temperate deciduous forest	Very hot in summer and very cold in winter	High rainfall spread evenly over the year. In winter, water may freeze for a short time	Deciduous trees like oak, hickory, and maple dominate the forest. In warmer seasons, a wide range of herbaceous plants grow and flower on the forest floor
Tropical rainforest	Very warm	Very high precipitation of more than 250 cm yr⁻¹	Plant diversity is high. A canopy of trees is the top layer. Next is a layer of shrubs. The ground layer is herbaceous plants and ferns. Large trees have vines climbing on them. Trees have orchids and bromeliads tucked in their branches
Tundra	Very cold; in summer, the upper layer of soil thaws but the lower layers remain frozen: this is permafrost	Little precipitation	Low-growing plants like lichen and mosses and a few grasses and shrubs. Permafrost prevents the roots from growing deeply. Continuous daylight in summer allows some plant growth and reproduction
Coniferous forest (taiga)	Slightly warmer than the tundra	Small amount of precipitation but wet due to lack of evaporation	Cone-bearing trees such as pine, spruce, fir and hemlock

Schmitt et al. 2011

Look at Figure 9.21.

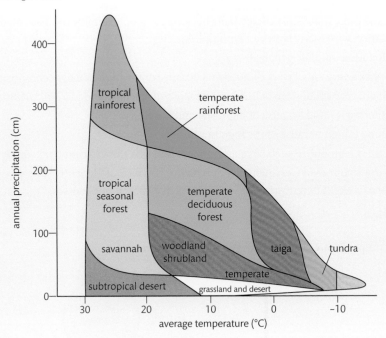

Figure 9.21 A climograph. This type of graph shows the relationship between temperature, rainfall, and ecosystem type. www.marietta.edu/-biol/biomes/desert.htm.

16 What is the average temperature range of a subtropical desert?

17 What is the highest amount of precipitation for a subtropical desert?

18 Compare the mean annual temperature for grasslands and tropical forests.

19 Compare and contrast the mean annual temperature for temperate deciduous forest and temperate rainforest.

Gersmehl diagrams

Another way of describing energy flows and nutrient recycling is to use Gersmehl diagrams of different biomes. These diagrams are a common method of demonstrating the cycling of nutrients within the main 'stores' of an ecosystem. As you will notice from the diagrams, the main stores of nutrients are soil, biomass (plants), and litter. Arrows of varying thickness represent nutrient transfer. Circles of varying size represent the size of the stores. Included in the diagrams are the following:

- input, such as of nitrogen, carbon, and minerals from weathered rock
- output, such as loses of nutrients by leaching and run-off
- flows, such as of leaf and needle fall from biomass to litter, and uptake of nutrients from the soil by plants.

Figure 9.22 shows a generalized model of a Gersmehl diagram.

Figure 9.22 A model of the mineral nutrient cycle.

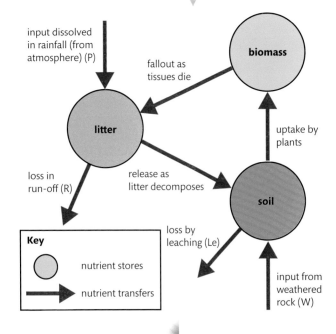

457

We will now look at a Gersmehl diagram for a specific biome, the tropical rainforest. First read this information about a rainforest, as it will help you make the diagram.

- Biomass is the main store of nutrients because the tropical rainforest has tall, dense vegetation with many layers and multiple species.
- Precipitation: rainfall is high all year.
- Litter has a very small store of nutrients because of the high rate of decomposition.
- Soil has a very small store of nutrients because of leaching and low soil fertility.
- Weathering is rapid because of high heat and humidity.
- Leaching is high because of the high rainfall.
- Run-off is high due to such large amounts of rain that the soil cannot absorb it all.

Try to draw your own Gersmehl diagram before you look at Figure 9.23. Be sure to make the circles different sizes and use arrows of different thicknesses.

Solution

Now compare your diagram with the actual diagram.

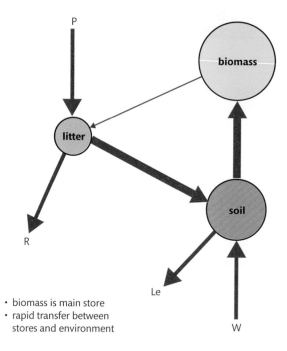

Figure 9.23 Gersmehl diagram of a tropical rainforest.

- biomass is main store
- rapid transfer between stores and environment

Worked example

We will now construct another Gersmehl diagram. This time the biome is taiga. Here are the specifics for taiga.

- Litter is the largest store of nutrients because of the low rate of decomposition as a result of low temperatures.
- Run-off is high. The ground is still frozen when the snow is melting.
- Biomass is relatively low because conifers have only one layer of needles and there is no undergrowth.
- Transfer from biomass to litter is high because of the constant supply of needles falling from coniferous trees.
- Soil stores are very small. Poor soil is formed from glacial deposits and so there is low soil fertility.
- Weathering of rocks is slow because of the cold.

Have a go at drawing your own diagram before looking at Figure 9.24; see if you are more accurate than you were with your first diagram.

Solution

Figure 9.24 shows the actual diagram for taiga.

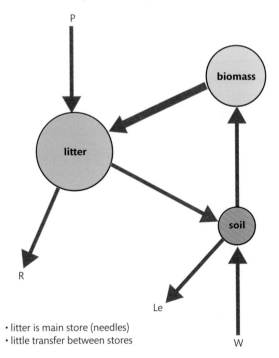

- litter is main store (needles)
- little transfer between stores

Gersmehl diagrams are models that predict and explain the natural world.

Figure 9.24 Gersmehl diagram of a boreal forest (taiga).

CHALLENGE YOURSELF

20 Draw a Gersmehl diagram for a desert biome. Here are the specifics you need:
- soil is rich in nutrients because there is little rain available to wash them away
- biomass is small because of the extreme heat and lack of water
- litter or topsoil is practically non-existent because it is eroded by the wind
- run-off is high because there is no litter to hold on to the water
- loss as a result of leaching is low.

An example of humans interfering with nutrient cycling

In a study published in 2011 in the journal *Ecological Applications*, researchers documented how the collapse of marine fisheries as a result of overfishing and habitat loss has affected nutrient recycling in the marine environment.

Fish have a functional role in ecosystems. Through consumption and assimilation, fish recycle nutrients, especially nitrogen and phosphates, into forms that can be taken up by microorganisms and plants. The role of fish as nutrient recyclers is critical.

Eighty per cent of the nutrients that are used by primary producers are supplied by fish. Removal of fish tissues by marine fisheries in areas where nitrogen is low has affected primary production by plants. This has a negative effect on the herbivores in that community. In this study, estimates of nitrogen excretions rates for grey snapper in the Bahamas were 456% higher in unfished areas compared with fished areas. The excretion rates of phosphates were 451% higher in unfished areas compared with fished areas. The concern of these authors is that the sea grass beds that are the key habitat for young fish may be affected by this lack of recycled nutrients. Loss of primary production in the sea grass beds could cause the loss of even more fish.

A closed ecosystem

Most ecosystems are open. In a forest ecosystem, light enters and is trapped by plants. Herbivores eat the plants and their faeces fertilize the soil. After a fire, the soil may blow away to another ecosystem. Minerals may be leached by water after rain and be carried down the river to a new ecosystem.

Closed systems exchange energy but not matter. No natural system on Earth is considered to be a closed system, but the entire planet can be considered 'almost' closed. Large amounts of light energy enter the Earth and eventually return to space as heat, but matter is not exchanged.

Some experimentation has been done with artificial closed systems. A closed ecological system (CES) could be a space station. A space station does not rely on exchange of matter with its surroundings. In a closed ecosystem, waste products made by a species must be used by at least one other species. Waste products such as urine, faeces, and carbon dioxide must be converted into oxygen, food, and water. This involves at least one autotroph (green plant), which can use the waste products to make food as long as sunlight is available. Energy can be exchanged, but not matter.

An example of a large CES is Biosphere 2. Biosphere 2 is a large research facility, the size of two football fields, owned by the University of Arizona, USA. The research done here demonstrates the conditions that can affect a closed system. This facility has its own farm under a glass dome, and experiments are carried out with week-long periods of full closure, where humans live in the closed environment.

Biosphere 2 Rainforest building.

Disturbances influence the structure and rate of change in an ecosystem

A disturbance is a new environmental condition that affects the structure and rate of change in an ecosystem. Examples of disturbances can be natural (for example fire, flood, wind, and insect invasion) or caused by humans (for example the clearing of a forest, building a road, ploughing a field, or clearing a natural area to build a housing development.)

In 1975, Joseph Connell proposed a new idea. His theory stated that disturbance is a common phenomenon that can actually have a beneficial effect on species diversity in a community. For example, fire in a forest affects the structure of the forest. By burning down the trees that shade the forest floor, the structure of the community is then changed, many more shade-intolerant plants can grow quickly, so the rate of change is affected.

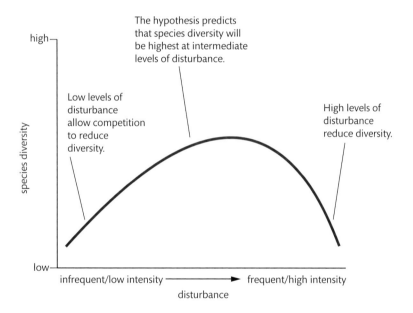

TOK The old paradigm of diversity in an ecosystem stated that the most diversity is found in the oldest ecosystem. The intermediate disturbance hypothesis changed the way that ecologists think about how disturbances affect ecosystems. This hypothesis predicts that intermediate levels of disturbance promote higher levels of diversity.

Figure 9.25 Graph of the disturbance hypothesis. Disturbance is a common phenomenon that may have a beneficial effect on species diversity in a community. Molles, Jr. 2010, Fig. 16.18.

Look at Figure 9.25 and the points below.

- High levels of disturbance (e.g. constant mowing) reduce diversity. The community will only consist of the few species that can complete their life cycle between disturbances.
- Low (infrequent) disturbances will cause a decline in diversity because the species that are the best competitors will dominate.
- Intermediate levels of disturbances, such as a fire every few years, are the most effective at maintaining diversity. There is enough time between disturbances for a number of species to colonize an area. It can also slow the growth of dominant species.

Section summary

- Pyramids of energy show how much energy is left at each trophic level in a food chain. Approximately 10% of the energy from one tropic level is transferred to the next level. For example, primary consumers receive only 10% of the energy from the producers that they eat. Ninety per cent of the energy in a food chain is lost as it travels from one trophic level to the next.

- Gross production is the amount of energy trapped in organic matter measured in kilojoules per metre squared per year. Net production is the gross production minus the energy lost through respiration. Biomass is the dry weight of the organism, measured in grammes per metre squared per year.

- A pyramid of biomass is similar in shape to a pyramid of energy. Each successive level of the ecosystem loses more and more biomass.

- The food conversion ratio (FCR) is a measure of the efficiency of an animal's ability to convert food mass into increased body mass. If 8 kg of food is eaten and 8 kg of body mass is gained, the FCR is 1. Such an animal would be very efficient. Some herbivorous fish have an FCR close to 1.

- Ecosystems change over time by primary and secondary succession. Primary succession takes place on a previously barren and lifeless area, while secondary succession takes place as a new group of organisms takes over following a natural or artificial upheaval.

- At the end of secondary succession, a stable climax community will develop based on the climate. For example, in the USA and Britain a temperate forest is the climax of a sand dune community.

- The living part of the Earth that you can see is called the biosphere. Biomes are divisions of the biosphere and are defined by their vegetation and community structure. A desert is a biome, as is a tropical rainforest.

- A Gersmehl diagram shows the energy flow and nutrient recycling in a particular biome.

- The disturbance hypothesis states that disturbances can actually have a beneficial effect on diversity in an ecosystem. It hypothesizes that, as the structure of the community is changed by the disturbance, more organisms can grow.

Exercises

4 Describe a method of representing the cycling of nutrients in an ecosystem.

5 Explain how the Earth is a closed ecosystem.

6 Compare and contrast two energy pyramids from two different ecosystems.

NATURE OF SCIENCE

Assessing risks and benefits associated with scientific research: the use of biological control has associated risk and requires verification by tightly controlled experiments before it is approved.

C.3 Impact of humans on ecosystems

Understandings:

- Introduced alien species can escape into local ecosystems and become invasive.
- Competitive exclusion and the absence of predators can lead to reduction in the numbers of endemic species when alien species become invasive.
- Pollutants become concentrated in the tissues of organisms at higher trophic levels by biomagnification.
- Macroplastic and microplastic debris has accumulated in marine environments.

Applications and skills:

- Application: Study of the introduction of cane toads in Australia and one other local example of the introduction of an alien species.
- Application: Discussion of the trade-off between control of the malarial parasite and DDT pollution.
- Application: Case study of the impact of marine plastic debris on Laysan albatrosses and one other named species.
- Skills: Analysis of data illustrating the causes and consequences of biomagnification.
- Skills: Evaluation of eradication programmes and biological control as measures to reduce the impact of alien species.

Biological control: risks and benefits

Biological control is the idea of using a natural predator to control unwanted or invasive species. There are powerful arguments for using biological control. One argument is that biological control is an environmentally friendly alternative to chemical control. In fact a report by the National Academy of Sciences in 1987 argued that biological control should be the primary pest control method in the USA. When an invasive species is affecting an entire community, even cautious observers would agree that biological control should be considered. However, there is always a risk when introducing a new organism into an ecosystem. Unexpected consequences may occur even though rigorous testing is carried out beforehand. Scientists look at risk–benefit analyses and make decisions based on those analyses.

Introduced alien species can become invasive

One of the classic examples of biological control 'gone wrong' is the introduction of cane toads, *Rhinella marina*, into Australia in the 1930s. The cane toad was imported from Hawaii and released in Queensland to control the beetle pests of sugar cane.

The larvae of the beetle pests of sugar cane eat the roots of the cane and the plants die. Cane growers were interested in controlling the beetle pests because sugar cane crops are a major income producer in Australia. Entomologists researched many solutions to the sugar cane pest problem, such as chemical insecticides, soil fumigation methods, and physical removal. After 25 years, none showed much promise in field trials.

In 1935 one entomologist was sure he had found the solution. In Hawaii, the cane toad was being used to control beetle infestations of sugar cane crops. This idea was quickly accepted in Australia. In June 1935, 2400 toads were released in an area of Queensland. Other entomologists had argued against this quick release. Risk assessments of the potential harm of introducing these toads had not been done. Unfortunately, the outcome has been that this poisonous toad has multiplied very rapidly, currently the population has grown to more than 200 million, yet the beetles that the cane toad was brought in to eradicate have not been affected. It seems that the beetle pests were not affected because in Australia, compared with Hawaii, the toads have found other food sources, such as smaller beetles and moths. By 1950 the cane toad was recognized as a pest in the Vermin Act, but it wasn't until the 1980s that the cane toad was recognized as a national issue. Lessons learnt from the cane toad debacle are probably one of the reasons why Australia today has very strict quarantine laws and tough risk-assessment procedures.

Australia is the only nation with a specific law for classical biological control, the Australian Biological Control Act of 1984. Most state laws in the USA encourage the use of biological control, but adequate supervision is lacking. There is an international organization, the International Organization for Biological Control (IOBC), working to promote environmentally safe practices around the world.

- Cane toads were brought to Australia to control the sugar cane beetles biologically.
- Cane toads have no natural predators in Australia because they are toxic to Australian crocodiles and large lizards.
- Cane toads reproduce rapidly.
- Cane toads have become more of a pest in Australia than the beetles they were meant to eat.
- Cane toads have found plenty of other species to eat in Australia, so they ignore the target beetle pests.
- The risk assessment carried out before the introduction of cane toads to Australia was not adequate.

Competitive exclusion can affect endemic species

The principle of competitive exclusion states that no two species can occupy the same niche. When two species have a similar need for the same resources, such as food, one will be excluded. In Australia, when the cane toads attain high population densities, they consume a large number of invertebrates. Individual cane toads are thought to consume 200 beetles, ants, and termites per night. A report from the National Cane Toad Task Force of Australia in June 2005 showed that a decline in some small reptile species has coincided with the increase in the cane toad population. Competition for food is inferred as the reason for the population declines. A burrowing frog, *Limnodynastes omatus*, shows no survival of tadpoles in ponds where cane toad tadpoles are present. Direct predation on tadpoles is not significant, which is why competition for food is inferred. Small skinks (blue-tongued lizards) begin to disappear once the cane toad arrives. Both species are insectivores, and it is hypothesized that the skinks are outcompeted by the cane toad for insects because of the voracious appetite of the toad. These examples are evidence that endemic species are being outcompeted by the cane toads. Many more studies are being carried out by scientists in Australia to discover what exactly the results are of this attempt at biological control.

The cane toad.

New research on cane toads in northern Australia has suggested that a good way to control the cane toad invasion is to use parasites that are specific to cane toads.

Will our knowledge of the damage that biological control can do, if not monitored well, change the methods we use in the future?

TOK

Absence of predators can affect endemic species

Cane toads are extremely poisonous. Behind the ears of cane toads are glands that contain a toxic substance. Predator species in Australia are seriously affected by eating cane toads. Seventy-five species of turtles are at risk because they can eat toads large enough to kill them with their toxin; 90% of large lizards die after eating cane toads. Other evidence has shown an impact on snakes and crocodiles that have eaten cane toads. The absence of a successful predator of cane toads is a significant factor in the population explosion of cane toads in Australia.

Kudzu: an introduced alien species

What we do to the environment today may have unforeseen consequences for future generations. Kudzu was introduced from Japan to the USA in 1876 at the Philadelphia Centennial Exposition as an ornamental plant. In the 1930s it was promoted by the Soil Conservation Service of the US government as a fast-growing plant that could solve the problem of soil erosion. From 1935 to 1950 it was planted by the Civilian Conservation Corp sponsored by the federal government. Then, in 1953, it was recognized by the US Department of Agriculture as a pest weed.

Currently, kudzu is common throughout the southeastern states of the USA. It is often called 'the plant that ate the South'. Here is the reason why: kudzu grows rapidly, as much as 20 m per season. Thirty stems can emerge from one root. It grows both horizontally and vertically. Kudzu spreads by runners that can make roots and produce more plants. Kudzu grows well in many conditions, although prolonged freezing will kill it. The thick growth crushes other plants as it covers them. Its weight breaks tree branches. In the USA, the effects of kudzu cost $500 million annually.

Kudzu, the plant that ate the South.

Biomagnification

Biomagnification is a process by which chemical substances become more concentrated at each trophic level.

When chemicals are released into the environment they may be taken up by plants. The plants may not be affected by the small amount of a chemical that they absorb or have on their surface. But when large amounts of the affected plants are eaten by a primary consumer, the amount of chemical the consumer takes in is much greater. Similarly, if numbers of the primary consumer are eaten by a secondary consumer, the amount of chemical taken in by the secondary consumer is magnified even more. Chemicals that are biomagnified in this manner are fat soluble. After ingestion, they are stored in the fatty tissue of the consumer. When the consumer is caught and eaten, the fat is digested and the chemical moves to the fatty tissue of the secondary consumer.

Causes of biomagnification

Some toxic chemicals have been put deliberately into the environment to kill insect pests. One of these pesticides is dichlorodiphenyltrichloroethane (DDT), which has been used to control mosquitoes and other insect pests. At the time it was first used, it was not known that DDT does not break down and can persist for decades in the environment. DDT was commonly sprayed on plants and eventually entered water supplies. There it was absorbed by microscopic organisms. These microorganisms were eaten by small fish, and the small fish were eaten by larger fish. DDT built up in the fatty tissues of the fish. When these fish were eaten by birds, the magnification of DDT was even greater (see Figure 9.26).

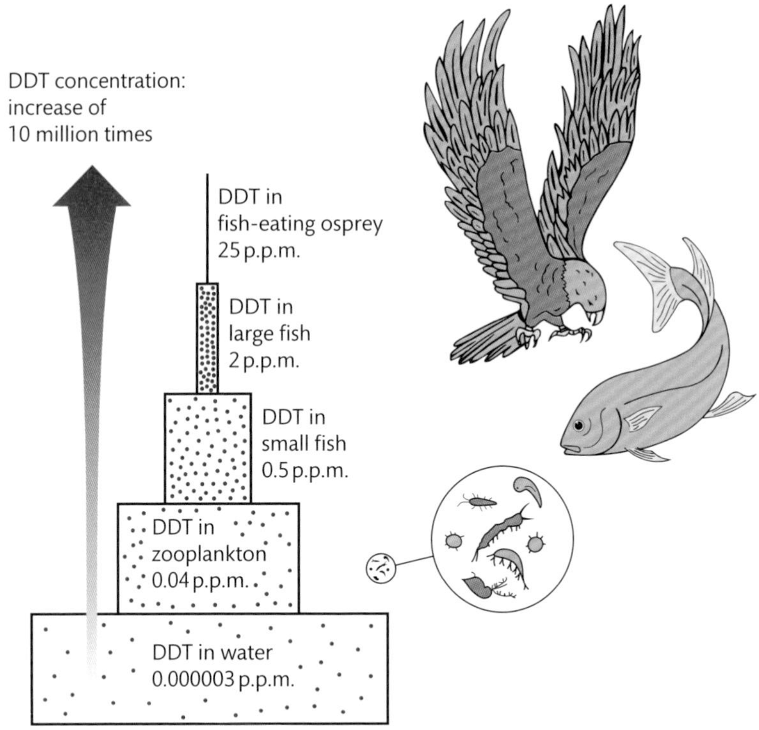

Figure 9.26 Biomagnification of DDT.

Consequences of biomagnification

The first sign of the problem with DDT was a decline in the number of predator birds. Studies showed that the eggs of these birds were easily cracked. In fact, the weight of the mother sitting on the eggs cracked them. It was finally discovered that DDT was building up in the tissue of the birds and interfering with the calcium needed for the shells to be hard. DDT was banned in the USA in 1971. The bird population has begun to recover following the ban. DDT was originally banned because of its effects on birds. However, It also affects humans who consume agricultural products and eat fish containing accumulations of DDT. Because DDT is stored in fat, levels of DDT in breast milk are often six times higher in a mother than in her blood.

Worked example

1 Define biomagnification.

2 What are the causes and consequences of biomagnification?

Solutions

1 Chemical substances become more concentrated at each trophic level. The chemicals may not be very concentrated in producers, but they become more concentrated in primary consumers, and even more concentrated in secondary consumers.

2 Causes:
- Toxic chemicals are released into the environment.
- Toxic chemicals do not break down.
- Toxic chemicals are fat-soluble and build up in the fatty tissues of organisms.

Consequences:

Organisms highest up in the food chain are harmed by the toxic chemicals because these chemicals are very concentrated at the top trophic level. For example, DDT built up in the bodies of birds of prey and caused their eggs to be easily cracked. The birds of prey began to die out. DDT was banned and the bird population has rebounded.

Many other toxic chemicals are in the environment and may be causing harm.

The trade-off between DDT pollution and malarial parasite control

What are the challenges that must be overcome as we face decisions over DDT pollution and malarial parasite control? Malaria is the most deadly vector-borne disease in the world. It kills more than 1 million people per year. In the past 25 years, there has seen a dramatic rise in cases of malaria, despite the use of insecticide-treated bed nets (ITNs), indoor resident spraying (IRS), and artemesin combination therapy (ACTs, an antimalarial drug). How can we overcome this challenge? Should the trade-off be the environment or human health?

DDT pollution

We have just looked at some of the problems caused by biological magnification of DDT. DDT is a persistent organic pollutant (POP). These pay-offs have followed the ban on DDT in the USA. Peregrine falcons have come off the endangered species list; bald eagles will soon follow. DDT levels in human blood samples have declined sharply. DDT has disappeared from the breast milk of nursing mothers.

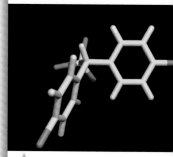

A feeding mosquito.

Control of malaria for large human populations

The difficulties of malaria control for some nations are significant. When IRS is used in houses, DDT can be found in the breast milk of nursing mothers. Without IRS, hundreds of mosquitoes can enter a house, compared with no mosquitos entering a house that has been sprayed. In Africa and Indonesia, malaria is more of a problem than human immunodeficiency virus (HIV). Many health officials would like to use DDT to ease the suffering of human populations, but donor governments refuse to allow DDT spraying. A new documentary movie shows the effect of refusing to spray DDT for human populations in underdeveloped countries; *3 Billion and Counting*, tells the story of the devastation of malaria on large populations of people.

DDT

The proposal to commit to a deadline for a worldwide ban on the pesticide DDT by 2020 was rejected at the Sixth Conference of the Parties to the Stockholm Convention on Persistent Organic Pollutants. India, the largest producer of DDT, strongly opposed the proposal. India is the only country still manufacturing DDT.

A Laysan albatross with regurgitated waste.

A sea lion caught in a fishing net.

The Marine Conservancy has published the estimated decomposition rates of most plastic debris found on coasts.

- Polystyrene cups: 50 years.
- Plastic drinks containers: 400 years.
- Disposable nappies: 450 years.
- Plastic bottles: 450 years.

Worked example

Discuss the pros and cons of not using DDT.

Solution

Pros:

- Peregrine falcons are off the endangered species list.
- There is less DDT in the breast milk of nursing mothers.
- There has been a decline in the amount of DDT present in samples of human blood.

Cons:

- Hundreds of mosquitos carrying disease can enter houses in Africa.
- Malaria is more of a problem in some nations than HIV.
- Malaria devastates large populations of people in tropical countries.

Macroplastics in the marine environment

Macroplastics are pieces of plastic bigger than 5 mm. The accumulation of macroplastics is very high adjacent to urban areas in the northern hemisphere. Macroplastic items such as plastic bottles, bags, nets, fishing lines, and many items of rubbish can pose a serious threat to marine wildlife.

- Marine mammals and turtles can ingest plastic bags and bottles, which then interfere with their digestive system.
- Drift nets can entangle birds, fish, and mammals.
- PCBs and other contaminants may be concentrated in pieces of plastic that are ingested by birds, fish, and mammals.

The Laysan albatross

Seabirds can mistake plastic floating on the surface of water as food and ingest it. Because most adult birds regurgitate food to feed their young, the plastic is passed on to the chicks. One study discovered that 98% of Laysan albatross, *Phoebastria immutabilis*, chicks had been fed beads, toys, golf tees, buttons, and many other plastic items by their parents. It seems that the albatross prefers pink items. It is hypothesized that pink items are the same colour as, and are mistaken for, shrimps. These items can obstruct a chick's digestive system, leading to starvation and death. One Laysan albatross chick had a piece of plastic 11 cm long embedded in its gut.

Microplastics in the marine environment

Microplastics are defined as plastic particles smaller than 5 mm. They are produced directly as abrasives and exfoliants, or indirectly as a consequence of the breakdown of larger plastic material. The amount and distribution of microplastic particles in the marine environment has increased steadily over the past 20 years because of the rise in the use of plastics by humans. It has been found that microplastics act like sponges and soak up toxic chemicals such as PCBs in the marine environment. Microplastics have a large surface area in relation to their size, so there is plenty of surface for the chemicals to stick to. The potential impacts of microplastics on the marine environment include:

- accumulation of more and more plastic debris, because these plastics do not break down
- ingestion of microplastic pieces by marine organisms, causing damage to their digestive systems
- absorption of components of the plastic, or chemicals adsorbed on the plastics, by the ingesting organism
- accumulation of those chemicals in the body of the ingesting organism.

Research is ongoing to determine whether microplastics themselves or the chemicals they contain are carried across trophic levels. For example, do PCBs or other POPs adsorbed onto plastic pieces build up in the bodies of fish and become magnified as the small fish are eaten by larger fish, etc.? Biomagnification of chemicals from plastics, either within the plastics or adsorbed onto the plastic pieces, may be occurring.

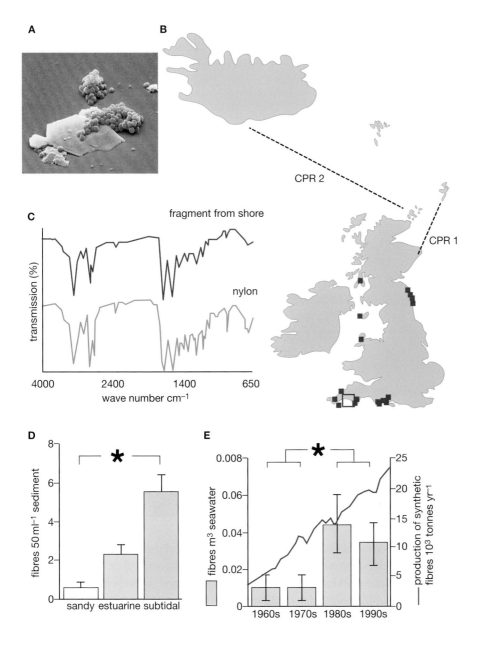

Figure 9.27 **A** Facial scrub particles shown in an electron micrograph are microplastics polluting the ocean. **B** Sampling locations in the northeast Atlantic, showing routes sampled by Continuous Plankton Recorder (CPR) 1 and 2 since 1960 and used to assess the abundance of microplastics in the water column. Red squares indicate the abundance of microplastics. **C** Example showing how FT-IR spectroscopy was used to identify fragments from the environment. Here an unknown fragment is identified as nylon. **D** There were significant differences in abundance of microplastics between sandy beaches and subtidal habitats, but abundance was consistent among sites within habitat type. **E** Accumulation of microscopic plastic in CPR samples revealed a significant increase over time when comparing the 1960s and 1970s with the 1980s and 1990s. Approximate figures for global production of synthetic fibres (red line) overlain for comparison. Microplastics were also less abundant along oceanic route CPR 2 than CPR 1. To read the article where this figure is adapted from ('Lost at sea: Where is all the plastic?'), go to the hotlinks site, and click on Chapter 9: Section C.3. http://www.kimointernational.org/MicroPlasticResearch.aspx.

A lugworm casting on a beach.

Mark Anthony Browne from the University of California at Santa Barbara has joined with UK scientists from Plymouth University to study lugworms as they feed on highly contaminated ocean sediments.

Impact of microplastic debris on lugworms

Lugworms, *Arenicola marina*, are called the earthworms of the sea. They are commonly found in the USA and Europe and are used as bait by fishermen. They feed on ocean floor sediments by striping the sediment of debris and organic matter. They can eat sand particles and digest the microorganisms and nutrients on the surface of the sand particles. Because they are basically 'eating' what has fallen to the bottom of the sea, their health can tell us about the health of the oceans, making them indicator organisms. In one experiment, a California scientist, Mark Anthony Browne, found that, when lugworms eat microplastic pieces contaminated with common chemical pollutants, those pollutants are found in high concentrations in the lugworm's tissues. These high concentrations make the lugworms vulnerable to pathogens. They cause the worms to have less energy for churning up the bottom sediments, which is one of their most important functions in the ocean ecosystem. This is a key finding because the current policy in the USA considers microplastics to be non-hazardous.

 International Pellet Watch (IPW) was founded in 2005 by Dr Hideshige Takada of Tokyo University. He has asked citizens across the globe to collect plastic pellets from the beaches they visit and send them to his laboratory. He analyses the POP content of the pellets and their global distribution. The results are sent back to donors by email and released on the web. So far pellet samples have been analysed from 200 locations and 40 countries. About 1000 pellets have been analysed, and POPs have been detected in every one of those 1000 samples.

Biological control and eradication programmes to reduce the impact of alien species

Water hyacinths are aquatic plants native to the Amazon basin, but are often considered to be an invasive species outside their native range.

Invasive alien species are recognized as a serious biological threat to the environment and to economic development. Without any natural predators, a plant or animal that has been moved out of its local ecosystem may multiply and threaten other species, agriculture, or public health. Many nations are grappling with the complex and costly problems caused by invasive alien species organisms, such as the black striped mussel and fire ants. The following examples describe some strategies that have been used to eradicate invasive alien species.

The black striped mussel, *Mytilopsis sallei*, was found to have invaded Cullen Bay in Darwin Harbor, Australia, in 1988. This mussel is capable of making a thick matt more than 10 cm thick and can foul anchors, pylons and buoys, storm water pipes, vessel hulls, and breakwaters. It is a very serious threat to tropical Australian waters. Regular surveys of Australian ports highlighted the discovery of the mussel within 6 months of its arrival. A rapid decision to eradicate it prevented the spread. The method of eradication was to close the gates to the marina where they were located and expose the entire area to copper sulfate and chlorine. These chemicals were poured into the water, killing the mussels and all other living organisms in the marina. The potential economic damage to the pearl industry from black mussels is $350 million a year, and damage to the prawn fishery catch is worth close to $120 million a year, at today's values.

Fire ants, *Solenopsis invicta*, are notorious because of their painful, burning stings. The stings result in pustules, which continue to itch intensively. Fire ants attack humans as they walk across lawns and golf courses. Red fire ants also attack livestock grazing in the fields of Florida. Fire ants were brought to Florida from South America. Use of insecticides kills native ants as well as fire ants, but fire ants return much more quickly than the native ants. Insecticides are the primary control of fire ants today in Florida. The estimated cost of red fire ant control in Florida is $36 per household.

A biological control agent that is being tested against fire ants is a fly of the genus *Pseudacteon*. If the fly catches an ant, it lays its eggs inside the head of the fire ant. When the eggs hatch, the larvae eat through the head of the fire ant. *Pseudacteon* flies might work but they might not control the fire ants. They could also become a pest because they have no predators. In South America, the fire ant population is only one-fifth the size of that in southern USA. Scientists hypothesize that the 24 species of *Pseudacteon* flies native to South America keep the fire ant under control. In 2011, one species of *Pseudacteon* fly was introduced to control fire ants in Florida. It was found that it did not have a significant impact on the fire ant population after its release. The study concluded that multiple species of flies would be required in order to replicate the conditions of natural fire ant control seen in South America. Would Florida be inviting new pests to the sunshine state, in the hope of ridding themselves of an old pest?

Imported red fire ants on a wooden stick.

The oriental fruit fly, *Bactrocera dorsalis*, was introduced into Okinawa Island in Japan in 1945. It damages fruit crops by laying eggs in the fruit: the larvae from the eggs eat the fruit. All Japanese territories were declared free of the oriental fruit fly in 1985, because of an 18-year eradication programme combining some insecticide use with sterile insect release (SIR). SIR entails raising large numbers of sterile male flies and releasing them to mate with wild females. The numbers of released sterile males are very high. In one study, 648 sterile males were released for every one wild male in the wild population. However, according to another study it is enough to release nine sterile males to one wild male. When the males are released and mate with wild females, the eggs from these females are not viable. After SIR release on one island, the percentage of infestation of host fruits decreased to zero in 3 months. The success of SIR and strict inspection of incoming produce that might contain this fruit fly means that Japan has been free of the oriental fruit fly for the past 20 years.

An adult female oriental fruit fly, *Bactrocera dorsalis*.

Whenever a question in an IB exam asks you to 'evaluate' something, it means to state both the risks and the benefits. It does not mean give just your opinion. Creating a table is a good way of answering this type of question.

Analysis of data illustrating the cause and effects of biomagnification

As we have learned previously, biomagnification is the build-up of heavy metals and POPs by successive trophic levels, resulting in higher concentrations in the predator organisms than in the prey. Bioaccumulation is the net accumulation over time of POPs or heavy metals (such as mercury, arsenic, and lead) within an organism from both biotic (other organisms) and abiotic (soil, water, etc.) sources.

CHALLENGE YOURSELF

The data you will analyse were collected from streams in the USA, from the state of Missouri, in an area called the Ozarks. The heavy metal that is causing concern there is mercury. It is hypothesized that mercury is bioaccumulating in several fish that are commonly caught and eaten by the people in this area.

Mercury (Hg) is a pollutant from both natural and human sources. Mercury found in aquatic systems comes from leaf litter: leaves accumulate atmospheric mercury when alive and then fall into streams when dead. Wet areas are conducive to changing the inorganic mercury in the leaves into methyl mercury (MeHg), which is subject to bioaccumulation and biomagnification. MeHg is highly toxic to fish, wildlife, and humans. In the USA, nationwide fish consumption guidelines have been developed. For example, Missouri guidelines suggest not consuming a fillet of fish that is more than 0.3 μg g⁻¹ wet weight of the whole fish because of MeHg accumulation. Recreational fishermen in the Ozarks catch hogsuckers and smallmouth bass. The fatty tissues of both these fish typically exceed the amount of MeHg recommended as safe in Missouri.

Figure 9.28 shows the food web for the study you are about to analyse, and an explanation of the organisms that are involved in the biomagnification process.

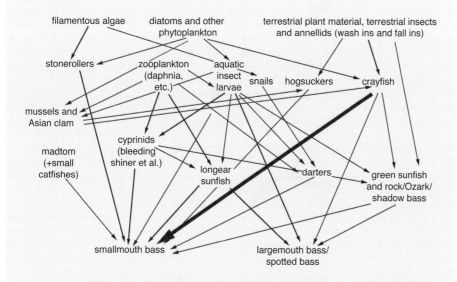

Figure 9.28 Simplified food web. Adapted from www.combat-fishing.com/ reproduced with permission

The organisms involved in this process are described below.

The Asian clam *Coribicula* is a filter-feeding mollusc that ingests fine particulate organic matter from leaf litter and algae.

Crayfish, *Cambarus*, are crustaceans that are omnivorous primary consumers; they eat leaf litter, and aquatic invertebrates such as clams and fish.

Hogsuckers, *Hypentelium nigricans*, are bottom-feeding fish that eat aquatic invertebrates such as crayfish, and organic matter from the stream bottom.

Smallmouth bass, *Micropterus dolomieu*, are fish that feed primarily on crayfish, along with other aquatic invertebrates and small fish.

Look at the map of sites (Figure 9.29) sampled by scientists from the University of Nebraska at Lincoln. Figure 9.29 and Table 9.9 tell you where the samples were taken and the name of the sites. You will need this information when you analyse the data from the following graphs.

TOK Can you use inductive reasoning to formulate a hypothesis about the effectiveness of biological control?

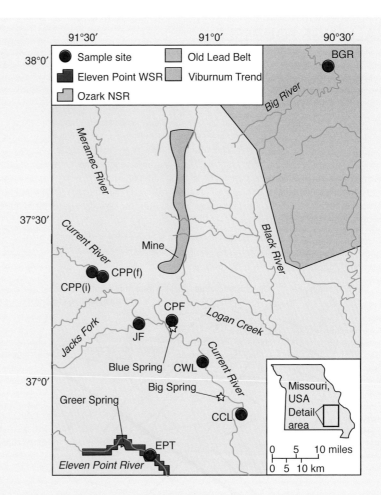

Figure 9.29 Map showing collection sites, lead-zinc mining area (Viburnum Trend and Old Lead Belt), and boundaries of the Eleven Point Wild and Scenic River and boundaries of the Ozark National Scenic Riverways. Schmitt et al. 2011, Fig.1.

Table 9.9 The collection sites for the fish

Collection sites for fish (f) and invertebrate (i; crayfish and *Corbicula*)

Site	River	Location	Latitude, longitude
$EPT_{i,f}$	Eleven Point	Turners Mill	36°45′56.7″N, 91°16′01.0″W
CPP_i	Current	Pulltite Landing	37°20′04.1″N, 91°28′33.8″W
CPP_f	Current	Presley Center	37°19′12.6″N, 91°26′14.6″W
$JF_{i,f}$	Jacks Fork	Shawnee Creek	37°10′21.3″N, 91°18′00.6″W
$CPF_{i,f}$	Current	Powdermill Ferry	37°10′48.0″N, 91°10′25.0″W
$CWL_{i,f}$	Current	Waymeyer Landing	37°03′15.1″N, 91°03′16.8″W
$CCL_{i,f}$	Current	Cataract Landing	36°53′22.2″N, 90°54′473″W
$BGR_{i,f}$	Big	St Francois State Park	37°57′23.7″N, 90°32′29.2″W

Schmitt et al. 2011, Tab. 1.

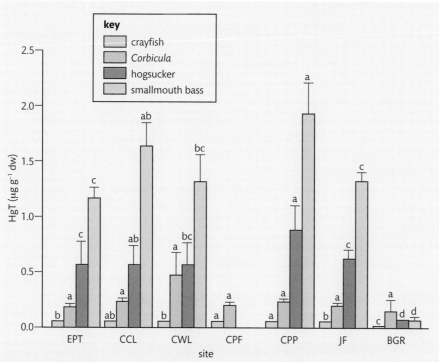

Figure 9.30 Total mercury (HgT) arithmetic site means (± standard errors) in *Corbicula*, crayfish, hogsuckers, and smallmouth bass. Within taxa, means sharing the same letter are not significantly different (ANOVA, $p < 0.05$). See Figure 9.29 and Table 9.9 for site names and locations. Schmitt et al. 2011, Fig. 2

Look at the graph Figure 9.30 of mercury build-up at these sites.

22 Distinguish between the concentration of HgT in crayfish and smallmouth bass at all the sites where both were collected.

23 Compare and contrast HgT at the two sites CPP and BGR.

24 Across all the sites, which organism had the highest concentration of HgT? Suggest a reason for this.

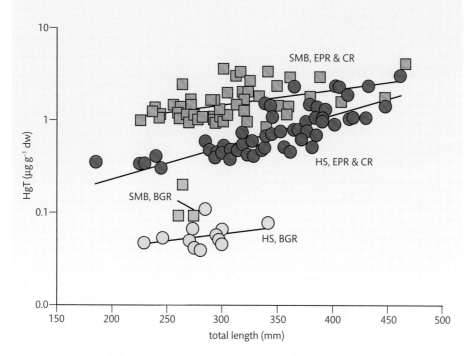

Figure 9.31 Total mercury (HgT; *y*) versus total length (*x*) in hogsuckers (HS) and smallmouth bass (SMB) from the Current River (CR), Eleven Point River (EPR), and Big River (BGR). Adapted from Schmitt et al. 2011, Fig. 3

25 Using Figure 9.31, was it length or site that contributed to HgT accumulation?

26 If you were an Ozark fisherman, at which site would you choose to fish? Explain your answer.

To learn more about the DDT controversy, go to the hotlinks site, search for the title or ISBN, and click on Chapter 9: Section C.3

Section summary

- Biological control uses a natural predator to control an unwanted or invasive species. There are both risks and benefits to biological control. The cane toad in Australia is an example of biological control 'gone wrong'.
- When introduced species have no predator their population can explode, outcompeting native species.
- Chemicals in the environment can become concentrated as they move up the food chain. This is called biological magnification. DDT is a pesticide that can be biologically magnified. High levels of DDT move up the food chain and eventually into human tissues.
- The trade-off for banning DDT is that mosquitoes, which carry disease, negatively affect some communities and can be killed by DDT. Do the risks outweigh the benefits?
- Macroplastics and microplastics are environmental hazards in the marine communities of the world. Microplastics are particles smaller than 5 mm and include things as common as facial scrub particles. Macroplastics are plastic bags, bottles, etc.
- Invasive species are a serious threat to both the environment and industry. Black striped mussel and fire ants are examples of invasive species.

Exercises

7 Explain how competitive exclusion can affect endemic species.

8 Describe the effect of microplastics on the marine ecosystem.

9 Discuss the trade-offs between DDT and control of malarial parasites.

NATURE OF SCIENCE

Scientists collaborate with other agencies: the preservation of species involves international cooperation through intergovernmental and non-governmental organizations.

C.4 Conservation of biodiversity

Understandings:

- An indicator species is an organism used to assess a specific environmental condition.
- Relative numbers of indicator species can be used to calculate the value of a biotic index.
- *In situ* conservation may require active management of nature reserves or national parks.
- *Ex situ* conservation is the preservation of species outside their natural habitats.
- Biogeographic factors affect species diversity.
- Richness and evenness are components of biodiversity.

Applications and skills:

- Application: Case study of the captive breeding and reintroduction of an endangered animal species.
- Application: Analysis of the impact of biogeographic factors on diversity limited to island size and edge effects.
- Skill: Analysis of the biodiversity of two local communities using Simpson's reciprocal index of diversity.

Guidance

- *The formula for Simpson's reciprocal index of diversity is:*

$$D = \frac{N(N-1)}{\Sigma\, n(n-1)}$$

D = *diversity index*, N = *total number of organisms of all species found, and* n = *number of individuals of a particular species.*

Indicator species and biotic indices

Do you remember reading stories of coal miners taking canaries into the mines? If the canary died, it indicated the presence of poisonous gas. In an ecosystem, some species are like those canaries. They are very sensitive to environmental change. They are called indicator species.

Some indicator species

A common indicator species is lichen. Lichens live on rocks and trees and are a reliable indicator of air quality. They are very sensitive to pollution in the atmosphere. Lichens are not usually found on trees in a city because the air is too polluted for them. Because lichens also retain metal in their tissues, they can show the presence of lead or mercury in the air.

Another group of indicator species are macroinvertebrates found in rivers and streams (see Figure 9.32). The presence or absence of these organisms can be used to judge the water quality.

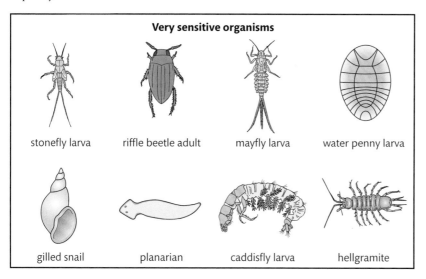

Very sensitive organisms

stonefly larva   riffle beetle adult   mayfly larva   water penny larva

gilled snail   planarian   caddisfly larva   hellgramite

Figure 9.32 Some macroinvertebrates that are indicator species.

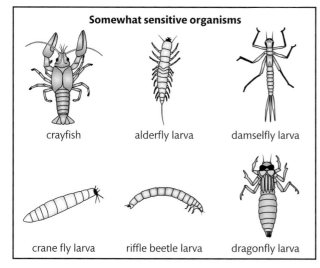

Somewhat sensitive organisms

crayfish   alderfly larva   damselfly larva

crane fly larva   riffle beetle larva   dragonfly larva

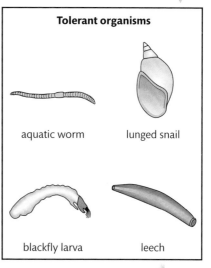

Tolerant organisms

aquatic worm   lunged snail

blackfly larva   leech

We are all interested in the quality of our rivers and streams. In the recent past, rivers and streams were often used as dumping grounds for toxic chemicals and unwanted materials. In Chicago, USA, around 1900, the river was a dumping ground for the waste products from the slaughter houses. All of the unwanted parts of the animals were thrown into the Chicago River. In fact, one branch of the river was named 'bubbly creek' because of all the fermentation that was taking place as the animal tissue decomposed in the water. Today, that river is a much cleaner place, with boats and canoes floating on it rather than waste. This change has come about because of our increased awareness that water and waterways are precious commodities to be treasured.

Freshwater indicator species have various levels of pollution tolerance. Organisms like leeches and aquatic worms are not very sensitive and can live in water with low oxygen levels and high amounts of organic matter. Organisms like the larvae of alderfly and damselfly are moderately sensitive, whereas the larvae of the mayfly and caddisfly are very sensitive to pollution. The very sensitive organisms must have high levels of oxygen and little organic matter in the water in order to survive. The cleaner the water, the higher the number of sensitive organisms present.

Figure 9.33 Stream study sampling form.

Stream study: Sample record and assessment

Stream _____ Site number _____

County or city _____ State _____

Collection date _____ Collectors _____

Weather conditions (last 3 days) _____

Average depth at site _____ Average width at site _____

Water temperature _____ °C _____ °F

Flow rate: ☐ High ☐ Normal ☐ Low

Appearance: ☐ Clear ☐ Cloudy ☐ Muddy

Macroinvertebrate count

Sensitive	Somewhat sensitive	Tolerant
☐ __ caddisfly larvae	☐ __ beetle larvae	☐ __ aquatic worms
☐ __ hellgramite	☐ __ clams	☐ __ blackfly larvae
☐ __ mayfly larvae	☐ __ crane fly larvae	☐ __ leeches
☐ __ gilled snails	☐ __ crayfish	☐ __ midge larvae
☐ __ riffle beetle adult	☐ __ damselfly larvae	☐ __ lunged snails
☐ __ stonefly larvae	☐ __ dragonfly larvae	
☐ __ water penny larvae	☐ __ scuds	
	☐ __ sowbugs	
	☐ __ fishfly larvae	
	☐ __ alderfly larvae	
	☐ __ watersnipe larvae	
boxes checked × 3 = _____ index value	boxes checked × 2 = _____ index value	boxes checked × 1 = _____ index value

Water quality rating
Total index count _____

☐ Excellent (>22) ☐ Fair (11–16)
☐ Good (17–22) ☐ Poor (<11)

Biotic index

When you perform a river or stream study, you count the number of macroinvertebrates collected in each sample and record the data on a stream study form (see Figure 9.33). The number of organisms in each group is multiplied by a factor that is determined by how sensitive the organism is to pollution. The presence of sensitive organisms is multiplied by a higher number. The more sensitive organisms you have in the sample, the higher the quality of the water in the river or stream. The total number is called the biotic index.

Periodic sampling gives an idea of the overall health of the river or stream. After a storm, there will be a lot of run-off from the areas surrounding the river. How does the run-off affect the biotic index? Is any sewage diverted into a river after a big storm? Is the biotic index different in winter and spring? Sampling provides us with biological data that can be used to answer these questions.

Richness and evenness are components of biodiversity

Biological diversity can be described in two ways: evenness and richness. The number of different organisms in a particular area is the richness. Evenness is how the quantity of each organism compares with the other. Richness only takes into account the kinds of species present in the ecosystem, while evenness take abundance into account.

For example, Table 9.10 compares the numbers of different larvae in samples from two interdunal ponds at the Indiana dunes.

Table 9.10 Dune samples

Larva species	Number of individuals in sample 1	Number of individuals in sample 2
Caddisfly larva	200	20
Dragonfly larva	425	55
Mosquito larva	375	925
Total	1000	1000

Both samples have the same number of individuals, but in sample 2 the numbers are not distributed evenly between the species. Both samples have the same species richness: each has three types of larvae. But they do not have the same evenness.

The individuals in sample 2 are mainly mosquito larvae. A community is not considered diverse if it is dominated by one species.

Analysis of the biodiversity of two local communities

A measure that takes into account both richness and evenness is Simpson's diversity index. To see how this works, let's consider the community of plants on the foredune at the Indiana dunes and the community of plants on the mature dune. Which would you hypothesize is more diverse and why? To calculate Simpson's diversity index, we need the formula

$$D = \frac{N(N-1)}{\text{sum of } n(n-1)}$$

where
D = diversity index
N = total number of organisms in the ecosystem
n = number of individuals of each species

So, for each community we need to know the number of organisms present and the number of individuals of each species present. This information is found by sampling the two dunes with quadrats as follows:

• record the number of plant species in each quadrat
• count the number of individuals of each species
• record the data for each area in tables.

Tables 9.11 and 9.12 record the plant species on the foredune and mature dune of the Indiana dunes.

Table 9.11 Plant species recorded on the foredune of the Indiana dunes

Plant species	Number of individuals, n	$n(n - 1)$
Marram grass	50	50(49) = 2450
Milkweed	10	10(9) = 90
Poison ivy	10	10(9) = 90
Sand cress	4	4(3) = 12
Rose	1	1(0) = 0
Sand cherry	3	3(2) = 6
Totals	$N = 78$	2648

Table 9.12 Plant species recorded on the mature dune of the Indiana dunes

Plant species	Number of individuals, n	$n(n - 1)$
Oak tree	3	3(2) = 6
Hickory tree	1	1(0) = 0
Maple tree	1	1(0) = 0
Beech tree	1	1(0) = 0
Fern	5	5(4) = 20
Moss	3	3(2) = 6
Columbine	3	3(2) = 6
Trillium	3	3(2) = 6
Virginia creeper	4	4(3) = 12
Solomon seal	3	3(2) = 6
Totals	$N = 27$	62

Using the formula given above, the calculation for the foredune is:

$$D = \frac{78(77)}{2648}$$

D = 2.27

The calculation for the mature dune is:

$$D = \frac{27(26)}{62}$$

D = 11.3

Was your hypothesis correct? According to the Simpson's diversity index, the mature dune is more diverse even though the total number of plants is less. The mature dune has a higher diversity index because it has a higher number of different species. Periodic sampling of an area and calculation of its Simpson's index provides an assessment of the health of an ecosystem.

Worked example

Choose from the following for each question: richness and or evenness.

1 One daisy has as much influence as 1000 buttercups.

2

| | Numbers of individuals | |
Flower species	Sample 1	Sample 2
Daisy	300	20
Dandelion	335	49
Buttercup	365	931
Total	1000	1000

3 Used in Simpson's diversity index.

Solutions

1 Richness.
2 Evenness.
3 Richness and evenness.

Investigation into the effect of an environmental disturbance in an ecosystem

Ecological disturbances remove biomass from an ecosystem. The general effect of an ecological disturbance is to shift the community to an earlier stage in succession, which may be more diverse. The aim of this lab it to compare the species diversity in a disturbed area with the species diversity in an area that has not experienced a disturbance, by taking a series of quadrat samples along a transect line in each area.

For this lab, you will take a trip to an ecosystem that has experienced some disturbance. You will use a combination of transect and quadrat sampling techniques to determine plant species diversity along a disturbance gradient. You will also use the same techniques to determine the plant species diversity along a similar gradient that has not been disturbed. Finally, you will calculate Simpson's index for each quadrat in the plant communities along the transect lines and compare the diversity along each transect.

At the site:

- determine the disturbance you will analyse (for example a path made in the dunes, trampling of an area by visitors, a fire, a blow-out, or a windy side of a dune)
- decide when it occurred (how long ago) and whether it is a repeated, intermediate, occurrence, or a one-time disturbance.

Based on the information you have learned about the effect of disturbances on an ecosystem, you can then make a hypothesis about the effect of the disturbance on this part of the ecosystem. Has the diversity of species increased, decreased, or remained the same as a result of the disturbance? Explain why you have made this hypothesis.

The materials you will need are:

- metre-square quadrats
- rolls of thick twine for the transects, or landscape paint
- soil hooks to hold the transect (twine) in place
- a data table to record the plants species present
- graph paper
- a digital camera
- metre sticks
- field guides.

The real cost of damaging nature, it turns out, is at least 10 times greater than the cost of maintaining an ecosystem. Using Simpson's index of biodiversity helps ecologists keep track of the changes in diversity that can indicate problems in an ecosystem.

TOK How do we justify our knowledge? Is an indicator organism sufficient evidence?

Follow these procedures.

- Work in teams.
- Lay out one transect along the gradient of the ecosystem to be examined where a disturbance has occurred (for example along a trampled area).
- Lay out another transect in parallel where no disturbance has occurred.
- Choose the sampling points along the transect.
- Record the distance along the transect at which you located each quadrat (make a map on graph paper).
- Each team should sample at least two transects, with a minimum of 10 quadrats per transect.
- At each quadrat:
  - identify each species within the quadrat
  - if you cannot identify every species, take a picture of it and give it a name of your own, count it, and, if you see it again, it can be counted again (later it may be identified, but the correct name is not necessary to calculate the diversity index)
  - count the number of each species present and record it
  - photograph each quadrat (make sure to label the photograph with the quadrat number and transect name, disturbed or not disturbed)
  - record qualitative observations at each quadrat site, such as the amount of shade and soil type
  - record as much qualitative data as you can about the disturbance.
- Each team can choose its own disturbance, or several teams can do the same disturbance. Working in teams on the same disturbance will allow more data points to be pooled and give a better estimate of the actual diversity.
- Calculate Simpson's diversity index for each quadrat by using the formula below and following the example shown based on the data in Table 9.13.

Table 9.13

Species	Number	$N(n-1)$
Lyme grass, *Leymus arenarius*	2	2
Sand couch grass, *Elytrigia*	8	56
Marram grass, *Ammophila arenaria*	1	0
Sea sandswort, *Honckenya*	1	0
European searocket, *Cakile maritime*	3	6
Total (*N*)	15	64

$$D = \frac{\text{sum of } n(n-1)}{N(N-1)}$$

$$D = \frac{64}{15(14)}$$

$$D = \frac{64}{210}$$

Where D = diversity index, N = total number of organisms in an ecosystem, and n = number of individuals in each species.

$D = 0.3$, which is Simpson's index

$1 - D = 0.7$, which is Simpson's index of diversity.

1 Construct a graph showing how Simpson's index of diversity is related to a factor in the ecosystem, such as the distance from the shore to the first dune for both the disturbed and undisturbed areas in the ecosystem.

2 Draw a conclusion a based on the data you (and your classmates) have collected. Restate the data supporting your conclusion. Discuss any uncertainties.

3 Describe how the design of the experiment or data collection method could be improved. Many websites discuss the pros and cons of various sampling methods. What improvements would you make?

As an alternative lab, you could perform a similar investigation of an aquatic environment, such as a river or stream where some disturbance has occurred. Sample benthic organisms along a disturbed and an undisturbed area. Calculate the species diversity using Simpson's index.

Another alternative would be to perform the entire investigation as a class so that repeat samples can be made at each point in the transect or each area of the river or stream. Or either investigation could be performed over time, returning to the site periodically to collect data.

Management of conservation areas

In order to maintain the beauty and diversity of a nature reserve, it is important to manage it effectively. Nature reserves cannot just be left to nature. Active intervention is required to restore areas and protect native species. Examples of good management practices are discussed below.

Restoration

Restoration attempts to return the land to its natural state. To restore land on which vegetation has been destroyed may require managers to use active management techniques such as scrub clearance, cutting or burning, and replanting. A UK project is restoring the heathlands within an area designated as a nature reserve in 2007: the Dorset Heathland Project set up in 1989 and completed in 2006, and regular monitoring is ongoing.

Recovery of threatened species

Threatened species are usually helped when we restore their habitat. Active management maintains the areas needed for the habitat of the endangered species. In a Florida nature reserve, the habitat of the endangered gopher tortoise is being restored. This tortoise lives in deep burrows in a sandhill ecosystem. As many as 350 other animal species live in the burrow with the gopher tortoise. Restoration of the sandhill ecosystem is necessary for the existence of all these species, not just the gopher tortoise. Some insects are obligates with the gopher tortoise, which means they are rarely found anywhere except in the burrow that the tortoise digs.

Removal of introduced species

Most of the exotic species (species that are not native to an area when it is introduced) that are introduced into an area die out because they do not have adaptations for the local ecosystem. However, when an exotic species can survive and takes over, it can have devastating results. In parts of the UK, plants called rhododendrons have taken over large areas and almost eliminated the native plants in those areas. Active management is needed to remove rhododendrons from nature reserves in the UK. In the southern USA, the kudzu plant is a very aggressive invader. Active management of kudzu requires removing it as soon as it is spotted.

The gopher tortoise is a keystone species. Many other species depend on it for survival.

▼

Legal protection against development or pollution

Nature reserves protected by the government or private organizations can prohibit activities that might harm the native animals and plants. Such activities might be extraction of minerals, development of recreational facilities, hunting of animals, or over-use by the public. Active management measures include posting warning signs and using security personnel to ensure the nature reserve is protected from harmful human activities.

Funding and prioritizing

Because all activities require funding, which should take priority? Should funds be used to remove all exotic species, or can we assume most exotics will die out? Should we repair the habitat of a few endangered species, or use the limited funds to maintain the habitat for the majority of organisms? Should we build footpaths for the public even though that will bring destruction to some of the habitat? Increasing public awareness of reserves can help provide the funds needed to support the reserves. Management of nature reserves requires a balance between the health of the ecosystem, maintenance of diversity, and the costs involved.

In situ conservation methods

Nature reserves help endangered species by maintaining their habitat and preventing competition from invasive species. Keeping these organisms *in situ* means putting them in the ecosystem where they belong. Organisms have adapted over hundreds of years to a certain set of conditions. These conditions include the other species present in the ecosystem as well as abiotic factors. It is the goal of *in situ* conservation to allow the target species to continue to adapt to conditions in the reserve without interference from outside influences, such as invasive species and human incursions.

Reserves can be terrestrial (land-based) and aquatic (water-based). Terrestrial reserves can be found in most communities. Lake and pond areas are also common. Marine reserves are rare and are lagging behind in their development. Terrestrial reserves have been around for centuries, but there is no tradition of conservation of species using marine reserves. The ocean is a large ecosystem that needs protection. The same *in situ* strategies as used in terrestrial reserves can be put into practice in a marine reserve.

In situ conservation aims to achieve the following:

• protect the target species by maintaining the habitat
• defend the target species from predators
• remove invasive species
• have a large enough area in the reserve to maintain a large population
• have a large enough population of the target species to maintain genetic diversity.

On occasion, the *in situ* area is unable to protect the targeted species. For example:

• the species is so endangered that it needs more protection
• the population is not large enough to maintain genetic diversity
• destructive forces cannot be controlled, such as invasive species, human incursion, and natural disasters.

Ex situ conservation methods

Ex situ methods are usually used as a last resort. If a species cannot be kept in its natural habitat safely, or the population is so small that the species is in danger of extinction, then *ex situ* methods of conservation are used. There are three methods: captive breeding of animals, cultivation of plants in botanic gardens, and storage of seeds in seed banks.

Captive breeding

Some zoos have large facilities devoted to breeding. They have staff trained in animal husbandry. Breeding programmes capture the interest of the public and can generate new funds for the zoo. The San Diego Zoo in California, USA, has devoted a large part of its resources to captive breeding programmes. The goal of captive breeding is to try to increase the reproductive output of a species and ensure survival of the offspring. Here are some of the techniques used.

- Artificial insemination. If the animals are reluctant to mate, semen is taken from the male and placed into the body of the female.
- Embryo transfer to a surrogate mother. To increase the number of offspring, 'test-tube' babies are produced and implanted in surrogate mothers. Sperm and eggs are harvested from each parent, respectively, and then joined together in a Petri dish. The resulting zygote is implanted in the female uterus. The mothers can be a closely related species.
- Cryogenics. Eggs, sperm cells, and embryos can be frozen for future use.
- Human-raised young. If a mother is not interested or able to care for her young, then staff can hand-raise the young in the nursery of the zoo.
- Keeping a pedigree. If artificial insemination is a common occurrence in the management of a species, it is important that the relatedness of the individuals is known, to keep inbreeding to a minimum.

One problem with captive-breeding programmes is that the introduction into the wild of captive-bred individuals can spread disease to a non-infected wild population. When some captive-bred desert tortoises were introduced to their native habitat, they infected the wild population with a respiratory disease. Another problem is that animals bred in captivity have not experienced the process of *in situ* learning that their wild relatives undergo. This may put them at a severe disadvantage in the wild.

Captive breeding and the reintroduction of an endangered animal species

Captive breeding has helped save the Mexican gray wolf from extinction. At the beginning of the breeding programme only five wolves, of which only one was a female, could be found in the wild. This lone female gave birth to one male and three females. One male and three females were captured and protected at a site for captive breeding. Today's wild Mexican gray wolves can all be traced back to those first wolves used for the captive breeding programme that began in 1981.

NATURE OF SCIENCE

The World Association of Zoos and Aquariums (WAZA) is the lead organization for the world zoo and aquarium community. Its mission is to provide leadership and support for zoos and aquariums. It is dedicated to the preservation of species and involves international cooperation in order to promote conservation of biodiversity around the world.

Mexican gray wolf.

485

Zoos play an important role in species preservation internationally. A zoo in South Carolina is supporting the preservation of species from all over the world.

To learn more about the Mexican gray wolf recovery programme, go to the hotlinks site, search for the title or ISBN, and click on Chapter 9: Section C.4.

In 2006 the Norwegian government established a global seed bank. The Millennium Seed Bank Project at the Royal Botanical Gardens in the UK aims to safeguard 24 000 plant species from around the globe.

In the western USA, during the early 1900s, the most important prey for wolves were bison and moose. However, these prey species were severely depleted by the actions of human settlers. As a consequence, the wolves began preying on sheep and other livestock. Pressure was put on the government to kill the wolves, and bounty programmes were established. Up until 1965, $50 was offered per wolf. As a result, the wolf population was devastated. After the US Congress passed the Endangered Species Preservation Act in 1966, the gray wolf made it on to the endangered species list. Studies in 2004 showed that when wolves were eliminated the elk population exploded, leading to overgrazing of plants, especially along rivers. A significant decline in plant species such as willow and aspen then led to a reduction in beaver and songbird populations. Evidence was collected showing that removal of wolves led to instability in some environmentally sensitive areas.

In 1997, because of the availability of wolves bred in captivity, the USA reintroduced the gray wolf into areas of Arizona and New Mexico. In 2010 there were 59 wolves living in these areas. Radio-tracking methods are used to monitor the population size and health of these important animals. Hopefully, their populations will continue to increase. This is a case where scientists have collaborated with government agencies and wildlife organizations to preserve a species and also to preserve biodiversity in an important ecosystem.

Botanical gardens

Plants are easily kept in captivity. They have simple needs and usually breeding them is not difficult. About 80 000 plant species are grown in private gardens, arboretums, and botanical gardens all over the world. It is much easier to take care of and breed plants outside their natural setting than it is to take care of and breed animals. One problem with the collections of botanical gardens, however, is that the wild relatives of commercial crops are under-represented. These plants may have genes that confer resistance to diseases and pests. Adding these wild plant relatives to collections at botanical gardens would provide gene banks for commercial crops.

Seed banks

Seeds in a seed bank are kept in cold, dark conditions. Under these conditions, the metabolism of the seed slows down and prevents it from germinating. Seed can be kept this way for decades. Some seeds are grown, allowed to mature, and their new seed collected. Currently, seeds from 10 000 to 20 000 plant species from all over the world are stored in seed banks.

Biogeographical factors affect species diversity

Species diversity is defined as the number of species and their relative abundance. Three factors influence species diversity: latitude gradient, elevation gradient, and the area effect.

- Latitude gradient is the effect of climate on species diversity. The farther you travel away from the equator, the fewer species you will find. For example, the growing season at the equator is five times longer than in a tundra community. Many more plants have an opportunity to grow in a much longer growing season. The short season of the tundra allows only a few plants to grow.

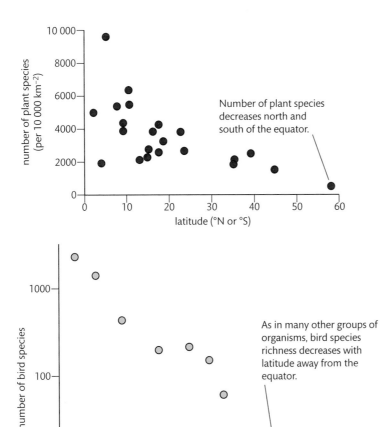

Figure 9.34A Graph of the number of plant species versus latitude.
Molles, Jr. 2010, p. 502, Fig. 22.15

Figure 9.34B Graph of the number of bird species versus latitude.
Molles, Jr. 2010, p. 502, Fig. 22.16

- Elevation gradient is the effect of altitude on species richness. As you travel up to higher altitudes, species richness increases until you reach a certain point, and then it declines again. That point is about half way up the elevation gradient and is called the mid-point bulge. At the mid-point bulge the diversity of species is at its greatest. After the mid-point bulge the species diversity declines.

- The area effect is the effect of area on species richness. The larger the geographic area, the more species it can support. Larger areas can offer a greater diversity of habitats than a smaller area. The area affect concept began with a study of islands: the larger the island, the more diverse the species on the island. The concept of 'islands' has been extended to mean any area that is so isolated it can be considered as an island. For example, a lake can be an island because it is an aquatic environment isolated from other aquatic environments by the surrounding land. A mountain peak, or a woodland fragment isolated from other woodlands by a housing development, can also be considered as islands.

CHALLENGE YOURSELF

In an experiment in 1962, Frank Preston examined the relationship between the areas of islands in the West Indies and number of species. Look at Figure 9.35.

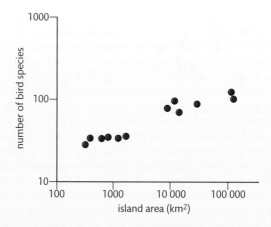

Figure 9.35 Island area versus number of bird species. Molles, Jr. 2010, p. 493, Fig. 22.2(a)

27 Interpret the results of the Preston experiment from the data shown in Figure 9.35.

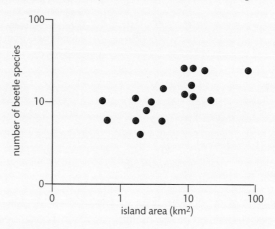

Figure 9.36 The relationship between island area and number of species. Molles, Jr. 2010, p. 493, Fig. 22.2(b)

28 Look at Figure 9.36, which shows the patterns of species richness in 17 lake islands in Sweden. Interpret the results of this experiment from the data shown on the graph.

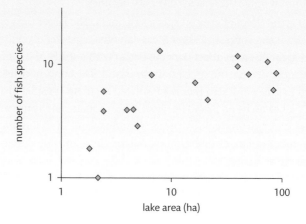

Figure 9.37 Lake area and the number of fish species in the lakes of northern Wisconsin. http://sky.scnu.edu.cn/life/class/ecology/chapter/Chapter22.htm

29 Look at Figure 9.37. Lakes can be considered as habitat 'islands'. Three scientists studied 18 lakes in Wisconsin. Interpret the results of their experiment from the data shown on the graph.

The impact of edge effect on diversity

Edge effect describes what occurs at habitat boundaries where two bordering communities influence each other. Factors that affect the edge can be:

• abiotic, such as more or less sunlight or moisture at the edge of a forest
• biotic, such as the presence of certain predators at the edge.

Does the edge effect promote species diversity in an ecosystem? Some species thrive only at the edges of a habitat because they depend on unique resources that are not present in the interior environment of the habitat. Other species thrive only in the interior environment. High habitat diversity, which includes both the interior and the edge of a habitat, promotes species richness in an ecosystem.

Edge effect plays an important role in the habitat suitability of the western meadowlark and other grassland birds. A study of how the edge effect affects the presence of the western meadowlark provided evidence that species diversity could be increased in the ecosystem if woody plant encroachment was curtailed so that populations of grassland bird species that live at the edge of the woodland could be maintained. A consistent decline in grassland bird populations because of woody plant encroachment decreases species diversity.

Worked example

Choose edge effect or island size to identify what each statement is describing.

1 Species number roughly doubles for every 10-fold increase in area.
2 Forest fires occur at the border of the forest where plants are dried out by the sun.
3 Species invade clear areas that they would not have previously been able to grow in, before the conditions changed.
4 Larger areas support more species than smaller areas.
5 Larger areas cause less large disturbances for a community than smaller areas.

Solutions

1 Island size.
2 Edge effect.
3 Edge effect.
4 Island size.
5 Island size.

CHALLENGE YOURSELF

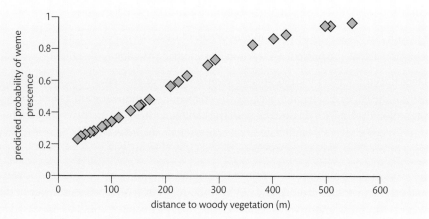

Figure 9.38 Scatterplot of the predicted probabilities from a logistic regression model of western meadowlark (weme) presence in relation to the distance to woody vegetation. http://nature.berkeley. edu/classes/es196/ projects/2013final/LeeL_2013. pdf

30 What is the effect of woody vegetation on the presence of the western meadowlark?

31 Give a hypothesis regarding the cause for this effect.

32 What other 'edge' factor that might affect grassland birds could be studied?

The western meadowlark.

Section summary

- Indicator species are very sensitive to environmental change. Lichen in forests and macroinvertebrates in rivers and streams are indicator species. The biotic index measures the presence of indicator species in rivers and streams.

- Richness and evenness are measures of biodiversity. Richness is how many different organisms are in a particular area, while evenness compares only the quantity of organisms from one area to another.

- Simpson's diversity index measures biodiversity.
- Nature reserves must be cared for and managed by restoration programmes, recovery of threatened species, removal of introduced species, protection against development, and raising funds.
- *In situ* conservation allows target species to live in the ecosystem where they belong. *Ex situ* conservation takes the organism out of its native habitat.
- Captive breeding programmes can restore a population of animals back into the community from which they disappeared.
- Species diversity is affected by biogeographic factors. For example, the further you travel away from the equator, the less species you will find.
- The edge effect also affects species diversity. A high diversity of habitat, in both the centre and the edge of an area, promotes species richness.

Exercises

10 Describe a case study of the captive breeding and reintroduction of an endangered animal species.

11 Explain how the edge effect affects species diversity.

12 Describe three factors that influence species diversity.

Practice questions

1 The brown-headed cowbird, *Molothrus ater*, is a parasitic bird that lays its eggs in the nests of other species. The parasitized hosts often raise the resulting cowbird offspring as their own. The true offspring may starve while the larger cowbird offspring consume most of the food brought by the parents.

The preferred habitat of the brown-headed cowbird is open agricultural areas.

The results of a study into the effects of deforestation on cowbird parasitism of four different host species are shown below.

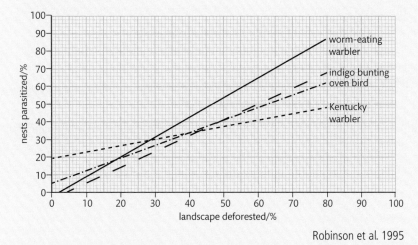

Robinson et al. 1995

(a) State the effect of deforestation on cowbird parasitism. (1)

(b) Compare the effect of deforestation on cowbird parasitism of the worm-eating warbler and the Kentucky warbler. (2)

(c) Determine the percentage of worm-eating warbler nests parasitized by cowbirds at a level of 60% deforestation. (1)

(d) Suggest reasons for the relationship between deforestation and cowbird parasitism. (2)

(Total 6 marks)

2 (a) Outline the use of Simpson's diversity index. (3)

(b) Explain the use of biotic indices and indicator species. (6)

(Total 9 marks)

3 Describe how distribution of species can be affected by limiting factors.

(Total 10 marks)

4 The energy flow diagram below for a temperate ecosystem has been divided into two parts. One part shows autotrophic use of energy and the other shows the heterotrophic use of energy. All values are kJ m^{-2} yr^{-1}.

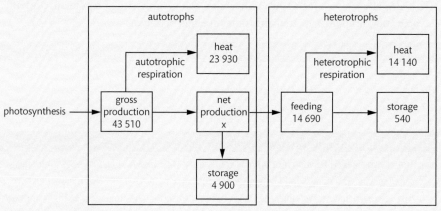

(a) Calculate the net production of the autotrophs. (1)

(b) (i) Compare the percentage of heat lost through respiration by the autotrophs with the heterotrophs. (1)

(ii) Most of the heterotrophs are animals. Suggest one reason for the difference in heat losses between the autotrophs and animal heterotrophs. (1)

The heterotrophic community can be divided into food webs based upon decomposers and food webs based upon herbivores. It has been shown that of the energy consumed by the heterotrophs, 99% is consumed by the decomposer food webs.

(c) State the importance of decomposers in an ecosystem. (1)

(d) Deduce the long-term effects of sustained pollution that kills decomposers on autotrophic productivity (2)

(Total 6 marks)

5 Seawater temperature has an effect on the spawning (release of eggs) of echinoderms living in Antarctic waters. Echinoderm larvae feed on phytoplankton. In this investigation, the spawning of echinoderms and its effect on phytoplankton was studied.

In the figure below, the top line indicates the number of larvae caught (per 5000 l of seawater). The shaded bars below show when spawning occurred in echinoderms.

☐ = 0% to 25%

▨ = 25% to 75%

■ = 75% to 100%

The concentration of chlorophyll gives an indication of the concentration of phytoplankton.

Note: the seasons in the Antarctic are reversed from those in the northern hemisphere.

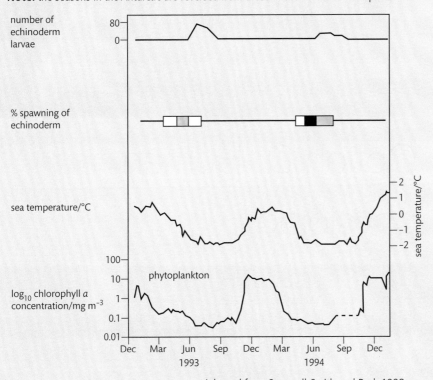

Adapted from Stanwell-Smith and Peck 1998

(a) State the trophic level of echinoderm larvae. (1)

(b) Identify the period during which the spawning of echinoderm lies between 25% and 75%. (1)

(c) Explain the relationship between the seasons and the concentration of phytoplankton. (2)

(d) (i) Outline the effect of seawater temperature on echinoderm larvae numbers. (2)

 (ii) Using the data in the figure, predict the effect of global warming on echinoderm larvae numbers. (2)

(Total 8 marks)

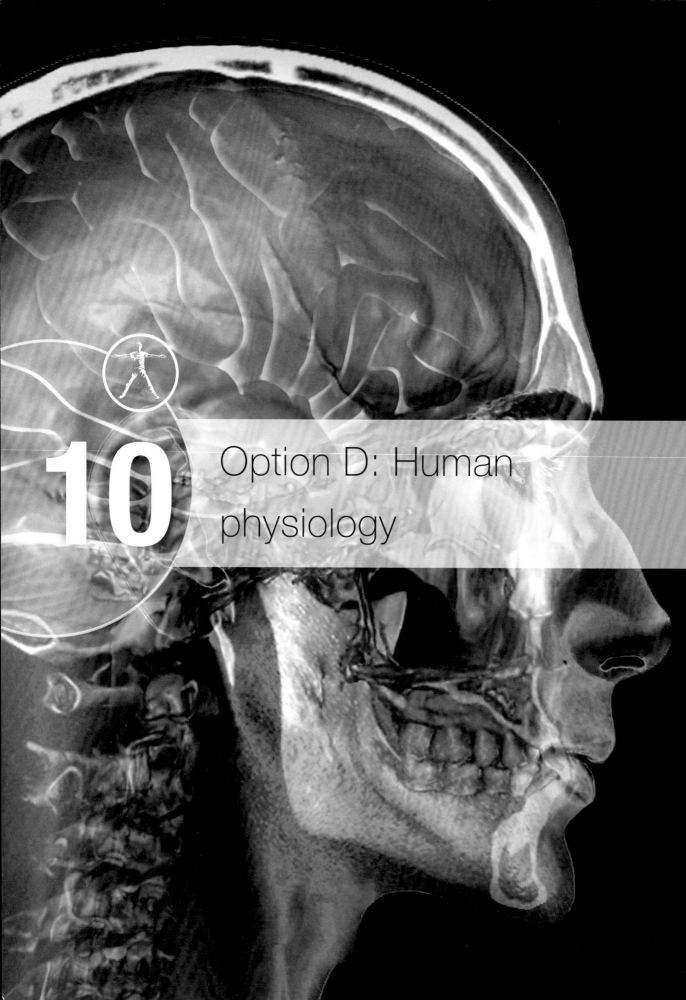

10

Option D: Human physiology

Essential ideas

D.1 A balanced diet is essential to human health.

D.2 Digestion is controlled by nervous and hormonal mechanisms.

D.3 The chemical composition of the blood is regulated by the liver.

D.4 Internal and external factors influence heart function.

There is no end to what one can learn about human anatomy and physiology. In this chapter you will learn more in-depth detail about several of the systems of the body. Whether you want to pursue a career in medicine or just want to know more about the inner workings of human beings, this material can be fascinating.

Coloured composite image of a magnetic resonance imaging (MRI) scan of the brain, and a three-dimensional (3-D) computed tomography (CT) scan of the head and neck, of a 35-year-old man.

D.1 Human nutrition

Understandings:
- Essential nutrients cannot be synthesized by the body, therefore they have to be included in the diet.
- Dietary minerals are essential chemical elements.
- Vitamins are chemically diverse carbon compounds that cannot be synthesized by the body.
- Some fatty acids and some amino acids are essential.
- Lack of essential amino acids affects the production of proteins.
- Malnutrition may be caused by a deficiency, imbalance, or excess of nutrients in the diet.
- Appetite is controlled by a centre in the hypothalamus.
- Overweight individuals are more likely to suffer hypertension and type II diabetes.
- Starvation can lead to breakdown of body tissue.

Applications and skills:
- Application: Production of ascorbic acid by some mammals, but not others that need a dietary supply.
- Application: Cause and treatment of phenylketonuria (PKU).
- Application: Lack of vitamin D or calcium can affect bone mineralization and cause rickets or osteomalacia.
- Application: Breakdown of heart muscle due to anorexia.
- Application: Cholesterol in blood as an indicator of the risk of coronary heart disease.
- Skill: Determination of the energy content of food by combustion.
- Skill: Use of databases of nutritional content of foods and software to calculate intakes of essential nutrients from a daily diet.

NATURE OF SCIENCE

Falsification of theories with one theory being superseded by another: scurvy was thought to be specific to humans, because attempts to induce the symptoms in laboratory rats and mice were entirely unsuccessful.

Essential nutrients: what are they?

A nutrient is a chemical substance found in foods and used in the human body. Nutrients can be absorbed to give you energy, help strengthen your bones, or even prevent you from getting a disease. You may recall from Section 2.1 that a handful of types of organic molecule make up all living organisms. Although some of these molecules, such as certain amino acids and lipids, can be synthesized by the human body, many cannot. Those that cannot be synthesized from other molecules, and thus must be a part of our diet, are called essential nutrients. They are:

- essential amino acids
- essential fatty acids
- minerals
- most vitamins.

Let's consider some examples of essential nutrients and the ramifications of a deficiency of those nutrients in the diet.

Dietary minerals: essential chemical elements

Minerals are the inorganic substances that living organisms need for a variety of purposes. Our world is full of minerals, but living organisms typically only need a very small intake of these elements to ensure good health. Each type of mineral has one or more specific role in making anatomical structures (e.g. calcium in bones) or a physiological role because it is incorporated into important molecules (e.g. iron within haemoglobin). These structures and molecules are typically 'long-lived' within the body, and thus the need for minerals is only for small amounts, but it is constant. The bones within our bodies require constant repair, requiring small amounts of calcium for that repair. Calcium ions are also used for other purposes within the body, and a small amount is always being lost and must be replaced. Red blood cells (erythrocytes) that contain haemoglobin have a cellular life span of only about 4 months. The components of erythrocytes are recycled within our liver, and much of the iron is recovered in order to produce more erythrocytes in the bone marrow. Some of the iron is inevitably lost, however, as the recycling is not 100% efficient. Females need more iron in their diet than males because the blood lost during menstruation leads to a loss of iron.

Many of the minerals required in our diet are known as electrolytes because they are easily dissolved in a fluid medium (e.g. blood, cytoplasm, and intercellular fluid) as charged ions. These charged ions include calcium (Ca^{2+}) and iron (Fe^{2+}), mentioned above, as well as sodium (Na^+), magnesium (Mg^{2+}), and chloride (Cl^-). Many of these electrolytes are particularly important in the mechanisms behind how we send action potentials along neurones, synaptic transmission between neurones, and muscle contraction. You may have experienced the pain involved in a 'muscle cramp' when an electrolyte imbalance occurs after strenuous exercise. This is just a small part of the story of minerals, as each has its own important role(s) within our physiology.

Vitamins: essential organic compounds

Unlike minerals, vitamins are organic (carbon-based) molecules. They are synthesized by living organisms, but many living organisms rely on an intake of vitamins from other organisms (especially from plants, in the form of fruits and vegetables). Like minerals, the intake of vitamins needs only to be in small quantities, as vitamins are typically used to create relatively long-lived substances within the body.

In many countries the food industries indicate the percentage of daily vitamins and minerals contained within a 'serving' of their products.

496

A perfect example to illustrate the idea of an essential versus a non-essential vitamin is vitamin C (ascorbic acid) in humans. Vitamin C is not an essential vitamin in most animals, including the vast majority of vertebrates. However, it is essential for humans and thus must be a part of our diet. Failure to ingest enough vitamin C over an extended period of time results in a serious deficiency disease known as scurvy. Humans, some other primates, and guinea pigs are the only known animals where vitamin C is an essential vitamin.

Vitamin C is produced from glucose in the kidney tissue in some animals, and in the liver in others. The synthesis of vitamin C from glucose requires four enzymes that are used in a step-by-step set of reactions. The gene coding for the fourth of these enzymes has been shown to be universally defective in all humans, thus making it essential that vitamin C is present in our diet.

Vitamin C should not be thought of as just a vitamin that prevents scurvy. Vitamin C is important in protection against infections, helping in wound healing, and in maintaining healthy gums, teeth, bones, and blood vessels.

NATURE OF SCIENCE

Linus Pauling was an American chemist and biochemist who, in his book, *How to Live Longer and Feel Better* (1986), suggested that large doses of vitamin C would protect people against colds. This was a radical idea because vitamin C is normally regarded simply as a substance only useful in very small quantities. Pauling's ideas were not supported by conclusive results from clinical trials, so he was criticized by other scientists. Are suggestions given by established scientists more likely to receive acceptance than suggestions from lesser known researchers?

To learn more about vitamin C, go to the hotlinks site, search for the title or ISBN, and click on Chapter 10: Section D.1.

Another essential component of the human diet is vitamin D. Vitamin D is an important nutrient for the proper formation of bones. Without a sufficient supply of vitamin D and/ or the mineral calcium, it is possible to develop rickets, a disease that leads to deformities in the bones. Rickets develops in children when the bones near the growth plates (areas at the ends of developing bones) do not mineralize properly. This often leads to irregular, thick, and wide bone growth. The bone plates in adults are already fully formed, so rickets cannot develop. Children with rickets do not reach their optimal height during growth, and their legs are often bowed inwards or outwards at the knees. Even though adults cannot develop rickets, they can develop a similar condition called osteomalacia (pronounced os'te-o-mah-la´shah), which means soft bones. Osteomalacia is also the result of a deficiency in vitamin D or calcium.

A person suffering from rickets with characteristic bowed legs as a result of improper bone plate growth. This develops in childhood and can be caused by vitamin D deficiency or calcium deficiency, or both.

The term precursor in biochemistry refers to a molecule that precedes another in a chemical reaction or metabolic pathway.

It is not possible to come up with a specific length of time that everyone should spend in sunlight to allow the synthesis of sufficient vitamin D. Factors such as latitude and sunlight intensity, seasonal variation, and genetic skin pigmentation have to be taken into consideration. However, typical suggestions range from about 5 to 30 minutes a day.

The epidermis of human skin contains precursors that are able to synthesize vitamin D when stimulated by the ultraviolet rays of the Sun. Exposure to ultraviolet radiation has its own dangers, specifically sunburn and skin cancer, so everyone needs to balance the risks and rewards of obtaining vitamin D from the Sun.

Fatty acids: two are essential

In Chapter 2 you learned that there are a variety of fatty acids that are components in triglycerides and phospholipids. If you recall, fatty acids all have a carboxyl functional group and a long hydrocarbon chain. Within that long hydrocarbon chain all of the carbon to carbon bonds may be single bonds (resulting in a saturated fatty acid), or one or more of the carbon to carbon bonds may be a double bond (resulting in an unsaturated fatty acid). The identity of the fatty acid is determined by its number of carbon atoms and the location(s) of the double bond(s). Two fatty acids are required in our diet because humans lack the enzymes to make these fatty acids from other fatty acids or precursors. These two fatty acids are omega-3 and omega-6. Both of these fatty acids are essential in the human diet and indicate that consuming fats is not necessarily bad for your health. The source and therefore the type of fat consumed is the key to good health.

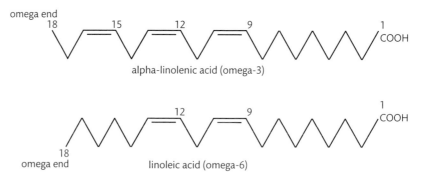

Figure 10.1 The two essential fatty acids shown in abbreviated form. Carbon number 1 is the carbon of the carboxyl group. Each angle change after that represents a carbon atom. Carbon atoms with double bonds are shown, and the first is numbered. Each carbon in the chain would have an appropriate number of hydrogens to make four bonds around each. The carbon on the far left of each structure is called the omega carbon. Counting from the omega carbon, you can easily see why these fatty acids are called omega-3 and omega-6, respectively. There is no reason to memorize these structures.

Cholesterol is a lipid substance needed in the body for a variety of reasons. Unfortunately, many people have levels of cholesterol circulating in their bloodstream that are excessive and can create problems within their blood vessels. Over time, as a condition called atherosclerosis develops, cholesterol can help form deposits called plaque on the inside of arteries. The inside of the artery slowly becomes smaller and smaller as the plaque continues to form. One of the more serious locations for this to occur is in the arteries that feed oxygenated blood directly into the heart muscle itself. These blood vessels are called the coronary arteries. The result is coronary heart disease, which can lead to a serious heart attack.

Amino acids: nine of 20 are essential

You would think it would be easy to specify the exact number of amino acids that are essential for humans. There is no doubt about nine of the 20: these nine are definitely essential, for everyone throughout their lives. After that it becomes a little less clear. For example, there are amino acids that are only essential for very young people, or for people who are suffering from a particular disease. Bear in mind what it means to be an 'essential' substance. Essential substances are no more important for our physiology than any other substances, but they are substances that cannot be synthesized from other molecules and thus must be a part of our diet. In the case of amino acids, a lack of one or more of the essential amino acids would mean that certain proteins could not be synthesized. The human body has no storage mechanisms for amino acids, so essential amino acids must be a part of your regular diet. People who live in cultures where their source(s) of protein comes from one or just a few food types can sometimes be in danger of a deficiency disease if their dominant protein source is low in one or more of the essential amino acids.

For example, some cultures are dependent on a single staple crop for much of their diet. One such staple crop is corn or maize. Corn is deficient in two essential amino acids, lysine and tryptophan. Populations that rely too much on maize as their primary source of protein can suffer from a variety of symptoms because of a low intake of these two amino acids. Researchers are developing an improved variety of maize that has increased levels of lysine and tryptophan.

Phenylketonuria (PKU)

Phenylketonuria (PKU) is a genetically inherited disease caused by a person's chemical inability to metabolize the amino acid phenylalanine. The inability to break down phenylalanine is a result of inheriting the mutated form of a gene that should be producing an enzyme (phenylalanine hydroxylase) that helps break down phenylalanine. Instead, phenylalanine builds up in tissues and the bloodstream. For a variety of biochemical reasons, excess phenylalanine can result in mental deficiency, behavioural problems, seizures, and other developmental problems. The allele for PKU is autosomal recessive (see Chapter 3 to remind yourself of these terms) and thus both parents must contribute an allele in order for the homozygous recessive condition to be expressed. Remember that both parents could be heterozygous individuals (carriers) who do not have PKU but do have a 25% chance of causing each of their children to have PKU. This gene defect is most common in European populations; it is much less common in Asians, Latinos, and Africans.

There is no cure for PKU, but there is a course of treatment that is effective as long as the disease is detected early. In countries where medical care is good, it is common for every newborn to be tested for PKU. If that test is positive, the treatment is based on a diet that limits proteins sources that are known to be high in phenylalanine. By simply limiting the intake of this one amino acid, the toxic levels characteristic of a 'normal' protein diet do not develop.

The incidence of PKU ranges between 1 in 2600 births in Turkey and 1 in 125 000 births in Japan.

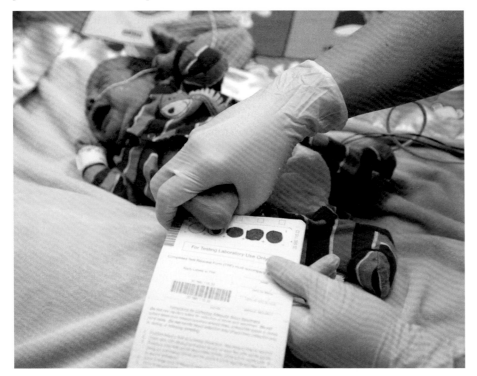

A baby having a small amount of blood drawn from his or her heel to test for the possibility of PKU. This test is typically done very soon after birth so that a limited protein diet can be implemented as soon as possible if needed.

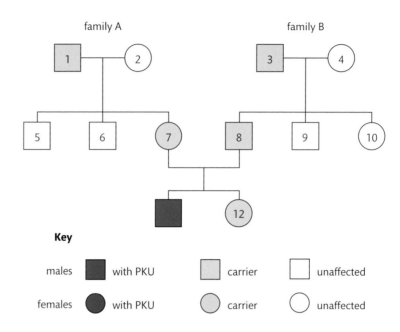

Figure 10.2 A pedigree showing the inheritance of PKU. Notice that the disease can be 'hidden' in families for several generations before manifesting itself when two carriers have children. The disease is not sex-linked, thus the male being shown with PKU was coincidental.

Key

males	■ with PKU	▢ carrier	□ unaffected
females	● with PKU	⬤ carrier	○ unaffected

Eating and nutrition disorders

There are a variety of disorders involving food that can affect humans. Some of these are the result of a lack of sufficient healthy food, while others are behavioural and physiological disorders. All aspects of eating and nutritional disorders are heavily influenced by a person's culture.

Appetite is controlled by the hypothalamus

Hunger is the body's way of expressing its need for food. Appetite is the desire to eat. It is quite possible to experience hunger and yet not feel the desire to eat (i.e. to be hungry but have no appetite), for example when you are sick. On the other hand, it is very common to not be hungry but see something that looks too good to resist.

At the end of a meal, when you have eaten a sufficient quantity of food, you have reached a state of satiety, and that is when most people stop eating. Although the mechanisms of appetite and satiety are quite complex and not fully understood, they seem to be a combination of feedback loops from the nervous system, the digestive system, and the endocrine (hormonal) system. For example, after a meal the pancreas releases hormones that reduce appetite. The question is, where do the feeling of hunger and the sensation of appetite originate in the body? To understand this, let's consider what happens when there is a problem with the system.

People who have medical complications that damage their hypothalamus (a part of the brain found at its base) can have severe appetite problems: some become very thin because of a loss of appetite, while others become very obese because of an insatiable appetite. From this evidence, it is clear that the hypothalamus plays an important role in regulating appetite. Although it has other functions as well, it can be said that the hypothalamus acts as your appetite control centre. During a meal, your stomach fills with food, expands, and stimulates cells of the vagus nerve. A signal is sent to the hypothalamus to stop eating. The intestines produce various hormones to send signals about hunger and satiety to the brain.

Anorexia is an eating disorder characterized by an obsession about body image, weight, and what foods to eat. Often sufferers of anorexia have an imagined 'ideal' body image that is far too underweight for good health. Sometimes the greatly restricted diet is accompanied by excessive exercise. The end result is not only a body that is far too thin, but a physiology that is in grave danger of collapsing because of a lack of essential nutrients. Even the heart muscle and internal valves can suffer damage that can be life threatening. If you know someone who appears to have the eating and exercise behaviours characteristic of anorexia, try to encourage him or her to get help because his or her life could be in danger.

In addition, the cells of adipose (fat) tissue produce a hormone called leptin that sends a message to the hypothalamus to suppress appetite. A person with more body fat produces more of this hormone, so that the brain knows there are adequate energy stores. If you fast, your level of leptin significantly decreases. But leptin is not the only hormone involved in the process of appetite; it would be an oversimplification to think that appetite was regulated solely by leptin, and other factors, such as compulsive eating and persuasive advertising, seem to be able to override leptin's effects.

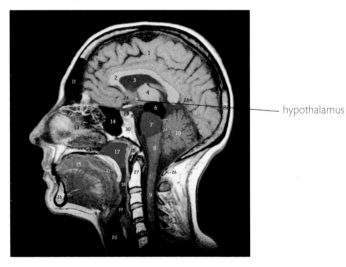

hypothalamus

The hypothalamus is found at the base of the brain as part of the brainstem. In addition to acting as the appetite control centre, the hypothalamus has a variety of other functions important to your physiology.

Consequences associated with being overweight

The perception of being underweight, normal, or overweight is highly biased by cultural and personal feelings about body shapes and expectations. A much better way to determine whether you have an appropriate weight is to calculate your body mass index (BMI). The BMI is a calculation of body mass that is corrected for height.

So, what are the health consequences of being overweight? Two of the more serious consequences are that people with high BMIs are much more likely to experience hypertension (high blood pressure) and develop type II diabetes.

Hypertension

There are many factors that can contribute to hypertension. Many of these factors are not controllable, such as age, ethnic origin, and family history. One of the factors that can be controlled is weight. There is a positive correlation between a higher BMI and hypertension. The more you weigh, the more blood you need to supply oxygen and nutrients to your cells. As the volume of blood circulated through your blood vessels increases, so does the pressure on the internal walls of your arteries.

Type II diabetes

Like hypertension, there are several factors that may contribute to the development of type II diabetes. But the data show that there is a positive correlation between developing type II diabetes and the occurrence of obesity. Type II diabetes used to be commonly called adult-onset diabetes because it was much more common to develop the symptoms of this disease later in life. As obesity has become more common in children and teenagers, the incidence of type II diabetes for these age groups has also increased, and thus 'adult-onset diabetes' is now an inappropriate name. Type II diabetes is most often characterized by body cell resistance to the normal effect of insulin, as well as a decrease in insulin production. Insulin is the hormone that allows cells to remove glucose from the bloodstream. The result is that blood glucose levels remain abnormally high because cells are not receiving the glucose for normal metabolic activity. People with type II diabetes must control their carbohydrate intake carefully to keep their blood glucose level reasonably stable.

Nutrition problems and their consequences

Food quantity and quality is a serious problem in many areas of the world. Malnutrition is a term that can be used for any of three possibilities: deficiency, imbalance, or excess of nutrients.

Deficiencies

Earlier in this chapter we considered situations in which one particular essential substance was missing from the diet, such as vitamin C or vitamin D. Very specific diseases, such as scurvy and rickets, are the result. Sometimes deficiencies can exist for many essential substances, including the calories (energy) from foods. When there is a lack of calories in the diet, a person's body will first draw upon any reserves that it has for substances that are needed. Glycogen stored in the liver and muscles will be exhausted very quickly as a source of glucose. Body fat will then be used. Many people who live in areas of the world where the availability of any type of food is severely limited will have neither glycogen nor body fat to make use of. Instead they will have to make use of protein within their body as a source of energy. We do not have storage mechanisms for protein: we need to have a regular intake of protein that can be digested to provide the amino acids needed for our own protein synthesis. When energy is not available from ingested carbohydrates, lipids, or proteins, the body's metabolism begins a series of reactions that digests body tissues for energy. One of the primary tissue types that is used first is skeletal muscle. Typically a single muscle does not completely 'disappear' when it is being used as a source of energy: the muscle just gets thinner and is therefore far less useful. When human beings are in the late stages of starvation they may be described as being 'just skin and bones'. The reason for this is that the skeletal muscle has become so thin it appears to be non-existent.

Weak muscle development in children because of poor nutrition. When the body has to 'choose' between energy needs and muscle development, energy needs become the priority for staying alive.

Imbalance

In areas of the world where there is a single staple crop providing most of the nutritional needs for a population, there can be an imbalance of nutrients in the population's diet. Depending on the species of staple crop being grown, this situation can lead to an overall imbalance of too many carbohydrates or a more specific deficiency of one or more essential nutrients. Even in areas of the world where excellent sources of nutrition are available, an individual's own choice of what is in his or her diet can lead to serious nutritional imbalances. The flourishing fast-food industry is a testament to how many people choose acquired tastes over good nutrition.

Excess of nutrients

An excess of nutrients leads to obesity. Back in 2005, the World Health Organization's Obesity Task Force estimated that 400 million people were obese and 1.6 billion were overweight. The World Health Organization (WHO) defines overweight and obesity as abnormal or excessive fat accumulation that may impair health. The degree of fat accumulation affects a person's BMI and determines whether someone is obese, overweight, or neither. You can review information on BMI in Section 2.3. The numbers of people overweight and obese have continued to increase in the last few decades. The causes for these ever-growing numbers are complex but the most obvious culprits are:

• change in the types and quantities of food people eat
• change in the amount of physical activity people do on a daily basis.

Just a few generations ago, most people in the world lived on farms. A family's daily routine involved a significant amount of physical activity to care for the crops and animals. Today, a migration towards urban centres has greatly reduced the amount of daily physical activity. In addition, the amount of time people devote to procuring and preparing their own food has dramatically decreased. The result is often low-nutrition, high-calorie choices being made from the many ready-to-eat food products available today.

To learn more about essential fatty acids and the Linus Pauling Institute, and about essential amino acids, go to the hotlinks site, search for the title or ISBN, and click on Chapter 10: Section D.1.

Section summary

• Some nutrients must be a part of our diet because they cannot be synthesized from other types of nutrients. Essential nutrients include some amino acids, some fatty acids, minerals, and vitamins.
• Minerals are non-organic substances that we need in very small amounts in our diet.
• Vitamins are a diverse group of organic compounds that we need in small amounts in our diet.
• Essential amino acids cannot be synthesized from other amino acids, and limit the production of some proteins unless they are included in our diet.
• Malnutrition can have several causes, including a deficiency of one or more nutrients, an imbalance of nutrients, or an excess of nutrients in the diet.
• The area of the brain known as the hypothalamus contains an appetite control centre.
• Type II diabetes is positively correlated with excess body weight.
• Hypertension (high blood pressure) is positively correlated with excess body weight.
• Starvation can lead to an individual self-digesting his or her own body tissue, including the breakdown of muscle tissue as a source of energy.

1 List four essential nutrients.

2 What is the fundamental difference between an essential nutrient and a non-essential nutrient?

3 For a long time, scurvy was thought to be unique to humans, as scientists could not replicate the symptoms of scurvy in rats and mice, even when these animals were denied vitamin C for a long period of time. Why did these experiments fail to produce symptoms of scurvy?

4 Why is rickets (a disease cause by insufficient intake of vitamin D) unique to children?

NATURE OF SCIENCE

Serendipity and scientific discoveries: the role of gastric acid in digestion was established by William Beaumont while observing the process of digestion in an open wound caused by gunshot.

D.2 Digestion

Understandings:

- Nervous and hormonal mechanisms control the secretion of digestive juices.
- Exocrine glands secrete to the surface of the body or the lumen of the gut.
- The volume and content of gastric secretions are controlled by nervous and hormonal mechanisms.
- Acid conditions in the stomach favour some hydrolysis reactions and help to control pathogens in ingested food.
- The structure of cells of the epithelium of the villi is adapted to the absorption of food.
- The rate of transit of materials through the large intestine is positively correlated with their fibre content.
- Materials not absorbed are egested.

- Application: The reduction of stomach acid secretion by proton pump inhibitor drugs.
- Application: Dehydration due to cholera toxin.
- Application: *Helicobacter pylori* infection as a cause of stomach ulcers.
- Skill: Identification of exocrine gland cells that secrete digestive juices and villus epithelium cells that absorb digested foods from electron micrographs.
  ### Guidance
  - *Adaptations of villus epithelial cells include microvilli and mitochondria.*

Exocrine secretions are fundamental to the digestive process

Exocrine glands are glands that produce a secretion that is useful in a specific location in the body and is taken to that location by a duct. Exocrine gland ducts lead to two general locations of the body. One location is the surface of the body. Examples of this type of secretion to the surface of the body are tears (lacrimal fluid) secreted from lacrimal glands and carried through ducts to the surface of the eye, perspiration produced by sweat glands and taken to the skin surface by small ducts, and milk produced by the mammary glands and taken through ducts to the nipple opening in lactating mothers. The second general location is the interior (lumen) of some part of the alimentary canal (gut). The secretions that fall into this second category are fluids that are necessary for digestion. All of these are needed at specific locations in the alimentary canal. Table 10.1 summarizes some of the more important digestive exocrine secretions.

Table 10.1 Important digestive secretions

Exocrine secretion	Exocrine gland	Ducts lead to	Function of secretion
Saliva	Salivary glands	Mouth	Moistens food; contains the enzyme amylase
Gastric juice	Three cell types found in pits in the stomach wall	Interior of the stomach	A mucus protects the stomach; hydrochloric acid (HCl) denatures proteins; pepsin is an enzyme
Pancreatic juice	Pancreatic cells	Duodenum	Trypsin, lipase, and amylase are all enzymes; a bicarbonate solution helps neutralize partially digested food entering from the stomach
Bile	Liver	Gall bladder and duodenum	Emulsification of lipids

Gastric secretions and their control

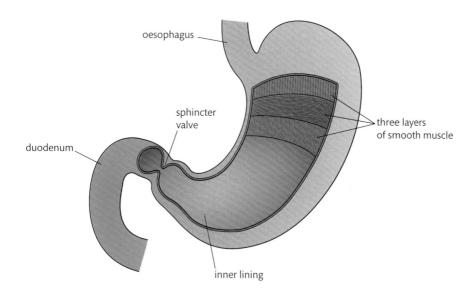

oesophagus

sphincter valve

duodenum

three layers of smooth muscle

inner lining

Figure 10.3 The term 'gastric' specifically refers to the stomach. Food enters the stomach from the tubular oesophagus. A valve located at the other end of the stomach remains closed for a period of time to allow gastric secretions to act upon the ingested food. In this sketch, you can see the three smooth muscle layers of the stomach that provide a churning action to mix the food thoroughly with the gastric juice.

As you learned in Section 6.1, the stomach is not only a 'holding place' for ingested food, but it is also the site where the early steps of digestion occur. In order to do this, some of the cells making up the inner lining of the stomach must be glandular and, as you have seen, they are exocrine glands. There are three types of glandular cells located in what are called pits (gastric pits) extending down into the inner lining of the stomach.

505

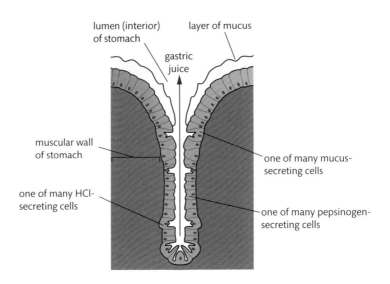

lumen (interior) of stomach

layer of mucus

gastric juice

muscular wall of stomach

one of many mucus-secreting cells

one of many HCl-secreting cells

one of many pepsinogen-secreting cells

Figure 10.4 One of the many gastric pits located in the inner lining of the stomach. Each pit is shared by each of the glandular cell types creating and secreting one of the components of gastric juice (hydrochloric acid, pepsinogen, or mucus). Note the thin duct leading to the lumen of the stomach; the presence of this duct qualifies each of these pits as an exocrine gland.

To learn more about protein pump inhibitors, go to the hotlinks site, search for the title or ISBN, and click on Chapter 10: Section D.2.

Late in the 20th century, researchers discovered a class of drugs that inhibit the production of acid by cells in the gastric pits of the stomach. Ever since then, these drugs have been available for people who suffer from conditions where the oesophagus becomes irritated by hydrochloric acid. This condition is generally known as acid reflux. In addition, some people develop ulcers, a condition where the stomach or duodenum has become irritated by acid as a result of a combination of thinned mucus and hydrochloric acid being in direct contact with the exposed tissue. By taking the acid-reducing drug(s) known as proton pump inhibitors (PPIs), the resulting decrease in acid production allows the irritated tissues to heal.

Even before eating food, your stomach is being prepared for digestion. The thought, smell, sight, or taste of food results in autonomic nervous system impulses being sent to the medulla oblongata of your brainstem. The medulla oblongata responds using the parasympathetic division of the autonomic nervous system. Action potentials are sent by a cranial nerve called the vagus nerve directly to the stomach. The stomach then begins hydrochloric acid (HCl) and pepsinogen production and secretion into the cavity of the stomach. The same action potentials from the vagus nerve also stimulate endocrine cells in the lower portion of the stomach to secrete a hormone known as gastrin. Gastrin enters the blood and is carried to other cells elsewhere in the stomach, and results in even higher secretion of HCl and pepsinogen. When pepsinogen enters the cavity of the stomach and comes into contact with HCl, the pepsinogen converts into its active enzymatic form known as pepsin. Pepsin is one of many protease (protein-digesting) enzymes.

When food enters the stomach, the walls of the stomach become distended (expanded as a result of internal pressure). This results in an autonomic nervous system signal being sent by the vagus nerve to the medulla oblongata. The medulla oblongata then sends impulses back to the glandular cells of the stomach to continue (and increase) production of HCl and pepsinogen.

Finally, when a valve at the lower end of the stomach opens and releases the partially digested food (called chyme) into the duodenum of the small intestine, a set of signals terminates the secretion of acid and pepsinogen from the gastric pits. This includes production of a hormone called secretin that enters the blood and results in lowered gastric pit activity.

What is the role of HCl during the digestive process?

Remember that digestion is a chemical process that generally converts macromolecules (like proteins) into smaller 'absorbable size' molecules (like amino acids). When proteins enter the stomach, they are in their three-dimensional fibrous or globular molecular shapes characteristic of the secondary, tertiary, and quaternary shapes of this type of molecule (see Section 2.4). If you recall, there are many internal bonds holding proteins in these three-dimensional shapes, including numerous hydrogen and ionic bonds between non-adjacent amino acids. Also remember that one of the environmental factors that denatures proteins is pH conditions outside a protein's norm (see Section 2.4). In the highly acidic environment of the stomach, most proteins are far outside their normal pH range, and thus become denatured. This means that many of the hydrogen and ionic bonds that help shape the molecule become broken. The result is that the protein 'opens up' and digestive (hydrolytic) enzymes are able to more easily access the peptide bonds between adjacent amino acids.

Pepsinogen is one of the enzymes that benefits from the activity of HCl. When pepsinogen is first secreted from the gastric pits into the cavity of the stomach, it is in an inactive form. When the pepsinogen comes into contact with the HCl, it undergoes a molecular modification that activates the enzyme. At that point the enzyme is called pepsin. The function of pepsin is to catalyse the hydrolysis of large polypeptide chains into smaller peptides. The smaller peptides will be acted on by other protein-digesting enzymes later in the digestive process. In addition to activating pepsin, the highly acidic environment of the stomach is the ideal pH for the enzymatic activity of pepsin.

One final function of HCl in the stomach is to help control the ingestion of some pathogens. Many foods contain bacteria and fungi, and the vast majority of these are not harmful within the alimentary canal. A small percentage are harmful (pathogenic), and the highly acidic environment of the stomach helps to kill many of these before releasing the chyme into the small intestine.

NATURE OF SCIENCE

In 1822, an American physician by the name of William Beaumont saved the life of a Canadian trapper who had suffered a shotgun wound at close range. The wound left a permanent hole in the man's abdomen and stomach wall, allowing Beaumont to make observations and take samples of the digestive process.

A cow fitted with a fistula for observing and taking fluid samples from the rumen (one of its stomachs). The fistula is a surgically implanted 'window' that does not harm the animal.

What causes stomach ulcers?

The answers to scientific questions sometimes change. Can anything live in the highly acidic environment of our stomach? Until fairly recently, the answer to that question was thought to be no. The fluid in the stomach can be as acidic as pH 2. The consensus among scientists was that no living organism could survive such a harshly acidic environment.

In the early 1980s, two researchers isolated living bacterial cells (*Helicobacter pylori*) from the stomach lining of patients suffering from stomach ulcers. The conventional wisdom at that time was that stomach ulcers were caused by excess production of HCl, perhaps brought on by stress. Here is a summary of the more recent scientific information concerning stomach ulcers and gastritis (inflammation of the stomach).

Hopefully, you have begun to view all sciences as a process, or perhaps a way of 'knowing'. Anyone who looks at a science topic as only a set of things to memorize is missing the much bigger and more important picture. Please don't memorize this.

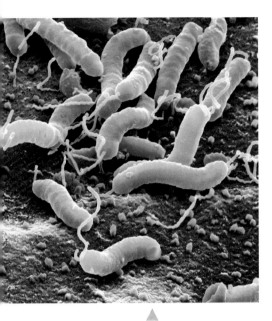

- *H. pylori* survives when introduced into the stomach, probably by burrowing beneath the mucus layer and infecting stomach lining cells.
- *H. pylori* employs the enzyme urease to create ammonia, and this helps to neutralize stomach acid.
- *H. pylori* infection of the stomach lining leads to gastritis and stomach ulcers.
- Patients treated with a selected range of antibiotics respond well to treatment.
- Patients with gastritis (and therefore infected with *H. pylori*) for many years (20–30 years, for example) are much more prone to stomach cancer than the general population.
- *H. pylori* infection may well be the most common bacterial infection in the world, as it is estimated that more than 3 billion people are infected.

A scanning electron micrograph (SEM) of *H. pylori* in the stomach. This bacterial infection can result in gastritis, stomach ulcers, and possibly even stomach cancer if the infection persists for many years.

Adaptations of villi epithelial cells for efficient absorption

An artist's representation of villi in the small intestine. Each villus contains a capillary bed and lacteal for the absorption of nutrients. The villi epithelial cells are the cells in contact with the nutrients inside the lumen of the intestine. Nutrients must pass through these cells in order to get to the capillaries and lacteal.

Digested molecules must pass through epithelial villi cells, and are absorbed into either a capillary or a lacteal on the interior of each villus. The surface of each villus cell that faces into the lumen (cavity) of the small intestine has many microscopic finger-like projections known as microvilli. The function of microvilli, like that of villi, is to increase greatly the surface area for absorption (compared with what it would be if the interior of the intestine was smooth).

Some of the molecules absorbed through the plasma membranes of the villi are absorbed using an active transport mechanism. The requirement of active transport mechanisms for adenosine triphosphate (ATP) partly explains why the epithelial villi cells contain mitochondria. In addition, near the plasma membrane surface, pinocytotic vesicles are often visible.

False-colour transmission electron micrograph (TEM) showing the microvilli of an epithelial cell extending into the intestinal lumen.

Pinocytosis is another active transport mechanism often used to absorb molecules from the lumen of the intestine into the interior of the villi cells, and also requires ATP from the mitochondria. Most cells in the body are surrounded by intercellular (interstitial) fluid. Even cells that make up the outer boundary of an organ typically allow molecules to move between cells. This would be an unacceptable situation for epithelial cells that make up villi. If intercellular fluid and dissolved molecules moved between adjoining cells, nutrients would have no selective barrier to pass through. It is the movement of digested molecules through the selectively permeable membrane of the villi epithelial cells that guarantees that the molecules have completed the process of enzymatic digestion. To this end, epithelial cells of villi are sealed to each other by membrane-to-membrane protein 'seals' called tight junctions (see Figure 10.5). The two cell membranes share some membrane proteins. This results in the two membranes being held so tightly together that most molecules cannot pass between them and must be transported first into and then out of the epithelial cells lining each villus.

On the side of the villi epithelial cell opposite where the microvilli are located (closer to the capillary bed), the plasma membrane has infoldings (invaginations) in order to increase the surface area for transport out of the epithelial cell. These invaginations are called the basal labyrinth and operate in the opposite direction but have a similar function as the microvilli.

When studying, ask yourself how well you know something. A general rule of thumb is, if you know it well enough to explain to someone else, then you know it well enough.

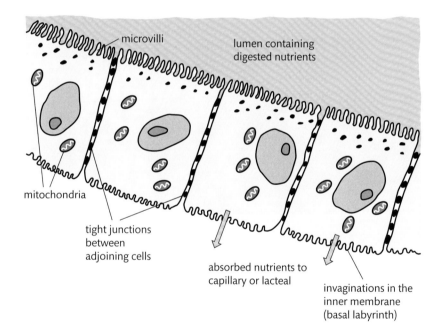

Figure 10.5 Individual epithelial cells of a villus. Digested molecules must pass through these cells in order to reach a capillary bed or lacteal.

Cholera is a disease caused by the bacterium *Vibrio cholera*; more specifically it is caused by the toxin secreted by *V. cholera*. The toxin results in a severe diarrhoea that leads to dehydration and is frequently fatal. Cholera is spread by drinking water or food contaminated with the bacterium. At one time cholera outbreaks occurred in almost every area of the world. Today, areas that have modern sewage processing and drinking water treatment rarely have problems with cholera. However, outbreaks still occur regularly in some areas of the world, and specifically in areas that have suffered catastrophic disasters such as tsunamis or major earthquakes.

To learn more about cholera go to the hotlinks site, search for the title or ISBN, and click on Chapter 10: Section D.2.

CHALLENGE YOURSELF

1 See if you can identify the epithelial cell adaptations described on the previous page on the electron micrograph on the right. The photo shows two partial epithelial cells. The photograph does not show the 'lower' portion of each of the cells where the basal labyrinth is located. A key for the letter abbreviations is provided in the caption.

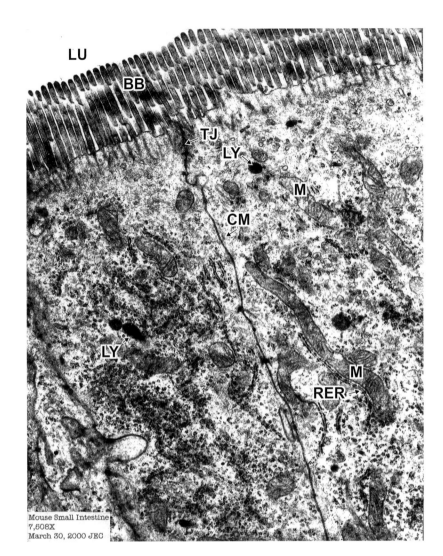

LU, the lumen of the small intestine (nutrients to be absorbed are found here); BB, brush border (the collective name for all the microvilli); TJ, tight junction; M, mitochondrion; RER, rough endoplasmic reticulum; LY, lysosome (organelles that contain digestive (hydrolytic) enzymes for use within the cell); CM, cell membrane.

Mouse Small Intestine
7,508X
March 30, 2000 JEC

Materials that are not absorbed are egested (become part of faecal matter).

The human large intestine is populated with billions of bacteria. These bacteria are mutualistic because they provide us with vitamin K and a normal intestinal environment, while we provide the bacteria with undigested food from the small intestine.

The importance of fibre in the diet

Almost all absorption of nutrients occurs in the small intestine. However, some ingested substances will never be digested and thus have no chance of being absorbed into the bloodstream. These substances continue into the large intestine and become a part of the solid waste (faeces). These substances include:

- cellulose, from the cell walls of ingested plant material
- lignin, another component of plant cell walls
- bile pigments, from bile, which give the characteristic colour to faeces
- bacteria, because a few survive the low pH in stomach and become a constantly regenerating population of billions of mutualistic inhabitants of our digestive tract.

How many times have you been told to 'eat up your vegetables'? Besides being a good source of vitamins and minerals, vegetables are an important source of fibre, although they are not the only fibre-rich foods. Fresh fruit and salads are also good sources of fibre.

Fibre, also referred to as dietary fibre (or, more informally, roughage), is composed mostly of the cellulose and lignin in plant material (see the list above). It helps the human digestive system function better by providing bulk. In order for peristalsis (smooth muscle contractions that propel material through the alimentary canal) to function optimally, the muscles that push 'food' along the intestines need to have a sufficient volume of material to apply pressure to. Not surprisingly, the rate of movement of material through the large intestine has a positive correlation with fibre content.

High-fibre diets also help people manage their body mass better. It is easier to lose excess weight with a diet that includes fruits and vegetables, in part because the fibre fills up the stomach, giving a feeling of satiety without introducing excess energy. A common criticism of modern diets, especially in industrialized countries, is that they do not contain enough fibre. One recommendation is to eat at least five servings of fruit or vegetables each day.

There is a positive correlation between the amount of fibre in a person's diet and the rate of movement of material through his or her large intestine.

Figure 10.6 To help you remember to eat at least five serving of fruits and vegetables every day, count them on your fingers.

Section summary

- Digestion requires secretions to be added to ingested foods.
- Exocrine glands secrete substances to the surface of the body or to the lumen of the alimentary canal.
- The volume and makeup of these exocrine secretions needed for digestion is under the control of both the nervous system and the endocrine (hormonal) system.
- The stomach secretes hydrochloric acid, which kills most ingested pathogens and creates a low pH environment for hydrolytic digestive reactions in the stomach.
- The numerous villi and microvilli within the small intestine create an incredible membrane surface area for the absorption of digested food.
- Fibre in food includes substances such as cellulose that cannot be digested. Substances not digested cannot be absorbed and are passed into the large intestine for elimination. In other words, they are egested as faeces.
- The rate of passage of waste through the large intestine is positively correlated with its fibre content.

Exercises

5 What are the three components of gastric juice? Summarize the function of each.

6 You are sitting at the dining room table with your parents. They both mention that they are worried about getting a stomach ulcer because of the stress they are under at work. What would you tell them?

7 What are some of the adaptations of epithelial villi cells that allow them to be efficient at absorbing digested nutrients and passing those nutrients on to the bloodstream or lymphatic system?

8 Explain the general function of an exocrine gland.

D.3 Functions of the liver

Understandings:

- The liver removes toxins from the blood and detoxifies them.
- Components of red blood cells are recycled by the liver.
- The breakdown of erythrocytes starts with phagocytosis of red blood cells by Kupffer cells.
- Iron is carried to the bone marrow to produce haemoglobin in new red blood cells.
- Surplus cholesterol is converted to bile salts.
- Endoplasmic reticulum and Golgi apparatus in hepatocytes produce plasma proteins.
- The liver intercepts blood from the gut to regulate nutrient levels.
- Some nutrients in excess can be stored in the liver.

Applications and skills:

- Application: Causes and consequences of jaundice.
- Application: Dual blood supply to the liver and differences between sinusoids and capillaries.

Circulation of blood to and from the liver

The liver receives blood from two major blood vessels, and is drained by one (see Figure 10.7). The hepatic artery is a branch of the aorta and carries oxygenated blood to the liver tissues. The hepatic portal vein is the other blood vessel supplying blood to the liver. These two blood vessels carry blood into the capillaries of the liver, called sinusoids. All sinusoids are then drained by the hepatic vein, which is the sole blood vessel taking blood away from the liver.

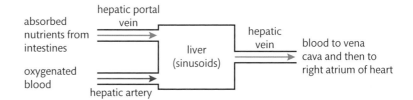

Figure 10.7 A schematic showing the blood circulation pattern to and from the liver.

The hepatic portal vein receives blood from the capillaries within all the villi of the small intestine. The blood within the hepatic portal vein varies in two ways from blood that normally arrives at an organ:

- it is low-pressure, deoxygenated blood because it has already been through a capillary bed
- it varies considerably in quantity of nutrients (especially glucose), depending on the types of food and the timing of ingestion, digestion, and absorption of food within the small intestine.

The blood within the hepatic vein is also low-pressure, deoxygenated blood, but it does not vary in nutrients as much as the blood within the hepatic portal vein. The stabilization of nutrients within the hepatic vein represents one of the major functions of the liver, specifically the storage of nutrients and the release of those nutrients when needed.

A portal system of circulation (like the hepatic portal system described here) is when blood travels through two capillary beds before returning to the heart to be re-pumped.

Sinusoids are the capillaries of the liver

The function of the liver is to remove some substances from the blood and add others to it. This removal or addition of a variety of substances is the job of the hepatocytes (liver cells). Oxygen-rich blood from the hepatic artery and (sometimes) nutrient-rich blood from the hepatic portal vein both flow into sinusoids of the liver. Sinusoids are where exchanges occur between the blood and the hepatocytes (see Figure 10.8).

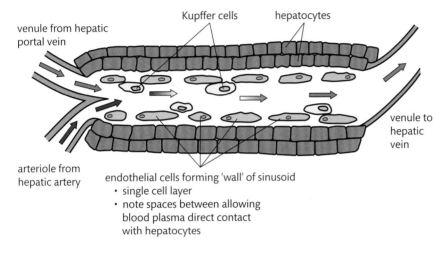

venule from hepatic portal vein

Kupffer cells   hepatocytes

venule to hepatic vein

arteriole from hepatic artery

endothelial cells forming 'wall' of sinusoid
- single cell layer
- note spaces between allowing blood plasma direct contact with hepatocytes

Figure 10.8 Sinusoids are the capillary beds of the liver, but their structure and action are different from capillary beds found elsewhere in the body.

Sinusoids differ from a typical capillary bed in the following ways:

- sinusoids are wider than capillaries
- sinusoids are lined by endothelial cells with gaps between them
- these gaps allow large molecules like proteins to be exchanged between hepatocytes and the bloodstream
- hepatocytes are in direct contact with blood components, making all exchanges with the bloodstream more efficient
- sinusoids contain Kupffer cells that help break down haemoglobin released from 'older' erythrocytes for recycling cell components
- sinusoids receive a mixture of oxygenated blood (from hepatic artery branches) and nutrient-rich blood (from hepatic portal vein branches), and this mixture eventually drains into small branches of the hepatic vein.

The liver does not extract all excess glucose, toxins, etc., on a single pass of the blood through the liver sinusoids. The hepatocytes act on the chemicals within the blood many times as the blood makes a continuous circuit through the liver.

The liver removes toxins from the blood

A typical human being ingests an amazing number of toxic substances every day. These toxins come in the form of pesticides and herbicides added to food produce, food preservatives, food flavour 'enhancers', medications, and alcohol, to name just a few. The reason we do not think of many of these substances as being toxic is because our bodies have efficient mechanisms in place to process and eliminate them. The liver contains two kinds of cells that are used in these processes.

1 Kupffer cells: these cells line the inside of sinusoids and use phagocytosis to remove old erythrocytes and bacteria from the blood. They are therefore phagocytic and contain many lysosomes. Kupffer cells are specialized leucocytes (white blood cells).

2 Hepatocytes: these are the most numerous cells in the liver, and are the most active in removing and processing chemical toxins from the blood. When blood

513

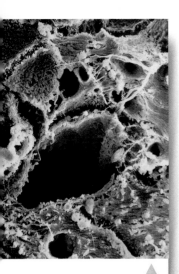

False-colour SEM of liver cells with cirrhosis. A sinusoid is visible (blue) surrounded by abnormal hepatocytes. Many fibres of connective tissue (light brown) have invaded the damaged area.

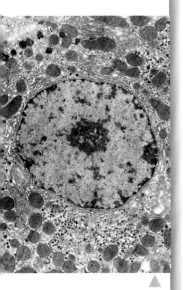

TEM of a section through a rat liver cell. At the centre is the nucleus, containing a single nucleolus. The dark ovoid objects spread throughout the cell are mitochondria surrounded by large numbers of endoplasmic reticulum. The small black dots are glycogen granules, the storage form of glucose.

flows through the sinusoids, hepatocytes are bathed with the liquid (plasma) component of blood. They extract toxins from the plasma and begin a two-step process to eliminate the toxins. First, they chemically modify the toxin to make it less destructive, and second, they add chemical components that make the (now modified) toxin water soluble. The water-soluble modified substance can be added back into the blood in order to be eliminated by the kidneys as a component of urine.

Alcohol consumption damages liver cells over time

People who drink alcohol, especially often and in high volume, can expect liver damage. As is the case with useful nutrients, the hepatic portal vein brings absorbed alcohol to the liver first. Any alcohol not removed the first time is brought back through the liver sinusoids by the hepatic artery. Each time the blood passes through the liver, hepatocytes attempt to remove the alcohol from the bloodstream. Thus alcohol has a magnified effect on liver tissue compared with other tissues in the body. It has been shown that long-term alcohol abuse results in three primary effects on the liver.

- Cirrhosis: this is the scar tissue left when areas of hepatocytes, blood vessels, and ducts have been destroyed by exposure to alcohol. Areas of the liver showing cirrhosis no longer function.
- Fat accumulation: damaged areas of the liver will quite often build up fat in place of normal liver tissue.
- Inflammation: this is the swelling of damaged liver tissue as a result of alcohol exposure, sometimes referred to as alcoholic hepatitis.

The liver can repair itself if the damage is not too severe, but long-term alcohol abuse can be fatal.

Regulation of nutrients in the blood

Solutes that are dissolved in blood plasma vary a little in concentration, but each type of solute has a normal homeostatic range. Any concentration below or above this normal range creates problems in the body.

Let's consider glucose as an example. For most people, the glucose levels in blood are lowest in the morning and highest soon after a meal. When you digest a meal that is high in carbohydrates, such as starch, your hepatic portal vein will contain blood with a very high concentration of glucose. When this blood enters the sinusoids of your liver, some of the excess glucose is taken in by the surrounding hepatocytes and converted to the polysaccharide glycogen. This keeps the glucose level in the normal range. Stored glycogen can be seen as large vesicles or 'granules' in electron micrographs of hepatocytes.

Now imagine you have not eaten any carbohydrates for a long time. Your blood glucose levels decrease as cells use the glucose for cell respiration. To keep the glucose level in the normal range, the stored glycogen in the granules is reconverted to glucose and added into the bloodstream in the sinusoids.

The homeostatic mechanisms at work are regulated by the production of the hormones insulin and glucagon from the pancreas. When blood glucose levels are towards the upper end of the normal range, insulin is produced and this stimulates hepatocytes to take in and convert glucose to glycogen. When blood glucose levels approach the lower end of the normal range, the pancreas produces glucagon and this hormone stimulates hepatocytes to convert glycogen back into glucose.

In addition to glycogen, other nutrients can be stored in the liver, as summarized in Table 10.2.

Table 10.2 Nutrients stored by the liver

Nutrient	Relevant information
Glycogen	A polysaccharide of glucose (sometimes called animal starch)
Iron	Iron is removed from haemoglobin, and later sent to bone marrow
Vitamin A	Associated with good vision
Vitamin D	Associated with healthy bone growth

The liver recycles components of erythrocytes and haemoglobin

Erythrocytes have a typical cellular life span of about 4 months. This means every erythrocyte needs to be replaced every 120 days or so by the blood cell-forming tissue of the bone marrow. This is necessary because erythrocytes are anucleate (they have no nucleus) and thus cannot undergo mitosis to form new blood cells, nor are they able to code for new proteins within the cell.

As erythrocytes approach the end of their approximately 120-day life, the cell membrane becomes weak and eventually ruptures. More often than not this occurs in the spleen or bone marrow, but it can happen anywhere in the bloodstream. The rupture leads to millions of haemoglobin molecules circulating in the bloodstream. As blood circulates through the sinusoids of the liver, these circulating haemoglobin molecules are ingested by Kupffer cells within the sinusoids. This ingestion is by phagocytosis because haemoglobin molecules are very large proteins.

Kupffer cells are a type of leucocyte that resides in the sinusoids of the liver. Besides ingesting haemoglobin, they can also ingest cellular debris and bacteria within the bloodstream.

Haemoglobin consists of four polypeptides (globins) and a non-protein molecular component at the centre of each globin called a haem group. At the centre of each haem group is an iron atom. Thus each haemoglobin consists of four globins, four haem groups, and four iron atoms. It is within Kupffer cells that haemoglobin is disassembled into its component parts. The key events are summarized in the following bullet list and in Figure 10.9.

• The four globin proteins of each haemoglobin are hydrolysed into amino acids.
• The amino acids are released back into the bloodstream and become available to any body cell for protein synthesis.
• The iron atom is removed from each haem group. Some of this iron is stored within the liver and some is sent to bone marrow to be used in the production of new erythrocytes.
• Once iron has been removed from the haem group, what remains of the molecule is called bilirubin or bile pigment. This is absorbed by the nearby hepatocytes and becomes a key component of bile.

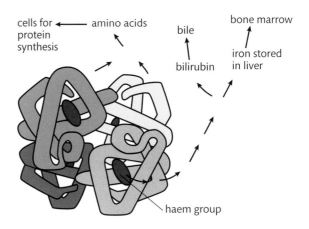

Figure 10.9 The molecular components of haemoglobin are recycled when erythrocytes die after about 4 months.

Cholesterol in our diet has a bad reputation. To some degree and in some food types this reputation is deserved. However, many people don't understand that there are different kinds of cholesterol and that they are used for different purposes in the body. You might remember that we need one type of cholesterol in our cell membranes to provide flexibility. When you have your cholesterol checked with a blood test, there is one type of cholesterol/lipid that is considered to be 'good cholesterol'. It is abbreviated as HDL, standing for high-density lipoprotein.

About 95% of the bile salts that enter the small intestine are reabsorbed into the blood in the last portion of the small intestine. These bile salts enter the bloodstream and attach to the plasma protein called albumin. They are returned to the liver to be reincorporated into more bile.

Hepatocytes produce and secrete bile and plasma proteins

One of the better-known functions of the liver is the production of bile. Bile is added to the duodenum when fatty foods are being digested in order to emulsify fats. Lipids (fats and oils) have a tendency to coalesce (clump) together because they are hydrophobic and thus not water soluble. This makes it difficult for the enzyme lipase to digest the lipids as very little surface area of the 'clump' is exposed. When bile is added into the duodenum, the resulting emulsification does not chemically change the lipids, but it does break up the coalesced clumps and increases the surface area for lipase to catalyse the digestion.

Hepatocytes within the liver produce bile by converting surplus cholesterol into a similar molecule known as a bile salt. These bile salts are added to bilirubin to make the substance bile. The bile salts are the emulsifying portion of bile.

Another well-documented function of hepatocytes is the production of many types of proteins that are added into the bloodstream. These are called plasma proteins because they circulate in the liquid portion of blood called blood plasma. There are many of these proteins produced by the liver, but two whose functions are documented elsewhere in this text are:

• albumin, which helps regulate blood osmotic pressure and acts as a carrier for bile salts and some other fat-soluble substances
• fibrinogen, which when converted to fibrin forms the mesh component of a blood clot.

Plasma proteins produced by the liver must also be secreted from hepatocytes. Thus the sequence of events is identical to that of any cell that produces and secretes a protein for use outside of that cell:

1 DNA within the nucleus of a hepatocyte synthesizes messenger (m)RNA for a particular protein (transcription).
2 mRNA exits the nucleus through a nuclear pore.
3 mRNA finds a ribosome located on rough endoplasmic reticulum (ER).
4 Plasma protein is synthesized (translation).
5 Plasma protein is transported by a vesicle to the Golgi apparatus.
6 The Golgi apparatus possibly modifies the protein and surrounds the protein with another vesicle.

7   The vesicle goes to the plasma membrane for exocytosis (secretion).

8   The plasma protein enters the blood plasma.

Causes and consequences of jaundice

Jaundice is a condition characterized by having too much bilirubin circulating in the bloodstream and thus within the body tissues. Bilirubin is a yellow pigment and so people with jaundice have a yellow tinge to their skin and a yellowing of the whites of their eyes. Bilirubin is formed when haemoglobin molecules are processed from dying erythrocytes. There are two main types of jaundice.

1   Infant jaundice is found in newborns. It most typically occurs in babies who are born prematurely because their livers are not yet capable of fully processing the bilirubin into bile. Up to the point of birth, bilirubin is processed by the mother through the placenta. Soon after birth, a newborn may begin showing the yellowing symptoms of jaundice. Except in very serious cases, the most common treatment is exposure to the blue and green portion of the light spectrum. The blue–green light changes the shape and structure of bilirubin molecules, and they can then be eliminated in the baby's urine and stools. This gives the baby's liver time to mature for full processing of bilirubin into bile. The most severe consequence of untreated jaundice is a brain condition called acute bilirubin encephalopathy. Excessive bilirubin levels are toxic to brain cells, which is why newborns with symptoms of jaundice must be treated promptly.

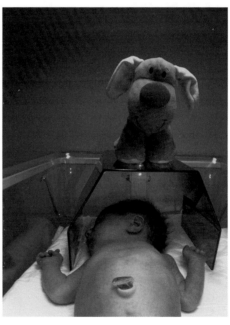

A newborn receiving phototherapy for infant jaundice. The light used emits blue–green wavelengths of the spectrum (not ultraviolet, as commonly believed).

2   Adult jaundice has many of the same symptoms and consequences as infant jaundice. The cause can always be traced back to liver function. The jaundice is therefore a symptom, and the underlying cause is whatever problem is leading to the liver not functioning properly. When the liver is not functioning properly, there are also likely to be many other symptoms.

Section summary

• The liver's capillary beds are called sinusoids. Each sinusoid is wider and much more permeable to substances compared with a typical capillary.

• The liver is responsible for filtering toxins out of the blood and detoxifying those substances.

• Sinusoids contain white blood cells called Kupffer cells that take in red blood cells and haemoglobin to be recycled for other purposes.

• One of the components of the recycling of haemoglobin is iron, which is sent to bone marrow to be incorporated into new haemoglobin molecules in new red blood cells.

• The liver recycles excess cholesterol into bile salts that are used to make bile.

- Hepatocytes (liver cells) produce a variety of proteins that circulate in our blood plasma, including albumin and fibrinogen.
- Nutrients, such as glucose, that are absorbed by the capillary beds within the villi of the small intestine are routed to the liver sinusoids before being released into the general body circulation.
- This allows the liver to remove and store some nutrients that are in excess. An example of this is excess glucose, which is stored in the liver as the polysaccharide glycogen.

Exercises

9 Briefly describe the blood supply into and out of the liver.

10 Explain why humans do not need excessive amounts of iron in their diet in order to make the millions of new erythrocytes that are formed each and every minute in the bone marrow.

11 Describe what would happen in the liver if a person was to go for an extended period of time without eating or exercised heavily for a long period of time.

12 Why does alcoholism lead to liver damage?

NATURE OF SCIENCE

Developments in scientific research followed improvements in apparatus or instrumentation: the invention of the stethoscope led to improved knowledge of the workings of the heart.

D.4 The heart

Understandings:
- Structure of cardiac muscle cells allows propagation of stimuli through the heart wall.
- Signals from the sinoatrial node that cause contraction cannot pass directly from atria to ventricles.
- There is a delay between the arrival and passing on of a stimulus at the atrioventricular node.
- This delay allows time for atrial systole before the atrioventricular valves close.
- Conducting fibres ensure coordinated contraction of the entire ventricle wall.
- Normal heart sounds are caused by the atrioventricular valves and semilunar valves closing, causing changes in blood flow.

- Application: Use of artificial pacemakers to regulate the heart rate.
- Application: Use of defibrillation to treat life-threatening cardiac conditions.
- Application: Causes and consequences of hypertension and thrombosis.
- Skill: Measurement and interpretation of the heart rate under different conditions.
- Skill: Interpretation of systolic and diastolic blood pressure measurements.
- Skill: Mapping of the cardiac cycle to a normal ECG trace.
- Skill: Analysis of epidemiological data relating to the incidence of coronary heart disease.
  Guidance
  - *Include branching and intercalated discs in structure of cardiac muscle.*

The heart is composed of cardiac muscle cells

Skeletal muscle is muscle that acts to move your bones to create various body motions. In skeletal muscle, many individual cells are fused together to make a fibre. The evidence for this is that the fibre contains many nuclei: it is said to be multinucleate. This arrangement makes it easier for the fibre to act as a single unit when contracting.

Cardiac muscle has some similarities with skeletal muscle, especially in the arrangement of the actin and myosin proteins in contracting units called sarcomeres. Cardiac muscle cells containing the sarcomeres remain as single cells joined together by interconnections called intercalated discs. These disc-shaped areas contain openings called gap junctions where cytoplasm from one cell freely passes to the next cell. This sharing of cytoplasm is what allows the cardiac muscle cells to pass an electrical signal so quickly from cell to cell. Without these gap junctions the impulse to begin a heart beat would spread too slowly through the muscle tissue to result in a unified event.

Cardiac muscle cells that are joined together by intercalated discs form fibrous units that repeatedly branch. The muscle tissue is dense with relatively large mitochondria, and has a very generous blood supply (it is said to be highly vascular). These adaptations help prevent cardiac muscle getting fatigued. The evolutionary design behind the repeated branches and individual cells joined by intercalated discs is based on getting the muscle cells to work together as a unit. All they need are signals to synchronize their contraction activity.

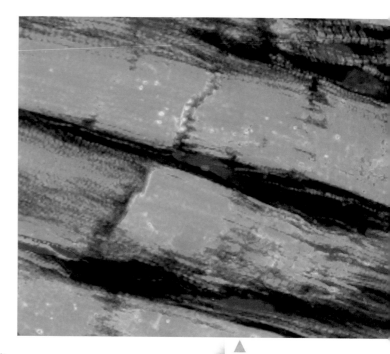

A light micrograph taken with fluorescent markers showing cardiac muscle cells. The light and dark green lines running horizontally are the sarcomeres. Two intercalated discs are shown (vertical orange lines). A variety of nuclei (blue) can be seen.

Illustration showing a small portion of cardiac muscle. Notice the branching between one area of muscle cells and another. There are several individual cardiac muscle cells shown, with two shown in section. The sections are shown with a portion of an intercalated disc cut in half. The sections also show sarcomeres and a large central nucleus (purple).

> **Intercalated discs contain structures known as gap junctions. Gap junctions are protein-lined channels that allow direct transmission of the nerve impulse from cell to cell so that cells contract in unison. Because of this, muscle cells are said to be 'electrically coupled'.**

The cardiac cycle

The cardiac cycle is a series of events that we commonly refer to as one heart beat. More properly, one cardiac cycle is all the heart events that occur from the beginning of one heart beat to the beginning of the next heart beat. The frequency of the cardiac cycle is your heart rate, and is typically measured in beats per minute. If you have a resting heart rate of 72 beats min^{-1}, you are performing 72 cardiac cycles each minute.

When a chamber of the heart contracts, it is because the cardiac muscle of the chamber has received an electrical signal that has caused the muscle fibres of the chamber to

Anatomical diagrams identify right and left sides as if it is your own body that is being shown. Most anatomical diagrams show a ventral view (from the front): so the left side of the body is on the right, and the right is on the left. Any diagram identified as a dorsal view (from the back) shows the right side on the right, and the left on the left.

contract. This causes an increase in pressure on the blood within the chamber, and the blood leaves the chamber through any available opening. This is called systole (pronounced sis-tol-ee). When a chamber is not undergoing systole, the cardiac muscle of the chamber is relaxed. This is called diastole (di-astol-ee). Both atria contract at the same time, therefore you can say that both undergo systole at the same time. Both ventricles also undergo systole simultaneously, just a little after the atrial systole.

Heart valves

Heart valves keep blood moving in a single direction. Each chamber of the heart has to have an opening to receive blood and another opening to allow blood to exit. When a chamber undergoes systole, it is imperative that the blood moves consistently in a single, useful direction (see Figure 10.10). The heart valves serve to prevent a backflow of blood.

The valves located between the atria and ventricles are called the atrioventricular valves (identified as right and left according to the side of the heart). The valves located where the blood exits the ventricles are called semilunar valves and are also identified as left and right (see Figure 10.10).

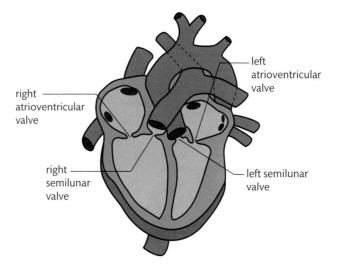

Figure 10.10 The location of the four heart valves.

Each of the heart valves has at least one other name that you may well come across in books and texts. In order to avoid confusion, some of the more common synonyms (alternative names) are given in Table 10.3.

Table 10.3 Different names for the valves of the heart

Heart valve	Synonym(s)
Right atrioventricular valve	Tricuspid valve
Left atrioventricular valve	Bicuspid valve, Mitral valve
Right semilunar valve	Pulmonary valve, Pulmonary semilunar valve
Left semilunar valve	Aortic valve, Aortic semilunar valve

You may have noticed that there are no valves where blood enters the atria. So what prevents blood from flowing back up into the vena cava and pulmonary veins when the atria undergo systole? The answer to this question is two-fold.

- Both the vena cava and pulmonary veins are veins, and thus have internal, passive flap valves characteristic of all veins. These are valves curved in the direction of blood flow that stay open as long as the blood is flowing in the proper direction within the vessel. If blood attempts to flow backwards in any vein, the passive flap valves use the force of the blood hitting the valve to close down and prevent blood from flowing in that direction.
- Atrial systole does not build up very much pressure. The muscular walls of the atria are very thin in comparison with the ventricles. Their force of contraction is slight in comparison with the ventricles. Thus the relatively low pressure exerted by the atria in combination with the passive flap valves within the supply veins means that no heart valve is necessary where the blood enters each atrium.

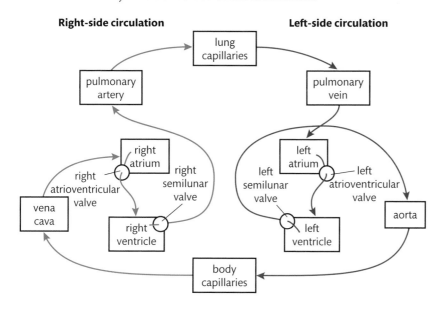

Figure 10.11 A flowchart showing the circulation pattern. Red arrows indicate oxygenated blood and blue arrows indicate deoxygenated blood.

Sometimes a faulty heart valve allows some blood to 'backflow'. The resulting sound when heard through a stethoscope is often described as a 'squishing' sound and is known as a heart murmur.

The sounds of the heart

When you listen directly to the heart using a stethoscope, you can hear a rhythmic set of sounds that most people describe as a series of 'lub dub' sounds. Each 'lub dub' is the sound of one cardiac cycle (one heart beat) and, for the most part, is the sound of the heart valves closing. Remember that the right and left sides of the heart are working in unison, therefore there are only two heart sounds even though there are four heart valves. The atrioventricular valves closing are heard as one sound, 'lub', and the two semilunar valves closing are heard as a second sound, 'dub'. Following these two sounds is a silence before the cycle is repeated.

Myogenic control of heart rate

If you are at your resting heart rate, your heart itself is controlling the frequency and internal timing of the events of each cardiac cycle. This is called myogenic control. Heart muscle is unusual in that it does not need nervous stimulation to contract. The only control needed from the nervous system is when the heart needs to change its rate of contraction because of increased body activity. The mass of tissue that acts as the living pacemaker for the heart is known as the sinoatrial (SA) node. This node of cells is located in the upper wall of the right atrium, close to where the superior vena cava enters.

Artificial heart valves can be surgically implanted to replace damaged natural valves. Artificial and natural valves open and close depending on which side of the valve has the higher blood pressure. The type of replacement valve shown is known as a ball-and-cage design.

The SA node is a group of modified cardiac muscle cells that are capable of generating action potentials at a regular frequency. If your myogenic heart rate is 72 beats min^{-1}, your SA node is generating an action potential every 0.8 seconds. The action potentials from the SA node spread out nearly instantaneously and result in the thin-walled atria undergoing systole. The SA node action potential also reaches a group of cells known as the atrioventricular (AV) node. This node is located in the lower wall of the right atrium, in the septum or partition between the right and left atria.

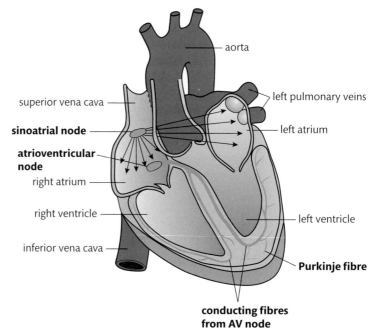

Figure 10.12 This drawing of the human heart shows you the location of the SA node, AV node, and the conducting fibres spreading out through the ventricles from the AV node. The black arrows represent action potentials from the SA node. Cardiac muscle cells are very good at conducting these action potentials through the gap junctions within the intercalated discs that join the cells together. There is a time delay before the AV node sends out action potentials through the conducting fibres that run down the septum between the two ventricles and then to various branches (called Purkinje fibres).

When you learn about a mechanism such as the timing of the SA node and the delay before the AV node sends an impulse, think about why the mechanism works in the way that it does. In other words, 'what is the benefit?' In this case, the benefit is to allow the atria time to send the blood down to the ventricles before the AV node 'fires'. This then results in the ventricles contracting and the atrioventricular valves closing, allowing the blood to exit the heart through the semilunar valves.

The AV node receives the action potential coming from the SA node and delays for approximately 0.1 second. The AV node then sends out its own action potentials that spread out to both ventricles. As you learned earlier, the walls of the ventricles are much thicker muscle than the walls of the atria. In order to get the action potentials to reach all of the muscle cells in the ventricles efficiently, there is a system of conducting fibres that begin at the AV node and then travel down the septum between the two ventricles (see Figure 10.12). At various points these conducting fibres have branches called Purkinje fibres that spread out into the thick cardiac muscle tissue of the ventricles. Finally, the gap junctions within the intercalated discs of the cardiac muscle cells finish conducting the impulse and both ventricles undergo systole simultaneously.

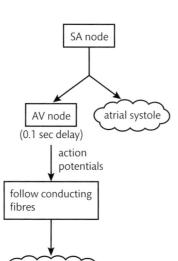

Figure 10.13 A flowchart of the events associated with one heart beat or one cardiac cycle.

Mapping the cardiac cycle to a normal ECG trace

An electrocardiogram (ECG) is a graph plotted in real time, with electrical activity (from the SA and AV nodes) plotted on the *y*-axis and time on the *x*-axis. Electrical leads are placed in a variety of places on the skin in order to measure the small voltage given off by these two nodes of the heart. Every repeating pattern on an ECG is a representation of one cardiac cycle. In the previous section you learned that a cardiac cycle is initiated by impulses given off by the SA node. This is where we will begin our 'mapping'.

How to 'read' a 'normal' ECG trace (Figure 10.14).

- P wave: this part shows the voltage given off by the SA node, thus it marks atrial systole.
- Point Q: this is the point at which the AV node sends its impulse.
- QRS complex: this is where the impulse from the AV node spreads down the conducting fibres and out to the Purkinje fibres within the ventricles, thus this shows the ventricular systole.
- T wave: the AV node is repolarizing (ions are returning to the resting potential), getting ready to send the next set of impulses for the next cardiac cycle.

It is important to be aware of the following.

- The SA node also has to repolarize, but the electrical activity is hidden 'behind' the QRS complex.
- An ECG clearly shows the delay between the firing of the SA node and the firing of the AV node. This shows the time separation between the systolic contractions of the atria and ventricles.

Common heart problems and their treatments

The heart is one of the hardest working organs in the body. The only rest that it gets is during the period within the cardiac cycle when any one chamber is not undergoing systole. It is also an organ that cannot stop working for any length of time. Many heart conditions have been studied, and there are now very effective treatments for several of those conditions. We will take a look at some of those conditions and treatments.

Use of artificial pacemakers to regulate heart rate

An artificial pacemaker is a small battery-operated device that is implanted under the skin, typically in the upper chest area. The pacemaker does what the name implies, which is to set the heart rate in the same way that a healthy SA node does naturally. The device is connected to one or more wires (leads) that are threaded into a blood vessel that leads directly into the interior of the heart. The placement of the lead(s) is

Individual cardiac muscle cells grown in a Petri dish contract in an independent rhythm. When heart muscle cells touch each other, they synchronize their contractions. The SA and AV nodes take advantage of this natural ability and provide the timing necessary to synchronize the entire heart.

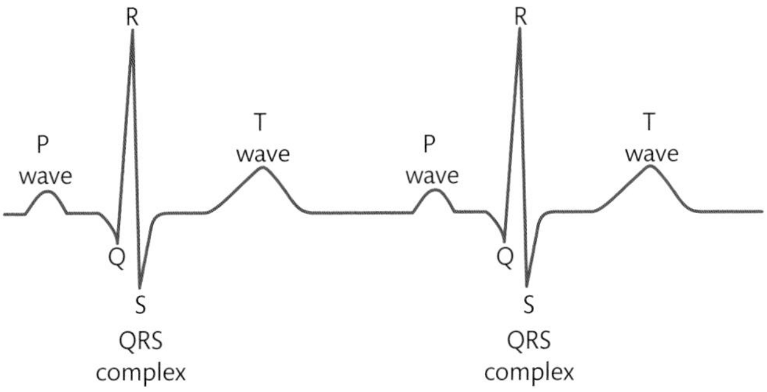

Figure 10.14 An electrical trace of two cardiac cycles (note the repetition from left to right side). Think of this as a graph with electrical activity (measured in millivolts) plotted on the *y*-axis and time plotted on the *x*-axis.

To learn more about the heart and ECG traces, go to the hotlinks site, search for the title or ISBN, and click on Chapter 10: Section D.4.

dependent on the patient's heart problem and how many leads are being placed. The battery-operated device gives off a very small electrical shock at regular intervals, each shock triggering a cardiac cycle. Pacemakers can be used for patients with slow heart rates, fast heart rates, irregular heartbeats, and a host of other problems. The battery life of pacemakers is currently on average 7 years. Patients typically receive an entire new pacemaker when the need arises to ensure that their current pacemaker is still well within the estimated battery life.

Use of defibrillation devices to treat life-threatening heart conditions

A person suffering from a 'heart attack' may well be suffering from a heart that has stopped (cardiac arrest) or a heart that is no longer in sequence with the set of electrical impulses typical of a cardiac cycle (a condition called arrhythmia). In either case, blood is not being pumped effectively to organs and tissues that are demanding oxygen. Defibrillation is a process carried out using a device that delivers an electric shock to the heart and resets the electrical signals starting with the SA node. When successful, the heart will continue beating on its own once the electrical shock has been delivered.

In recent years, small portable defibrillators have become available and are routinely carried by all medical first responders. These portable defibrillators are called automated external defibrillators (AEDs). It is becoming routine for AEDs to be located in many areas where large numbers of people are routinely found, such as shopping centres, sports stadiums, gymnasiums, etc. AEDs found in these areas are designed for anyone to use because they have audible instructions and the components are very easy to handle.

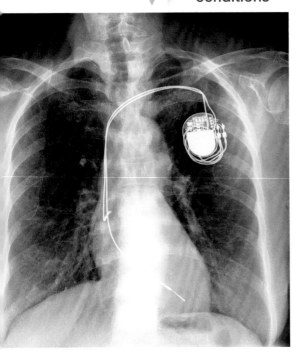

A coloured X-ray of the chest of a patient with a dual-lead artificial pacemaker. One lead extends into the right atrium and the other into the right ventricle.

Thrombosis

The term thrombosis refers to the condition when a clot (thrombus) forms within a blood vessel. Some people suffer from a condition called deep vein thrombosis (DVT), where a thrombus develops in one of the larger veins, usually in a leg. Often this occurs when a person has been sitting down for a long period of time, perhaps while travelling on a plane or in a car. The big danger with DVT is that all or a portion of the clot breaks loose and travels to a smaller vein, where a total blockage could occur. This is especially dangerous when the travelling clot lodges in a vein within a lung. DVT is often treated with anticoagulant medications. These are often called blood thinners, but they do not actually 'thin' the blood. Anticoagulants simply help prevent blood clotting from occurring as quickly.

Another form of thrombosis is called coronary thrombosis. Heart muscle needs a rich supply of oxygenated blood to maintain its non-stop action. Heart muscle is supplied with oxygen-rich blood by blood vessels known as coronary arteries. Over time a substance called plaque can build up in one or more of these coronary arteries to the point where a substantial narrowing of the lumen (inside) of the artery occurs. This can be a problem in itself, but the problems can be increased if a thrombus becomes lodged in the reduced lumen. This can easily lead to a myocardial infarction (heart attack).

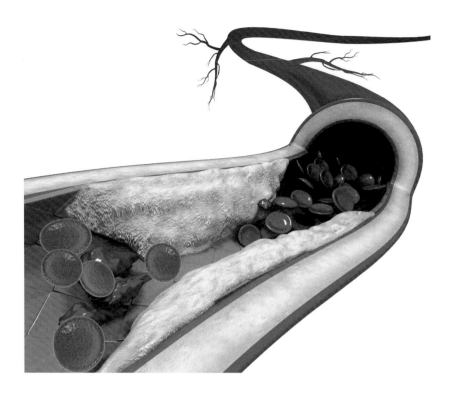

TOK

The classic heart symbol has become synonymous with 'love'. There are many ideas about how this association was made. One idea is that, in the 7th century BC, in a Greek and Roman city called Cyrene, the plant known as silphium was used as a form of birth control. The seedpod of the silphium plant has the classic heart shape that we recognize today.

Artwork showing an artery narrowed by plaque build-up over many years. If this blood vessel is feeding oxygenated blood to oxygen-demanding tissue like the cardiac muscle of the heart, a myocardial infarction could result.

Hypertension

Hypertension is higher than 'normal' blood pressure. There is no single blood pressure value that can be used to determine the norm, as a person's blood pressure can be highly variable depending on many factors. Because hypertension typically develops over a period of years, it is best to monitor your blood pressure regularly and look for any increasing trend. Blood pressure measures the force of the blood pushing outwards on the wall of the arteries. The more blood your heart pumps, and the narrower your arteries are, the higher your blood pressure. Loss of elasticity and a build-up of plaque in arteries are prime contributors to hypertension. Even though no single blood pressure reading can be considered to be the norm, the American Heart Association has released ranges of blood pressure values that can be used for advice on cardiovascular health (see Table 10.4). Let's look at what blood pressure is and how it is measured. A blood pressure reading is actually two values, one called the systolic pressure and the other called the diastolic pressure. A typical example might be:

Your blood pressure is typically measured each time you visit the doctor. Many people also monitor their own blood pressure at home with the use of digital sphygmomanometers. After applying the pressure cuff to the upper arm and inflating the cuff, the systolic and diastolic pressures are given by a digital readout.

115 (systolic)

---

68 (diastolic)

These values are read as 115 over 68 (both in mm of Hg).

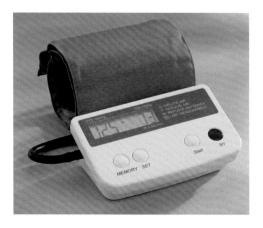

A digital sphygmomanometer designed for home monitoring of blood pressure.

- Systolic pressure: the top number measures the pressure in the arteries when the heart beats (when the heart muscle contracts).
- Diastolic pressure: the bottom number measures the pressure in the arteries when the heart muscle is resting and refilling with blood.

Table 10.4 The American Heart Association has released the following blood pressure ranges for guidance when interpreting blood pressure readings

Blood pressure category	Systolic mm Hg (upper number)		Diastolic mm Hg (lower number)
Normal	Less than 120	and	Less than 80
Prehypertension	120–139	or	80–89
High blood pressure (hypertension) stage 1	140–159	or	90–99
High blood pressure (hypertension) stage 2	160 or higher	or	100 or higher
Hypertensive crisis (emergency care needed)	Higher than 180	or	Higher than 110

Risk factors affecting coronary heart disease

Coronary heart disease (CHD) is the term used for the slow progression of plaque build-up in arteries and the corresponding problems that can result. Individuals can have CHD for many years without any obvious symptoms, because the early stages do not have noticeable symptoms. Not everyone builds up plaque in their arteries at the same rate. The factors that determine plaque build-up, and thus the eventual chances of heart-related problems, fall into two main categories: those that cannot be controlled or avoided, and those that can.

Most people will have to cope with at least some of the risk factors of CHD during their working life. It is very difficult to measure the effects of any one factor and its impact on the incidence of CHD. Almost all factors have an impact on one or more other factors. For instance:

- people who are overweight often have problems with high blood pressure and cholesterol
- a sedentary lifestyle may lead to obesity
- stress may lead to smoking and overeating, and thus high blood pressure, cholesterol problems, etc.

Researchers who attempt to isolate any one factor and study that factor's impact on CHD must take into account the cascading effect of one factor affecting another, making this type of study open to many interpretations.

Worked example

Epidemiology is defined as the branch of medicine that deals with the incidence, distribution, and possible control of diseases and other factors relating to health. Epidemiological data can be used to help individuals and societies make good choices concerning their own health. Below you will find a brief synopsis of some epidemiological data concerning the incidence of CHD in the UK.

- Coronary heart disease is the most common cause of death in the UK.
- Death rates from CHD have fallen by 45% for people under 65 years of age in the last 10 years.
- The incidence of CHD increases with increasing age.

- The incidence of CHD is higher in men, but is the leading cause of death in women as well.
- Smokers have a 60% higher incidence of mortality as a result of CHD than non-smokers.
- Exposure to passive smoking increases the risk of CHD by 25%.
- Diets high in saturated fat, sodium, and sugar increase the risk of CHD.
- Diets high in complex carbohydrates, fruits, and vegetables decrease the risk of CHD.
- Eating trans-fatty acids (see Section 2.3) increases the risk of CHD.
- Physical activity reduces the risk of CHD.
- High blood pressure may double the risk of mortality from CHD.
- Abnormal blood lipid levels significantly increase the risk of mortality from CHD.
- Obesity significantly increases the risk of mortality from CHD.
- Men with type II diabetes have as much as a four-fold risk of CHD compared with men without type II diabetes; women with type II diabetes have as much as a five-fold risk of CHD compared with women without type II diabetes.
- Ethnicity has a significant impact on CHD risk. People from India, Pakistan, Bangladesh, and Sri Lanka living in the UK have a 50% higher incidence of mortality from CHD compared with other ethnic groups.
- First-generation relatives of patients who have suffered a heart attack have double the risk of CHD compared with those whose parents did not suffer a heart attack.

After reading through this information, create a list of bullet points that offer advice to people to help them make good lifestyle choices in order to reduce their chances of developing CHD. Notice that some of the information given cannot be acted upon by an individual (e.g. age/gender/ethnic background/family history) and so this information cannot be used to help someone follow a healthy lifestyle, although it can make them aware of the importance of those factors that can be controlled.

Solution

In order to lead a healthy lifestyle, specifically designed to minimize the risk of CHD:

- do not smoke or be in an area where cigarette smoke is present
- eat a healthy diet minimizing saturated fats, trans-fats, salt, and sugar, while increasing your intake of fruits, vegetables, and complex carbohydrates
- attempt a reasonable amount of physical activity as often as possible
- attempt to lower high blood pressure by natural means or, if necessary, by taking prescription medicines
- keep cholesterol and other blood lipids in a normal range by eating a healthy diet and/or taking prescription medications
- make lifestyle choices that will lead to weight loss, if necessary
- avoid lifestyle choices that could lead to type II diabetes, or control the disease as much as possible.

Section summary

- Cardiac muscle cells electrically communicate with each other efficiently with the use of cell-to-cell connections called intercalated discs, through which openings called gap junctions permit an electrical signal to pass from cell to cell.
- The electrical signal from the sinoatrial node (the heart's pacemaker) spreads throughout the cardiac muscle cells of the atria, but cannot spread directly to the cardiac muscle cells of the ventricles.
- The electrical signal from the sinoatrial node is received by the atrioventricular node, which then delays a very short period of time before sending out its own electrical signal to the ventricles.
- The delay permits atrial systole to be completed before the increase in pressure as a result of the earlier ventricular systole closes the valves between the atria and ventricles (atrioventricular valves).
- The thick muscular tissue of the ventricles requires nerve fibres to conduct an impulse efficiently and quickly throughout the ventricles to ensure a unified ventricular systole.
- The sounds of the heart heard through a stethoscope are caused by the closing of two sets of valves, first the atrioventricular valves and then the semilunar valves.

Exercises

13 Artificial hearts and heart valves have been designed and surgically implanted into both test animals and humans. How do the valves within these artificial devices 'know' when it is time to close and open?

14 An ECG is a graph showing the electrical activity of the heart. The voltage can be traced back to the SA node and the AV node. When a person exercises and thus increases his or her heart rate, what is the expected change in a subsequent ECG?

15 Why is there a delay between the signal from the SA node and the signal from the AV node within one cardiac cycle?

16 Why are heart cells so efficient at passing an electrical signal from cell to cell?

Practice Questions

1 (a) Define the term nutrient. (1)

(b) Discuss the relationship between nutrition and rickets. (3)

(Total 4 marks)

2 Osteoporosis is a major health problem for many post-menopausal women. As the ovaries reduce their secretion of oestrogen, calcium is gradually lost from bones, weakening them and increasing the chance of fractures. To test whether diet influences the rate of calcium loss, ovaries were removed from groups of female rats and the rats were then either fed a control diet or the same diet with 1 g of a supplementary food per day. The rate at which the rats excreted calcium was measured. The ratio of calcium loss between the control rats and the rats that were given a supplementary food was calculated.

$$\left(\text{ratio} = \frac{\text{loss with supplementary food}}{\text{loss in control rats}} \right)$$

The results are shown in the graph on page 529.

(a) (i) Identify which supplementary food was most effective in reducing calcium loss. (1)

(ii) Identify which supplementary food was least effective in reducing calcium loss. (1)

(b) Among the ten foods shown in the graph, seven are plant products (vegetables) and three are animal products. Discuss whether the plant or the animal products were more effective at reducing calcium loss. (3)

(c) Suggest a trial, based on the results shown in the graph, that could be done to try to reduce osteoporosis in humans. (3)

(Total 8 marks)

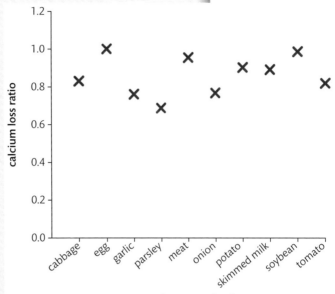

Nutrition: Effect of vegetables on bone metabolism *Nature*, 401, 23 September, pp. 343–344 (Roman C. Muhlbauer and Feng Li 1999), Copyright 1999. Reprinted by permission from Macmillan Publishers Ltd.

3 A major requirement of the body is to eliminate carbon dioxide (CO_2). In the body, carbon dioxide exists in three forms: dissolved CO_2, bound as the bicarbonate ion, and bound to proteins (e.g. haemoglobin in red blood cells or plasma proteins). The relative contribution of each of these forms to overall CO_2 transport varies considerably depending on activity, as shown in the table below.

CO_2 Transport in blood plasma at rest and during exercise

Form of transport	Arterial	Rest Venous	Exercise Venous
	mmol l⁻¹ blood	mmol l⁻¹ blood	mmol l⁻¹ blood
Dissolved CO_2	0.68	0.78	1.32
Bicarbonate ion	13.52	14.51	14.66
CO_2 bound to protein	0.3	0.3	0.24
Total CO_2 in plasma	14.50	15.59	16.22
pH of blood	7.4	7.37	7.14

Adapted from Geers and Gros 2000, Tab. 1 ©The American Physiological Society (APS). All rights reserved.

(a) Calculate the percentage of CO_2 found as bicarbonate ions in the plasma of venous blood at rest. (1)

(b) (i) Compare the changes in total CO_2 content in the venous plasma due to exercise. (1)

(ii) Identify which form of CO_2 transport shows the greatest increase due to exercise. (1)

(Total 3 marks)

4 Describe the process of erythrocyte and haemoglobin breakdown in the liver.

(Total 4 marks)

Theory of knowledge

An astronomer, a physicist, and a mathematician are on a train going to a conference in Edinburgh. Out of the window, they see a solitary black sheep.

Astronomer: That's interesting, sheep in Scotland are black.

Physicist: It would be more prudent to say that *some* of the sheep in Scotland are black.

Mathematician: To be more precise, we can say that in Scotland there exists at least one field in which there is at least one sheep, which is black on at least one side.

What does this story reveal about scientific observations, hypotheses, and conclusions? What does it reveal about the nature of each of the disciplines represented?

Is biology less exact than physics or mathematics? If there had been a biologist on board the train, what would he or she have said about the sheep?

What is this chapter all about?

This chapter has some ideas, quotes, anecdotes, case studies, and many unanswered questions, but very little factual information. Why? Because with Theory of knowledge (TOK), you are the knower. This concept should stimulate your brain. It should be exciting to think that you are the expert. You have had a decade or more of formal education, and even more years of life experience, giving you ideas in the form of knowledge, beliefs, and opinions.

You are the knower.

On the other hand, it is a bit intimidating to think that there are some things that no one will ever know the answer to. You are encouraged to explore, develop, and share your views, as well as actively seek the views of your classmates.

On the right track?

How will you know if you are answering TOK questions in the 'right' way, as the answers are not given in this book or by your teacher? Here are two guidelines to consider.

- If you think the question has a quick, simple answer, such as 'yes' or 'no', you can be pretty sure that you are not treating it like a TOK question. If you think the answer has many sides to it, is a debatable area, or leads to further questions, you are probably on the right track.

- Ask yourself, 'Am I pushing myself a little bit outside my comfort zone and exploring other ways of seeing an issue?' If so, you are on your way to scratching through the surface and getting to the interesting issues. That is the stuff of intellectual stimulation and growth. That is one of the challenges of the IB programme in general and TOK in particular.

Debates

To get your brain warmed up, consider the following two statements about the nature of all human beings on Earth.

A: We are all the same.

B: We are all different.

Use your biological knowledge to support or refute these two claims. Choose one, and try to imagine someone saying to you, 'That's not true! How can you say that?' How would you respond to that person? (Keep it polite, of course.)

Now try these two statements.

X: Biology is a collection of facts about nature.

Y: Biology is a system of exploring the natural world.

Use your critical thinking. Critical thinking is characterized by reflective inquiry, analysis, and judgement. Ask yourself, 'Should I believe this?' 'Am I on the right track?' 'How reliable is this information?' In short, you are deciding whether or not you should accept something as valid or not. Again, if you think it is an easy, quick decision, then you are not treating the question in the way that you should.

Critical thinking: Is this statement valid? What is its source? Is the person who said it a reliable person? Do they have a bias that I should know about? Bias is a good term to know in TOK. It refers to a type of prejudice whereby a person gives an unfair preference to one opinion over another, rather than giving a balanced argument.

More debates

Coming back to the pairs of statements above, what would lead someone to believe one or the other statement? In each pair, could it be possible that both statements are valid? Or are they mutually exclusive? What about the following two statements?

- There is only one scientific method that is universal throughout the world: only by following the same method can scientists reach the same results and conclusions.
- Different scientists and different cultures in different regions of the world use different versions of the scientific method to obtain valid results and conclusions.

The TOK framework

One of the most important skills students are asked to develop in the IB is analysis. The TOK framework is a useful tool for analysing knowledge issues. When analysing a particular scenario, students are not asked

A knowledge framework applied to the area of knowledge of the natural sciences.

Circular diagram with "Natural Sciences" at center surrounded by: scope, motivation, and applications; specific terminology and concepts; methods used to produce knowledge; key historical developments; interaction with personal knowledge.

to address each of the five points below exhaustively, but this framework can be a good place to start.

Try it out on the example of the scientists on the train looking at the sheep. There may be some aspects of the framework that apply nicely to the sheep example, and others that do not fit well, but give it a try. Throughout this chapter there are a certain number of case studies; as good practice, it is worth analysing some of them based on the knowledge framework.

Nature of science(s)

> All science is either physics or stamp collecting.
> Ernest Rutherford

What did Rutherford mean by the above? Is he justified in saying that chemistry, biology, or other branches of science, are only there to catalogue and classify phenomena in nature? What does his statement imply about the degree of prestige or respect each scientific discipline enjoys? Is it possible to understand all sciences by studying one of them?

Ernest Rutherford was a physicist: you probably identified the bias he had from his quote!

What is knowledge?

Below are some knowledge issues/knowledge questions to consider.

• What counts as knowledge in biology?
• How does biological knowledge grow?
• What are the limits of knowledge?
• Who owns knowledge?
• What is the value of knowledge?
• What are the implications of having or not having knowledge?

• Is there one way that is best for acquiring knowledge?
• Where is knowledge? Is it a 'thing' that resides somewhere: is it in books, in your head, in a computer database?

Look at the following images. Use the list of questions above and your critical thinking to evaluate whether some or all of these are valid as scientific knowledge. For example, does mythology count as scientific knowledge?

Mythology

Electronically stored data

A biology diploma

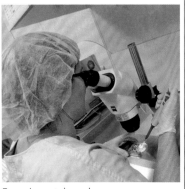

Experimental work

Ancient belief systems

Websites and email systems

Student discussions

Religious texts

Libraries

Copernicus is the scientist who mathematically showed that the Earth goes around the Sun, and not the other way round. This is an example of a paradigm shift, another good term to know in TOK. A paradigm shift is a fundamental change in the way we see or understand something.

> **"** To know that we know what we know, and to know that we do not know what we do not know, that is true knowledge. **"**
> Copernicus

How do we know?

Here is an example of scientific knowledge in biology: 'The organelle in a plant cell that is responsible for photosynthesis is the chloroplast.'

How could you verify that? How can you be sure that there is not another part of the cell that photosynthesizes? Is it a falsifiable idea? Such questions are second-order questions. They are not about the thing we want to know, they are about how we know it. Such knowledge questions are on a different level.

Epistemology is the study of the theory of knowledge and it raises the question: 'How do we know what we know?'

Case study 1 Life on Mars?

This is not a simple question. Despite several visits by space probes, no conclusive evidence has been discovered on Mars that can lead scientists to declare that there is life on its surface. And yet the search continues. The most compelling evidence that there was once life on Mars comes from a meteorite found in Antarctica that The National Aeronautics and Space Administration (NASA) claims came from Mars and contains fossils of bacteria.

If you apply your critical thinking to this, some knowledge questions should pop into your mind. How do we know that this chunk of rock is really from Mars? How did it get to Earth? How does NASA know that the 'fossils' are from bacteria? Could they have been formed from non-living chemical reactions? How important are such discoveries in ensuring funding for future missions?

Is NASA planning to collect more fossils from Mars directly, and bring them back to Earth to study? Could there still be colonies of bacteria living on Mars today, or is life extinct on the red planet?

From this specific example, two more general questions arise. Is it possible to really 'know' the truth? Is information absolute or relative?

Are you an empiricist or a rationalist?

Empiricism = the belief that our senses allow us to acquire knowledge. Rationalism = the belief that reason allows us to acquire knowledge.

Be careful: critical thinking does not mean you criticize everything. It means you are aware of questions of validity. You are not being negative, you are just being inquisitive and prudent.

Ways of knowing

In the list of TOK ways of knowing listed to the right, are there some that are better suited to the natural sciences than others? Are there any that can be completely eliminated from the list when dealing with the natural sciences? What about ones that are absolutely necessary?

Ways of knowing:

- language
- sense
- perception
- emotion
- reason
- imagination
- faith
- intuition
- memory.

Case study 2 Babies born on a full moon

Ask an experienced midwife 'Are more babies born on a night when there is a full moon?' and the chances are pretty good she will say yes. You would have no reason to challenge her: she is the expert. She is an eyewitness to this phenomenon.

But knowledge questions arise. Where is she getting her information? How does she know? Is it just a feeling, an intuition, a belief? Or is this knowledge claim based on carefully analysed statistics comparing birth numbers with a lunar calendar?

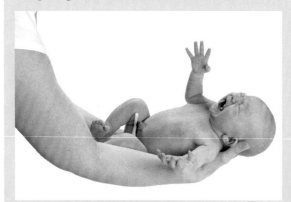

As it turns out, the statistics do not support this knowledge claim. The evidence from maternity ward numbers does not show a correlation between births and the full moon. So what is going on? Is the midwife lying? The chances are she is the victim of something we all are susceptible to: confirmation bias. Confirmation bias happens when we only remember the times when something confirmed our beliefs, and ignore the times when something refuted our beliefs. In the case of the midwife, on a busy night she might look out the window, see a full moon, and cry out to her colleagues, 'See? I was right! More babies on nights when there is a full moon.' Two weeks later, on another busy night, she looks out the window and what does she see? No moon at all because, it's the new moon. It is unlikely that she will now go around to all her colleagues and say 'Sorry, I was wrong: it's a busy night and yet there is no full moon.' It is more likely that she will forget this negative result and only remember the positive results, thereby showing a bias for confirmation.

As an afterthought: should we tell her she's wrong? It could be argued that she's not hurting anyone and that it's lots of fun to have these sayings in our culture. Having shared beliefs unites people and strengthens a sense of community and belonging. Is it better to be right or to belong?

Catching a cold

Despite the biological evidence that colds are caused by viral infections, many people believe that you can catch cold from being exposed to low temperatures or changes in humidity.

Who is right? Where does the truth lie? For something to be considered 'true', does it have to be formally proven using a scientific method? Is a profound conviction that something is true good enough to make it valid? If one person believes that something is true, does that make it true or does there have to be a certain number of believers before the idea can be considered true?

Phrenology

The pseudo-science of phrenology claimed that the shape of a person's skull, and the bumps and indentations on it, determined a person's intelligence, personality, and talents. More controversially, it was used by some to justify the superiority or inferiority of 'races' of humans.

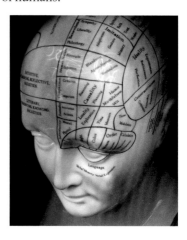

How do you think it was demonstrated that the 'laws' of phrenology were not, after all, scientifically valid?

Tongue map

As students and teachers, what do we claim to know about biology? Are we justified in making such claims? How?

What experiences have you had that give you insight concerning these issues? Consider the following example.

For decades, the idea of a 'tongue map' (that certain zones of the tongue relate to certain tastes) was propagated by biology textbooks, and taste-test investigations were suggested as lab work for students. It has since been shown that all parts of the tongue can taste sweet, sour, bitter, and salty.

> " There must be no barriers for freedom of inquiry. There is no place for dogma in science. The scientist is free, and must be free to ask any question, to doubt any assertion, to seek for any evidence, to correct any errors. "
>
> Robert Oppenheimer
> Barnett 1949

Art and imagination

Is there a place for imagination and creativity in science? Are there any parallels between biology and art? Could it be argued, that just as an artist sees things in his or her own way, so a scientist sees things in his or her own way? Or, on the contrary, are science and art diametrically opposed ways of interpreting nature?

Case study 3 Spirit/soul

In 1907, Dr Duncan MacDougall conducted experiments to determine whether or not people lost mass after death. His results seemed to suggest that they did, and led him to the conclusion that the human soul weighed 21 g. Since his experiments (some of which did not give conclusive results) were done with scales of questionable accuracy and he had only six subjects, his conclusions are widely criticized and are not taken seriously by the scientific community today.

Will questions about souls always remain beyond the capabilities of science to investigate or verify? Why hasn't anyone repeated this experiment in over a century? What do you think the reaction of the religious community would be if scientists repeated MacDougall's experiment?

Decisions, decisions …

Should experiments be performed to answer fundamental questions, or should they only be done if they have a useful application in our everyday lives?

Who should decide which research pursuits are of the most value? Who should decide on how funding is distributed, or the prioritizing of the use of laboratory space and resources? Universities? Governments? Committees of scientists? Taxpayers?

Should research about a tropical disease such as malaria be paid for by tax money from non-tropical countries?

Is there an end?

Is scientific knowledge progressive? Has it always grown? Imagine a graph with scientific knowledge on the y-axis and time on the x-axis. How would you draw the graph? Would it be a curve or would it be linear? Is it always increasing? What units would you use? Could the graph ever go down: in other words could scientific knowledge ever be lost (maybe because of war, a laboratory burns down, a famous scientist dies)?

Could there ever be an end to science? If there was an end, what would be the consequences?

> " Science knows no country, because knowledge belongs to humanity, and is the torch which illuminates the world. "
>
> Louis Pasteur

Doctor, which drug treatment is best for me?

How do doctors know which medication is the best for their patients? One way is for them to keep up with the latest breakthroughs and developments published in scientific and medical journals. Doctors put their faith in these prestigious peer-reviewed journals and, because they do not have the time or the budget to do all the clinical trials themselves, they trust that the researchers doing the work are following sound practice. The problem is, a large percentage of the studies are being funded by the companies who make the drugs and, according to epidemiologist Dr Ben Goldacre's 2012 book *Bad Pharma*, it is common practice in the pharmaceutical industry to use a wide variety of tricks and manipulations to make a new drug look good in clinical trials. One trick goes something like this: a company will set up a 2-year trial to test a new drug and then, after only 6 months, it decides to stop the trial and publish the data because the numbers show that its drug is performing well. This is advantageous to the company because it saves money (trials are very costly), and it reduces the chances that participants develop side-effects or show negative results after 6 months. Doctors reading about the clinical trials will never be informed, however, that the trials were stopped early. Another trick is to not report in the published study any participants who dropped out of the trial because they felt ill from side-effects. That way, by only mentioning the people who stayed in the study, they can report that, at the end of the trial, none of the participants complained of any major side-effects. In short, Goldacre says that the studies being published are not showing all the data and that, in order for doctors to decide whether a drug is safe to prescribe, they need to see both the positive and the negative results. What knowledge issues does Goldacre's book raise about the highly competitive $600 billion pharmaceutical industry? Do the practices he denounces sound like the kinds of things your biology teacher encourages you to do in your lab investigations? If you were a scientist working at one of these companies, and you decided to complain and point out that some of the trials seemed unfair, what do you think your boss's reaction would be? If a company decided to publish the positive as well as the negative results of its drug trials, what do you think might happen to the sales of their drugs? Lastly, as doctors find out more and more of the practices exposed, what will happen to their faith in the data presented by the medical journals? What kind of critical thinking or TOK questions should they pose when they pick up a medical journal and read about the latest breakthroughs in drug research?

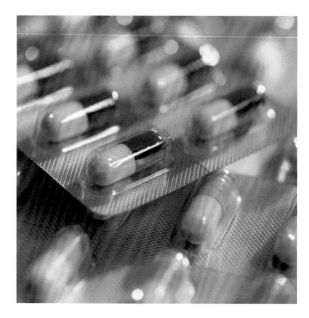

The placebo effect

One of the ways that scientists test a drug is to compare it with a placebo. A placebo is a pill that contains no active ingredients: it is often just a sugar pill. To find out if a new drug is effective, one group of volunteers in a study is given the new drug and another group is given a placebo. Neither group knows whether it is taking an active pill or a placebo. Surprisingly, even in the group taking the placebo, there are usually patients who report that they feel better. This is called the placebo effect.

Researchers studying the placebo effect have observed that the following things have a positive influence on how effective the patients thought the pill was:

- the doctor was wearing a white lab coat
- there were diplomas on the wall in the doctor's office
- the doctor sat down and listened attentively to the patient.

The medical community is essentially unanimous on the validity and power of the placebo effect, and yet the mechanism of how it works is poorly understood. For example, astounding as it may sound, placebos seem to have an effect even when people are told that they are receiving a placebo. Some participants still feel better, even when they are conscious that they have not been given any active drugs.

Inhabitants of industrialized countries often scoff at tales of traditional medicine men and healers in indigenous peoples. And yet, those same critics may very well accept the effectiveness of the placebo effect: an effect that appears to be produced essentially by ritual. What knowledge issues are raised by this puzzling effect? What does it say about the limits of modern medicine?

Models

The double-helix shape for DNA, and the fluid mosaic membrane model, are examples of models that were created in order to explain observed phenomena. Are such models just inventions? If so, how is it that they can be used to make predictions or explain natural phenomena?

Look at the false-colour electron micrograph (above right). The magnification and resolution are not good enough to see how the integral or transmembrane proteins and cholesterol are arranged in the membrane, but chemical tests reveal that they are there. This is why the fluid mosaic model was introduced. It is a proposed explanation for how the various components of

the membrane are arranged. If the model successfully fits the observed phenomena, does that validate it as being true?

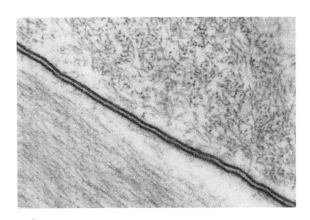

The double line in the centre of this photomicrograph shows the phospholipid bilayer of a membrane.

> " All models are wrong, but some are useful. "
> George E. P. Box (innovator in statistical analysis)
> Box and Draper, 1987. Copyright © 1987 by John Wiley & Sons, Inc.

Which of the following conceptual drawings best represent the interconnections between the ways of knowing and areas of knowledge? In what ways might these metaphors be useful?

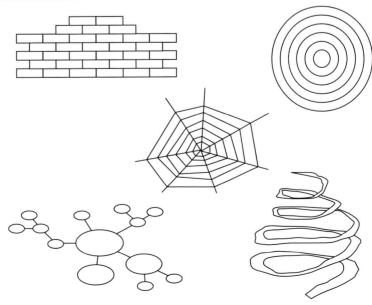

Who's right?

Among all the points of view that are available to you in the classroom, at home, in the media, on websites, how do you know which one is right?

Religion in an age of science

In what ways could someone's cultural or religious background influence his or her acceptance of certain scientific theories?

There was a time when scientists hesitated to publish their works out of fear of the church. Have the tables turned? Are there religious writers who fear scientific criticism if they publish their ideas?

If a student writes on an IB exam that he or she refuses to answer the questions about evolution by natural selection because of his or her religious beliefs, should he or she get any marks?

In 1663, the Roman Inquisition condemned Galileo for defending the idea that the planet Earth goes around the Sun and he remained imprisoned for nearly a decade before he died. In 2010, the Catholic Church formally apologized for Galileo's condemnation.

Ockham's razor

Simply put, the principle of Ockham's razor states that, all other things being equal, the simplest explanation should be preferred. This is reflected in the idea of parsimony: seeking out the least convoluted solution. Scientists take this principle very seriously and yet some aspects of science seem to be extremely complex. Is there a conflict here?

Limits of perception

> “ You cannot speak of the ocean to a well frog … ”
>
> Chuang Tzu Taoist text (written more than 2000 years ago)

Can we here on Earth possibly know of worlds beyond our own? Can we possibly know what the distant past was like, or what the distant future will hold? Or are we like a frog at the bottom of a well trying to understand what the ocean might be like?

The eye is not a camera

A fun activity to do in a classroom is to have someone unknown to the students barge in during a lesson, say something, take something off the teacher's desk, and leave, after which the teacher asks each student to take out a sheet of paper and write down a description of the person, and what he or she said and did. The students' observations are often astounding in their diversity, and the activity demonstrates how human perception is notoriously bad at picking up crucial details, and notoriously good at filling in missing information. 'The eye is not a camera' is a good example of a knowledge claim that can be explored and discussed after such an observation activity.

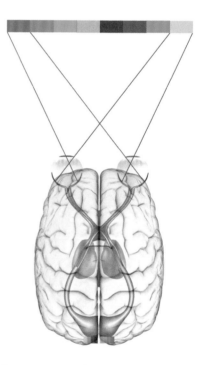

Although we associate the eyes with vision, truly seeing something means interpreting the signals that arrive at photoreceptors in the eyes. This interpretation is done in the brain, so in fact, do we see with our eyes or our brain?

Another knowledge claim on this theme also relates to eyewitnesses: 'all memories are reconstructed memories.' Have you ever had a story in your family that was told time and time again for years, and then one day you found out that the event in question never actually happened? And yet, you could swear that you can remember the event clearly. Or have you ever watched a video recording of something you experienced and thought to yourself, 'That's funny, I don't remember it being like that: my memory of that event is very different'. Such examples put into question the validity of eyewitnesses' testimonies in a court of law. Given that we ourselves know that our memories and observations can trick us, should we trust an eyewitness's account as irrefutable evidence during a trial? Are such testimonies reliable enough to put defendants in jail or to sentence them to death? This theme is explored well in Syndey Lumet's 1957 film *Twelve Angry Men*.

We were wrong, here's the real story …

In palaeontology, it seems that every time a new hominid fossil is dug up, we have to redraw the human family tree. If you search the internet for human phylogeny, you will probably find that few sources agree with each other. When are they ever going to make up their minds and get it right? Likewise, regarding questions of diet and nutrition, every few years nutrition experts change their minds about dietary advice.

Does this frequent revision give credibility to science, or does this make science less credible?

Argument for the question: It's important for scientists to be able to modify ideas as new evidence is revealed. This is how science grows and progresses and, without such a system, we would be intellectually stuck.

Argument against the question: Why can't these so-called experts make up their minds? One year they say one thing, and then a year or two later they say 'Oh, we were wrong, here's the real story.'

Archaeopteryx

Archaeopteryx is one of the most famous fossils in the world. It has some features of a dinosaur, such as reptile teeth and a bony tail, but it also has some bone structures like a bird and it has the most bird-like feature of all: feathers. It did not take long for some observers to jump to the conclusion that Archaeopteryx is the 'missing link' between dinosaurs and birds. Can we be so sure that this fossil is the transition between the two? Are physical

features enough to base such a decision on? What kind of evidence would give more credibility to this claim?

Many palaeontologists shy away from terms like 'missing link': what features of this use of language make the term unscientific?

For centuries, it was firmly believed that rats, maggots, and mould sprang from rotting meat and vegetable matter. This was called spontaneous generation. It took tireless experiments by Louis Pasteur and others to refute this idea and prove that the rats, maggots, and mould came from the surrounding environment.

The end of spontaneous generation

The idea of spontaneous generation has been shelved as unscientific. It has no value as biological knowledge, but it does have historical value and it helps to illustrate how science works.

This is a good example of an original hypothesis that was disproved and falsified by experimentation. It can be argued that, in order for something to be considered valid as scientific knowledge, it has to be verifiable. If experiments show that the results do not support the hypothesis or even refute it, the idea is falsified. This assumes that the experiment is repeatable. Other scientists should be able to do the same experiment and get similar results. Imagine the consequences of the following situation.

The colleague of a famous scientist dies unexpectedly and a student of his decides to publish extracts from the laboratory notebooks. The notes are filled with interesting ideas but also contain severe criticisms of the methods of the famous scientist. For example, only the experiments that gave evidence supporting the famous man's hypotheses were considered and the others that refuted the hypotheses were ignored. This goes against everything the scientific method is supposed to represent. This scenario happened when Claude Bernard died in 1878. He had been working with Louis Pasteur and it took a great amount of persuasion and force of personality for Pasteur to save his reputation. He had lots of both.

Case study 4 Science and government

Trofim Denisovich Lysenko was a Soviet biologist who opposed the ideas of Mendel and Morgan concerning genetics. Instead, he promoted the idea that acquired characteristics could be passed on from one generation to the next. Under Stalin, he was promoted to a high-ranking post in agronomy and given his own scientific journal for publishing his ideas. The agricultural techniques he developed were used to feed the Soviet population and the Red Army. Once Stalin and Khrushchev were no longer in power, however, his methods were widely criticized and his theories attacked for lack of scientific validity. An inquiry revealed that, in order to retain his powerful position and promote his ideas, he had intimidated and removed scientists who questioned his theories. He was finally fired from his post at the Institute of Genetics in 1965 and his reputation was crushed. What does this story reveal about the influence of politics on scientific theories? In what ways does it reveal scientific bias? How do we know that Lysenko's critics were not simply trying to push their own opposing political agenda?

Unprovable assumptions?

Does biology make any assumptions that are impossible to prove? Consider this: all events in nature are caused by physical phenomena.

In other words, every natural event can be explained by the interactions between atoms and molecules. Is such a statement provable? If we find enough examples of instances where this is true, can we proceed by induction that it is true for all phenomena? This seems reasonable, and yet the philosopher David Hume criticized induction, saying that there is no logical reason to assume that it is the case. Consider Karl Popper's quote about swans, which illustrates clearly the problem of induction.

> " No matter how many instances of white swans we may have observed, this does not justify the conclusion that all swans are white. "
> Karl Popper
> Popper 1992a

Scientific science

To what extent is there an overlap between biology and the social sciences? Are the latter 'less scientific'? Consider psychology, sociology, anthropology, and economics.

Knowledge claims

Compare the validity of knowledge claims of two categories of scientific disciplines. For example, you could think about a historical approach (evolution) versus an experimental approach (lab investigation).

Consider these two types of scientific investigation.

2   Controlled experiments in a biology lab.

What is nature?

Biology is a natural science, but what is meant by nature? Is it a clockwork machine? Or is it one big Gaia-type living organism? How useful are these metaphors?

1   An archaeological dig searching for evidence of the past.

Is this a useful image for 'nature'?

Science vocabulary

Does scientific language and vocabulary have a primarily descriptive or interpretive function? Consider the following expressions.

- Natural selection
- Concentration gradient
- Artificial intelligence.

Wiki

Online wikis are filled with user-generated content on a wide range of subjects, including scientific ones. Wikis have been created for scientist to upload their latest laboratory findings. In what ways is this useful to scientists wanting to publish their results? In what ways is this useful to the general public? In what ways does this go against the very nature of peer-reviewed scientific publications, which is the norm today for sharing experimental results? For example, are such wikis just as valid as traditional scientific journals?

What about a wiki or a scientific journal for failed experiments? Why is it that scientists only publish successful investigations and not their failures? If failures were published, couldn't scientists save time by not repeating the same mistakes? Or, could it be that, if another scientist reads what one team thought was a failure but sees it for what it really is, a breakthrough, wouldn't that help science advance?

> 〝 Prediction is very difficult, especially about the future. 〞
>
> Niels Bohr (a Danish physicist who helped us understand how atoms work)
>
> Ellis 1970

Seeing is believing: but what if you cannot see?

There is a story from Asia about a small group of blind men who encounter a tame work elephant, a creature none of them have ever had contact with before.

One blind man touches the elephant's side and says 'It's like a wall'. Another grabs the end of its tail and says 'It's covered in long hairs'. Another feels a leg and says 'Elephants are round and vertical like a pillar'. A fourth holds his ear and says 'It's like a sail'. A fifth holds the animal's trunk and exclaims 'Elephants are like snakes.'

None of the men is wrong but none is completely correct. This story illustrates how easy it is to jump to conclusions before having all the evidence. In science, is it possible to have all the evidence of any particular phenomenon?

Case study 6 A famous hoax: Piltdown Man

It's always exciting to find a fossil of a new species, especially if it is a hominid. But if you can't find one, should you make one up? In 1912, someone did just that, and called it Piltdown Man. The 'fossil' was made from a human skull and the jaw of an orang-utan. Amazingly, the fake fossil puzzled specialists for more than 40 years before it was finally exposed as a hoax.

This famous hoax demonstrates how important it is to double-check findings. Why did it take so long for the truth to come out? You may find useful online sources if you want to investigate this story.

The Piltdown Man hoax jaw.

Perception

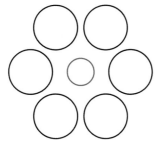

Which red circle is bigger? Judge using your eye first and then use a ruler to check your answer. What does this say about our perceptions and reality?

> " Science may be described as the art of systematic oversimplification. "
>
> Karl Popper
>
> Popper 1992b

What qualifies as an experiment?

Biology is an experimental science, but what constitutes an 'experiment'? Do you have to have a hypothesis, controlled variables, a laboratory? What if you just have people filling out questionnaires? Is that an experiment? What about digging up fossils?

Theory versus myth

In what ways are theories and myths similar and different? Consider the similarities and differences when comparing and contrasting the two.

Is it based on well-substantiated facts?

Is it passed on from generation to generation?

Can it be modified over time?

Can it be used to predict future events?

Has it been tested repeatedly?

Is it widely accepted as being true?

Is it considered to be a supposition?

Is it considered by many to be false?

> " Irrationally held truths may be more harmful than reasoned errors. "
>
> Thomas Henry Huxley

Biology and values

Do the ends justify the means? Consider the following domains of research in biology. What are the ethical issues?

- Gene therapy
- Vaccine tests
- Experimentation on human volunteers, notably prisoners
- Research involving human embryos.

Moral responsibility

Should scientists be held morally responsible for the applications of their discoveries? Is there any area of scientific knowledge the pursuit of which is morally unacceptable or, on the contrary, morally required?

- Cloning humans
- Eugenics
- Genetic engineering of crops
- Finding a cure for cancer.

> " Nothing in this world is to be feared ... only understood. "
>
> Marie Curie

Marie Curie was the first woman to be awarded a Nobel prize and the first person to get two.

Science and religion

To what extent should religion take note of scientific developments? For example, should religious communities keep abreast of scientific discoveries related to Darwin's theory of evolution by natural selection? Some people think that science and religion can coexist; others believe that they are mutually exclusive.

> " Science gets the age of rocks, and religion the rock of ages; science studies how the heavens go, religion how to go to heaven. "
>
> Stephen Jay Gould
>
> Gould 2002

Science and technology

Is scientific knowledge valued more for its own sake or for the technology that it makes possible?

Reading your mind

With modern technology tracking everything we do with our computers and smartphones, it can be argued that the kind of privacy our grandparents had no longer exists. Can we at least say that our private and personal thoughts are still safe within our minds and cannot be tracked and monitored?

Functional magnetic resonance imaging technology (fMRI) allows researchers to see which parts of the brain are active when a person is thinking a specific thing or performing a specific task. This has led to the possibility of identifying thoughts or, as some call it, 'mind reading'. For example, researchers have shown a series of images to participants and recorded the patterns that show up on the fMRI scanner for each image. Later, they pick an image at random and show it to the participant while he or she is still in the scanner. A computer can match the current brain scan pattern with one of the patterns observed before and can determine which image the person's brain is perceiving. Experts claim that they can use this technology to see whether someone is lying or to see whether someone recognizes a crime scene that they claim they have never visited. Marketing agencies are interested in seeing how the brain reacts to different advertising campaigns. Some major knowledge issues and knowledge questions arise from this. How can we know if such claims are valid? How do we test them and decide if the scanner and computer are accurate? Should evidence collected in this way be used legally in court as evidence? Could complex thought

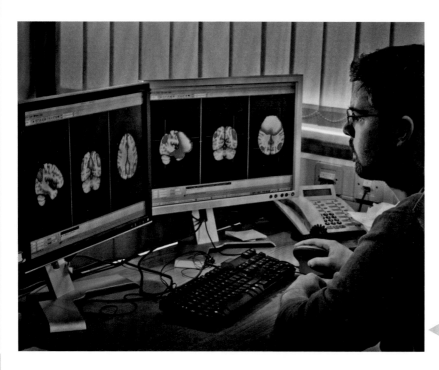

Researcher interpreting fMRI scans of the brain.

patterns be identified, such as musical creativity or cruel intentions? Who should decide whether such experimentation and exploration into our private thoughts should be pursued or banned? Would you want a scan done of your thoughts?

Inaccessible worlds

Some scientific fields of exploration have only been possible since suitable technology has been invented, for example genetic engineering has only been possible since technological developments in the 1970s and 1980s. Could there be problems with knowledge that are unknown now because the technology needed to reveal them does not yet exist? Remember that, despite the fact that bacteria are all around us, we were not able to see them until the microscope was invented in the 1600s. Perhaps there are other phenomena that we simply cannot observe because no one has invented an apparatus to detect them yet.

Is there any science that can be pursued without the use of technology?

“ The most important discoveries will provide answers to questions that we do not yet know how to ask … ”
John Bahcall (commenting on the Hubble space telescope's capabilities)
http://en.wikiquote.org/wiki/Science

“ My business is to teach my aspirations to conform themselves to fact, not to try and make facts harmonize with my aspirations. ”
Thomas Henry Huxley

Mathematics, and information and communication technology skills

An important part of being a good scientist and of being a citizen in today's information-rich world is to be number-savvy and tech-savvy. This chapter is divided into two parts: Part 1 Mathematics and statistical analysis, and Part 2 Information and communication technology (ICT) in biology.

In Part 1, we will explore the kinds of mathematical skills needed by a student of biology in order to understand some basic operations and ways of statistically analysing scientific data. Hopefully this section will make you to feel more comfortable with data and give you strategies for understanding graphs and statistical tests that will improve both your internal assessment (IA) work and your exam results.

In Part 2, we will look at how computers, tablets, data-logging devices, and software programs can help us work with numbers and statistics, notably for lab reports.

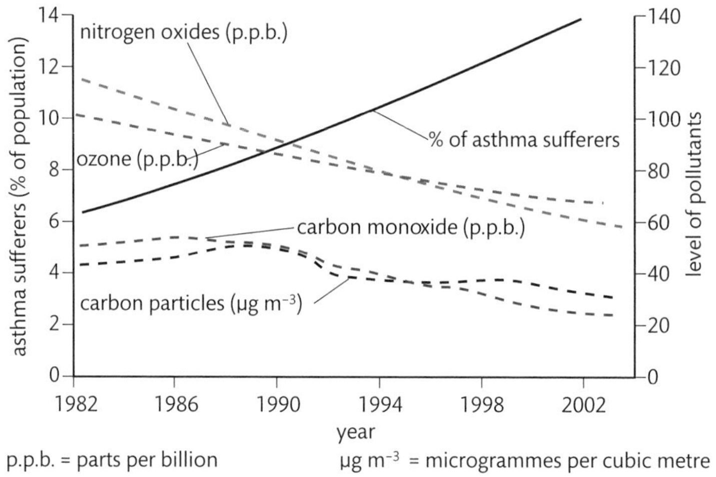

Figure 1 Large quantities of data give us superpowers: they allow us to see things other people cannot see. Being able to collect and process data are important skills but also students need to know how to interpret data, including reading graphs, grasping statistics, and understanding units and their uncertainties. This graph contains an impressive amount of information in just a few square centimetres – there are 20 years of measurements of five different things. The graph aims to answer the question of whether or not there is a link between asthma and air pollution. Try out your data analysis skills and your TOK critical thinking skills on this graph.

p.p.b. = parts per billion   μg m^{-3} = microgrammes per cubic metre

1 Mathematics and statistical analysis

In the first part of this chapter, you will learn how scientists analyse the evidence they collect when they perform experiments. You will be designing your own experiments, so this information will be very useful to you. You will be learning about:

• means
• error bars
• t-tests
• standard deviation
• significant difference
• causation and correlation.

Have your calculator with you to practise calculations for standard deviation and t-tests, so that you can use these methods of analysing data when you do your own experiments.

Mean

The mean is an average of data points. For example, suppose the height of bean plants grown in sunlight is measured in centimetres (cm) 10 days after planting. The heights for nine of the plants are shown below in cm. The sum of the heights is 56.7 cm. Divide 56.7 by 9 to find the mean (average). The mean is 6.3 cm. The mean shows the central tendency of the data.

3.2	9.5	4.4	6.2	7.9	4.4	9.4	7.3	4.4

In the ICT section of this chapter, you can learn how to use a spreadsheet to calculate the mean and many other values for your data.

Median

Simply put, the median is the number in the middle. It is the number that separates the higher half of the data from the lower half of the data. To find it, the data must first be put in order from the lowest to the highest value. The nine heights of plants have been put in order below.

Because there are nine values, the fifth value separates the lower four from the top four. In cases when there is an even number of data points, take the mean (average) of the two numbers in the middle. For example, if a tenth plant was added to the sample and it was the tallest at 9.7 cm, then the two values in the centre would be 6.2 and 7.3. The mean of those two is 6.75, so the median would be 6.75 cm. But in the example above with nine plants, the median is 6.2 cm.

Mode

The mode is the most frequently occurring measurement. In this case, 4.4 is repeated three times, and no other value is repeated, so the mode is 4.4.

Range

The range is the measure of the spread of data. It is the difference between the largest and the smallest observed values. In our example, the range is 9.5 − 3.2 = 6.3. The range for this data set is 6.3 cm. If one data point was unusually large or unusually small, this very large or small data point would have a big effect on the range. Such very large or very small data points are called outliers. In our sample there is no outlier. If one of the plants died early and had a height of only 0.5 cm, it would be considered to be an outlier. In a lab report, it is acceptable to exclude an outlier from data processing, but it is important to declare it and explain why it was excluded.

Error bars

Error bars are a graphical representation of the variability of data. Error bars can be used to show either the range of data or the standard deviation (SD) on a graph. Standard deviation is explored further on the next page. Notice the error bars representing standard deviation on the bar chart in Figure 2 and the graph in Figure 3.

The value of the standard deviation above the mean is shown extending above the top of each bar of the chart, and the same standard deviation below the mean is shown extending below the top of each bar of the chart. As each bar represents the mean of the data for a particular tree species, the standard deviation for each type of tree will be different, but the value extending above and below a particular bar will be the same. The same is true for the line graph. As each point on the graph represents the mean data for each day, the bars extending above and below the data point are the standard deviations above and below the mean.

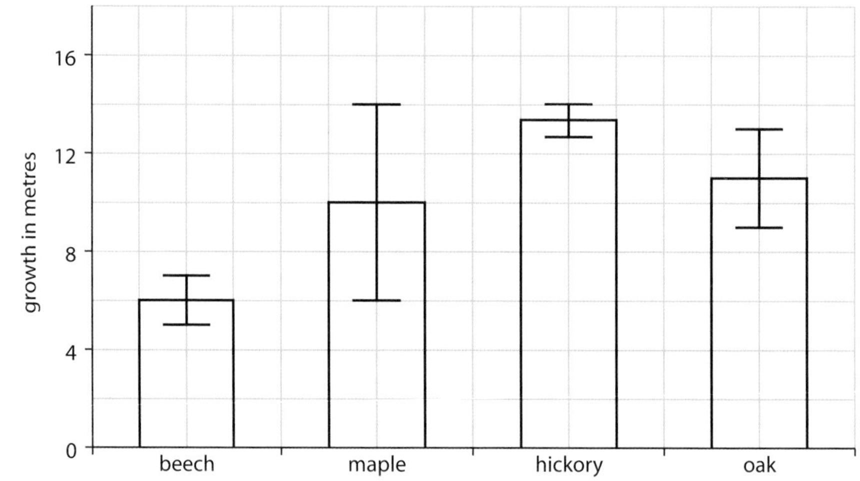

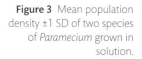

Figure 2 Rate of tree growth on an oak–hickory dune in 2004–05. Values are represented as mean ±1 SD of 25 trees per species.

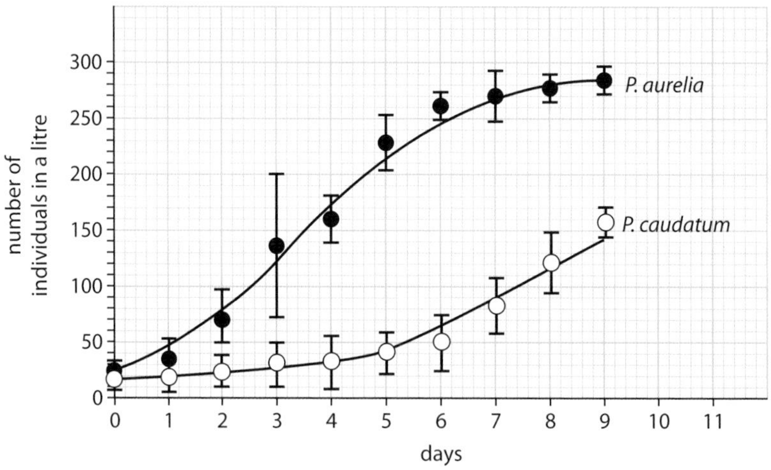

Figure 3 Mean population density ±1 SD of two species of *Paramecium* grown in solution.

Standard deviation

We use standard deviation to summarize the spread of values around the mean, and to compare the means and spread of data between two or more samples. Think of the standard deviation as a way of showing how close your values are to the mean.

In a normal distribution, about 68% of all values lie within ±1 SD from the mean. This rises to about 95% for ±2 SD from the mean.

To help understand this difficult concept, let's look again at the bean plants. Some bean plants were grown in sunlight, and some were grown in shade. Regarding the bean plants grown in sunlight: suppose our sample is 100 bean plants. Of those 100 plants, you might guess that a few will be very short (maybe the soil they are in is slightly sandier). A few may be much taller than the rest (possibly the soil they are in holds more water). However, all we can measure is the height of all the bean plants growing in the sunlight. If we then plot a graph of the heights, the graph is likely to be similar to a bell curve (see Figure 4). In this graph, the number of bean plants is plotted on the *y*-axis and the heights, ranging from short to medium to tall, are plotted on the *x*-axis.

Many data sets do not have a distribution that is as perfect as the middle part of Figure 4. Sometimes, the bell-shape is very flat. This indicates that the data are spread out widely from the mean. In some cases, the bell-shape is very tall and narrow. This shows that the data are very close to the mean and not spread out.

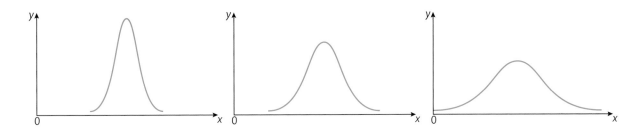

The standard deviation shows us how tightly the data points are clustered around the mean. When the data points are clustered together, the standard deviation is small; when they are spread apart, the standard deviation is large. Calculating the standard deviation of a data set is easily done on a calculator with mathematical functions.

For example, if all the students in a year group got 5s and 6s as their marks in a test, the standard deviation would be low, whereas if the results ranged from 2s to 7s, the standard deviation would be higher.

Look at Figure 5. This graph of normal distribution may help you understand what standard deviation really means. The dotted area represents one standard deviation (1 SD) in either direction from the mean. About 68% of the data in this graph are located in the dotted area. Thus we say that, for normally distributed data, 68% of all the values lie within ±1 SD from the mean. Two standard deviations from the mean (the dotted and the cross-hatched areas combined) contain about 95% of the data. If this bell curve was flatter, the standard deviation would have to be larger to account for the 68% or 95% of the data set. Now you can see why standard deviation tells you how widespread your data points are from the mean of the data set.

How is knowing this useful? For one thing, it tells you how many extreme values are in the data. If there are many extremes, the standard deviation will be large; with few extremes the standard deviation will be small. When processing your data for lab reports, calculating the standard deviation can help you to analyse the data.

Figure 4 Three different normal distribution curves. The first shows very little spread from the mean, the second shows a moderate amount of spread from the mean, and the third shows a wide distribution of data points from the mean.

Figure 5 This graph shows a normal distribution.

Key

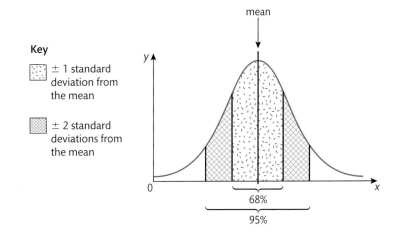

± 1 standard deviation from the mean

± 2 standard deviations from the mean

Comparing the means and spread of data between two or more samples

Remember that in statistics we make inferences about a whole population based on just a sample of the population. Let's continue using our example of bean plants growing in the sunlight and shade to determine how standard deviation is useful for comparing the means and the spread of data between two samples. Table 1 shows the raw data sets at the end of the experiment looking at bean plants grown in sunlight and in shade.

Table 1 Data from a bean plant experiment

Height of 10 bean plants grown in sunlight, in centimetres ±1 cm	Height of 10 bean plants grown in shade, in centimetres ±1 cm
125	131
121	60
154	160
99	212
124	117
143	65
157	155
129	160
140	145
118	95
Total 1310	Total 1300

Bean plants being grown for an experiment.

First, we determine the mean for each sample. As each sample contains 10 plants, we can divide the sum of all the heights by 10 in each case. The resulting means are 131 and 130 cm, respectively.

Of course, that is not the end of the analysis. Can you see that there are large differences between the two sets of data? The heights of the bean plants grown in the shade are much more variable than those of the bean plants grown in the sunlight. The means of each data set are very similar, but the variation is not the same. This suggests that other factors may be influencing growth, in addition to sunlight and shade.

How can we mathematically quantify the variation that we have observed? Fortunately, your calculator should have a function that will do this for you. All you have to do is input the raw data. As practice, find the standard deviation of each raw data set above before you read on.

The standard deviation of the bean plants grown in sunlight is 17.68 cm, while the standard deviation of the bean plants grown in shade is 47.02 cm. Looking at the means alone, it appears that there is little difference between the two sets of bean plants. However, the high standard deviation of the bean plants grown in the shade indicates a very wide spread of data around the mean. The wide variation in this data set makes us question the experimental design. What is causing this wide variation in data? Is it possible that the plants in the shade are also growing in several different types of soil? This is why it is important to calculate the standard deviation, in addition to the mean, of a data set. If we looked at only the means, we would not recognize the variability of data seen in the shade-grown bean plants.

Significant difference between two data sets using a *t*-test

In order to determine whether or not the difference between two sets of data is a significant difference, *t*-tests are commonly used. The Student's *t*-test (named after a scientist publishing his work under the pseudonym 'Student') compares two sets of data, for example the heights of the bean plants grown in sunlight and the heights of bean plants grown in shade. Look at the top of the table of *t*-values (Table 2) and you will see the probability (*p*) that chance alone could make a difference. If *p* = 0.50, it means the difference could be the result of chance alone 50% of the time.

Statistical significance refers to how probable it is that a relationship is caused by pure chance. If a relationship is statistically significant, it means that there is very little chance that the relationship is caused by chance. We can also use this idea to see whether the differences between two populations are random or not.

For example, a value of *p* = 0.50 (or 50%) is not a significant difference in statistics. It means that there is a 50% probability that the differences are caused by chance alone. However, if you reach *p* = 0.05, the probability that the difference is caused by chance alone is only 5%. This means that there is a 95% likelihood that the difference has been caused by something besides chance. A 95% probability is statistically significant in statistics. Statisticians are rarely completely certain about their findings, but they like to be at least 95% certain of their findings before drawing conclusions.

The formula when comparing two populations that are assumed to have equal variance is as follows:

Note: you will *not* be asked this formula on exams – it is presented here only as something that might be useful for processing the data collected in your laboratory investigations.

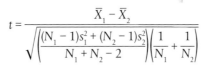

$$t = \frac{\bar{X}_1 - \bar{X}_2}{\sqrt{\left(\frac{(N_1 - 1)s_1^2 + (N_2 - 1)s_2^2}{N_1 + N_2 - 2}\right)\left(\frac{1}{N_1} + \frac{1}{N_2}\right)}}$$

$\bar{X}_1$ = the mean of population 1
$\bar{X}_2$ = the mean of population 2
N = sample size of the population
s = standard deviation

If you plug in the values from the above example with bean plants, you should get *t* = 0.06. You can use a table of critical *t*-values (Table 2) to find out what this number means. To do this, look in the left-hand column of Table 2, headed 'Degrees of freedom', then look across to the given *t*-values. For a two-sample *t*-test like the one we are doing, the degrees of freedom (d.f.) are the sum of the sample sizes of the two groups minus two: 10 + 10 - 2 = 18.

If d.f. = 18, we need to look at the row on the table of *t*-values that corresponds to 18. We see that our calculated value of *t* (0.06) is less than 0.69 on the table, indicating that the probability that the differences between the two populations of plants are due to chance alone is greater than 50%. In other words, we can safely declare that there is no statistically significant difference in the data collected from the bean plants in the sunlight and those from the shade. The differences are most likely due to chance. In order to be able to declare that our two populations showed a level of 95% significance in their differences, we would need a *t* value of 2.10 or more (see d.f. = 18 and *p* = 0.05 (5%) in Table 2). Interpretations of such data processing can be a crucial addition to an effective conclusion on a lab report.

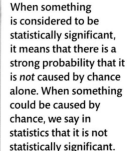

When something is considered to be statistically significant, it means that there is a strong probability that it is *not* caused by chance alone. When something could be caused by chance, we say in statistics that it is not statistically significant.

Table 2 *t*-values

		Probability (p) that chance alone could produce the difference					
		0.50 (50%)	0.20 (20%)	0.10 (10%)	0.05 (5%)	0.01 (1%)	0.001 (0.1%)
Degrees of freedom	1	1.00	3.08	6.31	12.71	63.66	636.62
	2	0.82	1.89	2.92	4.30	9.93	31.60
	3	0.77	1.64	2.35	3.18	5.84	12.92
	4	0.74	1.53	2.13	2.78	4.60	8.61
	5	0.73	1.48	2.02	2.57	4.03	6.87
	6	0.72	1.44	1.94	2.45	3.71	5.96
	7	0.71	1.42	1.90	2.37	3.50	5.41
	8	0.71	1.40	1.86	2.31	3.37	5.04
	9	0.70	1.38	1.83	2.26	3.25	4.78
	10	0.70	1.37	1.81	2.23	3.17	4.59
	11	0.70	1.36	1.80	2.20	3.11	4.44
	12	0.70	1.36	1.78	2.18	3.06	4.32
	13	0.69	1.35	1.77	2.16	3.01	4.22
	14	0.69	1.35	1.76	2.15	2.98	4.14
	15	0.69	1.34	1.75	2.13	2.95	4.07
	16	0.69	1.34	1.75	2.12	2.92	4.02
	17	0.69	1.33	1.74	2.11	2.90	3.97
	18	0.69	1.33	1.73	2.10	2.88	3.92
	19	0.69	1.33	1.73	2.09	2.86	3.88
Degrees of freedom	20	0.69	1.33	1.73	2.09	2.85	3.85
	21	0.69	1.32	1.72	2.08	2.83	3.82
	22	0.69	1.32	1.72	2.07	2.82	3.79
	24	0.69	1.32	1.71	2.06	2.80	3.75
	26	0.68	1.32	1.71	2.06	2.78	3.71
	28	0.68	1.31	1.70	2.05	2.76	3.67
	30	0.68	1.31	1.70	2.04	2.75	3.65
	35	0.68	1.31	1.69	2.03	2.72	3.59
	40	0.68	1.30	1.68	2.02	2.70	3.55
	45	0.68	1.30	1.68	2.01	2.70	3.52
	50	0.68	1.30	1.68	2.01	2.68	3.50
	60	0.68	1.30	1.67	2.00	2.66	3.46
	70	0.68	1.29	1.67	1.99	2.65	3.44
	80	0.68	1.29	1.66	1.99	2.64	3.42
	90	0.68	1.29	1.66	1.99	2.63	3.40
	100	0.68	1.29	1.66	1.99	2.63	3.39

Two groups of barnacles living on a rocky shore were compared. The width of their shells was measured to see whether there was a significant size difference depending on how close they lived to the water. One group lived between 0 and 10 m above the water level. A second group lived between 10 and 20 m above the water level.

The width of the shells was measured in millimetres (mm). Fifteen shells were measured from each group. The mean size of the group living closer to the water indicated that barnacles living closer to the water had larger shells. If the value of t is 2.25, is that a significant difference?

Solution

For one of the steps of the Student's t-test, we need to determine the degrees of freedom. In an example like this one, where the two sample sizes are equal and we can assume the variance in the two samples is the same, the degree of freedom is $2n - 2$. The letter n represents the sample size (the number of measurements made), and in this case $n = 15$. The degrees of freedom in this example is 28 because $(2 \times 15) - 2 = 28$. Looking along the row of Table 2 that shows the degrees of freedom of 28, we see that 2.25 is just above 2.05.

Referring to the top of this column in the table, $p = 0.05$: so the probability that chance alone could produce that result is only 5%.

The confidence level is 95%. We are 95% confident that the difference between the barnacles is statistically significant. In other words, the differences in mean size is very unlikely to be a product of pure chance.

Note: when calculating the t-test value using a spreadsheet program such as Microsoft Excel, be aware that the value obtained is the % chance rather than the value for t. As a result, you do not need to look up the critical values in the table.

Correlation does not mean causation

We make observations all the time about the living world around us. We might notice, for example, that our bean plants wilt when the soil is dry. This is a simple observation. We might carry out an experiment to see whether watering the bean plants prevents wilting. Observing that wilting occurs when the soil is dry is a simple correlation, but the experiment provides us with evidence that the lack of water is the cause of the wilting. Experiments provide a test that shows cause. Observations without an experiment can only show a correlation. Also, in order for these to be evidence of causality, there must be a mechanism to explain why one phenomenon might cause the other. Knowing the properties of osmosis and turgidity in plant cells would explain the causality associated with the correlation, thus giving it great scientific plausability.

Cormorants

When using a mathematical correlation test, the value of the correlation coefficient, r, is a measure of the degree of linear relationship or linear dependence between two variables. This can also be called the Pearson correlation coefficient. The value of r can vary from +1 (completely positive correlation) to 0 (no correlation) to −1 (completely negative correlation). For example, we can measure the size of breeding cormorant birds to see whether there is a correlation between the sizes of males and females that breed together.

A cormorant.

Table 3 Cormorant size data

Pair number	Size of female cormorants, cm	Size of male cormorants, cm
1	43.4	41.9
2	47.0	44.2
3	50.0	43.9
4	41.1	42.7
5	54.1	49.5
6	49.8	46.5
$r = 0.88$		

Correlation does not necessarily mean causality. Just because two things show a relationship and have a strong r-value, does not mean one causes the other.

The r-value of 0.88 shows a positive correlation between the sizes of the two sexes: large females mate with large males. However, correlation is not cause. To find the cause of this observed correlation requires experimental evidence. There may be a high correlation, but only carefully designed experiments can separate causation from correlation. Causality requires that the mechanism of exactly how X causes Y needs to be demonstrated. For example, the mathematics here does not explain whether it is the males choosing the females or the females choosing the males. Correlation says nothing about the direction of the influence.

Graphs

Scientists use graphs extensively because they are useful tools for presenting data and seeing relationships that might otherwise remain hidden. Graphs are instrumental in analysing data, and if you know how to make accurate and appropriate graphs your conclusion and evaluation will be greatly enhanced.

The most common forms of graphs you are expected to be able to use are:

- bar charts
- histograms
- line graphs
- scatter plots.

Occasionally, you may also need to use pie charts or box and whisker diagrams, but here we will focus on the four listed above.

Bar charts

Bar charts use rectangles to show the amount of data in a certain number of categories. The height of each rectangle corresponds to a quantitative value. The y-axis is quantitative, but the x-axis shows categories rather than incremental numerical values. The order of these categories could be changed and it would not make a difference. Empty spaces separate the rectangles along the x-axis. For example, Figure 6 is a bar chart showing the amount of vitamin C in various foods.

Figure 6 A bar chart showing vitamin C levels in different types of food.

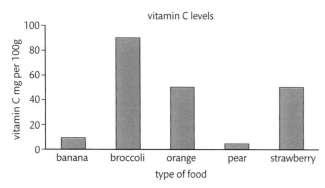

In a graph of this type, it is okay to rearrange the bars anyway you want. In Figure 6, the data are presented alphabetically, but there is no reason why you couldn't order the bars from the greatest to the smallest numerical values.

Histograms

Histograms have some similarities with bar charts, except that the x-axis has a quantitative scale marking off intervals of continuous data. In addition, the widths of the rectangles that make up the histogram represent specific incremental quantitative values. The histogram in Figure 7 shows the amount of time that 42 individuals of a particular species of animal spent drinking at a river.

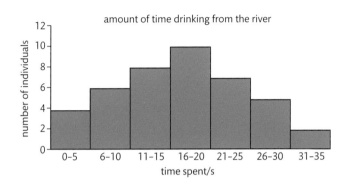

Figure 7 A histogram of the time spent by individuals of a species drinking from a river. Notice the lack of space between the categories, and the fact that the categories on the x-axis represent continuous incremental numerical values.

Histograms have no spaces between the rectangles because the data are continuous. This was not the case in the bar chart that we looked at in Figure 6. In Figure 7, we cannot rearrange the rectangles of the histogram so that the highest values are on the left and the lowest values are on the right, as we could have done for the bar chart. Histograms must follow the scale shown on the x-axis. If an animal drank for 24 seconds, the data must go in the range 21–25. These ranges can also be called bins, and you can think of a histogram as a series of bins that you fill up with the appropriate data as the data are sorted.

Line graphs

A line graph plots single points over regular increments such that each x-value has only one corresponding y-value. The dots are then joined with straight lines. The example in Figure 8 shows a newborn baby's body mass between the time of its birth and the age of 18 months.

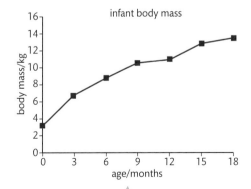

In line graphs, the x-axis is usually the independent variable, in which case the y-axis is the dependent variable. There is clearly a correlation in this graph: as age increases, body mass increases. There is a positive correlation. But remember, that does not mean there is causality. Ageing is not the mechanism that causes an increase in the child's body mass; on the contrary, good nutrition, genes, and growth hormones are more likely candidates for causing the increase. Line graphs can sometimes show discrepancies in the data. For example, a doctor might wonder why a child did not grow as fast between the ages of 9 and 12 months compared with the rest of the graph. Perhaps the child did not have access to proper nutrition during that interval.

Figure 8 A line graph of infant body mass. Notice that the data points are connected by straight lines rather than using a trend line or line of best fit.

Scatter plots

A scatter plot is used when two variables are involved, and they are plotted as *y* against *x* using Cartesian coordinates. Such graphs work well for situations where one *x*-value may have multiple *y*-values. As with line graphs, scatter plots are useful for trying to see a correlation. Figure 9 shows a scatter plot for the numbers of pairs of grey partridges (a type of bird) plotted against the number of sightings of birds of prey per square kilometre (km^{-2}).

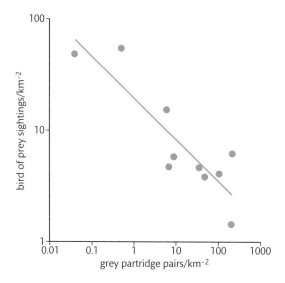

Figure 9 A scatter plot of grey partridge pairs against bird of prey sightings, with logarithmic scales on the *x*- and *y*-axes. M. Watson et al. 2007

Notice how the dots are a bit irregular: this scattering is where this type of graph gets its name from. Notice also how the data points are *not* connected by a line. Rather, a line of best fit or a trend line has been placed over the graph showing an overall trend in the data. Such lines or curves do not need to pass through each data point, as we saw in the line graph. The trend line in Figure 9 shows that there is a negative correlation. A negative correlation means that as one variable increases the other decreases.

Do you notice anything peculiar about the axes? They are shown using a logarithmic scale, which means that each increment is 10 times the size of the one before. This is relatively exceptional: most scatter plots have standard incremental scales on the *x*- and *y*-axes, the way the line graph does in Figure 8. Logarithmic scales are useful when you are trying to show distributions of data points that would not show up if they were put on a normally incremental scale. In this case, it is likely that the authors of the report in which this graph appeared wanted to show the correlation between the sightings of birds of prey and the number of couples of partridges. As we know that there is a logical mechanism for causality (birds of prey kill and eat partridges), it is not impossible to suspect that there is a causal relationship here. But this graph alone cannot prove that birds of prey cause the reduction in numbers of partridges.

Regression models and coefficient of correlation

When scientists measure something, often they are looking to see whether they can demonstrate that the phenomenon is following a law of nature. Sometimes laws of nature follow patterns that can be expressed in mathematical equations. For example, when measuring the light that a leaf might use for photosynthesis, a scientist knows that the intensity of the light varies according to an equation relating intensity with the distance to the light. You know from personal experience that holding a torch close to your eyes can be blinding, whereas seeing the same torch from far away does not hurt your eyes. In Figure 10, the graph on the left illustrates the 'pure' mathematical law about light intensity and distance from the light source. On the right is the same graph superimposed with measurements taken in a lab. Because of any number of things, including limitations in the equipment and human error, the lab measurements do not fit the mathematical model perfectly.

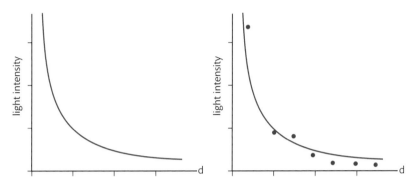

Figure 10 A model of what the data should show (on the left) and the actual collected data (dots on the right), of which only one point is actually where it was expected to be. The d on the x-axis of the graphs represents the distance from the light source.

Now imagine the opposite. A scientist takes some measurements and wonders if there is some kind of mathematical equation that could act as a model of her data. She makes a scatter plot and then sees if there is a trend line that fits her data reasonably well. She might start with a straight line because that is the simplest relationship between two variables. This is called a simple linear regression model. But if that does not fit her data well, she could try other regression models that are not straight lines. Fortunately, statistical functions in her calculator or spreadsheet program on her computer can do this for her in an automated fashion.

How can we know if the trend line's regression model is the best one for the data we collected? The squared correlation coefficient, r^2, also called the coefficient of determination, is used to see how well a regression model matches the data collected. A value of $r^2 = 0$ means the regression model does not fit the data at all, whereas a value of $r^2 = 1$ means a perfect fit. Note that r^2 cannot be a negative number. Here are some examples showing the r^2 values calculated by Microsoft Excel for three data sets and their trend lines.

Figure 11 Three examples of data that have been modelled with a linear regression. The r^2-value is then calculated to see how closely the linear regression model matches the data.

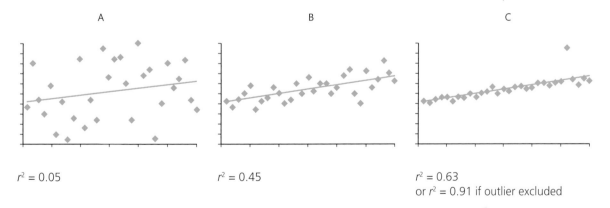

A

B

C

$r^2 = 0.05$

$r^2 = 0.45$

$r^2 = 0.63$
or $r^2 = 0.91$ if outlier excluded

Notice what happens to the r^2-value as the variability of the data points is reduced from A to B to C. This reveals that the regression model shown by the trend line matches the observed data better and better. Graph A's regression line suggests that there is very

- Trend lines are useful for seeing whether there is an overall pattern or tendency in the data points.
- The r^2-value, the coefficient of determination, is useful for seeing if the trend line matches the data points closely or not. It indicates how good the model is. The closer it is to 1, the better the model. Values close to 1 reveal that there is a strong correlation between the x- and y-values.
- If the regression model fits the data well, it can be used to predict values that were not measured.

little evidence of an agreement between the regression model and the data, whereas B and C show a stronger fit. Notice what happens in graph C: there is clearly an outlier at the top right. Fortunately, the investigator identified it as being a result of an error during the lab. It can safely be ignored, and therefore the value of 0.91 can be used for analysis purposes. Students are encouraged to used trend lines and r^2-values in their data processing, in order to analyse the data they have collected better.

In addition to simply seeing whether the data points follow a predictable pattern, a regression model can be used to predict values that were not measured. Knowing the equation of the line or the curve allows a researcher to plug in hypothetical values and get a prediction from the model. For example, changes in the human population in the coming decades can be predicted based on a regression model of current trends in the population. When using a regression model for prediction purposes, the r^2-value can help give a sense of how reliable the prediction will be. For example, predicting an outcome using graph A above would be extremely unreliable. However, using C's regression model would be more likely to give reliable results.

Before and after: by how much did this change?

Sometimes we need to analyse how something has changed over time, or we need to see whether there is a difference between what we expected and what we got.

The simplest way to see a difference is to subtract the 'after' value, V_2, from the 'before' value, V_1. However, it is often practical to calculate a percentage change:

$$\text{percentage change} = \left(\frac{V_2 - V_1}{V_1}\right) \times 100$$

Expected versus observed values: first application of the chi-squared test for goodness of fit

As we saw in Figure 10, we do not always get what we expect with our results. The difference between the expected values and the observed values may simply be caused by chance or, on the contrary, may be because an unexpected phenomenon is having an effect on the data. How can we know? One way to answer this question is to carry out a statistical test called the chi-squared (χ^2) test, which calculates how close our observed results are to the expected values. Chi is the Greek letter χ and is pronounced like the word 'sky' without the s at the beginning.

The first way we will use the χ^2 test is to compare our observed results with what we can theoretically calculate the results should be (the 'expected' results). To use this statistical test it is important to note down carefully all the observed results (O) and the expected results (E). In the case of genetics exercises, the expected results would be the proportions of phenotypes as determined by a Punnett grid, such as 25%/50%/25% or 25%/75%, although it is important to use the actual numbers of offspring rather than percentages or ratios. Setting up a table to help keep track of the numbers is helpful.

Table 4 Charting observed and expected results

	Possible outcome 1	Possible outcome 2	Sum
Observed numbers in each category of possible outcomes (O)			
Expected numbers in each category of possible outcomes (E)			
Difference (O – E)			
Difference squared (O – E)^2			
$\dfrac{(O - E)^2}{E}$			$\chi^2 =$

The third and fourth lines of this table are intermediate steps to see the difference between the observed and the expected values as well as their squared values.

The bottom right cell of the table is what we want: it shows the sum of the last row's values and this is the χ^2 value we are interested in. In effect, the contents of this table can be summarized in the generalized formula for calculating χ^2, which is:

$$\chi^2 = \Sigma \frac{(O - E)^2}{E}$$

where χ = Greek letter chi, O = observed values (the results of the experiment), E = expected values (calculated theoretically), Σ = sum of all the calculations for each type of outcome.

Interpreting the χ^2 value calculated

Once we know the χ^2 value, we need to know what it means. For this there are some concepts that need to be clarified. First of all, there is the concept of the null hypothesis (H_0). The H_0 in an experiment of this type is what we would expect: this is usually determined by mathematical calculations. The χ^2 value will help us to determine whether the null hypothesis can be rejected. Accepting the null hypothesis is a way of saying 'Yes, there is a high probability that any deviation from the expected values can be attributed to chance'.

Another two important concepts to understand are the idea of degrees of freedom (d.f.) and how the idea of probability (p) is used. When using the χ^2 test to determine whether there is a difference between the expected and the observed values, the degrees of freedom is determined by taking the number of categories into which the data fall and subtracting 1 from that number. In Table 4, there are two categories into which the data fall (possible outcomes 1 and 2, so there is $2 - 1 = 1$ degree of freedom). This number allows us to know where to look in the table of critical values for χ^2 (Table 5). Notice in Table 5 that, in addition to the degrees of freedom, there are probability values for p. It is a convention in biology to look for probabilities of 5%, or 0.05.

Do not confuse Tables 2 and 5. Although they both refer to probability and hypothesis testing, the former is for the *t*-test and this one is for the chi-squared test.

Table 5 Critical values for χ^2

		Probability values (*p*)				
		0.1	0.05	0.025	0.01	0.005
Degrees of freedom (d.f.)	1	2.706	3.841	5.024	6.635	7.879
	2	4.605	5.991	7.378	9.21	10.597
	3	6.251	7.815	9.348	11.345	12.838
	4	7.779	9.488	11.143	13.277	14.86
	5	9.236	11.07	12.833	15.086	16.75
	6	10.645	12.592	14.449	16.812	18.548
	7	12.017	14.067	16.013	18.475	20.278
	8	13.362	15.507	17.535	20.09	21.955
	9	14.684	16.919	19.023	21.666	23.589
	10	15.987	18.307	20.483	23.209	25.188

Look at Table 5 and find the critical value that is of interest to us: it is the one that lines up with a probability value of 0.05 and a degree of freedom of 1. You should get 3.841. This means that any value we calculate for χ^2 that is greater than 3.841 tells us to reject the null hypothesis.

Here is a summary of the steps.

1 Determine the expected values (although we sometimes like to use percentages or proportions in science, the χ^2 test requires numbers here: do not use percentages or ratios).

2 Note down the observed values and decide what the null hypothesis will be.

3 Calculate the value for χ^2 by determining the differences between the values $(O - E)$, then square them, $(O - E)^2$, and finally add them all up.

4 Determine the degrees of freedom (d.f.) by taking the total number of classes into which the data fall and subtracting 1.

5 Look at the table of critical values of χ^2 and use the d.f. and *p*-value (conventionally we use 0.05 for *p*) to determine which critical value ($\chi^2_{critical}$) to compare the calculated value of χ^2 ($\chi^2_{calculated}$) to.

6 Compare $\chi^2_{critical}$ to $\chi^2_{calculated}$ and decide if the null hypothesis can be rejected using these rules:

 $\chi^2_{calculated}$ < $\chi^2_{critical}$ < $\chi^2_{calculated}$

do not reject null hypothesis,

any deviations from the expected values are probably the result of chance alone

reject null hypothesis,

deviations from the expected values are *not* the result of chance alone

If the calculated value for χ^2 is less than the critical value, the null hypothesis cannot be rejected, whereas if the calculated value for χ^2 is greater than the critical value, the null hypothesis can be rejected.

Independent or correlated: second application of the chi-squared test as a test for independence

As seen in Chapter 4, sometimes we need to know whether it is likely that two phenomena are independent from each other or associated with each other. This next application of the χ^2 test will also compare expected and observed values, but this time the expected frequencies are not given in advance. The use of a contingency table like the one below is necessary to determine them. Table 6 shows the data relevant to the quadrat experiment described in Chapter 4, in which students wanted to see whether the distribution of ferns was random or whether they were found more commonly in sunny or shady areas.

Table 6 Quadrat data

Observed:		Area sampled		
		Sunlight	Shade	
Presence of ferns	Present	7	14	21
	Absent	13	6	19
		20	20	40

The cells in pink show the two columns and two rows of observed data; the yellow cells show the marginal totals for the two rows; and the blue cells show the marginal totals for the two columns. The number 40 represents the whole sample size of 40 quadrats (20 from the sunlit areas, and 20 from the shaded areas).

Determining the expected values

Unlike the previous use of the χ^2 test, we have no mathematical model to predict the theoretical 'expected' values. For that, we construct a new table by removing the observed values.

Table 7 Determining the expected values, step 1

		Area sampled		
		Sunlight	Shade	
Presence of ferns	Present			21
	Absent			19
		20	20	40

Now, to fill in the table with expected values, we multiply the marginal total of each row by the marginal total of each column.

Table 8 Determining the expected values, step 2

Expected:		Area sampled		
		Sunlight	Shade	
Presence of ferns	Present	$(20 \times 21) \div 40 = 10.5$	$(20 \times 21) \div 40 = 10.5$	21
	Absent	$(20 \times 19) \div 40 = 9.5$	$(20 \times 19) \div 40 = 9.5$	19
		20	20	40

There are some conditions that need to be met when using the χ^2 test.

- **This kind of statistical test works with data that you can put into categories and you want to find out whether the frequency that the results fall into a particular category is the result of chance alone.**

- **Make sure the categories into which the data can fall are exhaustive and mutually exclusive, such as yes/no, or red flower/white flower/pink flower. As with flipping a coin, heads/tails, all the data collected must fall into one or the other of the categories.**

- **Make sure the data sample is sufficiently large: with fewer than five data points in any one category, the result will not be very reliable.**

The null hypothesis is usually the opposite of the investigator's hypothesis. For example, if a doctor wanted to study the effects of a drug on her patients, she might have the hypothesis 'This drug has a positive influence on my patients' health. Compared with the control group not taking the drug, the experimental group will declare more often that they feel better.' In such a scenario, the null hypothesis would be: 'This drug has no influence on my patients' health. There is no difference between the control group and the experimental group: I can be confident that any observed differences will be due to chance alone.'

This is why researchers are happy and satisfied when they can reject the null hypothesis. They are glad to see that they can rule out the idea that the results are only caused by chance. But be careful: just because the null hypothesis can be rejected, it does not mean that the investigator's hypothesis has been validated.

Degrees of freedom

To determine the degrees of freedom, take the number of rows (r) minus one and multiply that by the number of columns (c) minus one. In this case, there are two columns (sunlight and shade) and two rows (ferns present and ferns absent), so the formula is:

$$\text{d.f.} = (r-1)(c-1)$$
$$\text{d.f.} = (2-1)(2-1) = 1$$

Calculate the chi-squared value

For most tables of contingency, the normal formula for χ^2 can be used:

$$\chi^2 = \Sigma \frac{(O-E)^2}{E}$$

Your calculator or spreadsheet program most likely has formulas to calculate this value quickly, but using tables like Table 4 can allow you to walk through the calculation step by step. You should get 4.91 as the critical value of t.

Test for independence: interpreting the chi-squared value

Now we need to look at the critical values table (Table 5). As we have 1 degree of freedom and we always look at $p = 0.05$, the critical value comes out as 3.841. As our calculated value (4.91) is higher than this critical value, we can safely reject the null hypothesis. What does this mean? It means that if the null hypothesis were true and the distribution of ferns was solely the result of chance, there would be less than a 5% chance of getting the results we observed. The fact that our calculated χ^2 value is high means that the relationship is statistically significant. It also means that the distribution of ferns and the presence of sunlight are not totally independent from each other. We can reject the idea that they are independent.

2 Information and communication technology in biology

In the second part of this chapter, we will look at how digital technology can be applied to biology. Thanks to advances in desktop computers, laptops, tablets, and smartphones, many tools that would have only been available to highly specialized labs a few decades ago are now available to everyone. In the 1980s, for example, three-dimension (3-D) animation was cutting-edge technology requiring a roomful of computer processors. Today, teenagers can sketch objects in 3-D on their smartphones. We will look at the following aspects of ICT that apply to biology:

- models
- simulations
- databases
- questionnaires and surveys
- data-analysis exercises
- fieldwork and data logging
- ICT skills as applied to lab reports.

Models

A model is a simplified representation of an object or a phenomenon that can be used to better explain or understand it. Physical models, such as a plastic model of a heart, might help a student to see how the valves work to keep the blood flowing in one direction between the chambers. Computer models, such as a 3-D animation of a beating heart or abstract models showing a flowchart of a process such as DNA replication, can help the learner grasp complex concepts by providing simplified visualizations. Computational models, such as climate models, might be used to help simulate Earth's true climate on a computer.

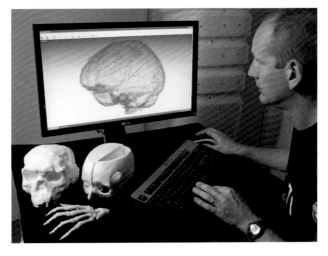

A computer model can be used to study 3-D objects. Once an object such as this skull is represented as a 3-D model, the data can be shared with other labs and be studied by multiple experts all over the world simultaneously.

Simulations

Models can be applied in simulations in order to represent a process or system. Because variables can be manipulated within them, simulations are often used to predict an outcome or to find out what the optimum parameters are for a system. For example, computer simulations use climate models to predict what will happen to Earth's climate if carbon dioxide levels increase. In the lab, some experiments are too dangerous, too time-consuming, or too costly to carry out; computer simulations of those experiments can be performed on a computer safely and in a time-saving fashion. Experiments mating fruit flies, for example, would take many weeks to do, or experiments on the effects of introducing predators into an ecosystem would take months or years, and not be very realistic for an IB student to undertake. However, computer simulations can allow a student to collect data and perform experiments virtually on screen. See the hotlinks section at the end of this chapter for examples of online simulations.

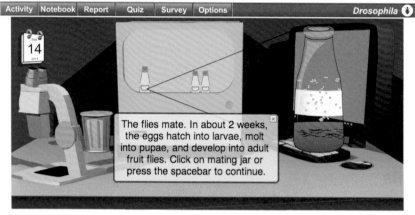

A simulation for mating fruit flies to see what kinds of genetic combinations are possible. Notice that this simulation uses models of a microscope, an incubator, glassware, and a lab bench to simulate this experiment with virtual flies that follow a genetic model.
sciencecourseware.org

Mating

See Background for more detailed information. When mating has completed, click on the mating jar animation or press the space bar to continue.

Entering data about blood plasma into a database using a bar code reader.

Databases

Students are often encouraged to compare the values they get in the lab investigations they carry out with values that scientists in other labs have obtained. In other instances, students do not have access to the lab equipment necessary to do certain experiments, such as finding gene sequences or measuring carbon dioxide concentrations over many decades. In either case, databases are available online for a variety of types of data, and students should take advantage of these resources. Hotlinks to some useful databases can be found at the end of the chapter.

Gathering your own statistics

Questionnaires and surveys can sometimes come in handy when students are looking for large quantities of data to analyse. Writing a good survey or questionnaire is an art as well as a science. As with many projects, once you have an idea for your research question, it is best to start with the end in mind and then work backwards.

1 Picture the kinds of graphs that you would want to see on your final data processing that would lead you to an interesting conclusion.

2 Then think of what kinds of data need to be collected in order to produce such graphs. For example, suppose you want to

find out whether the use of flashcards helps students perform better when doing biology multiple-choice questions. You would need to decide whether you want to ask how many flashcards students have made or how much time they spend reviewing them, or both.

3   Because you are trying to show the influence of X on Y, you would probably want to do some kind of scatter plot graph with a trend line to see whether there is a positive or negative correlation. Perhaps you could do some data processing to find out whether the number of cards and/or the amount of time they are used is independent of the students' test scores or not. You could calculate whether there was a statistically significant difference between one group and another in terms of test performance.

4   To see if there is an influence, you would need to obtain the test scores from the participants in your study. This raises some ethical questions because certain students might not want to give you that information. Every time you do a questionnaire, you must tell the students what information is being collected, why it is being collected, and what will be done with the information. They have the right to know, for example, if your data is going to be shared with other people. If your intent is to collect anonymous data, you can reassure your participants that their names will not appear anywhere in the data. Also, you should give the participants the opportunity to leave certain questions blank.

5   Use these helpful hints about setting up questionnaires and surveys.

   (a)   Even if your questionnaire is anonymous, be sure to collect some demographic information, such as female/male, age, year group, etc. Put such questions at the end of your questionnaire or survey rather than at the beginning. This information might prove useful later because you might see some unexpected trends in the data, such as which age groups use flashcards the most. Some of the best discoveries are the unexpected ones.

   (b)   So that the data are easier to use in a spreadsheet, use tick boxes or multiple-choice questions whenever possible. Avoid open-ended questions where participants write their own answers. For example, in an open-ended question about gender, some participants may write 'male' and others may write 'M'. A computer would see that as two different answers, even though we know they both mean male.

   (c)   Be sure that your categories do not overlap. For example, if you are asking students to tick their age group, do not put '13 to 15' as one category and '15 to 17' as another category because students who are 15 will not know which one to tick.

   (d)   Before you send out your questionnaire to all the participants, try it out on a few classmates and teachers. Often they can spot errors that you did not see or they might have suggestions for clarifying certain points.

Although it is possible to print out and photocopy sheets to collect data, it is very time-consuming to type in all the answers into a spreadsheet when you want to do your data processing. It is much quicker to set up an online questionnaire so that as soon as participants click 'submit' the answers are added to a spreadsheet. The hotlinks at the end of this chapter have some suggestions for online questionnaire and survey websites.

In addition to following the IB's guide concerning ethical questions applied to experimentation in the lab, students interested in writing questionnaires might want

Google Forms is a no-cost solution for making an online survey. Some online services for surveys limit the number of respondents or charge a fee if you get more than 100 respondents, but this is not the case for Google Forms.

to have a look at the diploma programme guide for psychology. In it, there are clear guidelines about what the IB considers to be acceptable practice when using human subjects for an investigation.

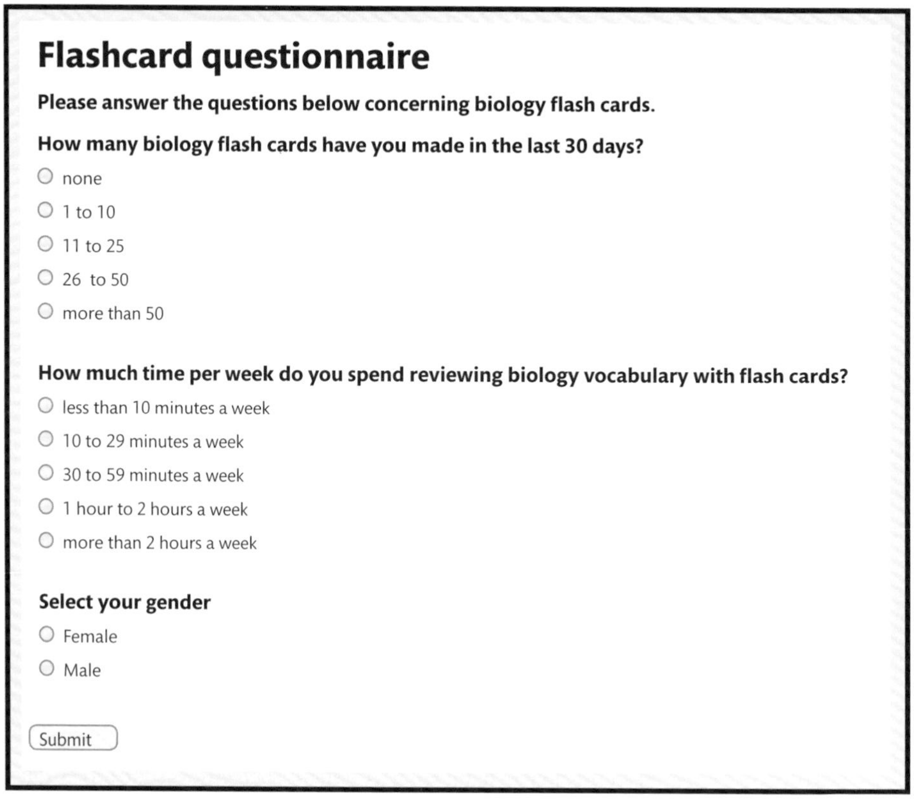

Flashcard questionnaire

Please answer the questions below concerning biology flash cards.

How many biology flash cards have you made in the last 30 days?

- none
- 1 to 10
- 11 to 25
- 26 to 50
- more than 50

How much time per week do you spend reviewing biology vocabulary with flash cards?

- less than 10 minutes a week
- 10 to 29 minutes a week
- 30 to 59 minutes a week
- 1 hour to 2 hours a week
- more than 2 hours a week

Select your gender

- Female
- Male

Submit

Figure 12 Example of three questions from an anonymous online questionnaire using multiple-choice questions from Google Forms. Other questions might gather data about students' results on their last biology test or whether they are taking HL or SL Biology.

Data-analysis exercises

Both for your IA work and in data-based sections of exams, you will be required to interpret sets of data presented either as tables or as graphs. Being able to extract scientific information from data is a key skill in biology.

The first thing to look for on a table or a graph is a title. When titles are not available, often the text before or after the tables and graphs will reveal some key information about what they are showing. The next clues to look for in order to interpret the data correctly are labels and units in the headings of tables, or labels and units on the axes of graphs. In both cases, the labels are often the dependent and independent variables of the investigation that generated the data. Knowing these will help you reach conclusions about the investigation. The units might be familiar to you, such as grams, millilitres, or °C, but sometimes they are units you have never heard of. In such cases, do not panic, just be sure to include those unfamiliar units in your answers and in your analysis. The same goes for arbitrary units, which are sometimes used to avoid employing confusing units.

Next, look at the scales on the axes of graphs. Do they show regular intervals (10, 20, 30, 40) or is there an atypical scale, such as a logarithmic scale (1, 10, 100, 1000)? If two graphs are being compared, do they use the same scales and the same maximum and minimum values? If not, be careful with how you compare the two because they may look the same but in fact be very different.

Analyse the graph below showing the sizes of wings of fruit flies in Europe, North America, and South America. Note that the original species of *Drosophila subobscura* lived in Europe and was introduced to the Americas in recent decades. What scientific information can be concluded from the graph? For example, can any predictions be made?

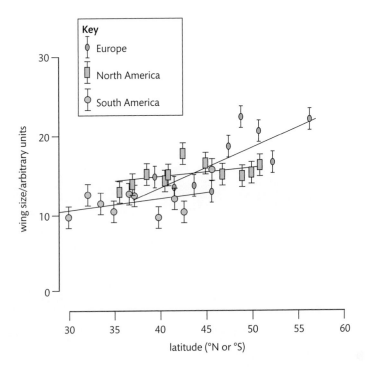

Figure 13 Graph showing fruit fly, *Drosophila subobscura*, wing sizes in different parts of the world.
Gilchrist et al. 2004

Solution

Reading the graph: look at the axes, showing latitude for the *x*-axis and wing size for the *y*-axis. Latitude is a measurement of how many degrees away from the equator something is: low numbers are closer to the equator, high numbers are further away from the equator. Next, look at the key: there are three different shapes and colours to analyse, depending on where the flies were observed. Associated with each group is a trend line. In addition, each data point has vertical error bars.

Analysis of the graph: all three trend lines increase as the latitude gets further from the equator, but the one from Europe has the greatest slope. If we look at the centre of each trend line, it appears that the South American population has the smallest wing size, the North American population has an intermediate wing size, and the European population has the biggest wing size. The European population has the widest range of wing sizes.

Conclusion: There is a relationship between latitude and wing size: they are positively correlated. We can predict that if the introduced populations of *D. subobscura* in the Americas were to spread to latitudes that are further away from the equator than the ones show in the graph, they should show an increase in wing size.

Throughout this book, there are examples of past paper questions, and some of them have graphs or tables of numbers that need to be interpreted and analysed. Be sure to practise analysing them because that is what you will be asked to do in exams.

Fieldwork and data logging

Biology investigations carried out in labs allow students to have a certain amount of control over the variables that they are manipulating. Fieldwork, however, does not offer such possibilities. Studying a forest, stream, grassland, or marine environment poses some unique challenges. Abiotic factors, such as temperature, air humidity, and light, can vary considerably, and could have an influence on what is being studied. For example, setting up pitfall traps is a wonderful way to collect invertebrates in a forest or grassland, but adverse weather conditions might greatly affect how active invertebrates are. Because they cannot be controlled, abiotic factors should be monitored and data should be collected to make sure that they do not have an adverse effect on the results.

A student using a hand-held data-logging device to measure the pH of a sample of water in a river.

Collecting large quantities of data can sometimes be tedious and prone to errors if done by hand. Instead of using a thermometer and writing down the temperatures, students can use temperature probes connected to data-logging devices that can automatically record temperatures at particular intervals. Such devices can be equipped with probes for:

- temperature
- light intensity
- relative humidity
- flow rate (to see how fast water is flowing)
- dissolved oxygen.

Data loggers can also have an integral global positioning system (GPS) (to record the exact location of each measurement).

Figure 14 A hand-held data-logging device with a probe measuring the temperature of a solution in a beaker.

Once the probes are plugged in, the data-logging device can be used in various modes depending on how the data are to be collected. Here are some examples:

- real-time (useful for monitoring measurements without recording them; in this mode, the device is used as a simple meter)
- events with entry (useful for measuring a certain factor every metre, or when another event happens; data will only be recorded when you tell the device to do so)
- time-based (useful for measuring something constantly over a fixed amount of time; in this mode, parameters can be adjusted to measure every minute, hour, second or fraction of a second).

Although the data can be transferred to a computer, many of these devices allow you to graph and analyse the data directly on screen. This is especially useful when doing fieldwork without a readily available computer.

ICT skills applied to your lab reports

To produce top-quality lab reports, it is expected that students have access to the following types of programs.

- Word processing software: programs such as Microsoft Word will help you with text, tables, footnotes, and chemical as well as mathematical formulas.
- Spreadsheet software: programs such as Microsoft Excel will help you with data processing to perform calculations such as averages, standard deviation, chi-squared tests, and more.
- Graphing software: in addition to its spreadsheet functions, Microsoft Excel also has graphing capabilities, to make line graphs, bar charts, histograms, and scatter plots, to which you can add trend lines and automatically calculate correlation coefficients.

Students who do not have access to Microsoft products can find other solutions, such as cost-free software packages available from OpenOffice.org, or online applications such as the ones available from Google. See the hotlinks section at the end of the chapter for more information.

The sections below list the functions and capabilities of the various software programs that students should consider learning about and using in their lab reports. To find out how to use them, look through the menus of whichever program you are using. The way the lists are set out below, the first word suggests which menu or tab to start to looking in, although many programs have icons with some of the more frequently used functions. Examples have been provided for some functions.

Word processing

Students should know how to do the following things with a word processor.

- Format: changing text formatting, such as putting species names in *italics*.
- Format: turning numbers into subscripts (e.g. H_2O) and superscripts (e.g. cm^3).
- Table: setting up tables, merging cells, aligning text horizontally/vertically within cells, rotating text 90°.
- Table/ruler/tabs: aligning decimal points within columns of a table.
- Table: adding borders around the cells so that they show up clearly.
- Insert: adding bulleted lists and numbered lists.

If you cannot find a feature in a program you are using, do not hesitate to go online. Do a search for 'how do I …?' and type in the function you are looking for, and finish the search with 'in …' and type in the name of the software and the version. If it is important that the solution is specifically for Mac, say so in your search otherwise there is a good chance the solutions you find will be for non-Mac users. For example, 'How do I insert footnotes in Microsoft Word for Mac?'

- Insert: adding a photo and resizing it to fit, and including a legend with the photo. Students should know how to adjust the quality or resolution of images to avoid the problem of the file size of their documents being too big. This can be a particular issue when submitting a document electronically.

- Edit: pasting a graph copied from a graphing program; if the lab report is going to be submitted electronically, is best to paste the graph as an image rather than as a linked object.

- Insert: using shapes such as arrows or boxes to annotate an image.

- Insert: adding notes such as footnotes at the bottom of a page, or endnotes at the end of the document.

- Insert: adding formulas using formula editors to produce well-presented equations to show how you processed your data. Note that some versions of word processors do not have the formula editors pre-installed so they need to be added manually.

- Insert: adding symbols such as $\pm$, Δ, λ, or $\leq$ where necessary.

- Insert: using page breaks to avoid having a section start at the bottom of a page or to avoid having a table split over two pages.

- Tools: selecting the text and setting the proofing language for the language you are using.

- Edit: using paste special for pasting text or numbers without the formatting.

Spreadsheets

Students should know how to do the following things with a spreadsheet program.

- Understand the system of identifying cells as A1, B2, C3, etc. (see screenshot 2 on the next page).

- Format: changing the format of the cell to match the type of data, such as number, date, percentage, text, time, scientific notation, etc.

- Format: changing the number of decimal places after the decimal point to correspond to the desired degree of precision.

- Insert: using math operations by inserting an equals sign '=' followed by a formula using 'A1 + A2' to add, or 'B3/B2' to divide, or '(A1 + A2 + A3)*B1' to combine more than one operation in the same formula.

- Insert: inserting predefined formulas such as sum, average, maximum or minimum, standard deviation, chi-squared, etc. Example for Excel: typing '=max(A1:A100)' in cell A101 finds the maximum value between A1 and A100. Replacing the term 'max' with 'min' in the formula finds the minimum value. Note: if your software is installed in a language other than English, the commands may be different. For example, 'sum' is 'somme' in French versions of spreadsheet software.

- For a repeating operation, copying the formula down a column or across a row rather than re-typing it separately each time.

- Converting a relative reference into an absolute reference by adding $, for example B2 does not behave the same way as $B2 or B$2 or B2 when it is copied and pasted to another place on the sheet.

- With international settings, the decimal point can sometimes be a full point (.) and sometimes be a comma (,) so if the decimals in your data do not seem to be recognized by the program, it is possible that you need to switch from one to the other. Instead of doing this manually, use the find and replace feature in the edit menu.

Use a spreadsheet program to calculate the mean, mode, and median of the data mentioned earlier in the chapter.

Solution

Be sure a spreadsheet program is installed on the computer or tablet you are using, such as Microsoft Excel or the spreadsheet programs available in software packages such as NeoOffice, LibreOffice, and Apache OpenOffice. The screenshots in this chapter are from OpenOffice Calc, which is available at no cost online.

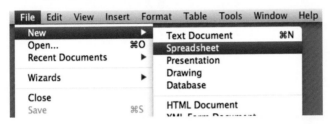

Screenshot 1 Creating a new spreadsheet in OpenOffice.

By typing in the values into the cells A1–A9 of your spreadsheet, you can then enter a formula to calculate the mean in cell A10. See screenshot 2.

	A	B
1	3.2	
2	9.5	
3	4.4	
4	6.2	
5	7.9	
6	4.4	
7	9.4	
8	7.3	
9	4.4	
10	=AVERAGE(A1:A9)	
11		

Screenshot 2 Calculating the mean (average) by using the '=average' function and either selecting cells A1–A9 by manually selecting them or typing A1:A9 in the parentheses. When you hit the ENTER key, it should calculate 6.3.

If you get an error message, be sure your program is not expecting a comma (,) instead of a full point (.) for the decimal point. In certain international versions of spreadsheet programs, the default is for a comma.

To find the median in the spreadsheet program, first select the nine values, then go to the Data menu and select Sort.

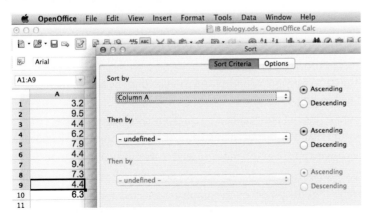

Screenshot 3 Using the sort feature to put numbers in order. Notice how cell A10 is purposely left out of the selection, as it is not part of the data (it is the calculated mean).

You could find the median manually by counting the data points and finding the one in the middle, or you could let the computer calculate it: type in the formula '=median(' and select the data between A1 and A9.

MEDIAN	▼	𝑓x ✖ ✓	
	A	**B**	
1	3.2		
2	4.4		
3	4.4		
4	4.4		
5	6.2		
6	7.3		
7	7.9		
8	9.4		
9	9.5		
10	6.3	average	
11	=MEDIAN(A1:A9)		

Note that the median function works even if you do not sort the data as we did in screenshot 3.

Screenshot 5 shows finding the mode.

Function Wizard		Function result	
Functions Structure			
Category	MODE		
All	MODE(number 1; number 2; ...)		
Function			
MODE	Returns the most common value in a sample.		
MONTH			
MONTHS			
MROUND			
MULTINOMIAL			
MUNIT			
N			
NA			
NEGBINOMDIST			
NETWORKDAYS			
NOMINAL	Formula	Result Err:520	
NOMINAL_ADD	=		
NORMDIST			
NORMINV			
NORMSDIST			
☐ Array	Help	Cancel	<< Back	Next >>	OK

Graphing

Students should know how to do the following things with graphing software.

- Entering the data in proper columns and rows so that the computer recognizes the data with its headings.
- Defining which data will be graphed by carefully selecting the correct rows and lines (it is important that there are no blank rows or blank columns in the selected data).
- Insert: selecting a type of graph that will lead to useful analysis.
- Insert: once the data points on a scatter plot are selected, a trend line can be inserted.
- Options: once the data points on the graph are selected and a trend line added, graphing programs often suggest options such as inserting the formula for the trend line or calculating the r^2-value.
- Options: once data points on the graph are selected, error bars can be added.

- Format: adding a title to the graph as well as labels to the axes. Many graphing programs suggest a legend, but legends are only necessary if two or more colours are used.
- Options: Once the numbers on the *x*- or *y*-axis are selected, it is often possible to alter the maximum and minimum values (useful for zooming in on a part of the graph that is interesting) or changing the scale (sometimes it is clearer to show every fifth value or every tenth value rather than every number on the scale).
- Options: for graphs showing two values for *y* measured in two different units, it is sometimes necessary to add a second *y*-axis using a different scale to avoid the problem of one variable's graph being squashed and unreadable.

As with all skills, it will probably take some time to learn the software the first time you use it. But with practice and perseverance, you should become proficient. Learning these skills will undoubtedly help you in your future studies after IB, and many will help you later in your career.

Worked example

Make a scatter plot graph using the following data points of abiotic factors measured by students doing fieldwork between an open grassy area (towards the 0 m side) and a woodland (towards the 24 m side).

	A	B	C
1	Distance / m	Soil Temp / °C	Light / lux
2	0	22.5	1582
3	2	23.0	1336
4	4	22.4	1063
5	6	21.4	780
6	8	21.0	407
7	10	20.2	351
8	12	18.4	171
9	14	18.2	198
10	16	17.8	132
11	18	18.3	119
12	20	17.8	107
13	22	16.7	117
14	24	17.4	95

Screenshot 6 The raw data.

Solution

First, enter the data as shown in columns A, B, and C. Second, select the cells A1–C14: it is recommended that you include the labels of the data in row 1 when graphing data. Note: too many students look at data like this and decide to do two separate graphs, one for soil temperature and another for light levels. However, it saves space and allows a better comparison if both variables are graphed together. Third, indicate to your spreadsheet program that you want to insert a graph. Fourth, choose the graph type, in this case a scatter plot, in order to plot y against x.

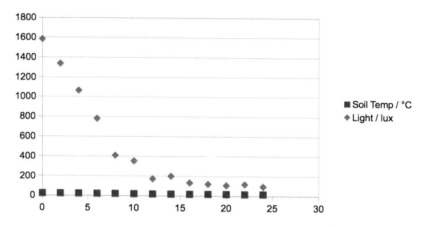

Screenshot 7 A graph that is not very useful.

What you have at this point (screenshot 7) is far from satisfactory, and you need to work through quite a few options in order to obtain a graph that will allow you to analyse the trends.

By selecting the blue data points (the soil temperature), it is possible to right-click on them and ask OpenOffice to change the format of the data series. Select 'secondary Y axis' for the blue data points. This will create a second y-axis on the right.

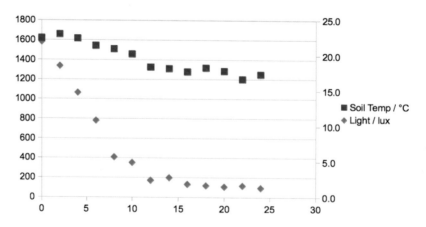

Screenshot 8 Creating a secondary y-axis.

This solves the problem of not being able to see any changes in the soil temperature in °C because it is on the same scale as the light readings in lux. But the graph is still not finished. To add a title to the graph and labels on the axes, make sure the graph is selected (by double-clicking on it) and choose 'Titles' from the options.

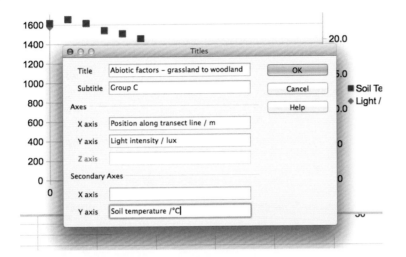

Screenshot 9 Adding a title and labels for the axes.

Now the graph should look like screenshot 10.

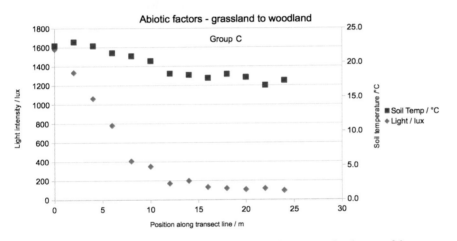

Screenshot 10 Labels added.

To finish data processing, a trend line could be added to one or both sets of data points. Here is an example of a trend line being added to the soil temperature by right-clicking on the selected data points.

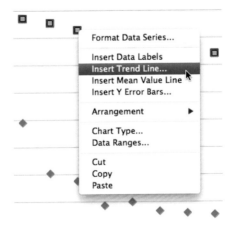

Screenshot 11 Using a drop-down menu to insert a trend line.

The r^2-value can been added by right-clicking on the selected trend line and choosing the format options. Do not be surprised if the graphing software writes r^2 as R^2.

Screenshot 12 The graph is now ready to interpret.

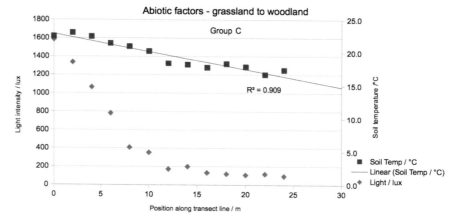

To learn more about maths and ICT skills, go to the hotlinks site, search for the title or ISBN, and click on Mathematics, and information and communication technology skills.

There is a trend in the temperature that goes from warmer temperatures in the open grassland near the 0 m mark, and cooler temperatures in the woodland towards the 24 m mark. The light levels seem to be a good indication of where the tree line starts to block out the sunlight after 10 m. This graph might inspire you to see the correlation from 0 to 10 m and compare it to 11 to 20 m.

Just because you spend time making a graph look great does not mean it is worth including in a lab report. Sometimes it will inspire you to look for other patterns. In this example, further processing could be done by plotting soil temperature against light levels to see whether they are correlated. It is advisable that you not wait until the night before an assignment on data processing is due before learning how to graph. Remember when you were a child and you first learned how to tie your shoelaces? Remember how long it took the first time? This is true for many skills, and preparing graphs for data processing is no exception. The first few times you make a graph will take a long time. Once you are an expert, it will take much less time.

Here is a closing thought about your smartphone: have you ever considered using it as a measuring device for lab work? Smartphones have microphones to measure sound levels, accelerometers that can be used for detecting vibrations or measuring angles as a spirit level, a camera that can be used as a lux meter or to make slow motion videos, a GPS that can measure your position, and many other things. Check out app stores online for the ones available for your phone. Ideas include a click counter, decibel meter, timer, tape measure, 'radar' speed gun, and many more. When doing microscope work in the lab, certain smartphone cameras work quite well for taking photos of what you are observing. Different teachers have different philosophies about the use of smartphones in the lab or during fieldwork but it is a shame not to take advantage of this powerful computer in your pocket. Whether or not you become a scientist later in life, the maths and ICT skills you learn in the IB will help you throughout your life.

One of the requirements of the IB diploma is to write an extended essay. This in-depth study of a limited topic within a particular subject area provides you with the chance to carry out independent research within a subject of your choosing. This essay is restricted to 4000 words and is expected to involve about 40 hours of work. Most schools introduce this requirement during the last portion of the first year of the IB programme. The essay is then completed and handed in during the second year.

The extended essay is awarded marks according to a very specific set of criteria and, in conjunction with the theory of knowledge (TOK) essay, can contribute to your overall diploma score through the award of bonus points. These points can be quite helpful in gaining your IB diploma. If excellent marks are obtained on both essays, you may be awarded a bonus of three points. However, if you do very badly in both essays, you will not be eligible for an IB diploma.

One of the subjects often selected for the extended essays is biology. It is particularly popular because many of the topics discussed in class and researched in laboratory activities provide unique ideas for the essay. Most successful extended essays in biology involve experimental work. However, some literature-based essays have scored well. Many submitted essays include both approaches.

An important requirement of the extended essay is that it should represent a new or unique approach to addressing a specific research question. Creativity and an individualistic approach are important to achieve a high mark. The table that follows offers you some guidance on writing your essay. However, there is no set formula that guarantees success in this important requirement.

Before you start, you must be aware of the criteria on which your essay will be marked. You will be assigned a supervisor (a teacher at your school) who will be available to discuss your progress with you. He or she will also help you ensure the safety and appropriateness of your work.

Advice on criteria for assessing your extended essay

Criterion	Advice
Research question	A good research question is essential to a good extended essay. It should be stated early in the introduction and should be focused for a 4000-word essay. Adequate time and thought must be spent in writing the research question.
Introduction	This should provide an explanation of the research question. The introduction should include discussion of the significance of the research question.
Investigation	The procedure is the key. Is it unique? Does it allow for adequate data collection? Are controls used? Is the procedure truly biological in nature? Is the procedure relevant to the research question? If the paper is library based, this criterion involves a detailed look at how the data to be analysed were obtained.

Criterion	Advice
Knowledge and understanding of the topic studied	Is an academic context evident? Have you shown that you clearly understand all aspects of the essay? Do your analyses represent an obvious understanding?
Reasoned argument	In your quest to confirm your hypothesis, are you logical and methodical in your approach and explanation? Is a convincing argument presented?
Application of analytical and evaluative skills	If library based, has there been careful analysis of all sources? Have all aspects of the experiment been evaluated for appropriateness? Is the presentation of data logical? Has there been adequate data analysis?
Use of language appropriate to the subject	Is the language appropriate to the topic and is it correctly used? Is it clear and precise? Does the terminology represent understanding?
Conclusion	Does the conclusion flow logically from the arguments in the essay? Is the conclusion relevant to the research question and does it relate to the original hypothesis? Does the conclusion include unresolved questions and potential future research?
Formal presentation	This includes elements such as a title page, table of contents, page numbers, appropriate illustrations, proper citations and bibliography, and appropriate appendices, if used.
Abstract	This is written last and includes three elements: • the research question • the investigative approach • a conclusion. Is it within 300 words?
Holistic judgement	This criterion is used to reward creative and unique approaches. It also involves depth of understanding, insight, and apparent interest in the topic.

These criteria are the key to a strong extended essay. It is important to remember that a biology extended essay must be clearly related to biology. Ethical considerations are extremely important and should be discussed with your supervisor. Discuss all aspects of your procedure with your supervisor before beginning, so that safety issues are not a concern.

The emphasis on this essay is independent research. Select a topic that is interesting to you and do substantial library research before beginning the process of writing the research question and formulating a hypothesis. Obtain samples of past successful extended essays from your supervisor for basic ideas on how to approach the task ahead.

The completion of your extended essay is followed by a viva voce (concluding interview). This is a 10–15 minute interview with your supervisor. It provides an opportunity to reflect on successes and on what has been learned.

Enjoy your research.

Suggestions for course study and strategies for the IB biology exam

To be successful as an IB biology student, you should achieve the following.

- Develop a body of knowledge that characterizes the concepts of biology, and the methods and techniques necessary to carry out basic experimentation in the subject.
- Demonstrate the ability to apply this body of knowledge in explanations, analyses, and evaluations.
- Communicate this knowledge and ability in proper, acceptable ways.
- Appreciate the ethical aspects of our subject area, as well as an understanding of the possibilities and limitations of biology and science in general.
- Utilize mathematical skills accurately and efficiently. These skills include basic mathematical functions, data table preparation and understanding, graph plotting and interpretation, and basic statistical analysis.

These suggestions/requirements will involve a great deal of dedication on your part. It will be essential to listen carefully and participate fully in your class activities. Practical experiences (laboratory activities) are essential in your full development as an IB biology student.

General suggestions for course study

The following is a list of study habits that have helped many students become successful in biology.

1. Study at the same time and place every day until it becomes automatic.
2. Pick an area to study in that is well lit and uncluttered, to minimize distractions.
3. Use a method to keep track of major assignment and test dates. This will help avoid the need for last minute emergency cramming.
4. Start your study sessions with the most difficult material first, then go to the easier materials. End the study session with a quick review.
5. By including several subjects in your study sessions, you may avoid loss of concentration on one particular subject.
6. Be as active as possible in your study. For example, you could include outlining, re-wording, condensing, and reciting facts aloud. Discussions with partners and groups are often beneficial.
7. Take notes on main ideas in class discussions and from reading to help you concentrate and grasp the material better.
8. Leave space when taking notes on paper to add information when reviewing the information at a later time.
9. Re-read and revise your notes as soon as possible after taking them. This means the information is fresh in your mind, and it is easier to complete or edit phrases.
10. Mnemonic devices (assisting the memory) are extremely effective. Make up a sentence or word with the same initials as the material you need to memorize or understand.

11 Break up larger projects into smaller tasks spread over many days. This helps make the project less intimidating.

12 Always strive to see the 'big picture'. Try to see the material you learn each day as part of the whole picture of biology. Realize that each day's material is a small segment of the interconnected parts that comprise biology.

13 Complete assignments and any class work as neatly as possible. Make certain you order materials as they are covered in class. One suggestion is to consider your notebook as a publishable work of knowledge!

14 Always begin test preparation early. This gives you time to seek help if necessary. It is more effective to study in short sessions (perhaps 20–30 minutes) than in long single study sessions, such as the infamous 'all-nighters'.

15 Have a designated plan for each study session. Do not wander aimlessly through your studies.

16 Choose appropriate sources on the internet to supplement your biology knowledge.

17 Note or flash cards are a highly recommended form of study at any level. It involves active learning that is highly effective in gaining knowledge.

18 Plan physical activity, recreation, and quiet time for yourself, as well as your studies.

Specific suggestions for IB biology course study using this text

This book has been designed to help you achieve success in IB biology. It provides guidance to allow you to fulfil the suggestions/requirements presented earlier in this section. Some key features to note include the following.

1 Essential ideas are presented at the beginning of each chapter. These should focus your thoughts on the general concepts to be discussed in the chapters.

2 Statements labelled Nature of science are included at the beginning of each section. These allow you to grasp the overarching theme in the study of all the major sciences. They often present major improvements in scientific investigations that have occurred during the 21st century.

3 Understandings and Applications and skills are extremely important and are clearly presented at the beginning of each section.

4 Understandings present a detailed description of the knowledge you should achieve. It is vital to study the text and e-text information carefully so that these Understandings can be mastered. Background building is essential to master these statements.

5 Application and skills statements outline the specific applications and skills to be developed from the understandings. These statements represent higher levels of thought and are often quite demanding.

6 When you come across Hints for success in the book, take special note. These present activities or suggestions that will make you a better IB biology student.

7 The extracts marked International mindedness present essential material that may be very helpful in the exams.

8 Utilization information and lab or practical activities will be of great value in being successful in the IB exams.

9   Other sections/features presented in the book that should be carefully noted for course success include Key points, Animations, Theory of knowledge, hotlinks, and Interesting information.

By focusing on these features during the course and as a revision activity near the exam, you will become a much more effective IB biology student.

Strategies for success when answering questions in the IB exams

IB exams for both standard level (SL) and higher level (HL) biology are dominated by four types of questions:

- multiple-choice questions
- data-based questions
- open-ended questions
- short-answer questions.

Strategy for success when answering multiple-choice questions

SL exams contain 30 multiple-choice questions, and HL exams contain 40 multiple-choice questions. All multiple-choice questions have four choices (A–D) and there is no penalty for guessing. Therefore you should answer every question.

The content for multiple-choice questions comes from the core material for SL students, and the core and additional higher level (AHL) material for HL students. No material from the options appears in multiple-choice questions.

Strategies for success when answering data-based questions

Data-based questions present you with data in some form and then ask you questions about that data. Some questions will ask you to read the data displayed, and some will ask you to draw conclusions from it.

Pay close attention to the number of marks for each question. The examiner is comparing your answer to acceptable answers on a mark scheme. You can write as much as you like as long as you do not contradict yourself. Grading is positive so, if you write something wrong, no marks are deducted. But if you contradict yourself, you receive no mark.

You are expected to use the data given within the question. Make it a habit to reference the data when you practise data-based questions; this will make it natural to do the same when taking the exam. Become familiar with unit expressions such as $kJ\ m^{-2}\ yr^{-1}$ (read as kilojoules per metre squared per year). If you are not comfortable with the unit expressions you see in data-based questions in this book, ask your instructor for help.

A glossary of 'command terms' is provided in the eBook that accompanies this text. You should be very familiar with the meaning of each command term and respond appropriately when they are used in exam questions.

If the question has the command term 'calculate', you must show your work.

Questions that use the command term 'compare' require you to relate clearly the similarities *and* differences between two sets of data. In most situations, an answer that involves numeric data will not achieve a mark unless a unit is given with the number. Do a full comparison and be sure to state whether any difference is an increase or decrease.

When encountering command terms such as 'describe' or 'outline', provide a general or big-picture summary of the data presented. Include a numerical value or values when asked to 'describe' a data pattern.

When directed to 'explain the results', be certain to write the reasons or mechanisms that produced the results.

'Suggest' questions indicate that you are to use your knowledge from throughout the course to provide causes for the data presented.

Use a ruler when answering data-based questions because the graphs are often small and the degree of precision required in your answers is often quite demanding. A ruler can be used to draw lines on the graph to help you increase your chance of being within the degree of tolerance allowed by the mark scheme.

Practise the questions given at the end of each chapter in this book. They are from past exam papers and a mark scheme is provided. Write out the answers as you would during an exam. Give yourself a set time to answer all of the questions in a section. Finally, grade yourself with the answer key (the mark scheme) provided in the eBook.

Strategies for success when answering open-ended questions

As with data-based questions, it is essential you are familiar with the meaning of the command terms when answering open-ended or extended-response questions. These types of questions often involve a larger number of possible marks than other questions.

'Explain' or 'discuss' command terms typically cannot be done with a brief response. There is never a penalty for writing too much. The problem here is that you could spend too much time answering one question at the expense of another. Look at how many marks the question is worth. If one question is worth 6 marks, it is worth spending more time on it than a question worth only 2 marks. When answering a 'discuss' question, make sure you present at least two alternative views. For example, imagine a discussion about conserving the rainforest. You must give opposing views on why the rainforest should and should not be conserved.

When a question includes the command term 'list', you must give the exact number of things asked. For example, if the question is 'List three factors that affect the distribution of plant species', you should list only three factors. If you list four, the fourth answer will not be scored. However, if a specific number is not specified, you may list more than the number of marks calls for.

Remember these tips.

- The examiner does not know you. You must communicate fully what you know and not expect the examiner to 'fill in the blanks' with information that you do not relate clearly.
- State the obvious in your answers. Many of the items in a mark scheme will be information that is very basic in relation to the question.

- Do not use abbreviations that may be unfamiliar to someone else. Be clear and concise with your choice of words.
- If you have handwriting that is very small or unclear, *print* your response. If the examiner cannot read your writing, you will not get a mark.
- Make sure to use the 'supplemental booklets' at the test site for continuing answers if you run out of space in the exam booklet. Do not write outside the boxes provided on the exam booklets. This is because the exams are being e-marked, and any writing outside the lines provided will not be visible to the examiner. Number the remainder of the response in the 'supplemental booklet' so that the examiner knows where the response continues.

If a question requires you to 'draw and label', follow these directions.

- All drawings need to be done within the boxes provided. These boxes are of adequate size to represent the complexity required.
- Coloured pens, pencils, and highlighters should not be used because the papers will be marked electronically. Use a black pencil for the drawing, and use black ink for the labels.
- Horizontal labelling is recommended.
- Use a ruler to draw a line from the label to the item in the drawing, and be sure the line touches exactly the part that it is labelling (if the examiner has any doubt about the structure that you are naming, no marks will be awarded).
- There should be no gaps in the lines when drawing closed shapes such as cells or organelles.
- Structures should be positioned correctly within the drawing. Connections between included structures within drawings should be clearly and properly shown.
- Correct proportions of structures included in a drawing is required.

Strategies for success when answering short-answer questions

Short-answer questions involve fewer marks per question than data-based or open-ended/extended-response questions. However, the command term involved is just as important with this type of question as with data-based or open-ended/extended-response questions. This type of question is often divided into parts, and is usually answerable in the few lines provided. Separate distinct ideas from one another: this decreases the chances of the examiner missing the different parts of your answer.

And finally

Remember that the three papers of the written IB exam account for 80% of your overall score. The other 20% is based on your performance in the internal assessment (lab work) portion of the course. This internal assessment portion is graded by your instructor and moderated by an examiner.

The exam papers are based on the requirements and direction presented in the course subject guide. It is therefore vital that you become very familiar with the requirements and directions that relate to the material for your level of study (SL or HL).

In the exam

1   The first day of the exam presents papers 1 and 2. These papers test your knowledge of the core material (plus AHL material for HL students). No option material is tested on the first day.

2   The second day of the exam presents paper 3. This paper tests the option material plus questions based on the experimental work carried out as directed in the course subject guide. Paper 3 will include questions from the core (also from the AHL for HL students) particularly relating to skills and techniques, and data analysis and evaluation.

3   It is highly recommended that you read each question twice before beginning to write. Examiners report a disturbing number of students who write an answer that does not correspond to the question (often indicating poor understanding of command terms). In addition, when you have finished, if time allows, re-read the questions and your answers one more time just to be certain everything is in order. Make sure you cross out clearly any work that you do not want the examiner to mark.

A

ABCC11 gene   123
abiotic   188
ABO blood type   156–7
absorption   285–92, 508–10
acetyl-CoA   104
acetylcholine   322
acid reflux   506
acquired immune deficiency *see* AIDS
actin   55, 518
action potential   317–18
activational energy   57
active transport   31, 35–9, 291
    endocytosis   18, 37–8, 291
    endocytosis/exocytosis   37–8
    sodium–potassium pump   35–7
acute bilirubin encephalopathy   517
adaptation   244–5
    and survival   246–7
adaptive radiation   234, 235–6
adenine   89, 90
adenosine diphosphate *see* ADP
adenosine triphosphate *see* ATP
adhesion   64–5
adipocytes   74
ADP   57
adrenal glands   296
adult-onset diabetes   502
aerobic respiration   104–6
aestivation   278
agricultural uses of biotechnology   397–410
    genetically modified crops   81, 173,
        398–410
Agrobacterium tumefaciens   401, 406
AIDS   304–5
alanine   78
albedo   217
albinism   152–4, 158, 162
albumin   516
alcohol, and liver damage   514
alcoholic fermentation   103
algae   24, 41
alien species   463–4
    eradication   470–2
    kudzu   465, 483
    removal of   483
alimentary canal   287–8
alleles   121–4, 162
    co-dominant   151, 154
    dominant   151, 154
    multiple   156–7
    recessive   151
    sex-linked traits   159–60
alveoli   309, 311–12
Alzheimer's disease   11, 355
Amflora potato   402
amino acids   66, 78–9, 498–9
    orientation   272
    polarity   68
    see also proteins
ammonia   192, 508
amniocentesis   148

amniotes   267
Amoeba amazonas   256
amphibians   266–7
    heart   293
amphipathic   27
Amphiprion ocellaris (clownfish)   434
amylase   288, 289
anabolism   58–60
anaerobic respiration   102–4
    alcoholic fermentation   103
    lactic acid fermentation   103–4
analogous traits   274–5
anaphase
    meiosis   144, 145–6
    mitosis   45, 46–7
anatomy   270
    digestive system   287
ancestry   161, 169, 229, 234, 254, 257, 260,
        262, 272, 275, 278
Anemonia sulcata (sea anemone)   434
Angiospermophyta   264
animal experiments   354–5
animal phyla   264–6
animalcules   4
Annelida   265
anorexia   501
anosmia   375
anoxic   207
antagonistic pairs   308, 310, 314, 326
anterior pituitary   332, 351
anthropoids   236
antibiotics   305–7
    resistance   249–51, 306–7, 416, 417
antibodies   303–4
anticodon   99, 100
antigens   304
antimalarial drugs   387
antiparallel strands   90
anucleate cells   515
anus   287
aorta   294
aortic valve   520
aphasia, post-stroke   348
Apis mellifera (honey bee)   256
apomorphic traits   271
appetite   500–1
apple tree (*Malus domestica*)   256
Aptenodytes patagonicus (king penguin)   256
aquaporins   54
aquatic ecosystems   204
aqueous humour   370
aqueous solutions   65–6
Archaea   257
    biogas production   393–4
    classification   393
Ardea herodias (blue heron)   433
area effect   487
Arenicola marina (lugworms)   470
arginine   78
Armasillidium vulgare (pill bug; woodlouse)   260
arrhythmia   524
artemisinins   387, 467

arteries   292–3
    plaque build-up   298–9
Arthropoda   265
artificial pacemakers   523–4
artificial selection   233
asbestos   313
Asclepias syriaca (monarch butterfly)   433
Ascomycota   434
ascorbic acid   497
asparagine   78
aspartic acid   78
Aspergillus niger   391
atherosclerosis   298–9
atmosphere   191, 215
    greenhouse effect   217–18
ATP   19, 31, 56, 57, 88, 198, 508
    production   101–4
atria   294
atrioventricular node   295, 522
atrioventricular valves   520
auditory association area   363
auditory cortex   363
autoimmune disease   328
automated external defibrillators (AEDs)   524
autonomic nervous system   287, 356–8
    parasympathetic division   357–8, 359
    sympathetic division   357–8
autopsy   356
autoradiography   140–1
autosomal genetic disease   128, 158
autosomal recessive disease   158
autosomes   139, 140
autotrophs   185, 187, 191, 197
    carbon cycle   203–4
axon growth   344–5

B

B lymphocytes   307
bacteria   24
    antibiotic resistance   249–51, 306–7
    biofilms   414–19
    biogas production   393–4
    cell wall   395
    gene number   122
    Gram staining   394–6
    intestinal   510
bacteriophages   419
Bactrocera dorsalis (oriental fruit fly)   471–2
basal labyrinth   509
base changes   123
base substitutions   126–8
Beaumont, William   504, 507
benzene bioremediation   412
bicuspid valve   520
bile   505, 516–17
    pigments   510, 515
    salts   516
bilirubin   515
    jaundice   517
binary fission   14, 241
binomial nomenclature   253–7
bioaccumulation   472

prosimians   236
prostate gland   329
proteases   506
proteins   56, 76–82, 286
  denaturation   81–2, 84
  formation   77–9
  membrane   30–1
  polypeptides   81
  structure   79–80
protein synthesis   96–101
  transcription   97–8
  translation   98–101
protein therapy   132
proteome   81, 398
prothrombin   302
Protista   5
proton pump inhibitors   506
Pseudacteon   471
Pseudomonas spp.
  mercury bioremediation   413
  oil bioremediation   412
Pseudomonas aeruginosa   416
puberty   332
pulmonary circulation   294
pulmonary valve   520
Punnett grid   152–4, 155
pupil   370
pupil reflex   358, 359
Purkinje fibres   522
pyramids of biomass   446–7
pyramids of energy   199, 200, 441–6, 448–9
  construction of   445–6
pyruvate   102

Q

QRS complex   523
quadrats   188–90
quarantine   250
quorum sensing   415

R

rabbit (*Oryctolagus cuniculus*)   433
radiation damage   163, 164–5
radioisotope dating   232–3
random orientation   144
random sampling   188
rapid oxidation   101
rats, pesticide resistance   248–9
realized niche   436–7
recessive alleles   151
reclassification of species   260–2, 277–9
recombinant DNA   408–9
rectum   287
recyclable resources   198
red blood cells   302, 496
  recycling   515–16
red fox (*Vulpes vulpes*)   432–3
red-green colour blindness   372
Redi, Francesco   40
reduction division   142
repolarization   318
reproduction   5, 328–30
  cellular   10–12
  female reproductive system   330
  in vitro fertilization   334–5

male reproductive system   329
menstrual cycle   332–4
puberty   332
sex determination   139–40, 331
sexual   14, 243–4
reproductive cloning   176
reptiles   267
resistance
  to antibiotics   249–51, 306–7, 416, 417
  to pesticides   248–9
respiration   386
  aerobic   104–6
  anaerobic   102–4
respiratory system   307–14
  anatomy   308–9
  gas exchange   311–12
  ventilation   309–11
respirometry   105–6
resting potential   316–17
restoration of land   483
retina   370, 371
Rhinella marina   423, 463
Rhizobium   192, 434
rhodopsin   79
ribonucleic acid *see* RNA
ribose   89
ribosomal RNA (rRNA)   98
ribosomes   14, 15, 18, 22, 77
  plant cells   16
rice plant, gene number   77, 122
rickets   497, 502
RNA   88–91, 97–8
  mRNA   97, 98
  rRNA   98
  structure   89–91
  tRNA   98, 99
RNA polymerase   97
rods   370, 371
rough endoplasmic reticulum   15, 17–18, 22
rubisco   79
Ruderman, Joan   43
runaway greenhouse effect   216

S

salamanders   235
saliva   505
saltatory conduction   319–20
saltmarsh cordgrass (*Spartina alterniflora*)   237
sand dunes, species diversity in   451–2, 453
  foredune   451
  grey dune   452
  mature dune   452
  yellow dune   451
Sanger technique   130
saprotrophs   186–7, 191–2
sarcomere   518
satiety   500
saturated fatty acids   72
scale bars   8
Schleiden, Matthias   4
Schwann, Theodor   4
Schwann cells   319
sclera   371
scrotum   329
scurvy   497, 502

sea anemone (*Anemonia sulcata*)   434
secondary succession   450–1
secretin   506
sedimentation rate   18
seed banks   486
selective breeding   233
selective pressure   237
semen   329
semicircular canals   374
semilunar valves   520
seminal vesicles   329
sensory association cortex   363
sensory receptors   367
serine   78
sessile organisms   264
set point   324
sex chromosomes   139–40
  genes carried on   159
sex determination   139–40, 331
sex-linked genetic disease   128, 159–62
  alleles and genotypes   159–60
  carriers   152, 160
  inheritance   160–2
sexual reproduction   14, 243–4
sheep, FCR   449
Shelford, Victor   425
sickle cell disease   127–8, 158
Simpson's diversity index   479–81, 482
Singer, Seymour J.   28
sinoatrial node   295, 521–2
sinusoids   449, 512, 513
sister chromatids   137
skeletal muscle   357, 502
skin   301
  pigmentation   122
slime moulds   40
slow oxidation   101
small intestine   287, 288, 289–91
smoking and cancer   49–50, 313
smooth endoplasmic reticulum   15, 17–18, 22
smooth muscle   287, 288
sodium   496
sodium chloride, polarity   68
sodium–potassium pump   35–7
Solenopsis invicta (fire ant)   471
solvents   65–6
somatosensory cortex   364
sound perception   372
soybeans
  genetically modified   398
  glyphosate resistance   400–1
Spartina alterniflora (saltmarsh cordgrass)   237
spatial habitat   431
speciation   230
species   183–5, 258–9, 423–40
  binomial nomenclature   253–7
  common ancestral   259–60
  competition   432–3
  competitive exclusion   435–6
  divergence   235
  hybrids   184
  interactions   187, 432–5
  keystone   430, 483
  new, naming of   255–6
  niche   431–5, 436–7